Beyond the Death of God

Beyond the Death of God

RELIGION IN 21ST CENTURY INTERNATIONAL POLITICS

Edited by
Simone Raudino and Patricia Sohn

University of Michigan Press
Ann Arbor

Published in the United States of America by the
University of Michigan Press
Manufactured in the United States of America
Printed on acid-free paper
First published May 2022

A CIP catalog record for this book is available from the British Library.

Library of Congress Cataloging-in-Publication data has been applied for.

Library of Congress Control Number: 2022931576

ISBN 978-0-472-07515-7 (hardcover : alk. paper)
ISBN 978-0-472-05515-9 (paper : alk. paper)
ISBN 978-0-472-90268-2 (open access ebook)

DOI: https://doi.org/10.3998/mpub.11866503

An electronic version of this book is freely available, thanks to the support of libraries working with Knowledge Unlatched (KU). KU is a collaborative initiative designed to make high quality books Open Access for the public good. More information about the initiative and links to the Open Access version can be found at www.knowledgeunlatched.org.

The University of Michigan Press's open access publishing program is made possible thanks to additional funding from the University of Michigan Office of the Provost and the generous support of contributing libraries.

Cover illustration: Early in the morning at Tong La, October 2004. Photograph by Jan Reurink. Courtesy Wikimedia Commons, https://creativecommons.org/licenses/by/2.0/deed.en

Simone would like to dedicate this volume to Caroline:
"To err is human; to forgive, divine."

Patricia would like to dedicate this volume to religious freedom and religious pluralism; to her Father; and to the 14th Dalai Lama.

Acknowledgments

The editors would like to acknowledge the support of several institutions and individuals who were critical in the publication of this volume. First, Charles Watkinson, Elizabeth Demers, Hailey Winkle, and Kevin Rennells at the University of Michigan Press ensured a seamless, pleasant, and most professional editing, revising, copyediting, and production process at every stage. We would like to extend our thanks to Charles Watkinson in making possible our volume's participation in the Knowledge Unlatched international open access program, which we hope will make this volume freely available to many graduate and undergraduate students. We are grateful to the University of Michigan Press.

Many thanks to Mark Tessler for his generous commentary on this volume, and for what turns out to have been some years of moral and intellectual support in the making of this volume. His confidence in the project was critical at many stages. He read drafts of the editors' introduction, and his commentary gently helped to suggest a highlighting of certain points there, and in the religion-section introductions, which strongly enhanced the final product of the volume. Thanks are also due to all of the contributors to this volume, well-established voices and new, who joined at various stages; who were steadfast in the face of the long process, from start to finish, of making an edited volume on a cross-disciplinary topic; and whose works, collectively, add to our understanding of the place of religion in politics, and in sociopolitics, on at least three continents with insights far broader. Moreover, the contributors, while never gathered as a group in person before publication, and working throughout the Covid-19 period almost entirely remotely, joined across religious concentrations in ways that give credit to the academic project. All magnanimously contributed their time and skills to framing their diverse arguments, cases, and methodologies in order to relate them to one central theme for the volume. It is the triangulation of those diverse studies into one collective theme, and argument or finding, that is the result of this collective project. Thank you very much to Gad

Barzilai for reading drafts of the volume and for his support of the project at important moments.

The Kyiv School of Economics provided Simone with institutional support and affiliation while he worked on the publication and development of the volume. Simone would also like to acknowledge the indirect contribution of the many academics involved in the interfaith dialogue network linked to the "Bridging Gaps" Society in Hong Kong, who, over a period of 10 years, have provided an invaluable breeding environment for many of the ideas collected, and further elaborated on, in this volume. Simone is also thankful to Patricia Sohn for her initiative, detailed work, and unfaltering dedication to this project.

Patricia would like to acknowledge the University of Florida, Department of Political Science, and Center for Jewish Studies, for institutional support, a sabbatical, and research leave. These were used in helping to lay the groundwork for the project in the mid-2010s and, later, in the development of the volume and manuscript. Thank you to several departmental graduate students or junior fellows who read a draft of her case study chapter: Eyup Civelek, Katrina Siason, and Victoria Puerto. Portland State University, International and Global Studies, and Washington State University–Vancouver, Public Affairs, also provided important institutional support in the early stages of this project. She would like to thank Simone Raudino for his countless hours devoted to securing no fewer than three contracts for the volume, a diplomatic feat in itself; as well as for his persistence, steadfast work, and easy relays of division of labor in a protracted editing process that resulted in what they hope to be a volume that offers some small contribution to the cross-disciplinary field of religion and politics. That process included their co-authorship of the editors' introduction and religion-section introductions; their own chapter contributions; many hours of communications with contributors via Zoom, telephone, and email; conference meetings with one or two contributors at a time; and three iterations of volume-wide editing before the publication process. For her part, she dedicates the volume to religious freedom and religious pluralism; to her Father; to the spiritual teachings of H.Em. Gyalwa Rinpoche, the 14th Dalai Lama, which have sustained her in good times and bad; and to world religious and spiritual leaders who work tirelessly, daily, with little public acclaim or reward to make the lives of billions of individuals better and more meaningful.

Contents

PART I: INTRODUCTION AND COMPARATIVE THEMES

Editors' Introduction: Religion and Politics 3
Patricia Sohn, University of Florida—Gainesville
Simone Raudino, Kyiv School of Economics—Kyiv, Bridging Gaps—Hong Kong

Commentary: Modernization, Comparison, and Religion 31
Mark Tessler, University of Michigan—Ann Arbor

Religion and Conflict: Theoretical Perspectives and Empirical Evidence 45
Simone Raudino, Kyiv School of Economics—Kyiv, Bridging Gaps—Hong Kong

PART 2: THEORETICAL AND EMPIRICAL CASES ACROSS REGIONS

CHRISTIANITY IN EUROPE—INTRODUCTION 67

On the Genealogy of Populist Morals 75
Marco Ferraro, Orta Doğu Teknik Üniversitesi—Ankara

Belief in Politics and the Politics of Faith: The Case of the 2019 Presidential Elections in Ukraine 97
Antoine Arjakovsky, Collège des Bernardins—Paris

Secularism and Sectarianism in Christianity: The Case of Northern Ireland during the Troubles 120
C. K. Martin Chung, Hong Kong Baptist University

ISLAM IN AFRICA AND THE MIDDLE EAST—INTRODUCTION 147

The Politics of Islam in the Sahel: Between Quiescence and Violence 155
Abdourahmane (Rahmane) Idrissa, Leiden University—Leiden

Religious Freedom: The Case of Apostasy in Islam 173
Mutaz Al-Khatib, College of Islamic Studies, Hamid Bin Khalifa University—Doha

The Politicization of Islamic Humanitarian Aid: The Case of Islamic NGOs 200
Ibrahim Yahaya Ibrahim, Crisis Group—Dakar

JUDAISM IN THE MIDDLE EAST—INTRODUCTION 227

Global Trends in Religion and State: Secular Law and Freedom of Religion in Israel 232
Patricia Sohn, University of Florida—Gainesville

The Balancing of Democratic and Jewish Values in the Israeli Court System, 1983–2006 259
Eti Peretz and Jonathan Fox, Bar Ilan University—Ramat Gan

Psychology in Religion and Politics: The Role of Cognitive Dissonance in Religious Readings of the Israeli Disengagement Plan 281
Mordechai (Motti) Inbari, University of North Carolina—Pembroke

HINDUISM, BUDDHISM, AND SYNCRETIC RELIGIONS IN ASIA—INTRODUCTION 305

Diaspora Hinduism and Hindutva: A Historiography of Modern Indian Politics 314
Pratick Mallick, Acharya Prafulla Chandra College—New Barrackpore

Multiculturalism and Revolution: An Analytical History of the Chinese Communist Party's Relationship with Syncretic Religious Movements 337
Wasana Wongsurawat, Chulalongkorn University—Bangkok

"Trading Western Suits for Monastic Robes": Remaking Tibetan Buddhism in the Chinese Religious Revival 360
Jue Liang, Denison University—Granville

Distancing the Other: Religious Violence and Its Absence in South Korea 380
Manus I. Midlarsky and Sumin Lee, Rutgers University—New Brunswick

Contributors 411

Index 417

Digital material related to this title can be found on
the Fulcrum platform via the following citable URL:
https://doi.org/10.3998/mpub.11866503

PART I

Introduction and Comparative Themes

Editors' Introduction

Religion and Politics

Patricia Sohn and Simone Raudino

University of Florida; Kyiv School of Economics, Bridging Gaps

In 1882, Friedrich Nietzsche announced that "God is dead." However, that was not the end of his speculations on the subject. He continued: "And we killed him. How shall we comfort ourselves, the murderers of all murderers" who brought God to die "under our knives."[1] In Nietzsche's text it is, in fact, "the madman" who cries in an open marketplace filled with atheists: "I seek God!" And then, later, in despair: "Whither is God? . . . I will tell you. *We have killed* him—you and I. All of us are his murderers. But how did we do this? How could we drink up the sea? . . . Whither are we moving? Away from all the suns? Are we not plunging continually? Backward, sideward, forward, in all directions?" Finally, after visiting many churches with the same rant, ignored and mocked by the crowd, the madman concludes: "I have come too early."[2]

Nietzsche is writing about his own society as he witnesses science murdering religion.[3] The seventeenth-century's scientific advances, turned into "revolution" by the eighteenth century and steadily gaining terrain through-

1. Friedrich Nietzsche, *The Gay Science: With a Prelude in Rhymes and an Appendix of Songs*, trans. and commentary by Walter Kaufmann (New York: Vintage, 1974), 181–82.

2. Nietzsche, *Gay Science.*

3. Nietzsche was born and raised near Leipzig, Prussia, which later became part of Germany. He was educated in Prussia and Germany, and he taught at the University of Basel in Switzerland. Lesley Chamberlain, *Nietzsche in Turin: An Intimate Biography* (New York: Picador [Macmillan], 1997); and Walter Kaufmann, *Nietzsche: Philosopher, Psychologist, Antichrist* (Princeton: Princeton University Press, 1975).

out the nineteenth century, had, by the time Nietzsche wrote, already unraveled for many the widely held belief that God exists in some ontological form. With God apparently dead, Nietzsche asks whether we now become gods to replace this being, "the holiest and mightiest of all that the world has yet owned."[4] Is our becoming God to replace that which we have killed an achievable goal? In answer, it seems that Nietzsche's primary concern is that the death of God will cause the death of all absolute principles of appeal based on a divine order and reason. He predicts that these will give way, instead, to *nihilism*, or a will to nothingness. Meanwhile, the lack of divine order and otherworldly authority undergirding the worldly order of monarchy and the divine right of kings would be replaced by something decidedly less preferable.

Nihilism, for Nietzsche, is both a social and a psychological condition. It is both the result of the downfall of the temporal power of Christianity and an outcome of too many centuries of absolute certainty on moral questions, or what Nietzsche calls "fanatical faith."[5] In Nietzsche's analysis, fanatical certainty, over time, inevitably leads to an equally fanatical disbelief in any moral good whatsoever, or a throwing of one's hands in the air on moral questions. And, now, "All is False."[6]

How are we humans, then, to live alone, ourselves, with no divine entity (or divinely appointed monarch) to lead us? Can we abandon the safe shores of "true world" beliefs—of the type that Christianity had provided for centuries—while maintaining social order, individual purpose, and our very psychological sanity?

Nietzsche does not have final answers to these questions. Yet Nietzsche's speculations on how modernism killed the idea of God left fundamental ramifications for both the inner and outer spheres of human thought. The introspective, speculative world of philosophy and psychology, on the one side, and the outwardly directed efforts at understanding and organizing societies, through sociology or political science, on the other, are equally affected. In fact, in Nietzsche's thought, the two spheres are so intimately intertwined as to effectively become mutually constitutive: anthropological speculations on the different natures of men, and on their capacity to react to the death of God, ultimately led him to a theory of society. By walking the

4. Nietzsche, *Gay Science*, 181.

5. Friedrich Nietzsche, *The Will to Power*, trans. and ed. with commentary by Walter Kaufmann (New York: Random House, 1973), 7.

6. Nietzsche, *Will to Power*.

treacherous path linking psychology to action, Nietzsche simultaneously spoke to the two provinces of religion: as an intimate belief and as a source of political power.

FROM PSYCHOLOGY TO POLITICAL PHILOSOPHY

Nietzsche's path to a social theory based on the concept of (the death of) God begins from his intimate knowledge of human psychology. Nietzsche is well aware of people's fundamental need for a meaningful existence, and he anticipates that, without God and the prospect of an afterlife,

> nihilism . . . [will] appear . . . not [because] the displeasure of existence has become greater than before but because one has come to mistrust any "meaning" in suffering, indeed in existence. . . . It now seems as if there is no meaning at all in existence, as if everything were in vain.
>
> *The Will to Power*

The lack of the idea of a god brings out human primordial fears: living without a cause, a reason, or an aim—what ultimately amounts to life without meaning. In particular, it raises the ghastly prospect of going through one's life sufferance without any anchoring hope or belief that can help face such sufferance. Nietzsche believed that men could only overcome the dreadful state of *personal nihilism* by finding meaning in something else.

And what is this "something else"? According to Nietzsche, it depends upon the defining qualities of the single person facing the death of God. Fundamentally, he identifies two categories of men.

The *Übermensch*—Superior Men or Super Men—will find such "something else" in the acceptance that personal nihilism is the result of a misguided and sterile desire to find objective meaning in life, and subsequently in coming to terms with the absence of such objective meaning or absolute truth in life. These people will accept existence as a subjective experience to be fostered through life-promoting actions. They will find the inner resources necessary to navigate their existential fears and to achieve their own life-affirming morality, consisting in giving themselves their *own* good and evil as *laws*. These are superior beings who will manage to move from the "death of God" to "becoming God" by realizing that the need to find meaning in life's suffering is what had originally brought humanity to externalize its highest values and ideas of perfection into God. These superior beings will now recognize themselves as the legitimate creators of such values and renounce their dependency upon external institutions and creeds. Nietzsche makes a mission of incentivizing this process by creating an ethic of self-deification:

> To lure many away from the herd, that is why I have come. . . . I teach you the superman. Man is something that should be overcome. What have you done to overcome him? All gods are dead: now we want the superman to live.
>
> *Thus Spoke Zarathustra*

Yet, this approach is not for everyone. Not all men are equal and not all men are *Übermenschen*. Not everyone can react to the skepticism stemming from the death of God by turning themselves into a new god. The masses that have been guided for centuries by religious morality, by the drive to obey socially accepted norms, and by the need to be given a fixed designation of what is good and what is bad will remain the majority. Herd morality will continue to have the better of them, instilling the idea that mediocrity is strength rather than weakness, and that the qualities that the herd lacks are evil:

> High and independent spirituality, the will to stand alone, even a powerful reason are experienced as dangers; everything that elevates an individual above the herd and intimidates the neighbors is called evil.
>
> *Beyond Good and Evil*

For these people, the "something else" that will allow overcoming personal nihilism will come from the ideology of the day. The more pervasive the ideology, the more reassuring the result to its followers. These people will avoid personal and social nihilism by becoming the Last Man, the man who, like Candide in Voltaire's novel of the same name, believes he already lives in the best of all possible worlds. As his religious predecessor, the secular Last Man lives a quiet life of psychological comfort without thoughts for individuality or personal growth. Ultimately, this conformation process will be so entrenched and encompassing as to shape a world where there is

> no herdsman and one herd. Everyone wants the same thing, everyone is the same: whoever thinks otherwise goes voluntarily into the madhouse.
>
> *Thus Spoke Zarathustra*

As the Super Men are the few and the Last Men are the many, this condition is the world Nietzsche *sees* coming throughout his lifetime. He experiences a tumultuous nineteenth century, witnessing the consolidation of nationalism and imperialism, the rise of anarchism, trade unionism and socialist movements, and the first signs of feminism. Nietzsche did not live long enough to see the totalitarianisms of the twentieth century; yet the Nietzschean reader has often recognized in the Last Men's mentality the ideal psychological and social ground for such movements to breed, wherein masses of Last Men stood ready blindly to follow an encompassing, ready-to-use, secular, and high modernist *Weltanschauung*. Others have noticed a return to the Last Man's herd mentality on occasion since World War II. It has seen its influence in some movements on both the left and the right in Western democracies, particularly in those contexts in which efforts to standardize results within society have been characterized rather by homogenization than by merit or the encouragement and raising of the exceptional. Under such conditions, talent becomes suspicious, possibly associated with the charismatic, and therefore conceptually tied to superstition, religion, or even divine gift, which is then seen as unfair. There is a conceptual contradiction, of course, in acknowledging divine gift enough to see it as unfair, all the while denying God as relevant to the social or political order (e.g., "God is dead").

There is little scholarly agreement as to where Nietzsche's social analysis has led—or should have led—his normative political theory. This scholarly impasse arises because the large literature on Nietzsche's purported political philosophy is effectively built upon limited ground, to the extent that many question whether Nietzsche had any political philosophy at all.

On the one side, the proclamation that "God is dead" has often been understood by advocates of secularism in the West, to use Geertzian terms, as a *model for*[7] rather than a *model of* late-modern society and politics. That is, the death of God became for some a rallying cry, providing a blueprint for action rather than an empirical map.[8] For such fans, it became one foundation for the notion that secularization was part of the modernization process, while also being a normative justification of such a process. The followers of this understanding had their view reinforced by a wide range of especially rationalist liberal Enlightenment and post-Enlightenment think-

7. Clifford Geertz, *The Interpretation of Cultures* (New York: Basic Books, 1973), 93–95.

8. Geertz, *Interpretation of Cultures*, 93.

ers, including Karl Marx, who began writing before Nietzsche, Max Weber, and Émile Durkheim, all of whom conveyed in various ways the normative idea that the world's progress toward secularization was to be welcomed.[9] Thus, the *secularization thesis*, whose origin, in hindsight, can be seen as strictly entangled with the origin of the modern disciplines of sociology and political science, could confidently posit that, as societies modernize, and as nation-states expand their reach over societies, religion will decline. In this particular *Weltanschauung*, Nietzsche's analysis of European society echoed with a fairly common nineteenth-century belief that religion "would gradually fade in importance and cease to be significant with the advent of industrial society."[10]

A *secularization thesis* reading of Nietzsche's work might also conclude that, by Nietzsche's time, such ideas could rely on a strong and reputable track record in government. For example, the French Revolution, which predates *The Gay Science* by almost a century, had already created, through a difficult, protracted, and nonetheless successful process, a praxis of secularization in the public administration. The French Revolution led to a practical roadmap for "how to" modernize the state machine, its officials, the populace, and the (urban and rural) landscape, taking its bureaucratic and technocratic efficiencies to new levels.[11] In this sense, the French revolutionary state contributed

9. See, for example, Pippa Norris and Ronald Inglehart, *Sacred and Secular: Religion and Politics Worldwide*, 2nd ed. (New York: Cambridge University Press, 2011), 3–5, 7, 9; Craig Calhoun, "Secularism, Citizenship, and the Public Sphere," in *Rethinking Secularism*, ed. Craig Calhoun, Mark Juergensmeyer, and Jonathan Van Antwerpen (New York: Oxford University Press, 2011), 77–78; Saba Mahmoud, *Religious Difference in a Secular Age: A Minority Report* (Princeton: Princeton University Press, 2016), 33; Jocelyne Cesari, *The Awakening of Muslim Democracy: Religion, Modernity, and the State* (New York: Cambridge University Press, 2014), 5–6; Jonathan Fox, *Universal Human Rights: Political Secularism, Religion, and the State: A Time Series Analysis of Worldwide Data* (New York: Cambridge University Press, 2015), 18; Elizabeth Shakman Hurd, *The Politics of Secularism in International Relations* (Princeton: Princeton University Press, 2008), 25–28. For a critique of the historical development of the idea of the death of God in the United States, and particularly its connection with secularism as well as notions of scientific progress and what might be called, in contemporary terms, extreme production, see Denis Lacorne, George Holoch, and Tony Judt, *Religion in America: A Political History* (New York: Columbia University Press, 2011; first published as *De la religion en Amérique* [Paris: Editions Gallimard, 2007]), 106, 119, 122.

10. Norris and Inglehart, *Sacred and Secular*, 3.

11. See James C. Scott, *Seeing Like a State: How Certain Schemes to Improve the Human Condition Have Failed* (New Haven: Yale University Press, 1999). See also Michael Mann,

a material precedent: societies that wanted to be modern and efficient must secularize. For these views, Nietzsche's tragic cry that "God is dead" became one of the foundations for justifying the secularization process.

Yet, from a historical perspective, such clear-cut exegesis of Nietzsche's thought is unwarranted. To begin with, the description of the death of God does not strike the Nietzschean reader as an entirely good thing, at least from a sociological perspective:

> When one gives up the Christian faith, one pulls the right to Christian morality out from under one's feet. This morality is by no means self-evident. . . . Christianity is a system, a whole view of things thought out together. By breaking one main concept out of it, the faith in God, one breaks the whole.
>
> *Twilight of the Idols*

Just as the individual finds himself struggling with the psychological consequences of losing the idea of God, so a society needs to find new sources of legitimacy in order to organize itself. Yet, herein lies a paradox: What is the nature of this new legitimacy? If society drops the idea of the ontological existence of God—if "everything is false"—subsequently to embrace a new credo, is not society substituting one false belief for another (as Nietzsche feared, God for nihilism—or relativism)? And what is this other belief that should be embraced in exchange for God? Nietzsche attacks all the modern moral or political surrogates for God—trade unionism, democracy, feminism, socialism—*and the state*. Nietzsche does not trust the *state*, and even less so the secular social contract upon which it is ostensibly based. On the contrary, his hostility is evident:

> A state? What is that? . . . State is the name of the coldest of all cold monsters.
>
> Coldly lies it also; and this lie creeps from its mouth: "I, the state, am the people." It is a lie! . . . Destroyers, are they who lay traps for many, and call it the state.
>
> *Thus Spoke Zarathustra*

The Sources of Social Power Volume II: The Rise of Classes and Nation-States, 1760–1914 (New York: Cambridge University Press, 1993); and Theda Skocpol, *States and Social Revolutions* (New York: Cambridge University Press, 1979).

Nietzsche could hardly be seen as an advocate of secularism, at least in the sense of being a proponent of a modern and centralized state founded upon a contract. To the contrary, he saw the state's effort to appropriate the space and authority that religion had once held as just that—negative appropriation.[12] Many agree in crediting Nietzsche with skepticism for rationalist forms of political power held by the state,[13] including Tamsin Shaw, who stresses Nietzsche's hostility toward the state.[14]

With this skepticism of secular power in mind, it seems legitimate to the current analysis to read Nietzsche's death of God as presenting a violent and illegitimate crime of the secularists against monarchy and its religious foundations. With the disposal of the divine right of kings, which had characterized the *ancien régime*, first in France and later in Nietzsche's Prussia, as well as other European countries swept by regime change in 1848,[15] Nietzsche warns that traditional slavery to a potentially false God only risks being substituted by even more irrational and uncertain beliefs.

THE ORIGIN OF SECULAR POLITICAL POWER

While the normative interpretation of Nietzsche's political philosophy remains controversial, there is no doubt as to the centrality that Nietzschean thought on psychology and social organizations has acquired in subsequent debates on religion and politics. For, if human nature is congenial to superior aims, if the hunt for meaning is the defining feature of the human condition, and if the vast majority of people remain incapable of finding such meaning within themselves, having to rely instead on externalized authori-

---

12. Tamsin Shaw, *Nietzsche's Political Skepticism* (Princeton: Princeton University Press, 2009).

13. Elizabeth Shakman Hurd, *The Politics of Secularism in International Relations* (Princeton: Princeton University Press, 2008), 45.

14. See Tamsin Shaw, *Nietzsche's Political Skepticism*, 12: "Nietzsche had . . . come to the conclusion that religious belief had been discredited and was destined to die out. But we do not find in his work any celebration of victory on behalf of the secular political powers. Instead we find an increasingly cautious and even hostile attitude to the state and its ideological approach."

15. See Karl Polanyi, *The Great Transformation: The Political and Economic Origins of Our Time* (New York: Beacon Press, 2001), and Eric Hobsbawm, *The Age of Revolution: 1798–1848* (New York: Vintage Books, 1996).

ties embodying superior values, then the question of the alternative to God is the question of the alternative to traditional sources of political legitimacy. Hence, the question of what could become a functional alternative to the ontological existence of God is intrinsically linked to the question of what political order is there beyond God.

By the time that Nietzsche began writing about religion and society, the interpretative question of the origin and legitimacy of secular power had already been debated by social contract theorists for over two centuries. In *The Leviathan,* which was published only three years after the signing of the Peace of Westphalia, Thomas Hobbes had firmly underpinned the sovereign's right to impose civil society even against his subjects' own will. In a post-Westphalian world freed from the yoke of the two universal authorities who had commanded spiritual and temporal authority throughout the Middle Ages—the pope and the emperor—absolute sovereignty was justified upon people's pragmatic desire to escape the prospect of living a "solitary, poor, nasty, brutish, short" life outside of society. Because of the importance of the matter at stake, the subjects of the Leviathan have no right to revolution. Moreover, Hobbes asserts that even when the sovereign's laws occasionally contradict God's *prophetical* laws, his subjects must still obey the sovereign's laws.

While the work of subsequent social contract theorists—most notably, John Locke and Jean-Jacques Rousseau—maintained more balanced approaches to the rights and duties of the citizen and the state, notably establishing the citizens' right of rebellion against the state, this refitting continued to be done at God's expense. In particular, Locke explicitly refuted the idea that kings rule according to divine right, arguing that human beings have human rights upon which no one can infringe. He also maintained that neither knowledge nor faith demand the use of force against persons who differ intellectually or religiously. Writing almost a century later, Rousseau considered the advantages and drawbacks of different types of religion upon societal organizations, eventually concluding in favor of a religious tolerance in which religion was effectively relegated to the sphere of matters of private conscience.

Thus, in the 200 years separating the Peace of Westphalia from Nietzsche, the international political system had already placed the legitimacy of political power above the emperor and beyond God (the pope). Mainstream political philosophy, on its side, had sanctioned the view that the state was the depository of original (e.g., not derived), absolute (*superiorem non reco-*

gnoscens), inalienable, and imprescriptible power. To this extent, Nietzsche's death of God is considerably more original in portraying the revolutionary changes existent in the belief systems of contemporary European societies leading up to his time, as they moved toward *modernism* understood as a particular type of social development,[16] than it was involved in justifying any alternative, subsequent political system emerging from these processes.

The "death of God" is the expression of a new age and a new cultural movement, Romanticism, describing in three words how this new era related to both the dismissal of the idea of the ontological existence of God and the percolation of such an idea through the European low and middle classes, a process otherwise known as the *secularization thesis*.

This was a process happening over several generations. Karl Marx, who was one generation older that Nietzsche, held the belief that religion was a symptom of all that was wrong in society and thought that it would eventually die out when a perfect socialist state would eventually be achieved. Durkheim, who was a contemporary of Nietzsche, thought that, as society modernizes, the role of religion, which is primarily to bind people together, was progressively becoming redundant. The fundamental social bonds that religion constituted in villages were destined to be broken as people moved to cities. As with Nietzsche, Durkheim expressed some concern about this process and was not a wholesale advocate of all changes related to it, as seen in his works on suicide, anomie, and the lost social solidarity of the extended patriarchal family. Max Weber, who was a generation younger than Nietzsche, reflected upon the sociological consequences of the rise of scientific knowledge, concluding that the application of rational and bureaucratic standards in life would eventually create a way of reasoning destined to take the magic out of religion.[17] In different ways, all these thinkers were evolutionary—their theories are tied to the idea of progress toward an ulti-

---

16. Steve Bruce, who is explicitly indebted to Max Weber, has defined modernization as "the rationalization of thought and public life; increasing individualism, egalitarianism, and social diversity; industrialization and growth in technological consciousness; structural-functional differentiation; increased social differentiation; increased literary and education; democratization; the demographic transition from high fertility and high death rates to low death rates and low fertility; and urbanization." Steve Bruce, "Secularization Elsewhere: It Is More Complicated Than That," in *Política & Sociedade* 16, no. 36 (2017): 196–97.

17. While we do not claim to have a deep expertise on Weber's extensive works in comparative sociology of religion, we note that some parts of the general framework we mention can be found in Max Weber, *The Sociology of Religion*, introduction by Talcott Parsons, foreword by Ann Swidler (Boston: Beacon Books, [1963] 1993).

mate ideal of modernism. For some of them, in their own turn, the ideas of modernism and progress become bound up with the idea of nation-states expanding their reach in society.

The secularization thesis survived throughout the first half of the twentieth century, and arguably strengthened in its second half, sustained by a number of theoretical refinements. Writing from the 1960s onward, Brian Wilson of Oxford University points to key distinctions between different types of secularization, suggesting that "religion—seen as a way of thinking, as the performance of particular practices and as the institutionalization and organization of these patterns of thought and actions—has lost influence."[18] Wilson thus traces this loss of influence at three levels: (1) the societal; (2) the individual; and (3) the institutional and organizational levels.[19] Typically referring to the Catholic Church, Wilson notices that religion has lost authority over people's private lives, the organization of their communities, and its own capacity to propose substantive values that give social significance to religion and that allow people to socialize. David Martin, a British sociologist of religion, also worked on refining secularization theory in the 1960s; in particular, he analyzes "under what conditions religious institutions, like churches and sects, become less powerful and how it comes about that religious beliefs are less easily accepted."[20] He does so by looking at the specific role played by religion in specific societies and at specific historical junctures. Martin argues that religion has a tendency to be identified with a particular political position and concludes that, by observing the role of churches in defending national identities and in relating to reactionary and revolutionary forces, it is possible to explain the amount of influence they hold over society.

Steve Bruce's work portrays the secularization paradigm as not a "single concept," while bringing powerful empirical evidence to the general idea that "a long-term decline in the power, popularity and prestige of religious beliefs and rituals [caused] individualism, diversity and egalitarianism in the context of liberal democracy."[21] In particular, Bruce brings hard data into the debate, showing how the declining importance of religion in the West can be measured empirically.

18. Karel Dobbelaere, "Bryan Wilson's Contribution to the Study of Secularization," *Social Compass* 53, no. 2 (2006): 141–46.

19. Dobbelaere, "Bryan Wilson's Contribution to the Study of Secularization."

20. David Martin, *A General Theory of Secularization* (New York: Harper and Row, 1978).

21. Steve Bruce, *God Is Dead: Secularization in the West* (Oxford: Blackwell, 2002).

THE EPISTEMOLOGY OF RELIGION AND POLITICS

Until the 1980s, while remarkable analytical works on religion persisted in many disciplines,[22] religion was somehow segregated to second-class status in political science and international relations. Throughout the twentieth century, Western political scientists and international relations theorists continued to treat religion as an anomaly to be corrected rather than to be studied by unpacking its impacts upon, interactions with, or influences from society and politics. The presumed anomaly of religion came in part because the prevailing theories in these disciplines continued reading the world through the prism of social contract and the secularization thesis under the assumption that, at least in the West, the separation between religious beliefs and political legitimacy was a manifest, unambiguous fact.

In these academic disciplines, the death of God was seen as an accomplished phenomenon, the natural arrival point of an ideational trajectory that, from the Reformation through the European religious wars, the Peace of Westphalia, the rise of modern science, the French Revolution, the creation of modern state bureaucracies, and to the present had shaped the ultimate model of secular society. These standards have since been presented through international organizations of various types as the standard to which nondemocratic societies should strive to conform.

During the Cold War years, socialist alternatives from the Soviet Union to the People's Republic of China, as well as their many satellite allies scattered across Eastern Europe, Asia, Africa, and Latin America, only seemed to confirm such prevailing views on the separation between religion and politics, even competing with Western rhetoric in representing the expression(s) of the people in governments. During these years of bipolar confrontation, some religious societies across the world—particularly across the Middle East and Asia—effectively renounced their primary religious identity and accepted secular political institutions (at least formally, and not without internal conflict) in order to access support from one or the other camp.

---

22. Complementary to the works mentioned so far, see also Mircea Eliade, *The Sacred and the Profane: The Nature of Religion* (New York: Harcourt Brace, 1959); Claude Levi-Strauss, *The Savage Mind* (Chicago: University of Chicago Press, 1962); Mary Douglas, *Purity and Danger: An Analysis of the Concepts of Pollution and Taboo* (New York: Routledge, 1966); Victor Turner, *The Ritual Process: Structure and Anti-Structure* (New York: Aldine de Gruyter, 1969); and Clifford Geertz, *The Religion of Java*, erev. ed. (Chicago: University of Chicago Press, 1976).

As a result, throughout the twentieth century, the default epistemological approach in mainstream political science and international relations remained an "unquestioned acceptance of the secularist division between religion and politics."[23] Within this narrative, the existing contact points between religious and state institutions—including religious-inspired political parties and state-recognized or state-controlled churches—were understood as carefully defined and strictly regulated by the state itself. All indications of a persistent religious meddling in politics were either downplayed or seen as exceptions to be corrected.

It is only recently, with the crisis of the secularization theory itself, that it has appeared increasingly evident that the very conceptual arena inhabited by the idea of a separation between religion and politics had always been socially and historically constructed rather than ontologically given. Moreover, these socially and historically constructed concepts owed far more to religious structures and worldviews than the secularists were ready to accept.

First, the very "ideological conditions that give point and force to the theoretical apparatuses employed to describe and objectify" the secular and the religious[24] were themselves religious. They came from what Elizabeth Hurd defines as "Judeo-Christian secularism," that is, the idea that religion can be disentangled from social action, that its principles pertain to specific religions rather than to all religions, and that it is unthinkable to assume that such a Judeo-Christian-West-oriented worldview might be compatible with or even comparable with other religions, particularly including Islam. Far from being religiously or ideologically neutral, secular political authority as it emerged in Europe was historically constructed and was "deeply" Christian from its origins in the Peace of Westphalia onward.[25] Indeed, some of the forms that it has taken have been precisely dominating rather than creating a liberating neutrality, particularly vis-à-vis religious traditions for which separation of religion from the public sphere is antithetical to foundational principles or to people's lived existence, or both.[26]

Second, long-held epistemological positions in political science and international relations had affirmatively answered the question of whether

23. Hurd, *Politics of Secularism*, 1.

24. David Scott and Charles Hirschkind, "Introduction: The Anthropological Skepticism of Talal Asad," in *Powers of the Secular Modern: Talal Asad and His Interlocutors*, ed. David Scott and Charles Hirschkind (Palo Alto: Stanford University Press, 2006), 3.

25. Hurd, *Politics of Secularism*, 1, 3, 5–6, 25.

26. Hurd, *Politics of Secularism*, 3, 27. See also Mahmoud, *Religious Difference*.

purposefully using secularization as a blueprint for changing societies and states (e.g., in a normative view) was the only possible approach to studying religion and politics. That is, the question of whether secularization could be an empirical phenomenon simply to be observed, analyzed, and commented upon in the same way that other political phenomena are treated (e.g., a non-normative analytical view), did not arise until recent years. Instead, Western political scientists have long been more concerned with normative political theory, by implementing a modernization always understood inherently to include secularization, than with comprehending or theorizing religion and politics on their own terms throughout various religious, cultural, national, and regional empirical contexts.[27] These academic perspectives have been mirrored in many Western foreign policy efforts bent on establishing pro-Western secular governments, often in otherwise overwhelmingly religious societies.

With the end of the Cold War and the growing importance of nationalist centrifugal forces backed by religious components—in the former Soviet

27. Elizabeth Shakman Hurd explains in some detail that the US government did include religion in international policy considerations even in the mid-twentieth century when modernization theory and the secularization thesis were predominant. According to Hurd, these policies occurred mainly in the context of the Cold War and involved the encouragement of certain forms of religion that would be peaceful and supportive of US interests. The American Political Science Association was, at the time, cognizant of these efforts and formally supported certain of these policy initiatives. Contrary to the implicit claims in some of the works in this volume, Hurd argues *against* the inclusion of religion as an organizing principle around which some human rights frameworks should be structured in the international legal arena. See Elizabeth Shakman Hurd, *Beyond Religious Freedom: The New Global Politics of Religion* (Princeton: Princeton University Press, 2015), 69–70, and chapter 6. Regarding the tendency of disciplinary research in the mid-twentieth century through at least the 1980s to address religion in terms of modernization and secularization, see, for example, Daniel Lerner, *The Passing of Traditional Society: Modernizing the Middle East* (New York: Free Press, 1958); Gabriel A. Almond and Sidney Verba, *The Civic Culture: Political Attitudes and Democracy in Five Nations* (Princeton: Princeton University Press, 1963); David E. Apter, *The Modernization Process* (Chicago: University of Chicago Press, 1965); Donal Cruise O'Brien, "Modernization, Order, and the Erosion of a Democratic Ideal: American Political Science 1960–70," *Journal of Development Studies* 8, no. 4 (1972): 351–78; Dean Tipps, "Modernization Theory and the Comparative Study of National Societies: A Critical Perspective," *Comparative Studies in Society and History* 15, no. 2 (March 1973): 199–226; and Zehra F. Arat, "Democracy and Economic Development: Modernization Theory Revisited," *Comparative Politics* 21, no. 1 (1988): 21–36.

Union as in the Balkans and other regions—some scholars reevaluated the weight of religion in comparative politics. Scholars such as Mark Tessler[28] and Samuel Huntington[29] were in the vanguard of changing the predominant epistemology regarding religion and politics by making the rather Weberian[30] suggestion that religion and culture could have a great impact not only on local or national dynamics but on international affairs as well. Tessler, for example, was among the first political scientists to note, as early as 1980, that religion in the Middle East was on an upsurge, in contravention to the expectations of the secularization thesis.[31] Tessler pioneered the field of religion and public opinion research in the Middle East and North Africa (as well as public opinion in other topical areas in the region); his work on Islam, Judaism, gender, identity politics, and democracy has sought to establish statistical and causal relationships between religion, national politics,

28. See Mark Tessler, "The Identity of Religious Minorities in Non-Secular States: Jews in Tunisia and Morocco and Arabs in Israel," *Comparative Studies in Society and History* 20, no. 3 (1979): 359–78; Mark Tessler, "Political Change and the Islamic Revival in Tunisia," *Maghreb Review* 5, no. 1 (1980): 8–19; Mark Tessler, "The Political Culture of Jews in Tunisia and Morocco," *International Journal of Middle East Studies* 11, no. 1 (1980): 59–86; Jamal Sanad and Mark Tessler, "Women and Religion in a Modern Islamic Society: The Case of Kuwait," in *The Politics of Religious Resurgence in the Contemporary World*, ed. Emile Sahliyeh (Albany: State University of New York Press, 1990); and Mark Tessler, "The Origins of Popular Support for Islamist Movements: A Political Economy Analysis," in *Islam, Democracy, and the State in North Africa*, ed. John P. Entelis (Bloomington: Indiana University Press, 1997).

29. See Samuel Huntington's highly controversial work on the "clash of civilizations," positing a potential "Islamo-Confucian Bloc" with which Western secularists may have to contend: Samuel P. Huntington, "The Clash of Civilizations?," *Foreign Affairs* 72, no. 3 (1993): 22–49. See also Samuel Huntington, "Religion and the Third Wave," *National Interest* 24 (1991): 29–42; Samuel Huntington, "Transnational Organizations in World Politics," *World Politics* 25, no. 3 (1973): 333–68; and Samuel Huntington, *Who Are We? The Challenges to America's National Identity* (New York: Simon and Schuster, 2004). For work on the vanguard of bringing religion into the study of American politics, see Kenneth D. Wald, Dennis E. Owen, and Samuel S. Hill, "Political Cohesion in Churches," *Journal of Politics* 52, no. 1 (1990): 197–215; Clyde Wildox and Ted Jelen, "Evangelicals and Political Tolerance," *American Politics Quarterly* 18, no. 1 (1990): 25–46; David C. Leege and Lyman A. Kellstedt, eds., *Rediscovering the Religious Factor in American Politics* (Armonk, NY: M. E. Sharpe, 1993); and Kenneth D. Wald and Corwin E. Smidt, "Measurement Strategies in the Study of Religion and Politics," in Leege and Kellstedt, *Rediscovering the Religious Factor*.

30. Max Weber, *The Protestant Ethic and the Spirit of Capitalism*, trans. with commentary by Stephen Kalberg (Oxford: Oxford University Press, 2010).

31. Tessler, "Political Change and the Islamic Revival in Tunisia," 1980.

cultural factors, and international politics in those contexts.[32] And, while Samuel Huntington's work has been at times controversial, he was one of the early scholars to bring the attention of comparative political scientists to religion and politics as an empirical area of study. Like Weber, Huntington's work presents religion and cultural variables as potentially causal in world-historical political analysis. In many ways, Huntington,[33] like John Esposito in religious studies,[34] energized the field in the 1990s. The rise of terrorist-linked organizations such as Al Qaeda in the early 2000s, moreover, contributed to creating interest around religion and security studies, and, more broadly, around cross-national studies, effectively highlighting the continuing universality of religion in society and politics.[35]

THE ONTOLOGY OF RELIGION AND POLITICS

While the twentieth century's commanding epistemology on the subject of "religion and politics" was coming from scholars imbued with Western secularism, it appears increasingly evident that the ontology of their studies was deeply, and increasingly, removed from such a vision. The Western—and, especially, the US and French—emphasis on the strict separation of religion and state have made these countries outlier cases rather than average models

32. For work in more recent decades, see Mark Tessler and Eleanor Gao, "Gauging Arab Support for Democracy," *Journal of Democracy* 16, no. 3 (2005): 83–97; Mark Tessler and Michael D. H. Robbins, "What Leads Some Ordinary Arab Men and Women to Approve of Terrorist Acts against the United States?," *Journal of Conflict Resolution* 51, no. 2 (2007): 305–28; Mansoor Moaddel, Mark Tessler, and Ronald Inglehart, "Foreign Occupation and National Pride: The Case of Iraq," *Public Opinion Quarterly* 72, no. 4 (2008): 677–705; Mark Tessler, "Religion, Religiosity and the Place of Islam in Political Life: Insights from the Arab Barometer Surveys," *Middle East Law and Governance* 2, no. 2 (2010): 221–52; Mark Tessler, Amaney Jamal, and Michael Robbins, "New Findings on Arabs and Democracy," *Journal of Democracy* 23, no. 4 (2012): 89–103.

33. Huntington, "Clash of Civilizations?"

34. See, for example, John Esposito, *Voices of Resurgent Islam* (Oxford: Oxford University Press, 1983); John Esposito, "Sudan's Islamic Experiment," *Muslim World* 76, nos. 3–4 (1986): 181–202; John Esposito, ed., *The Islamic Revolution: Its Global Impact* (Gainesville: University Press of Florida, 1990); John Esposito and James Piscatori, "Democratization and Islam," *Middle East Journal* 45, no. 3 (1991): 427–40; and John Esposito, "Political Islam: Beyond the Green Menace," *Current History* 93, no. 579 (1994): 19–24.

35. Norris and Inglehart, *Sacred and Secular.*

of religion, society, and politics around the world.[36] One need only think of the dozens of religious-inspired political events throughout the twentieth century—both toward the secular, as in Mustafa Kemal Ataturk's Turkey, and toward the religious, as in Ayatollah Ruhollah Khomeini's Iran—to realize that such a world could not be understood without factoring religious determinants into the equation.

The weight of religion in politics is arguably even more evident in the twenty-first-century international community, where more than 20 percent of countries have an official state religion, and a further 20 percent have a preferred or favored religion—while 5 percent of states either tightly regulate religious institutions or actively ostracize them.[37] That is to say, almost half (45%) of the world's governments have an official religion, a preferred religion, or tight regulations against religion; at the same time, these figures do not reflect some of the more nuanced ways in which religion and politics may interact or affect one another in the remaining 55 percent of countries worldwide.

As expected, the two-in-five states that have a privileged relationship with religious institutions are primarily located in developing regions, including the Middle East, North Africa, and Latin America. Because of the contrasting demographic trends between these regions and the developed regions of the world, there are today more people with a religious *Weltanschauung* than ever before. Crucially, these constituencies also represent an ever-growing proportion of the world's population.[38]

This empirical datum is also what indirectly emerges from this collection: the broad summa of the different contributions to this volume is that, while Nietzsche's "death of God" might have given momentum to secular forces in the West throughout the nineteenth and twentieth centuries, God was proliferating in the rest of the world to a far greater extent.

Outside Europe, very few countries were witnessing secularization

36. Norris and Inglehart, *Sacred and Secular*, 4.

37. Pew Research Center, "Many Countries Favor Specific Religions, Officially or Unofficially" (Washington, DC: Pew Research Center, 2017).

38. "With rising levels of existential security, the publics of virtually all advanced industrial societies have been moving toward more secular orientations during at least the past fifty years. Earlier perceptions of this process gave rise to the mistaken assumption that religion was disappearing. 'God is Dead,' proclaimed Nietzsche more than a century ago. A massive body of empirical evidence points to a very different conclusion." Norris and Inglehart, *Sacred and Secular*, 240.

phenomena,[39] while even in the West religion was playing more continuing institutional and political roles than normative accounts of modernization often suggest. Inside Europe, the expression of this continuing salience has taken different shapes.

First, belief in the traditional God is still prominent in a number of countries, ranging from 95 percent in Roman Catholic Malta to 16 percent in Lutheran Estonia.[40] Generally speaking, Roman Catholic countries in Europe have high degrees of religious belief, excepting France, in which belief (34%) is almost the same as nonbelief (33%).[41] Salience can be found in countries in which religious communities and institutions have formalized relationships with the (secularized) institutions of the state,[42] as well as in cases in which formal separation corresponds with a powerful historical legacy associated with one religion.[43]

Second, religion and religious identities have continued to show a predominant role in the relatively few conflicts the continent has witnessed after 1945—from Northern Ireland to the Balkans to the multiple fracture lines inside the former Soviet Union: Abkhazia, Chechnya, and, more recently, between Russia and Ukraine.

Third, religion has an overwhelming presence in identity and material exclusion, a phenomenon that continues to be used as a basis for domestic national unity: in a number of European democracies, it is the norm to see strong divisive patterns along overlapping ethnic, religious, social, economic, and professional cleavages, to the extent that segregation has brought some metropolitan areas to vast protests, or even riots, as happened in Paris

---

39. José Casanova mentions New Zealand and Uruguay as possibly the only countries with a similar development to Europe. In José Casanova, "Religion, European Secular Identities and European Integration," in *Religion in an Expanding Europe*, ed. Timothy Byrnes and Peter Katzenstein (New York: Cambridge University Press, 2006).

40. See *Special Eurobarometer*, "Social Values, Science, and Technology" June (Brussels: European Commission, 2005).

41. *Special Eurobarometer*, "Social Values, Science, and Technology."

42. Silvio Ferrari and Rosella Bottoni, "The Institutionalization of Islam in Europe," in *The Oxford Handbook of European Islam*, ed. Jocelyne Cesari (Oxford: Oxford University Press, 2015). See also Christopher Sopher and Joel Fetzer, "Religious Institutions, Church-State History, and Muslim Mobilization in Britain, France, and Germany," *Journal of Ethnic and Migration Studies* 33, no. 6 (2007): 933–44.

43. See John Richard Bowen, *Why the French Don't Like Headscarves: Islam, the State, and Public Space* (Princeton: Princeton University Press, 2007), 60, 20.

in 2005.[44] With some caveats, the terror wave that has swept the US and Europe since 2001 can also be framed as one of correlation between religious communities and the socioeconomic exclusion of the groups or subgroups they represent.[45]

Fourth, as noticed by Peter Berger, since the post-Reformation era, religion has also taken different and less orthodox forms of manifestation. For example, indications of religious influence in Europe can increasingly be found in loosely constrained, and nonetheless highly pervasive, attitudinal factors, such as belief in some type of "spirit" or "life-force" (a sort of "new age" way of talking about divinity). Such views remain high in Estonia, 54 percent; the Czech Republic, 50 percent; Sweden, 53 percent; and, to a lesser degree, France, 27 percent. In some states, belief in God and belief in "spirit" or "life-force" combines in high degrees: Slovenia, 37 percent God / 46 percent spirit (a combined 83% belief in God or spirit); Latvia, 37 percent God / 49 percent spirit (a combined 86%); and the United Kingdom, 38 percent God / 40 percent spirit (a combined 78%).[46]

The third and fourth points above are also to be found in the United States, where religious institutions are strictly separated from state institutions. In particular, religiosity remains high (approximately 83% certain or fairly certain belief in God in 2014).[47] These numbers are even higher in

---

44. The 2005 French riots saw thousands of youth, mostly from the Maghreb and sub-Saharan Africa, engaging in the burning of 10,000 cars and the ransacking of 300 public buildings. These were only the latest episodes of a long string of violent demonstrations by Muslim minorities in France. See Fabien Jobard, "An Overview of French Riots: 1981–2004" (HAL, 2015), https://hal.archives-ouvertes.fr/hal-00550788/document

45. The poverty-terrorism link is highly contested. Recently, while noticing how "most individual-level studies of terrorist groups have concluded that these groups are composed of people wealthier and better educated than the average member of the societies from which they recruit," political scientist Alexander Lee has concluded that "members of violent groups . . . tend to be lower status individuals from the educated and politicized section of the population." That is, compared to the population as a whole, terrorists tend to be wealthier and better educated; however, compared to the politically involved and nonviolent subgroups pertaining to similar ideologies, terrorists tend to have a lower social status measured by education and employment. In Alexander Lee, "Who Becomes a Terrorist? Poverty, Education, and the Origins of Political Violence," *World Politics* 63, no. 2 (2011): 203–45.

46. See *Special Eurobarometer*, "Social Values, Science, and Technology."

47. "2014 Religious Landscape Study (RLS-II), Main Survey of Nationally Representative Sample of Adults, Final Questionnaire," May 30 (Washington, DC: Pew Research Center, 2014).

the US South (approximately 87% certain or fairly certain belief in God in 2014).[48] Nationally, religious practice in the United States is moderate to high (approximately 36 percent weekly service attendance, and another 33 percent twice a month to a few times per year service attendance, meaning 69 percent religiously engaged to some degree in terms of religious practice);[49] while religious practice, per se, tends to be lower in Europe.[50]

Thus, even in paradigmatic Western cases of "secularism," religion remains important either directly in relation to political institutions or in the various forms of interaction among specific communities (religious or secular, or both), local, and national political issues. It is a truism today, for example, to note the significance of Christianity in US politics since the late 1960s.[51] While scholars have tended to address the impact of religion and migration on national and regional politics as being more salient for Europe than for the United States,[52] such an assessment may change in coming years.

Ignoring these trends due to normative proclivities—or, perhaps, only to habits of mind—that suggest modernizing is inherently tied to secularization makes opaque an empirical world that it is important to know. The notion advocated in some religious contexts that modernism and religion are *not* inherently oppositional bears serious consideration, and deserves more attention than only the dismissive turn of the hand.[53] Indeed, the continuing

---

48. "2014 Religious Landscape Study." See summary results, religion in the US South.

49. "2014 Religious Landscape Study." See summary results, religious service attendance (national).

50. Parts of the discussion of the Eurobarometer and Pew Research Center surveys herein has been presented previously in a blog piece, Patricia Sohn, "Inhabiting Orthodoxy: Discussing Islam and Feminism, Continued," *E-International Relations*, December 9, 2016. It is presented here with permission.

51. Andrew Lewis, *The Rights Turn in Conservative Christian Politics: How Abortion Transformed the Culture Wars* (New York: Cambridge University Press, 2018).

52. See Jocelyne Cesari, *Why the West Fears Islam: An Exploration of Muslims in Liberal Democracies* (New York: Palgrave Macmillan, 2013); Paul Sniderman, Michael Pedersen, Rune Slothuus, and Rune Stubager, *Paradoxes of Liberal Democracy: Islam, Western Europe, and the Danish Cartoon Crisis* (Princeton: Princeton University Press, 2014); Joel Fetzer and Christopher Soper, *Muslims and the State* (New York: Cambridge University Press, 2005); Christian Joppke, *The Secular State under Siege: Religion and Politics in Europe and America* (Cambridge: Polity Press, 2015; and Claire de Galembert, "The City's 'Nod of Approval' for the Mantes-la-Jolie Mosque Project: Mistaken Traces of Recognition," *Journal of Ethnic and Migration Studies* 31, no. 6 (2005): 1141–59.

53. See Saba Mahmood, *Politics of Piety: The Islamic Revival and the Feminist Subject*

salience of religion in politics—even in the West—appears to bear out some parts of this basic idea simply on the empirical merits. That is, the reality of the place of religion in politics today is significant for hard geopolitical reasons of "failures of imagination,"[54] as well as for more lofty reasons of pure science seeking to know the real world as it exists rather than as we wish to imagine it.[55] Indeed, the two may well be related in various contexts—that is, we are only as good as our scholarship.

THE VOLUME

This volume is based upon the qualitative methodology of *triangulation*—that is, the use of multiple themes, data sources, and data analyses as a deliberate methodology to enhance the comprehensiveness of the discussion. Triangulation is one methodological answer to addressing complex and difficult topics, or controversial claims. It calls for the use of multiple methods and types of data in order to achieve sufficient methodological leverage in regard to the question at hand: if all—or most—arrows point in the same direction, then we have increased the degree of confidence in the claim being made. While these degrees of confidence are not numeric in qualitative case study research, they are, nonetheless, the tangible difference between compelling or not compelling, as arguments go. Thus, while the contributors to the volume differ in their methodological approaches, the architecture of the collection remains geared to the ultimate finality of discussing the common question: How, where, why, and through which

(Princeton: Princeton University Press, 20015), 117, and Lara Deeb, *An Enchanted Modern: Gender and Public Piety in Shi'i Lebanon* (Princeton: Princeton University Press, 2006), 19, 25, 143. In Fazlur Rahman, *Islam and Modernity: Transformation of an Intellectual Tradition* (Chicago: University of Chicago Press, 1982), 67, 74, see, for example, schools of thought seeking to rediscover "modernity" in the origins of Islam, as well as modern scientific disciplines emerging from medieval Islamic sciences.

54. Erik Dahl, *Intelligence and Surprise Attack: Failure and Success from Pearl Harbor to 9/11 and Beyond* (Washington, DC: Georgetown University Press, 2013); see also Thomas H. Kean and Lee H. Hamilton, *The 9/11 Commission Report: Final Report of the National Commission on Terrorist Attacks upon the United States* (Washington, DC: Superintendent of Documents, Government Publishing Office, 2004).

55. See Thomas Kuhn, *The Structure of Scientific Revolutions, 50th Anniversary Edition*, introduction by Ian Hacking (Chicago: University of Chicago Press, 2012), 111.

modalities does religion matter across different sociopolitical micro and macro contexts?

What unites an otherwise heterogeneous set of chapters is therefore the discussion of how religion affects, interacts with, and transforms society and politics throughout the many thematic, theoretical, geographical, and historical intersections analyzed in the volume. It is the similar conclusion across regions, cases, theories, and modalities of analysis that strengthens the basic finding: religion matters, and it matters increasingly, not decreasingly, to politics.

We see *triangulation* as an opportunity to bring together multiple perspectives around the many facets of the rich and controversial relation between religion and politics. We see this multipoint, multilayered, and multicontextual approach as a resource in bringing strength to the collection's ultimate claim: the grip of religion over politics is strong and clearly on the rise, both outside and inside the Western world.

The collection offers case study analyses looking both at Western and non-Western cases, as well as including "East meets West" political and cultural debates. All chapters are unified by the methodological question of building theory—in this case, theories regarding the relationship between religion and politics—using case study research.

Authors build "theory" in various ways. Some case studies develop theories regarding patterned institutional, social, or individual dynamics or factors in which religion affects or is affected by politics. That is, the arrow may go in either direction depending upon the study; religion may be an independent or a dependent variable. Others link their case studies to social theory and ask how their cases may expand upon that social theory, or may reinforce it. Still others suggest ways in which their cases may require that we ask jarring new questions of existing social theories with which we have become perhaps too comfortable. Others yet again remain more comfortable with existing social theories but use their case studies to stretch those theories further than before, or in ways that are surprising to the current generation. There may be historical antecedents for this "stretching," or periods in which it was the norm; so, such conceptual "stretching" may not be so much *nouveau* as a renewal of past interpretations. Some chapters test hypotheses against empirical data, be those data qualitative or quantitative in nature, while others make the theoretical attempt to draw broad operating principles from the qualitative or quantitative data before them. In all of these ways, the case studies in this volume offer new empirical information regarding the panoply that is religion and politics in the world today, drawing upon cases from Europe, the Middle East, Africa and Asia.

The ethos of this volume strives to step beyond the assumption that "either a country is prodemocracy, pro-Western, and secular, or it is religious, tribal, and theocratic."[56] By leveraging empirical research, the volume offers, instead, detailed studies of how, where, and why religion matters in contemporary sociopolitical (thematic or country) contexts, and what we might be able to learn from the patterns discerned therein.

The volume is organized into six sections: Introduction and Comparative Themes; Christianity in Europe; Islam in Africa and the Middle East; Judaism in the Middle East; and Hinduism, Buddhism, and Syncretic Religions in Asia. Each section begins with an introduction by the editors framing the methodological, substantive, and theoretical contributions of each chapter, and the relation of the section as a whole to the volume. A commentary by one veteran scholar of religion and politics in the Introduction and Comparative Themes section offers insights into how this volume fits into current debates regarding religion and politics within political science.

In all, the studies in this volume present a nuanced picture of specific cases, and a broadly global or theoretical picture of the phenomenon of religion and politics through country and thematic case studies. They draw upon social theory, offer taxonomies, and bring our attention to variations in the specific mechanisms, variables, institutional, and ideational factors through which religion matters to politics in different country cases and regions. For example, theological debates are significant in some places, whereas communal issues are more prominent in others. Factors internal to religion itself are significant in some cases, whereas exogenous or international trends relating to religion and politics are more critical in others, depending on locale and time period. Local context matters in all cases. Quantitative and material analyses are used in some case studies together with qualitative data and analyses, while many draw upon qualitative data only. Most studies use some form of causal (or, perhaps, neo-Positive) analysis. Broad philosophical questions are raised and—tentatively or conclusively—answered.

This volume contributes to the claim that the weight of religion in twenty-first-century international politics has been on the rise. It is suggestive of *how* religion matters in different ways in a number of specific polities at specific junctures in their histories. Far from upholding the thesis that

56. Hurd, *Politics of Secularism*, 5.

"God is dead," proffered by Nietzsche's madman, and perhaps suggested by Nietzsche himself as a more empirical than normative claim, the volume suggests that an appreciation of divinity as holding a significant place in the hearts, minds, social orders, and political organizations of many polities around the world is a more apt empirical conclusion from the works found herein.

References

"2014 Religious Landscape Study (RLS-II), Main Survey of Nationally Representative Sample of Adults, Final Questionnaire." May 30. Washington, DC: Pew Research Center, 2014.

Almond, Gabriel A., and Sidney Verba. *The Civic Culture: Political Attitudes and Democracy in Five Nations*. Princeton: Princeton University Press, 1963.

Apter, David E. *The Modernization Process*. Chicago: University of Chicago Press, 1965.

Arat, Zehra F. "Democracy and Economic Development: Modernization Theory Revisited." *Comparative Politics* 21, no. 1 (1988): 21–36.

Bowen, John Richard. *Why the French Don't Like Headscarves: Islam, the State, and Public Space*. Princeton: Princeton University Press, 2007.

Bruce, Steve. *God Is Dead: Secularization in the West*. Oxford: Blackwell, 2002.

Bruce, Steve. "Secularization Elsewhere: It Is More Complicated Than That." *Política & Sociedade* 16, no. 36 (2017): 195–211.

Calhoun, Craig. "Secularism, Citizenship, and the Public Sphere." In *Rethinking Secularism*, edited by Craig Calhoun, Mark Juergensmeyer, and Jonathan Van Antwerpen. New York: Oxford University Press, 2011.

Casanova, José. "Religion, European Secular Identities and European Integration." In *Religion in an Expanding Europe*, edited by Timothy Byrnes and Peter Katzenstein. New York: Cambridge University Press, 2006.

Cesari, Jocelyne. *The Awakening of Muslim Democracy: Religion, Modernity, and the State*. New York: Cambridge University Press, 2014.

Cesari, Jocelyne. *Why the West Fears Islam: An Exploration of Muslims in Liberal Democracies*. New York: Palgrave Macmillan, 2013.

Chamberlain, Lesley. *Nietzsche in Turin: An Intimate Biography*. New York: Picador (Macmillan) USA, 1997.

Cruise O'Brien, Donal. "Modernization, Order, and the Erosion of a Democratic Ideal: American Political Science 1960–70." in *Journal of Development Studies* 8, no. 4 (1972): 351–78.

Dahl, Erik. *Intelligence and Surprise Attack: Failure and Success from Pearl Harbor to 9/11 and Beyond*. Washington, DC: Georgetown University Press, 2013.

Deeb, Lara. *An Enchanted Modern: Gender and Public Piety in Shi'i Lebanon*. Princeton: Princeton University Press, 2006.

De Galembert, Claire. "The City's 'Nod of Approval' for the Mantes-la-Jolie Mosque Project: Mistaken Traces of Recognition." *Journal of Ethnic and Migration Studies* 31, no. 6 (2005): 1141–59.

Dobbelaere, Karel. "Bryan Wilson's Contribution to the Study of Secularization." *Social Compass* 53, no. 2 (2006): 141–46.

Douglas, Mary. *Purity and Danger: An Analysis of the Concepts of Pollution and Taboo*. New York: Routledge, 1966.

Eliade, Mircea. *The Sacred and the Profane: The Nature of Religion*. New York: Harcourt Brace, 1959.

Esposito, John. *The Islamic Revolution: Its Global Impact*. Gainesville: University Press of Florida, 1990.

Esposito, John. "Political Islam: Beyond the Green Menace." *Current History* 93, no. 579 (1994): 19–24.

Esposito, John. "Sudan's Islamic Experiment." *Muslim World* 76, nos. 3–4 (1986): 181–202.

Esposito, John. *Voices of Resurgent Islam*. Oxford: Oxford University Press, 1983.

Esposito, John, and James Piscatori. "Democratization and Islam." *Middle East Journal* 45, no. 3 (1991): 427–40.

Ferrari, Silvio, and Rosella Bottoni. "The Institutionalization of Islam in Europe." *The Oxford Handbook of European Islam*, edited by Jocelyne Cesari. Oxford: Oxford University Press, 2015.

Fetzer, Joel, and Christopher Soper. *Muslims and the State*. New York: Cambridge University Press, 2005.

Fox, Jonathan. *Universal Human Rights: Political Secularism, Religion, and the State: A Time Series Analysis of Worldwide Data*. New York: Cambridge University Press, 2015.

Geertz, Clifford. *The Interpretation of Cultures*. New York: Basic Books, 1973.

Geertz, Clifford. *The Religion of Java*. Rev. ed. Chicago: University of Chicago Press, 1976.

Hobsbawm, Eric. *The Age of Revolution: 1798–1848*. New York: Vintage Books, 1996.

Huntington, Samuel P. "The Clash of Civilizations?" *Foreign Affairs* 72, no. 3 (1993): 22–49.

Huntington, Samuel P. "Religion and the Third Wave." *National Interest* 24 (1991): 29–42.

Huntington, Samuel P. "Transnational Organizations in World Politics." *World Politics* 25, no. 3 (1973): 333–68.

Huntington, Samuel P. *Who Are We? The Challenges to America's National Identity*. New York: Simon and Schuster, 2004.

Hurd, Elizabeth Shakman. *Beyond Religious Freedom: The New Global Politics of Religion*. Princeton: Princeton University Press, 2015.
Hurd, Elizabeth Shakman. *The Politics of Secularism in International Relations*. Princeton: Princeton University Press, 2008.
Jobard, Fabien. "An Overview of French Riots: 1981–2004." HAL, 2015. https://hal.archives-ouvertes.fr/hal-00550788/document
Joppke, Christian. *The Secular State under Siege: Religion and Politics in Europe and America*. Cambridge: Polity Press, 2015.
Kaufmann, Walter. *Nietzsche: Philosopher, Psychologist, Antichrist*. Princeton: Princeton University Press, 1975.
Kean, Thomas H., and Lee H. Hamilton. *The 9/11 Commission Report: Final Report of the National Commission on Terrorist Attacks upon the United States*. Washington, DC: Superintendent of Documents, Government Publishing Office, 2004.
Kuhn, Thomas. *The Structure of Scientific Revolutions, 50th Anniversary Edition*. Introduction by Ian Hacking. Chicago: University of Chicago Press, 2012.
Lacorne, Denis, George Holoch, and Tony Judt. *Religion in America: A Political History*. New York: Columbia University Press, 2011 (first published as *De la religion en Amérique* [Paris: Editions Gallimard, 2007]).
Lee, Alexander. "Who Becomes a Terrorist? Poverty, Education, and the Origins of Political Violence." *World Politics* 63, no. 2 (2011): 203–45.
Leege, David C., and Lyman A. Kellstedt, eds. *Rediscovering the Religious Factor in American Politics*. Armonk, NY: M. E. Sharpe, 1993.
Lerner, Daniel. *The Passing of Traditional Society: Modernizing the Middle East*. New York: Free Press, 1958.
Levi-Strauss, Claude. *The Savage Mind*. Chicago: University of Chicago Press, 1962.
Lewis, Andrew. *The Rights Turn in Conservative Christian Politics: How Abortion Transformed the Culture Wars*. New York: Cambridge University Press, 2018.
Mahmood, Saba. *Politics of Piety: The Islamic Revival and the Feminist Subject*. Princeton: Princeton University Press, 20015.
Mahmoud, Saba. *Religious Difference in a Secular Age: A Minority Report*. Princeton: Princeton University Press, 2016.
Mann, Michael. *The Sources of Social Power Volume II: The Rise of Classes and Nation-States, 1760–1914*. New York: Cambridge University Press, 1993.
Martin, David. *A General Theory of Secularization*. New York: Harper and Row, 1978.
Moaddel, Mansoor, Mark Tessler, and Ronald Inglehart. "Foreign Occupation and National Pride: The Case of Iraq." *Public Opinion Quarterly* 72, no. 4 (2008): 677–705.
Nietzsche, Friedrich. *The Gay Science: With a Prelude in Rhymes and an Appendix of Songs*. Translation and commentary by Walter Kaufmann. New York: Vintage, 1974.

Nietzsche, Friedrich. *The Will to Power*. Translated and edited with commentary by Walter Kaufmann. New York: Random House, 1973.

Norris, Pippa, and Ronald Inglehart. *Sacred and Secular: Religion and Politics Worldwide*. 2nd ed. New York: Cambridge University Press, 2011.

Pew Research Center. "Many Countries Favor Specific Religions, Officially or Unofficially." Washington, DC: Pew Research Center, 2017.

Polanyi, Karl. *The Great Transformation: The Political and Economic Origins of Our Time*. New York: Beacon Press, 2001.

Rahman, Fazlur. *Islam and Modernity: Transformation of an Intellectual Tradition*. Chicago: University of Chicago Press, 1982.

Sahliyeh, Emile, ed. *The Politics of Religious Resurgence in the Contemporary World*. Albany: State University of New York Press, 1990.

Sanad, Jamal, and Mark Tessler. "Women and Religion in a Modern Islamic Society, the Case of Kuwait." In *Religious Resurgence and Politics in the Contemporary World*, edited by Emile Sahliyeh. Albany: State University of New York Press, 1990.

Scott, David, and Charles Hirschkind. "Introduction: The Anthropological Skepticism of Talal Asad." In *Powers of the Secular Modern: Talal Asad and His Interlocutors*, edited by David Scott and Charles Hirschkind. Palo Alto: Stanford University Press, 2006.

Scott, James C. *Seeing Like a State: How Certain Schemes to Improve the Human Condition Have Failed*. New Haven: Yale University Press, 1999.

Shaw, Tamsin. *Nietzsche's Political Skepticism*. Princeton: Princeton University Press, 2009.

Skocpol, Theda. *States and Social Revolutions*. New York: Cambridge University Press, 1979.

Sniderman, Paul, Michael Pedersen, Rune Slothuus, and Rune Stubager. *Paradoxes of Liberal Democracy: Islam, Western Europe, and the Danish Cartoon Crisis*. Princeton: Princeton University Press, 2014.

Sohn, Patricia. "Inhabiting Orthodoxy: Discussing Islam and Feminism, Continued." *E-International Relations*, December 9, 2016.

Sopher, Christopher, and Joel Fetzer. "Religious Institutions, Church-State History, and Muslim Mobilization in Britain, France, and Germany." *Journal of Ethnic and Migration Studies* 33, no. 6 (2007): 933–44.

Special Eurobarometer. "Social Values, Science, and Technology." June. Brussels: European Commission, 2005.

Tessler, Mark. "The Identity of Religious Minorities in Non-Secular States: Jews in Tunisia and Morocco and Arabs in Israel." *Comparative Studies in Society and History* 20, no. 3 (1979): 359–78.

Tessler, Mark. "The Origins of Popular Support for Islamist Movements: A Political Economy Analysis." In *Islam, Democracy, and the State in North Africa*, edited by John P. Entelis. Bloomington: Indiana University Press, 1997.

Tessler, Mark. "Political Change and the Islamic Revival in Tunisia." *Maghreb Review* 5, no. 1 (1980): 8–19.

Tessler, Mark. "The Political Culture of Jews in Tunisia and Morocco." *International Journal of Middle East Studies* 11, no. 1 (1980): 59–86.

Tessler, Mark. "Religion, Religiosity and the Place of Islam in Political Life: Insights from the Arab Barometer Surveys." *Middle East Law and Governance* 2, no. 2 (2010): 221–52.

Tessler, Mark and Eleanor Gao. "Gauging Arab Support for Democracy." *Journal of Democracy* 16, no. 3 (2005): 83–97.

Tessler, Mark, Amaney Jamal, and Michael Robbins. "New Findings on Arabs and Democracy." *Journal of Democracy* 23, no. 4 (2012): 89–103.

Tessler, Mark, and Michael D. H. Robbins. "What Leads Some Ordinary Arab Men and Women to Approve of Terrorist Acts against the United States?" *Journal of Conflict Resolution* 51, no. 2 (2007): 305–28.

Tipps, Dean. "Modernization Theory and the Comparative Study of National Societies: A Critical Perspective." *Comparative Studies in Society and History* 15, no. 2 (March 1973): 199–226.

Turner, Victor. *The Ritual Process: Structure and Anti-Structure*. New York: Aldine de Gruyter, 1969.

Wald, Kenneth D., Dennis E. Owen, and Samuel S. Hill. "Political Cohesion in Churches." *Journal of Politics* 52, no. 1 (1990): 197–215.

Wald, Kenneth D., and Corwin E. Smidt. "Measurement Strategies in the Study of Religion and Politics." In *Rediscovering the Religious Factor*, edited by David C. Leege and Lyman A. Kellstedt. Armonk, NY: M. E. Sharpe, 1993.

Weber, Max. *The Protestant Ethic and the Spirit of Capitalism*. Translated with commentary by Stephen Kalberg. Oxford: Oxford University Press, 2010.

Weber, Max. *The Sociology of Religion*. Introduction by Talcott Parsons, foreword by Ann Swidler. Boston: Beacon Books, [1963] 1993.

Wildox, Clyde, and Ted Jelen. "Evangelicals and Political Tolerance." *American Politics Quarterly* 18, no. 1 (1990): 25–46.

Commentary

Modernization, Comparison, and Religion

Mark Tessler

University of Michigan, Ann Arbor

The introductory essay by this volume's editors, Simone Raudino and Patricia Sohn, emphasizes the continuing salience of religion in present-day social and political affairs, including international political affairs. Accordingly, the volume both assumes and argues, as its title makes explicit, that it is necessary to move "beyond the death of God" when thinking about whether religion, or particular dimensions of religious belief and experience, have explanatory power. Aspects of religion will not always be relevant, of course. But the volume's point is that religion matters. Conceptualized and expressed as variables, either independent variables, dependent variables, or both in more fully elaborated explanatory models, dimensions of religion should not be ignored in the mistaken belief that modern societies are increasingly secular and that religion no longer has whatever political and sociological importance it may have had in the past. On the contrary, aspects of religion may have, and almost certainly will have in the future, explanatory power in inquiries seeking to map and account for variance in the normative orientations and behavior of individuals, communities, and nations.

MODERNIZATION THEORY AND RELIGION

In advancing their argument, the editors lay a foundation for this volume by pointing out that scholars of political science and international relations have, in recent decades, "missed the significance of religion to local, national, and international politics." Prominent among the reasons for this, they state, are the influential but at least partially flawed assumptions about social change and human development that are posited by modernization theory. This is a provocative claim, provocative in the constructive sense of encouraging additional reflection and research. The contributions to this volume make abundantly clear that religion is present and connected to politics, and that this is the case for all major religions and in a diverse array of political and social settings. This assertion is also supported by findings from my own research on Islam and political Islam in the Middle East and North Africa and, to a lesser extent, on Judaism in Israel. Without going into detail about my research, much of which incorporates insights derived from original public opinion surveys, I can report, and this will not be surprising to those familiar with the MENA region, that attitudes and behavior related to Islam are important determinants of the views about political and policy concerns held by ordinary citizens.[1] Further, moving from the individual level to the societal level of analysis, the connection between a country's identity and the religion of the majority of its citizens plays a role both in shaping political processes and political affairs within that country and in accounting for variance in political life across societies and countries.[2]

Against this background, it is worth taking a quick look at modernization theory and asking to what extent and on what basis it equates modern and secular. These questions are of particular interest to me since modernization theory was particularly influential during the years in which I began my academic career. And, indeed, my early research used data from North Africa to test some of the hypotheses that are central to modernization theory.

Among the reasons that modernization theory has been persuasive, and

1. Mark Tessler, "Assessing the Influence of Religious Predispositions on Citizen Orientations Related to Governance and Democracy: Findings from Survey Research in Three Dissimilar Arab Societies," *Taiwan Journal of Democracy* 1 (2006): 1–12; and Mark Tessler and Hafsa Tout, "Religion, Trust, and Other Determinants of Muslim Attitudes toward Gender Equality: Evidence and Insights from 54 Surveys in the Middle East and North Africa," *Taiwan Journal of Democracy* 12, no. 2 (2018): 1–29.

2. Mark Tessler, "What Kind of Jewish State Do Israelis Want? The Nature and Determinants of Israeli Attitudes toward Secularism and Some Comparisons with Arab Attitudes toward the Relationship between Religion and Politics," in *Judaism and Jewishness: The Evolution of Secular and Religious Jewish Identities*, ed. Zvi Gittelman (New Brunswick, NJ: Rutgers University Press, 2008).

to a considerable extent remains influential, is the attention it pays to both societies and their members and to the connections and interaction between these two levels of analysis. It is against this dynamic and multilevel model of change and development that we may consider the point at which, and the reasons for which, modernization theory has expected there to be movement from the importance of religion to the importance of secularism. At the societal level, modernization is the process of social change brought on, or intensified, by such agents of change as urbanization, education, and the expanded diffusion of communication media. These agents of change often, and probably more often than not, reinforce one another, such that their societal impact is one in which the whole is more than the sum of the parts.

Much of the early research motivated by modernization theory's ideas and agenda, beginning as early as the 1960s and in a few cases even earlier, sought to identify and describe the underlying mechanisms and pathways through which these and other agents actually produced change. Some studies explored the impact on relatively isolated and traditional societies, such as a study of a remote oasis village in southern Tunisia.[3] Change was introduced when one of the community's young men who had served in the army returned with a radio. Soon some in the village, particularly young men, were eagerly listening to broadcasts from the capital and discussing the meaning and significance of the news they were hearing. Other studies focused on the consequences, not necessarily intended, of changing lifestyles associated with new economic and employment patterns. Introduced or reinforced through even menial jobs were particular, and essentially modern, notions of time, money, hierarchy, and more.

All of this brought, or deepened, the involvement of societies and communities in a sociological and economic environment to which the name "modern" might be applied. Movement in this direction might be bumpy and uneven, as indeed it was and still is. There are digressions and tangents and local or temporal variations, or both, in the relative importance of particular change agents. Nevertheless, modernization theory argued that ordinary men and women were increasingly residing in settings that were less isolated, settings in which more information, and information from more diverse sources, was available and consumed. To those residing in such settings, change was familiar and advancement was possible, or at least could be

3. Jean Duvignaud, *Chebika: Mutations dans un village du Maghreb* (Paris: Gallimard, 1968).

imagined. This is the social and economic order that would be produced by the agents of change to which modernization called attention. Such transformations might produce losers as well as winners. The material conditions of some might not improve. Indeed, the conditions of some might worsen. But even in such instances, isolation would recede, new information would penetrate, and change as well as stasis would be the order of the day.

Interestingly, early modernization theory did not give much attention to political considerations. Its primary focus was on social and economic change, both the process and its consequences. Political scientists nevertheless engaged with its assumptions and findings, as I did in my own research during the late 1960s and the 1970s.[4] A particularly important political science contribution was made by Samuel Huntington's *Political Order in Changing Societies*.[5] Huntington convincingly argued that the consequences of social and economic change—change that undermined traditions and often unsettled populations—could not be understood without attention to the character of the prevailing political system. More specifically, he hypothesized that change would be destabilizing and lead away from, rather than toward, a modernity equilibrium if a society's political institutions were not strong and robust enough to absorb and respond productively to the preferences of an increasingly energized and demanding population.

Modernization theory has come a long way since the heyday of its influence in the 1960s, 1970s, and to some extent the 1980s. Its assumptions and propositions for the most part remain the same, however, at least with respect to aggregate, or system-level, social change and economic development. But in addition to the story that modernization theory tells about communities, societies, and states, it has, from the beginning, connected these system-level trends to the circumstances and behavior of ordinary citizens, to the lives of the men and women who are members of the communities, societies, and states that are modernizing. And this brings us back, finally, to the matter of religion.

The individual-level analyses spawned by modernization theory are illustrated particularly well by an important early study by Alex Inkeles and

4. Mark Tessler, "Cultural Modernity: Evidence from Tunisia," *Social Science Quarterly* 52 (1971): 290–308; Mark Tessler, "Le concept de modernité au miroir des sciences sociales," *Cultures et Développement* 5 (1973): 779–93.

5. Samuel Huntington, *Political Order in Changing Societies* (New Haven: Yale University Press, 1968).

his associates.[6] Entitled "Making Men Modern: On the Causes and Consequences of Individual Change in Six Developing Countries" and published in the *American Political Science Review* in 1969, Inkeles reports that "since 1962 a group of my colleagues and I at Harvard University have been working to understand the impact on the individual of his participation in the process of modernization." An even earlier study is the poorly titled but empirically useful analysis of Leonard Doob. In his data-rich 1960 book, *Becoming More Civilized: A Psychological Exploration,* Doob talks about the normative and behavioral orientations that an individual is likely to embrace and display to the extent that he or she resides in a modernizing, or "modern," environment and is personally impacted by such change agents as urbanization, education, and the consumption of new media and information sources.[7]

It is in this connection that we see the proposition that modernization pushes toward secularism: individuals are more likely to be less personally religious and to attach less importance to religious institutions and religion's role in societal affairs to the extent they are exposed to and participate in the process of modernization. As the present volume makes clear, this often has not been the case, and it is at the nexus of macro-level change and individual-level attitudes and behavior that the origins of this dubious, or at least overly generalized, proposition can be found. While the system-level change agents emphasized by modernization theory may be operating very broadly, giving societies and national communities on the whole more in common with one another than they had in the past, the argument that individuals would also increasingly become similar to one another, and that this would give rise to a universal modern culture, was at best only partially accurate.

The limitations and challenges to this argument are nicely summarized by Inkeles himself in a thoughtful 1977 article, "Understanding and Misunderstanding Individual Modernity."[8] Inkeles offers a conceptual and empirically informed response to many of the questions raised about individual modernity, but the article also makes clear that there are indeed limitations to both the content and the applicability of the concept of individual modernity. And to the extent that disagreements about content and appli-

6. Alex Inkeles, "Making Men Modern: On the Causes and Consequences of Individual Change in Six Developing Countries," *American Journal of Sociology* 75 (1969): 208–25.

7. Leonard Doob, *Becoming More Civilized: A Psychological Exploration* (New Haven: Yale University Press, 1960).

8. Alex Inkeles, "Understanding and Misunderstanding Individual Modernity," *Journal of Cross-Cultural Psychology* 8 (1977): 135–76.

cability apply specifically to religion and to secularism, the present volume offers powerful evidence that modernization—institutional or system-level modernization—has not caused religiosity and religion to occupy what is at best a marginal place in the lives of most men and women and the societies in which they reside.

This assessment is cogently and persuasively expressed by Terrance Carroll in a 1984 article entitled "Secularization and States of Modernity." Carroll writes that "apparent contradictions between the findings of at least some studies of the role of specific religions in particular countries and the more general literature on political modernization raise the possibility that the relationship between religion and political change may be considerably more complex than is usually suggested. In this article I argue that there is no *necessary* relationship between secularization and the development of a modern state."[9] The contributions to the present volume offer additional evidence and insight about this relationship, and they demonstrate in particular that religion continues to matter in societies and polities and in the lives of their populations around the world.

COMPARISON IN THE STUDY OF RELIGION

A study of the same phenomenon at multiple points in space or time, or both, may have an essentially descriptive objective. It may seek to provide information to interested consumers with the understanding that none of these consumers seeks information and insight about the phenomenon at more than a single time or place. In other words, the investigation offers multiple but segmented thick descriptions, each intended for a different audience. There is no reason to question the value of such a collection. Moreover, the study may offer within-case explanatory insights as well as descriptive information for some or even all of the cases included in the collection. However, the value of its contribution notwithstanding, such a collection, even though it includes and juxtaposes a number of case-specific reports, is not analytical, and it certainly is not comparative. The primary goal in this instance is not a whole that is more than the sum of the parts, meaning generalizable understandings that shed light on causal stories and scope conditions applicable to

9. Terrance Carroll, "Secularization and States of Modernity," *World Politics* 36 (1984): 362–82.

the subject more broadly. Its contribution instead resides in the parts themselves, each of which may be rich and instructive but will, nonetheless, be of primary interest to an audience seeking case-specific rather than generalizable information and insights.

The chapters in this volume, organized by religion, in many cases provide information and insights that are essentially descriptive. Frequently original and almost always instructive, the value and utility of the information provided is not in doubt. But to the extent that these chapters offer case-specific descriptions, or thick descriptions, value and utility will primarily accrue to readers with an interest in the particular religion, or the particular aspect or dimension of the religion, to which each chapter is devoted.

But, in fact, the contribution that this volume and its chapters make is not only or even primarily in the domain of description. On the contrary, the chapters can and should also be read with attention to comparison,[10] including comparison both within sections devoted to a particular religion and across sections devoted to different religions. The three chapters on Islam nicely illustrate the potential for instructive within-section comparison. The chapters focus broadly on what, for present purposes, may be called Islamic activism in the domain of politics, or Islamic political activism. This invites us to locate the degree of activism in each case at a point on a continuum ranging, as expressed by one contributor, from quiescence to violence. Activism may thus be understood as a variable, as indeed it is, and it may be treated as either, or both, a dependent or an independent variable. As a dependent variable, it tells us what some of the variance associated with activism looks like, and it then asks how to account for this variance—on what does it depend, in other words. Conversely, as an independent variable, it becomes a determinant—a cause rather than an effect—and asks what difference an increase or decrease in activism makes.

Further, as either a dependent variable or an independent variable, the opportunity for comparison invites us to formulate hypotheses about the determinants or consequences, or both, of Islamic political activism and then to test these propositions, at least preliminarily, with the information provided by the chapters on Islam. In this way, it is possible not only to observe variation in degree of Islamic political activism but also to develop

10. For a useful overview of comparative research on religion, see Anna Grzymala-Busse, "Why Comparative Politics Should Take Religion (More) Seriously," *Annual Review of Political Science* 1 (2012): 421–42.

or derive causal stories that tell us, or purport to tell us, to which other politically salient phenomena Islamic political activism is connected, and what then is the direction and structure of these explanatory relationships.

Finally, in addition to variance and causal stories, comparison leads us to think about scope conditions, what is sometimes also called the locus of applicability. Hypotheses put forth a causal story that needs to be tested in order to establish, or at least estimate, the likelihood that it is correct. But it is possible, indeed likely, that a confirmed hypothesis has explanatory power under some conditions but not under others. From this follows the need for attention to scope conditions, and here again the path forward involves comparison. What are the characteristics, described in terms of concepts and variables, of the places, times, and issues that specify when an established causal story fits the facts and is correct? Answers to this question are themselves propositions. The confirmed hypothesis with its embedded causal story is the dependent variable; the factors that condition applicability, the scope conditions, in other words, are the independent variables.

Additionally, it is of course possible that scope conditions are specified by the religion itself. In other words, to continue the example of religious political activism, not only might we ask under what conditions do hypotheses about Islamic political activism fit the facts and not fit the facts, such that the hypotheses are confirmed, but also whether confirmed hypotheses pertaining to Islamic political activism specify causal stories and relationships that also have explanatory power when they involve political activism in the name of Christianity, Judaism, or an Asian religion. Although not addressed directly in this volume's chapters on Christianity, Judaism, and Asian religions, the circumstances, actions, and trends discussed in some of these chapters do involve what might loosely be called political activism. Thus, even within the framework of this volume, as well as more broadly, it is possible to ask whether patterns initially identified through research on Islam also apply when the religion is not Islam but is rather Christianity, Judaism, or an Asian religion. If the answer is yes, there is evidence that the pattern is generalizable, that what has been discovered is not an Islam-specific causal story. But if the answer is no, then it *is* an Islam-specific causal story and Islam is in fact a scope condition.

The delineation of variance, causal stories, and scope conditions is an ongoing and cumulative endeavor; very few single studies, if any, do more than initiate or carry forward a line of inquiry that seeks to discover the patterns and relationships that make up the "theory" of a given phenomenon or dynamic. This is the case for broad and multidimensional research frameworks and agendas, such as modernization theory. It is also the case for lines of inquiry that are at least somewhat more narrow and focused, such as Islamic political activism in the previously discussed example. But the point to be noted here is that the pursuit of theory, whether initiating it or pushing forward work done by others, is carried out through comparison at each stage, the stage of delineating variance, the stage of formulating and evaluating causal stories, and the stage of identifying and specifying scope conditions.

These formulations about the role of comparison in research devoted to explanation as well as description apply to comparison both across this volume's chapters in a section devoted to a particular religion and across the sections themselves, across a group of sections each of which is devoted to a different religion. In this case, attributes of the religion or its real-world interpretations and practices, again considered as concepts and variables, are either independent variables or scope conditions or both. This can be illustrated by some of the research, including some of my own research, that asks whether Islam, or dimensions of Islam, are either drivers or conditionalities with significant explanatory power. There is research along these lines at both the system level of analysis and the individual level of analysis. In the former, country is very frequently the unit of analysis. In the latter, the ordinary citizen is very frequently the unit of analysis.

Studies by Michigan's Ronald Inglehart and Harvard's Pippa Norris provide examples of system-level research in which country is the unit of analysis.[11] Among their analyses based on World Values Survey data is a cross-national study of the relationship between gender equality and democracy that also considers religion, including Islam, in their explanatory model. More specifically, they argue, and subsequently find, that "the trend toward gender equality is intimately linked with the broader process of democratization" but also that "culture," meaning aggregate religiosity or a strong connection between religion and politics at the national level, is "a major reason why many nations with a strict Islamic background have often ranked at the bottom of the list worldwide" in terms of gender equality. A

11. Ronald Inglehart and Pippa Norris, *Rising Tide: Gender Equality and Cultural Change around the World* (Cambridge: Cambridge University Press, 2003). The quoted passages are from Inglehart, Norris, and Christian Welzel, "Gender Quality and Democracy," 2004, pages 2–4, https://wcfia.harvard.edu/files/wcfia/files/814_gender_equality_democracy.pdf

discussion of how to conceptualize and measure "strict Islamic background" is beyond the scope of the present chapter, as is a discussion of how to assess whether a chosen measure is valid and reliable. Rather, what is to be noted here is that religion is hypothesized to be part of a system-level causal story when the dependent variable is gender equality, democracy, or the relationship between gender equality and democracy.

I tend to give examples relating to Islam since this is the religion on which some of my own research has focused. But there is no shortage of comparative research in which the focus is on a religion or its dimensions other than Islam. Nor, as will be seen shortly, is there an absence of studies that offer different conclusions about the explanatory power or conditioning effects of normative orientations or institutional arrangements, or both, associated with Islam. For example, a study of gender equality in the political realm cited by Inglehart, Norris, and Christian Welzel found, based on a comparison of 180 nation-states, that "the greatest contrasts were between dominant Christian countries (whether Protestant or Catholic) and all other religions, including Islamic, Buddhist, Judaic, Confucian and Hindu."[12] The study considered the proportion of women in legislative and cabinet positions and found, in other words, that countries with a significant Islamic connection, while low on these measures of gender equality, were not any lower than those of countries with a significant connection to one of many other religions.

Individual-level comparative research that considers religion, or attitudes and behavior associated with religion, as independent variables or conditionalities is the focus of some of my own research on the explanatory power of Islamic attachment. With "Islamic attachment" conceptualized as one or more variables ranging from strong to weak, I have used data from cross-national surveys of Middle Eastern Muslim populations to test hypotheses in which the dependent variables are attitudes toward democracy, toward gender equality, toward international conflict, and toward terrorist acts against the United States.[13] The findings from this research are

12. Andrew Reynolds, "Women in the Legislatures and Executives of the World: Knocking at the Highest Glass Ceiling," *World Politics* 51, no. 4 (1999): 547–72.

13. Mark Tessler and Michael Robbins, "What Leads Some Ordinary Men and Women in Arab Countries to Approve of Terrorist Acts against the West: Evidence from Survey Research in Algeria and Jordan," *Journal of Conflict Resolution* 51 (2007): 305–28; Mark Tessler, "Islam and Democracy in the Middle East: The Impact of Religious Orientations on Attitudes toward Democracy in Four Arab Countries," *Comparative Politics* 34 (2002): 337–

not easily summarized. Nor is the methodology and analysis on which the findings are based. But while I leave these matters to those who may wish to consult the published research reports, it can be noted here that the findings from these studies contradict negative stereotypes alleging that Islam is hostile to democracy and predisposes adherents toward violence.

One of the comparisons in these individual-level studies is between ordinary citizens in Muslim-majority Middle Eastern countries who are more devout and observant and those in these same countries who are less devout and observant. A major finding is that personal religiosity very rarely accounts for variance on the dependent variables mentioned above. In other words, men and women who are more religious and men and women who are less religious do not differ significantly in their views about democracy, women's status, international conflict, and terrorism against the United States. Other religion-related attitudes, such as support for political Islam, sometimes do but very often do not bear a statistically significant relationship with these same dependent variables. Overall, this body of research offers strong evidence that essentialist culture-based or religion-based explanations for the most part do not fit the facts and that other explanatory models, in this case those emphasizing political and economic factors, do a much better job of accounting for variance and are much more important shapers of attitudinal and behavioral predispositions among Muslims.

These examples remind us that failing to accept a research hypothesis and being forced to accept the null hypothesis are not without value. On the contrary, empirical determinations of when a religion and its attributes are not drivers or conditionalities can be as instructive, and sometimes more instructive, as empirical determinations of when a religion and its attributes do play a role in shaping attitudes and behavior. This is certainly the case with respect to Islam, a religion about which there are many pejorative stereotypes that systematic and rigorous social science research has shown to be inaccurate.

Individual-level comparative analysis may not connect with the chapters in this volume as well as does system-level or country-level comparative analysis. But in fact, a number of this volume's chapters do present and discuss findings from studies of popular attitudes and values. These findings

54; Mark Tessler and Jodi Nachtwey, "Islam and Attitudes toward International Conflict: Evidence from Survey Research in the Arab World," *Journal of Conflict Resolution* 42 (1998): 619–36. See also the reports cited in footnote 1.

can be compared to those from other individual-level studies in order to assess their generalizability or, if the findings are not very generalizable, to lay a foundation for identifying and specifying scope conditions, with the possibility that the religion itself, or religious affiliation, will be a limiting conditionality.

✦ ✦ ✦

The two sections of this reflective chapter connect in ways that are pertinent for the present volume. Modernization theory posits many instructive hypotheses, some at the system-level and some at the individual-level. These propositions are for the most part plausible and they are also very frequently persuasive; over the half century that modernization theory has been an influential analytical framework, and at times a dominant one, social and political science research has offered evidence that many of these hypotheses are essentially correct. But this research has also shown that many are in need of revision and that some, or perhaps even many, are actually incorrect. The place of religion, and more broadly of culture, in modernization theory's network of causal stories and conditionalities has been at the center of questions and debates about the applicability and accuracy of modernization theory. And as the chapters in the present volume make clear, religion and attitudes and behavior associated with religion have been and remain potent parts of the story that modernization theory aspires to tell.

Testing and refining the parts of this network is, as indeed it should be, a cumulative endeavor with contributions over time and from many sources. Accordingly, as a framework for theorizing as well as a set of specific variable relationships, modernization theory responds to and incorporates the research findings of a continuously expanding community of investigators, and the result is that its understandings and explanations evolve in response to new ideas and new evidence. Comparative analysis, broadly defined, is the method by which this is carried out.

As illustrated previously with the example of Islamic political activism, variance on key dimensions is identified and mapped, sometimes involving new conceptualizations as well as new empirical observations. This then requires the articulation of explanatory causal stories, hypotheses that to varying degrees may be original and, whether original or not, are tested and evaluated through comparison at the appropriate level of analysis. All of this applies to religion and the associated circumstances, attributes, and manifestations to which the chapters in the present volume are devoted.

Whether the comparison is of different instances of the same religion or of comparable circumstances involving different religions, contributions like those assembled here enable comparisons both within and across religious experience.

The chapters in the same way also lay a foundation for the delineation of scope conditions involving religion. Findings reported in any chapter or set of chapters can be tested against findings from the existing body of relevant research, and that of future research as well, to determine the extent to which the information and insight provided by these chapters are generalizable. And if generalizability is limited, comparison may make it possible to identify the relevant scope conditions, the conditions under which a particular insight, or causal story, fits the facts and has explanatory power. Religion is among the factors that may constitute scope conditions. Research may show, and the present volume invites and encourages reflection on the matter, that observed patterns fit the facts for one religion but not for others, or for certain combinations of religion but, again, not for others.

References

Carroll, Terrance. "Secularization and States of Modernity." *World Politics* 36 (1984): 362–82.

Doob, Leonard. *Becoming More Civilized: A Psychological Exploration.* New Haven: Yale University Press, 1960.

Duvignaud, Jean. Chebika: Mutations dans un village du Maghreb. Paris: Gallimard, 1968.

Grzymala-Busse, Anna. "Why Comparative Politics Should Take Religion (More) Seriously." *Annual Review of Political Science* 1 (2012): 421–42.

Huntington, Samuel. *Political Order in Changing Societies.* New Haven: Yale University Press, 1968.

Inglehart, Ronald, and Pippa Norris. *Rising Tide: Gender Equality and Cultural Change around the World.* Cambridge: Cambridge University Press, 2003.

Inglehart, Ronald, Pippa Norris, and Christian Welzel. 2004. "Gender Quality and Democracy." Pages 2–4. https://wcfia.harvard.edu/files/wcfia/files/814_gender_equality_democracy.pdf

Inkeles, Alex. "Making Men Modern: On the Causes and Consequences of Individual Change in Six Developing Countries." *American Journal of Sociology* 75 (1969): 208–25.

Inkeles, Alex. "Understanding and Misunderstanding Individual Modernity." *Journal of Cross-Cultural Psychology* 8 (1977): 135–76.

Reynolds, Andrew. "Women in the Legislatures and Executives of the World: Knocking at the Highest Glass Ceiling." *World Politics* 51, no. 4 (1999): 547–72.

Tessler, Mark. "Assessing the Influence of Religious Predispositions on Citizen Orientations Related to Governance and Democracy: Findings from Survey Research in Three Dissimilar Arab Societies." *Taiwan Journal of Democracy* 1 (2006): 1–12.

Tessler, Mark. "Cultural Modernity: Evidence from Tunisia." *Social Science Quarterly* 52 (1971): 290–308.

Tessler, Mark. "Islam and Democracy in the Middle East: The Impact of Religious Orientations on Attitudes toward Democracy in Four Arab Countries." *Comparative Politics* 34 (2002): 337–54.

Tessler, Mark. "Le concept de modernité au miroir des sciences sociales." *Cultures et Développement* 5 (1973): 779–93.

Tessler, Mark. "What Kind of Jewish State Do Israelis Want? The Nature and Determinants of Israeli Attitudes toward Secularism and Some Comparisons with Arab Attitudes toward the Relationship between Religion and Politics." In *Judaism and Jewishness: The Evolution of Secular and Religious Jewish Identities*, edited by Zvi Gittelman. New Brunswick, NJ: Rutgers University Press, 2008.

Tessler, Mark, and Jodi Nachtwey. "Islam and Attitudes toward International Conflict: Evidence from Survey Research in the Arab World." *Journal of Conflict Resolution* 42 (1998): 619–36.

Tessler, Mark, and Michael Robbins. "What Leads Some Ordinary Men and Women in Arab Countries to Approve of Terrorist Acts against the West: Evidence from Survey Research in Algeria and Jordan." *Journal of Conflict Resolution* 51 (2007): 305–28.

Tessler, Mark, and Hafsa Tout. "Religion, Trust, and Other Determinants of Muslim Attitudes toward Gender Equality: Evidence and Insights from 54 Surveys in the Middle East and North Africa." *Taiwan Journal of Democracy* 12, no. 2 (2018): 1–29.

Religion and Conflict

Theoretical Perspectives and Empirical Evidence

Simone Raudino

Kyiv School of Economics (Kyiv) & Bridging Gaps (Hong Kong)

This chapter addresses the question of the relation between religion and conflict. More specifically, it asks whether religion has a strong correlation with conflict, and whether this could be defined in terms of positive (incentivizing) or negative (defusing) causation. The article considers important methodological and metaphysical questions attached to the debate and subsequently proposes a virtual methodology for answering the research question from a positive epistemological angle. Finally, it provides a set of references as to how the scholarship has carried out similar exercises, and it offers a discussion of their results.

THE SPIRITUAL AND TEMPORAL POWER OF RELIGIONS

"Religion" is often understood as a dual concept. On the one side, religion represents the intimate world of beliefs in transcendental being(s) above the realm of the normal. The codification of this "world" along with the organization of its rites and customs represents a key function of any religious tradition and results in the very essence of the religious experience for the believer. In the Christian world, this understanding of religion corresponds to the *spiritual* "authority" or "realm" of the Church, indicating both moral stewardship of the believer, and, more crucially, what French philosopher

René Guénon called "knowledge free of all contingency."[1] According to Guénon, this is the character that truly gives sacredness to the religious function, that of preserving and transmitting "the traditional doctrine, in which all regular social organization finds its fundamental principles."[2]

On the other side, common understandings of religion also include the socially organized manifestations of such spiritual authority, resulting in social authority manifesting via (1) theocracies and other forms of government resting upon divine rights in nondemocratic regimes; (2) religious political parties in democratic regimes; (3) the institutional and administrative structures of churches; and (d) religiously inspired civil society organizations.

Both popular understandings and the religions' own conceptualization of the two provinces varied greatly across different traditions, following different historical patterns and timelines. For any religion, the interplay between these two constitutive elements is at the very core of their ever-evolving identities, and marked profoundly the history of the polities in which they propagated. In Christianity, the province of religious governmental action, represented by military but also economic, administrative, judicial, diplomatic, and social activities, has traditionally been identified with the *temporal* "power" or "realm" of the church. Although traditional Islam originally had no concept of separation between the church and the state, it later experienced such separation with the creation of secular regimes ruling Islamic societies, as has been the case in Turkey since Kemalism or in Iran between the reign of Reza Shah Pahlavi and the Iranian Revolution. Similarly, while the creation of Israel in 1948 may be seen as the culmination of a religious process, its Declaration of Independence establishes a secular state, where the religious power is by and large separated from the state power, so much so that Israel has no laws restricting freedom of religion, nor, for that matter, forbidding the act of execrating religion. To this extent, all the three major Abrahamic religions have developed, at different points in time, understandings of the separation between spiritual and temporal authority and power. This has also been the case for Buddhism, which, having been born out of a total renunciation of worldly interests and organizations, has subsequently exerted remarkable political influence in polities throughout South, East, and Southeast Asia.

Thus, while the word "religion" conveys an element of personal ethical

1. René Guénon, *Spiritual Authority and Temporal Power* (Ghent, NY: Sophia Perennis, 2001).

2. Guénon, *Spiritual Authority and Temporal Power*, 18.

significance, it also captures a host of meanings related to the myriad social organizations leveraging *spiritual authority* to claim *temporal power*; or, differently said, an active role in the worldly businesses of politics, economics, and societal organizations more generally. The global sum of belief systems and worldly institutions run in the name of God constitutes a powerful network of interrelated institutions actively shaping local, national, and global systems of governance, much along the lines of institutions behind phenomena such as capitalism, globalization, or democratization.

For millennia, the two souls of religion—the provinces of *Spirituality* and *Temporality*—have posed fundamental ethical questions to billions of believers around the world: Should the Church's moral guidance translate into political legitimacy? And, if so, how should the relay mechanism be organized? These questions apply both to the "domestic" struggle within any religion—between the different leaders of its own two provinces—and, even more importantly, to the more general relationship between religious organizations on the one side and secular organizations on the other.

French philosopher Alain de Benoist explores this question by analyzing the work of several authors writing on the relationship between spiritual authority and temporal power. De Benoist highlights Guénon's observation that "history, like myth, constantly stages an opposition or rivalry between temporal and spiritual powers."[3] Eventually, he identifies two strongly minded and vehemently opposed lineages of thinkers. On the one side are the advocates of the primacy of knowledge over potency, thought over action, the contemplative over the constitutive, and intellectualism over sovereignty. De Benoist concludes, in relation to these thinkers, that the "royal-warrior function needs to be subordinated to the sacerdotal function, just as potency should be subordinate to knowledge and action to thought."[4]

On the other side, de Benoist identifies the supporters of activist volunteerism. These thinkers believe that ideas are the reflection of sociohistorical practices and not the other way around. They are promoters of the sacred nature of action; the spiritual meaning of royalty; the primacy of action over contemplation; and the overall belief that the "king should always have the last word," and that "the sacerdotal castes should naturally be dominated by a warrior tradition."[5]

3. Alain de Benoist, "Autorité spirituelle et pouvoir temporelle," in *L'Empire intérieur* (Saint Clément de rivière: Fata Morgana, 1995).

4. de Benoist, "Autorité spirituelle et pouvoir temporelle."

5. de Benoist, "Autorité spirituelle et pouvoir temporelle."

While this debate cannot be settled on normative accounts (what ought to be), it can have a solution from a praxis perspective (what could be attributed to whom), in the interest of empirical analysis. For example, this volume considers policy areas and legislative provisions as the responsibility of a given religion any time that applicable state laws establish so (e.g., when the state grants religion official authority), or where religious representatives demonstrate enough influence to impose their de facto authority upon state laws. Drawing such a neat line about the supremacy of one or the other of the two provinces is relatively easy in theocracies, or in states where the government controls the church.[6] It is more difficult in secular contexts, where religious authorities may hold considerable covert influence upon the political process and the shaping of popular culture and, vice-versa, state authorities may control much of intrachurch politics. More often than not, these influences can, however, still be identified. Politically, state institutions often make legal provisions for the applicability of religious laws in specific matters relating, for example, to family law, education, or ecclesiastical property. Culturally, epistemological techniques such as genealogy and discourse analysis allow uncovering many of these power relations and mutual influences, as several authors have shown in this volume.

METHODOLOGY OF RELIGION AND CONFLICT

René Descartes wittingly mused upon how agreements on definitions could spare the world half of its illusions. Approaching a subject as vast as the linkages between the worlds represented by the words "religion" and "conflict," one can only feel sympathetic toward such a remark. Breaking down comprehensive philosophical concepts into sequences of analytical definitions and conceptual passages is an ungrateful task. Yet it remains a necessary evil if we are to apply a positive epistemology to the topic, and if we can, thus, establish some firm points in a complex field charged with

6. The Pew Research Center recognizes today seven polities as full theocracies (the Vatican, Yemen, Saudi Arabia, Sudan, Iran, Mauritania, and Afghanistan). It further recognizes 43 countries with an official state-endorsed faith, where linkages between the church and the state can assume very different connotations, including the possibility of governmental control of religion, such as in the United Kingdom, Greece, Norway, and Turkey. See K. Kishi, A. Cooperman, and A. Schiller, "Many Countries Favor Specific Religions, Officially or Unofficially," Pew Research Center, October 3, 2017.

millennia of opposing theories, belief systems, and, ultimately, both vital and deadly interests.

The first of these points draws upon the boundaries of the term "religion" in either its spiritual or temporal understanding. Definitions of "religion" have, at times, been stretched to include all sorts of social movements, including political ideologies (Marxism and various fascisms); national movements (nationalism); unorganized or extinct beliefs (witchcraft, paganism); cultural movements (theosophy); and esoteric organizations (Masonry). On the other side, radical preachers such as evangelist Jimmy Swaggart have restrained the concept of religion within their own denomination, denouncing any deviation from traditional readings of the Bible as "shamanism" or "occultism," thus implying that, at par with "positive thinking" and "internal healing," liberal interpretations of the Bible are "mental gymnastics" and not religion.[7]

The empirical methodology used in this volume suggests that social movements that do not refer to transcendental matters (e.g., that do not rely on unscientific claims) or are not institutionalized (e.g., do not have a bureaucratic and hierarchical organization) should not be categorized as "religion." As arbitrary as it might be, this definition has the advantage of being fairly recognizable and clear-cut. It leaves the door open to hundreds—perhaps thousands—of monotheistic and polytheistic religions. These include doubtful movements such as *Scientology*, which purposefully relies upon unscientific claims while having built a powerful organization; but not mundane organizations such as the Church of Satan, which preaches to followers that they are "their own Gods." This would certainly be comprehensive of what most of the world's population believes in: to keep things in perspective, it should be recalled that four religions alone (Christianity, Islam, Hinduism, and Buddhism) represent some 5.5 billion believers, or three-fourths of the world's population.[8]

---

7. The theology of Swaggart is well represented in the work of Dave Hunt, who suggests that evangelists straining away from biblical fundamentalism are unwittingly promoting the work of the devil, while urging a return of old-fashioned evangelical fundamentalism. See Dave Hunt, Thomas A. McMahon, and Shirley Cauthen, *The Seduction of Christianity* (Eugene, OR: Harvest House, 1985), and Lloyd Grove, "Jimmy Swaggart's Controversial Crusade," *Washington Post*, April 8, 1987.

8. Thus, any definition like the one adopted here, capable of capturing the top 10 religions by number of adepts, would likely do enough statistical justice to any quantitative correlation between religion and other phenomena.

On the other side of the equation, the term *conflict* can be defined as a struggle or contest between people or societal groups with opposing needs, ideas, beliefs, values, or goals.[9] *Violence* is the physical or psychological manifestation of such struggle or contest. While conflict primarily implies a dynamism in which opposing parties engage in physical or psychological violence—a more or less violent struggle or contest—conflict can also reflect a relatively static situation in which the conflicting parties rest on different positions and refuse or postpone engagement. For the methodology suggested in this chapter, the most immediate operationalization of conflict and violence would be a standardly agreed upon definition of *violent conflict*.[10]

The opposite of conflict is *peace*, typically defined as a state or period of mutual concordance among different people or societal groups. Peace, too, can have an active or passive connotation. In particular, Norwegian sociologist Johan Galtung, founder of the discipline of peace and conflict studies, has famously distinguished between negative and positive peace, defining the former as the mere absence of war or visible conflict, and the latter as the

9. More detailed definitions include (a) "struggle over values or claims to status, power, and scarce resources, in which the aims of the groups or individuals involved are to neutralize, injure or eliminate rivals"; (b) "two or more parties with incompatible interests who express hostile attitudes or pursue their interests through actions that damage the other(s). Parties may be individuals, small or large groups or countries. Interests can diverge in many ways, such as over access to and distribution of resources (e.g., territory, money, energy sources, food); control of power and participation in political decision making; identity (cultural, social and political communities); status; or values, particularly those embodied in systems of government, religion, or ideology." See Payson Conflict Study Group, "A Glossary on Violent Conflict: Terms and Concepts Used in Conflict Prevention, Mitigation, and Resolution in the Context of Disaster Relief and Sustainable Development" (Tulane, LA: Tulane University, 2001).

10. "The use of armed force by two parties, of which at least one is the government of a state that results in at least 25 battle-related deaths per year. Armed conflicts are grouped into three categories: minor armed conflicts, in which the battle-related deaths during the course of the conflict are below 1,000; intermediate conflicts, in which there are more than 1,000 battle-related deaths recorded during the course of the conflict, and in which between 25 and 1,000 deaths have occurred during a particular year; and wars, in which there are more than 1,000 battle-related deaths during one particular year. The two latter categories are sometimes referred to as major armed conflicts." Peter Wallensteen and Karin Axel, "Conflict Resolution and the End of the Cold War, 1989–1993," *Journal of Peace Research* 31, no. 3 (1994): 333–49.

qualitatively superior product of cultivating institutions and sociopolitical structures necessary to maintain and promote a state of *sustainable* peace.[11]

METAPHYSICS OF RELIGION AND CONFLICT

Empiricism has clear limits. The methodological exercise by which each term of an equation is defined and operationalized, and in which borderline cases are clarified by recurring to arbitrary assumptions, cannot do justice to a complex and intricate relation as the one between "religion" and "conflict." Some theoretical knots cannot simply be untied through a definition, an operationalization, or an assumption. How much religion, for example, can be detached from other aspects of the human experience, including the interpretation of reality and the search for purposeful agency, is a question with no effective answer. This typology of questions pertains to the realm of metaphysics, investigating the fundamental nature of reality. They also thread into the realms of epistemology and norms, questioning what we really know and what we ought to do.

In particular, theory around religion and conflict needs to deal with three major issues relating to foundational controversies[12] as to the nature of the relation between religion and the human experience understood both in terms of consciousness and agency. I call these questions "metaphysical fractures," as they pose alternative options deeply embedded in opposing readings of human nature, to such an extent that they often lead to divisive interpretations with little possibility for resolution. These include the following questions: (1) How does religion (or any other belief system for that matter) frame people's experience of life and, consequently, how does it influence their societal behavior? (2) What is the role of religion—and particularly of the universal spiritual authority it purports to represent as opposed to the contingent interpretations and actions it often leads to—in nurturing conflict and violence? (3) What should be the role of spiritual and temporal religion in administering the use of violence?

---

11. Johan Galtung, "Violence, Peace, and Peace Research," *Journal of Peace Research* 6, no. 3 (1969): 167–91.

12. I use the term "foundational" as knowledge or belief that rests on a foundation of noninferential knowledge, for example, as self-standing, self-justified knowledge or belief, much in the same way the term "axiom" is used in math. Thus, foundational controversies are intrinsically incompatible worldviews, each based on beliefs that cannot be empirically proved.

The first fracture relates to the role of religion in framing people's experiences of life, by influencing their phenomenological perceptions, belief systems, world visions, and, ultimately, personal and social behavior. Over and beyond the two understandings of religion as *spiritual* and *temporal* phenomena, the question here is the extent to which both people's perceptions of reality and societies' political, economic, and social features can be analytically untwined from the religious beliefs and institutions inhabiting these worlds.

Theologian Peter Ochs laments that the reading of religion and conflict introduced by the Enlightenment is deeply reductionist. This is because it has reduced the impact of one phenomenon over the other to a cold, causal, mechanic sequence of analytical processes.[13] Ochs believes it is not: religion does not float in a cultural vacuum, and its roots and branches cannot be detached from the trunk of its psychological and societal aspects. Referring to the work of theologian William Cavanaugh,[14] he notices that the same idea of religion as an isolated variable within the social context is a product of post-Enlightenment rationalism, and that the term "religion" has been imposed "from the outside" by Western thinkers upon communities that hitherto had holistic views of life, ethics, family, and work. Quoting a sizeable body of literature, Ochs concludes that there is little evidence for the secularist presumption of the existence of a discrete activity that can be called "religion"; it is therefore not possible to ascribe to this ostensibly isolated activity the responsibility for inciting conflict or violence.

If we agree with Ochs's view that the religious identity for many believers cannot be separated from other defining identities, including, for example, those of gender or ethnicity, then a dualistic view of religion, claiming a separation between thought and action, or between knowledge and potency, cannot really be justified. Yet it is clear that different people rely to different degrees upon their respective religious identities—provided that they have one in the first instance. Similarly, no set of two persons can easily be compared when it comes to their personal reliance upon religion, whether in terms of world vision or any specific item in their behavioral portfolio.

13. Peter Ochs, "The Possibilities and Limits of Inter-Religious Dialogue," in *The Oxford Handbook of Religion, Conflict, and Peacebuilding*, ed. Atalia Omer, R. Scott Appleby, and David Little (Oxford: Oxford University Press, 2015).

14. William T. Cavanaugh, *The Myth of Religious Violence: Secular Ideology and the Roots of Modern Conflict* (New York: Oxford University Press, 2009).

To this extent, the question of the relation and impact of religious identity upon human agency is destined to remain without a pragmatic answer.

The second, strictly interrelated fracture relates to the source of religion-inspired behavior, including conflictual behavior. The question here is whether tension originates from the very essence of religion, its inherent character, or whether it should be ascribed to the contingent and instrumental interpretations of religious teachings. Should we accept the former interpretation, then we would obviously be led to believe that, among dozens if not hundreds of religious traditions, some could be more conflict-prone than others.

How could such a claim be established in positive terms? An example could be to carry out a comparative study of the lexicon used by the Bible and the Quran. While the Old and New Testament of the Bible, King James version (roughly 840,000 words), use the word "kill" 240 times, the word "peace" 452 times, and the word "trade" or "money" 152 times, the Quran (roughly 150,000 words) uses the word "kill" 95 times, the word "peace" 55 times, and the word "trade" or "money" 15 times. This means that in the Bible references per page to "peace," "money," and "trade" occur twice as much as in the Quran. Conversely, references to "kill" are more frequent in the Quran than in the Bible.[15] On this basis, some esteem that more comprehensive but similar textual analyses can provide substantial insights as to similarities and differences in religions' underlying propensity to enjoin or legitimate violence and conflict.

Would such analysis hold to empirical and historical testing? It would be hard to prove, as it would require contextualized translations in which words, concepts, and principles are all weighted against the historical and cultural context in which they were used. Besides, one would only have to think at the order of magnitude of death and looting perpetrated in history in the name of the Christian God, or even in the name of Buddhism in the contemporary history of countries such as Sri Lanka, Myanmar, and Thailand, to sense that the amount of references to violence in religious texts cannot be easily put in direct positive correlation with actual conflicts.

Such qualitative methodological remarks would seem to strengthen the position of those scholars who, on the other side, insist on the necessity

15. In the Bible, the average use of the word "kill" is 1 in every 3,500 words; "peace," 1 in 1,860; "trade" or "money," 1 in 5,530. The same values for the Quran are, respectively, 1 in 1,580; 1 in 2,730, and 1 in 10,000.

of using techniques such as *genealogy* and *discourse analysis*, that is, historically interpretative readings of concepts. This is because hermeneutics—a contextual understanding of the religious ethos, rather than an analytical reading of its textual logos—can do justice to the relative characters of religions. This approach implies attention to the historical unfolding, transformation, adaptation, tension, and contradiction inside each tradition, and it would need to be done across long time periods. Such analysis would need to take into account the historical and empirical foundations of religions, and the original conditions from which they developed, as all this has influenced the genesis of their founding beliefs and customs, as well as their historical patterns of adaptation and compromise. All this engenders complexity and suggests cautiousness in adopting any plain interpretation. For example, the Quran extensively documents warfare between early Muslim communities and the Meccan pagan elites, who persecuted and prevented them from practicing their new religion. Hence, the Quran's high number of references to "kill" could be interpreted differently if such war-intensive social context was to be taken into consideration. Others would claim that early-day Christians had to endure just the same levels of ferocious persecutions, while nonetheless resorting to less violent reactions.

Indirectly, giving centrality to hermeneutics also means believing that what matters is not what is written in religious texts or what is said by religious preachers; what matters is how believers interpret them, and how they decide to turn those interpretations into behaviors. Should this approach be preferred, then any religion claiming a mission of peace and forgiveness should be taken at face value and portrayed on an equal footing, irrespective of what it is written in its sacred texts or preached by its priests. At the same time, anthropologists and psychologists would not easily agree with such an approach, as they would suggest that it is nearly impossible to detach the analytical from the interpretative, and the interpretative from the normative: what one reads and hears oftentimes leads to what one believes and that upon which one acts.

The debate on the dichotomy between the interpretive agency of individual believers, on the one hand, and the power of the normative context over the individual, on the other hand, goes back a long time. It appears to be reflected in the argument of religious people against the contention that the most sacred texts are riddled with references and invitations to violence. To this claim, they often answer that it is not what religious texts say; it is how believers interpret them, and how believers decide to turn interpretations into behaviours. R. Scott Appleby draws on this same distinction by referring to the dualist view of *strong religion*—holding religion accountable for violence authorized or enacted by religious actors—versus *weak religion*—laying the blame on secular actors who manipulate religious sensibilities and symbols toward nonreligious ends.[16] According to this distinction, most works on the topic of religion and conflict could be positioned on a continuum rather than in compartmentalized chambers. As an example, Appleby positions some of the work of sociologist of religion Mark Juergensmeyer closer to the *strong religion camp*, as he makes reference to concepts such as *cosmic war*, whereby the true believer sees himself as engaged in a metaphysical struggle, justifying "endless self-renewing, ultra-violent enactments of divine wrath."[17] Such a Manichean worldview would hardly happen if the believer were not given a chance to find clear references in religious texts as to the foundational, teleological, and normative superiority of this or that religion, along with a motivated justification of the use of violence.

On the other side, in the *weak religion camp*, Appleby ascribes to "innumerable books and articles" the tendency to "modify the category 'religious violence' by embedding religious agency within encompassing nationalist and ethnic narratives."[18] In these interpretations, religious motivations, violent dynamics, and religious roles are always seen as dependent upon secular dynamics; somehow, religious leaders and institutions fall prey to "the manipulations of state, nationalist, and ethnic forces" in the societies they inhabit. In other words, "the religious element is weak." Appleby positions some of Juergensmeyer's later work closer to the weak religious camp because it is premised upon the claim that twentieth-century militant religious actors have adopted secular ideologies such as nationalism.[19]

Interestingly, Appleby relies on epistemology as a tool to explain the dif-

16. R. Scott Appleby, "Religious Violence, the Strong, the Weak and the Pathological," in *The Oxford Handbook of Religion, Conflict, and Peacebuilding*, ed. Alalia Omer, R. Scott Appleby, and David Little (Oxford: Oxford University Press, 2015).

17. Mark Juergensmeyer, *Terror in the Mind of God: The Global Rise of Religious Violence* (Berkeley: University of California Press, 2000).

18. R. Scott Appleby, "Religious Violence, the Strong, the Weak and the Pathological," in *The Oxford Handbook of Religion, Conflict, and Peacebuilding*, ed. Atalia Omer, R. Scott Appleby, and David Little (Oxford: Oxford University Press, 2015).

19. Appleby classifies as closer to the weak religious camp Mark Juergensmeyer's "The New Cold War? Religious Nationalism Confronts the Secular State," in *The New Cold War?* (Berkeley: University of California Press, 1993), which was updated and reissued in 2008 under the title *Global Rebellion: Religious Challenges to the Secular State, from Christian Militias to Al Qaeda* (Berkeley: University of California Press, 2008).

ferent worldviews inhabiting the two interpretative approaches. Scholars and believers in the *strong religion* camp rely upon a positive epistemology of neatly defined ontological worlds that easily lends itself to the clear-cut distinction between right and wrong. Thinkers in the *weak religion* camp would rather rely on the centrality of hermeneutics, that is, the importance of (methodologically rigorous) interpretations, and the weak divide between observing subjects and observed objects.

The third fracture relates to how responsibility (understood in analytical, legal, and normative terms) in causing and using violence is shared—or *should* be shared—between the state, on the one hand, and social organizations, including religious organizations, on the other hand. Do people need to fear the judgment and punishment of the state, or of God, and its representatives, only? Do people maintain their right of recurring to violence against the state in any circumstance at all? Behind these questions lie the issues of the legitimacy of the use of violence and, a theoretical step further, the encompassing realms of foundational concepts in the history of philosophical ideas, including those of *just war* and *state of emergency*.

Here, the main intellectual juxtaposition lies between the cultural references of the Renaissance and part of the Enlightenment, including the almighty concept of the *state* and its exclusive right to recur to *violence*, as defined in the philosophical lineage of Nicolò Machiavelli and Thomas Hobbes. On the other side is the right of revolution, as espoused by Enlightenment thinkers such as Locke and Rousseau, and later embraced by more exquisitely Romantic ideas, with their ultimate references to the superiority of transcendental rights, liberty and equality. The first lineage of thinkers portrays the state as the result of a social contract whereby the Leviathan is given the exclusive monopoly on the legitimate use of force. The second, by contrast, understands moral superiority as an independent realm from the province of politics, managing to bring together seemingly irreconcilable movements, often animated by sentiments of democracy and social justice, but also higher divine principles than those governing humans, thus envisioning the possibility of a state of exception and the right to revolution.

RELIGION AND CONFLICT: MEASURING ISSUES

Each of these "metaphysical fractures" pits a non-connotational understanding of "religion" against an equally generalized understanding of "society" or the "state."

However, below each of these theoretical fractures there are very concrete cases of conflict between contingent declinations of "religion," "society," and the "state." That is, each specific temporal and geographical instance of violent conflict may see the role of a specific religion being measured and assessed differently. Indeed, varying religious communities perceive that they are treated disparately when it comes to being judged against their relation with conflict and violence. This two-weight and two-measure perception results in both simmering and overt religious tensions, contributing themselves to the cycle of conflict and violence.

A. Rashied Omar takes the view that there is a biased tendency to attribute deadly violence as an almost exclusive purview of nonstate religious actors, and to obscure state involvement in deadly conflicts. He also stresses the importance of the toxic role played by double standards of judgment across different religions.[20] He notices, for example, that every time Islam is involved in violence, there is a general tendency to assign to the religious component a more important role than to the state component, whereas the contrary happens when Christianity or Judaism are involved. He describes relevant examples, including the war in Bosnia and Herzegovina (1992–95) and apartheid in South Africa (1948–94), to show that Christian churches held very clear responsibilities in providing moral justifications for the systematic use of violence, and that these justifications were kept out of media discussion for long periods of time. To the contrary, religious aspects are always publicized in case of conflicts involving Islamist camps, including in the case of contemporary Lebanon.

By drawing attention to the double standards both between religion and the state—appearing in the general perception that terrorism is the exclusive preserve of nonstate actors—and among different religions, which appears in the mainstream perception that some religions are more violent than others, Rashied Omar indirectly poses the question of the robustness of any empirical finding around the relation between religion and conflict.

RELIGION IN CONFLICT: CORRELATION AND CAUSATION

Mindful of the above methodological and metaphysical discussion, as well as the limitations of any empirical finding on the subject, the question of

20. A. Rashied Omar, "The Possibilities and Limits of Inter-Religious Dialogue," in *The Oxford Handbook of Religion, Conflict, and Peacebuilding*, ed. Atalia Omer, R. Scott Appleby, and David Little (Oxford: Oxford University Press, 2015).

how religion relates to conflict can be articulated via two subsets of questions: (1) How strong is the empirical correlation between religion and conflicts, and (2) How can such a relation best be described?

The academic literature addressing the correlation between *religion* as an independent variable and *violent conflict* as a potentially dependent variable is rich. While the largest body of the empirical literature looks at the topic by analyzing data from specific time periods and geographies (study cases), some reviews adopt a more comprehensive approach. For example, American political scientist R. J. Rummel quantifies the number of people killed as a result of state-orchestrated violence for any reason, an act he names *democide* to differentiate it from the more circumscribed policy of *genocide*.[21] He eventually places the number of deaths caused by democide somewhere in-between 174 and 340 million people in the twentieth century alone, roughly corresponding to four times the number of people killed in all twentieth-century national and international wars, including the two world wars.[22] Rummel defines as *Megamurderers* those regimes that have caused more than 10 million deaths: the Soviet Union (1917–87); the People's Republic of China (1949–87); Germany (1933–45); and the Chinese Kuomintang (1928–49), which are collectively responsible for some 130 million deaths. Below them, he enlists the *Lesser Megamurderers*, each responsible for the death of less than 10 million people; the *Suspected Megamurderers*; and the *Centi-Kilomurderers*, responsible for less than 1 million deaths.[23]

Were religious organizations involved in these acts of *democide*? If anything, the role of religion in organized mass murders in the twentieth cen-

21. "*Democide* is a government's murder of people for whatever reason; *genocide* is the murder of people because of their race, ethnicity, religion, nationality, or language." In Rudolph J. Rummel, *Death by Government* (New Brunswick, NJ: Transaction, 1997), 145. Thus qualified, democide can be taken as an indicator for violent conflict.

22. The number of deaths caused by governments fomenting wars seems nonetheless to be counted in Rummel's democide statistics.

23. *Lesser Megamurderers:* Japan (1936–45); Maoist Soviets (1923–49); Cambodia (1975–79); Turkey (1909–18); Vietnam (1945–87); Poland (1945–48); Pakistan (1958–87); Yugoslavia (1944–87). *Suspected Megamurderers*: North Korea (1948–87); Mexico (1900–1920); Russia (1900–1917). *Centi-Kilomurderers*—Chinese warlords (1917–49); Turkey under Ataturk (1919–23); United Kingdom (1900–1987); Portugal (1926–82) and Indonesia (1965–87). Altogether, these add an extra 20 million people to the list. Rudolph J. Rummel, *Death by Government* (New Brunswick, NJ: Transaction, 1997).

tury was conspicuous by its weakness. The Holocaust contributed 6 million deaths to the 21 million caused by Nazi Germany. Yet, while Holocaust victims were chosen on an ethnic-religious basis, it would be difficult to argue that the Holocaust itself was motivated or justified, directly or indirectly, by reference to religious or theological arguments.[24]

Arguably, the Turkish genocide of Armenians had a religious connotation attached to it; yet many interpret it as part of a wave of a state terror finalized with the goal of creating ethnically homogenous states in an era of growing nationalism.[25] Similarly, while state violence in China was particularly harsh against the non-Han population, such as the Tibetans and the Uighurs, these groups were primarily distinguished on ethnic, cultural, and linguistic—rather than religious—grounds. In the Balkans, the national wars that erupted after the dissolution of multinational Yugoslavia in 1991 are mostly interpreted as multicause, with religion only representing one of these causes. While religion has been generally recognized as a force seeking the division of Yugoslavia into ethnically and religiously homogenous states, and therefore a factor galvanizing conflict and helping in rationalizing its outcomes, it was less prominent in national discourse than references to ethnic and ideological propaganda. At the same time, religious organizations were also promoting activities aimed at preventing violence and healing postconflict societies.[26]

24. To confirm this, one should consider that in the era of the Holocaust, alongside the six million Jews, the Nazi also systematically exterminated twice as many people among Slavs, Roma, people of color, communists, trade unionists, homosexuals, the mentally and physically handicapped, and more. Among religious communities, Jehovah's Witnesses and Baha'is were systematically targeted. Relations with Catholics and Protestants were not good, either: in 1935, the Nazi regime reneged on a concordat it had signed with the Vatican two years earlier, and begun persecuting and killing Catholic leaders. Meanwhile, the Lutheran Church was being both infiltrated and sidelined by establishing a Reich Church under the leadership of Ludwig Müller in 1933. More generally, religion was put under the state's control via the Ministry for Church Affairs established in 1935, generally driven by policies aimed at undermining the influence of religion on the German people.

25. Before 1915, Muslim Turks and Christian Armenians had coexisted for centuries in a multiethnic and multireligious Ottoman Empire. By 1915, the rebellion of Ottoman-ruled Christian peoples of the Balkans, including Serbs, Greeks, and Bulgarians, had already led to the creation of new nation-states, which also had resorted to ethnic cleansing, often against Muslims.

26. See, for example, Vjekoslav Perica, "Religion in the Balkan Wars," in *Oxford Handbooks Online*, October 2014.

Rummel is not alone in seeing a limited role for religious motivations in most of the twentieth-century violence. American social activist George Weigel reminds us that "it was not religion that has made the twentieth the most bloody century. Lenin, Stalin, Hitler, Mao Tse Tung, Pol Pot and their apprentices maimed and murdered millions of people . . . in the name of a policy which rejected religious or other transcendent reference points for judging its purposes and practice."[27] This suggests that, at least in the twentieth century, secularist ideologies were responsible for more violence than religious ideologies.

More nuanced pictures of the correlation between religion and conflict emerge with more granular investigations of specific regions and time periods. Many quantitative study cases, thus, conclude that religious discourse and actors *can* influence conflict, albeit their influence is always a concurrent factor, often limited in time and mostly subordinated to other leading players and narratives. For example, while dissecting Middle Eastern conflicts between 1945 and 2001, Jonathan Fox concludes that after 1980, religious nationalist ethnic groups were responsible for a higher level of violence than nonreligious nationalist groups, although the religious determinant was not the only influence.[28] By looking at interstate conflicts in the same region and in the same period (1950–92), Brian Lai similarly concludes that religion does matter in conflict, specifying, however, that religious identity alone is more predictive of the propensity of leaders to perceive and manipulate identity to rally support, rather than predictive of conflict itself.[29]

Similarly, looking at sub-Saharan Africa during the period 1990–2008 in an effort to establish a link between religion and conflict by arguing that particular religious structures are prone to mobilization once politicized, Matthias Basedau, Georg Strüver, and Johannes Vüllers conclude that "quantitative research has failed to find support for the *significant* causal influence of religious factors on the onset of armed conflicts in Africa and

27. Quoted in Luc Reychler and Arnim Langer, ed., *Luc Reychler: A Pioneer in Sustainable Peace Building Architecture* (Leuven: KU Leuven, 2020).

28. Jonathan Fox, "The Rise of Religious Nationalism and Conflict: Ethnic and Revolutionary Wars, 1945–2001," *Journal of Peace Research* 41, no. 6 (2004): 715–31; Mark Juergensmeyer, *Terror in the Mind of God: The Global Rose of Religious Violence* (Berkeley: University of California Press, 2000).

29. Brian Lai, "An Empirical Examination of Religion and Conflict in the Middle East, 1950–1992," *Foreign Policy Analysis* 2, no. 1 (2006): 21–36.

elsewhere."[30] They nonetheless emphasize that religious and ethnic *identities* are predictors for religious armed conflicts. The underlying idea that in specific circumstances religion is a permissive, and therefore predictive, cause of conflict, particularly when it overlaps with other identities, was confirmed in later studies based on new data from developing countries more generally.[31]

In a comprehensive empirical study on the subject, the Institute for Economics and Peace recently suggested that, while religion did not stand as a single cause of conflict in any of the 35 active conflicts it reviewed in 2013, it did remain as one of the most common causes *contributing* to conflict worldwide, along with "identity," "self-government," and "opposition to the system." Religion played a role in 60 percent of all the reviewed conflicts. Within this 60 percent, religion represented one of three or more reasons for conflict in 67 percent of the cases.[32] These results are complemented by a few other findings in the same study, including a weak correlation between levels of religious belief and peace (as measured by the Global Peace index). In statistical terms, this finding likely comes as a result of the fact that the overwhelming majority of people in the world have a religious belief, independently of the level of conflict in the region they inhabit. The overall conclusion of the study is that there is no clear correlation between religious beliefs and peace. On the contrary, religion plays a significant role in many conflicts and is a feature of many violent confrontations. Yet, when analyzing the determinants of peace and conflict through an empirical analysis, there are other factors that are statistically more relevant, including economic inequality, corruption, political terrorism, and political instability.

30. Matthias Basedau, Georg Strüver, Johannes Vüllers, and Tim Wegenast, "Do Religious Factors Impact Armed Conflict? Empirical Evidence from Sub-Saharan Africa," *Terrorism and Political Violence* 23 (2011): 752–79.

31. In particular, the authors underline how "overlapping religious and other identities form a particular conflict risk [thus showing] that religious identities, rather than being socially insulated, are actually embedded in other social relationships. When these identities run parallel, and possibly are amplified and dichotomized through economic and political inequalities, fertile ground for conflict emerges." In Matthias Basedau, Birte Pfeiffer, and Johannes Vüllers, "Bad Religion? Religion, Collective Action, and the Onset of Armed Conflict in Developing Countries," *Journal of Conflict Resolution* 60, no. 2 (2016): 226–55.

32. Institute for Economics and Peace, *Five Key Questions Answered on the Link between Peace and Religion*, 2014, www.economicsandpeace.org

CONCLUSIONS

The question of the relation between religion and violent conflicts elicits methodological and metaphysical issues that have no straightforward answers. While these issues cannot be solved in methodological, metaphysical, or normative terms, it is nonetheless possible to adopt a number of simplifying assumptions allowing for some empirical analyses.

The evidence collected in a literature review of empirical analyses suggests that "religion" can only be scantly associated with *major* acts of orchestrated violence in the twentieth century. The reason for such low correlation might well be read through the structure of the international system during this period, as nationalism remained the major driving force of political disruption in the first half of the century, while the Cold War and the distinct possibility of a nuclear holocaust in a MAD (mutual assured destruction) scenario left relatively little space to major ethnic, religious, or national conflicts in the second half of the century.

On the other side, several studies looking at specific geographic regions or shorter time periods, or both, suggest that, under specific circumstances, religious factors were positively correlated to violence in some of the less deadly conflicts of the twentieth century. This is particularly the case with the overlapping of religious identities with other social identities in difficult economic or political contexts.

This review leaves open the question of the role of religion in major conflicts before the twentieth century, when religion played a more prominent role in driving the political agenda in polities across the world, and particularly throughout ancient history and the Middle Ages. In this sense, Charles Derber and Yale R. Magrass notice that there is strong evidence supporting the contention that religion and war were intertwined from the earliest time, with sacred texts justifying or legitimizing war among pre-Christian Scandinavian Norsemen (11th–8th century BC); inhabitants of China during the Zhou dynasty (11th–3rd century BC); ancient polytheist Greeks (9th century BC); early Hinduist believers (4th–2nd century BC); and the Aztecs of Mexico (14th to 16th century AD).[33]

Religion, thus, certainly plays a role in permitting, generating, and sustaining conflict, but the weight and quality of that role have been both weak and spurious in the twentieth century. These findings are strongly suggestive

33. Charles Derber with Yale R. Magrass, *Morality Wars* (New York: Routledge, 2010).

of the need for more systematic reviews allowing a clarification of the significance of religion in violent conflicts before the twentieth century.

References

Appleby, R. Scott. "Religious Violence, the Strong, the Weak and the Pathological." In *The Oxford Handbook of Religion, Conflict, and Peacebuilding*, ed. Alalia Omer, R. Scott Appleby, and David Little. Oxford: Oxford University Press, 2015.

Basedau, Matthias, Birte Pfeiffer, and Johannes Vüllers. "Bad Religion? Religion, Collective Action, and the Onset of Armed Conflict in Developing Countries." *Journal of Conflict Resolution* 60, no. 2 (2016): 226–55.

Basedau, Matthias, Georg Strüver, Johannes Vüllers, and Tim Wegenast. "Do Religious Factors Impact Armed Conflict? Empirical Evidence from Sub-Saharan Africa." *Terrorism and Political Violence* 23 (2011): 752–79.

Cavanaugh, William T. *The Myth of Religious Violence: Secular Ideology and the Roots of Modern Conflict*. New York: Oxford University Press, 2009.

de Benoist, Alain. "Autorité spirituelle et pouvoir temporelle." In *L'Empire intérieur*. Saint Clément de rivière: Fata Morgana, 1995.

Derber, Charles, with Yale R. Magrass. *Morality Wars*. New York: Routledge, 2010.

Fox, Jonathan. "The Rise of Religious Nationalism and Conflict: Ethnic and Revolutionary Wars, 1945–2001." *Journal of Peace Research* 41, no. 6 (2004): 715–31.

Galtung, Johan. "Violence, Peace, and Peace Research." *Journal of Peace Research* 6, no. 3 (1969): 167–91.

Guénon, René. *Spiritual Authority and Temporal Power*. Ghent, NY: Sophia Perennis, 2001.

Hunt, Dave, Thomas A. McMahon, and Shirley Cauthen. *The Seduction of Christianity*. Eugene, OR: Harvest House, 1985.

Institute for Economics and Peace. *Five Key Questions Answered on the Link between Peace and Religion*, 2014, www.economicsandpeace.org

Juergensmeyer, Mark. *Terror in the Mind of God: The Global Rise of Religious Violence*. Berkeley: University of California Press, 2000.

Kishi, K., A. Cooperman, and A. Schiller. "Many Countries Favor Specific Religions, Officially or Unofficially." Pew Research Center, October 3, 2017.

Lai, Brian. "An Empirical Examination of Religion and Conflict in the Middle East, 1950–1992." *Foreign Policy Analysis* 2, no. 1 (2006): 21–36.

Ochs, Peter. "The Possibilities and Limits of Inter-Religious Dialogue." In *The Oxford Handbook of Religion, Conflict, and Peacebuilding*, ed. Atalia Omer, R. Scott Appleby, and David Little. Oxford: Oxford University Press, 2015.

Omar, A. Rashied. "The Possibilities and Limits of Inter-Religious Dialogue." In *The Oxford Handbook of Religion, Conflict, and Peacebuilding*, ed. Atalia Omer, R. Scott Appleby, and David Little. Oxford: Oxford University Press, 2015.

Payson Conflict Study Group. *A Glossary on Violent Conflict: Terms and Concepts Used in Conflict Prevention, Mitigation, and Resolution in the Context of Disaster Relief and Sustainable Development*. Tulane, LA: Tulane University Press, 2001.

Perica, Vjekoslav. "Religion in the Balkan Wars." *Oxford Handbooks Online*, October 2014. https://www.oxfordhandbooks.com/view/10.1093/oxfordhb/9780199935420.001.0001/oxfordhb-9780199935420-e-37

Reychler, Luc, and Arnim Langer, eds. *Luc Reychler: A Pioneer in Sustainable Peace Building Architecture*. Leuven: KU Leuven, 2020.

Rummel, Rudolph J. *Death by Government*. New Brunswick, NJ: Transaction, 1997.

Wallensteen, Peter, and Karin Axel. "Conflict Resolution and the End of the Cold War, 1989–1993." *Journal of Peace Research* 31, no. 3 (1994): 333–49.

PART II

Theoretical and Empirical Cases across Regions

Christianity in Europe

Introduction

Christianity is popularly assumed—often incorrectly—to play little role in European politics. The Nietzschean proclamation that "God is dead" is routinely accepted by many Europeans, with measures of religiosity or churchgoers being showcased as indicators of religion as a phenomenon of the past—except, perhaps, as a reflection of cultural heritage. Yet religiosity in Europe is more complex than any one-sided picture would suggest: even in paradigmatically "secular" European cases, religion may have official ties with the state, and statistics suggest that people believe in spirituality or a life force in higher numbers than might be expected from accounts emphasizing Europe's strong secularism. Stronger political engagement from minority Christian denominations in specific local contexts—such as Christian Anglicans and Christian Orthodox—contribute to reflecting Christianity as significant in European politics. The case studies in this section show that Christianity marks its presence in Europe through philosophical and theological debates; active, albeit subdued roles in century-old political conflicts; vibrant contemporary political elections; and deep-seated visions of politics and communal life.

The studies in this section of the volume suggest a number of important lessons in terms of both social theory and empirics. First, religion and populism have joined in Europe in what Marco Ferraro calls *populist religions*. These are antirationalist movements that in philosophical terms may fall within Nietzsche's concept of *priestly type*, which emphasizes ideas, essences, spirit, and knowledge. This contradiction stands as a level at which populist religion shares something in common with scholars, even as it decries scholars, intellectuals, sciences, and other knowledge elites. Second, scholarship, like the *Übermensch*, may constitute, for Nietzsche, alternative esoteric and material strategies to manage the historical death of God, normatively and institutionally speaking, in the West. Third, the Christian world still struggles, normatively and philosophically, with Greek moral models, such as the Greek concept of the slave mentality *versus* the warrior mentality. These models run counter to more typical Christian thinking (traditional and contemporary): in the Greek model, modesty and humility are slave-like and are, literally, conceived of as evil; whereas (consequence-challenged) life-seeking exuberance and aggressiveness is perceived to be an unqualified good. Fourth, there appears to be a masking, in Europe, historically, of religion through ideology or ideology through religion, or of religion through philosophy and religion through scholarly pursuits and institutions, or both. It is not always clear the extent to which Nietzsche is advocating this transition, or is simply reflecting and recording it in his writing.

Fifth, religion remains a key player among social and political actors in both Eastern and Western Europe. The case studies in this section address Ukraine and Ireland in this regard. In the former case, religious imagery and rhetoric were deeply influential in elections as recently as 2019. In the latter case, religion was critical in sectarian conflict among Catholics and Protestants for at least 300 years, ending only in 1999. Sixth, scholarly attention to religious variables among political scientists, including theological principles, would increase the likelihood of our correct conceptualization of religious conflicts, patterns of conflict resolution and coexistence, and the predictability of the same. Seventh, there are alternative philosophies to neoliberalism, populism, and postmodernism. The scholars in this section of the volume outline several important options among these on philosophical and political grounds, including attention to their relationship with religious precepts and world religions. And, eighth, religion appears to matter *profoundly* to some Europeans, particularly relating to emphases on the arenas of morals, values, spirit, essences, refusing a mind-body dialectic, and perhaps refusing a spiritual-material dialectic as normatively *better* alternatives for achieving peace, coexistence, and for ending political corruption within the state.

Marco Ferraro examines Nietzsche's *On the Genealogy of Morals* and its relationship with developments in the Western European political scene. He addresses Nietzsche's critique of the death of God and the rising divine authority in Europe as a normative crisis in which something is offered to replace it (typically, secular science, progress, and so on), and sets out, nonetheless, on a Nietzschean critique of the current relationship among populist politics and religion. When populist movements draw upon religion, they tend to use religion as a peculiar marker of identity, Ferraro argues, in service of a civilizational divide. This identity, in turn, links moral struggle with struggles in regard to institutional religious hierarchies, and possibly political hierarchies and institutions as well. Thus, Ferraro draws upon Nietzsche's *On the Genealogy of Morals* to examine the role of "knowledge economies" as used by populists in Europe to attack the existing political order. An interesting link between political populism and religion is made possible by the secularization process in the West, which affects both religion and politics.

Addressing both metaphysics and the *priestly type* in Nietzsche's thinking, Ferraro suggests that the link between (secular) populism and *political religions* in the twentieth century—in which the ascetic instinct was, in a sense, secularized or vulgarized—has confirmed Nietzsche's analysis of the death of God as a historical and normative fact or process in European (and Western) history. The normative need for metaphysical and moral debates, however, continues to present itself in both religion and politics, linked, paradigmatically, in populist religions in politics, or what Ferraro calls *political religions*.

In particular, debates regarding where normative moral good lies are addressed: Is the moral good to be found in the Greek notion of life lived energetically without care for consequences; or, in what the Greeks would call the "slave" mentality, in being passive, docile, humble, and domesticated, embodying a good-things-come-to-those-who-wait ethic, and the like? And, what are the traits of its opposite, evil? The Greek notion of evil would be precisely passivity or slave-like behavior, whereas the Christian notion of evil is precisely living without care for consequences. The Western Christian world "inverted" the Greek principle, according to Nietzsche, creating the *priestly type*, someone who substitutes self-abnegation for life-affirming (and consequence-challenged) exuberance. The *priestly type* is contrasted with the Greek ideal, the *warrior type*. This analysis relates to the construction of political meaning as a contested terrain with specific constituencies who benefit, each and differently, from disparate configurations of moral philosophy in practical, political application, and in distinct formations of meaning.

The death of God in Europe, then, was none other than the disappearance of the metaphysical foundation for the lives of Westerners as humans. The source of meaning was gone, as was the source of authority. For Ferraro, God is not a necessity in Nietzsche's thinking, however. Both philosophy and religion, for Nietzsche, can be used to turn humans away from "the real" and to "the fictional"—that is, away from things that are life-affirming and toward the worlds of either (philosophical) *ideas* or (spiritual) *afterlife* (metaphysics having once combined them, as well as the material disciplines, into one). For Nietzsche, Ferraro tells us, metaphysics is a statement, "No," to life pertaining to people who are in a position of weakness in the world. Because of their relative physical, psychological, or resource-related weaknesses, they find solace in the worlds of ideas, essences, spirit, and knowledge. Abstractions take on meaning as "true," leaving us wafting in a world of theory, while life-affirming material conditions are less important, and so "the world as given suffers a loss of reality" for Ferraro. The qualities of material realities are, likewise, taken away and replaced (ideologically) with the world of ideas—or scholarly theories in general. Through this process, (secular) ideology appears to replace God, historically, in the European context. In twentieth-century *political religions*, the process comes full circle; ideology, which remains politicized in the sense of being enacted in political movements and institutions, has become at once sanctified and, perhaps, vulgarized in populist religious movements. Or, perhaps, ideology is sanctified by association with religion, and religion is vulgarized by the same. Indeed, for Ferraro, where ideology is the ideational-essential-spiritual replacement for religion after the death of God, veiling its true intent as such, in twentieth-century *political religions* ideology becomes veiled yet again by its association with *political religion* in a sort of double-masking.

The ascetic instinct is, nonetheless, a trait of the *priestly type*, who may, for this analysis, include the range from religious specialists (e.g., actual priests, rabbis, imams, and monks) to scholars in any discipline to cult leaders, and the like. That is, it includes some categories that may be normatively valid for Nietzsche, who is unlikely to be suggesting a strict materialism in which philosophy does not matter. Indeed, for Nietzsche, scholarship, like the *Übermensch*, may be a strategy that is both esoteric and material to manage the historical death of God, normatively and institutionally speaking, in the West. That is, among other things, concepts play the role of replacing God as a source for constructing meaning in the European normative imagination. For Ferraro, both Apollonian order and rationality and Dionysian artistic intoxication are necessary, in some balance, to both efforts (e.g., the building of conceptual frameworks for the construction of meaning, and religious efforts building meaning through God). Populism, for its part, presents itself (probably incorrectly) as antirationalist. It instrumentalizes religion, in Ferraro's analysis, despite its antirationalist position. It publicly denies, in a sense, the common esoteric ground of the *priestly type* in intellectual, spiritual, and other types of nonmaterial endeavors centered upon ideas, essences, spirit, and knowledge.

Antoine Arjakovsky suggests that fundamentalism can come in laicist or religious forms. For Arjakovsky, the two share in common the desire to separate faith and reason; to deny transcendence and immanence (that is, related to divinity, or divinity-oriented states of being, consciousness, or existence that we typically associate with world religions); and to foreground their own "civilizational project at the expense of the expression of difference." Arjakovsky commends the argument of Jean Birnbaum in noting that movements such as Islamic *jihadism* have forced European civilization to define, in Arjakovsky's words, those "living symbols of deep choices" that Europeans have made—"from socializing in coffee shops to use of municipal pools"—in terms not laic but, rather, of transcendence and immanent experience. Both the agnostic state and cultural values emerging from European philosophers of *noumena* were unable to "resist the rise of totalitarianisms," for Arjakovsky, as well as religious fundamentalism. The key to reconciliation among them, then, is to find the meanings or gateways that unite them.

Today's world is one characterized by a neo-gnosticism, with its emphasis on the esoteric, and the precedence of ideas over matter, as well as extreme (material) violence, according to Arjakovsky. It is the irony of the juxtaposition of these two (competing or mutually reinforcing?) impetuses that he addresses through the case study of the 2019 presidential elections in Ukraine with an eye to its implications for contemporary Christian societies, and for tensions among neoliberal and neopopulist beliefs and forces. The campaign of one candidate (the incumbent Petro Poroshenko) weaved Christianity into a neopopulist narrative regarding the Ukrainian people, sovereign rights, language, and God with campaign slogans such as "Army, Language and Faith." It reflected deep convictions on the part of the candidate himself, which drew effectively, in Arjakovsky's analysis, upon the religious consciousness of a large majority of the Ukrainian people, as approximately 72 percent of the Ukrainian population define themselves as believers.

The other leading candidate in the 2019 Ukrainian elections, Volodymyr Zelensky, was raised within Judaism and expressed an identity and politics that included strong religious convictions, which were, nonetheless, largely separated from traditional institutional religion. In his comic and political writings (he was a television personality and a comedian by profession), Zelensky presented a cosmogony in which "God is alone in the Heavens," and humans on earth know only a thirst for power and the ability to engage in the destruction of God's creation. The political characters who ruled Ukraine since independence, in his framework, were nothing but adventurists: corrupted from within by the lust for power, capable of leaving the people with naught but the struggle for survival. Imagery including heavens, hearts betrayed, and others were powerful parts of his campaign. The candidate, for his part, presented himself as the avenger, according to Arjakovsky, "who, like God the Father in person, is going to avenge the political personnel in power in Ukraine since 1991." Arjakovsky characterizes Zelensky's discourses as "gnostic," that is, as emphasizing the ethereal, and as not offering a complete political program, per se, but, rather, a hotly rhetorical and cosmically purifying alternative to corruption. While Arjakovsky offers a gentle critique of the relative lack of programmatic specifics in Zelensky's campaign, he is the candidate who ultimately won the 2019 elections and stands as the current president of Ukraine.

Arjakovsky explains this passage in the context of the enormous political, economic, and military pressures from the military confrontation with Russia; Western pressures for the liberalization of the economy; and low domestic economic indicators. The current president presented himself, in Arjakovsky's words, as a man "without experience and, thus, not contaminated by the corruption of the elites, ready to travel by bicycle to his presidential palace just like his personage on television." This strategy, combined with his highly charged religious imagery, was the best option in the eyes of the Ukrainian people. That is, he offered the people hope. Arjakovsky analyzes these developments in the context of debates among neoliberals and neopopulists, a debate reflecting the "sickness of the postmodern soul." He offers a combination of *emergentist* and *neo-personalist* approaches as alternatives. *Emergentist* approaches reject a Cartesian strict separation of mind and body together with the emphasis on a voluntarist vision of the world, and suggest, instead, the neo-gnostic emphasis on the resonance of the Spirit in the world, perhaps metaphysics, and a sort of Taoist-Christian vision of divine humanity. Such a vision allows for the purification of both religion and politics at the institutional and philosophical levels. *Neo-personalist* approaches uncouple the division between subjective and objective worlds; reintegrate identity and otherness; and suggest a number of different levels of reality, including, following the French philosopher Jean-Marc Ferry, that which we associate with images, imputations, differentiation, and counterfactual suppositions; in such a view, authentic religion should not wait for divine intervention to act within the world.

C. K. Martin Chung addresses conflict and efforts at coexistence among Catholic and Protestant populations in Northern Ireland; or, what some locals call, the "unfinished Reformation." A form of Christian secular framework has developed as a result of—or in order to foster—intercommunal attempts to eschew the "sin of sectarianism." Secularism, in this context, has been viewed by disparate Christian communities as a common threat; on the other hand, it has been welcomed inasmuch as it aided in the achievement of peace across sectarian lines. In this study, Chung also seeks to shed light on the question of the relative benefits and shortcomings of a theologically informed analysis vs. a purely secular political science approach to these questions. Indeed, Chung joins the two in a fascinating inquiry.

While Northern Ireland has remained part of the United Kingdom since 1920–21, conflict among Catholics and Protestants has been informed by a history of British colonial rule in Ireland, which, as a whole, became part of the United Kingdom since the Acts of Union in 1800. The status of Northern Ireland has remained a question ever since. Moreover, the sectarian religious cleavages have run parallel with ethnic difference in this case. These factors complicate the religion question into one of ethno-religious cleavage as well as "colonial injustice, existential fear, and historical traumas," according to Chung. The Thirty Years' War of 1618–48 ran together in the minds of the parties with the Troubles of 1968–98—that is, the history reflects a long, sometimes violent memory on both sides, centered upon a melee of ethnicity, religion, and conflicts over the distribution of power, both political and economic. That is, the conflict among Catholics and Protestants in Northern Ireland has been unusually persistent over time. Indeed, Chung notes, when Nietzsche was proclaiming the death of God in the European imagination and political order, Northern Ireland was (still then/already then) experiencing vandalism of churches and religious statues, as well as other acts of violence.

The case of North Ireland has been used both as a *sui generis*, or exceptional, case, and as a case with universal applicability in terms of religious or ethno-religious conflict, or both. Within the Christian European world, Chung tells us, it is a case that demonstrates the longevity of the influence of religion within the (ostensibly) secular political sphere. Chung asks how, during the Troubles, were faith, politics, and secularization viewed in Northern Ireland? Moreover, he suggests that these factors—all part of the conflict—were, ultimately, mobilized to achieve peace and reconciliation in 1998. It is the process of the intentional invoking of these factors to lead from conflict to reconciliation that Chung details in the chapter. Contrasting his argument to those who have suggested that conflict in Northern Ireland persisted precisely because of a refusal to engage, sufficiently, in a secularization process, Chung contends that "Christian secularists" combined theology and secularism, in various and specific parts, giving them the impetus for peace, negotiation, and reconciliation.

Indeed, secularization itself played the role of uniting factor for religious parties on both sides over time, as it became viewed as a common threat; and, the "sin of sectarianism" was raised in contrast to those arguments based upon historical, ethnic, religious, political and economic distributions of power, which had previously been used to justify and support political violence. Chung analyzes the role of secularism in this case in terms of Elizabeth Hurd's concept of "Judeo-Christian secularism." He argues that Christian communities did not provide concrete political (that is, secular) plans for constitutional reform; rather, they drew upon theological traditions within their respective religions in order to develop the foundations for peace. Inasmuch as political science tends to be laicist (that is, *laic*, or, roughly, strictly secularist) and to lean away from analysis of factors such as religious theology, Chung suggests, it may have a difficult time accounting for the processes that led to the historic peace and reconciliation in the Northern Ireland context.

IN SUM, religion appears to matter significantly more in Europe than popular, and even some scholarly, accounts would suggest. Some of the ways in which religion matters in Europe are outlined in the chapters in this section of the volume in political, philosophical, cultural, normative, theological, and electoral contexts in various parts of the region.

On the Genealogy of Populist Morals

Marco Ferraro

Orta Doğu Teknik Üniversitesi (METU)—Ankara

This chapter addresses contexts and methods through which populist movements in Western Europe employ religion. It does so through a Nietzschean critique of the present relationship between populist politics and religion in Western Europe. When populists employ religious discourse, we witness a peculiar form of the interaction between politics and religion: religion is used as a "marker" of identity or as part of an effort to impose a civilizational divide, or both. The conjunction between populism and religion in Western Europe is visible through populism's discourse on élites and "the people." This discourse does not favor an alignment of populist politics with institutional religious hierarchies but rather it favors an appropriation by populist politics of religious themes. Because populism articulates a strongly moral discourse on the values of élites and the people, such a moral tone allows populist leaders to disguise themselves as quasi-religious leaders, speaking on behalf of the people: these, in populist discourse, are treated as "sacred." In fact, populist leaders from Marine Le Pen to Matteo Salvini to Geert Wilders have consistently referred to the "people" as absolutely sovereign, as an entity from which all legitimacy and power comes, and whose interests should trump any opposition. Populists present all limitations to the unhindered expression of popular sovereignty, like constitutional checks and balances, as entrapments prepared by the corrupted "liberal" élites to keep the "people" under control.[1]

As much as populist discourse concerns a moral struggle of some sort,

1. Cas Mudde, "The Populist Zeitgeist," *Government and Opposition* 39, no. 4 (2004): 541–63.

Friedrich Nietzsche's *On the Genealogy of Morals*[2] provides a useful framework through which to understand the case of populism in Western Europe. This region is also the most secularized[3] globally: it is again worth borrowing some of Nietzsche's ideas to understand how secularization managed an (incomplete) expulsion of religion from the public sphere, while the *ascetic* ideal remained a fundamental part of Western European societies.

Asceticism is connected to morals, particularly in the form of religion and knowledge. The present analysis posits that, in our current "knowledge economies,"[4] it is precisely the value of certain types of knowledge claims or epistemologies that populists wage their moral attack against.

A specific configuration of the politics-religion connection is extant in the case of European populism. Populism utilizes religious discourse and religious elements to supplement its own ideolog(ies). This marriage is possible in current postmaterial times, ironically, precisely because of the secularization process, which affects both religion and politics as experienced in the West. Religion features centrally in much Western European populist discourse, though not as a coherent and unitarian force, but rather as an "archive" or as a toolbox: populist leaders are not advocating for a "pious" society, instead they use religious references, symbols, and tropes as markers of an identity, as a separation line between an "us" and a "them," and "us" is never defined more clearly than the "people." Populist discourse, conveniently, does not develop an ideology or even a myth of this "people," so according to the context this "us" can be stressed as secular or as Christian, depending on the "them" it opposes: if it is the liberal cosmopolitans, then "us" means the genuine people, inheritor of the Christian legacy of Europe. If it is the Muslim immigrants, then "us" means the emancipated Europe that has properly emasculated the role of religion in public life.[5]

The relation between populist politics and religion in Western Europe is therefore informed by the advanced secularized character of most societies in this region of the world.

2. Friedrich Nietzsche, *On the Genealogy of Morals*, translated by Water Kaufmann and R. J. Hollingdale (New York: Vintage Books, 1989). Hereafter, Nietzsche, GM.

3. Peter Berger, "Secularism in Retreat," *National Interest* 46 (1996).

4. Peter F. Drucker, *The Age of Discontinuity* (Oxford: Butterworth-Heinemann Oxford, 1969).

5. Andrea Molle, "Religion and Right-Wing Populism in Italy: Using 'Judeo-Christian Roots' to Kill the European Union," *Religion, State & Society* 47, no. 1 (2019): 151–68.

THE INVERSION OF VALUES AND THE PRIESTLY TYPE

In addressing the "death of God," Nietzsche highlights the crisis of a metaphysical foundation, which may be represented by God or by other equivalents (e.g., science, progress, humanity). While he decried the death of God in Western societies more than one century ago, his analysis remains relevant for much of the story of the past century, and perhaps also for the current one: Nietzsche's observation of the nearly ubiquitous ascetic ideal, found across space and time, has taken new forms in the secular era. It has engaged in a sort of transference, moving the sacred to be included in ostensibly secular politics, as *political religions*[6] in the twentieth century have shown.

Nietzsche introduced the concept of the death of God to describe the transformation that he witnessed in his own time, and which he thought would be increasingly manifest in the future. It is in his *On the Genealogy of Morals* (GM) that we can trace the elements to understand what this divine death meant for him. In this work, Nietzsche presents the genealogical method as a means to reconstruct the processes through which humans came to have moral concepts. This method weaves together concepts pertaining to human value-making and also to the ways in which religion and the sacred are situated, conceptually, by human societies in relation to life experience. The Nietzschean genealogical method can allow us to develop insights into changes in the relationship between politics and religion in contemporary global societies.

The genealogical method is used to trace the emergence of Christian morality. The process that led to it, for Nietzsche, was one of inversion, replacing a "noble" with a "slave" morality.[7] For an example of the noble morality, we can refer to pre-Socratic Greeks, the paradigmatic case of a noble morality for Nietzsche: Greek morality was based upon the opposition between the concept of "good" and "bad." It called good what it saw as life-affirming: the healthy, the strong, the energetic, and that which led to a youthful expenditure of energies without care for the consequences of the expenditure itself. This latter point is key in identifying this type of morality as aristocratic: it is exactly the trait of the careless self-expenditure that was

6. Emilio Gentile, "Political Religion: A Concept and Its Critics—a Critical Survey," *Totalitarian Movements and Political Religions* 6, no. 1 (2005): 19–32.

7. Friedrich Nietzsche, *On the Genealogy of Morals*, GM I:7–11.

seen as the mark of a full embracement of life.[8] Defined as bad was the opposite, that which is weak, sickly, incapable of self-expression, and concerned with subsistence. An inversion of the duality, good-bad, had already begun with Socrates,[9] but reached completion with Christianity: the dyad "good-bad" came to be replaced with the dyad "evil-virtuous."[10]

This replacement meant that the previous Greek concept of good was now taken to be evil in Christianity, and the previous concept of bad was now taken to be virtuous. The antinomy of evil and virtuous managed to assert itself and replace the Greek noble morality for the Christian virtuous morality. Thus, while the concept of "good" in the Christian morality pertains to what is weak, tame, docile, domesticated—the mark of the "slave" morality for the Greeks—this becomes with Christianity that which is assumed to be virtuous. In parallel, what previously was "good" under the Greek noble morality is now taken to be "evil" under Christianity: the old Greek virtues of physical and moral health and activity are now viewed as aggression, prevarication, excess, and violence.

This historical development of inversion of moral types, Nietzsche explains, substitutes a "life-affirming" morality with a "life-negating" morality, and is enacted by the priestly type of individual. Nietzsche's concept of the priestly type pertains to the Christian religion, but, beyond that, it aims to describe a type of individual who lives in a relation of opposition to the world ("*in order to exist, slave morality first needs a hostile external world*"[11]). This individual type (unlike the ancient Greeks) exists in a position of weakness in the world and intentional inferiority to "nobles," in the sense of limited physical strength and resources. The priestly type therefore develops what Nietzsche calls *ressentiment* (resentment): a bad conscience channel-

8. A key point here is that "accumulation" of ever increasing resources (capital) or protection of one's own physical health (personal safety) do not for Nietzsche pertain to the noble morality: for him, again visible in the Greek ethos, the noble can take (resources, life) and can give, being detached from what he may lose: "to be incapable of taking one's enemies, one's accidents, even one's misdeeds seriously for very long—that is the sign of strong, full natures in whom there is an excess of the power to form, to mold, to recuperate and to forget" (GM I:10).

9. Friedrich Nietzsche, *Twilight of the Idols*, trans. Richard Polt (Indianapolis: Hackett, 1997), 12–18. See also Paul S. Loeb, "The Priestly Revolt in Morality," *Nietzsche Studien* 47, no. 1 (2018): 100–139.

10. Nietzsche, *On the Genealogy of Morals*, GM I:13–14.

11. Nietzsche, *On the Genealogy of Morals*, GM I:10.

ing will into the negation of life-affirming qualities—strength, energy, self-expression, self-expenditure. As such, he cultivates a morality of opposition to those qualities. Under the instinct of *ressentiment,* the previously "bad" traits by Greek standards are sublimated in a new concept of Christian good. This is, for Nietzsche, the pattern according to which the "priestly type" of humans have managed to subvert the moral system and orient it to a life-negating set of values (humility, abstinence, passivity, weakness).

What is relevant here for the discussion of our current political situation in contemporary societies is the political meaning of the philosophical story that Nietzsche tells us. That is, Nietzsche's analysis suggests that morality is a contested terrain wherein different configurations can serve the interests of different (and, perhaps, opposing) groups; and when some groups do not have sufficient resources to compete in certain domains, they may try to gain an upper hand by moving the normative moral struggle to another field. Religion has been used strategically to carry out this political struggle on the appropriate center of the normative moral ground. Moreover, when this struggle for the moral ground takes place, it is also mirrored by a contestation of the foundational basis of society (the "slave revolt" Nietzsche presents in *The Genealogy of Morals* led to the expansion of metaphysics). Below, this type of analysis will be applied to the "insurgency"[12] that populist movements carry out against the established liberal-democratic order in Western Europe, and the strategic use they make of religion. However, before moving to that task, the next section addresses the metaphysical side of the question, because of its relevance for understanding the context in which populism draws upon religion in its opposition to political order.

THE ASCETIC IDEAL

The inversion of morality from one cultural and historical vantage point as explained by Nietzsche is accompanied by a twin phenomenon: the expansion of metaphysics, which, in most cases (but not necessarily), takes the form of religion. When Nietzsche declares that "God is dead," he is indicating that the metaphysical foundation of our life has disappeared. The

12. Marco Brunazzo and Mark Gilbert, "Insurgents against Brussels: Euroscepticism and the Right-Wing Populist Turn of the Lega Nord since 2013," *Journal of Modern Italian Studies* 22, no. 5 (2017): 624–41.

Christian God carried the function of metaphysical foundation for Europe over the course of many centuries. However, Nietzsche does not see in metaphysics—and in a transcendental, all-powerful God—a conceptual necessity. In pre-Platonic times, ancient Greeks posited the experience of a flourishing of culture and life and lived without the constraint of an overarching metaphysical signification system, and the possibility of such a life is what Nietzsche assumed from the Greeks as his ideal. However, according to Nietzsche, the same life-negating instinct of the priestly type was responsible for shifting the meaning of life away from itself, away from the world (e.g., the world of experience) and toward a fictitious, metaphysical other world. The priestly type—who, unlike the warrior type, cannot obtain in the given world any satisfaction for his will to power—devised the world of ideas (as in Platonism) or the afterlife (as in Christianity). This world was accessible not by the virtues of the "nobles" but by those of the "slaves": humility, abstinence, piety, and so forth.

Metaphysics is, for Nietzsche, the equivalent of a "No" to life.[13] The logic

13. While this point goes partially beyond the scope of this article, my reading of the relation between Nietzsche and metaphysics is one where Nietzsche's thought does not aim to offer a new metaphysics replacing the other metaphysics that Nietzsche criticizes.

While a significant part of the scholarship maintains the opposite position, I think that Nietzsche did not intend to elaborate a new metaphysics and that the concepts that are usually assumed to point to a Nietzschean metaphysics (the will to power, the Overman/Superman, the eternal recurrence) are not offered by Nietzsche as elements of a discipline, but as maieutic experiments.

Martin Heidegger initiated the traditional interpretation of Nietzsche's thought as a new metaphysics, arguing that the reversal of Platonism enacted by Nietzsche would still amount to a metaphysics (Martin Heidegger, *Nietzsche*, ed. Franco Volpi [Milan: Adelphi, 1994]). In his analysis Heidegger also relied extensively on the posthumously published "Will to Power" of which he believed that Nietzsche had himself planned the structure in four books, and the titles of the same (this was later proved wrong by Giorgio Colli and Mazzino Montinari; see Giuliano Campioni, *Leggere Nietzsche: Alle origini dell'edizione Colli-Montinari: Con lettere e testi inediti* [Pisa: ETS, 1992]).

Heidegger poses the question of metaphysics as the question of the "truth of the being in itself and as a whole" (Heidegger, *Nietzsche*): he sees Nietzsche as answering this question by saying that the being is the will to power, and therefore logically this describes the nature of being as a whole, and this description amounts to a metaphysical statement. This influential tradition has been developed and elaborated since then to account for the contradictions that this interpretation would necessarily detect in Nietzsche's thought or to develop the Heideggerian criticism of Nietzsche's thought as part of the metaphysical Western tradition. John Richardson, for example, has reconnected Nietzsche's thought to the Platonic distinction between being and becoming and ascribed Nietzsche's thought to the latter category, and interpreted it as an ontology based on processes rather than on real objects (John Richardson, *Nietzsche's System* [New York: Oxford University Press, 1996]). Peter Poellner has discussed Nietzsche's "anti-essentialism" and his conception of reality as made up of "quanta of force" (Peter Poellner, *Nietzsche and Metaphysics* [Oxford: Oxford University Press, 1995]).

This traditional interpretation of Nietzsche is very influential: however, I think it does not take into account the low value Nietzsche accorded philosophical truth, and at the same time it is overenthusiastic in interpreting Nietzsche's unpublished works. I do not think, in fact, that when Nietzsche refers to the will to power in his published works he has the intention to present it as a doctrine.

In this I am sympathetic to the reading of Maudemarie Clark (*Nietzsche on Truth and Philosophy* [Cambridge: Cambridge University Press, 1990]), who sees in the will to power not a cosmological doctrine but a projection of Nietzsche's own life-affirming ideal. Clark is also conscious that "the cosmological doctrine of the will to power is the kind of construction of the world Nietzsche claims philosophers have self-deceptively engaged in. The difference is that Nietzsche knows perfectly well it is not the truth and that he gives us the clues we need to figure out that it is actually a projection of his life-affirming (and self-affirming) ideal."

In fact, as George J. Stack argues (*Nietzsche's Anthropic Circle: Man, Science, and Myth* [Woodbridge: Boydell and Brewer, 2005]), Nietzsche is not offering the will to power as a description of reality but as an "exoteric fable." I agree with this and more precisely I think that Nietzsche's apparent metaphysical claims are maieutic linguistic tools; they are not meant as truth statements but as thought experiments producing a change in the reader.

The concept of the Overman has also been taken to signal a metaphysical project in Nietzsche's thought. A recent formulation of the argument, initiated by Heidegger, is offered by Daniel A. Dombrovsky: he argues that the project of the Overman is the apex of the development of modern subjectivism and as such it aims to absolute dominion over the earth. The same subjectivism is also responsible for the current notions of Caesarism and charismatic leadership. This interpretation of the Overman is in line with previous accounts of the thought of Nietzsche as being protofascist. Opposite interpretations of the Overman as self-overcoming have also been proposed in the literature (for a recent source, see Jacob Golomb, "Will to Power: Does It Lead to the 'Coldest of All Cold Monsters'?," in *The Oxford Handbook of Nietzsche*, ed. John Richardson and Ken Gemes [Oxford: Oxford University Press, 2013]).

More than that, I think that the concept of the Overman is not related to dominion over the earth: Gilles Deleuze considers that Nietzsche aims to free thought from nihilism and asks what a man would be "who would not accuse or depreciate existence," and in the answer to this question I think it is possible to meet the Overman (Gilles Deleuze, *Nietzsche and Philosophy*, trans. Hugh Tomlinson [New York: Columbia University Press, 1983]). Moreover, and in conclusion, I think Nietzsche did not intend to offer a new metaphysics and that the elements of his thought that are interpreted in that direction should not be taken to point to an ontology but to a praxis: as Clark notes, "Nietzsche's point is that though philosophers claim otherwise, their theories are not even designed to arrive at truth. They are attempts to of this "No" is to be traced to the prototype of individuals choosing a position of existential weakness in the world, a "contemplative" position turning "them away from action" (GM I:6). According to Nietzsche, this prototype of man (GM III:10) is the priestly type, which includes philosophers, intellectuals, and individuals cultivating ascetic beliefs. Their physiological drive to affirm their selves (their "will to power") cannot be satisfied in the world due to their comparatively lesser physical, psychological, or material resources, which make them unable to compete with the more powerful nobles (as Bernard Reginster notes, "*ressentiment* is a response not to the loss of a good or to violation of a right, but to a lack of power: it bears an essential connection to the feeling of impotence"[14]). Slavish morality develops only in reaction to this hostile situation. This reaction results in a "slave revolt" in morality:[15] morally, it enacts an inversion of values, while existen-

---

construct the world, or an image of the world, in terms of the philosopher's values" (Clark, *Nietzsche on Truth and Philosophy*).

14. Bernard Reginster, "The Psychology of Christian Morality: Will to Power as Will to Nothingness," in *The Oxford Handbook of Nietzsche*, ed. Ken Gemes and John Richardson (Oxford: Oxford University Press, 2013), 708. On the feeling of impotence as a fuel for ascetic values, see also Ken Gemes, "We Remain of Necessity Strangers to Ourselves: The Key Message of Nietzsche's Genealogy," in *Nietzsche's "On the Genealogy of Morals": Critical Essays*, ed. C. D. Acampora (Lanham, MD: Rowman and Littlefield, 2006), 191–208.

15. According to the traditional interpretation, the slave revolt originates, entirely or mainly, out of oppressed classes. See, for example, David Owen, *Nietzsche's Genealogy of Morality* (Montreal: McGill-Queen's University Press, 2007); Brian Leiter, *Routledge Philosophy Guidebook to Nietzsche on Morality* (London: Routledge, 2002); Robert Pippin, "Lightning and Flash, Agent and Deed (GM I: 6–17)," in *Nietzsche's "On the Genealogy of Morals": Critical Essays*, ed. Christa Davis Acampora (Lanham, MD: Rowan and Littlefield, 2006); R. Jay Wallace, "*Ressentiment*, Value and Self-Vindication: Making Sense of Nietzsche's Slave Revolt," in *Nietzsche and Morality*, ed. Brian Leiter and Neil Sinhababu (Oxford: Oxford University Press, 2007). Other readings of the slave revolt have instead given a more preeminent role to priests as members of the noble class and as creators of (reactive) values: in this interpretation, the slave masses do not necessarily develop reactive values against the nobles until priests, as a split faction of nobility, exert their influence over them. See Bernard Reginster, "Nietzsche on *Ressentiment* and Valuation," *Philosophy and Phenomenological Research* 57, no. 2 (1997): 281–305; R. Lanier Anderson, "On the Nobility of Nietzsche's Priests," in *Nietzsche's "On the Genealogy of Morality": A Critical Guide*, ed. Simon May (Cambridge: Cambridge University Press, 2011); Avery Snelson, "The History, Origin, and Meaning of Nietzsche's Slave Revolt in Morality," *Inquiry: An Interdisciplinary Journal of Philosophy* 60, nos. 1–2 (2017): 1–30. However, this seems contrary to what Nietzsche writes about natural differences resulting necessarily in dominant and passive types and the second ones suffering

tially it develops as an escape strategy from the world of life, answering to an "aversion to life" (GM III:28). Therefore, this type of individual needs to find better conditions for his life than those available to him in the world: "*every animal—therefore la bête philosophe, too—instinctively strives for an optimum of favourable conditions under which it can expand all its strength*" (GM III:7). And this type of man finds optimal conditions for living in a world of ideas, of essences, of religion, and of knowledge.[16] This world of abstractions, which is metaphysics, is then also assumed to be the "true" world, while the world as given suffers a loss of reality. Here too we see an inversion, whereby the quality of reality is taken away from the world as given and is attributed to the (now artificial) platonic world of ideas.[17]

The consequence is that—as with the point indicated clearly in Plato's "myth of the cavern"—our common world (the only one we have, according to Nietzsche) loses its capacity of having a meaning of its own; it loses, in fact, significance altogether, becoming just a world of "shadows." Meaning and significance become the purview of the world of ideas, which are located outside of the world, outside of the cavern. The ascetic ideal locates the key condition of the priestly type—seeking an optimal condition for expressing life away from the frustrations of the physical world—in the "No" it says to the world of experience.

Now some qualifications of what has been said so far are necessary before we can move to the next logical passage. The priestly type, as hinted, is for Nietzsche an abstract type not limited to priests. In the genealogical method, Nietzsche broadens the scope of inquiry to include the "intellectuals" among the priestly types. As we discuss later, this category may be seen to have dramatically expanded since the time of Nietzsche's writing and may have become so inflated as to be all-pervasive in our current service-oriented "knowledge economies."

---

because of that (GM III:18). It also neglects the fact that Nietzsche indicates that slavish revolts have been at times instigated and have succeeded without the involvement of priests-as-nobles (see Loeb, "The Priestly Revolt in Morality," who recalls Nietzsche's references to the peasant Luther and the nonpriest Socrates; caustically Loeb also calls this attempt to negate the slaves' principal role in creating reactive values as a new expression of *ressentiment* against the oppressors).

16. Gemes, "We Remain of Necessity Strangers to Ourselves: The Key Message of Nietzsche's Genealogy."

17. Friedrich Nietzsche, *Twilight of the Idols*, translated by Richard Polt (Indianapolis: Hackett, 1997).

SCIENCE AS ASCETICISM

Thus, the ascetic ideal is something that priests and intellectuals share. This reflection is central to Nietzsche's discussion of our metaphysics and morals, and it is illuminating of the enduring nature of the sacred, even in a secularized society. In fact, *On the Genealogy of Morals* opens with a reference to the readers, to the men of knowledge: "we are unknown to ourselves, we men of knowledge."[18]

It is exactly the modern intellectuals who are the audience for whom Nietzsche writes these considerations: modern individuals dedicated to science and knowledge are those who realized the falsity of the ascetic ideal, and the hollowness of religious claims.[19] However, and this is very much relevant for us, contemporary men and women, and especially people reading Nietzsche among academics, have not yet managed to realize in science and in knowledge what we have managed to realize and dismiss in the (human-made) nature of religion and God. That is, we continue to mythologize our own will to power in science and in our (nonreligious, humanly originated) knowledge systems.[20] Thus, even we, modern secular individuals, are still very much infected by the ascetic ideal: while the body hosting the disease has changed, the ascetic ideal is still very much alive.

By seeing and eliminating the asceticism present in religion and God, we have not managed to get rid of asceticism itself. In fact, we have failed precisely because in the moment when we thought that our emancipatory impulse was at its peak, that is, during the Enlightenment, we were sowing the seeds of a new asceticism, this time in the guise of science and knowledge.

What has not changed, through the ages, is what Ken Gemes calls the "latent meaning of our commitment to truth."[21] This meaning is very much a physiological instinct, which pushes us to escape pain, suffering, and to seek optimal conditions for our life activities.[22] Therefore, as men of knowledge, we instinctively feel aligned to ascetic values: they conform to us, they

18. Nietzsche, *On the Genealogy of Morals*, GM I:2.

19. Gemes, "We Remain of Necessity Strangers to Ourselves."

20. "Our faith in science is still based on a *metaphysical faith*,—even we knowers of today, we godless anti-metaphysicians, still take *our* fire from the blaze set alight by a faith thousands of years old, that faith of the Christians, which was also Plato's faith, that God is truth, that truth is *divine*," GM III:24.

21. Gemes, "We Remain of Necessity Strangers to Ourselves."

22. Nietzsche, *On the Genealogy of Morals*, GM III:7.

conform to our fear of life, and they conform to our feeling of impotence toward that fear. As those inspired by religious ascetic values, "the modern scholar similarly removes himself from life by telling himself that what is of ultimate value is not acting in this world . . . but understanding the world."[23] Incidentally, this "neutrality" of knowledge is one of the assumptions upon which our current liberal globalization rests. Knowledge of economic "laws" is, by itself, knowledge of a disincarnated and unchangeable "idea": economic knowledge, therefore, can only help humans to describe liberal globalization and adapt to it, but it cannot challenge its "natural" logic.

Returning to the status of knowledge in modern societies, we see two unchanging elements. First, ascetic ideals, although in different forms but not in different roles, continued to exist even after the "death of God." And, they continue even in the contemporary age. Science, knowledge, and ideology, by being hypostatized, assume the same role (although not the same appearance or attributes) as that of God in prior ages. They constitute a meaning, a sense, a description of reality that is beyond humanity, that is above humanity. While Europeans rid themselves of the vestiges of "God," God's place, space-marker, and conceptual content remains there; it has not been abolished. And, as long as it is there, it can be filled by a disparate range of concepts and frameworks.

Second, the "ascetic ideal" remains a peculiar trait of a certain type of man and woman: at the time *On the Genealogy of Morals* was written, this type was the intellectual, modern incarnation of the priestly type. In our contemporary societies, this category has been replaced by that of the expert: a much wider and pervasive group, whose size matches the pervasiveness of knowledge in our economies. The criticism of the value of knowledge and science in our world should take into account the hypostatization or metamorphosis of science as a "new host" for the ascetic infection. As long as a "metaphysical" place remains, any type of object will fill it: science, progress, the subject, materialism, liberalism, and so forth. We may devise the most critical, humanly "body of knowledge," and, still, that would not solve the "ascetic problem." The problematic aspect is the relationship that we have with the body of knowledge. As long as we attribute to it (our own body of knowledge) any value that situates it in a status above life, we will continue to manifest a higher meaning and cultivate an ascetic ideal, something more serious than just life as experience.

23. Gemes, "We Remain of Necessity Strangers to Ourselves."

The criticism of the ascetic nature of our commitment to knowledge comes with the criticism of the subject itself, the "knower." This criticism entails a breaking down of the rationalist, unitary, "Apollonian" conception of the subject, and the revaluation of its irrational, "Dionysian" constitution. Knowledge no longer has the status of an "essence," as what we know is not a distinct object existing independently from us. It is, rather, very much of a construct of our own instinct and physiological pulse, a product that fulfils our need to exist under optimal conditions. Likewise, the subject of the action of knowledge is no longer an "individual," clearly constituted, who is gifted with a soul (as in Christianity) or at least with the potential for a pure rationality (as in the traditions stemming from the Enlightenment), useful for building political or economic (*homo economicus*) social rationalities. In fact, rationality is never pure if we look at its genealogy, Nietzsche would argue.

KILLING THE "LIBERAL" GOD?

The previous paragraph argued that the ascetic ideal can also be hypostatized as science, as knowledge, as liberalism: but then, if so, could this latest version of asceticism also be subject to contestation, as already happened to other secular asceticisms (e.g., Marxism)? For populists, the answer is unequivocally positive: populist leaders across Western Europe have repeatedly spoken of European societies as dominated by an overarching and global ideology. For radical right populists, people in Western Europe are living within a political situation analogous to the *political religions* of the twentieth century, where only one ideology exists and is reproduced (this time, globalist liberalism).

Over several decades, Western European populists have consistently worked to take a discourse previously repeated by marginal groups into the mainstream. In particular, populist leaders have identified the European Union (EU) as a primary target in their struggle against the liberal ideology. It is paradigmatic that populist leaders across the region—like Le Pen of the National Front, Salvini of the Lega Nord, Nigel Farage of the UK Independence Party—have compared the EU to the Soviet Union and spoken of a "European Soviet Union."[24] In the discourses of these populist parties,

24. Marine Le Pen, "I Don't Want This European Soviet Union," *Der Spiegel* (Hamburg),

the EU—emblem of the global liberal ideology—is often criticized for its "secular" qualities: pluralism, internationalism, and insistence on the rule of law and human rights. The EU is also sometimes criticized for not defending the Christian roots of the continent, or even for positively planning the de-Christianization of European societies.

The last three decades have seen an adjustment of the populist discourse in articulating opposition to the secular values issued out of the Enlightenment: while the anti-European theme has become traditional, more recent Western European populist narratives have expanded their discourse to include anti-science and anti-expertise positions. This adjustment is exemplified by the populist support for the "no vax" positions:[25] indeed, populism provides antivaxxers with political validation for a mental attitude of distrust toward élites and experts. Just like in the case of global warming denialism,[26] populists came to articulate an opposition to the value of scientific expertise and rationality: by opposing the value of science and expertise, especially on transnational and global issues, populists pursue their contestation of global liberalism, of which experts and knowledge "élites" represent building blocks.

The shift in populist discourse indirectly reflects changes in the discourse on "liberalism": compared to the liberalism that was common in Western Europe until the 1990s, the current global liberalism has a more manifest insistence on the value of "knowledge" as a pivotal factor for both human and societal development. In fact, global competition is certainly a public good, as actors can give value to their competencies. Over the last decades, the transformation of liberal-democratic societies into "knowledge economies" has been presented as a positive and inevitable development, and

June 3, 2014; Nigel Farage, "Intervention in the Debate at the European Parliament, Preparation of the European Council Meeting of 18–19 October 2018," October 2, 2018, European Parliament, Brussels, https://www.europarl.europa.eu/doceo/document/CRE-8-2018-10-02-INT-2-020-0000_EN.html; Matteo Salvini, "Unione Europea come l'Unione Sovietica, se non si svegliano usciranno tutti," *CorriereTV* (Milan), June 25, 2016, https://video.corriere.it/salvini-unione-europea-come-unione-sovietica-se-non-si-svegliano-usciranno-tutti/df39f91e-3ae3-11e6-a019-901bc4c9f010

25. Jonathan Kennedy, "Populist Politics and Vaccine Hesitancy in Western Europe: An Analysis of National-Level Data," *European Journal of Public Health* 29, no. 3 (2019): 512–16.

26. Matthew Lockwood, "Right-Wing Populism and the Climate Change Agenda: Exploring the Linkages," *Environmental Politics* 27, no. 4 (2018): 712–32.

the tertiarization[27] of European economies has followed suit. National governments have widely adopted the economic models proposed by liberal and reformist economists, often brewed in academic circles. The logic of "economic transition"—which, in the 1990s was an analytical framework applied to postcommunist countries—has now expanded to include the rest of the world. Now Western European societies, too, are conceived of as in a state of permanent transition.

The logic of neoliberal models applied to these transitions has obfuscated the fact that these models, particularly in the domain of financial integration, were not "cameras" presenting a picture of the situation. Quite to the contrary, they contributed actively to creating the conditions for their application.[28]

Knowledge, as said, has come to the fore as the key element of the new form of global liberalism; it constitutes an essential element of the ideology of global liberalism, much like science constituted an essential element of Marxism in the twentieth century. In fact, knowledge has been conceptualized as the common element in both traditions, liberalism and Marxism, the origins of both of which lie in the Enlightenment.[29] Together with the increased relevance of knowledge in the global economies, we also notice the emergence of global élites based upon knowledge capital. These may be élites in the wider sense, as they represent social strata that are more integrated in the global societies by virtue of their educational, professional, and technological resources. And they participate in networks made up of similar individuals who are, likewise, transnational in nature (e.g., networks may be created around educational institutions or professional affiliations).

Populist leaders are carrying out a radical contestation of the political tradition of Western liberalism, born out of the Enlightenment: their discourse speaks of the wish to bring down the liberal order. While there is an attempt to kill the liberal god, the secularization process of the past two centuries has left religion without the former role of being a foundational element for society as a whole—and without much autonomous political agency. Religion has been relegated to the personal domain or to the cultural

27. E.g., a move to the tertiary sector, or service sector, in economic terms.

28. Donald MacKenzie, *An Engine, Not a Camera: How Financial Models Shape Markets* (Cambridge: MIT Press, 2006).

29. Eric Voegelin, *The Collected Works, Vol. 5, Modernity without Restraint* (Columbia: University of Missouri Press, 2000).

sphere, as politics, science, and morality—which, under the *ancien régime*, depended on it—are now autonomous spheres of human life. A more tenuous hold of religion over society in a secularized and postmodern context provides a good combination for the appropriation of religion by political agents. Indeed, it is exactly a relation of instrumental use that populists have developed with religion in Western Europe.

POPULIST MORALITY

Populism has been on the rise in Western societies, and in Europe, over the last two decades; it has also received increasing attention in academia. Several attempts at describing it have stressed its nature as a "political style,"[30] a tactic for "political mobilization,"[31] and a thin (e.g., not robust) ideology creating an opposition between the "good people" and the "corrupted élites."[32] The most peculiar element of populism, a point around which there is a broad consensus, lies precisely in the fact that populism describes society as divided into two opposing groups, people and élites, who it presents, in turn, as carriers of opposing moral values.[33] The nature of this opposition, which, for populists, is grounded in moral judgments, remains understudied. Moreover, the focus on the "thin" ideological center of populism, as well as its promethean nature, has so far not allowed scholars to properly understand the radical opposition of current populist movements to the established European political order, with some exceptions, such as Marco Brunazzo and Mark Gilbert, who present the idea of a "populist insurgency."[34]

The Nietzschean critique of morality and asceticism can thus be usefully applied to the analysis of the current forms of populist insurgency against the European order. In this analysis, I think it is necessary to take seriously the "moral" character of the opposition that populists establish between the élites and the people. This opposition is one that aims to turn upside-down

30. Margaret Canovan, "Populism for Political Theorists," *Journal of Political Ideologies* 9, no. 3 (2004): 241–52.

31. Ernesto Laclau, *On Populist Reason* (London: Verso Books, 2007).

32. Cas Mudde, "The Populist Zeitgeist," *Government and Opposition* 39, no. 4 (2004): 541–63.

33. Jan-Werner Müller defines populism as "moralised anti-pluralism." Jan-Werner Müller, *What Is Populism?* (Philadelphia: University of Pennsylvania Press, 2016).

34. Marco Brunazzo and Mark Gilbert, "Insurgents against Brussels."

the classical understanding of "élite"—originally an appreciative qualification associated chiefly with positive values and functions in a society—into an opposite qualification, associated with negative values such as "corrupted" and "inimical to the people." We are seeing, in the current period, an attempted inversion process similar to that in Nietzsche's *On the Genealogy of Morals*, in which the aims are to replace one set of binary oppositions with the other. That is, populists are trying to replace and invert the moral antinomy "knowledgeable/good" and "uneducated/bad"; hence, their self-presentation as antirationalists.

Knowledge is the ascetic ideal that has been left standing after the secularization process has removed religion, and then ideology, as metaphysical foundations: it is the quality of global liberalism that has increasingly been promoted in the last two decades as a path for both individual and collective salvation. That is, education, economic success, and development, as linked with well-being, have taken the place, in the rhetoric of global liberal powers/instruments, of salvation.

In its opposition to globalization and liberalism, populism is clearly signaling that it wants to challenge the domination of the "experts," be it on questions such as climate change, economic growth, vaccination, infrastructures, or other issues. The views of the scientific community are understood to be just opinions and are lumped together in the same basket with the opinions of politicians from the "establishment." The challenge that populists bring to the liberal-democratic system is, therefore, against élites not only of a political nature, but to the wider élites of knowledge (including professional experts, as well as those parts of the population with higher educational capital).[35]

Like power and physical strength in the case of the inversion between slave and noble morality, in the case of populists and global liberals knowledge is the element creating a gap between the two groups. Morality becomes the ground upon which this asymmetry can be circumvented. Populism, likewise, attempts to signal that the morality of the "weak" in globalization is higher in value than the morality of the "experts." In this sense, populist leaders are acting as a new kind of *priestly* type, in Nietzschean terms. In fact, they develop a discourse, which is charged with moral tones of guilt and resentment. Therefore, to the dyad "knowledgeable/good" and "unedu-

35. Michael Gove, interview on "EU: In or Out?," Sky News (London), June 3, 2016, https://www.youtube.com/watch?v=t8D8AoC-5i8

cated/bad," populist morality responds (and tries to replace) with the couple "knowledgeable/evil" and "uneducated/good."

The devaluation of expertise and knowledge also has the effect of eroding the domain of reason in the public sphere. As experts are no longer—or less—trusted in their role of judges of what constitute reasonable opinions in policy debates (from medicine and public health to climate change to technology and more), the rise of populist movements in the political arena is accompanied by the concurring spread of conspiracy theories, antiscientific beliefs, and, more generally, by the increase of emotionality (self-interested rather than empathic), and the reappearance of political myths. These factors are generally described under the definition of "post-truth." In our Nietzschean critique, we may even say that populism is showing its "Dionysian" character in a face-off with the "Apollonian" nature of the liberal appreciation for reason.

RELIGIOUS POPULISM

The de-secularizing effect of populist discourse also has a more properly "religious" effect. It concerns both institutionalized religion (the church) and other forms of religiosity within the political domain. The relationship between populism and the church is instrumental. The "death of God," with its immediate effect on Christianity and its delayed effect on political religions, has left politics incapable of presenting itself with a consciously developed metaphysical foundation. It has left religion essentially retreated into the domain of private life, or, where present in politics, in the diminished role of "cultural heritage." Populism, therefore, the "thin" ideology *par excellence*, moves, agile, in this postmodern landscape from which grand narratives have retreated. On its way, it may borrow elements that it encounters, now-abandoned themes of theistic and political religions that populism recycles. This instrumental logic leads Western European populist movements to use Christian religious themes and symbols as part of their propaganda.[36]

However, the utilization of religious themes and symbols by populists does not mean that religion acquires a larger role in the political domain; not if, with religion, we mean its institutional presence, for example, the Catholic

36. Petr Kratochvil, "Religion as a Weapon: Invoking Religion in Secularised Societies," *Review of Faith and International Affairs* 17, no. 1 (2019): 78–88.

Church. Populists, in fact, are capable of having an apparently contradictory attitude toward the church. For example, they can, at once, display religious symbols prominently in crowded political meetings, and then criticize the pope for his too-soft stances on some policy issues. One such case includes Matteo Salvini, head of the Italian Lega Nord, displaying a large cross in a political meeting of his party and then criticizing Pope Francis for his stance on migration.[37] The same ambivalence toward the Catholic Church has been highlighted in relation to the Front National in France.[38]

The logic of opposition between élite and people is at play also in the populists' relation with the Christian religion: institutional religious hierarchies are often seen as part and parcel of the hated "élites," and there is no automatic loyalty from populist leaders toward clerical institutions. On the other hand, religious themes are sometimes appropriated by populists, although it is an instrumental logic that serves the purpose of lending cultural themes to the populist discourse. In particular, the utilization of Christian references is meant to mark an identity.[39] And, for what concerns Europe, Christianity is used by populists to trace a dividing line between an "us" and a "them." The "us" in this discourse is a confused—and mythical—construction, a conflation of a "Western" civilization encompassing (a selective conceptualization of) both its Christian and secular incarnations. That is, the two aspects are sometimes mobilized separately, sometimes jointly; and they are sometimes opposed and at other times used in concert. In largely secularized societies like those of Western Europe, populists—conscious of the context they are doing politics in—often present religion in cultural terms, therefore being able to equate religion with national history and national culture.[40] The ethical or evangelical aspects are not as relevant for the populist logic, only its capacity to work as a marker of identity/difference.

For populists, the "them" is often identified, in the contemporary period,

37. Matteo Salvini (@salviniofficial): "Papa Francesco si lamenta perchè, quando lui prendeva l'autobus a Roma e salivano degli zingari, gli autisti dicevano ai passeggeri 'Attenti al portafoglio' . . . ," Facebook, June 6, 2014, https://www.facebook.com/salviniofficial/posts/papa-francesco-si-lamenta-perch%C3%A8-quando-lui-prendeva-lautobus-a-roma-e-salivano-/10152182717518155/

38. Olivier Roy, "The French National Front: From Christian Identity to Laicité," in *Saving the People: How Populists Hijack Religion*, ed. Nadia Marzouki, Duncan McDonnell, and Olivier Roy (London: Hurst and Publishers, 2016), 79–93.

39. Olivier Roy, "The French National Front."

40. Petr Kratochvil, "Religion as a Weapon: Invoking Religion in Secularised Societies."

with Muslim peoples.[41] The populist discourse presents "Western" civilization as superior both in its religious and secular forms, which are capitalized upon and seen interchangeably. Notably, there is scarce to no emphasis on personal behaviors such as sexual conduct, although in some cases the "individual freedoms" of Western societies are juxtaposed to the (ostensible or misunderstood) lack of freedom of the "others." Another instance of the "them" is the "secular élites," often impersonated by supranational organizations such as the European Union. In populist discourse, these specters are bent upon corrupting the genuine nature of the "people." In this case, religion is used as a marker of "the genuine" in opposition to the artificial progressivism of the élites.

An exemplary case of opposition between populists and the EU is found in the domain of gender, where populists across Europe accuse the European Union of conspiring to corrupt the natural (e.g., here, morally righteous) customs of the people, either by promoting gender equality, reproductive rights, or LGBT "propaganda." With migration, populist leaders denounce immigration of Muslims as an attack on the Christian heritage of Europe. Often, this argument puts them at odds with clerical hierarchies, since the anti-immigration stance of populists hardly matches the universalist and ecumenical languages of the church.[42]

Not only can populist leaders instrumentalize religious themes and act independently of institutionalized religion, they often assume for themselves some of the qualities of religious leaders. In fact, they can wear the charisma of religious leaders themselves: populist discourse is highly charged in moral terms, since, as we have seen, its function is to operate an inversion in the prevailing attributions of moral values. Because it sets a Manichean opposition between the élites and the good people, it also articulates a notion of the people as sacred.[43] In the background of these elements, and with the promise to protect and vindicate the people, the capacity to assume a "religious aura" is a potential that is within the reach of most populist leaders. Notably, it is also something that has rarely occurred to Christian Democratic and Christian conservative leaders. The political leaders of those affiliations had

41. Olivier Roy, "The French National Front: From Christian Identity to Laicité."

42. Luca Ozzano, "Religion, Cleavages, and Right-Wing Populist Parties: The Italian Case," *Review of Faith and International Affairs* 17, no. 1 (2019): 65–77.

43. Daniel Nilsson DeHanas and Marat Shterin, "Religion and the Rise of Populism," *Religion, State & Society* 46, no. 3 (2018): 177–85.

and continue to have a clearer focus on Christian ethics and doctrine; but, in their case, they also have a stronger link with institutionalized religious hierarchies, while articulating non-Manichean views of society. For these reasons, and despite the "Christian" denomination of their political parties, Christian Democrats do not normally enjoy the potential of assuming the charisma of religious leaders in the way that populist politicians do.

Populism, therefore, appears as an antirationalist movement, which, by its discursive logic, erodes secularism and public reason without trying to replace it with a substitute (religion or other forms of metaphysics). Instead, populism fills the cracks that it, itself, has opened in public reason. It provides its own myths and its own populist religiosity: small narratives and not metaphysical promises. As the trajectory of contemporary European populism is still happening, it is not possible to divine where it will lead. It is, however, clear that the inversion of moral values attributed to the élites and the experts is not a departure from the logic of *ressentiment* that Nietzsche described in *On the Genealogy of Morals*. It is still a reconfiguration within the same dynamic of a slave-master normative opposition played on the moral ground.

The connection between populism and religion is a relation between two domains that are both weakened—by secularization, earlier, and by technological globalization, later. The domain of politics has seen the failure of political religions and is now hosting only ideologies that are either disguised as scientific objectivity (global liberalism) or are extremely thin and fungible (populism). The domain of religion has lost its centrality as the cornerstone of society, politics, and science that it had enjoyed under premodern times. It is increasingly limited to the private or cultural spheres, although within those fields it may still enjoy a notable vitality. The metaphysical place of God is still present, however, and filled with other conceptual variants and frameworks, including science and philosophy.

For the current moment, the relationship between populism and religion in Western Europe is one in which populism is instrumentalizing religion and borrowing from its themes and tones. Despite the higher visibility of religious themes in populist politics, this visibility does not mean that religion, per se, is in the process of acquiring a new political impetus; not, at least, as we are concerned with Western European societies. The visibility of religious themes hides, instead, the fact that politics is assuming religious connotations, specifically due to the moral and antirationalist nature of populist discourse.

CONCLUSIONS

This chapter has used a Nietzschean framework of analysis, based on *On the Genealogy of Morals*, to give an account of the operative modality of the populist struggle in Western Europe. The aim of this struggle is the contestation of the incumbent order in Europe, which populists identify in the ideology of global liberalism. Against this ideology, populist leaders activate the anti-elite resentment of social groups that, in the current global knowledge economies, are marginalized or less well-off. As in the account given by Nietzsche in *On the Genealogy of Morals*, populist *ressentiment* also elicits a "No" to the world as given. In Nietzschean terms, knowledge remains—among the ruins of *political religions* and ideologies—as the last form of public asceticism. Populism, in opposing liberal-democratic systems, attacks the value of knowledge and expertise through a highly morally charged discourse on the opposition of the people and élites. So intense is the nature of this moral discourse that populism verges, ironically, given its antirationalist stance, on the religious. Indirectly, populism borrows themes and symbols from institutionalized religions, and, directly, it assumes traits of a quasi-religious phenomenon. Populist leaders may obtain the aura, even, of charismatic religious leaders. So combined, religious populism wages a battle against "global knowledge asceticism," as defined herein, advocating that the voices of those who cannot rise to those pinnacles shall be more important than those who commune with "knowledge."

Populists endeavor to reframe expertise and knowledge as indicators of moral corruption rather than moral distinction. Resentment against the élites of knowledge features prominently in populist discourse, and so populist leaders are operating in a way akin to a new form of "priest" in Nietzschean terms. As the attack on knowledge goes on, the role of reason and expertise in solving problems of our public sphere is challenged. Some ground is lost to emotionality and myth in science and policy debates, and we notice a de-secularizing effect in place, induced by populist discourse.

The relation between populism and religion remains influenced by the mostly secular nature of Western European societies: the appropriation of Christian religious symbols by populist leaders is normally done at a superficial level, for political communication and for using them as "markers" of identities and differences with other groups. Populist leaders show little or no conscious interest in promoting the evangelical or ethical behaviors deriving from Christian doctrine, and they certainly do not advocate a pious society: this would contradict the fungible use populist leaders make of religious symbols.

Populism seems to herald different things: a turn toward irrationalism and myth, especially as a result of the current post-truth climate (itself a result of "the death of God"); a vehicle for the return of religion to center stage; and compromise with other forces, such as nationalism. The solution depends upon whether, in the longer term, the "thinness" of populism continues to suffice as ideological content for this politics, or whether populist politics will need to rely to a greater extent than it currently does on religion, thereby altering the present balance between populism and religion in favor of the latter.

Belief in Politics and the Politics of Faith

The Case of the 2019 Presidential Elections in Ukraine

Antoine Arjakovsky

Research Director, Collège des Bernardins (Paris), and
Founder, Institute of Ecumenical Studies (Lviv)

In a recent essay, *La religion des faibles* (The religion of the weak), Jean Birnbaum has shown that the rediscovery of the power of *jihadist* beliefs has impelled Europeans, especially since the 2015 wave of terrorist attacks, to defend the religious postulates of European civilization. We imagined ourselves as modern, liberated from any dependence on a transcendent god, and immune from any belief system. On the contrary, as Peter Berger, Charles Taylor, Marcel Gauchet, and Jürgen Habermas have recognized, we are discovering that our lifestyle, from socializing in coffee shops to the use of municipal pools, are living symbols of deep choices that have been stored away in the depths of our collective subconscious for a long time. We must recover the metaphysical significance of these symbols if we want to preserve and enrich their role in European culture.

Birnbaum reminds us that, as early as 1955, Albert Camus suggested that the task of intellectuals was to give "a content to European values even though European unity will not happen tomorrow."[1] As Christian philosopher Remi Brague has explained, the difficulty of such an endeavor consists in how the value of secular beliefs can fluctuate according to the whims of collective passions and seasonal ideologies; whereas the foundations of religious faith are linked to relatively stable bodies of doctrine and inter-

1. Jean Birnbaum, *La religion des faibles* (Paris: Seuil, 2018).

pretative traditions.[2] The major characteristic of fundamentalism, be it *laic* or religious, is wanting to separate faith and reason; to deny the sense of transcendence and that of immanent experience; and to foreground the civilizational project at the expense of the expression of difference. As Antoine Fleyfel puts it, "criminal gods" cannot be wiped out by simply using military force.[3] In order to counterbalance fundamentalist violence, of the caliphate or of the secular state, it is indispensable to rediscover the gateways, invisible to the naked eye, that unite the two meanings—those of religious conviction and those of rational postulates—in a reciprocal movement toward one another.

Yet, before all this can be done, we should leave behind *presentism*, a vision that imposes present ideas and perspectives into depictions or interpretations of the past; and maintain, instead, some historical distancing. Our postmodern age is marked by disillusionment with the continual progress of civilization. It suffers from a narcissistic wound: the loss of belief in the humanistic values defined by the modern epoch. In spite of the efforts of certain philosophers, from Edmond Husserl to Immanuel Kant, bent on preserving the world from the *noumena* of practical reason, these values were unable to resist the rise of totalitarianisms.

In order to avoid wallowing in the weakness of this disenchanted age, it is first necessary to recognize the return of belief in politics, that is, the gnostic sign of our convictions and of our political, economic, and cultural practices. Often ignored by Western analytical academic traditions, it certainly exists over and beyond the mere comprehensive knowledge, a "saving wisdom"—according to Philippe Sollers—or, at any rate, something that presents itself as such. Then, in a second moment, once this task of autocritical lucidity has been accomplished, we Europeans should ask ourselves what are the safest paths to safely cross the neognostic and ultraviolent[4] era that is opening up before our eyes.[5]

---

2. Rémi Brague, *Du Dieu des chrétiens et d'un ou deux autres* (Paris: Flammarion, 2008).

3. Antoine Fleyfel, *Les dieux criminels* (Paris: Cerf, 2017).

4. In addition to the 50 or so conflicts going on over this planet, we must add the increasing systematic dangers beginning with global warming, and the growing awareness, through mediatic extension, of increasing inequalities generated by the ultraliberal mode of development.

5. For more information on this epoch, the reader could consult the literary review *Ligne de risque* edited by Francois Meyronnis and Yannick Haenel, in particular no. 24, "La sagesse qui vient," February 2009.

Confronted with this task, this chapter will begin with the discussion of a study case, the 2019 presidential elections in Ukraine. The chapter addresses this event to show how the religious factor played out in the political campaigns of the two leading candidates, Petro Poroshenko and Volodymyr Zelensky. In a second step, I propose potential healing remedies to the wounds of Ukraine, but also of many contemporary Christian societies, such as they appear through the ongoing ideological struggle between neoliberal and neopopulist beliefs.

RELIGION AND THE 2019 UKRAINIAN PRESIDENTIAL ELECTIONS

The Campaign of President Petro Poroshenko

The religious factor was central in the 2019 political campaign of incumbent president Petro Poroshenko. The slogan "Army, Language and Faith" presented Poroshenko as the father of the nation, capable of reconciling the Ukrainian people through a powerful army, the defense of the Ukrainian language, and the affirmation of a sole faith in a transcendent God. The Ukrainian president's move to obtain for the Ukrainian Orthodox Church a "decree of autocephaly" from Patriarch Bartholomew of Constantinople strengthened his nationalistic credentials.[6] Religious discourse by Poroshenko corresponded to personal convictions but was also well tuned with a rising national religious consciousness among Ukrainians.[7]

According to a 2018 study, out of an overall population of 44 million people, almost 30 million (67.3%) of Ukrainians are Orthodox Christians.[8]

6. Irma Bekechkina, a Ukrainian sociologist, has demonstrated that the Ukrainian president gained 4 percentage points in support from voters after this move.

7. President Poroshenko does not hide his membership in the Orthodox Christian Church. Yet his personal faith tends to be ecumenical. On the one hand, his initial membership in the Patriarchate of Moscow changed after the annexation of Crimea by Russia in March 2014. On the other hand, he has also manifested his attachment to the Catholic Church to the point of going to communion during a Greek Catholic liturgy. From the beginning of his mandate, he attempted to carry forward the initiatives of President Viktor Yushenko in favor of granting autocephaly to the Ukrainian Orthodox Church and facilitating reconciliation among different branches of this church.

8. Among the non-Orthodox Christians, the Ukrainian population also counts 9.4%

Among these, 15.3 million belonged to the Patriarchate of Kyiv, a church created in 1992 by Metropolitan Filaret after the Patriarchate of Moscow refused to grant autocephaly to the Ukrainian Orthodox Church; 6.9 million declared themselves as "just Orthodox"; 5.6 million belonged to the Patriarchate of Moscow; and the remainder pertained to other Orthodox autocephalous churches. Thus, while the Patriarchate of Moscow had the greatest number of parishes in Ukraine and was the only Orthodox Church recognized by the communion of Orthodox churches, it only had a minority of Ukrainian adepts.

The Orthodox Church has a complex governance system. The communion comprises 14 separate autocephalous churches recognizing each other as "canonical," the patriarch of Constantinople being the first among equals. Since the rupture with Rome and, above all, since the failure of the reception of the 1439 Council of Florence (which was rejected by Constantinople in 1484), the patriarch of Constantinople has the right of appeal in the regulation of inter-ecclesial conflicts and the right to convene pan-Orthodox councils. Claiming to be the direct heir of the Apostle Andrew, the "first-called" among the apostles of Christ, the patriarch of Constantinople benefited from the support of the Byzantine emperors since the foundation of Byzantium as the capital of the empire in the fourth century AD. Moreover, the ecumenical councils recognized him as having the second place in the hierarchy of the Christian Church, after Rome. The role of the Patriarchate of Constantinople is thus crucial not only in the Greek-speaking world but also among the churches that it founded, including the Church of Kyiv in 988 AD, and among the Orthodox diasporas throughout the world.

In 2016, the Patriarchate of Moscow—which had been founded in 1686 and throughout the centuries had risen to become today's richest and most populous church in the Orthodox world—openly challenged the leadership of Constantinople by refusing to send a delegation to the pan-Orthodox Council of Crete. The dissidence of the patriarch of Moscow, joined by the churches of Bulgaria, Georgia, and Antioch, was likely related to the fear of seeing Constantinople grant autocephalous status to the Ukrainian Church, which he considered as part of Russia's canonical territory. This move con-

Greek Catholics, 2.2% Protestants, 1.1% Muslims, 0.8% Roman Catholics, and 0.4% Jews. Only 3% of Ukrainians consider themselves "atheists," with 11% "non-religious." See Mykhailo Mischenko, "Society's Expectations of Church and Interchurch Relations," public opinion survey, Razumkov Centre, https://risu.ua/en/razumkov-center_t2420

vinced Patriarch Bartholomew that the Mother Church should have solved the ecclesial disorders reigning in Ukraine since 1992, with three churches coexisting in a conflictual disunity.

In the spring of 2018, after several meetings with President Poroshenko, Patriarch Bartholomew eventually decided to grant autocephaly to the Ukrainian Church, hoping that the religious communities belonging to different jurisdictions (Moscow, Kyiv, and the new autocephalous church) would progressively reconcile. President Poroshenko, who had been waiting for this moment since his election in 2014, hailed the event as historic.[9] After the many religious reforms suggesting that a consolidation of a Ukrainian national church was underway,[10] and after the political revolutions of 1991, 2004, and 2014, Poroshenko interpreted the feelings of the majority of Ukrainians, who sensed that the time had come to affirm their ecclesial independence vis-à-vis both Moscow and Constantinople.

The evolution of the religious *cum* political consciousness displayed by Ukraine is specifically modern in the Orthodox world. It follows the path traced since the nineteenth century by other Orthodox churches, such as those of Greece, Bulgaria, and Albania. It consists in the affirmation of the fractal constitution of the Church of Christ, and, consequently, the link between the sacramental life of Christians (baptism, Eucharist, ministry) and the corporeity that it institutes. In this perspective, modern secular visions, consisting in systematically excluding the head of state from ecclesial affairs, and vice-versa, is not acceptable. If Christ is the Head of the spiritual body formed by the Church, and if the ecclesial community lies at the heart of the national community (as it was the case in Greece and Ukraine), the political head cannot be entirely dissociated from the national body, even if the latter is multinational and pluri-religious. From this per-

9. Poroshenko addressed the nation, affirming that "after the Resurrection of Christ, the faith of the Orthodox Church is to consider that the heavens had opened and since all the prayers of the most just can find their fulfillment, the time has come to dedicate ourselves to the establishment of an autocephalous Ukrainian Orthodox Church."

10. A new vote of the Ukrainian deputies in favor of the recognition; the attribution of the *tomos* (decree); the decision to break off communion with Constantinople; the wait-and-see position of the rest of the Orthodox churches; the adoption of a new status for the Church of Kyiv that would be open both to clerics and laity of different jurisdictions; the election of a new patriarch of Kyiv in January 2019; the subsequent change of jurisdiction for more than 400 communities, most of them from the Patriarchate of Moscow, in favor of the new Ukrainian Orthodox Church.

spective, the Ukrainian president has the duty to protect the national community as a whole from Russia's geopolitical ambitions as found in ecclesiastical authority.

There are limits to this approach. As the theologian John Erikson has pointed out, such an approach is not exempt from the intrusion of political power into the internal affairs of the Orthodox Church, thus affecting the Orthodox Church's consciousness and spiritual authority. The Orthodox Church, in fact, lacks a more recent body of law envisaging the separation between the kingdom of God and the kingdom of Caesar, while establishing a necessary cooperation framework between political authorities and national religious communities.

The Myth of the Savior in Zelensky's Campaign

Petro Poroshenko was not the only presidential candidate whose political discourse drew legitimacy from the religious world. Volodymyr Zelensky, who had been raised as a Jew and who subsequently moved some distance from his cultural roots, also relied on a strong religious narrative. Known as a comic actor and the producer of the program *Neighborhood 95*, which aired on the most popular TV channel in the country, Zelensky's caustic and desacralizing humor is rooted in a vision of the world that has broken away from traditional religious institutions.

This can best be seen in an article entitled "The Bleeding Heart of the Motherland" in which the author "V. Z." presents an anthropomorphization of contemporary Ukrainian politics.[11] The tale is an original interpretation of the book of Genesis, whereby, to the extent that "God is alone in the Heavens," he should have been able to create a perfect world. The result, however, was the opposite, with humans driven by power and essentially bent on destroying what God had created. Then, without much of a transition, the author evokes the failure of the Soviet state in 1991 and the first chaotic postcommunist years of Ukraine, when "people were abandoned by the state." The state, in its own turn, was overwhelmed by "adventurists"—a reference taking aim at Yuliia Timoshenko, the founder of the "Fatherland" party—accused of washing their hands from any responsibility toward the Ukrainian people, who eventually were "sold . . . to the International Mon-

11. Volodymyr Zelensky, "The Bleeding Heart of the Motherland," personal blog of author, V-zelenskiy.com, ze2019.com/blog

etary Fund." People were left obliged to fight, tooth and nail, for survival, often reduced to slavery: "It was then that corruption seized the heart of Ukraine." The article ended with a threatening interrogation directed at Timoshenko and Poroshenko: "Should not justice treat these adventurists like they have treated the people?" The conclusion, which is a repetition of the introductory sentence—influenced more by Stoicism than the Bible—reminds the reader of the author's fatalistic vision:

> Everything happened as it should have happened. For God is Unique, He does not have to share power, to buy judges or to lie to the people. What counts for God is man's conscience but when man replaces it with a bloody heart in the name of the Motherland, can God bless such a man? It is probably simpler to lead such a person, through sufferings, to an awareness of his faults, just as this man made his people suffer for many years.[12]

When reading this article, one understands how right René Girard was in pointing out the centrality of the *mediator*, from Miguel de Cervantes to Stendhal, in the creation and evolution of *mimetic desire*. When the mediator, who arouses the impulse of desire among his followers, is no longer distant but rather part of the space and time of the man who desires, the latter can turn from a disciple into an avenger. That is what happened to Zelensky, who, having been one of Poroshenko's supporters in 2014, later felt deceived. His admiration turned into anger, then resentment. Girard defined this state with the title of one of Max Scheler's books, *L'Homme du Ressentiment*:

> Passionate admiration and the desire to emulate come up against the apparently unjust obstacle that the model opposes to his disciple and they fall upon this latter in the form of a powerless hatred, provoking a sort of psychological auto-poisoning.[13]

Thus, Zelensky presents himself as the avenger, the man who, like God the Father, will avenge the average Ukrainian citizen against the political class that reigned since 1991. In a debate between Zelensky and Poroshenko in April 2019, the former, after evoking certain corruption scandals during the last few years, publicly repeated such threats to the latter. President Porosh-

12. Zelensky, "Bleeding Heart of the Motherland."
13. René Girard, *Mensonge romantique et vérité romanesque* (Paris: Grasset, 1961), 25.

enko tried to fight back by reminding people that Zelensky was linked to Igor Kolomoisky, himself one of the richest oligarchs of the country, the owner of television chain 1+1 and a leading figure of the old guard—to no avail. The electorate did not care: Ukrainians voted massively in favor of the television hero (73% of votes) because he promised to fight corruption, to strike a peace deal with Russia, and to bring national unity.[14] Looking at Zelensky's campaign, one might notice the extent to which the *spin doctors* of the Ukrainian comedian leveraged both Raoul Girardet's myth of the *Savior*[15] and Girard's processes of *mimetic rivalry*.[16] It was done in a twofold manner. On the one hand, in the absence of a political program, Zelensky's campaign created a strategic mirror that allowed each voter to recognize herself in the new Ukrainian president, and to believe that he will take up her own aspirations. On the other hand, the campaign counted on the most irrational hopes of peoples who, in a period of economic upheaval and international war, desperately needed a message of hope, peace, and purification. This makes us understand better the insistence of gnostic discourses in Zelensky's messages, particularly concerning the vengeance that will fall upon the old political class.

Understanding the Wounds in the Ukrainian Soul

It would be tempting to conclude this brief presentation of the 2019 Ukrainian presidential elections by agreeing with Karl Marx's adage that religion is the opium of the people. Such a move would correspond with interpreting religious narratives in the Ukrainian presidential elections as yet another instance of an instrumental politicization of the religious culture, discourse, and unconscious.

---

14. Much of Zelensky's popularity had been built on television. Since 2016, tens of millions of Ukrainians watched the episodes of the television series *Servant of the People*, in which Zelensky played the role of Vassili Holoborodko, a high school history teacher, who, through completely fortuitous circumstances, becomes the president of the Ukrainian Republic. This television series constituted the heart of Zelensky's campaign, which did not have any political and economic program other than some manifest measures taken by the character he was playing on TV, such as the suspension of parliamentary immunity. Zelensky was eventually elected president of Ukraine.

15. Raoul Girardet, *Mythe et mythologies politiques* (Paris: Seuil, 1986).

16. René Girard, *Mensonge romantique et vérité romanesque* (Paris: Grasset, 1961).

Yet, if we were to consider Ukraine's recent political and social evolution, we would realize that the need for hope, more than anything else, played significantly into these developments. Between 2014 and the elections of 2019, Ukraine had already confronted military aggressions, first denied, then assumed by Vladimir Putin. By 2019, the annexation of Crimea, followed by the destabilization of Donbass, had left 13,000 dead among the Ukrainians, tens of thousands of people gravely wounded, and more than two million displaced. Moreover, during this period, Ukrainians lived with the knowledge that hundreds of Russian tanks were stationed at their eastern border and that, at any moment, they might be summoned to war, which eventually tragically happened in February 2022. Russian propaganda in Ukraine continued on a massive scale; the progressive multiplication of *fake news* prevented people from believing in the state of law. This agonizing situation included a growing economic pressure from the state, which was itself under pressure from European and American allies and their international financial institutions. The result was a demand to raise prices for communal tariffs and utilities, such as gas and electricity. In the years between 2014 and the 2019 elections, the national currency lost half of its value, the average wage remained around 300 euros a month, and inflation experienced a double-digit increase.

This background explains the success of Zelensky's intuition in spite of his total lack of political experience. His success came precisely from the fact that he introduced himself as a simple man, without experience, uncontaminated by the corruption of the elites. Just like his character on television, Zelensky was the one presidential candidate willing to travel by bicycle to his presidential palace.

As for Marx himself, who had been a victim of his own materialist illusions, so the Ukrainian peoples' thirst for hope, often against any semblance of rationality, is not necessarily an issue of faith. It is, above all, an issue of modern rationality, which seems to be increasingly less capable of discernment. While it is hard to imagine a movie actor being made the captain of an airliner, this is an increasingly frequent choice made by national communities for their state leadership, from Ukraine to Pakistan, and from the United States to Italy. Such rational blindness is also behind two extreme intuitions of our epoch—neoliberalism and populism.

THE SICKNESSES OF THE POSTMODERN SOUL

The Neoliberal Vision

Let us consider the liberal myth of the invisible hand, such as often presented in classic narratives on Adam Smith. This belief in the auto-regulatory power of the markets through the mediation of the prices of supply and demand is an illusion: as the ultraliberal businessperson Georges Soros recognized in 2008, prices never represent a just balance, for there is never perfect transparency among market players. For the Christian economist Gael Giraud, prices, at best, only represent the opinion that investors have of the anticipation of their colleagues on a certain number of variables that each has agreed to consider fundamental. Since the wave of financial liberalization of the 1980s, the financial markets have worked to develop financial assets—including credit default swaps and collateralized debt obligations—that are mostly detached from real economy mechanisms, while artfully hiding the risky and unsustainable mechanisms through which they produce rents. In 2007, the total derivative market represented a value of some USD 600 trillion, or 10 times the global GDP. The stock market collapse of 2008 and the subsequent economic recession showed the dramatic failure of neoliberal theories, and the ever growing disconnect between real people's interests and the "market," an entity increasingly dominated by purely financial assets and logics.

As René Passet has argued, the neoliberal vision as supported by "prophets" such as Friedrich Hayek and Milton Friedman—based on the dogma of deregulation, disintermediation, and de-compartmentalization—led to the illusion that the victory of neoliberalism over communism was a pacifying victory toward everyone's best interest. The subsequent propagation of the famous Washington Consensus, the "ten commandments," a theory of John Williamson in favor of free circulation of goods, people, and capital, was indeed presented as a "consensus"—an intersocially agreed truth on the best way forward.

However, the theory has been heavily criticized from several camps, including from mainstream economists, such as Passet[17] and Michel Cam-

---

17. In 2003, Passet suggested: "Capital, freed from the controls of the State that dominated it, could now concentrate itself on a global level within powerful financial institutions—banks, insurance companies, pension funds, speculative funds—which were able to impose

dessus, a former director at the International Monetary Fund. The latter revealed the naivete of the rational underpinnings of the Washington Consensus, deriving from a specific religious substructure: a raw, unitarian, unquestioned focus on one element—the "market." For Camdessus, a convinced Christian economist, economic progress is instead based upon the product of three separate hands rather than one: next to the "invisible hand of the market," there must be "the regulatory hand of the State"—for "markets can be mistaken and there are also many predators"—and, as markets cannot solve the problem of poverty, it is necessary to have a "hand of solidarity" capable of introducing gratuities in economic transactions.[18]

Thus, Camdessus suggests that the Presbyterian theses of Adam Smith suffered, above all, from a Christocentric and non-Trinitarian vision of the divine-humanity. Unfortunately, the ultraliberal reaction to the failure of Communist thought has not been to propose more of a rational criticism to the ensemble of nineteenth-century gnostic thought; on the contrary, such reaction has been to introduce more contrarian beliefs.

The Postliberal Populist Vision

Imbalances between faith and reason can also be found in populist intuitions, such as those formulated by former Donald Trump chief strategist Steve Bannon and by Vladislov Surkov, former first deputy chief of the Russian presidential administration. Bannon explains populism as consisting in being opposed to elites and favorable to the principle of solidarity. He defends his conviction in the necessity of a Westphalian system of sover-

their law on the ensemble of the economy and society through the great international financial and economic institutions such as the International Monetary Fund, the World Bank and the World Trade Organization. Capitalism, become 'shareholding,' would henceforth be ruled by an essentially financial logic. It was explained to us that this was something positive, that by seeking maximum results, finance would push the economy towards the optimization of its performances; the prices of national currencies, fluctuating freely, would adjust themselves to the level of the parity of the powers of purchase and, in the case of a disparity, would constantly bring back the sales or purchases of currencies to parity. . . . this would mark the end of the great speculative movements susceptible of throwing economies off balance." In *Sortir de l'économisme*, ed. P. Merant, Rene Passet, and J. Robin (Paris: Editions de l'Atelier, 2003), 11–12.

18. M. Camdessus, *La scène de ce drame est le monde* (Paris: Les Arènes, 2014), 136.

eignty (in which each state has exclusive sovereignty over its territory), to the profit of nation-states, without even realizing that this has historically been in internal contradiction with the principle of subsidiarity to which both the US and the EU are strenuously attached. According to Bannon, the common points among Donald Trump, Matteo Salvini, Viktor Orbán, and Jair Bolsonaro consist in the defense of national populism and a return to the traditional social structures of nations, families, and cultures. For Bannon, neoliberal globalization has led to depriving peoples of their democratic choices.

In a typically mythological way, Bannon, a former influential member of the Tea Party, lumps all the "elites" together without any distinction of currents of thought, generations, or nationalities. He glides rapidly over the fact that he himself attended Harvard's School of Business and worked at Goldman Sachs on Wall Street. As the producer of Breitbart News, which was at the origin of much of the phenomenon of *fake news*, Donald Trump's former campaign manager assumes that facts can be manipulated into "alternative truths." A study of his intellectual references reveals that he has been marked by the gnostic and millenarianism theses of Neil Howe and William Strauss, but also by Jean Raspail, the author of *The Camp of the Saints*, an apocalyptic novel imagining the invasion of France by a multitude of migrants. Here, too, it is the absence of historical rationality that pushes Bannon into an undifferentiated mythological vision of the world.

The Post-Soviet Populist Vision

While Steve Bannon remains attached to democracy, Vladislav Surkov, a former deputy prime-minister in the Russian government and special advisor to Putin, believes that democracy is a "Western thing" that prevents access to reality. Among the key theorists of the Putin regime over a period of 20 years, he believes that democracy is an illusionary system, for it rests on the deception of free choice.[19] His autocratic vision of power is also found on a quaternary vision of history in which the reign of Putin appears as the continuation and final term of the construction of the imperial Russian state, and even as the "ideology of the future." Any contradictory or nonse-

19. V Surkov, "Dolgoe gosudarstvo Putina," *Nezavisimaja Gazeta*, February 11, 2019.

quential vision is excluded: Surkov simply ignores the period from Mikhail Gorbachev to Boris Yeltsin. He points out, moreover, that he is not the only one to develop a mythological vision of the genealogy of the state, since the United States also refers to its "half-legendary founding fathers." He suggests that this representation remains in contradiction with the reality of American politics, assimilated in its entirety to the *House of Cards* television series. According to Surkov this cynical ideology, hostile to any freedom of choice and based upon the idea that most politicians are corrupt anyway, should be exported.

An assiduous reader of the Russian writer Victor Pelevin, an author who had anticipated the current evolution of the postmodern world, Surkov assumes that his concept of power can be designated as populism "for lack of better word." However, he explains that this term is itself illusory. With disarming simplicity, he explains that the propaganda of the Kremlin is very well organized and aimed at reaching the minds of Western citizens. The time when Russia was humiliated has ended, he goes on to say, and Russia is not alone in the defense of nationalism. He maintains that the Russians were the first, notably in Putin's 2007 speech in Munich, to understand that every state has to ask itself whether it is a "spider or a fly" in the global web.[20] Thus, he defends the Russian "deep State"—a nondemocratic organization of power, founded on violence and masked behind the exterior appearances of democratic institutions and civil society—without any complication. Surkov believes that the West is going to turn to Russia as the source of salvation, not necessarily because of its virtues, but because of its power and realism: the virtuous Russian people alone can bring the cosmopolitan elites back to the realities of the earth, thanks to the state structure created by Putin, which is "adequate for the people."[21] In his conclusion, Surkov wants to make his reader believe that this type of government, opposed to Western models, reposes on confidence, not dictatorship.

---

20. Antoine Arjakovsky, *Russia/Ukraine: From War to Peace? (2013–2015)* [in French], trans. Jerry Ryan, Lucy Collard, and Stefanie Hugh-Donovan (Paris: Parole et Silence, 2014).

21. Surkov also has a theory about a new form of fascism with, on the one hand, an effective leader called to rule for a long period, capable of reuniting the different branches of power and, on the other hand, a "deep people," not to be confused with the purely sociological definition of "population," which would be wary of Western institutions but which would, on the contrary, adhere to a vertical and monarchical concept of power.

The Possible Healing Paths

A lucid rediscovery of belief in politics allows us to anticipate and counter the dominant illusions of postmodernity. The awareness of the causal connection between skepticism and postmodern relativism, on the one hand, and the surge of extremes in the "ultraliberalism" and "populism" cycles, on the other, is, in itself, a powerful remedy. However, that is not sufficient to treat the wounds of postmodern consciousness.[22]

As suggested by Jean Birnbaum, the defense of European civilization against religious and secular fundamentalisms is not sufficient if it is not accompanied by a new philosophical and theological reflection. Nor can we remain satisfied with the proposition of Alain Caille, one of the authors of the *Manifeste du Convivialisme*, who pretends to "substitute the anthropology of man moved by the desire of recognition for the anthropology of *homo economicus*."[23] For, as he himself recognizes, this tilt can be for the better if the desire of recognition leads to a deeper sense of community, or for the worse, if the desire is auto-centered.

Hence, it is the time to present some of the recent philosophical theories trying to rehabilitate an authentic theological-political thought, theories capable of auto-criticism in regard to confessional religious thinking and modern rational thought. They may shed light on the nebulous Gnosticism of today.

The Theological Criticism of Modern Anthropology

For many, postmodern cynicism has its origin in the pessimistic vision of modern political thinkers, from Machiavelli to Thomas Hobbes. John Milbank and Adrian Pabst have authoritatively demonstrated this connection in their book *The Politics of Virtue*.[24] The materialist philosophies of fascism were only able to appear at the beginning of the twentieth century because of the vacuum created by the procedural formalism of liberalism. After the

---

22. See Vincent Delecroix, *Apocalypse du politique* (Paris: DDB, 2016), who considers that "the kingdom, the power and the glory are archaic theological-political productions."

23. A. Caille, *Manifeste du convivialisme* (Paris: Le bord de l'eau, 2015), 123.

24. John Milbank and Adrian Pabst, *The Politics of Virtue* (London: Rowman and Littlefield, 2016).

collapse of fascism, liberalism insisted once again on its own latent materialism. This latter tendency took the form of naturalism and scientism. It is enough to read a few pages of Yuval Noah Harari's book to be convinced that this new vision—which has the support of such influential figures as Mark Zuckerberg, the founder of Facebook, and Ray Kurzweil, the chief ideologist of Google—no longer fears to present itself under the visage of *dataism*.

Such a vision announces, in a messianic fashion, the proximate "singularity," that is, the synthesis of biological data with numerical data.[25] For Milbank and Pabst, only a rediscovery of the soul, of the psyche, could offset this monistic flattening of human consciousness.[26] Several contemporary intellectuals have revealed the origins of this monism in a new flattening of the already deficient binary anthropology characterizing modern times. In the opinion of Michel Fromaget, Judeo-Christian anthropology was initially trinary, as with many religious traditions. In this anthropology, the soul and the spirit are united, without separation but also without confusion: "any more than the form, the color and the taste of a lemon are parts of the fruit. Experience shows that, in fact, there is *no living body other than a body animated by a soul, a soul that animates such and such a body, and of a spirit that spiritualizes the soul and the body*." Fromaget thinks that Thomas Aquinas, in the thirteenth century, was at the origin of the first deviation from Eastern patristic theology when he postulated that the human soul was eternal by nature, and this led to confusion with the spirit. In fact, Evangelical theology believed that it was only possible for the human being, body and soul, to be

25. Y. N. Harari, *Homo deus* (London: Harvill Secker, 2018).

26. "According to this perspective (monist), the human spirit is only a series of chemical processes regulated by instrumental rationality and the body is only an assemblage of cells belonging to an owner (a la Locke) now defined as a physical brain. Not only has the spirit disappeared, but the subject as well, in such a way that the private biological property necessarily tends progressively towards a code that regulates the functioning of a centralized technological control." Due to the lack of emergence of a postliberal movement based on a democracy of the psyche, it is very possible that quasi-fascist tendencies will become more attractive and come to power throughout Europe and even in the United States as we are seeing already. For these insurgencies could be described as brute and imitative versions of postliberalism but responding to some of the same needs, notably a popular turning against the excesses of liberalism, the culture of success at the expense of the majority of people, amoral and narrow criteria that define this success, and a cosmopolitan scorn of rooted identity and the need to belong. Milbank and Pabst, *Politics of Virtue*, 18.

reborn because of the recognition of the divine spirit shining into him. But, according to Fromaget, it was René Descartes who was at the origin of the passage from ternary anthropology to dualist anthropology.[27]

Dany-Robert Dufour agrees that the anthropological deficiencies of seventeenth-century philosophers are the source of the uneasiness currently experienced by our neoliberal, and even libertarian, Western civilization.[28] Dufour denounces the progressive passage from a Puritan philosophy to a pornographic philosophy in a movement that began with Blaise Pascal and ended in Adam Smith, with Bernard de Mandeville in-between.

In his *Pensees* (fragment 48), Blaise Pascal affirms that the original sin, by separating God and man, transformed self-love into a criminal attitude. Everything happens as if man was henceforth abandoned by God. Without divine help, man's will is only capable of evil. In this anthropodicy, good comes from evil. Even a man's conversion does not wipe away the sin, a stain that must be unceasingly expiated. For Pascal, virtue comes only from God's love, while vice is the fruit of self-love. Pascal's whole life was marked by this constant alternation between the desire of a worldly life marked by vice and the thirst of a virtuous conversion. This tension deepened over the course of centuries to the point that Pierre Klossowski made the Marquis de Sade an heir of Pascal, a sort of perverse Puritan discovering that an admirable order can be founded on concupiscence. Simultaneously, in 1714, Bernard de Mandeville, a French Protestant intellectual who lived as a refugee in Holland, published his famous collection *La Fable des Abeilles*. Beginning from his reading of Pascal, the author added his own observations, drawing a conclusion that proved decisive for the whole history of modern, liberal, economic thought:

---

27. "Descartes abased the spirit to the psychic stage by having it signify man's faculty of thinking and reasoning. Now the spirit, in its original and ternary meaning, signifies something infinitely other; it designates, in man, a dimension that is ineffable and unconceivable which cannot be reduced to any precedents, a dimension that is specifically religious and spiritual and, in fact, extremely mysterious. This is why the great mystics affirm that the spirit cannot be defined in any way. Shankara, who lived in the 8th century, the Master of advaita, the doctrine of non-duality, put it nicely: 'The spirit is that before which words retreat.'" From M. Fromaget, "Apercus sur la signification et les implications de l'anthropologie ternaire 'Hic et Nunc,'" a conference presentation at the College of the Bernardins, April 2019. I thank the author for having given me the text of his presentation. Quotatión in text, emphasis added.

28. Dany-Robert Dufour, *La cité perverse* (Paris: Denoël, 2009), 102.

> The attitudes, characters and behaviors, considered as the disastrous effects on the individual by one of three concupiscences or libidos, (the passion to see, to know and to be able) are the source of general prosperity for the collectivity and promote the development of arts and sciences.[29]

It would be necessary to await the coming of the personalist thought of such authors as Nicolas Berdiaev before a new anthropodicy was proposed, and, along with that, a new concept of the libido, and notably the idea of sexuality. The Russian philosopher began by basing himself on the "genial vision of Boehme" to remind us that, according to God's design, man is a being who is integral, androgynous, both solitary and earthly, logical and elementary. He is complete and wholesome only in the measure in which he is chaste and wise. As a sexual being, he is reduced to disharmony. Only the rediscovery of Eros as a relationship constitutive of humanity united to God allows the recovery of the peaceful and creative vocation of the human being. But the phenomenon of the sublimation of the sexual energy does not correspond to an attitude of rejection of the world, much less its destruction. It is based on men and women's awareness of their condition not as fallen from the grace of God but, on the contrary, as divine-humanity.[30]

The Response of the Emergentist Vision

According to Jean-Michel Besnier, the concept of emergence expresses a refutation of the Cartesian principle that there is never more reality in the effect than there is in the cause. Quantum mechanics has enabled us to free ourselves from a mechanistic and determinist conception of the world. Jean-Pierre Dupuy, the author of *Pour une catastrophisme eclaire,* is one of the gnostic intellectuals seeking to go beyond a purely conceptualist, auto-organizational, and, ultimately, voluntarist vision of the world. The book reveals phenomena of auto-transcendence and the emergence of new opacities that are invisible to the modern eye. His work, marked by the thought of Girard, seeks to valorize the phenomena of resonance, and, equally, an opening to the work of the Spirit in the world. This system is really a gno-

29. Dufour, *La cité perverse,* 133.

30. Nicolas Berdiaev, *De la destination de l'homme* (Paris: Je Sers, 1935).

sis in the measure in which the question of evil is central, as it becomes evident in his *Petite metaphysique des tsunamis*. It blows apart strictly secular philosophies such as that of John Rawls, the troubadour of a liberalism that presents contemporary societies as "rational zombies." This thought is as much open to Taoist conceptions as it is to the Christian vision of divine-humanity. Dupuy, in fact, tends to rehabilitate a restrained conception of free will, which places each individual decision into a global vision of the world. This move leads to a rehabilitation of the prophet, even when he fails, as was the case with Jonas.

In addition, the doctrine can lead as much to a resigned vision of the power of metahuman mechanisms as to a jubilant vision of the world. It is for that reason that certain contemporary biologists, such as Jean-Claude Ameisen, speak of a "mysticism of emergence." For the latter, human liberty is at the foundation of this doctrine of emergence. It is the source of creation and relational co-construction. It bears testimony to the inalienable dignity of human beings and reveals, as in a negative, the reality of transcendent forces. Some physicists, such as Philippe Guillemant, use the concept of emergence to propose a new physics of consciousness, reestablishing the future alongside the past in a definition of the present.

This new gnostic vision enables the purification of certain aspects of confessional religious philosophy. The philosopher François Jullien advocates a rediscovery of the still unexploited resources of Christianity in order to envisage the world according to a postmodern model. At his turn, he uses the expression of auto-revelation to understand what Christ wanted to say when He spoke of the Kingdom of God on earth.[31]

31. What John wants to say when he speaks of the royalty of Christ, which is not of this world, is that the subject, when it affirms its originality or, better, auto-reveals itself, necessarily de-coincides with that world. But since he "ex-ists," outside of the enclosure of this world, without being integrated into it, he can effectively "witness" against the oppression that the world can impose or against the judgment of this world. That is why by ex-isting in this way, he can pass from the regime of the *psyche*, from his attachment to his vital being in this world, to the *zoe*, *life* in sur-abundance that effectively exceeds the measure of this world. Thus, there is in the world, as Jesus is in the world, something that does not belong to the world that cannot be reduced to it; this is what "ex-istence" is, most literally. F. Jullien, *Ressources du christianisme* (Paris: L'Herne, 2018), 114–15.

The Neopersonalist Vision

This concept of de-coincidence between the subject and the objective world enables us to extract ourselves from a religion of reason that has marked modern states since at least the nineteenth century.

Scientists and philosophers agree with theologians on the fact that, as Jean-Marc Ferry wrote, "the concept of the real goes beyond that of the tangible existence we run up against." The French philosopher proposes a new grammar of human intelligence, which does not separate identity and otherness, but reveals the emergence of people dependently from their confrontation with different levels of reality. He distinguishes among four types of "grammar"—archaic architectures of language existing from long before the creation of languages themselves: the grammar of the associations of images (grammar 1); that of the role of imputation (grammar 2); that of propositional differentiation (grammar 3); and, finally, that of counterfactual suppositions (grammar 4).[32] Each of these grammars opens a facet of the world according to a specific mode—respectively, luminous, erotic, pragmatic, and compassionate—and directs human trust in specific fashions dependent upon the forces of attraction: natural manifestations, providential interventions, rational explanations, and personal testimonies. The new vision of Jean-Marc Ferry, inspired by the thought of Georg Wilhelm Friedrich Hegel and Jürgen Habermas, suggests that authentic religion should not only focus upon the providential interventions. For Ferry, the ethical charity of reconstructive ethics, characteristic of grammar 4, is the only one able to embrace the collection of human experiences, from the most immanent to the most transcendent. It leads to a new personalist vision:

> A person's fulfillment does not separate the corporeal from the spiritual nor nature from rationality. Each being gives itself to a pluri-dimensional entirety of reality, invests in the diversity of the grammatical spectrum; it is there that reason and religion, overcoming their prior antagonism, finally come together, accomplishing one another thanks to having passed through a confidence of reality in its entirety, a passage which is as intelligent as it is "charitable," and thus serves as a universal language of faith.[33]

32. Jean-Marc Ferry, *Le grammaires de l'intelligence* (Paris: Passages, 2004).
33. Jean-Marc Ferry, *La raison et la foi* (Paris: Agora, 2016), 256.

This vision of the world, as "postliberal" as it is "postpopulist," grants renewed importance to the mediation of rights. Since the time has come to bring private convictions into public space, the new society—which could be qualified as ecumenical—and which will have to be reconstructed on the ruins of postmodernism, has the right to translate narrative and interpretive discourse into arguments, and vice versa.

This personalist vision also implies leaving to one side the liberal vision of Rawls, which includes an attitude of simple tolerance for individual convictions. For Michael Sandel, a vital democracy cannot last if it does not allow an in-depth dialogue on its citizens' existential and religious orientations regarding the good life. Such an approach supposes the ecumenical organization of a series of interreligious dialogues at a global level. Here we see again the work carried out over decades by Catholic, Protestant, and Orthodox intellectuals such as Hans Küng, Jürgen Moltmann, and Olivier Clément in view of creating a new ecumenical and global ethic. Within this context, in 1993 the Parliament of World Religions signed a charter seeking to complete, on an ethical level, what the United Nations had legally proclaimed in the 1948 Universal Declaration of Human Rights. This new planetary ethic was decidedly personalist:

> By planetary ethic we are not referring to a new ideology nor a global unifying religion above and beyond all existing religions; less still do we mean the domination of one religion over the others. For us, planetary ethics signifies the fundamental consensus concerning constraining values, irrevocable criteria and essential attitudes of the person. Without such a radical ethical consensus, each community will, sooner or later, run the risk of chaos or dictatorship and leave individuals in the shadows of despair.[34]

For, as Paul Tillich has shown, authentic convictions can never be disconnected from social practices. On the contrary, they should be ordered, in their diversity, to the common good. This notion makes more understandable what Milbank and Pabst have to say about a policy of virtue. It seeks, in fact, to favor "individual realization and mutual fulfillment in an objectively valid sense, in the respect of natural equity, although always properly negoti-

34. "Declaration for a Planetary Ethic," Parliament of World Religions, Chicago, 1993, 6.

ated through local specificities and traditions."[35] Thus, the rehabilitation of virtue is not a neomoralism but rather an attempt to go beyond the materialist and populist egoisms through the coordinated valorization of individual and collective efforts such as courage, honesty, generosity, and altruism.

CONCLUSION: FROM BELIEF IN POLITICS TO THE POLITICS OF FAITH

During the medieval period of their political consciousness, Christian churches attempted to establish a coercive Christian order. In modern times, Christian churches have shown a tendency to disengage from the management of public affairs, while recentering on themselves. And, during the recent ecumenical period of their histories, the time of reconciliation between faith and reason, some Christian denominations have proposed new forms of cooperation with states, while respecting their differences.

This cooperation could be mutually beneficial for states and churches. It would enable states to avoid reactions from fundamentalism to secular neutrality. In an analogous manner, this respectful cooperation could also help religions to avoid the trap of communitarian isolation and the temptation to suspend their mission of bringing justice in the world. Recently, Popes John-Paul II, Benedict XVI, and Francis have considerably rehabilitated the political commitment of the Catholic Church. Faith cannot live its vocation of keeping the flock united if it is eroded by division and vice. Unity is not the final horizon of monotheistic faith; in this, it differs from the coming of the kingdom of God on earth. The Gospel pericope (Mark 5:1–20) of the herd of pigs running off the cliff's edge and into the sea following the healing of a single person by Christ has, on the contrary, the tendency to show that Christianity privileges the salvation of souls to the social status quo. It implies religious courage in politics, as has been shown by Christian heroes and martyrs, in both the East and the West, throughout history.

It is at this point that we should limit the political commitment of Christianity, and begin relying on the millenary experience of European history. Indeed, each of us can think about the contemporary reappearance in politics of the most fundamentalist religious currents, be they in Russian Orthodoxy or in Moslem Wahhabism. Christians concluded their trajec-

35. Milbank and Pabst, *Politics of Virtue*, 520.

tory by defending democracy and liberty of conscience, basing themselves on Christ's plea that the good grain and the weeds be allowed to grow side by side, leaving to the Father the task of sorting them out when the moment arrives (Matthew 13:24–30). For their part, liberal Muslims have accepted the fundamental principles of the Universal Declaration of Human Rights. They make reference to the early interreligious project of the Prophet with the Jews and the Christians. They are, then, aware that cooperation between the state and the Islamic religion can and should be carried out with other religious traditions.

In the case of Ukraine, the ecumenical and interreligious dialogue has allowed the nation to constitute itself around European values such as the constitutional rule of law, justice, and respect for dignity. Simultaneously, the noncritical acceptance of the gnostic principles of liberalism has brought about much frustration among the majority of the population. Similarly, the overexpectations placed upon the administration of Zelensky will likely cause a new period of troubles and divisions within Ukrainian society. It is up to every single political community to find a formula capable of associating the state's vocation to establish a nation; to satisfy the postmodern aspirations of its peoples for openness and protection; the religious imperative of establishing an ecumenical civilization capable of creating a renewed anthropology; and a community of nation-states founded on a new juridical grammar. The search for this formula is not the task of the Ukrainian nation alone.

References

Arjakovsky, Antoine. *Russia/Ukraine: From War to Peace? (2013–2015)*. [In French.] Translated by Jerry Ryan, Lucy Collard, and Stefanie Hugh-Donovan. Paris: Parole et Silence, 2014.
Berdiaev, Nicolas. *De la destination de l'homme*. Paris: Je Sers, 1935.
Birnbaum, Jean. *La religion des faibles*. Paris: Seuil, 2018.
Brague, Rémi. *Du Dieu des chrétiens et d'un ou deux autres*. Paris: Flammarion, 2008.
Caille, A. *Manifeste du convivialisme*. Paris: Le bord de l'eau, 2015.
Camdessus, M. *La scène de ce drame est le monde*. Paris: Les Arènes, 2014.
"Declaration for a Planetary Ethic." Parliament of World Religions, Chicago, 1993.
Delecroix, Vincent. *Apocalypse du politique*. Paris: DDB, 2016.
Dufour, Dany-Robert. *La cité perverse*. Paris: Denoël, 2009.
Ferry, Jean-Marc. *Le grammaires de l'intelligence*. Paris: Passages, 2004.
Ferry, Jean-Marc. *La raison et la foi*. Paris: Agora, 2016.

Fleyfel, Antoine. *Les dieux criminels*. Paris: Cerf, 2017.

Fromaget, M. "Apercus sur la signification et les implications de l'anthropologie ternaire 'Hic et Nunc.'" Conference workshop, College of the Bernardins, April 2019.

Girard, René. *Mensonge romantique et vérité romanesque*. Paris: Grasset, 1961.

Girardet, Raoul. *Mythe et mythologies politiques*. Paris: Seuil, 1986.

Harari, Y. N. *Homo deus*. London: Harvill Secker, 2018.

Jullien, F. *Ressources du christianisme*. Paris: L'Herne, 2018.

Merant, P., Rene Passet, and J. Robin, directors. *Sortir de l'économisme*. Paris: Editions de l'Atelier, 2003.

Meyronnis, François, and Yannick Haenel, eds. "La sagesse qui vient." *Ligne de risque* 24 (February 2009).

Milbank, John, and Adrian Pabst. *The Politics of Virtue*. London: Rowman and Littlefield, 2016.

Mischenko, Mykhailo. "Society's Expectations of Church and Interchurch Relations." Public opinion survey, Razumkov Centre, https://risu.ua/en/razumkov-center_t2420

Surkov, V. "Dolgoe gosudarstvo Putina." *Nezavisimaja Gazeta*, February 11, 2019.

Zelensky, V. "The Bleeding Heart of the Motherland." In personal blog of author, V-zelenskiy.com, ze2019.com/blog.

Secularism and Sectarianism in Christianity

The Case of Northern Ireland during the Troubles

C. K. Martin Chung

Department of Government and International Studies, Hong Kong Baptist University, & Centre for the Study of Ethnic Conflict, Queen's University Belfast

> But Jesus was not proclaiming a political program or a model society.
>
> —INTERCHURCH GROUP ON FAITH AND POLITICS, *LIVING THE KINGDOM: FAITH AND POLITICS IN THE NORTHERN IRELAND CONFLICT*

This chapter examines the ways that Christian communities in Northern Ireland perceived and grappled with the problem of violence between and among the Catholic and Protestant populations during the Troubles (1968–98). On the one hand, there is strong evidence of secularism being practiced by the communities in their intercommunal attempts to turn away from the "sin of sectarianism" committed against each other. On the other hand, however, within this "Christian secular" framework,[1] the communities involved also sought to make active political contributions to resolving the conflict, rather than consigning it to "the world." It is to the clarification of this apparent contradiction in Christianity—by way of the Northern Ire-

---

This work was supported by a grant from the Research Grants Council of Hong Kong (project no. 22612318).

1. On "Judeo-Christian secularism" as an accommodationist discursive tradition vis-à-vis the separationist narrative of laicism as two varieties of secularism, see Elizabeth Shakman Hurd, *The Politics of Secularism in International Relations* (Princeton: Princeton University Press, 2008), 5.

land example, the "unfinished Reformation," as some locals call it[2]—that this chapter is dedicated. It argues that while in general secularization as a historical process was seen by Christian communities in conflict as a common threat, it was also consciously *welcomed* if not promoted in specific instances to achieve peace. Hence the ambiguous nature of the relationship between the religious and the secular in Christianity, as reflected in the Northern Ireland conflict. Going beyond the question of "Christian secularism," the chapter will also highlight the possible contributions and shortcomings of a theologically informed analysis of intercommunal conflict, namely, the sin-structural approach, vis-à-vis a secular sociopolitical analysis.

I. THE CONFLICT

Devastating to local communal life as it was, the Troubles in Northern Ireland, which has remained part of the United Kingdom since the partition of the island of Ireland in 1920/1921, was but one of the latest episodes of violent confrontation involving Catholics and Protestants ever since the Reformation in the sixteenth century. Compounded by British colonialism on the island across the Irish Sea and, later as a response, Irish nationalism, the "ethnic frontier" in the region was the product of centuries of colonial injustice, existential fear, and historical traumas.[3] The history of violence in the region was both universal and unique: universal because violent conflicts between different Christian sects, not to mention different religious groups, were not only found here both in space and in time. It was unique, however, not only because of the specific colonial and ethnic dimensions layered on top of the religious, but also because of the unusual longevity of the enmity. When Nietzsche was famously proclaiming "God is dead" in 1882, Ireland, as part of the United Kingdom since the Acts of Union in 1800, was only beginning to be engulfed in the Irish Home Rule movement to wrestle more autonomy from Westminster, to which those Protestants against the idea taunted: Home Rule means Rome Rule, or

2. Alf McCreary, "Almost 500 Years on from Luther, Can We Manage Our Own Reformation in Northern Ireland?" *Belfast Telegraph*, September 23, 2017.

3. Frank Wright, *Northern Ireland: A Comparative Analysis* (Dublin: Gill and Macmillan, 1988).

the tyranny of the pope.[4] When Catholics and Protestants in Germany were celebrating *together* the fifth centennial anniversary of the Reformation in 2017 and speculating about possible reunification in the distant future,[5] communities in Northern Ireland still had to bear with suspected sectarian vandalism of churches and statues on a regular basis.[6] As a local academic told the author in 2018, "here, the Reformation is an everyday experience."[7]

Regardless of the uniqueness or universality of the Northern Ireland experience, it is a prime example in contemporary Christianity of the longevity of religious influence in the supposedly secular political sphere. The 30-year conflict, which ultimately claimed more than 3,500 lives among civilians, paramilitaries, and security forces before a tortuous process of transformation and compromises culminating in the Good Friday/Belfast Agreement of 1998 delivered a closure to the bloodshed,[8] is a most relevant "site" to explore the evolving relationship between the Christian faith and politics in a context of conflict. The purpose of this chapter is to elucidate the ways through which the relationship of faith and politics in general, and the phenomenon of secularization in particular, was perceived and shaped by the Christian communities in the sectarianized region struggling to achieve peace and, ultimately, reconciliation. If, as "laicists" claim, that religion was partly if not mainly responsible for the "tribal" nature of the conflict (i.e., the failure to modernize politics lies with religion), what was the response of "Christian secularists"?[9] Did they try to negate that the conflict had any-

4. Brendan O'Leary and John McGarry, *The Politics of Antagonism: Understanding Northern Ireland* (London: Athlone Press, 1996), 87.

5. Hannes Leitlein and Raoul Löbbert, "Sieht so die Wiedervereinigung aus?," *Die Zeit*, no. 6 (2017).

6. Leona O'Neill, "Community's Shock after Londonderry Church Vandalism," *Belfast Telegraph*, September 14, 2017; "Anger and Shock as Tyrone Statue of Mary Defaced," *Belfast Telegraph*, October 9, 2017.

7. Personal communication in Belfast, April 2018.

8. For a breakdown of the victim profiles, see the Conflict Archive on the Internet maintained at Ulster University, https://cain.ulster.ac.uk/sutton/tables/index.html. The region has still been suffering from "low-intensity" violence, however, in the post-Agreement period up to the present. Laia Balcells, Lesley-Ann Daniels, and Abel Escribà-Folch, "The Determinants of Low-Intensity Intergroup Violence: The Case of Northern Ireland," *Journal of Peace Research* 53, no. 1 (2016).

9. Hurd, *Politics of Secularism*, 23.

thing to do with religion, that is, it was in fact a *secular* problem? Or did they own up to their responsibilities and deal with those doctrines and biblical interpretations in their traditions leading to a politics of antagonism instead of accommodation? If so, how did they navigate between the spheres of politics and faith in the context of spiraling violence pitting one Christian community against another and the security personnel of a purportedly secular, but perceived to be one-sided, state? To answer these questions, which should prove instructive not only for reflecting on the furtherance of the reconciliation process in Northern Ireland amid political instability and a resurgence of sectarianism, but also possibly for dealing with sectarian conflicts in other religions, this chapter proceeds with the examination of "interchurch" dialogues[10] conducted and publicized between the 1970s and the 1990s. It will first answer whether Christian communities in the island of Ireland,[11] Catholic and Protestant alike, "behaved" as expected to practice what Elizabeth Hurd calls "Judeo-Christian secularism," that is, a narrative tradition that appreciates the functional separation of church and state but does not advocate for the complete separation the religious and the political spheres, as laicism does.[12] It then explores their joint strategies for peace, especially focusing on their (lack of) proposals in the area of constitutional reform. It argues that despite the "failure" of Christian communities in general to provide concrete plans for change in terms of political structure, their detailed and sustained analysis of "sins" and "structures of sin" in relation to intercommunal conflicts was able nonetheless to complement the secular political-scientific approach by pointing to the social structure of sectarianism and the moral responsibility for its dismantling.

---

10. To better focus on Christianity as a whole and for the sake of brevity, intrachurch dialogues and their products—no less important as these were—are not analyzed in this chapter. See, for example, Evangelical Contribution on Northern Ireland, *For God and His Glory Alone: A Contribution Relating Some Biblical Principles to the Situation in Northern Ireland*, 2nd ed. (Belfast: ECONI, 1998).

11. Dialogue partners were not confined to Northern Ireland alone for all the major churches—Anglican, Catholic, Methodist, and Presbyterian—organize on an all-island basis. For a brief introduction of these traditions in the context of Northern Ireland, see Nukhet Sandal, *Religious Leaders and Conflict Transformation: Northern Ireland and Beyond* (Cambridge: Cambridge University Press, 2017), 43–47.

12. Hurd, *Politics of Secularism*, 6.

Introduction to the Primary Sources

Interchurch dialogues, as a manifestation of ecumenism, were not new to Northern Ireland,[13] especially after the Second Vatican Council (1962–65), but it took a while before they actually focused on the Troubles and the politics of antagonism. The first directly relevant work of the Irish Council of Churches/Roman Catholic Church Joint Group on Social Questions, that is, the official Protestant-Catholic cooperation,[14] was the report *Violence in Ireland*, first published in 1976.[15] It was more than seven years into the Troubles, among which five (1972–76) saw the most casualties with annual deaths over 200.[16] It was thus not only a theological assessment of the ongoing carnage but also a historical document of the hopes and frustrations of the religious struggling to overcome their centuries-old intercommunal rift. The next relevant document of the official interchurch dialogue, now institutionalized as the Irish Inter-Church Meeting, *Sectarianism: A Discussion Document*, would have to wait until 1993,[17] just before the "complete" ceasefire of the Provisional Irish Republican Army (IRA) in 1994.[18] It was the most thorough cross-denominational theological reflection on the phenomenon of sectarianism in the period, or the "complex of attitudes, beliefs, behaviors and structures in which religion is a significant component," as the Irish Inter-Church Meeting Working Party defined it.[19]

---

13. On the "hesitant, yet hopeful" development of ecumenism in the island of Ireland before the Troubles, see Eric Gallagher and Stanley Worrall, *Christians in Ulster 1968–1980* (Oxford: Oxford University Press, 1982), 21–38, 130.

14. On the Protestant side, the three major traditions in the island were represented: the Church of Ireland (part of the Anglican Communion), the Irish Presbyterian Church, and the Methodist Church in Ireland. The notable exception is the Free Presbyterian Church founded in 1951 by Ian Paisley (1926–2014), who had a long history of vilifying "ecumenical clergymen" and "ecumenical churches." See Gallagher and Worrall, *Christians in Ulster 1968–1980*, 24–25; also Sandal, *Religious Leaders and Conflict Transformation*, 44.

15. Joint Group on Social Questions, *Violence in Ireland: A Report to the Churches*, rev. ed. (Belfast: Christian Journals; Dublin: Veritas Publications, 1977), 6. On the setting up of the Joint Group, see Gallagher and Worrall, *Christians in Ulster*, 134–35.

16. According to the Conflict Archive on the Internet, https://cain.ulster.ac.uk/sutton/tables/index.html

17. Working Party on Sectarianism, *Sectarianism: A Discussion Document* (Belfast: Department of Social Issues of the Irish Inter-Church Meeting, 1993).

18. David McKittrick and David McVea, *Making Sense of the Troubles: A History of the Northern Ireland Conflict*, rev. and updated ed. (London: Viking, 2012), 232.

19. Working Party on Sectarianism, *Sectarianism*, 8.

In the intervening years, unofficial groups of Protestants and Catholics carried on the interchurch discussion and produced several documents for wider consumption. One of these unofficial groups was the Inter-Church Group on Faith and Politics (ICGFP), "a group of Protestants and Catholics, Northerners and Southerners," which grew out of an ecumenical conference in 1983 and published *Breaking Down the Enmity*, their first "draft issued for discussion and response" in early 1985,[20] the year when a major political breakthrough was realized in the Anglo-Irish Agreement, which *inter alia* institutionalized the role of the Republic of Ireland in the affairs of Northern Ireland. Over the next few years the group would continue to comment on the Anglo-Irish Agreement and the new situation created by it. Their documents produced in this period together with those by the official dialogues are the primary basis of the analysis in this chapter.

II. CHRISTIAN SECULARISM DURING THE TROUBLES

It is clear from rereading the interchurch discussions on violence that it was no easy task for the churches to speak about politics during the Troubles. It was not only that the relationship between the two communities—more or less congruently labeled Catholic/Irish/nationalist and Protestant/British/unionist[21]—has been burdened by a long history of violence, which is always in need of narrative elucidation before any serious discussion on the present can begin. It was also because the churches themselves were not "independent observers." From the paramilitaries to the civilians to the security personnel involved in the conflict, more likely than not, they were all members—however close or distant—of different churches.[22] On the back cover of *Violence in Ireland*, it was thus stated that all Catholic and Protestant participants in the Joint Group had to go through a "considerable travail

20. ICGFP, "Breaking Down the Enmity," in *Living the Kingdom* (Belfast: Interchurch Group on Faith and Politics, 1989), 17–19.

21. On the more or less "perfect" ethno-religious and sociopolitical cleavages, see James Tilley, Geoffrey Evans, and Claire Mitchell, "Consociationalism and the Evolution of Political Cleavages in Northern Ireland, 1989–2004," *British Journal of Political Science* 38 (2008); and Jocelyn Evans and Jonathan Tonge, "Catholic, Irish and Nationalist: Evaluating the Importance of Ethno-National and Ethno-Religious Variables in Determining Nationalist Political Allegiance in Northern Ireland," *Nations and Nationalism* 19, no. 2 (2013).

22. According to a UK census in 2001, 46% of Northern Ireland is Protestant, 40% Catholic. Cited in Sandal, *Religious Leaders and Conflict Transformation*, 42.

of conscience" in order to come to an agreed historical account and speak with one voice, which was in itself no small achievement.[23]

The difficulty or reluctance to say anything directly political could also be glimpsed in the belated discussion on violence. Earlier Joint Group reports preferred to instead talk about drug abuse (1972), housing (1973), teenage drinking (1974), and underdevelopment in rural areas (1976), thus "social questions" rather than political affairs like one-party devolution, direct rule, or power sharing, during which time Northern Ireland politics had gone through all three (failed) arrangements, and the annual death toll peaked in 1972 with 480 casualties.[24] When the interchurch group finally spoke squarely on political violence the clearest message that came out was its condemnation. "There is absolutely no justification for the campaigns of violence that have characterized the situation in recent years," the Joint Group emphasized.[25] Indeed, an entire chapter in *Violence in Ireland* is dedicated to examining the "results of violence," which denounces in no uncertain terms the violent tactics of the "Republican Movement"—in contrast to the nonviolent "Civil Rights Movement."[26] "The sanctity of human life, which is a central Gospel principle as well as a basic human value, has been seriously eroded" in the Irish experience, which was also a "conclusive demonstration of both the evil and the ineffectiveness of violence as a means to desirable social change."[27]

Condemning Violence

If condemning violence and explicitly judging it as un-Christian and unscriptural is the least religious actors can do in an intercommunal conflict,

---

23. By comparison, official joint history-writing exercises by historical enemies often fail to agree on a single account but produce two (or more) separate and irreconcilable histories. See C. K. Martin Chung, "From Nation to Region: Comparing Joint History Writing in Europe and in East Asia," in *States, Regions and the Global System: Europe and Northern Asia-Pacific in Globalised Governance*, ed. Andreas Vasilache, Reimund Seidelmann, and José Luis de Sales Marques (Baden-Baden: Nomos, 2011).

24. Joint Group on Social Questions, *Violence in Ireland*, 6.

25. Joint Group on Social Questions, *Violence in Ireland*, 18.

26. Joint Group on Social Questions, *Violence in Ireland*, 42.

27. Joint Group on Social Questions, *Violence in Ireland*, 49.

the interchurch group, together with the leadership of the churches, never failed to do so. However, whether it is *enough* is another question. Contemporary church critics saw rather in this perhaps self-uncritical position of the churches vis-à-vis violence the problem of self-irrelevance. "'There is a lot of violence. Violence is not Christian' and the result of this is that 'the [Catholic] Church has no role in this problem because there is no historical analysis of what has been causing these problems.'"[28] Looking back, former Republican prisoner and Sinn Féin politician Jim McVeigh also found this attitude of his church not helpful: "It was our experience that the [Catholic] Church seemed only too willing to condemn the actions of Republicans while turning a blind eye to State violence and injustice,"[29] or "institutional violence," as some prefer to call it, which the interchurch authors of *Violence in Ireland* found problematic as such naming could be used to justify violence as reaction.[30]

Indeed, going beyond the mere condemnation of violence, there seems to be little on offer by the interchurch groups in terms of ideas about or proposals for constitutional or political structural changes. It is in fact in this area where the churches' secularist reflexes were most apparent. It is not the case that the churches and their "working parties" did not have any historical or structural analyses of the causes of violence, as their critics accused them; rather, it is their *principled* refusal to commit themselves to any logical conclusion out of these analyses (e.g., whether the 1920/1921 partition was legitimate or not) and to provide them with their theological justifications and religious blessings (e.g., to unionism or republicanism) that characterized their approach.[31] As the unofficial Faith and Politics group asserted—

28. Paedar Kirby quoted in Sidney Garland, "Liberation Theology and the Ulster Question," *Foundations* 15 (1985): 24.

29. Jim McVeigh, "The Irish Church and Republicanism: The Need for Liberation Theology," *The Furrow* 50, no. 1 (1999): 3. Given the anticlerical tradition of revolutions in Europe, the relationship between the Catholic hierarchy and revolutionary movements has long been contentious. From being disapproving of the 1916 Easter Rising to naming the IRA a "sinful and irreligious society" as early as the 1940s, the Catholic Church leadership has distanced itself from any violent attempts to change the constitutional status of the island of Ireland (Joint Group on Social Questions, *Violence in Ireland*, 118–19).

30. *Violence in Ireland*, 12.

31. Following the convention in the literature and except in direct quotations, "nationalism," "unionism," "republicanism," and "loyalism" in lower case refer to their respective political

quoting Catholic bishop Cahal (later cardinal) Daly (1917–2009), one of the two joint chairmen of the official interchurch group—in their very first fruit of collaboration published in 1985, *Breaking Down the Enmity*: "It is neither the right nor the competence of a churchman to propose constitutional or political blueprints."[32] The group was determined not to provide "a blueprint for a new political structure within Northern Ireland," but only "moral parameters" to frame those "blueprints."[33]

Justifying Christian Secularism

The unofficial interchurch group justified their "Christian secular" approach by referring to the primary example of the Lord himself: "Jesus was not proclaiming a political program or a model society. He was proclaiming the approaching Kingdom of God . . . [which] was not to be brought about by political action or by coercive power."[34] This view of Jesus without any specific "political program" was also shared by the official group, which bluntly stated—to the chagrin of republicans—that Jesus' revolution was not the zealot's.[35] But going beyond the Joint Group's condemnation of violence, the Faith and Politics group accused fellow Christians who did not share their "Christian secular" conviction of having committed a particularly grave sin: "Christians cannot identify any particular political program unconditionally with obedience to the will of God otherwise they fall into *idolatry*."[36]

Idolatry, rather than violence, was in fact the primary focus of *Breaking Down the Enmity*, of which I will say more in the next section exploring various theological readings of the Troubles. In the meantime, I will clarify further dimensions of "Christian secularism" as expressed by the interchurch

ideologies/convictions, whereas the same in upper case refer to particular party or organizational identities.

32. ICGFP, "Breaking Down the Enmity," 4.2.2, 43.

33. ICGFP, "Breaking Down the Enmity," 4.2.2, 43; 6.11, 53.

34. ICGFP, "Breaking Down the Enmity," 4.2, 42.

35. Joint Group on Social Questions, *Violence in Ireland*, 62. The authors did not refer to any specific biblical text in support of their statement. Possible sources include John 6:15 and Matthew 26:52.

36. ICGFP, "Breaking Down the Enmity," 4.2, 42. Emphasis added.

groups in Northern Ireland,[37] its scriptural basis, and the perceived problems and opportunities offered by increased secularization.

On the secular world, including its politics, the interchurch dialogues reiterated and reflected the great divergence of models and views within Christianity. On the one hand, they recognized that there was an interpretive tradition linking Paul's Letter to the Romans (13:1–7) to Christians' default obedience to the state, hence their basic conservatism.[38] On the other hand, they also expressed later Christian suspicion of secular government, seeing it as an instrument of evil rather than a godly creation, as reflected in Revelation 13.[39] The selfsame Jesus who did not have a "political program" was also the one who had "challenged the foundations of Jewish religious and political structures."[40] Though there was not to be a territorial Kingdom of God on earth before the Final Judgment, Christians could only accept the principle of territorial sovereignty with qualification because all lands belong to God (Psalm 24:1; Isaiah 40:28).[41] As it were, Christian secularism is built on multiple biblical sources, and contains multiple seeming paradoxes if not outright contradictions. In the assessment of the Faith and Politics Group, solving the problem in Northern Ireland was all about getting the *right* connections between faith and politics.[42] While Christian "blueprints" for constitutional and political structures are not to be expected, Christian *intervention* in the political sphere is considered a duty of the faithful, as we will see later.

---

37. Though the interchurch "reports" and "discussion drafts" were approved and endorsed by all the representatives of the participating churches, there is some anecdotal evidence of differences in opinion when it comes to "Christian secularism," with the Catholic Church (under William Cardinal Conway) appearing somewhat against secularism while the Protestant churches were more ready to explore and appreciate the "positive elements" of the spirit of secularism and the process of secularization. Cahal Daly and Stanley Worrall, *Ballymascanlon: An Irish Venture in Inter-Church Dialogue* (Belfast: Christian Journals; Dublin: Veritas Publications, 1978), 81–82.

38. Joint Group on Social Questions, *Violence in Ireland*, 56.

39. Joint Group on Social Questions, *Violence in Ireland*, 58.

40. ICGFP, "Breaking Down the Enmity," 2.4.1, 31.

41. "A Declaration of Faith and Commitment," in *Living the Kingdom* (Belfast: Interchurch Group on Faith and Politics, 1989), 66.

42. "Towards an Island That Works: Facing Divisions in Ireland," in *Living the Kingdom* (Belfast: Interchurch Group on Faith and Politics, 1989), 73.

Secularization: Opportunities and Threats

While in general critical of increasing secularization, the interchurch groups nonetheless saw opportunities for improved relations between Protestants and Catholics offered by the secularizing tendencies of Irish society. In *Toward an Island That Works: Facing Divisions in Ireland* (first published in 1987), the southerners (i.e., those from the Republic of Ireland) in the Faith and Politics Group bemoaned that "secularization has grown steadily" from the 1960s to the 1980s.[43] Among other things, this meant that the Catholic Church had "almost no influence on [Irish people's] attitudes towards Northern Ireland," thus bespeaking the political irrelevance of church teachings.[44] Nevertheless, when it was reported that some politicians in the Republic were increasingly willing "to differ publicly with Catholic Church leaders on certain issues," and the Catholic bishops in Ireland expressed that they actually "do not expect or desire that the law of the land should conform in all particulars to Roman Catholic teaching," the ICGFP welcomed the realization of this development of a more pluralistic society in the south, which they hoped would in turn lessen Protestant fear in the north of "Catholic domination" in Northern (or united) Ireland.[45]

The area in which secularization was seen as a threat rather than an opportunity was the surmised separation of faith and politics in republican paramilitarism. As the southerners in the unofficial group reflected on the rise of political violence among the Catholic laity:

> The Catholic Church . . . has consistently opposed the use of violence in Northern Ireland. But the fact is that the IRA would not exist unless enough people in the Catholic/nationalist community wanted or at least tolerated them. Perhaps a basic reason for this is that so many militant Republicans do not see *any connection* between their faith and questions of politics.[46]

In other words, this purported internal secularization of Catholics had possibly created a spiritual vacuum that republicanism had filled. As it were,

43. "Towards an Island That Works," 77.
44. "Towards an Island That Works," 78.
45. "Towards an Island That Works," 83, 101–2.
46. "Towards an Island That Works," 96. Emphasis added.

there was no contradiction for some to be Catholic and to be a supporter of violent revolution at the same time. The irrelevance of church teachings to political issues, which was partly a consequence of the political agnosticism of "Christian secularism," once again dawned on the interchurch dialogue partners. For them, this kind of *private secularism* on the part of Christian believers, vis-à-vis the *public secularism* of official churches and their leaders mentioned above, was part of the deeper structural realities of the Troubles.[47] As we shall see below, the unofficial interchurch group was convinced that internal secularization had left room for *idolatry* in Northern Ireland to grow—or the "over-identification" of Christians to this or that ideology, to this or that political structure—which, together with social injustice, had brought the problem of spiraling violence upon themselves.

III. THEOLOGICAL READING OF THE TROUBLES

"Churches have neither the task of drawing up constitutional blueprints nor of implementing them. Such tasks belong to politicians."[48] The unofficial Faith and Politics Group was adamant in their emphasis on "Christian secularism" in dealing with the Troubles, citing in support the relevant official documents from all four major Christian traditions in the island. But what then are the tasks of the theologians? In general, the tasks that the cross-denominational Christian groups took upon themselves involved providing a *theological* reading of the Troubles, making it possible for the wider Christian communities to *make sense* of what had befallen them in the eyes of their faith and to strike out on a new course of action, to effect a change of mind and heart, that would eventually lead them out of their predicament. In short, it was the perspective of *repentance* (*metanoia* in Greek) that the interchurch groups sought to propagate with the help of scripture.[49] This

47. See Johann Baptist Metz's discussion of the "danger of the self-privatization of Christianity" in his *Memoria passionis: Ein provozierendes Gedächtnis in pluralistischer Gesellschaft* (Freiburg: Herder, 2017), 188–90.

48. ICGFP, "Breaking Down the Enmity," 4.2.6, 44.

49. *Metanoia*, literally "change of mind," or *tshuvah* ("turning") in Hebrew, is among the quintessential teachings of the biblical traditions of Judaism and Christianity, which can have profound transformative effects when applied in post-atrocity situations of "coming to terms with the past." See Mark Boda and Gordon Smith, eds., *Repentance in Christian Theology* (Collegeville, MN: Liturgical Press, 2006), and C. K. Martin Chung, *Repentance for the Holo-*

section seeks to outline the main features of this perspective: from classifying the Troubles as divine judgment, to identifying the sins of idolatry, social injustice, and sectarianism. It will also connect the interchurch reflections with contemporaneous reflections in the wider Christian world on the *structural* problems underlying social conflicts.

Social Injustice and Idolatry

As mentioned in the previous section, the unofficial interchurch group went beyond their official counterpart to not only issue a condemnation of violence as un-Christian but to also accuse fellow Christians (and themselves) of having committed grave sins that were ultimately responsible for the Troubles. "It is our belief that the conflict in Northern Ireland is in part a judgement of God on the failure of Christians in Northern Ireland, Britain and the Republic to witness to the indiscriminate love of God, the God who has no favorites . . . (Mt 5:45)."[50] There was divine judgment because of the preexisting twofold sins of idolatry and social injustice in Britain and Ireland. "The conflict is something we in these islands have brought on ourselves by the ways in which we have practiced *injustice* in politics . . . by worshipping the *false God of sectarian interests* and not the God who is revealed in Jesus Christ."[51] In terms of social injustice, the group made clear that one of the two communities was the victim, and the other not. "In Northern Ireland we hear and see the judgement of God in the way that humanity has been distorted, that the Roman Catholic Community has not received full parity of treatment and esteem."[52] This is in sharp contrast to some other narratives that try to make the point that when it comes to social injustice, the dividing line is not religious but social, not between Catholics and Protestants but between the haves and the have-nots, who also counted underprivileged Protestants among them. In the Old Testament, the authors warned, prophets like Amos (5:10–13) never failed to criticize social injustice in terms of oppression of the poor, obstruction of justice, and silencing critics. "There

---

caust: Lessons from Jewish Thought for Confronting the German Past (Ithaca: Cornell University Press and Cornell University Library, 2017).

50. ICGFP, "Breaking Down the Enmity," 1.2, 20.
51. ICGFP, "Breaking Down the Enmity," 1.2, 20–21. Emphases added.
52. ICGFP, "Breaking Down the Enmity," 5.5, 45.

will be no peace in Northern Ireland until both communities feel included," the Faith and Politics Group counseled.[53] Because of this, they objected to the simplistic principle of majority rule held sacrosanct by some, whether within the Northern Irish context or with the island of Ireland as a whole. "Democracy is not only about majority rule; it is also, and perhaps more fundamentally, about individuals and minorities having a say and having their interests recognized and protected."[54] In its stead, they seemed inclined to support power-sharing arrangements but were pessimistic—perhaps also in view of the failed experiment[55] in 1974—that such "political devices" would ever work without first overcoming intercommunal enmity.[56]

In terms of idolatry, Christians in Northern Ireland were accused of having bowed down to "idols" and chosen leaders without divine approval, just like in Hosea 8:4.[57] In *Towards Peace and Stability: A Critical Assessment of the Anglo-Irish Agreement* (first published in 1988), the Faith and Politics Group reiterated their theological reading of the Troubles as partly the result of idol worship: "Idolatry . . . *necessarily* results in violence. . . . in our worship of the gods of nationalism, of loyalism and republicanism, we have forced others to fit into our 'space' or have been happy to have them expelled."[58] Aside from ideologies, the group also stressed that national identities,[59] political structures,[60] political programs,[61] and traditional cultures could "very quickly become idols" when there is "over-identification" with them.[62]

> Roman Catholicism in Ireland has been over-identified with what many Protestants have seen as an exclusivist Gaelic/Nationalist culture.

---

53. ICGFP, "Breaking Down the Enmity," 5.5, 45–46.

54. ICGFP, "Breaking Down the Enmity," 5.6.2, 46.

55. The first power-sharing government instituted by London broke down in a few months because of opposition within unionism/loyalism. O'Leary and McGarry, *Politics of Antagonism*, 197–201.

56. ICGFP, "Breaking Down the Enmity," 5.6.1, 46.

57. ICGFP, "Breaking Down the Enmity," 2.2, 29.

58. ICGFP, "Towards Peace and Stability: A Critical Assessment of the Anglo-Irish Agreement," in *Living the Kingdom* (Belfast: Interchurch Group on Faith and Politics, 1989), 7:136. Emphasis added.

59. ICGFP, "Towards Peace and Stability," 4:122.

60. ICGFP, "Breaking Down the Enmity," 3.8.7, 39.

61. ICGFP, "Breaking Down the Enmity," 4.2, 42.

62. ICGFP, "Breaking Down the Enmity," 4.1, 42.

> Northern Irish Protestantism has been over-identified with the Unionist Ascendancy in Northern Ireland and with the Orange Order. We need, with God's Grace, to find ways of releasing ourselves from these captivities.[63]

The way to extricate oneself from such "over-identification," according to the Faith and Politics Group, is to return to the true faith of Christianity, which requires one to completely reorient oneself with God as the center, not this or that political arrangement, be it union with Britain, or unification with Ireland. This requires collective repentance, which involves also overcoming private secularization. Taking inspiration from the promised efficacy of collective repentance in 2 Chronicles 6:38–39, the group reminded fellow Christians in Northern Ireland that "repentance is an admission of our true condition; that of being sinners who have turned away from God in pursuit of selfish idols and in exploitation of other people. It means a turning towards God."[64] By prioritizing the existing union or the longed-for unification over God, Christians in the divided region also risked "destroying the things they hold most dear," they warned, just as the Gospels (Mark 8:35; Matthew 10:39; Luke 9:24; John 12:25) had taught them, "there is a way of seeking to save life which ultimately means losing it."[65] In other words, what applies to the personal life of Christians also applies to their political life as a community.

Concerning private de-secularization, the official and unofficial interchurch groups were in agreement. The same authors who greeted the public secularism of Catholic bishops and politicians in Ireland, seeing in this development something conducive to lessening Protestant fear of Catholic dominance, now expressed the conviction that "we must attempt seriously to apply Christian principles to the political sphere."[66] The official Joint Group also opined that when it comes to the classic separation of church and state, or what belongs to God and what belongs to Caesar (Matthew 22:21), both are, in the final analysis, God's instruments, and the individual should therefore know where her ultimate allegiance lies—that is, neither blind loyalty to the secular political leaders nor blind faith in religious

63. ICGFP, "Breaking Down the Enmity," 3.3, 34.

64. ICGFP, "Towards an Island That Works," 85.

65. "Understanding the Signs of the Times: A Christian Response to the Anglo-Irish Agreement," in *Living the Kingdom* (Belfast: Interchurch Group on Faith and Politics, 1989), 3.5, 57.

66. "Towards an Island That Works," 106.

ones. "It would have been easier for us if Jesus had made a distinction between 'the things that are Caesar's and the things that are Caiaphas's'. For if both State and Church are instruments of God's will *in their respective spheres*, then all things are God's, and if God declares what is Caesar's, it is also God who declares the sphere of ecclesiastical authority. . . . There is *no part of his life* for the Christian in which Jesus Christ is not Lord."[67] The distinction between public and private secularization is obvious: whereas religious leaders are advised to refrain from forcing secular governments and politicians to implement policies *fully and always* in conformity with their religious doctrines, thus allowing for the development of a more pluralistic society that is less threatening to minority religious communities, individual believers are required to leave no separate sphere beyond the reach of faith so that there will be no space for political idolatry, which "necessarily" results in violence.[68] The first separation is *willed* by God, the latter is to be avoided by Christians. The two are supposed to work together and not contradict each other.

Structure of Sectarianism

That there were "spheres" shielded from faith in the personal and communal life of the faithful was the *structural* problem preoccupying subsequent interchurch dialogues. When the churches convened another official working party in 1991 to look at the "politico/religious conflict" in Northern Ireland,[69] the church representatives revisited the point about the actual irrelevance of religion in a supposedly (and originally) theological conflict in an increasingly secular age:

> A story was circulating a few years ago of two young men in masks stopping a man. "Are you a Catholic or a Protestant?" "Er . . . er . . . a Catholic." "Say a Hail Mary!" When the man does so, one youth turns to the other: "Did he say that right, Sean?" Like much of the black humor in

67. Joint Group on Social Questions, *Violence in Ireland*, 57. Emphases added. The mention of Caiaphas is interesting, for this priestly figure in the Gospels is indeed the paradigmatic religious leader who prioritizes national survival over doing justice: "it is expedient for us, that one man should die for the people, and that the whole nation perish not" (John 11:50). See also the divine act of separating kingship from judgeship in 1 Samuel 8.

68. ICGFP, "Towards Peace and Stability," 7:136.

69. Working Party on Sectarianism, *Sectarianism*, 7.

> Northern Ireland, the story makes a shrewd point about the part that religion plays in the conflict. In a sense religious issues are irrelevant; yet denominational allegiance is the most important question one can ask about a person.[70]

Yet unlike the unofficial interchurch group, who would then go on to label such "denominational allegiance" as idolatrous,[71] the official Working Party took a different approach to render the particular problem of what they called "sectarianism" visible by revealing the structure of this social phenomenon in Northern Ireland. According to their definition:

> Sectarianism is a complex of attitudes, beliefs, behaviors and structures in which religion is a significant component, and which (i) directly, or indirectly, infringes the rights of individuals or group, and/or (ii) influences or causes situations of destructive conflict.[72]

The authors chose to focus on the consequences of different religious beliefs, rather than on the beliefs themselves, for they wanted to stress that "acts and attitudes with no sectarian intent can have sectarian consequences," for which "we are responsible" as well, and that a religious belief could be "maintained as long as it does not damage my relationship with my neighbor."[73] Furthermore, while taking the impetus from the first official Joint Group that had seen in the 1970s that "concern for *sectional* interest has weakened the witness of some Christians" in Northern Ireland, and called sectarianism "the frame of mind that exploits denominational differences to promote a sense of superiority, a denial of rights, a justification of conflict,"[74] the later Working Party also sought to go beyond the definition of sectarianism as a "frame of mind," which is, according to them, "extremely difficult to judge," unlike *consequences*, which can be observed and measured.[75]

---

70. Working Party on Sectarianism, *Sectarianism*, 13.

71. ICGFP, "Towards an Island That Works," 85.

72. Working Party on Sectarianism, *Sectarianism*, 8.

73. Working Party on Sectarianism, *Sectarianism*, 9.

74. Joint Group on Social Questions, *Violence in Ireland*, 20, 71.

75. Working Party on Sectarianism, *Sectarianism*, 9. See also a further development of the concept and thorough analysis of the phenomenon in Joseph Liechty and Cecelia Clegg, *Moving Beyond Sectarianism: Religion, Conflict, and Reconciliation in Northern Ireland* (Dublin: Columba Press, 2001). Liechty was the Mennonite member of the Working Party on

Building on the insights of *Violence in Ireland*, which raised the point about the possible *continuity*, rather than a clean break, between the terrorists and ordinary Christians ("How far are the terrorists of both sides '*extensions of us*'... ? Is terrorism a rejection of the ethos of our society? Or is it . . . a manifestation of that ethos?"),[76] the Working Party asserted that "the structure of sectarian attitudes is like a pyramid," in which there was "no real break" between the conspicuous atrocities committed by the extremists at the top and "the daily actions of many ordinary people" at the bottom.[77] Compared with the double-sin perspective of the unofficial interchurch group, namely, the sin of idolatry and the sin of social injustice, this way of perceiving and framing the problem in Northern Ireland during the Troubles as *one* problem of sectarianism is much more far-reaching, for even "ordinary people" who were not active supporters of various *isms* (hence not "idolatrous") and who did not oppress the poor and the weak are now shown their hidden links with "sectarianism at the top." Analyzing the *unity* of sectarianism as a social phenomenon has also the advantage of revealing the myriad of connections between individual attitudes, beliefs, behaviors, and societal structures—a problem the unofficial group encountered when they were at pains to argue the case for the "close relationship" between idolatry and social injustice.[78] Hence with *Sectarianism*, the decades-long interchurch reflection on the conflict in Northern Ireland reached a new quality just as the Troubles entered the final phase.

"The structure of sectarian attitudes in our society is like a pyramid," the Working Party insisted. But just as Eve blamed the serpent for the forbidden fruit and Adam blamed God for giving him Eve in the book of Genesis (3:12–13), "it is a feature of this pyramid that people at each level . . . disclaim responsibility for the words and actions of the layer above."[79] It is not only the problem of denial and finger-pointing, however, but each level—knowingly or not—provides "a model and justification" for the level above it:

> At the apex are the actions of the "mad dog" . . . [whose atrocious attacks] are condemned by almost everyone in the layers beneath. . . . But such

Sectarianism.

76. Joint Group on Social Questions, *Violence in Ireland*, 50–51. Emphasis added.

77. Working Party on Sectarianism, *Sectarianism*, 13.

78. ICGFP, "Breaking Down the Enmity," 2.2.2, 30.

79. Working Party on Sectarianism, *Sectarianism*, 23.

> atrocities grow out of the hatred expressed in sectarian rioting and attacks. . . . This level of bigotry is sometimes condemned by the main paramilitary groups . . . but many of their actions have had a sectarian character. . . . The paramilitary level in its turn rests upon that of the people who use platform, pulpit or the pages of the press to express bigoted and inflammatory sentiments. . . . And this level could not survive without the tacit support of many "ordinary, decent people" who have some sympathy for their views. . . . they encourage by vote, religious view and private opinion the layer above them. . . . it is not hard to see how each individual stone supports the *total structure*.[80]

The structural analysis of sectarianism thus seeks to uncover the links between the outrageous and the ordinary, the openly confrontational and the privately supportive, with the obvious assumption that by owning up to the responsibility for what happens at the top, and by withdrawing support for the immediate level above, each layer of people—from the decent individuals to the bigots—can contribute to the dismantling of the sectarian pyramid. Borrowing this insight from Quaker luminary John Woolman (1720–72), the group urged their readers and fellow Christians to not only condemn and abhor the terrible sectarianism in the extreme but also to turn away from their own sectarianism in "more refined appearances."[81]

Structures of Sin

This kind of structural analysis of social problems and conflicts appears to be characteristic of Christian practices at the time. In the Catholic Church, for instance, the Social Doctrine of the Church, which is an evolving body of Catholic teachings on social issues based primarily on a number of papal encyclicals,[82] has seen a number of inputs by Pope John Paul II in the 1980s and early 1990s. Among these, *Sollicitudo Rei Socialis* (The Social Concern), issued in 1987, proposed the analytical concept "structures of sin" as an alternative to mere "sociopolitical analysis."[83]

80. Working Party on Sectarianism, *Sectarianism*, 23. Emphasis added.

81. Working Party on Sectarianism, *Sectarianism*, 13.

82. See Pontifical Council for Justice and Peace, *Compendium of the Social Doctrine of the Church* (London: Burns and Oates, 2005).

83. Pope John Paul II, "Sollicitudo Rei Socialis (30 Dec. 1987)," 36, accessed February 24, 2019, http://w2.vatican.va/content/john-paul-ii/en/encyclicals/documents/hf_jp-ii_enc_30121987_sollicitudo-rei-socialis.html

"Structures of sin," previously called "social sins" in his *Reconciliatio et Paenitentia* (Reconciliation and Penance),[84] are the "fruit of many [personal] sins,"[85] which is "difficult to remove" and goes far beyond the actions and brief life span of an individual."[86]

> It is a case of the very personal sins of those who cause or support evil or who exploit it; of those who are in a position to avoid, eliminate or at least limit certain social evils but who fail to do so out of laziness, fear or the conspiracy of silence, through secret complicity or indifference; of those who take refuge in the supposed impossibility of changing the world and also of those who sidestep the effort and sacrifice required, producing specious reasons of higher order.[87]

When left unconquered, these structures of sin "grow stronger, spread, and become the source of other sins, and so influence people's behavior."[88] These self-propelling, expanding, cyclical or spiraling social sins include not only interpersonal sins but also sins affecting the "relationships between the various human communities."[89] Though individual repentance is still the primary act to overcome these structures,[90] it is no longer enough if it is only accomplished by a few individuals. It requires collective repentance to unravel the intricate structures of sin jointly committed by so many in society—perhaps even across generations—"so that each may shoulder his or her responsibility seriously and courageously in order to change those disastrous conditions and intolerable situations."[91]

In the context, John Paul II was applying the sin-structural analysis on the contemporaneous situation of the Cold War in the 1980s, with "nations and blocs" succumbing to different structures of sin, obstructing the "development of peoples."[92] However, if one follows the way the Working Party analyzed the ongoing Troubles at the time, it is not difficult to see the "pyra-

84. Pope John Paul II, "Reconciliatio et Paenitentia (2 Dec. 1984)," 15–16, accessed February 24, 2019, http://w2.vatican.va/content/john-paul-ii/en/apost_exhortations/documents/hf_jp-ii_exh_02121984_reconciliatio-et-paenitentia.html

85. Pope John Paul II, "Sollicitudo Rei Socialis," 37.

86. John Paul II, "Sollicitudo Rei Socialis," 36.

87. John Paul II, "Reconciliatio et Paenitentia," 16.

88. John Paul II, "Sollicitudo Rei Socialis," 36.

89. John Paul II, "Reconciliatio et Paenitentia," 16.

90. John Paul II, "Sollicitudo Rei Socialis," 38.

91. John Paul II, "Reconciliatio et Paenitentia," 16.

92. John Paul II, "Sollicitudo Rei Socialis," 37.

mid of sectarianism" in Northern Ireland as one such "sin structure," as a social sin complex collectively constructed and maintained by many, from "mad dogs" at the top to "ordinary, decent people" at the bottom.

Contributions to Peacebuilding

What is more difficult to gauge is the contributions—if any—of such sin-structural analyses, or, more generally, the endeavors of the interchurch groups to conflict resolution in Northern Ireland. To what extent have these endeavors helped the contemporaneous political process of ending the Troubles? Have the interchurch discourses on sectarianism, political "idolatry," and social injustice brought about actual change in these "attitudes, beliefs, behaviors and structures"? Is there empirical evidence to sustain the unofficial interchurch group's assertion that the churches played "a significant stabilizing role" and that they were "one of the reasons why our society has not gone over the edge"?[93] These are challenging questions; perhaps some of them are not answerable with any degree of certainty. What can be shown, however, is how these interchurch dialogues *reflected* and provided theological justifications for some of the Christian actions known to have contributed to the Northern Ireland peace process.

To begin with, the version of "Christian secularism" displayed in the dialogues reflected in a way the respective roles played by the official churches and individual "religious actors" in peacebuilding.[94] On the one hand, aside from expressing a clear and united "no" to violence, the major official churches also staunchly refused to be associated too closely with either political projects, unionist or nationalist.[95] Despite repeated attempts by some paramilitary groups to label their killing "actions" and "reactions" as "Protestant" or "Catholic," all-out wars between large Christian groups of different denominations did not come about. Had the different church leaders taken a more antagonistic position, the escalation of

93. ICGFP, "Towards Peace and Stability," 4:122.

94. Sandal, *Religious Leaders and Conflict Transformation*, 42.

95. One obvious exception, of course, was Ian Paisley's Free Presbyterian Church and the affiliated Democratic Unionist Party. See Jonathan Tonge et al., *The Democratic Unionist Party: From Protest to Power* (Oxford: Oxford University Press, 2014), 133–42.

violence could have imaginably "gone over the edge," as the unofficial interchurch group said. On the other hand, individual religious actors often took up active roles to "interfere" in the political sphere in order to move the peace process forward. These actions took various forms, including venturing into "politically impossible" dialogues, such as the Feakle talks of December 1974, in which Protestant representatives such as Rev. Eric Gallagher (Methodist) and Rev. Jack Weir (Presbyterian) met with IRA representatives and Sinn Féin leaders,[96] and mending intrabloc wounds, such as Fr. Alec Reid's mediation between nationalism and republicanism in the 1980s and 1990s.[97] Without a nuanced understanding of Christian secularism, such "interventions" could have been inhibited by the self-imposed confines of the religious sphere.

Furthermore, the propensity to dialogue or to create conditions for dialogue, even with political untouchables such as "terrorists" and "mass murderers," did not seem to be only a matter of personal preference or the courage of the religious actors in question. Gallagher, who was a member of both official and unofficial interchurch discussions, could count on the Faith and Politics Group for theological support for unpopular conversations. "The cycle of violence cannot be broken by talking down to people," they asserted in their very first document, *Breaking Down the Enmity*, "but if a real dialogue can be initiated then people can become open to the Spirit."[98] They then used the example of Jesus' dialogue with the woman at the well (John 4) to make the point that dialogues can bring about life-changing encounters, which would not have happened "if Jesus had simply condemned her [im]moral behavior."[99]

It is outside the scope of this chapter to exhaust all such "indirect" contributions of the interchurch dialogues to the wider peace process in Northern Ireland. In an extended study one might discover that there is not only a pyramid of sectarianism, but perhaps also a pyramid of peacebuilding: the most conspicuous on top are political leaders such as Tony Blair and Bertie

---

96. Sandal, *Religious Leaders and Conflict Transformation*, 64–65.

97. Martin McKeever, *One Man, One God: The Peace Ministry of Fr Alec Reid C.Ss.R.* (Dublin: Redemptorist Communications, 2017), 30–35.

98. ICGFP, "Breaking Down the Enmity," 3.6.1, 37.

99. ICGFP, "Breaking Down the Enmity," 3.6.1, 37. See also C. K. Martin Chung, "Facilitated Dialogue: The Political Theology of Fr. Alec Reid," *Glencree Journal*, Inaugural Issue: Dealing with the Legacy of Conflict in Northern Ireland through Engagement and Dialogue (2021): 67.

Ahern concluding peace agreements, supported by the layer of individuals such as religious actors below paving the way to the agreement through difficult dialogues; these are in turn shored up by interchurch initiatives to provide theological support; at the bottom are local churches, parishes, and "ordinary Christians" responding to these initiatives positively, offering their cooperation.

IV. CONCLUSION

Unfortunately, it was precisely in the layer below the interchurch initiatives that sufficient and sustained support seemed not to be forthcoming. Observers following up on these dialogues found that the recommendations of *Sectarianism* were not properly followed through, and the Irish Inter-Church Meeting remained nothing more than a "debating club."[100] Gallagher himself also felt disappointed that the local churches' response to *Violence in Ireland* was less than enthusiastic: "The secular world took more notice of it than did the Churches for whom it was commissioned."[101] Hence even as the overall cross-denominational discourse on the problem of political violence has been hailed as "theological innovation of major public significance,"[102] how far this ethos succeeded in reaching down the church membership is doubtful.

One might argue that the seeming failure of such a discourse to penetrate the wider communities of the faithful in Northern Ireland has to do with a core problem in Christian secularism and the sin-structural approach to political problems of the Irish interchurch groups: namely, the entrenched perception that faith is irrelevant to politics. If church leaders object in principle to providing "constitutional blueprints," then obviously those who *expect* such blueprints will not pay much attention to what they have to say. The discourse on the "sectarian pyramid" can also prove disappointing for those who look for expedient solutions to pressing political problems, such as the trilemma of delivering a clean Brexit, upholding the Good Friday Agreement, and preserving the union of Great Britain and Northern

100. Maria Power, "'Of Some Symbolic Importance but Not Much Else': The Irish Inter-Church Meeting and Ecumenical Dialogue in Northern Ireland, 1980–1999," *Journal of Ecumenical Studies* 43, no. 1 (2008): 119.

101. Gallagher and Worrall, *Christians in Ulster*, 135, 204–5.

102. Sandal, *Religious Leaders and Conflict Transformation*, 100.

Ireland. By contrast, secular political-scientific approaches, such as consociationalism, have been relied on to provide precisely those "blueprints" and hence dominate the discussion on Northern Ireland as a "model" of conflict transformation.[103]

However, the interchurch groups might counter—as they did—that Jesus himself was also "disappointing" for those followers and spectators *expecting* him to be a political leader who would challenge the Roman domination over the oppressed Jewish people, which he did not, at least not in the way the "zealots" had in mind, and his "hard teaching" also turned many people away (John 6). The Christian dialogue partners would also counsel against an overly optimistic belief in the consociational approach alone, for powerful traditions "may be capable of upsetting the strongest power-sharing machinery that can be devised."[104] In the final analysis, it is in rerouting these powerful undercurrents below political structures that the real contributions of the interchurch dialogues may be found.

References

"Anger and Shock as Tyrone Statue of Mary Defaced." *Belfast Telegraph*, October 9, 2017.

Balcells, Laia, Lesley-Ann Daniels, and Abel Escribà-Folch. "The Determinants of Low-Intensity Intergroup Violence: The Case of Northern Ireland." *Journal of Peace Research* 53, no. 1 (2016): 33–48.

Boda, Mark, and Gordon Smith, eds. *Repentance in Christian Theology*. Collegeville, MN: Liturgical Press, 2006.

Chung, C. K. Martin. "From Nation to Region: Comparing Joint History Writing in Europe and in East Asia." In *States, Regions and the Global System: Europe and Northern Asia-Pacific in Globalised Governance*, edited by Andreas Vasilache, Reimund Seidelmann, and José Luis de Sales Marques, 229–42. Baden-Baden: Nomos, 2011.

Chung, C. K. Martin. *Repentance for the Holocaust: Lessons from Jewish Thought for Confronting the German Past*. Ithaca: Cornell University Press and Cornell University Library, 2017.

Chung, C. K. Martin. "Facilitated Dialogue: The Political Theology of Fr. Alec Reid." *Glencree Journal*, Inaugural Issue: Dealing with the Legacy of Conflict in Northern Ireland through Engagement and Dialogue (2021): 62–76.

---

103. Rupert Taylor, ed., *Consociational Theory: McGarry and O'Leary and the Northern Ireland Conflict* (London: Routledge, 2009).

104. ICGFP, "Towards Peace and Stability," 2:114.

Daly, Cahal, and Stanley Worrall. *Ballymascanlon: An Irish Venture in Inter-Church Dialogue*. Belfast: Christian Journals; Dublin: Veritas Publications, 1978.

Evangelical Contribution on Northern Ireland. *For God and His Glory Alone: A Contribution Relating Some Biblical Principles to the Situation in Northern Ireland*. 2nd ed. Belfast: ECONI, [1988] 1998.

Evans, Jocelyn, and Jonathan Tonge. "Catholic, Irish and Nationalist: Evaluating the Importance of Ethno-national and Ethno-religious Variables in Determining Nationalist Political Allegiance in Northern Ireland." *Nations and Nationalism* 19, no. 2 (2013): 357–75.

Gallagher, Eric, and Stanley Worrall. *Christians in Ulster 1968–1980*. Oxford: Oxford University Press, 1982.

Garland, Sidney. "Liberation Theology and the Ulster Question." *Foundations* 15 (Autumn 1985): 21–34.

Hurd, Elizabeth Shakman. *The Politics of Secularism in International Relations*. Princeton: Princeton University Press, 2008.

ICGFP. "Breaking Down the Enmity." In *Living the Kingdom*, 17–53. Belfast: Interchurch Group on Faith and Politics, 1989.

ICGFP. "A Declaration of Faith and Commitment." In *Living the Kingdom*, 63–69. Belfast: Interchurch Group on Faith and Politics, 1989.

ICGFP. *Living the Kingdom: Faith and Politics in the Northern Ireland Conflict*. Belfast: Interchurch Group on Faith and Politics, 1989.

ICGFP. "Towards an Island That Works: Facing Divisions in Ireland." In *Living the Kingdom*, 71–106. Belfast: Interchurch Group on Faith and Politics, 1989.

ICGFP. "Towards Peace and Stability: A Critical Assessment of the Anglo-Irish Agreement." In *Living the Kingdom*, 107–36. Belfast: Interchurch Group on Faith and Politics, 1989.

ICGFP. "Understanding the Signs of the Times: A Christian Response to the Anglo-Irish Agreement." In *Living the Kingdom*, 55–62. Belfast: Interchurch Group on Faith and Politics, 1989.

John Paul II, Pope. "Reconciliatio et Paenitentia (2 Dec. 1984)." Accessed February 24, 2019. http://w2.vatican.va/content/john-paul-ii/en/apost_exhortations/documents/hf_jp-ii_exh_02121984_reconciliatio-et-paenitentia.html

John Paul II, Pope. "Sollicitudo Rei Socialis (30 Dec. 1987)." Accessed February 24, 2019. http://w2.vatican.va/content/john-paul-ii/en/encyclicals/documents/hf_jp-ii_enc_30121987_sollicitudo-rei-socialis.html

Joint Group on Social Questions. *Violence in Ireland: A Report to the Churches*. Rev. ed. Belfast: Christian Journals; Dublin: Veritas Publications, 1977.

Leitlein, Hannes, and Raoul Löbbert. "Sieht so die Wiedervereinigung aus?" *Die Zeit*, no. 6 (2017).

Liechty, Joseph, and Cecelia Clegg. *Moving Beyond Sectarianism: Religion, Conflict, and Reconciliation in Northern Ireland*. Dublin: Columba Press, 2001.

McCreary, Alf. "Almost 500 Years on from Luther, Can We Manage Our Own Reformation in Northern Ireland?" *Belfast Telegraph*, September 23, 2017.

McKeever, Martin. *One Man, One God: The Peace Ministry of Fr Alec Reid C.Ss.R.* Dublin: Redemptorist Communications, 2017.

McKittrick, David, and David McVea. *Making Sense of the Troubles: A History of the Northern Ireland Conflict*. Rev. and updated ed. London: Viking, 2012.

McVeigh, Jim. "The Irish Church and Republicanism: The Need for Liberation Theology." *The Furrow* 50, no. 1 (1999): 3–7.

Metz, Johann Baptist. *Memoria passionis: Ein provozierendes Gedächtnis in pluralistischer Gesellschaft*. Freiburg: Herder, 2017.

O'Leary, Brendan, and John McGarry. *The Politics of Antagonism: Understanding Northern Ireland*. London: Athlone Press, 1996.

O'Neill, Leona. "Community's Shock after Londonderry Church Vandalism." *Belfast Telegraph*, September 14, 2017.

Pontifical Council for Justice and Peace. *Compendium of the Social Doctrine of the Church*. London: Burns and Oates, 2005.

Power, Maria. "'Of Some Symbolic Importance but Not Much Else': The Irish Inter-Church Meeting and Ecumenical Dialogue in Northern Ireland, 1980–1999." *Journal of Ecumenical Studies* 43, no. 1 (2008): 111–23.

Sandal, Nukhet. *Religious Leaders and Conflict Transformation: Northern Ireland and Beyond*. Cambridge: Cambridge University Press, 2017.

Taylor, Rupert, ed. *Consociational Theory: McGarry and O'Leary and the Northern Ireland Conflict*. London: Routledge, 2009.

Tilley, James, Geoffrey Evans, and Claire Mitchell. "Consociationalism and the Evolution of Political Cleavages in Northern Ireland, 1989–2004." *British Journal of Political Science* 38 (2008): 699–717.

Tonge, Jonathan, Máire Braniff, Thomas Hennessey, James W. McAuley, and Sophie A. Whiting. *The Democratic Unionist Party: From Protest to Power*. Oxford: Oxford University Press, 2014.

Working Party on Sectarianism. *Sectarianism: A Discussion Document*. Belfast: Department of Social Issues of the Irish Inter-Church Meeting, 1993.

Wright, Frank. *Northern Ireland: A Comparative Analysis*. Dublin: Gill and Macmillan, 1988.

Islam in Africa and the Middle East

Introduction

The Islamic world commonly perceives religion as salient to politics. The case studies in this section of the volume—ranging geographically and historically—affirm those perceptions. Fewer readers might begin with the assumption that twenty-first-century politics directly affect the role of Islam in politics, as more common perceptions assume that Islam is a rather fixed target, perhaps hardened against change, and certainly resistant to modern politics in its various permutations and demands for secular, institutional, or ideological compliance.

Several points worthy of mention emerge from the studies in this section of the volume. First, Muslims vary in their approaches to religion in terms of practice, theological orientation, cultural content, and definitions of ideal-typical relationship with politics and the state. Likewise, Islam is varied in the institutions, social movements, and interest groups associated with it in different national contexts; the extent to which it is intertwined with politics (that is, religion as an independent variable); and the extent to which politics affects its daily practice—or even theological-legal and political philosophies (that is, religion as a dependent variable).

Second, these chapters suggest that the relationship that we often assume to be bifurcated between Sunni and Shia Muslims does not appear to be so in areas outside of the Islamic heartland of the Middle East (if, indeed, it is so there). Local populations in more distant regions may well seek to synthesize theological, jurisprudential, and philosophical frameworks and ideas from both, particularly with relation to Saudi Arabian (Sunni) and Iranian (Shia) models. Indeed, for regions such as the Sahel in Africa, "*synthesis*" appears to be an overarching approach to religion on a number of levels. Third, the Iranian effort to wed Western political institutions (that is, a multibranch government, constitution, separation of powers) with Islamic institutions (and, perhaps, with local Persian cultural norms and practices) has been viewed by at least some Afro-Islamic communities as a positive model and creative example of integrating Islamic, Western, and local political and cultural forms. This finding is in keeping with earlier research in Middle East and North African public opinion in which 90 percent or more report a preference for democracy in a form that includes a significant Islamic cultural and political component.[1] Fourth, peoples in Muslim majority regions outside of the Islamic heartland maintain contact with it in a number of identifiable ways, including via political and religious thinkers, social movements, humanitarian organizations, and theological-jurisprudential debates. Indeed, *ideas* matter a great deal in these interactions and continue to be a source of robust and creative discussion and debate within and across Muslim regions.

Abdourahmane (Rahmane) Idrissa's chapter centers upon Salafism in the Sahel region of Africa, that is, those states inhabiting the space on the southern edges of the Sahara Desert, west to east, roughly from Mauritania to Sudan and Eritrea. Rather than addressing only the question of terrorism or *jihadism* in the region, and its origins or causes, Idrissa argues that these forms of militant action are *given meaning* to local peoples through a specific political and theological ideology originating in the late-modern era—political Salafism. Similarly to other modern ideologies—liberalism, socialism, or conservatism—political Salafism adopts conceptual lenses and parameters of action that make it different from earlier forms of political thought. Like these other modernist movements, political Salafism in the Sahel region approaches the world as a puzzle to be solved; its answer differs from Western and Christian answers in offering an Islamic state and Islamic laws as suitable solutions to creating a meaningful and well-functioning society out of that puzzle. For most of the Sahel, Islamist projects unfold under paradigmatically late-modern conditions, that is, "within the politics of the nation-state and upon stages opened up by political liberalization or democratization."

Idrissa's analysis centers upon Niger (*adj.* Nigerien) as its primary case study of political Salafism seeking an Islamic state for a Muslim nation. It begins in the last decades of the twentieth century. The story of political Salafism in Niger originates in bordering Northern Nigeria (*adj.* Nigerian) with Abubakar Gumi, a theological and political thinker from the late colo-

1. Mark Tessler and Eleanor Gao, "Gauging Arab Support for Democracy," 2005.

nial and early postcolonial eras, who, although very critical of British rule, started his career in Nigeria's Islamic judiciary with the assistance of the British colonial apparatus. His teachings radicalized in the years immediately after the brutal demise of his postcolonial patron, Ahmed Bello. However, he remained a notable national figure in Nigeria with some international presence as well, particularly in connection to Saudi Arabia. When he began preaching in the local vernacular of Hausa, which expanded his message to social groups that were more liable to be radicalized by it, his teachings made their way almost immediately to Niger, where about 52 percent of the population speaks Hausa as its mother language. His speeches were extremely effective among the popular classes, but also with merchant elites. As political discourse, these speeches concentrated on Nigeria's Christians, perceived as the enemy within; Sufi leaders, followed popularly, he viewed only as adversaries.

In Niger, Idrissa indicates, Sufi and other so-called traditional Islamic leaders had close relations with the secular postcolonial state with whom they worked easily. Indeed, they dominated Islam for Niger, theologically and in popular following. The Sufi establishment was part of a national association that was, for all intents and purposes, the "religious arm of Niger's secular state." It included reformist elements; however, they tended to be generally affiliated with more traditional orthodox forms of Islam rooted in local practice and cultural context. When the movement from Nigeria mentioned above reached Niger, under the name of *Izala*, this state-connected Islamic establishment attempted to keep it from taking root. Economic conditions likely mitigated in the *Izala* movement's favor, as did the aftershocks of the (Shia) Islamic Revolution in Iran in 1979 and the (Sunni) Saudi response, bringing this now clearly Salafist and Saudi Arabian–influenced form of orthodoxy to Niger. After 1987, with the relaxation of authoritarian rule, the Nigerien state ceased to view it as part of its agenda to restrict the *Izala* movement. While in other parts of the Sahal Salafism came from the upper classes, in Niger and Nigeria it came through the popular classes in the form of the *Izala* movement and worked its way upward toward the elites.

Another form of Islamist movement, Idrissa tells us, made its way to Niger in the aftermath of the Iranian Revolution through a small group of Western-educated Francophone communities in Niger. By the late 1980s, they established an Islamist newspaper named *Iqra*. It was a forum for Islamist thought and included the idea of Iran as a fruitful model for joining

Western-style state institutions with Islam. These were not Shia communities; they were Sunni middle classes and elites who looked up to the Iranian model. The electoral wins of the *Front Islamique du Salut* in neighboring Algeria strengthened their resolve as well as their public standing. In a fascinating story of ebb and flow between Shia and Sunni religious models, Idrissa suggests that when the *Front Islamique du Salut*'s wins were overturned by the Algerian military, this (Nigerien) Iran-inspired constituency felt it had nowhere to turn except to Saudi Arabia and Qatar for support. Soon *Iqra* ceased to appear and was replaced by a dedicated Salafi newspaper, *As-Salam*. *Political Salafism* in Niger tends not to be violent with some rare exceptions; and, while Niger, as explained in the chapter, experienced some degree of re-Islamization, it has not been of the particular form(s) most preferred by the *political Salafist* movement in Niger.

Mutaz Al-Khatib takes a theological, jurisprudential, and philosophical approach to the controversial question of apostasy in Islam. The debate is extraordinarily pertinent to the volume, as apostasy remains today at the center stage of a heated controversy regarding human rights and modernist framings of Islam. As of 2021, more than twenty states with Islam as an official religion and some ten Islamic nonstate actors criminalize public apostasy, with some allowing for the death penalty.[2] The debate regarding apostasy, together with contiguous debates relating to blasphemy and heresy, engages the issue of religious freedom and the lack thereof, which are topics addressed in the chapter.[3] As the legislative, judicial, and security apparatuses adopting and applying apostasy legislation pertain to state administrations, the debate has implications vis-à-vis issues of state power and definitional questions regarding intersections of ethics and law.

Al-Khatib approaches the thorny question of apostasy and its consequences through traditional forms of analysis in Islam, including *fiqh* (that is, Islamic jurisprudence). He begins by placing the notion of *freedom of religion* in its modern Western context and suggests that the concept has some

2. Humanists International, *Freedom of Thought Report*, 2020, and US Commission on International Religious Freedom, *Annual Report*, 2020.

3. The US Commission on International Religious Freedom and the US State Department recognize 29 countries with worrying limitations to religious freedom, out of which 14 are categorized as "Countries of Particular Concern" (engage in or tolerate particularly severe religious freedom violations) and 15 are on a "Special Watch List Countries" (engaging in or tolerating severe violations of religious freedom). Source: US Commission on International Religious Freedom, *Annual Report*, 2020.

antecedents in premodern Islamic thought. In general, Al-Khatib suggests that freedom in Islam reflects a dual concept, as it can be defined as freedom from servitude, as well as freedom to organize one's personal affairs without opposition. It is based upon three principles: reason; free choice (or lack of duress); and real capacity (that is, meaningful ability to achieve a certain duty). The notion of freedom in Islam, Al-Khatib emphasizes, is also related to the five *maqasid* (that is, "the five collective needs," or, preservation of religion, human life, intellect, lineage, and wealth). For a number of contemporary Muslim scholars, he tells us, freedom of religion is included as one of the *maqasid*, that is, as necessary to the basic needs of life and to human dignity. Outlining its Quranic roots, Al-Khatib separates freedom of religion into two parts: freedom of belief (which includes freedom from compulsion in religion) and freedom of expression (that is, religious practices).

The theological principles relating to freedom of religion raise the question of apostasy (*riddah*), that is, the notion that leaving a religion under certain conditions can be unacceptable or subject to sanction. Al-Khatib argues that the Quran does not call for any specific temporal (that is, *this-worldly*) punishment for apostates, and certainly not in general. To summarize from Al-Khatib's analysis, the Quran looks down upon apostates; suggests that apostates' deeds in this life and the afterlife are cursed and subject to hellfire; asks that believers not obey apostates but, most importantly, commands that believers *forgive* apostates.

Al-Khatib, therefore, turns to the major legal precedents in regard to apostates in the early Muslim period. He finds that capital punishment is used only in times of war and in cases of traitors; in cases in which the primary crime being punished is an act of outrage in that cultural context (such as, robbery and terrorizing of civilians—what we might call banditry, murder, and destroying the livelihood of a community); and, with rare exceptions primarily relating to treason, it has been used for men and not women. Apostasy, then, was usually seen, historically speaking, primarily as a separation from the community, which, in times of war, might take on special significance related to treason.

Al-Khatib outlines the parameters of current debate among scholars of *fiqh* in which some scholars view apostasy as akin to robbery and terrorizing of civilians (such as banditry); that is, as a form of civil strife worthy of punishment. For some, capital punishment is optional, not required. For others, no punishment is required at all. For some, women are to be punished. For others, punishment comes only during times of war; women do not participate in war and therefore are not included in punishment. For some thinkers, punishment is discretionary. For all, capital punishment is problematic, theologically; particularly so in relation to the well-accepted value of freedom of religion, which has modern as well as Quranic roots.

Al-Khatib asks, can belief be defined simply as belief in God and doing good deeds (as with the works of Muhammad Abdu), or support of Islam and Muslims (as with the works of Jawish)? For him, these two solutions are not sufficient to resolve the inherent freedom of religion–apostasy tension. If the effective, although not necessarily actionable, causes for capital punishment in apostasy are high treason or a sort of active disloyalty rooted in radical alterity, he asks, how can these principles be applied in the diaspora and in the nation-state, where loyalty may be defined by principles other than religion, such as citizenship? Whatever the answer, for Al-Khatib, the essential issue is rooted in questions of loyalty and betrayal, identity and alterity, and in the Islamic values of diversity and pluralism.

Ibrahim Yahaya Ibrahim constructs a taxonomy of Islamic humanitarian organizations (IHOs) informed by detailed fieldwork in the Maghreb region, Sahel, and case studies of three organizations established in the Middle East, as well as one in the United Kingdom. He suggests that the post-9/11/2001 approach to IHOs in the West was bifurcated into two main camps, one approaching them as an arm of terrorism, and one viewing them as organizations that "politicize aid" in ways similar to Western humanitarian organizations.

Yahaya categorizes IHOs into four main types based upon the variable spectrum of transnational-national and fundamentalist-moderate. The objectives of each resulting type vary in patterned ways. One follows an internationalist *Umma*-centric approach; one a global civil-society approach; one a national (e.g., domestic) religious revival approach; and one a (domestic) development-centric approach. He advances case studies of (1) the International Islamic Relief Organization, Saudi Arabia; (2) Islamic Relief Worldwide, United Kingdom; (3) the charitable wing of the Egyptian Muslim Brotherhood, Egypt; and (4) the Islamic Council for Development and Humanitarian Services, Ghana.

The concept of Islamic humanitarianism comes from an effort, beginning in the 1960s, in parts of the Muslim world to "hybridize" the Western notion of humanitarian action with the Islamic notions of charity, the latter based upon the principles of *zakat* (that is, roughly, tithing, or religiously obligatory alms); *waqf* (that is, religious charitable endowment, usually based in a local community); and *sadaqa* (this is, roughly, acts of loving kindness, including smiling when greeting people; offering knowledge without payment through education and offering of skills, or both; talking softly; giving time to family and others; giving respect to elders, and the like).

IHOs, according to Yahaya, began to be noted by Western scholars as significant after the Afghan-Soviet war (1979–89), and were, in fact, used by the United States during that war to channel humanitarian and military support to Mujahedeen forces. IHOs were, thereafter, suspected of channeling funds and support on behalf of international *jihadist* groups. Others disagree, Yahaya tells us, viewing such examples, while accurate, as rare or exceptional and as not representative of the range and corpus of IHOs. Many Western scholars admit a similarity between Western and Islamic charities in practice, and in the patterned ways in which aid is politicized.

THESE CHAPTERS TELL A STORY of religious constituencies as often providing meaningful (and, in some cases, exclusive) alternative models to secular policies, governments, and state actions. The authors highlight specific ways in which Islam may represent both an independent and a dependent variable in politics. Social and political Islam, and even religious Islam, may be changeable under varying conditions, and the authors indirectly remind us how diverse the religion is as community and as religion, per se. Their discussions include a range of theological precepts, which may be differently important in different regions, and, particularly, may have different emphases or findings. That is, there is not one Sharia; it is a matter of debate among experts of Islamic law and legislation, and from theorists and practitioners of quite varied Islamic legal schools of thought. Muslim peoples come from a wide range of cultural and political contexts, which may affect Islam as a dependent variable, or may be changed by Islam acting as an independent variable. Furthermore, the chapters tell us that different Islamist organizations, social movements, and interest groups organize differently, have disparate goals, ideological orientations, and varying theological proclivities and policy orientations. They may even be organized—if only initially—by class or economic status, and some of these varying tendencies are categorized into taxonomies and conceptual frameworks by scholars in this section.

Finally, these studies demonstrate that regions with majority Muslim populations outside of the Middle East may have different trajectories, but, nonetheless, often remain part of or in meaningful contact with the Middle Eastern heartland of Islam in a range of ways. In the cases in this section of the volume, local Muslims remain in contact with the Islamic heartland through individual thinkers, social movements, and institutional development. Individual thinkers may travel to the Middle East, give speeches or sermons at home and abroad, and lead local peoples to develop full-fledged social movements. They may draw upon institutional models from Middle Eastern states.

The Islamic heartland also continues to be important to Muslims in regions outside of the Middle East through theological, jurisprudential, and philosophical discussions and debates, as with the case study of the question of apostasy. Ideas move freely—but also in ways structured by ancient (that is, traditions as many as 15 centuries old) Islamic exegetical and jurisprudential forms—from the Middle East, outward, and back again. Indeed, we learn from these case studies, at the simplest level of abstraction, that Muslims are people who vary; they mobilize, organize, and campaign in a range of ways; they seek synthesis in regard to theological, jurisprudential, and institutional questions, questions of local culture, and questions related to tradition and modernity; and ideas matter to them and to their local religious and political contexts a great deal.

The Politics of Islam in the Sahel

Between Quiescence and Violence

Abdourahmane (Rhamane) Idrissa

Leiden University—Leiden

In the early 2000s, an Internet search linking the words "Sahel"—the bio-geographic region conventionally covering parts of Senegal, Mauritania, Mali, Burkina Faso, Niger, and Nigeria—and "security" would promptly pull up dozens of web links on "food security" and pictures of malnourished children. Ten years later, in the early 2010s, the same search led to many more links on "terrorism" and "Jihad" "in the Sahel," illustrated with images of AK-47-toting turbaned men and off-road vehicles speeding in dusty and craggy environments. During the course of a decade, the descriptor "insecurity in the Sahel" has been taken over and monopolized by events of a very different nature from recurring droughts, food deficit, or locust invasions.

A fame, peste et bello libera nos domine ("Free us from hunger, disease and war, O Lord") went the old European medieval prayer: hunger and disease might not be gone from the Sahel, but war has arrived. A whole new specialist literature, covering the range from consultancy briefs to academic journal articles through reports, working papers, and monographs has grown out of this phenomenon, mainly taking its cue from the fact that official geopolitical analysis—especially American—has defined the Sahel as an "Arc of Terrorism" in Africa. From the vantage point of such analysis, the Sahel is a region under fire, where "failed states" are confronted by "terrorists" and "jihadists" who are able to recruit their militants from a vast pool of "desperately poor" young men or inside "marginalized communities." It thus appears to be a particularly vulnerable region in a struggle that is seen as developing at the global level. While many scholars—especially Islam-focused anthropologists—endeavor to place the issues of insecurity in the Sahel within a more nuanced and complex perspective, their work often relates to the question of violence as well.

In this chapter, I argue that by making terrorism and jihadism-caused violence the entry point in the study of insecurity in the Sahel, we miss the forest for the trees. More specifically, by isolating terrorism and jihadism as the primary object of a study on regional insecurity, we narrow the field of investigation to looking only for a small set of clues that would tell us something about the origins and nature of the manifestations of violence, but which in fact draw their meaning from a much larger story. That story has to do with the rise, in the Sahel, of that which is called "political Salafism." To be sure, terrorism, in the Sahel as elsewhere, is generally understood to be a violent manifestation of the larger story of "political Islam." But the phrase "political Islam" does not refer to any identifiable phenomenon that can be approached as a self-contained object for research in ways that would lead to conclusive results. Rather, it is a broad and somewhat vague backdrop against which scholars and analysts may set a great diversity of phenomena and events through which the religion of Islam could be seen as being politicized. In that sense, "political Salafism" is related to "political Islam," but it is something which is both much more specific in meaning and yet much less discussed or studied in the literature. Political Salafism is, in the Sahel, understood to be a political ideology that draws its discourse and appeal from the religious reformist movement of Salafism that developed within Sunni Islam in the twentieth century, with roots going back at least to the Wahhabi movement in Arabia in the eighteenth century.[1] Despite these religious roots, it is a *political* ideology, as such closer in nature to other political ideologies of the modern world, such as liberalism, socialism, or conservatism. In ways similar to these ideologies, political Salafism views the world as a riddle to be solved in a comprehensive manner. It offers as a solution the rule of Sharia, seen as a wide-ranging code for regulating social interactions and economic exchanges and for governing one's personal conduct. The fact that it draws its frame of meaning, concepts, and discourse in large part (though not exclusively) from the theology of Salafism does not belie the homology with other ideologies. They too similarly have their own intellec-

1. For a good recent history of Salafism, see Alexander Thurston's *Salafism in Nigeria: Islam, Preaching and Politics* (Cambridge: Cambridge University Press, 2016), which also offers, in part 1, a precise definition of the movement.

tual foundations within traditions of philosophical thought that have been simplified and appropriated for ideological mobilization and action.

Ideally, for political Salafis, governmental power should take the form of an "Islamic state"—a "caliphate" or an "Islamic republic"—whose contours and distribution of powers presumably would take inspiration from the conventional principles of governance that have been historically accepted in states governed the "orthodox" Sunni way. There were experiments in that direction in the Sahel in the eighteenth and nineteenth centuries, all of them undertaken by militant members of the Fulbe clerical status group known as *Torodo*. The states born from these episodes—the Imamate of Futa Jallon, the Sokoto Caliphate, the "Diina" (a Fulbe word meaning "religious government") of Hamdallaye, and others—were founded following wars of conquest or jihads. In the modern Sahelian context, however—with the *apparent* exceptions of Mali and Nigeria—this kind of project unfolds within the politics of the nation-state and upon stages opened up by political liberalization or democratization in recent decades.

This chapter addresses Niger as a primary case study in political Salafism in the Sahel. Niger is a typical Sahelian country located at the center of the region and featuring all of the region's most typical socioeconomic characteristics. This chapter first chronicles the advent of political Salafism, seeking to explain how it came about and grew; it then offers a typology of its manifestations and a concise analysis of the several ways in which political Salafis tried (and still try) to advance their cause. It ends with some concluding thoughts on the nature and future of political Salafism in the region.

AN ISLAMIC STATE FOR A MUSLIM NATION

The ideas that developed into political Salafism at the turn of the 1990s first appeared in Niger a decade earlier, in the early 1980s. At that stage, they had two different forms and orientations. First, the Nigerien extension of a movement of religious reform with strong political undertones was born in Northern Nigeria in the course of the 1970s from the teachings of the religious scholar Abubakar Gumi. Second, a Nigerien response to Iran's Islamic Revolution in the early 1980s eventually led to the growth of politicized Salafism. The two phenomena were initially different in terms of organization, sociological makeup, and goals. They were also potentially antagonistic, given that the first was close to Saudi Wahhabism, a part of Sunni Islam, while the second took inspiration from an Iranian-inspired Shi'ite political agenda. Nonetheless, by the turn of the 1990s, they had coalesced into a single movement that can be called Niger's "political Salafism." To understand why and how this happened, we begin by looking at the emergence, in Niger, of *popular* and *Francophone Salafism*.

Those of the Sunna: The Birth of Popular Salafism in Niger

In the mid-1970s, Abubakar Gumi, a prominent religious figure in Northern Nigeria, started to address the popular classes in that region. He employed *tafsir* (e.g., scriptural exegesis) preaching with strong political connotations. Gumi was a religious ideologue.[2] He believed that Northern Nigeria was in essence a Sunni land that ought to be ruled by Sharia law. Referring to the historical fact that a version of Sharia law used to rule people in the region in the nineteenth century, under the Sokoto Caliphate, Gumi held that all of the social, economic, and political problems in Northern Nigeria would find their solution through a return to the ideal situation that, in his opinion, existed at the time. In his telling of this story, Sharia law was adulterated and ruined by the intervening British colonialism, and Northern Nigerians needed to rise from the "mental slavery" imposed by the colonial concoction of secularism and Christianity in which the nation of Nigeria incubated during decades of British rule. Ironically, and quite unlike the French in neighboring Niger, the British pretended to rule Northern Nigeria largely through laws based on Sharia. And, yet, Gumi's attacks on them as enemies of Sharia were on some level pertinent, since their policy was an instrumentalization of Sharia law, which limited its compass to serving British interests in keeping the peace. Otherwise, Sharia law was subjected to modern British conceptions of law and legal procedure, often in ways that went against both its letter and its spirit as traditionally known and accepted in the region. On the other hand, British dedication to use Sharia law as an instrument of colonial governance did lead them to create the institutions that made the education and career of Gumi possible. Gumi was trained in

2. On Abubakar Gumi as an ideologue, see his own book, *Where I Stand* (Ibadan: Spectrum Books, 1992), and the analyses in Roman Loimeier's *Islamic Reform and Political Change in Northern Nigeria* (Evanston: Northwestern University Press, 2011) and Rahmane Idrissa's *The Politics of Islam in the Sahel: Between Persuasion and Violence* (London: Routledge, 2017).

Arabic and Sharia law and became a teacher and a Sharia judge under the British in the 1930s and 1940s. He was thus able to acquire both the formal law training and the position that he needed in order to develop an attractive ideology—attractive in the context of Northern Nigeria—directed against what he thought the British represented. A story like his would have been impossible in French-ruled Niger.

In the early phase of Nigeria's independent history, Gumi was able to channel his ideological project—that is, returning Northern Nigeria to Sharia rule—through government work. He had been appointed grand kadi of Northern Nigeria by the regional premier, Sir Ahmadu Bello, a kindred spirit intent on making Islam the basis of his government in what was then known as the Northern Region. Backed by the power of the state, Gumi's only political problem was to win over other Muslim leaders whose visions of the religion were different from his own. His vision was, in particular, less esoteric, less defined by those Sufi theologies—often reflected in local popular forms of Islamic practice—of which he disapproved, and more focused on implementing literal judicial precepts. He engaged adversaries via polite and erudite debate in Arabic, far from the ears of the popular classes. But, in 1966, his benefactor, Bello, was killed in a coup. Subsequent events in Nigeria wrecked Bello and Gumi's agenda for the north. As a result, Gumi became gradually more radical, and by the mid-1970s, he had turned, through his *tafsir* in the vernacular Hausa language of Northern Nigeria, into the rabble rouser that he had carefully avoided being before that time. The evolution was, however, methodical, owing to the fact that he remained throughout a respected figure with strong connections in national politics and on the international stage—the latter, particularly in regard to Saudi Arabia.

Hausa is the majority language in Northern Nigeria, but also the mother tongue of 52 percent of Niger's population, settled over about 1,000 km along the border with Nigeria—and it is more generally a lingua franca across Niger. Gumi's militant preaching in Hausa reached Niger almost instantly, and many Nigeriens from the Hausa border areas crossed into Nigeria to attend his teachings. The style of Gumi's preaching appealed especially to members of the popular classes in towns and cities, although he also knew how to address the elite thanks to his long career in government. In Niger, his impact was felt especially among the urban middling classes of shopkeepers, small business owners, and market retailers. It was also felt among the upper classes of great import-export traders, who had a large economic as well as social clientele. At first weak and diffuse, Gumi's impact waxed stronger after 1978, when he supervised the creation of an association that organized his following into a structured movement called the *Jama'at Izalatul Bidi'a wa Iqamatus Sunnah* (i.e., "the people who cut off bad innovations and bind themselves to prophetic tradition"; innovation, particularly meaning fast and unnecessary theological changes, can be seen negatively in some parts of Islamic theology). "Yan Izala" ("the cutters"), or "Izala" as the movement was known in shorthand, crossed immediately into Niger, importing into the country the main tenets of Gumi's ideology.

That ideology had changed over time in the context of postcolonial Nigeria. The old enemy, the British government, was gone. But in Gumi and his followers' views, it had left behind the Christians, who formed half of the population of the country, living mostly in the south. As the legatees of British colonial rule, they were therefore the new enemy. Sufi Muslim leaders, who were somewhat cowed under Bello's rule, became critical of Gumi's positions and were defined as adversaries. Unlike the enemy, who needed to be subdued by coercion and hostility, if not violence (something that Gumi ultimately would not condone), the adversary could be converted by persuasion. Indeed, while the Sufi leaders themselves could not be turned into "Gumists," Gumi was successful in attracting large numbers of their followers to his side.

At the time, Niger's Islam was also dominated by a Sufi establishment. Moreover, and unlike Northern Nigeria, this Sufi establishment enjoyed cozy relations with the secular state, which had enrolled Muslim notables across the territory in a powerful government-sponsored institution, the Association Islamique du Niger (AIN). AIN may be defined as a religious arm of Niger's secular state. It helped governments to practice a form of control over Islamic expressions in exchange for state support for the national religious establishment. The aims of the Nigerien state in working with AIN included keeping the peace and preventing the rise of disruptive ideologies with a religious basis, always with a worried eye on what was happening in Nigeria. (As a country, Nigeria had been confronted in the late 1970s and early 1980s by the "Maitatsine war," a violent religious Islamic uprising that was in some ways similar to the "Boko Haram war" of more recent years.) One must note that AIN had a two-tiered structure in terms of its membership: on the one hand, a provincial establishment of traditional religious notabilities chiefly interested in maintaining their status while preserving old-style Nigerien Islam as it had evolved from local history; and on the other hand the leading staff of the organization, primarily based in Niamey, the capital, and made up of men who had studied abroad (mainly in Arab countries but some in France).

The AIN's take on the religion was reformist. It viewed old-style Nigerien Islam as flawed by lack of religious knowledge and too much mixing with local, non-Islamic beliefs. It nurtured the agenda of improving its quality. This reformist agenda was potentially subversive, but the reformist movement within AIN moved carefully, going only as far in their reformist zeal as the state permitted. Since the Nigerien state strongly upheld political secularism—despite occasional public discourse on the Islamic nature of the country—the leeway the AIN had was limited. The importance of this detail will appear in the next section.

The *Izala* movement arrived on this Nigerien scene. As in Nigeria, *Izala* in Niger was vocally critical of Sufi Islam and the traditional Islamic establishment tied to it, and it sought to grow by attracting people away from these adversaries, who were described as waylaying the faithful into a form of idolatry masquerading as Islam. Inevitably, this effort led to clashes and confrontation. By the late 1980s, the growth of *Izala* in Niger was checked by the support that the state offered to the traditional establishment, in particular in the control of public prayer and preaching. *Izala* progressed, nonetheless, especially among the urban popular classes. In part, its irresistible success with this section of the populace was due to the changing economic circumstances in the country, which were marked by a persistent fiscal crisis of the state and generalized economic depression, especially after the drought of 1984. In such parlous circumstances, *Izala*'s stress on hard work, forbearance, and frugality was a welcome message for those who sought social integration on the cheap, including low-cost marriage and baptism. Its insistence on the superiority of religious learning over traditional gerontocracy played into the intergenerational crisis that was a consequence of the economic disarray in the country. Moreover, after 1987, the Nigerien state relaxed its authoritarian control over society, also scaling down, as a result, the official restrictions on *Izala*.

Although *Izala* was the progeny of Gumi—who tirelessly worked to promote the organization behind the scenes, and sometimes squarely on stage, until his death in 1991—it was also shaped by specific events that impacted both the Nigerian and the Nigerien scenes in the 1980s and later. One of these events was the Islamic Revolution of Iran in 1979 and the Saudi response to it, which consisted in stepping up efforts to promote Wahhabi theology across the Sunni world as a bulwark against the possible progress of Shi'a Islam. Initially, *Izala* was not fully a Salafi movement. Although Gumi's theology was a form of Salafism, especially in its attacks against Sufism, the movement he masterminded was focused on the promotion of Sharia law more so than on the broader Salafi ideals of Sunni exoteric orthodoxy. But Saudi promotion of Wahhabism orientated many *Izala* toward more distinctly Salafi attitudes. By the mid-1990s, *Izala* spawned, both in Nigeria and Niger, new movements that were fully wedded to Salafi ideals, calling themselves names such as *Alh as Sunna* ("Those of the Orthodox Tradition"), *Kitab wa Sunna* ("the Book and the Orthodox Tradition"), or, in local languages, *Yan Sunna* (Hausa) and *Sunnance* (Songhay), that is, "the Sunnites."

What happened in this way was something peculiar to Northern Nigeria and Niger. In the other countries of the Sahel—Burkina Faso, Mali, and Senegal—Salafism came down from the top of the social pecking order. It was imported by wealthy merchants with connections in Saudi Arabia and former students in Arab countries. It had to fight its way toward the masses against the control exerted by older Muslim leaderships, who were typically Sufi in orientation. By contrast, in Northern Nigeria and Niger, *Izala*, which was from the outset a mass movement of the urban working classes, had cleared the ground for the emergence of popular Salafism. Salafi ideals could reach the masses—in the urban areas at least—through the organization and mobilization that had been achieved among them by *Izala*'s chapters across the two lands. However, while in Northern Nigeria this development ultimately led to the policy of "Sharia implementation" after democracy was restored in the federation in 1999, there has been no analogous affirmative policy outcome in Niger. We shall later see several key reasons behind this comparatively lackluster result of the development of popular Salafism in Niger.

Emergence of Francophone Salafism

Iran's Islamic Revolution had an impact in Niger within a very specific social stratum, the Francophones—the small Western-educated middle class—which, in the early 1980s, was employed almost entirely by the state. It gave to some in that section of the populace the notion that it was feasible to ground state rule in Islam. Niger's second national census, in 1988, showed that 98 percent of the population was Muslim; but the vision of Niger as essentially an Islamic nation was affirmed in official discourse decades before that census. Thus, for instance, in September 1974, Niger's head of state, Seyni Kountché, uttered, in his speech founding AIN, a kind of collective *shahada* (the Islamic profession of faith) in the name of all Nigeriens. He declared that he was "proud to proclaim that we know no other God but Allah; we know no other Prophet of God but Mohammed; we have no other holy book but the Qur'an."[3] But, in practice, Niger's government upheld the norm of *laïcité* (state secularism) inherited from the French, which fenced religious authorities out of the public square even as it associated them to service in certain areas of government, as was shown above. Moreover, until 1987, Niger was under a "regime of exception," meaning that the liberal freedoms of multiparty democracy were suspended and political expression in the public square was curtailed. In this context, the dream of an Islamic republic took form only as an object of living room conversations in informal networks, just as other ideological aspirations that existed in the country's middle class.

After 1987, political liberalization emerged and middle-class ideologues clamored for multiparty democracy. The "Islamists," as they were soon to be known, also started to organize to enter the political fray, stressing the very high percentage of Muslims in the population. Thus, in 1989, Ali Zada, a man whose open admiration for the Iranian Revolution had led many in the country to believe him to be a Shi'ite, founded a newspaper propagating Islamist views among the Francophones, *Iqra* ("Read," in Arabic, and also the first word uttered by the angel Gabriel to the illiterate Muhammad). *Iqra* reflected the dominant mood among Niger's Islamists and offered the first public forum in which religion was presented as the basis for political change and progress. Although Zada and his friends did not adhere to Shi'a theology, they saw Iran at the time as a model in which modern democratic institutions were successfully wedded to religion. They looked up to the Iranian regime. Yet, there was also, in this group, a tendency to stress Sunni culture that drew inspiration from Egyptian Salafism.

In 1990, the victory in Algerian elections of the Salafi party, the Front Islamique du Salut, strengthened that tendency. Even though the Front's victory was overturned by the Algerian military, the event bolstered Salafism as a viable political proposition in the eyes of Niger's Islamists, especially

3. Quoted by Jean-Louis Triaud, "L'Etat et l'Islam en République du Niger," in *L'Islam et l'Etat dans le monde d'aujourd'hui*, ed. Oliver Carré (Paris: PUF, 1982), 249.

given that its theology was more in tune than Iran's political shi'ism with the prevalence of Sunni Islam in Niger. One can imagine that, had the Front Islamique du Salut gone on to rule Algeria, Niger's Islamists would have sought its support for their own national agenda, given the fact that Algeria was a geographic neighbor and a French-speaking country. As things stood, however, the Salafi "wing" of Niger's Islamism had no other international patrons to turn to but Saudi Arabia and Qatar, the two leading Wahhabi powers in the Islamic world. Within a few years, *Iqra* ceased to appear—its promoter, Ali Zada, found a new career in the organization of trade shows featuring Iranian products—and was succeeded by *As-Salam*, a Salafi paper slanted toward both modernist Salafism (à la the Muslim Brothers) and Wahhabism.

The Political Ideology

Thus, in the early 1990s, Salafism came of age in Niger under the forms of a popular movement and a network of middle-class sympathizers. The two groups were separated, however, by their different sociological makeups and their goals. The movement was largely made up of members of the urban small business class, in the main people who were illiterate in French (and not often literate in Arabic), and whose objective was a moral reform of society so that a purified practice of Islam—as prescribed by Salafi doctrines—would remake Niger as a truly Muslim *nation*. The network, on the other hand, was, as mentioned above, a middle class affair (civil servants and clerical workers in the private sector), French-speaking—with a smattering of *Arabisants*, as students of Arabic are known in Niger—and with their main objective being a political reform of government that would seek to Islamize the Nigerien *state*. The convergence of these two groups, which I examine in the next section, birthed Niger's ideology of political Salafism, which may be defined as the project of offering an Islamic state to a Muslim nation. On the way to achieving this goal, they had to confront Niger's secularists.

RISE AND STALLING OF POLITICAL SALAFISM

Due to their different sociological makeups and objectives, Niger's Salafis, in the early 1990s, resorted to different methods of action that seemed to increase the divergence between them. If they reached a certain unity by the late 1990s, it was mainly due to the actions and policies of their common adversary, the secularist middle class that led Niger's democratization project on the basis of the separation of state and religion. In this section, I briefly describe the confrontation of each of the two groups with the secularists, show how this led to some unity of method and purpose between them, and ponder the key outcomes of this evolution.

United against Secularism

In 1991–93, Niger embarked in a political process that gave the country its first multiparty, democratic constitution since the 1960s. The changeover was led by politicized members of the Francophone middle class whose goal was to institute a liberal democracy on the French model, inclusive, therefore, of a solid wall between state and religion. Many among these people prided themselves, at the time, with the name of *laïciste*, that is, secularist. For their part, Francophone Salafis were, like other Francophones, keen on political reform and new bases for the Nigerien state. But, unlike the secularists, Francophone Salafis wanted these new bases to be religious. Like other Francophone factions, they duly created a political party, the Front de la Oumma Islamique (FOI, a French acronym for "Islamic Umma Front" that gestured to *foi*, the French word for "faith," and also to the Algerian Islamic Salvation Front). But the party's application for registration was denied because the new constitution prohibited parties based upon religion. In fact, the Francophone Salafis should have seen that eventuality since they had earlier been barred from participation in the National Conference—the broad-based congress of representatives of Niger's social forces that debated and organized the transition to democracy—when they had sought invitation as the "representatives of Islam."

If democratization was, thus, defined from the outset as a secularizing process, it also came with the freedoms and liberties that were part of its liberal substance. Under the new constitution, there was extensive freedom of association, and when their attempt at creating an Islamist political party failed, the Francophone Salafis focused on setting up the second best thing, Islamist associations. Interestingly enough, the popular Salafis had resorted to that method before them, founding in 1991 the first *Izala* association under the leadership of a wealthy merchant from Maradi. Maradi was a large city an hour away from the Northern Nigerian border. Former students of Gumi were legion there, and Gumi himself briefly stayed in town in his youth. The merchant, Rabé dan Tchadoua, also founded a madrasa and funded *Izala dawa* (conversion drives) in Maradi and its countryside. With these actions, dan Tchadoua had defined the methods of action of the popular Salafis: mobilization through formal associations, and religious propaganda through education and public preaching. In the course of the subsequent decade, these methods were amplified and intensified, but their basic form had been outlined by dan Tchadoua as soon as democratization had opened up the public space for religion.

When the Francophone Salafis also started to mobilize through formal associations, they left the section of the public space that was occupied by political parties and entered the one that was populated by civil society, so much so that their strategies also shifted. In this part of the public space, they found that their adversaries were rights-defending associations, especially those that promoted women's rights,[4] as defined by the philosophies of liberalism, and that their allies were popular Salafi associations. Moreover, the secularist handlers of Niger's democratizing state had committed the strategic blunder of marginalizing AIN for ideological reasons. They could not accept that an *Etat laïc* would consort with a religious body, clearly unaware of the fact that AIN was an instrument of the state to be made use of, not an autonomous agent of which to be wary. As a result, there was a dangerous (for secularism) rapprochement between Niger's religious establishment and the new religious forces that also felt marginalized, that is, the Francophone and popular Salafis. This rapprochement was all the easier because the top tier of AIN was—as we have seen—made up of people with reformist proclivities.

As a result, by the late 1990s, Niger had a strong and relatively unified Islamic faction with a largely Salafi coloration. To be sure, much of AIN was not Salafi, and even its reformist tier did not harbor Salafi views. But the Salafis were the organizing force of the faction, and it was they shaping its political agenda. The difference between popular and Francophone Salafis had been turned into a source of strength. Popular Salafis proved impressively adept at "Islamizing" or "re-Islamizing" Nigerien society. That is, they

4. For a nuanced analysis of these struggles, see Alice Kang's *Bargaining for Women's Rights: Activism in an Aspiring Muslim Democracy* (Minneapolis: University of Minnesota Press, 2015).

were successful at propagating generic Salafi attitudes, especially in the urban areas, in an ambiance, moreover, of prolonged economic decline, rendering a religious compass desirable to large numbers of pauperized people. In this way, Salafism gained a large popular base in the country and became part of mainstream religion. Since—unlike the Sufis—the Salafis had a very active militant wing, this base could and was several times mobilized for street protest against parts of the secularist state's policies, especially those related to family life and the status of women. In the 1990s, at least, state leaders usually backed down when faced with such protests.

On another level, the Francophone Salafis found their way back into the political arena by integrating political parties as individuals, since they could not create a Salafi party. In these new roles, they were able to influence state policies, especially during the critical times when *coups d'état* (there were three between 1996 and 2010) reopened the constitutional question. They were never able to tear down the wall between the state and religion, despite many attempts in the 1990s. However, they were successful in considerably weakening the practice of secularism by Niger's state organizations. For instance, while it was unthinkable at the beginning of the 1990s that an official state site—such as a police station, a city hall, a public university campus—would include a mosque, it has become routine and practically obligatory two decades later. It is a privilege not extended to Christians, who might wish to have a chapel on-site. Also, during much of the 1990s, AIN not only could not play the role of the regulator of the Islamic scene that it held under the previous regime, its leadership (although not its provincial cadres) became more open to the Salafi presence. This change occurred, in part, because they also came to enjoy largesse from Wahhabi benefactors and connections in the Persian Gulf. As a result, Salafism became a major force on Niger's religious scene. But the political gains accruing from such success were ambiguous and limited. Victories were scored especially against associations that promoted women's rights, while *laïcité* was put on the defensive. However, the projects of "Islamizing" the nation and the state stalled.

Disappointments

While Niger Salafi militants were successful in putting secularists on the defensive, they failed in the higher agenda of turning their country into an Islamic republic ruling a Muslim nation. One must note here that, by

"Islamizing" or "re-Islamizing," Salafi militants meant a general adherence to their particular conception of Islam. In that sense, they, in fact, achieved a limited degree of success, more so than in other French-speaking countries of the Sahel, although less than in Northern Nigeria. There are no quantitative studies on "Islamization" as measured by increased practice of the religion in Niger, but it can be easily assessed by the number of mosques and praying spots that have become much more ubiquitous in Niger's towns and cities than in other agglomerations in the French-speaking Sahel. The dress code—especially for women—tends also to be more observant in the Salafi view of sartorial conventions in Niger than in Burkina Faso, Mali, and Senegal; and the radio and television channels, both private and public, offer vastly more religious programs. In their great majority, such religious programs are Salafi-slanted more so than in these other countries. On the state front, secularists in Niger often fret that the state apparatus is in the process of being overrun by Salafi networks. While this fear is clearly a form of ideological panic, the impressions that gave rise to it correspond to a greater Salafi presence within the precincts of the state than used to be the case in the past.

These changes have some political expressions. Niger is, for instance, unique among the French-speaking Sahel country in witnessing recurring "Islamist"—that is, Salafi—riots that challenge the state on some occasions. They generally put forward the ideal of the "Sharia-compliant" lifestyle that Salafis wish to impose in the country. There were such riots in Maradi and Niamey in 2001, in Zinder in 2012, and in Zinder and Niamey in 2015. Maradi and Zinder are both large Hausa cities on the border with Nigeria, and the capital, Niamey, is both the seat of government and the largest recipient of people migrating out of Zinder and Maradi. Moreover, Niger's constitution no longer uses the word *laïcité*, and the country not only has apparently given up on adopting a liberal "family code," it is also among a few not to have ratified the African Union's liberal convention on women's rights. These outcomes, however, are in fact signs of the weakness of Salafi militancy in Niger.

The riots were opportunistic and did not develop into a larger, more enduring movement. They were, in large part, a consequence of the government's somewhat mishandling of the situation. All of them had negative repercussions on public opinion. In 2001, the opportunity for rioting was provided by the organization of a fashion festival in the desert city of Agadez. Salafi militants protested against it and wanted to organize a demonstration, as they often did in the 1990s, against things like the "family code"[5] or the use of the condom. By the turn of the 2000s, however, government policy had changed. After a decade of neglecting the religious field, the state was making a comeback and had, since 1998, rekindled its sponsorship of AIN. In 2001, the government refused to "cave to the Islamists"; it forbade the demonstrations. While demonstrations were subsequently canceled in Zinder, they went ahead in Maradi and Niamey. Repression turned them into riots. In the aftermath, the government dissolved dozens of Islamic associations, and, some years later, set up a national Islamic council. That council allowed it to exert patronage toward the docile among the Salafi associations.

The riots in Zinder in 2012, and in Zinder and Niamey in 2015, were especially shocking for the larger public opinion because, in addition to the "normal" targets of Salafi militants intent on removing from the urban space the sites of anti-Sharia behavior, many churches were also torched and there were casualties among Christians. Sites of anti-Sharia behavior included betting kiosks, bars, and places considered as "brothels," such as small hotels. Christians, a very small minority in Niger, do not represent a political stake in the country. The attack on them was a straightforward manifestation of the continued influence of Nigerian Salafism, in which Christians have been considered as the enemy since the time of Gumi, over Niger's popular Salafism. However, it also startled the majority of Niger's Muslims, who were not Salafi militants and had absorbed the Salafi message only as a way to improve their practice of the religion. In other words, the riots showed that there was a chasm between "generic" Salafism, which has become a prevalent approach to Islam in urban Niger, and the militant Salafism of more organized groups, which has been strongly ideological and political.

The riots were militant events that built upon the fact that, in this moment in Niger's history, Salafi discourse could be appropriated in a general protest discourse against governmental policy and conduct. But, for nonmilitants, it only applies to very specific subjects, all related to family life. Salafi militants were supported in their protest against liberal women's rights, mainly because of the impact that such rights would have on the organization of family life, which, across Niger, has been traditionally codified by a set of

5. For a history of Niger's failed adoption of a "family code," see Leonardo Villalón's "The Moral and the Political in African Democratization: The *Code de la Famille* in Niger's Troubled Transition," *Democratization* 3, no. 2 (1996): 41–68.

customary and Islamic rights and obligations. More recently, in 2017, laws by the government to broaden the tax base were first criticized on the subject of succession duties. These are rejected by Maliki jurisprudence as an immoral imposition on the orphaned. In all other areas of governance, public protest has consistently resorted to referents other than religion. Institutionally, if Niger's constitutions (there have been three since the one in the early 1990s) have stopped using the inflammatory word *laïcité*, they all upheld the "separation of state and religion." Moreover, the current constitution affirms that the secularism clause is not subject to revision or amendment. Compared with some of the outcomes of Salafi militancy in neighboring countries, these results are strikingly lackluster: in Northern Nigeria, Sharia has been fully integrated with the rule of law; in Mali, a "family code" has been adopted after having been revised by a Salafi-controlled high Islamic council; and, even in Senegal, where Salafis are much weaker than Sufis, the government failed in 2016 to pass a law that would have enshrined the inviolability of the secularism clause in the constitution.

In Niger, the state thus remains firmly secular, and if the nation has been "re-Islamized," this has not been fully in the way that Salafi militants had wanted. One key point to emphasize is that, even in the countries where they have been markedly more successful (i.e., Northern Nigeria and Mali), Salafi militants have been disappointed. These states remain a far cry from the "Islamic state" or "republic" that Salafi militants envision. In Mali and Northern Nigeria, the disappointment has led some to embrace the violence of "jihad" and terrorism as an extreme method to achieve their ideological dreams. One could, therefore, wonder why the much greater disappointment of Niger's Salafis has not similarly led to the endemic violence of jihadism and terrorism there.

CONCLUSION

To return to the question on the origin of terrorism and violence caused by jihadism that led to the discussion on political Salafism in Niger, there are some elements indicating that violence can only be found at the extreme end of a spectrum of ideological and political methods. While this has been happening, the cursor has more often stayed toward the center of the spectrum instead of sliding off at the extreme. Like all political ideologies, political Salafism harbors a possibility for violence, as the riots in Niger indicate.

But endemic violence depends on specific conditions, both structural and contingent. These conditions rarely mature in any given case, at least in the context of the Sahel. Salafi militants in the Sahel typically stick to the political game as it was opened up by democratization in the 1990s. The behavior of Niger's political Salafis, trying to found a political party, moving toward the civil society when that path was blocked, and subsequently trying to voice their grievances and requests through the accepted channels of street demonstrations and lobbying, is characteristic of how Salafis have generally pursued their agenda in the Sahel countries. The endemic violence of jihadism and terrorism, as opposed to the fragmentary violence of rioting, rose at the margins of the Salafi movement. It occurred in remote or isolated regions, including Boko Haram in Nigeria, Ansar Dine and the Movement for Unicity and Jihad in West Africa (and other related movements) in Mali.

In fact, when the movements do have roots within Sahelian populations, many experts analyze them as simple grievance movements, not as ideological movements bearing a political project.[6] In my view, this interpretation is not entirely accurate. Violence from the fringe can be and is a serious threat to the Sahel. As they fail to advance their project into impervious majorities and bump against military resistance, violent minorities increasingly resort to more extreme forms of violence, shifting from targeting security personnel to assailing civilians, as is now happening in Mali. They may take inspiration from large-scale civilian-focused attacks in the Middle East and Somalia. However, violence from the margins lacks the destabilizing potential that inheres in (potential) violence from the center. The case of Niger provides evidence that, in the Sahel, the center "holds." Niger is, with Nigeria, the Sahel country where political radicalization at the center has been the most advanced. While Niger's political Salafis lack a leader of the stature of Mali's Mahmoud Dicko, the man who single-handedly gave political relevance to Mali's comparatively small political Salafi movement, they have penetrated the social mainstream much more so than in Mali (although less so than in Northern Nigeria). Yet, as we have seen, the outcome, thus far, has been a reassertion of the secular state in addition to a tarnishing of their message in the eyes of Salafi supporters. The fact that the center still holds has another significant implication: it creates a situation that gives fuel to a propagation of violence from the margins. Nigeria is certainly the best example of this

6. This is especially the case for successive offerings from the International Crisis Group on Mali, Burkina Faso, and Niger.

phenomenon, given that the long-lasting endemic violence of Boko Haram has remained confined to the northeastern states despite years of inefficient response from the Nigerian federal state.

Finally, violence at the margins does a disservice to the nonviolent agenda of political Salafism at the center. The fact that this agenda has all but stalled in Niger is not only due to weak leadership, but, also, and perhaps chiefly, to the surge of patriotism against Boko Haram and other jihadist groups after they started killing large numbers of Nigerien troops in recent years.[7] Nonviolent Salafi militants are tainted by association, in this new spirit of self-defense patriotism. "Islamism" in general appears, in this frame, as the enemy of Niger. A public opinion backlash, which may not be limited to Niger and may characterize other parts of the Sahel, is, thus, quietly sending political Salafis into a spell in the wilderness from which it is very possible they might not return.

References

Gumi, Abubakar. *Where I Stand*. Ibadan: Spectrum Books, 1992.

Idrissa, Rahmane. *The Politics of Islam in the Sahel: Between Persuasion and Violence*. London: Routledge, 2017.

Kang, Alice. *Bargaining for Women's Rights: Activism in an Aspiring Muslim Democracy*. Minneapolis: University of Minnesota Press, 2015.

Loimeier, Roman. *Islamic Reform and Political Change in Northern Nigeria*. Evanston: Northwestern University Press, 2011.

Mueller, Lisa. "Religious Violence and Democracy in Niger." *African Conflict and Peacebuilding Review* 6, no. 1 (2016): 89–104.

Thurston, Alexander. *Salafism in Nigeria: Islam, Preaching and Politics*. Cambridge: Cambridge University Press, 2016.

Triaud, Jean-Louis. "L'Islam et l'Etat en République du Niger." In *L'Islam et l'Etat dans le monde d'aujourd'hui*, edited by Olivier Carré. Paris: PUF, 1982.

Villalón, Leonardo. "The Moral and the Political in African Democratization: The *Code de la Famille* in Niger's Troubled Transition." *Democratization* 3, no. 2 (1996): 41–68.

7. On Niger's patriotism as a response to jihadist violence, see Lisa Mueller's "Religious Violence and Democracy in Niger," *African Conflict and Peacebuilding Review* 6, no. 1 (2016): 89–104.

Religious Freedom

The Case of Apostasy in Islam

Mutaz Al-Khatib

Hamid Bin Khalifa University, Doha

This chapter provides some critical analysis of the prescribed punishment (*ḥadd*) for apostasy and is divided into three main parts. First, it explains the *fiqhī* (juristic) sys tem as a basis for the prescription of punishment for apostasy. Second, it explains how this *fiqhī* ruling can serve as an archetype demonstrating the need to rethink *ijtihād* (independent legal reasoning) and its mechanisms. Third, it underscores the impact of the change in moral values and the evolution of concepts, such as that of freedom, on the *fiqhī* reasoning.

Since the late nineteenth century, there were countless attempts to address the issue of apostasy. The approaches to this controversial issue have varied in terms of motives, orientations, and contexts. The concept of religious freedom proved central to orientalist debates as well as the debates of the traditionalist and the reformist.[1] Freedom, and specifically religious

---

A longer version of this chapter has been published in Arabic under the title "al-Ḥurriyyah al-Dīniyyah wa Qatl al-Murtadd: Madkhal li-I'ādat al-Tafkīr fī al-Ijtihād al-Fiqhī" in *Al-Ḥurrīyya fī al-Fikr al-'Arabī al-Mu'āṣir*, ed. Murād Dayyānī (Doḥa: al-Markaz al-'Arabī li al-Abḥāth wa Dirāsat al-Siyāsāt, 2018),), 369–406. Here I want to thank Mariam Taher and Rasha Badr for their assistance in editing this English version. I also would like to thank Yara Abdelbasset for her help in putting together the bibliography in this English version.

1. It would be fruitful to look into the context in which 'Abd al-'Azīz Jāwīsh wrote his book *al-Islām Dīn al-Fiṭra* and how the idea of the book was born while addressing some students at Oxford University. It is also intriguing to note how he presented it and talked about religious freedom and killing the apostate in an orientalist conference in 1950 before publishing it in 1952. Of additional note is the argument between 'Abd al-Muta'āl al-Ṣa'īdī and 'Īsā

freedom, is one of the key modern values that is unanimously accepted as a universal human value. It is worth noting that even traditionalist scholars eventually acknowledged the principle of religious freedom. However, their claim was that the prescribed punishment for apostasy does not contradict the value of religious freedom.

FREEDOM: CONCEPT AND MEANINGS

The discussion of religious freedom dates back to the early modern times,[2] in line with the spread of the values of modernity which are essentially premised on individualism and individual freedoms. Such notions later became part of a universal set of human values, raising several questions and concerns when read against the Islamic religious texts and the jurisprudence literature. Prior to the modern period, the Islamic tradition had not explored freedom in the modern philosophical sense in which the various spheres such as the civil, political, and social are treated as separate.[3] Instead, the Islamic tradition treated these spheres as closely relevant to one another but did examine a number of dimensions relevant to freedom. In the discipline of *fiqh* (jurisprudence), freedom was used in contrast to slavery/serfdom.[4] In the discipline of *kalām* (theology), freedom was used in contrast to fatalism under the binaries of fatalism and free will, and that of human action and Divine action. In the discipline of *Ṣufism*, some *ṣūfī* scholars, such as Abū al-Qāsim al-Qushayrī (d. 465/1074), devoted

Mannūn, a member of the council of senior scholars in Egypt, about religious freedom and apostasy in *al-Siyāsah al-Usbūʿiyyah* (Weekly Politics) magazine in the 1930s. These arguments were later compiled in al-Ṣaʿīdī's books: *al-Ḥurriyyah al-Dīniyyah fī al-Islām* (Religious Freedom) and *al-Ḥudūd* (Prescribed Punishments).

2. Napoleon's campaign in Egypt was one of the channels through which the concept of political freedom, for instance, was introduced to the Islamic world. The campaign's first Arabic statement laid out the foundation on which a republic is established and that is "freedom and equality."

3. Michael Cook has argued that political freedom is "not an Islamic value" but is in tension with Islam. In contrast, David Decosimo has argued that Cook is mistaken, and political freedom is an "Islamic value." See Michael Cook, "Is Political Freedom an Islamic Value?," in *Freedom and the Construction of Europe*, vol. 2, ed. Quentin Skinner, 283–310 (Cambridge: Cambridge University Press, 2013), and David Decosimo, "Political Freedom as an Islamic Value," *Journal of the American Academy of Religion* 86, no. 4 (December 2018): 912–52.

4. Muḥammad ʿAlī al-Tahānawī, *Mawsūʿat Kashshāf Iṣṭilāḥāt al-Funūn wa al-ʿUlūm*, vol. 1 (Beirut: Maktabat Lubnān Nāshirūn, 1996), 641.

a chapter to freedom. In this context, freedom was used to denote liberty from domination by creatures through the true submission to God alone. In the works on ethics, freedom was used to indicate a virtue of the self which falls under chastity, a value that makes a person keep to good practices and lawful gains, as found in the writings of Miskawayh (d. 421/1030) and al-Rāghib al-Iṣfahānī (d. 5th/11th).[5] In summary, freedom has two *meanings* in the Islamic tradition: the first is liberty from slavery and serfdom, and the second is the exercise of free will in personal affairs without any interference or opposition.

Even *jihād* is justified in the Quranic discourse as being a means to promote the freedom of belief and prevent compulsion, where the Quran states that "And fight them until persecution is no more, and religion is for God" (Quran 2:193). *Jihād* was thus legislated to prevent persecution, where persecution in this context refers to compelling people to follow a certain belief. This allowance comes in response to the historical context where the polytheists broadly persecuted Muslims and denied them freedom of religion.[6] Some contemporary jurists have even incorporated freedom of religion under *maqāṣid al-sharī'a* (the higher objectives of Sharia), as in the works of al-Ṭāhir Ibn 'Āshūr (d. 1393/1973),[7] Yūsuf al-Qaraḍāwī, and Rāshid al-Ghannūshī. In the context of modern Arab revolutions, al-Qaraḍāwī and al-Ghannūshī state that freedom is one of the basic necessities of life, and that human life has no dignity without it.[8] Indeed, each of the "the five collective necessities" is inseparable from freedom since the preservation of religion, human life, intellect, lineage, and property is impossible under compulsion and enslavement. This is why Muslim jurists continuously highlight the

5. See Abū 'Alī Aḥmad ibn Muḥammad Miskawayh, *Tahdhīb al-Akhlāq wa Taṭhīr al-A'rāq* (Cairo: Maktabat al-Thaqāfa al-Dīniyya, 1998), 29; Abū al-Qāsim al-Ḥusayn ibn Muḥammad al-Rāghib al-Iṣfahānī, *al-Dharī'ah ilā Makārim al-Sharī'a*, ed. Abū al-Yazīd Abū Zayd al-'Ajamī (Cairo: Dār al-Salām, 2007), 117.

6. For the objectives of *jihād*, see Muḥammad Rashīd Riḍā, *Tafsīr al-Manār*, vol. 10 (Cairo: al-Hay'ah al-Miṣriyyah al-'Āmmah li-l Kitāb, 1990), 270.

7. See Muḥammad al-Ṭāhir ibn 'Āshūr, *Maqāṣid al-Sharī'a*, ed. Muḥammad al-Ḥabīb Bilkhūjah, vol. 3 (Doha: Wizārat al-Awqāf wa al-Shu'ūn al-Islāmiyyah, 2004), 372–85. Ibn 'Āshūr has addressed the issue of freedom in detail in his books *Maqāṣid al-Sharī'a* and *Uṣūl al-Niẓām al-Ijtimā'ī fī al-Islām*. Also see the study of ibn Khūjah in which he introduced *Maqāṣid al-Sharī'a*, vol. 1, 690–93, vol. 2, 130–32.

8. See Yūsuf al-Qaraḍāwī, *al-Sharī'a wa al-Ḥayāt*, a program on Al Jazeera, an episode entitled "al-Ḥurriyyah wa Ḍarūratuhā fī al-Islām," (September 22, 2011); Rāshid al-Ghannūshi, *al-Sharī'a wa al-Ḥayāt program*, a program on Al Jazeera, an episode entitled "al-Ḥurriyyah wa Muqāwwimāt al-Istibdād" (May 24, 2012).

Lawgiver's zeal for that freedom stating that "The Lawgiver (God) ardently promotes all means to freedom" (*al-shāri' mutashawwif ilā al-ḥurriyya*).[9]

FREEDOM OF BELIEF IN THE QURAN

It is not within the scope of this chapter to explore the general concept of freedom; the focus here is on religious freedom only, which in essence draws upon the freedom of religious belief and the freedom of religious practice. In this context, we can highlight two groups of Quranic verses:[10] the first group speaks to the freedom of belief while the second speaks to apostasy and disbelief after belief.

In respect to the first group, the Quran includes several verses that serve as foundations for religious freedom. Some have explicit indications while others have only tacit indications. Two Quranic verses are central:

> "There is no compulsion in religion; right-mindedness has already been evidently (distinct) from misguidance." (Quran 2:256)

> "And if your Lord had (so) decided, whoever is in the earth would indeed have believed, all of them, altogether. Would you then compel mankind until they are believers?" (Quran 10:99)

These two verses are of paramount importance for a number of reasons: (a) they explicitly and directly affirm the freedom of religion; (b) they assume a form similar to that of general laws, universal rules, or cosmic norms; and (c) they are both in the form of predicates (*khabarī*), and predicates are the most apt pronouncement for laws and general norms. The two verses speak of the Divine will to allow people free choice for two reasons: guidance and

9. Al-Ṭāhir ibn 'Āshūr has clarified that the application of this rule includes Sharia has obstructed slavery, the issue of slavery was gradually treated by increasing the reasons that necessitate emancipation along with motivating emancipation while forbidding mistreatment. He has also highlighted that Islam is keen on achieving freedom of belief, expression, learning, teaching, writing, and working. See Muḥammad al-Ṭāhir ibn 'Āshūr, *Maqāṣid al-Sharī'a*, vol. 3, 372–83.

10. See a detailed study on the religious freedom verses in 'Abd al-raḥmān Ḥelalī, *Ḥurriyyat al-I'tiqād fī al-Qur'ān al-Karīm: Dirāsah fī Ishkāliyyat al-Riddah wa al-Jihād wa al-Jizyah* (Beirut: al-Markaz al-Thaqāfī al-'Arabī, 2001).

truth are clearly distinguished from misguidance and falsehood; and God wills to entrust humankind with duties, freedom of choice, and responsibility. Accordingly, not all people are believers since God did not will to make them believe by force.

In respect to the second group, the Quran includes six verses in which the term *riddah* (apostasy) appears explicitly (2:109, 217; 3:100, 149; 5:54; 47:25). The Quran also speaks of the concept of *riddah*, rather than the term, per se, in nine contexts (3:72–73, 86–90; 4:88–89, 137; 5:5; 6:88; 9:73–74; 16:106; 39:65). It is noticeable that all of these verses speak of only three themes. First, they speak of apostasy and apostates: the apostasy of a believer is ardently sought by both the disbelievers and the hypocrites, and apostates seem to form a distinguishable group in the community. Second, the destiny and punishment of apostates: their deeds are void in this life and in the afterlife and they are cursed and doomed to eternal punishment in hellfire, but no temporal worldly punishment is stated for this life. The third theme is a call to the believers: after pointing out the ardent desire of the People of the Book to make believers apostates, God commands the believers to forgive and to pardon. The Quran also asks the Messenger to disregard the attempts by the People of the Book to cast doubt on the faith of the believers, and calls on the believers not to obey disbelievers and hypocrites.

The Quran clearly asserts the freedom of religion as an absolute general rule and includes no indication of any temporal worldly punishment for apostasy. This fact implies that it is not a temporal crime (as was considered in other religions) and poses a problematic question. Indeed, this question was not put forth in the premodern jurisprudential tradition for two main reasons. The first is the absence of the particular formulation of the concept of freedom as found in the modern period. The second is relevant to the juridical deductive approach, how jurists traditionally envisioned the relationship between the Quran and Sunnah, and the various methods they used to synthesize and reconcile the two. Thus, since any punishment for apostasy constitutes an infringement on the freedom of religion, we will explore it in some detail.

PUNISHMENT FOR APOSTASY IN ISLAMIC JURISPRUDENCE

The punishment for apostasy can be traced in two distinct stages: the classical period and the modern period.

1. Apostasy from the Perspective of Premodern Jurists

The four *Sunnī* schools of jurisprudence (the Ḥanafī, Mālikī, Shāfiʿī, and Ḥanbalī schools) are in agreement that the apostate must be executed unless he repents and abandons apostasy.[11] They cite the Quran, Sunnah, and *Ijmāʿ* (Consensus) in support of this ruling.

For a proof from the Quran, some cite the Quranic verse: "You will soon be called against a people endowed with strict violence to fight them, or they surrender" (48:16). It is said that the "people" mentioned here are the apostates of Yamāmah and others. As for the proof from the Sunnah, they cite the Hadith (prophetic report) "he who changes his religion, kill him"[12] which is the most authentic and the strongest evidence with regard to the punishment of the apostate. Additionally, they cite the Hadith: "The blood of a Muslim cannot be shed except in three cases . . . and the one who renounces his religion and abandons his people (or community)."[13] Further proof comes from the Prophet's order that ʿAbdullāh ibn Abī Sarḥ, ʿAbdullāh ibn Khaṭal, and others be killed. Moreover, ibn ʿAbd al-Bar (d. 463/1071), ibn Daqīq al-ʿĪd (d. 702/1302), al-Nawawī (d. 676/1277), and ibn Qudāmah (d. 620/1223) relayed the consensus on killing the apostate.[14]

11. See Abū ʿUmar Yūsuf ibn ʿAbdullāh ibn ʿAbd al-Barr, *al-Istidhkār al-Jāmiʿ li-Madhāhib Fuqahāʾ al-Amṣār wa ʿUlamāʾ al-Aqṭār fī mā Taḍammanahu al-Muwwaṭṭaʾ min Maʿānī al-Raʾy wa al-Āthār wa Sharḥ dhālika Kullihi bi-l-Ījāz wa al-Ikhtiṣār*, ed. ʿAbd al-Muʿṭī Qalʿajī, vol. 22 (Damascus: Dār Qutaybah; Ḥalab: Dār al-Waʿy, 1993), 135 onward. See also ibn ʿAbd al-Barr, *al-Tamhīd lima fī al-Muwaṭṭaʾ min al-Maʿānī wa al-Asānīd*, ed. Muṣṭafā ibn Aḥmad al-ʿAlawī and Muḥammad ʿAbd al-Kabīr al-Bakrī, vol. 5 (Ribat: Ministry of Endowment and Islamic Affairs, 1986), 306–20; ibn Ḥazm, *al-Muḥallā bi-l Āthār* (Beirut: Dār al-Fikr, n.d.), vol. 12, 108–9; Abū Muḥammad ʿAbdullāh ibn Aḥmad ibn Qudāmah al-Maqdisī, *Al-Mughnī*,, vol. 9 (Cairo: Maktabat al-Qāhira, 1968), 3, and Muḥammad ibn ʿAlī al-Shawkānī, *Al-Sayl al-Jarrār al-Mutadaffiq ʿalā Ḥadāʾiq al-Azhār*, vol.1 (Beirut: Dār Ibn Ḥazm, 2004), 868.

12. Narrated by al-Bukhārī in al-Ṣaḥīḥ: Abū ʿAbdullāh Muḥammad ibn Ismāʿīl al-Bukhārī, *Al-Jāmiʿ al-Musnad al-Ṣaḥīḥ al-Mukhtaṣar min Umūr Rasūl Allāh Ṣallā Allāhu ʿalayhi wa Sallam wa Sunanihi wa Ayyāmih*, ed. Muḥammad Zuhayr ibn Nāṣir al-Nāṣir, vol. 4 (Beirut: Dār Ṭawq al-Najāh, 2002), 61, and other places.

13. al-Bukhārī, *Al-Jāmiʿ al-Musnad al-Ṣaḥīḥ al-Mukhtaṣar*, vol. 9, 5; Abū al-Ḥusayn Muslim ibn al-Ḥajjāj, *al-Musnad al-Ṣaḥīḥ al-Mukhtaṣar bi-Naql al-ʿAdl ʿan al-ʿAdl ilā Rasūl Allāh Ṣallā Allāhu ʿalayhi wa Sallam*, ed. Muḥammad Fuʾād ʿAbd al-Bāqī, vol. 3 (Beirut: Dār Iḥyāʾ al-Turāth al-ʿArabī, n.d.), 1302.

14. See Ibn ʿAbd al-Barr, *al-Tamhīd*, vol. 5, 306; Abū Zakariyyā Yaḥyā al-Nawawī, *al-Minhāj Sharḥ Ṣaḥīḥ Muslim ibn al-Ḥajjāj*, vol. 12, 2nd ed. (Beirut: Iḥyāʾ al-Turāth al-ʿArabī,

In this regard, al-Shāfiʿī (d. 204/820) said: "Muslims have all agreed that it is not permissible for an apostate to be saved by blood money (*diyah*), and he cannot be pardoned . . . unless he reverts to Islam or gets killed."[15] It is possible, however, that this relayed consensus was based on the first caliph Abū Bakr's fight against the apostates without being opposed by any of the companions of the Prophet, even though some of them initially argued against it.

This juridical induction is grounded in three methodological principles. The first is acting upon the Prophet's tradition when it fulfills the conditions set by Muslim scholars, even if it is an indecisive solitary report (*khabar al-āḥād*) narrated by a number that does not meet the standardized minimum number of narrators for *tawātur*; the condition necessary to beget certainty and decisiveness. The second is that the solitary report is acceptable in the area of *ḥudūd* (the prescribed penalties or punishments) in which blood is shed, as Abū Ḥāmid al-Ghazālī (d. 505/1111) confirmed.[16] The third, is the principle that a solitary report can qualify the general declarations of the Quran, a principle that the jurists employed to render the prophetic reports on killing the apostate as qualifiers for the Quranic general declaration "there is no compulsion in religion" (2:256) and other verses that assert the freedom of belief. Under this principle, the treatment of the case of the apostate constitutes an exception to the general rule.

Accordingly, the punishment for apostasy seems consistent with the *fiqhī* system—its foundations (*uṣūl*) and branches (*furūʿ*)— which renders it immutable with no room for the least divergence. However, delving deeper into these proofs exposes significant variability in processes and citations at the time that the ruling was concluded, but that is not the focus of this chapter.

1973), 208. Ibn Ḥazm has relayed the consensus on killing the apostate. See Ibn Ḥazm, *al-Muḥallā*, vol. 12, 112; ibn Qudāmah al-Maqdisī, *al-Mughnī*, vol. 9, 3. It is worth mentioning that the general consensus on killing the apostate is not mentioned in the books that specialized in consensuses, such as *Marātib al-Ijmāʿ* by ibn Ḥazm, *al-Awṣaṭ* by ibn al-Mundhir, and *al-Iqnāʿ* by ibn al-Qaṭṭān, despite mentioning other rulings related to the apostate.

15. Abū Bakr ibn Ḥusayn al-Bayhaqī, *Maʿrifat al-Sunan wa al-Āthār*, ed. ʿAbd al-Muʿṭī Amīn Qalʿajī, vol. 12 (Damascus: Dār Qutaybah, Dār al-Waʿī, 1991), 239.

16. See Abū Ḥāmid al-Ghazālī, *Al-Mustaṣfā min ʿIlm al-Uṣūl*, ed. ʿAbd al-Salām ʿAbd al-Shāfī (Beirut: Dār al-Kutub al-ʿIlmiyyah, 1993), 117.

Claim of *Ijmā*ʿ

An in-depth analysis of the wars against apostasy in the time of Abū Bakr (d. 13/634) is made possible through the chronicles by ibn Jarīr al-Ṭabarī (d. 310/923) who asserts that this was not an individual apostasy but rather a collective one.[17] Thus, it is unfit to be cited in this particular legal context as a proof for *ijmā*ʿ in support of the killing of the apostates. The act of *riddah* was in fact an act of insurgence and dissent against the caliph that endangered the unity and solidarity within the established state shortly after the death of its leader, Prophet Muhammad.

Reflecting on the viewpoints of the successors of the companions of the Prophet unveils that there are two leading successors who maintained that an apostate should not be killed but should rather be called to repent until the end of his time.[18] These are Ibrāhīm al-Nakhaʿī (d. 96/714) the leading jurist of Iraq and Sufyān al-Thawrī (d. 161/778) the famous leading authority in *fiqh* and Hadith. This view is also attributed to ʿUmar Ibn al-Khaṭṭāb (d. 23/644) and ʿUmar ibn ʿAbd al-ʿAzīz (d. 101/720). This opinion survived through later times, where it appears in the works of Ibn Ḥazm who devoted a considerable section of his book *al-Muḥallā* to argue against this opinion.

Remarks on the Inference from the Quran

In the context of *riddah* punishment, inference from the Quran is not of great significance for the following reasons. First, there is no indication of any punishment in this world for apostasy, thus the Quran is not cited in arguments supporting this ruling. Second, since the Quran does not address

---

17. See Abū Jaʿfar Muḥammad ibn Jarīr al-Ṭabarī, *Tārīkh al-Rusul wa al-Mulūk*, vol. 3, 2nd ed. (Beirut: Dār Iḥyāʾ al-Turāth al-ʿArabī, 1968), 249 onward.

18. ʿAbd al-Razzāq al-Ṣanʿānī (d. 211/826) has narrated this, citing Ibrāhīm al-Nakhaʿī in ʿAbd al-Razzāq ibn Hammām al-Ṣanʿānī, *al-Muṣannaf*, ed. Ḥabīb al-Raḥmān al-Aʿẓamī, vol.10, 2nd ed. (Beirut: al-Maktab al-Islāmī, 1983), 166. Ibn Abī Shybah (d. 235/849) has also cited Ibrāhīm al-Nakhaʿī, "the apostate is to be asked for repentance whenever he renounces Islām": Abū Bakr ʿAbdullāh ibn Muḥammad ibn Abī Shybah, *al-Kitāb al-Muṣannaf fī al-Aḥādīth wa al-Āthār*, ed. Kamāl Yūsuf al-Ḥūt, vol. 6 (al-Riyadh: Makatabat al-Rushd), 1989, 440. Ibn Abī Shyba has also attributed another narration to Ibrāhīm, saying: "He [the apostate] is to be asked for repentance. If he agrees, he is to be left alone. If he refuses, he is to be killed." Ibn Ḥajar has strengthened this narration, but books on *fiqhī* controversies have held on to the first narration. See Shihāb al-Dīn Aḥmad ibn Ḥajar al-ʿAsqalānī, *Fatḥ al-Bārī bi-Sharḥ Saḥīḥ al-Imām abī ʿAbdillāh Muḥammad ibn Ismāʿīl al-Bukhārī*, ed. ʿAbd al-Qādir Shybah al-Ḥamad, vol. 12 (Al-Riyadh: N.p., 2001), 280.

the details of rulings, citing it with respect to legal details is not conclusive in juristic debates.

Indeed, citing the Quran in support of the *riddah* punishment was first invoked by al-Shāfi'i in his book *al-Umm.*[19] However, his inferences are not conclusive and are mostly irrelevant to the essence of this controversy, since, as we have emphasized in this chapter, the Quran has no indication of any temporal punishment for apostasy. Al-Ṭabarī also asserted that the verse "there is no compulsion in religion" (2:256) was to be qualified by the prophetic tradition on the killing of apostates and that compulsion is impermissible before accepting Islam. However, according to him, the case is different if a person wants to leave Islam. This controversy stems from the problematic relationship between the Quran and the Sunnah that we will address later.

The insistence of reformists (*iṣlāḥiyyūn*) on the absence of a temporal worldly punishment for apostasy in the Quran drove some of their contemporaries to go to extremes to prove it. This trend started with al-Ṭāhir ibn 'Āshūr, who built his inference on the verse "and whoever of you reverts from his religion [to disbelief] and dies while he is a disbeliever—for those their deeds have become worthless in this world and the hereafter" (2:217). Building on the use of the *fa* in *fayamut,* which denotes a sequence whereby death follows reversion, and according to ibn 'Āshūr since everyone knows that most of those who revert do not die right after reversion, he therefore inferred that the apostate is to be punished by death and that the verse is to be deemed a proof for killing the apostate.[20] This type of induction is methodologically problematic as will be shown later.

Some contemporary scholars cited the Quranic verse "you will soon be called against a people endowed with strict violence to fight them, or they surrender" (48:16). Ibn Kathīr mentioned a number of probable interpretations for this verse. It is said that the "people" in question refer to the people of the Hawāzin, Thaqīf, or Banū Ḥanīfah tribes, to the Persians, or to the Romans. For 'Aṭā' (d. 114/732), Ibn Abī-Layla (d. 83/703), al-Ḥasan al-Baṣrī (d. 110/728), and Qatāda (d. 118/736), the passage refers to the Persians and

19. See Muḥammad ibn Idrīs al-Shāfi'ī, *al-Umm,* ed. Rif'at Fawzī 'Abd al-Muṭṭalib, vol. 2 (Cairo: Maktabat al-Khānjī, n.d.), 568–69 and 573–74.

20. Muḥammad al-Ṭāhir ibn 'Āshūr, *al-Taḥrīr wa al-Tanwīr,* vol. 2 (Tunisia: al- Dār al-Tūnisiyyah li al-Nashr, 1984), 335.

the Romans. Mujāhid (d. 104/722) maintained that it refers to the pagans.[21] This diversity in interpretations makes any inference concerning the punishment for apostasy problematic, since a text open to several probabilities is not valid as a proof. Al-Qaraḍāwī maintained that the Quran indicated the punishment for apostasy in the following verse: "Indeed, the penalty for those who wage war against Allah and His Messenger and strive upon earth [to cause] corruption is none but that they be killed or crucified or that their hands and feet be cut off from opposite sides or that they be exiled from the land" (5:33). Al-Qaraḍāwī's claim builds on the interpretation by some predecessors where the verse is believed to refer to the apostates, ibn Taymiyyah's argument that fighting by spreading apostasy is more serious than fighting by creating turmoil, and his own inference from verse (5:54) that apostasy will be fought with force.[22]

All of these inferences are weak and distorted and thus cannot be the base for *fiqhī* rulings. Consequently, there is no decisive text from the Quran in support of a temporal worldly punishment for *riddah*.

Remarks on the Inference from the Sunnah

With respect to the cited prophetic traditions, the Prophet never killed anyone for apostasy. For example, there is no authentic proof that al-Aswad al-ʿAnsī (d. 11/632) accepted Islam to make possible the claim that he later abandoned it. Similarly, when Ibn Abī Sarḥ (d. 36/656) joined the disbelievers and the Prophet commanded that he be killed, Uthmān (d. 35/656) interceded in his favor and the Prophet accepted that intercession.[23] Since intercession, as per the prophetic report, is not to be accepted in the case of a prescribed punishment (*ḥadd*), then these cannot be treated simply as incidents of apostasy.

---

21. See Ismāʿīl ibn ʿUmar ibn Kathīr, *Tafsīr al-Qurʾān al-ʿAẓīm*, ed. Sāmī ibn Muḥammad Salāma, vol. 7 (al-Riyadh: Dār Ṭybah, 1999), 338.

22. See Yūsuf al-Qaraḍāwī, *al-Sharīʿa wa al-Ḥayāt*, a program on Al-Jazeera, an episode entitled "al-Ḥurriyyah al-Dīniyyah wa al-Fikriyyah" (February 1, 2005).

23. Narrated by Abū Dāwūd Sulaymān ibn al-Ashʿath al-Sijistānī, *Sunan Abī Dāwūd*, ed. Shuʿayb al-Arnāʾūṭ & Muḥammad Kāmil, vol. 6 (Amman: Dār al-Salām al-ʿĀlamiyyah, 2009), 414; Abū ʿAbd al-Raḥmān ibn Shuʿayb al-Nasāʾī, *al-Mujtabā min al-Sunnan: al-Sunan al-Ṣughrā*, ed. ʿAbd al-Fattāḥ Abū Ghuddah, vol. 7, 2nd ed (Ḥalab, Syria: Maktab al-Maṭbūʿāt al-Islāmiyyah, 1986), 107, and Abū ʿAbdullāh Muḥammad Ibn ʿAbdullāh al-Ḥākim al-Naysābūrī, *al-Mustadrak ʿalā al-Ṣaḥīḥayn*, ed. Muṣṭafā ʿAbd al-Qādir ʿAṭā, vol. 2 (Beirut: Dār al-Kutub al-ʿIlmiyyah, 1990), 388.

Examining all the examples that are cited in this regard reveals that the accounts spoke of people who, after abandoning Islam, "dissented and joined the disbelievers" in times of war between two distinct camps: that of belief and that of disbelief.[24] As for the people of ʿUkl and ʿUraynah, who are mentioned in the Hadith, they committed a number of crimes such as killing shepherds and stealing camels. Thus, what the Prophet applied in these situations was the punishment of *ḥirābah* (banditry; armed robbery and terrorizing civilians) not of *riddah*. He had their hands and feet cut off, their eyes blinded, and left them in the Ḥarrah (a very large volcanic field) to die as per the narration of al-Bukhārī.[25] Following the narration of Anas Ibn Mālik (d. 93/711) the Prophet ordered the blinding because these bandits had blinded the eyes of the shepherds.[26] According to Ibn Taymiyyah, "in addition to apostasy they killed and robbed, and thus became bandits and aggressors against God and His Messenger."[27] These narrations thus indicate that they were killed because of their criminal activity not because of apostasy per se.

As to Miqyas ibn Ṣubābah (d. 8/630), he came to take revenge from the killer of his brother Hāshim ibn Subābah (who was inadvertently killed). To do so, Miqyas feigned Islam and took the blood money (*diyah*) of his brother, but later revenged against the one who killed his brother and fled while boasting of his treachery in poetic lines. It was on those grounds that the Prophet ordered that Miqyas be killed.[28] As for Sārah, the female wailing singer, she came from Mecca and feigned Islam in Medina. The Prophet was very benevolent to her, but she later returned to Mecca (the abode of disbelievers at the time of war) and was singing satire of the Prophet. Consequently, she was killed.[29] Likewise, ʿAbdullāh ibn Khaṭal (d. 8/630) accepted Islam and migrated to Medina. The Prophet entrusted him with

---

24. Mutaz al-Khatib, "al-Riddah fī al-Sunnah al-Nabawiyyah: Ḥafr ʿan al-Muṣṭalaḥ" (unpublished).

25. Al-Bukhārī, *Al-Jāmiʿ al-Musnad al-Saḥīḥ al-Mukhtaṣar*, vol. 5, 129.

26. Muslim ibn al-Ḥajjāj, *al-Musnad al-Ṣaḥīḥ al-Mukhtaṣar bi-Naql*, vol. 3, 1298.

27. Abū al-ʿAbbās Aḥmad ibn ʿAbd al-Ḥalīm ibn Taymiyyah al-Ḥarrānī, *al-Ṣārim al-Maslūl ʿalā Shātim al-Rasūl*, ed. Muḥammad Muḥyī al-Dīn ʿAbd al-Ḥamīd, vol. 1 (al-Riyadh: al-Ḥaras al-Waṭanī al-Suʿūdī, 1983), 325.

28. See his story in Abū al-ʿAbbās Aḥmad ibn Yaḥyā al-Balādhurī, *Jumal min Ansāb al-Ashrāf*, ed. Suhayl zakkār and Riyāḍ al-Ziriklī, vol. 1 (Beirut: Dār al-Fikr, 1996), 358.

29. See al-Balādhurī, *Jumal min Ansāb al-Ashrāf*, 360; also see Abū Muḥammad ʿAbd al-Malik ibn Hishām, *al-Sīrah al-Nabawiyyah*, ed. Muṣṭafā al-Saqqā, Ibrāhīm al-Abyārī and ʿAbd al-Ḥafīẓ al-Shalabī, vol. 2, 2nd ed. (Cairo: Maṭbaʿat Muṣṭafā al-Bābī al-Ḥalabī, 1955), 410.

collecting charity money and sent a man from the Khuzā'ah tribe with him. However, Ibn Khaṭal killed the man of Khuzā'ah and apostatized, making his way to Mecca with the charity money. In Mecca, he said to the Meccans: "I found no religion better than yours" and took two female singers who would regularly sing satire of the Prophet.[30] These are the incidents cited by those claiming that the Prophet killed apostates. However, in their arguments the proponents overlooked the details in these cases that uncover the other crimes committed by those individuals, crimes that are proven to warrant the death punishment irrespective of the accompanying act of apostasy.

Reviewing the reality of the Prophet's Sunnah and the above-cited incidents makes it clear that the Prophet's statement "the one who forsakes his religion and separates from the community" is a multidimensional description. During the lifetime of the Prophet, anyone who left Islam joined the disbelieving community of the enemy. Clearly, incidents of apostasy, in general, occurred before the conquest (*fatḥ*) of Mecca. Here, the narration of 'Ā'ishah (d. 58/678) is of special significance as it comes to describe the existing state of affairs: "a man who abandons Islam and fights against Allah and His Messenger, in which case he should be either killed, crucified, or exiled."[31]

We are left with the Prophet's tradition "he who changes his religion, kill him," which is deemed the strongest proof in support of this viewpoint. Some contemporaries, who are not specialized scholars, attempted to reject this tradition on grounds of inauthenticity. In fact, it is authentic and was reported by al-Bukhārī. However, citing it in support of this punishment is controversial since scholars raised three concerns. The first concern is whether the conditional phrase "*man*" (i.e., he who) applies to males and females. For the Ḥanafī jurists, women are not included and should not be killed. They argue that this conditional phrase does not apply to females and cite the Prophet's proscription against killing women in times of war.[32]

The second concern is whether "*dīnahu*" (i.e., his religion) is general and applies to any religion. For Mālik ibn Anas (d. 179/795), it applies only to the

30. See al-Balādhurī, *Jumal min Ansāb al-Ashrāf*, vol. 11, 41, and ibn Hishām, *al-Sīrah al-Nabawiyyah*, vol. 2, 410.

31. Narrated by Abū Dāwūd, vol. 6, 409, and al-Nasā'ī, vol. 7, 101.

32. Muḥammad ibn Muḥammad al-Bazdawī, *Ma'rifat al-Ḥujaj al-Shar'iyyah*, ed. 'Abd al-Qādir ibn Yāsīn ibn Nāṣir al-Khaṭīb (Beirut: Mu'asasat al-Risālah, 2000), 203–4.

one who renounces Islam and does that openly.[33] Some Shāfi'ī jurists understood the Prophet's statement "he who changes his religion" to apply to anyone who leaves one religion to another, regardless of whether it is a religion whose followers are subject to *jizyah* (poll tax levied on non-Muslims). This is one of two opinions attributed to al-Shafi'ī as well as Aḥmad ibn Ḥanbal (d. 241/855). The other opinion of Aḥmad is that if a disbeliever leaves one religion for a better one, this change is accepted, but if she or he converts to an inferior religion, this should not be approved. For example, Judaism and Christianity are equal but Magianism is inferior to both of them.[34] The Ḥanafī jurists held the view that all false beliefs are equal and this tradition only applies to the renunciation of Islam.[35] Despite these differences, all schools are in agreement that the literal meaning of any change of religion is not intended and that one who changes his religion and accepts Islam is not included in the Hadith.[36]

The third concern relates to the command of "*faqtulūh*" (i.e., kill him). Does it entail immediate killing without *istitābah* (calling someone to repent from his or her sin/crime) or does it necessitate *istitābah*? Various views exist on this point. Some jurists allowed a three-day limit for *istitābah*, others specified fewer or more days, while still others maintained that *istitābah* applies until the end of the apostate's time on earth.[37] According to Al-Nawawī, "they disagreed on the ruling of *istitābah*: is it obligatory or recommended? They also disagreed on the allowed period and whether repentance will be accepted."[38]

In the light of this debate, it is evident that the ruling on killing the apostate is deeply controversial. Differences exist with respect to the killing itself, the sources for inference and proof, whether it applies to both

33. Mālik ibn Anas, *Muwaṭṭa' al-Imām Mālik*, ed. Muḥammad Fu'ād 'AbdulBāqī, vol. 2 (Beirut: Iḥyā' al-Turāth al-'Arabī, 1985), 736.

34. Al- Shāfi'ī has clarified that the one who changes religions that do not involve Islam is not to be killed. This is because they converted from falsehood to falsehood. See al-Shāfi'ī, *al-Umm*, vol. 2, 569, and Abū 'Umar ibn 'Abd al-Barr, *al-Istidhkār*, vol. 22, 138–39. As for the elucidation of the *madhhab* (legal opinion) of Aḥmad, see ibn Qudāmah al-Maqdisī, vol. 7, 133.

35. Muḥammad ibn Aḥmad al-Sarakhsī, al-Mabsūṭ, *al-Mabsūṭ*, vol. 5 (Beirut: Dār al-Ma'rifah, 1993), 48.

36. Al-Bazdawī, *Ma'rifat al-Ḥujaj al-Shar'iyyah*, 204.

37. See ibn 'Abd al-Barr, *al-Istidhkār*, vol. 22, 139–45.

38. Al-Nawawī, *al-Minhāj*, vol. 12, 208.

men and women, and whether repentance applies and if so how to apply it. These differences are a result of the absence of explicit and decisive evidence, which keeps the door to *ijtihād* (independent legal reasoning) open. Moreover, the narrations cited on this issue are speculative in terms of their chains of transmission,[39] forms of acceptable documentation, and meanings. As seen, it is widely agreed that the main narration on the issue is not literally applied and should be broadly interpreted—and the realm for such interpretation is vast.

2. Rethinking Apostasy in Modern Times

The reconsideration of the punishment for apostasy would not have been invoked without coming in contact with Western thought, the principles of the French Revolution, secularism, the modern conceptions of freedom, and the conventions on human rights. Thus, the reformist approach of Muḥammad ʿAbduh (d. 1905) revisited the ruling and engaged in rethinking the cited proofs, responding to them, and at times reinterpreting them. This was also the approach adopted by others later on as they rethought this issue. To the best of my knowledge, ʿAbduh was the first in the contemporary times to revisit this issue.

ʿAbduh approached the issue through the Quran, building on his conviction that with the Quran's eloquence we are in no need for other means to understand its discourse.[40] Accordingly, he concluded that the verse "there is no compulsion in religion" (2:256) establishes one of the fundamental rules in Islam and for organizing the society. It does not allow compulsion in accepting Islam, nor does it allow anyone to coerce another to leave Islam. This is in contrast, according to ʿAbduh, to what was customary in other religions—especially Christianity—regarding forcing people into accepting the religion.[41] Al-Īmān (faith), according to ʿAbduh, is essentially the submission of the self, and submission cannot be by com-

39. Al-Qaraḍāwī has contended, in the episode mentioned earlier, that the Hadiths previously mentioned are *mustafīḍah* (narrated by a group from a group, so they are at a higher level than the solitary report). On the other hand, Maḥmūd Shaltūt and others regarded these Hadiths as solitary reports.

40. Rashīd Riḍā, *Tafsīr al-Manār*, vol. 1, 282.

41. Rashīd Riḍā, *Tafsīr al-Manār*, vol. 3, 33.

pulsion and coercion but is only through elucidation and proof.[42] ʿAbduh was aware of the conflict between this verse (2:256) and the Hadith, "he who changes his religion, kill him," but he opined that the issue at hand was political rather than religious given his assertion that believing can only be voluntary.[43] Thus, he believed the Hadith should be interpreted in light of this general rule set by the verse. In this regard, the Prophet has commanded the killing of the apostate to intimidate those who were scheming to cast doubt on Islam and cause people to renounce it, where such schemes might deceive the weak in faith whose hearts are yet to be fully assured. In this way, rather than conflicting with the verse, the Hadith complements it in rejecting compulsion.[44]

Rashīd Riḍā (d. 1935) adopted ʿAbduh's opinion in which he rejects compulsion in religion. Riḍā argued that killing apostates during the Prophet's time was to prevent the evil of the pagans and the scheming of certain Jewish communities who were at war with the new Muslim community at the time.[45] In that sense, it was a political decision and was not meant to persecute people for their religion. In commenting on the verse "And whoever of you reverts from his religion [to disbelief] and dies while he is a disbeliever—for those, their deeds have become worthless in this world and the Hereafter, and those are the companions of the Fire, they will abide therein eternally." (2:217), Riḍā expanded the conception of the revoked religion in this verse without making any reference to the punishment of apostasy. For Riḍā, the term "*al-dīn*" (religion) has three fundamental components: belief in Allah, belief in the Last Day, and good deeds, and thus renouncing these three fundamentals is a renunciation of religion.[46]

ʿAbd al-ʿAzīz Jāwīsh (d. 1929) also followed ʿAbduh's and Riḍā's in their opinion, stating that he had researched the issue of apostasy in the Sunnah and found that the Prophet only commanded the killing of fighter apostates. In his argument, the prophetic report commanding the killing of the apostate does not constitute a prescribed punishment (*ḥadd*). Instead, it should be interpreted contextually, not literally, as addressing a situation where

42. Rashīd Riḍā, *Tafsīr al-Manār*, vol. 3, 31.

43. Rashīd Riḍā, *Tafsīr al-Manār*, vol. 3, 31.

44. Rashīd Riḍā, *Tafsīr al-Manār*, vol. 3, 275.

45. Rashīd Riḍā, *al-Manār*, vol. 10, 285.

46. Rashid Riḍā, *Tafsīr al-Manār*, vol. 2, 253. Riḍā (vol. 1, 94) deems this understanding as one of the principles that *Sūrat al-Baqarah* contains.

apostasy was accompanied by joining the enemy's camp, thus the punishment is inclusive of *ḥadd al-ḥirābah*.[47]

Maḥmūd Shaltūt (d. 1963) hesitated to offer a judgment and believed that the view on this issue is open to change if we take the following into consideration: that many scholars do not accept establishing prescribed punishments on grounds of solitary report, that they do not simply hold disbelief as a justification for shedding blood but rather believe that it is the aggression against Muslims and the attempt to sway them away from Islam that counts as a justification, and that many verses of the Quran reject any compulsion in religion.[48]

In recent decades, the debate surfaced again in parallel to the heated debates on human rights, especially in light of the incidents of apostasy in Egypt and other countries for which *fatwās* were issued.[49] In their pursuit to prove that Islam is in conformity with the freedom of belief and human rights, some lawyers and writers in Syria and Egypt declared that an apostate should not be killed, and that freedom of belief must be asserted. In response, some scholars stressed that this debate was groundless given that the ruling did not stir doubt in the past centuries, and was only questioned by those attempting to undermine Islam.[50] Thus, while accepting the ruling of the early scholars, the modern endeavors were devoted to formulate new justifications that align with the values of modernity. For some, apostasy was seen as equivalent to *ḥirābah*, where publicly renouncing Islam and persistently promoting anti-Islamic ideas was seen as a premeditated act of *ḥirābah* that translates into scheming against Islam and Muslims, planting the seeds of misguidance, and casting doubt about Islamic beliefs and prin-

47. See ʿAbd al-ʿAzīz Jāwīsh, *al-Islām Dīn al-Fiṭra wa al-Ḥurriyyah* (Cairo: Dār al-Kitāb al-Maṣrī; Alexandria: Alexandria Library; Beirut: Dār al-Kitāb al-Lubnānī, 2011), 228–36.

48. Maḥmūd Shaltūt, *al-Islām ʿAqīdah wa Sharīʿah*, 18th ed. (Cairo: Dār al-Shurūq, 2001), 281.

49. It started with the execution of Maḥmūd Muḥammad Ṭāha in Sudan due to apostasy (in 1985) and Al-Khūmaynī's fatwā to execute Salmān Rushdī because of apostasy (in 1989). Incidents in Egypt that were described as apostasy soon followed (Faraj Fūdah in 1992, Naṣr Ḥāmid Abū Zayd in 1993, and Nawāl al-Saʿdāwī in 2001). Other incidents in other countries have also occurred; for example: an Afghani called ʿAbd al-Raḥmān had converted from Islam to Christianity in 2006 whose case caught international attention.

50. Muḥammad Saʿīd Ramadān al-Būṭī, *al-Jihād fī al-Islām: kazfa nafhamuh wa kazfa numārisuh?*, 6th ed. (Damascus: Dār al-Fikr, 2008), 210. However, al-Būṭī's opinion regarding apostasy later changed.

ciples. Advocates of this view included Muḥammad Saʿīd Ramadān al-Būṭī (d. 2013) and others.[51]

Others held the view that apostasy is worse than *ḥirābah*, since it constitutes "insurgency against the Muslim state" equivalent to treason that is embodied in the attack on "the social and political order of the state and the custodians (*al-qāʾimīn*) of Islam." This opinion builds on the premise that apostasy is the changing of loyalty and affiliation from Islam to its adversaries as adopted by Sayyid Quṭb (d. 1966) and Muḥammad al-Ghazālī (d. 1996).[52] Al-Qaraḍāwī argues that "apostasy is a change of loyalty, an alteration of identity, and a redirection of affiliation, where the apostate turns his loyalty and affiliation from one nation to another, and from one homeland to another; that is from the abode of Islam to another."[53] As for Muḥammad Salīm al-ʿAwwā, he argues that this penalty is "disciplinary in nature left to the discretion of the pertinent authorities in the Islamic state to decide on the appropriate punishments, and the authorities are not blameworthy if execution is decided as a penalty."[54] According to his view, the Prophet's statement, "kill him," indicates permission, not obligation.

In summary, several interpretations were offered for the punishment for apostasy. Some revisited the ruling on the basis of the general rule of no compulsion in religion. Others accepted the ruling but sought to elaborate new justifications that are aligned and compatible with modern thought. However, what is common to all these approaches is that they do acknowledge that the ruling is somewhat problematic in contemporary times in light of the prevailing values of freedom of belief and freedom of religion in general.

---

51. al-Būṭī, *al-Jihād fī al-Islām* 212. Al-Būṭī changed his opinion later on via a televised episode and argued that punishment for apostasy is determined by *al-Siyāsah al-Sharʿiyyah* (politics/leadership), meaning that it is not a fixed ruling; Riḍā and ʿAbduh hold the same opinion.

52. See Muḥammad al-Ghazālī, *Ḥuqūq al-Insān bayna Taʿālīm al-Islām wa Iʿlān al-Ummam al-Muttaḥadah*, 4th ed. (Cairo: Nahḍat Miṣr, 2005), 81; Sayyid Quṭb, *Fī Ẓilāl al-Qurʾān*, vol. 2, 17th ed. (Cairo: Dār al-Shurūq, 1992), 908–17, and Muḥammad ʿĀbid al-Jābirī, "Ḥukm al-Murtad fī al-Islām," in *al-Ittiḥād*, August 14, 2007.

53. See Yūsuf al-Qaraḍāwī, *Jarīmat al-Riddah wa ʿUqūbat al-Murtad fī Ḍawʾ al-Qurʾān wa al-Sunnah* (Beirut: Muʾasasat al-Risāalah, 2001), and the televised episode previously mentioned.

54. See Muḥammad Salīm al-ʿAwwā, *Fī Uṣūl al-Niẓām al-Jināʾī al-Islāmī: Dirāsah Muqāranah* (Cairo: Nahḍat Miṣr, 2006), 191–95. The book was also published by Dār al-Shurūq several years ago.

JURIDICAL DISCOURSE: METHODOLOGY, HISTORY, AND VALUES

This rigorous tracing of the punishment for apostasy and the pertaining classical and modern *fiqhī* arguments demonstrates the complex challenge for *fiqh* in light of the modern nation-state, and for which there are three dimensions: the methodological, the historical, and the governing moral values.

First, the methodological dimension pertains to the mechanisms through which *fiqhī* rulings are generated, which eventually become "Divine rulings" (*aḥkām* Allah). There are various mechanisms starting from the scripture and what derives from it (such as the techniques for interpretation and the methods of induction), and concluding with juristic *ijmāʿ*. These mechanisms constitute the *fiqhī* system, which deems any generated ruling categorical and leaving no room for reconsideration of the ruling, its premises, or the historical and methodological context in which it was derived.

The modern and classical discussions of the punishment for apostasy reveal the potential for multiple interpretations of the scripture and of the historical context. Yet, the classical *fiqhī* interpretations seem more consistent and cohesive given their formation under a methodological and conceptual *fiqhī* system that has its own foundations and applications in the discipline of *fiqh*,[55] and within an ethico-legal system that departs from that of the modern nation-state. The modern interpretations attempt to reconcile a legal ruling that belongs to premodern law with the modern context that builds on secular norms to redefine societal relationships, freedoms, and rights. Apostasy, here, becomes essentially connected to state power (*al-sulṭah*) for it entails several rulings and laws, rather than being an individual concern that can be resolved by a *fatwā* or an individual application.

Modern scholarship has endeavored to rationalize the *fiqhī* ruling in alignment with the modern context, a context that is essentially different from that in which the *fiqhī* ruling was originally concluded. To that end, scholars invoked modern justifications to rationalize it and integrate it with modern norms. Yet, this exercise neglected the interconnections with a set

---

55. Our research is focused only on the temporal punishment for apostasy. However, there are several other rulings concerned with apostasy, including the punishment in the hereafter, marriage, inheritance, rights, and the children of the apostate.

of other rulings and issues within the *fiqhī* system such as marriage and inheritance, and treated the punishment for apostasy as a stand-alone ruling that can be dealt with independently of this network. Accepting that the effective (although perhaps not the actionable) reason for killing the apostate is "high treason" or "the change of loyalty and alteration of identity" from Islam to another belief creates real problems in application, as in European context. If loyalty and identity are only based on religion, how would that apply in the case of Western Muslims who live in Western countries and carry those nationalities? Would that understanding of loyalty, identity, and treason apply to them by virtue of their citizenship in a non-Muslim state? Does this kind of argument entail an equal legal standing of the one who converts to Islam and then forsakes it and the one who has not accepted Islam in the first place? In this case, the meaning of compulsion materializes in both entering and leaving the religion, since the issue here would be based on loyalty and betrayal, making it difficult to explain the religious plurality that has been a constant characteristic of the Muslim society.

If we were to accept the view that openly adopting and promoting apostasy is a form of *ḥirābah* and rebellion against the social fabric, then such an argument will render any call be it political, social, ideological, or religious a form of *ḥirābah* in the eyes of its adversaries. This in turn will endanger the future of the Islamic *daʿwa* (call/invitation) itself, building on reciprocity, as there can be no plausible legal justification to make the Islamic *daʿwa* an exception. Such arguments presume that religion is the only foundation on which social communities form, and thus create problems for communities in the Muslim world as well as in the West.

Despite the agreement among Muslim jurists on the primacy of the Quran over the Sunnah in theory, the actual practice in the case of apostasy proved otherwise, where the reason behind the absence in the Quran of a temporal worldly punishment for apostasy, in spite of declaring a punishment in the hereafter, was not explored. Thus, the reconsideration of the punishment of apostasy elevates the methodological significance of: returning to the specifics of the legal cases involved, reexamining the operational legal principle applied in the juristic process in a given case, the divergence in the practice of juristic deduction, and the relationship between the Quran and Sunnah as they get invoked by jurists in each case. Thus, as always, historical context matters, as do the specifics of the law and the details of the legal cases themselves.

The general Quranic rule that asserts the freedom of belief and absolutely rejects any form of religious compulsion was sacrificed in favor of some prophetic reports that state that the killing of the apostate is acceptable. This has given rise to a form of reconciliation between the evidence from the Quran and that from the Sunnah: that the Sunnah qualifies the general statements of the Quran, or that the Quran is qualified by the Sunnah. Eventually, this leads to the conclusion that there is no compulsion to accept Islam but it is acceptable to compel someone to remain Muslim. This compulsion has been accepted as valid by both premodern scholars, such as al-Ṭabarī, and modern ones, such as al-Ṭāhir ibn ʿĀshūr.

In revisiting the methodology, upholding the centrality and dominance of the Quran over the past scripture and over the Sunnah is indispensable and the starting point. More studies and examination are necessary to determine the relationship between the Quran and the Sunnah. If it is concluded that freedom is one of the *maqāṣid al-sharīʿa* or a general Quranic rule, then other proofs are to be evaluated and understood in light of that rule not the opposite. It is inapt to render the Quranic proof a malleable reference that can be subjected to inconclusive interpretations as is practiced in *fiqhī* induction. Instead, it is necessary to introduce an interpretation that harmonizes all different narrations of the same Hadith, or of the related prophetic Hadiths and incidents with careful consideration of their historical contexts, to avoid misinterpretation and misapplication such as misjudging the relative as absolute or treating the historical as timeless. Thus, these interpretations should be judged in light of *maqāṣid al-sharīʿa*, or universal principles, in order to give rise to a consistent and harmonious system that is most fit for working with the divine revelation that is free of contradiction and divergence.

The second dimension, the historical, is concerned with how the *fiqhī* rulings were dealt with independently of the historical context, how they were judged as conclusive and immutable, and how the diverging opinions were marginalized and excluded. This exclusion of certain opinions has contributed to the rigidity of the ruling in the contemporary times and the misperception that rethinking the *fiqhī* ruling constitutes a "distortion of Islam." Another consequence is that the *fiqhī* ruling has turned into a symbol in the ideological and intellectual struggles and a tool in political struggles. It is for this reason that the historical context was given considerable weight in this study.

The third dimension is that of the governing moral values that underlie the *fiqhī* rulings. Previous studies focused on defending the punishment for apostasy or objecting to it, but overlooked the change in governing moral values with the advent of modern times. While one can infer some of the moral values underlying the argumentation in both the classical and reformist texts, the focus of the contemporary studies has been mainly on the traditional *fiqhī* argumentation and its tools (starting with the early works such as *tafsīr al-manār* and the work of ʿAbd al-Mutaʿāl al-Ṣaʿīdī [d. 1966] up to the contemporary writings of Ṭāha al-ʿIlwānī [d. 2016] and others).

According to the premodern Muslim jurists, the governing ethical value underlying the *fiqhī* ruling of killing the apostate is that of "coercion into the true religion" or "rightful compulsion." Identifying this underlying value explains their preoccupation with the discussion on changing religions which revolved around the binary of the true religion—Islam—and false religions for which the jurists provided some gradation (some religions were considered to be acknowledged by Islam such as Judaism and Christianity, while others were not, such as paganism [*wathaniyyah*] and atheism [*zandaqah*]). Thus, classical jurists categorized changing religions into three categories: converting from a false religion to a false religion (with some gradation), converting from the true religion (Islam) to a false religion (*ridda*), and converting from a false religion to the true religion (Islam).[56]

The *fiqhī* reasoning was accordingly based on the abovementioned categorizations. For example, al-Shāfiʿī argues: "He who converts from a religion other than Islam to any other religion converts from falsehood to falsehood, and should not be killed for abandoning falsehood. He should only be killed for abandoning the Truth."[57] The governing moral value in the classical times was that of the permissibility of coercing those who did not belong to an acknowledged religion into the true religion. For this reason, Qatāda interpreted the verse "there is no compulsion in religion" by arguing that "Arabs did not have a religion and thus they were coerced into Islam by the sword," and added that "the Jews, Christians and Magans are not to be

56. One of the oldest texts concerning changing one's religion is Anas ibn Mālik's comment on the Hadith of "he who changes his religion" in *al-Muwwaṭṭa*ʾ; and al-Shāfiʿī's text in Al-Shāfiʿī, *al-Umm*, vol. 2, 569. See also ibn ʿAbd al-Barr, *al-Istidhkār*, vol. 22, 138–39, and *al-Mawsūʿah al-Fiqhiyyah al-Kuwaytiyyah*, vol. 10 (Kuwait: Ministry of endowment and Islamic Affairs, n.d.), 294–95.

57. Al-Shāfiʿī, *al-Umm*, vol. 2, 569.

coerced provided they pay *jizyah*."[58] The Shāfiʿī jurist Abū Bakr al-Qaffāl (d. 365/976) concurred: "The benefit of fighting over religion cannot be denied. This is because most people are attached to their false religions by habit and familiarity. This prevents them from contemplating the proofs that are presented to them. When they enter into the true religion due to fear of being killed, the love for their false religion starts to weaken and their love for the true religion starts to get stronger. They eventually fully convert from falsehood to truth and from deserving eternal punishment to deserving eternal reward."[59] It is worth noting that scholars are in agreement on the permissibility of compulsion in religion since even those who are for abandoning the punishment for apostasy did not realize that demanding repentance is a form of compulsion even if it does not involve killing. The constant demand for repentance can be a proof against killing the apostate, but it cannot be used to negate compulsion in principle.

Thus, the essence of the disagreement is the underlying moral value. In light of this, Rashīd Riḍā refuted the opinion of Fakhr al-Dīn al-Rāzī (d. 606/1210) and al-Qaffāl regarding compulsion in religion, saying: "The argument for compulsion is false and is founded upon shaky foundations ... compulsion in religion is rejected in Islam by the Quran, and the Prophet did not fight anyone, be it Arab or other, to coerce them into Islam but rather fought in self-defense. How can he coerce anyone when the verse tells him, "would you compel the people in order that they become believers?" (10:99). He further added that the scholars who defend compulsion do so in imitation but then manipulate the scripture to serve as proof, rather than having it serve as a source, at the time when compulsion is in clear violation of the explicit verses of the Quran. Despite this, these scholars continue to assert that the greatest characteristic of Islam is following the proof and abandoning imitation.[60] However, the essence of this disagreement is essentially beyond what Riḍa captured. Al-Qaffāl and al-Rāzī are Shāfiʿīs, and the reasoning for *jihād* and fighting in their school builds on *kufr* (disbelief), which is also the stance of other schools except for the Ḥanafīs. Thus, the

58. Ibn Abī Ḥātim, *Tafsīr al-Qurʾān al-ʿAẓīm*, ed. Asʿad al-Tayyib, vol. 2 (Mecca: Maktabat Nizār Muṣṭafā al-Bāz,1419/1998), 493–94.

59. Al-Rāzī, Fakhr al-Dīn al-Rāzī, *Mafātīḥ al-Ghayb*, vol. 8 (Beirut: Dār Iḥyāʾ al-Turāth al-ʿArabī, 1420/1999), 326.

60. Rashīd Riḍā, *Tafsīr al-Manār*, vol. 4, 50–52.

application of this governing moral value reaches beyond apostasy to other rulings. The Ḥanbalīs, for instance, build on "rightful compulsion" other *fiqhī* rulings such as the coercion of the husband into rightful divorce by a judge.[61]

CONCLUSION

This chapter presented the different discussions on religious freedom and on compulsion in religion in two distinct periods: the classical period, and the modern and contemporary period. In addition, it expounded the dimensions of the debate around the value of religious freedom and the bases upon which it was argued that it is ethical to coerce people into religion. For such an analysis, the chapter looked into the historical contexts in which different arguments appeared.

In this chapter, religious freedom and the punishment for apostasy were used as exemplars through which to demonstrate the *fiqhī* thinking, its foundations and bases, and its tools for induction and argument. In response, the chapter proposed to revisit this thinking through a critical approach with three dimensions: the methodological, the historical, and the ethical. Under the ethical dimension, the chapter demonstrated how the change of ethical values left its mark on the *fiqhī* discussions even if these values where not explicitly addressed and the discussions seemed to focus on *fiqhī* linguistics and interpretation. This dimension was largely missed in previous works.

Such a critical approach is poised to have a significant effect in revisiting other areas of *fiqh*, such as that of *maqāṣid al-sharīʿa*. The five objectives (preservation of religion, human life, intellect, lineage, and property) were concluded from the five prescribed punishments for apostasy, killing, drinking alcohol, theft, and adultery. Accordingly, some contemporaries justify the punishment for apostasy by the threat it poses to the first objective of Sharia that Islam is keen on protecting—that is, religion. Should we uphold religious freedom and extend this critical approach to other punishments, such

61. See Muḥammad ibn ʿAbdullāh al-Zarkashī, *Sharḥ al-Zarkashī ʿlā Mukhtaṣar al-Khiraqī fī al-Fiqh ʿalā Madhhab al-Imām Aḥmad ibn Ḥanbal*, ed. ʿAbdullāh ibn ʿAbd al-Raḥmān ibn ʿAbdullāh al-Jibrīn, vol. 5 (Al-Riyadh: Maktabat al-ʿUbaykān, 1993), 392; ibn Qudāmah al-Maqdisī, *al-Mughnī*, vol. 7, 383, and Muṣṭafā ibn Saʿd al-Ruḥaybānī, *Maṭālib Ulī al-Nuhā fī Sharḥ Ghāyat al-Muntahā*, vol.3, 2nd ed. (Beirut: al-Maktab al-Islāmī, 1994), 10.

as stoning (*rajm*) for adultery, then it is inevitable that this connection of prescribed punishments to *maqāṣid al-sharīʿa* will be problematized. This might entail the need to separate *maqāṣid al-sharīʿa* from prescribed punishments, redefine this relationship, or reformulate the notion of *maqāṣid al-sharīʿa* in the first place, since limiting the objectives to five and only reconsidering some of them will prove problematic.

References

Abū Zakariyyā Yaḥyā al-Nawawī. *al-Minhāj Sharḥ Ṣaḥīḥ Muslim ibn al-Ḥajjāj*. Vol. 12, 2nd ed. Beirut: Iḥyāʾ al-Turāth al-ʿArabī, 1973.

Al-ʿAsqalānī, Shihāb al-Dīn Aḥmad ibn Ḥajar. *Fatḥ al-Bārī bi-Sharḥ Saḥīḥ al-Imām Abī ʿAbdillāh Muḥammad ibn Ismāʿīl al-Bukhārī*. Vol. 12. Edited by ʿAbd al-Qādir Shybah al-Ḥamad. Al-Riyadh: N.p., 2001.

Al-ʿAwwā, Muḥammad Salīm. *Fī Uṣūl al-Niẓām al-Jināʾī al-Islāmī: Dirāsah Muqāranah*. Cairo: Nahḍat Miṣr, 2006.

Al-Balādhurī, Abū al-ʿAbbās Aḥmad ibn Yaḥyā. *Jumal min Ansāb al-Ashrāf*. Edited by Suhayl zakkār and Riyāḍ al-Ziriklī, vol. 1. Beirut: Dār al-Fikr, 1996.

Al-Barr, Abū ʿUmar Yūsuf ibn ʿAbdullāh ibn ʿAbd. *al-Istidhkār al-Jāmiʿ li-Madhāhib Fuqahāʾ al-Amṣār wa ʿUlamāʾ al-Aqṭār fī mā Taḍammanahu al-Muwwaṭṭaʾ min Maʿānī al-Raʾy wa al-Āthār wa Sharḥ dhālika Kullihi bil-Ījāz wa al-Ikhtiṣār*. Edited by ʿAbd al-Muʿṭī Qalʿajī, vol. 22. Damascus: Dār Qutayba; Ḥalab: Dār al-Waʿy, 1993.

Al-Barr, Abū ʿUmar Yūsuf ibn ʿAbdullāh ibn ʿAbd. *al-Tamhīd li mā fī al-Muwaṭṭaʾ min al-Maʿānī wa al-Asānīd*. Edited by Muṣṭafā ibn Aḥmad al-ʿAlawī and Muḥammad ʿAbd al-Kabīr al-Bakrī, vol. 5. Ribat: Ministry of Endowment and Islamic Affairs, 1986.

Al-Bayhaqī, Abū Bakr ibn Ḥusayn. *Maʿrifat al-Sunan wa al-Āthār*. Edited by ʿAbd al-Muʿṭī Amīn Qalʿajī, vol. 12. Damascus: Dār Qutaybah, Dār al-Waʿī, 1991.

Al-Bazdawī, Muḥammad ibn Muḥammad. *Maʿrifat al-Ḥujaj al-Sharʿiyyah*. Edited by ʿAbd al-Qādir ibn Yāsīn ibn Nāṣir al-Khaṭīb. Beirut: Muʾassasat al-Risālah, 2000.

Al-Bukhārī, Abū ʿAbdullāh Muḥammad ibn Ismāʿīl. *Al-Jāmiʿ al-Musnad al-Saḥīḥ al-Mukhtaṣar min Umūr Rasūl Allāh Ṣalla Allāhu ʿAlayhi wa Sallam wa Sunanihi wa Ayyāmih*. Edited by Muḥammad Zuhayr ibn Nāṣir al-Nāṣir, vol. 4. Beirut: Dār Ṭawq al-Najāh, 2002.

Al-Būṭī, Muḥammad Saʿīd Ramadān. *al-Jihād fī al-Islām: kayfa nafhamuh wa kayfa numārisuh?* 6th ed. Damascus: Dār al-Fikr, 2008.

Al-Ghannūshī, Rāshid. *al-Sharīʿa wa al-Ḥayāt*. A program on Al Jazeera, an episode entitled "al-Ḥurriyyah wa Muqāwamat al-Istibdād." May 24, 2015.

Al-Ghazālī, Abū Ḥāmid Muḥammad ibn Muḥammad. *Al-Muṣtaṣfā min ʿIlm al-Uṣūl*. Edited by ʿAbd al-Salām ʿAbd al-Shāfī. Beirut: Dār al-Kutub al-ʿIlmiyyah, 1993.

Al-Ghazālī, Muḥammad. *Ḥuqūq al-Insān bayna Ta'ālīm al-Islām wa al-I'lān al-Ummam al-Muttaḥidah*. 4th ed. Cairo: Nahḍat Miṣr, 2005.

Al-Ḥajjāj, Abū al-Ḥusayn Muslim ibn. *al-Musnad al-Ṣaḥīḥ al-Mukhtaṣar bi-Naql al-'Adl 'an al-'Adl ilā Rasūl Allāh Ṣallā Allāhu 'Alayhi wa Sallam*. Edited by Muḥammad Fu'ād 'Abd al-Bāqī, vol. 3. Beirut: Dār Iḥyā' al-Turāth al-'Arabī, n.d.

Al-Ḥarrānī, Abū al-'Abbās Aḥmad ibn 'Abd al-Ḥalīm ibn Taymiyyah. *al-Ṣārim al-Maslūl 'alā Shātim al-Rasūl*. Edited by Muḥammad Muḥyī al-Dīn 'Abd al-Ḥamīd, vol. 1. al-Riyadh: al-Ḥaras al-Waṭanī al-Su'ūdī, 1983.

Al-Iṣfahānī, Abū al-Qāssim al-Ḥusayn ibn Muḥammad al-Rāghib. *al-Dharī'ah ilā Makārim al-Sharī'a*. Edited by Abū al-Yazīd Abū Zayd al-'Ajamī. Cairo: Dār al-Salām, 2007.

Al-Jābirī, Muḥammad 'Ābid. "Ḥukm al-Murtadd fī al-Islām." *al-Ittiḥād*, August 14, 2007.

Al-Maqdisī, Abū Muḥammad 'Abdullāh ibn Aḥmad ibn Qudāmah. *Al-Mughnī*. Vol. 9. Cairo: Maktabat al-Qāhirah, 1968.

Al-Mawsū'ah al-Fiqhiyyah al-Kuwaitiyyah. Vol. 10. Kuwait: Ministry of Endowment and Islamic Affairs, n.d.

Al-Nasā'ī, Abū 'Abd al-Raḥmān ibn Shu'ayb. *al-Mujtabā min al-Sunnan: al-Sunan al-Ṣughrā*. Edited by 'Abd al-Fattāḥ Abū Ghuddah, vol. 7, 2nd ed. Ḥalab, Syria: Maktab al-Maṭbū'āt al-Islāmiyyah, 1986.

Al-Naysābūrī, Abū 'Abdullāh Muḥammad ibn 'Abdullāh al-Ḥākim. *al-Mustadrak 'alā al-Ṣaḥīḥayn*. Edited by Muṣṭafā 'Abd al-Qādir 'Aṭā, vol. 2. Beirut: Dār al-Kutub al-'Ilmiyyah, 1990.

Al-Qaraḍāwī, Yūsuf. *al-Sharī'a wa al-Ḥayāt*. A program on Al-Jazeera, an episode entitled "al-Ḥurriyyah al-Dīniyyah wa al-Fikriyyah." February 1, 2005.

Al-Qaraḍāwī, Yūsuf. *al-Sharī'a wa al-Ḥayāt*. A program on Al-Jazeera, an episode entitled "al-Ḥurriyyah wa Ḍarūratuhā fī al-Islām." September 22, 2011.

Al-Qaraḍāwī, Yūsuf. *Jarīmat al-Riddah wa 'Uqūbat al-Murtadd fī Ḍaw' al-Qur'ān wa al-Sunnah*. Beirut: Mu'assasat al-Risālah, 2001.

Al-Rāzī, Fakhr al-Dīn. *Mafātīḥ al-Ghayb*. Vol. 32. Beirut: Dār Iḥyā' al-Turāth al-'Arabī, 1420/1999.

Al-Ruḥaybānī, Muṣṭafā ibn Sa'd. *Maṭālib Ulī al-Nuhā fī Sharḥ Ghāyat al-Muntahā*. Vol. 3, 2nd ed. Beirut: al-Maktab al-Islāmī, 1994.

Al-Ṣa'īdī, 'Abd al-Muta'āl. *al-Ḥurriyyah al-Dīniyyah fī al-Islām*. With introduction by 'Iṣmat Naṣṣār. Cairo: Dār al-Kitāb al-Maṣrī; Beirut: Dār al-Kitāb al-Lubnānī, 2012.

Al-Ṣan'ānī, 'Abd al-Razzāq ibn Hammām. *al-Muṣannaf*. Edited by Ḥabīb al-Raḥmān al-A'ẓamī, vol. 10, 2nd ed. Beirut: al-Maktab al-Islāmī, 1983.

Al-Sarakhsī, Muḥammad ibn Aḥmad. *al-Mabsūṭ*. Vol. 5. Beirut: Dār al-Ma'rifah, 1993.

Al-Shāfi'ī, Muḥammad Idrīs. *al-Umm*. Edited by Rif'at Fawzī 'Abd al-Muṭṭalib, vol. 2. Cairo: Maktabat al-Khānjī, n.d.

Al-Shawkānī, Muḥammad ibn ʿAlī. *Al-Sayl al-Jarrār al-Mutadaffiq ʿalā Ḥadāʾiq al-Azhār*. Vol. 1. Beirut: Dār Ibn Ḥazm, 2004.

Al-Ṭabarī, Abū Jaʿfar Muḥammad ibn Jarīr. *Tārīkh al-Rusul wa al-Mulūk*. Vol. 3, 2nd ed. Beirut: Dār Iḥyāʾ al-Turāth al-ʿArabī, 1968.

Al-Tahānawī, Muḥammad ʿAlī. *Mawsūʿat Kashshāf Iṣṭilāḥāt al-Funūn wa al-ʿUlūm*. Vol. 1. Beirut: Maktabat Lubnān Nāshirūn, 1996.

Al-Zarkashī, Muḥammad ibn ʿAbdullāh. *Sharḥ al-Zarkashī ʿalā Mukhtaṣar al-Khirqī fī al-Fiqh ʿalā Madhhab al-Imām Aḥmad ibn Ḥanbal*. Edited by ʿAbdullāh ibn ʿAbd al-Raḥmān ibn ʿAbdullāh al-Jibrīn, vol. 5. Al-Riyadh: Maktabat al-ʿUbaykān, 1993.

Anas, Mālik ibn. *Muwaṭṭaʾ al-Imām Mālik*. Edited by Muḥammad Fuʾād ʿAbd al-Bāqī, vol. 2. Beirut: Iḥyāʾ al-Turāth al-ʿArabī, 1985.

ʿĀshūr, Muḥammad Al-Ṭāhir ibn. *al-Taḥrīr wa al-Tanwīr*. Tunisia: al- Dār al-Tūnisiyyah li al-Nashr, 1984.

ʿĀshūr, Muḥammad al-Ṭāhir ibn. *Maqāṣid al-Sharīʿa*. Edited by Muḥammad al-Ḥabīb Bilkhūjah, vol. 3. Doha: Wizārat al-Awqāf wa al-Shuʾūn al-Islāmiyyah, 2004.

Cook, Michael. "Is Political Freedom an Islamic Value?" In *Freedom and the Construction of Europe*, vol. 2, edited by Quentin Skinner, 283–310. Cambridge: Cambridge University Press, 2013.

Dāwūd, Abū. *Sunan Abī Dāwūd*. Edited by Shuʿayib al-Arnāʾūṭ and Muḥammad Kāmil, vol. 6. Amman: Dār al-Salām al-ʿĀlamiyyah, 2009.

Decosimo, David. "Political Freedom as an Islamic Value." *Journal of the American Academy of Religion* 86, no. 4 (December 2018): 912–52.

Ḥātim, Ibn Abī. *Tafsīr al-Qurʾān al-ʿAẓīm, ed. Asʿad al-Tayyib*. Vol. 2. Saudi Arabia: Maktabat Nizār Muṣṭafā al-Bāz,1419/1998.

Ḥazm, Ibn. *al-Muḥallā bi-l Āthār*. Vol. 12. Beirut: Dār al-Fikr, n.d.

Ḥilalī, ʿAbd al-Raḥmān. *Ḥurriyyat al-Iʿtiqād fī al-Qurʾān al-Karīm: Dirāsah fī Ishkāliyyat al-Riddah wa al-Jihād wa al-Jizyah*. Beirut: al-Markaz al-Thaqāfī al-ʿArabī, 2001.

Hishām, Abū Muḥammad ʿAbd al-Malik ibn. *al-Sīrah al-Nabawiyyah*. Edited by Muṣṭafā al-Saqqā, Ibrāhīm al-Abyārī, and ʿAbd al-Ḥafīẓ al-Shalabī, vol. 2, 2nd ed. Cairo: Maṭbaʿat Muṣṭafā al-Bābī al-Ḥalabī, 1955.

Jāwīsh, ʿAbd al-ʿAzīz. *al-Islām Dīn al-Fiṭrah wa al-Ḥurriyyah*. Cairo: Dār al-Kitāb al-Maṣrī; Alexandria: Alexandria Library; Beirut: Dār al-Kitāb al-Lubnānī, 2011.

Kathīr, Ismāʿīl ibn ʿUmar ibn. *Tafsīr al-Qurʾān al-ʿAẓīm*. Edited by Sāmī ibn Muḥammad Salāmah, vol. 7. al-Riyadh: Dār Ṭaybah, 1999.

Miskawayh, Abū ʿAlī Aḥmad ibn Muḥammad. *Tahdhīb al-Akhlāq wa Taṭhīr al-Aʿrāq*. Cairo: Maktabat al-Thaqāfah al-Dīniyyah, 1998.

Quṭb, Sayyid. *Fī Ẓilāl al-Qurʾān*. Vol. 2, 17th ed. Cairo: Dār al-Shurūq, 1992.

Riḍā, Muḥammad Rashīd. *Tafsīr al-Manār*. Cairo: al-Hay'ah al-Miṣriyyah al-'Āmmah li al-Kitāb, 1990.

Shaltūt, Maḥmūd. *al-Islām 'Aqīdah wa Sharī'ah.*. 18th ed. Cairo: Dār al-Shurūq, 2001.

Shybah, Abū Bakr 'Abdullāh ibn Muḥammad ibn Abī. *al-Kitāb al-Muṣannaf fī al-Aḥādīth wa al-Āthār*. Edited by Kamāl Yūsuf al-Ḥūt, vol. 6. al-Riyadh: Makatabat al-Rushd, 1989.

The Politicization of Islamic Humanitarian Aid
The Case of Islamic NGOs

Ibrahim Yahaya Ibrahim
Crisis Group—Dakar

After the 9/11 attacks, the view of Islamic charities polarized between those who view them as the non-sword arm of terrorism and those who consider them as typical humanitarian organizations that politicize aid in the same way as their Western counterparts. Although each of these views captures a certain reality of Islamic charities, they downplay the diversity and complexity that characterize these charities and fail to adequately capture the ways in which this diversity affects the politicization of aid within some Muslim contexts. This chapter seeks to unpack the notion of Islamic charities by creating a taxonomy of Islamic humanitarian organizations (IHOs). It suggests patterned ways in which each ideal type of organization politicizes humanitarian aid.

In particular, the chapter suggests that IHOs can be categorized into four types according to their scale of intervention and religious pervasiveness. These types are (a) transnational-fundamentalist; (b) transnational-moderate; (c) national-fundamentalist; and (d) national-moderate. Each of these types of IHO has different objectives and therefore mobilizes and politicizes aid in a different manner. Whereas transnational fundamentalist IHOs follow an *ummah-centric* politics, transnational-moderate IHOs lean more toward a global civil-society approach. And while national-fundamentalist IHOs use humanitarian aid as a means of campaigning for the adoption of an Islamic way of life at a national level, national-moderate IHOs follow a national development-centric approach. Each of these four ideal types will be defined in detail in this chapter and elaborated through an analysis of four respective case studies: the International Islamic Relief Organization, Saudi Arabia (IIROSA, known since 2018 as the International Organization for Relief, Welfare and Development); the Islamic Relief Worldwide (IRWW), United Kingdom; the charitable branch of the Egyptian Muslim Brotherhood, Egypt; and the Islamic Council for Development and Humanitarian Services (ICODEHS), Ghana.

ISLAMIC HUMANITARIANISM AND JIHAD FINANCING

Islam, like many other religions, encourages believers to be generous toward those in need. A strong tradition of charitable giving evolved across the 15 centuries of Islamic history. Islamic charity, however, did not embody the "humanitarian" label until the 1960s and 1970s. In taking that label, it followed a general trend of adapting Western concepts of modernity to Islamic teachings and principles in significant parts of the Muslim world during that period. The notion of Islamic humanitarianism comes as a result of an effort to "hybridize" the concept of humanitarianism, which refers generally to the "technical delivery of relief in zones of disaster or conflict" and the practice of Islamic charity, which is based upon the Islamic principles of *zakat*, *waqf*, and *sadaqa*.[1]

Although this effort of hybridization started in the late 1960s as part of the process of Islamic revivalism (*an-nahdha al-Islamiyya*), it was not until the Afghan-Soviet War (1979–89) that IHOs became salient and recognized as important actors within the field of global humanitarianism.[2] In fact, throughout the Afghan-Soviet War, the US and Saudi governments

1. *Zakat*, meaning "that which purifies," or alms-giving. Zakat is the third of the five pillars of Islam. It is an obligatory payment imposed annually upon Muslims who have accumulated a certain level of wealth. It is used to ease economic hardship for others and eliminate inequality. See, for example, Lloyd Ridgeon, "Islam," in *Major World Religions: From Their Origins to the Present*, ed. Lloyd Ridgeon (New York: Routledge, 2003), 258. *Waqf* is an Islamic endowment, typically managed locally. It can include real estate, art, books, monies, and other forms of property. It is intended for use to support the local community and religious infrastructure. *Sadaqa* is a voluntary donation or a charitable act toward others. Contrary to *zakat*, which is mandatory, *sadaqa* is a voluntary act of giving to confirm the giver's true devotion and service to Allah.

2. Jonathan Benthall and Jerome Bellion-Jourdan, *The Charitable Crescent: The Politics of Aid in the Muslim World* (London: I.B.Tauris, 2003).

used a number of IHOs as channels to convey humanitarian and military support to the Afghan and international Mujahideen forces who fought against the Soviet army. In the years following this early collaboration with Mujahideen, IHOs have been suspected of serving as funnels of jihad financing in many places in the world, including the Balkans, the Caucasus, Southeast Asia, Europe, Sudan, and Palestine. However, the relationship between IHOs and international jihad remained largely mysterious until the 9/11 attacks, when efforts to dismantle Al Qaeda brought its sources of financing under intensive scrutiny. Following that, the US Department of Treasury established a task force to track the foreign terrorist institutions that financed them. US investigators identified Islamic charities as the main channel through which money flowed to Al Qaeda. The United States government designated 46 Islamic charities as foreign terrorist organizations, and some authors asserted that avowedly Islamic groups have supported "tens of thousands of terrorist attacks."[3]

Although the US government has failed to provide legal proof sufficient for the conviction of these Islamic charities in court, many observers have still continued to view mainstream Islamic charities as venues for terrorist financing, or, at least, they tend to see support of terrorism by Islamic charities as the rule rather than the exception.[4] The outbreak of Islamic insurgencies in the Sahel is often correlated with the proliferation of IHOs in the region.

While this view dominated the debate in the post 9/11 era, there is an opposing view that challenged these allegations against IHOs. A group of Saudi scholars, for instance, wrote a book entitled *Letter to the West: A Saudi View*, in which they respond to the post-9/11 criticism against Saudi Arabia, its version of Islam, and its charitable organizations accused of supporting terrorism. The argument of the Saudi scholars was that the activities of Saudi charities are not different from those of any other charity in the world. They are apolitical organizations that aim at offering help and assistance for the poor, the needy, the homeless and the refugees . . . "exactly the same objective as charities have in the West."[5] The alleged connection

3. Jon B. Alterman and Karin von Hippel, eds., *Understanding Islamic Charities* (Washington, DC: Center for Strategic and International Studies, 2007).

4. Alterman and von Hippel, *Understanding Islamic Charities*.

5. Mohammed Ben Saud Al-Bishr, *Letter to the West: A Saudi View* (Ghaina'a Publications, 2008), 197–98.

to terrorism is only the result of rare cases of infiltration of some Islamic charities by radical elements. They argue that these rare cases "do not at all justify generalization or campaigning against particular charitable institutions [since] penetration does occur even in the most cautious and highly trained intelligence services."[6] Many Western scholars admit the idea of similarity between Western and Islamic charities and warn against the risk of overgeneralization.

Each of these views captures a certain reality of Islamic charities. The seeming contradiction between them comes from the fact that they consider Islamic humanitarianism as a homogeneous unit of similar and like-minded organizations; or, when they acknowledge diversity among IHOs, they fail to identify the characteristics of this diversity and systematically examine the way this diversity affects the process of their politicization of relief assistance. Sometimes the analysts are careful to recognize that not all Islamic charities are related to terrorist activities. However, the distinction between those that are related, and those that are not, is blurred by the overemphasis on the former, or even by the temptation to generalize the former over the latter, or by both.[7]

THEORETICAL FRAMEWORK: UNDERSTANDING POLITICIZATION OF ISLAMIC HUMANITARIAN AID

The debate regarding political versus apolitical humanitarianism is echoed in the literature on IHOs as well. According to one view, Islamic NGOs are apolitical because they do not participate in formal political institutions, lobby state officials, or engage in overt protests. They are devoted to development issues and cultural awareness.[8] Moreover, the legal codes governing

6. Al-Bishr, *Letter to the West*, 198.

7. According to both Victor Comras and Robert Looney, even if Islamic NGOs do not directly finance terrorism, the very activities of conversion in which they are engaged are supportive to al-Qaeda. See Victor Comras, "Al Qaeda Finances and Funding to Affiliated Groups," in *The Political Economy of Terrorism Finance and State Responses: A Comparative Perspective*, ed. Jeanne K. Giraldo and Harold A. Trinkunas (Palo Alto: Stanford University Press, 2006), and Robert Looney, "The Mirage of Terrorist Financing: The Case of Islamic Charities," *Strategic Insights* 5, no. 3 (2006).

8. Quintan Wiktorowicz and Farouki S. Taji, "Islamic NGOs and Muslim Politics: A Case from Jordan," *Third World Quarterly* 21, no. 4 (2000): 685–99.

NGO work throughout the Middle East strictly prohibit transgressions into the political arena. As a result, Islamic NGO volunteers and activists claim that they do not have a political agenda, program, or purpose.[9] Instead, their activities are framed in terms of religious obligations of charity and *da'wa*—missionary work. Alternatively, some argue that this interpretation limits the scope of "the political" to institutions, actors, and behavior that are directly engaged in the state or public policy.[10] Such scholars suggest that groups and organizations that are apolitical in their identity can engage in very politically charged activities such as mobilizing, encouraging political participation, distribution of goods and services, and advocacies. Therefore, even though Islamic NGOs are not part of state institutions and do not participate in protests, the nature of their activities places them at the heart of politics.

The analysis of Islamic NGOs' politicization of humanitarian aid involves a debate between scholars who emphasize the role of Islam as a determinant factor in the conception and delivery of Islamic humanitarianism, on the one hand, and those who view Islamic charity through the prism of humanitarianism in general Islamic political theories, on the other hand. Scholars who build on essentialist theories, such as the clash of civilizations or *ummatic* transnationalism, approach IHOs from a particularistic point of view. In contrast, those who build on what should be called "contingencist" theories place Islamic NGOs in the broad context of humanitarian organization.

The essentialist-based analysts approach IHOs through the impact of the Islamist ideology over their humanitarian activism. Three major trends can be identified within this school. First, the relationship between terrorism and Islamic charities became a prominent topic especially after the events of 9/11 and following several governmental reports.[11] In their widely discussed book, *Alms of Jihad*, Millard Burr and Robert Collins[12] demonstrate that the most important Islamic charities were associated with terrorist activism and that "money from Islamic charities has funded conflicts across the world."

---

9. See Janine Clark, *Islam, Charity, and Activism* (Bloomington: Indiana University Press, 2004), and Wiktorowicz and Taji, "Islamic NGOs."

10. Wiktorowicz and Taji, "Islamic NGOs."

11. See, for example, Millard J. Burr and Robert O. Collins, *Alms of Jihad: Charity and Terrorism in the Islamic World* (New York: Cambridge University Press, 2006); Comras, "Al Qaeda Finances and Funding to Affiliated Groups"; Rachel Ehrenfeld, *Funding Evil: How Terrorism Is Financed—and How to Stop It* (New Rochelle, NY: Multieducator, 2003), and Looney, "Mirage of Terrorist Financing."

12. Burr and Collins, *Alms of Jihad*.

Second, Islamic NGOs are considered to participate in the revival of the spirit of *ummah* among the Muslim community worldwide using charity.[13] Jawad Rana[14] argues that "unlike ordinary forms of taxation or insurance, *zakat* is supposed to cement the sense of fellow feeling between Muslims and bind together the ummah." Third, some scholars consider the development and expansion of Islamic humanitarianism as a conscious reaction of some Muslim elites to the Westernization of Muslim societies by secular and Christian humanitarian organizations.[15]

On the other side, contingencist scholars downplay the Islamist particularism of IHOs and prefer approaching them from the perspective of mainstream humanitarianism. For example, Jonathan Benthall and Jerome Bellion-Jourdan[16] consider IHOs to be similar to Christian and secular organizations. They argue that the political and military use of aid is not a monopoly of Islamic charities: Christian charities used humanitarian channels to convey military support to the Irish Free State in 1921 and to Biafran rebels in Nigeria.[17] Secular NGOs have also supported the Afghan Mujahideen during the Soviet invasion of Afghanistan. Extremist Zionists and Hindus have also been raising funds for extreme political ends. IHOs are, rather, similar to all kinds of humanitarian organizations. They conclude that aid "[has] never existed in a political vacuum."[18]

I argue that none of these approaches is entirely false, and, yet, neither are they entirely true. They each suffer from the same problem of generalization. While it may be true that some Islamic NGOs have politicized aid in ways that support Islamist military groups, it is also

13. Ismail Yaylaci, "Communitarian Humanitarianism: The Politics of IHOs," paper presented at the Workshop on Religion and Humanitarianism, American University of Cairo, June 3–5, 2007; Jawad Rana, "Social Welfare and Religion in the Middle East: A Lebanese Perspective," *Social Policy & Administration* 44, no. 7 (2010): 872–74; M. Kaag, "Transnational Islamic NGOs in Chad: Islamic Solidarity in the Age of Neoliberalism," *Africa Today* 54, no. 3 (2008): 3–18; Marie Juul Petersen, *For Humanity or for the Ummah? Ideologies of Aid in Four Transnational Muslim NGOs* (Copenhagen: University of Copenhagen Press, 2011).

14. Rana, "Social Welfare and Religion," 60.

15. See Jonathan Benthall, "Humanitarianism and Islam after 11 September," in *Humanitarian Action and the 'Global War on Terror': A Review of Trends and Issues*, ed. J. Macrae and A. Harmer (London: Overseas Development Institute, 2003), and Wiktorowicz and Taji, "Islamic NGOs."

16. Benthall and Bellion-Jourdan, *Charitable Crescent*.

17. Benthall and Bellion-Jourdan, *Charitable Crescent*, 155.

18. Benthall and Bellion-Jourdan, *Charitable Crescent*, 154.

true that many Islamic NGOs operate in the same way as their Christian and even secular counterparts. The seeming contradiction between these approaches is the cumulative effect of the thus far (misleading) generalizations regarding IHOs. In fact, these approaches describe, and may conflate, different types of IHOs, while failing to specify the traits of this diversity (in general or in particular cases) and the particulars of how that diversity affects the politicization of relief assistance in each instance. Overall, I argue that the analysis of the politicization of Islamic humanitarian aid suffers from the lack of a theoretical framework—or a taxonomy of cases—to encapsulate the Islamic charities in all their diversity and complexity. Instead, as most studies already mentioned demonstrate, scholars identify some particular patterns within certain Islamic charities, which they examine through well-selected case studies. This approach is too narrow and does not allow for (valid) generalization. In the pages below, I attempt to parse the notion of IHOs by classifying them into four categories, based upon the variables (a) *degree of religious pervasiveness*[19] and (b) *scale of social intervention*.[20] I define each below and examine how organizations within each of the four resultant categories politicize humanitarian aid.

TYPOLOGIES OF ISLAMIC HUMANITARIAN ORGANIZATIONS

IHOs are considered to be "religious NGOs." I define them, paraphrasing the definition of religious NGOs provided by Kerstin Martens[21] as *for-*

19. By *degree of religious pervasiveness*, I mean the degree to which religion, per se, is a critical component of the organization's social programing. Religious programs, activities, or goals refers to theological, doctrinal, spiritual, and other specifically religious activities and goals. It may include the giving of books, the building of mosques or community centers, or other types of religious programs of a humanitarian nature.

20. By *scale of social intervention*, I mean national *versus* transnational charity and other humanitarian activities. Social intervention itself refers to humanitarian interventions in society. Social interventions may be religious or nonreligious (e.g., the providing of food and clothing, on the one hand, or of books, mosques, and community centers, on the other hand). The critical component of this variable is to be found in the word *scale*: Is the IHO's social intervention found at the national level, or is it transnational in nature?

21. Kerstin Martens, "Mission Impossible? Defining Nongovernmental Organizations," *International Journal of Voluntary and Non-Profit Organizations* 13, no. 3 (2002): 271–85.

mal organizations whose identity and mission are self-consciously derived from the teachings of Islam and which operate on a nonprofit, independent, voluntary basis to promote and realize collectively articulated ideas about the public good at the national or international level. Thus, IHO is a generic term that encompasses an array of organizations that share some commonalities in terms of the voluntary nature of their activity, the belief in the core values of Islam, the reliance on the same major sources of funds (*zakat*, *waqf*, and *sadaqa*),[22] while, at the same time, they vary on several other issues, such as their scale of intervention, religiosity, and sectarian and geographical characteristics.

Many typologies of IHOs can be created using different variables; however, in order to understand the politicization of humanitarian aid, two variables appear particularly determinant: the scale of intervention (whether the organization is national or transnational) and the religious pervasiveness (whether the organization follows a fundamentalist or moderate Islamic ideology). In fact, despite their self-identification as religious organizations, IHOs do not have the same level of religiosity. Some organizations follow a strict religious doctrine, their mission statement contains a powerful ideological message, and they engage in activities that have clear religious objectives; others are Islamic in name or by community, but they do not pursue any Islamic theological or spiritual objectives.

Also, whereas some IHOs intervene only at the national level, others have a global or transnational reach. National organizations pursue objectives at the national level and their activities are circumscribed within the nation-state boundaries, while transnational organizations follow interests at the global level and their activities cross the borders of the nation-states. My argument is that these differences in terms of religious pervasiveness and scale of social intervention result in a diversity of objectives and activities that determine the way aid is politicized.

I use these two variables to create a typology of two ideal-typical pairs of IHOs, which helps to explain the politicization of relief assistance. These two types are, on the one hand, transnational-fundamentalist IHOs and transnational-moderate IHOs, and, on the other hand, national-fundamentalist IHOs and national-moderate IHOs. Each of these types of organization differs in terms of their mission, discourse, and objective. Each engages in different kinds of activities to achieve their objectives. And each politicizes aid differently.

---

22. See note 1.

TABLE 1. Typology of International Humanitarian Organizations

		Religious Pervasiveness	
		Fundamentalist	Moderates
Scale of Intervention	Transnational	Transnational-Fundamentalist	Transnational-Moderate
	National	National Fundamentalist	National-Moderate

Summarily, IHOs politicize aid as follows:

(1) **Transnational-fundamentalist IHO:** the scope of its objectives and activities are transnational. Its objectives and activities are religiously oriented. Transnational-fundamentalist IHOs are the most likely to use aid as an instrument to achieve Islamic political goals at the transnational level. It tends to be *ummah-centric* in its aid activities, as defined in more detail below.

(2) **Transnational-moderate IHO:** it is not motivated by Islamic politics or religion, despite its self-identification as a Muslim[23] organization. Its politicization may be understood in terms of its struggle to concretize the idea of a moderate Islamic universalism. That effort may be found in its social interventions, particularly when related to improving the image of Islam, transmitting a message of peace in a transnational context, and so forth. It is most likely to use aid in the service of *global civil-society* activities.

(3) **National-fundamentalist IHO:** it pursues objectives at the national level with high Islamic political content. Its humanitarianism activities aim at displaying an alternative form of political, economic, and social governance based upon the framework of its Islamic values. It is the most likely to use humanitarian aid as an instrument of politics, populism, and political campaigning for the *adoption of an Islamic way of life at the national level.*

(4) **National-moderate IHO:** it is nationally limited in its presence and scope of activities. Its objectives are bounded within state territorial

23. Islamic is generally a modifier referring to concepts, principles, or other things inanimate (e.g., texts, architecture, art, law, theology, philosophy), although it is also used to describe communities (where community is a concept). Muslim is usually a modifier referring to humans who belong to the religion, Islam.

boundaries. It is nonreligious in orientation, making it neutral and professional. Yet its humanitarian action may, at times, inadvertently have a political function in terms of the dissemination of its Islamic values because its membership is primarily Muslim, as is its social context. These groups participate in national civil society activities as (usually unofficial) representatives of moderate local Muslim communities. It is most likely to use aid in a *development-centric* approach.

The categorization of IHOs into these four types is far from obvious. The borders between these ideal types is not rigid. There is fluidity between types. Indeed, owing to the fact that religious pervasiveness is not a clear-cut concept, this distinction between IHOs is better understood as a continuum. Moreover, NGOs themselves encounter difficulties in defining their position regarding religion.[24] In sum, the creation of these ideal types stems from a theoretical need to grasp a specific reality concerning these organizations. That is, theoretically, we must have categories as a conceptual tool from which to begin a more valid analysis. The method of ideal typing with all of its methodological benefits and drawbacks appears particularly useful in constructing these (taxonomical) categories, which are intended as a starting point for analysis.

KEY VARIABLES

The most defining variables in this IHOs classification are: (a) *religious pervasiveness*, and (b) *scale of intervention*. In the following paragraphs, I define these variables and provide indicators to measure them.

(a) Religious Pervasiveness

The variable "religious pervasiveness" is intended to capture the degree of religiosity of an organization from "fundamentalist" to "moderate." Fundamentalism is understood here as a strict adherence to theological doctrine, distrust of modern institutions, and a strong distrust of secularism. Funda-

24. Julia Berger, "Religious Nongovernmental Organizations: An Exploratory Analysis," *Voluntas: International Journal of Voluntary and Nonprofit Organizations* 14 (2003): 20–22.

mental Islam would sit on one end of a spectrum in this context. It might hold itself in contrast to modern, Western values and modern, Western institutions, particularly where those values and institutions insist upon *secularism* as a part of their philosophical core or of their *raîson d'être*. Moderate, by contrast, refers to something closer to a more daily-pragmatic approach to religious practice, and looser definitions, in as much as attention is only given to major doctrinal questions within Islamic theology.

How does one measure the religiosity of an organization? What criteria define an organization as fundamentalist or moderate? In order to measure the religious pervasiveness of IHO, I employ Rachel McCleary's (2009) five criteria:

- The presence of a notably religious person or clergy member in a leadership role of the organization, such as president or executive director, or on the board of directors (captures decision-making processes)
- The quote of religious text displayed prominently on the organization's website, annual report, or as part of the mission and values (material resources)
- The support of projects with a faith component, including Quran distribution, Quran classes, mosques planting, religious education, and *da'aw* (missionary actions)
- The use of religious terms, names, or a "Statement of Faith" on the organization's website, annual report, or as part of the mission and values (self-identity)
- The use of religious criteria in employment and/or volunteering, including the requirement of a statement of faith, description of religious beliefs, or a reference from a religious leader (participants)

Organizations that meet these criteria are likely to have a strong and overtly religious commitment; their discourse is likely to hold a doctrinal component that emphasizes the religious nature of their objectives; and the doctrines that they follow are described above (e.g., strongly following of theological doctrines in their activities, and skeptical of modern, and particularly secularized institutions). Their activities may have a religious content as well. Such organizations can be considered *fundamentalist*. The humanitarian actions of such organizations are likely to be a subterfuge for achieving religious goals.

In contrast, organizations that do not consider these criteria as critical for their work may be called *moderate*. Because of their Islamic identity, they may have a moderate or minor presence of a religious clergy in their administrative structure or may quote religious text in their website or their report, but they do not do so prominently enough to emphasize religion as the primary goal for their humanitarian action. Their discourse is clearly directed toward the primacy of humanitarian objectives, the necessity of alleviating suffering and fostering economic development. They may have a positive orientation toward modern institutions, although their approach to secularism may reflect either suspicion or ambivalence.

(b) Scale of Intervention

The variable "scale of intervention" captures the scope of the organization in terms of whether it intervenes at the global and transnational level or whether it is limited to the local and national level. Borrowing from Huntington (1973), I define the main characteristics of transnational, by contrast to national organizations, as follows:

- Transnational organizations are organizations that "transcend" the idea of a nation-state. An organization is "transnational" rather than "national" if it carries on significant centrally directed operations in the territory of two or more nation-states.
- A transnational organization has its own interests that inhere in its organization and functions; those interests may or may not be closely related to the interests of its constituent national groups.
- Transnational organizations focus on the heightened interconnectivity between people all around the world and the loosening of boundaries between countries. Transnationalism has social, political and economic impacts that affect people all around the globe.
- The constraints on a transnational organization are largely external, stemming from its need to gain operating authority in different sovereign states.

IHOs that operate in more than one nation, try to convey their message at the global level, and pursue the goal of establishing interconnectivity cross-nationally are called *transnational organizations*. On the contrary, IHOs that are confined within the nation-state's institutional or territorial control and are involved in action for the social and economic advancement of their countries may be considered *national organizations.*

IHOS IN PRACTICE: CASE STUDIES

Transnational Fundamentalist IHOs: The Case of International Islamic Relief Organization (IIRO), Saudi Arabia

The International Islamic Relief Organization, Saudi Arabia, is a charity organization established by the Muslim World League in 1979. It is a transnational organization that intervenes permanently in more than 30 countries; but it has also become reputed for its presence as one of the major humanitarian organizations worldwide. Its presence has been visible in relief operations in Yemen, Niger, Libya, Haiti, and Syria through the provision of tents, clothes, food items, and other relief items to victims of political conflict or natural disasters. Recently, an effort by the Saudi's authorities to further monitor the country's charitable organizations led to a significant reduction of IIRO's activity. Since 2018, the name of the International Islamic Relief Organization officially changed to International Organization for Relief, Welfare and Development (IORWD).

Religion is a fundamental aspect of the intervention of IIRO. The board of trustees and general assembly of the organization consists of Muslim dignitaries such the secretary general of the Muslim World League, who holds the position of chairman. Some of the personalities that led the organization—including Farid Al-Qurashi and Adnan Khalil Basha—have been prominent Muslim scholars with strong relationships with ruling families and religious authorities in Saudi Arabia and in the Gulf region in general.[25] The regular staff of IIRO are all practicing Muslims.

Although the organization is officially nondiscriminatory in its provision of aid, it has been accused of prioritizing Muslims as primary beneficiaries of its services. Furthermore, there is an overwhelming presence of citations from Islamic texts within the organization's website as well as in its

25. Jonathan Benthall, "The Rise and Decline of Saudi Overseas Humanitarian Charities," Center for International and Regional Studies, Georgetown University in Qatar, Doha, 2018.

official reports. For example, most of its reports start with a quote from the Quran. Finally, IIRO sponsors many projects that have clear religious objectives including the Holy Quran and Da'wa program. Notably, the organization was accused by the US government of supporting Al Qaeda, although the evidence provided has not resulted in a conviction in court.[26]

One way to analyze the overall humanitarian aid provided by IIRO is to approach it through the *ummatic* conceptualization of the Muslim community worldwide. The *ummah* is an ideological belief that refers to an "identity politics or a politics of communitarianism" (Yaylaci 2007). It is a concept that aims at bringing the Muslim community together in a unified political entity. Contrary to the mainstream transnationalism that is based on an economic and political argument, the *ummatic* transnationalism is based on a religious rationale. It builds on the Islamic conception that all the people who believe in the Islamic faith belong to the same community, referred in the Quran as "*ummahtan waahida*" (one unique community). As such, the Islamic community worldwide is supposed to be unified and behave as one body, with the consequence that "when a part is unwell, it is the whole body that suffers" (Yaylaci 2007).

Today's Islamic humanitarian approach has largely adopted the *ummatic* vision of the Muslim community by considering the suffering of the Muslims everywhere as the burden of the ummah and that the ummah has the duty and responsibility to address it. Yaylaci (2007), among others, argues that many IHOs act as an "imagined state" on behalf of its "imagined community"—the *ummah*.

According to Petersen (2011: 139), the underlying motivation of the humanitarian engagement of IIRO can be understood as a response to the feeling that the *ummah* is threatened from both outside and inside. The threats from inside include poverty and ignorance, which fosters immorality and sometimes extremism. From outside, the *ummah* is threatened on the one hand by "an organized invasion" of Christian NGOs, trying to take Muslims away from their religion; and, on the other hand, by the allegations of terrorism launched by some Western media and governments against individual Muslims and organizations. The IIRO's *ummatic* vision

26. Petersen, *For Humanity or for the Ummah*, 103; see also Jonathan Benthall, "Islamic Charities, Faith Based Organizations, and the International Aid System," in *Understanding Islamic Charities*, ed. J. Alterman and K. Von Hippel (Washington, DC: Center for Strategic and International Studies, 2007), 6.

of humanitarianism brought its leaders to think that it is the responsibility of the organization to address these challenges of the Islamic community. They consequently defined three ultimate objectives to pursue in order to address these challenges: (a) the spiritual education or re-Islamization of Muslims; (b) the promotion of the economic and social development of the *ummah*; and (c) the protection of Muslims against Christian evangelism.

This mission is compatible with the Islamic perspective whereby all the failures and challenges of Muslim societies have one general cause: the disconnection of Muslims from their religion. A project manager of the International Islamic Charity Organization, the Kuwaiti equivalent of the IIRO, argues: "If the Islamic ideas were being inserted [in everyday practice of Muslims], then society would be happier, more secure, there would be an abundance of wealth—both psychologically and materially."[27] There is a strong notion that prosperity in Muslim societies is conditioned by a belief in Islam and good practice of its rituals, both of which are conditioned by a good knowledge of Islam. The rationale here comes from the belief that if Muslims can get to know their religion and hold on to its teaching and practice, then Allah will ensure prosperity for them here and in the afterlife. The other part of the argument is related to linkages between ignorance and violence. As Marie Juul Petersen[28] mentions, IIRO officials perceive Islam as a religion of peace, and ignorance or misunderstanding of Islamic scripts drives some Muslims to engage in violence. For these reasons, IIRO officials emphasize the restoration or renaissance of Muslims' faith through religious education as part of a comprehensive strategy to combat ignorance, violence, and poverty. Islamic education also aims at raising "the consciousness of people about the magnificence of the true Islam" with the purpose of helping them to "preserve their culture and identity" and "boost the[ir] morale spiritually."[29]

The IIRO believes that addressing the spiritual shortcoming of the *ummah* is reinforced by curing the symptoms of poverty, through the creation of a network of solidarity exclusively targeting Muslims worldwide. In particular, the IIRO mentions in its statement of establishment that it motivates its donors "to assist their needy and suffering *brothers* in the world in order to help maintain their faith in Islam and relieve them from the

27. Petersen, *For Humanity or for the Ummah*, 147.

28. Petersen, *For Humanity or for the Ummah*, 147.

29. Petersen, *For Humanity or for the Ummah*, 153.

suffering."[30] This brotherhood explicitly reveals, beyond the simple act of giving and receiving, the vow of strengthening belief in Islam. Solidarity is about mutual interdependence among people, stemming from what they have in common, and Muslims are invited to engage in the provision of aid to the poor, because they are part of the same religious community, the *ummah*, and, as such, they are obliged to help one another.[31]

Transnational Moderate IHOs: The Case of Islamic Relief Worldwide (IRWW), UK

The Islamic Relief Worldwide (IRWW) is a Muslim international relief and development organization founded in the United Kingdom in 1984 by Dr. Hani El-Banna, a young Egyptian who had migrated to the UK a few years earlier. Inspired by Islamic values, IRWW aims to alleviate the suffering of the world's poorest people, envisaging a world where communities are empowered, social obligations are fulfilled, and people respond as one to the suffering of others.

The Islamic Relief Worldwide works in over 45 countries in the world and also intervenes in major humanitarian emergency crises worldwide. IRWW provides humanitarian aid regardless of religion, ethnicity, or gender. The recruitment of personnel is not conditioned on adherence to Islam but is rather determined by "aptitude and ability," hence the organization employs several non-Muslim staff members (Peterson 2011: 187–88). Its orphan sponsorship program includes Christian children and donors, several recipients of microfinance loans are Hindus, and Ramadan food packages are distributed to non-Muslims as well (Peterson 2011: 198). IRWW has never been subject to allegations of 'terrorist' connections. Though the organization is self-identified as Islamic, neither its objective nor its activities display a strong commitment to Islam as religion per se. On the contrary, the organization defines its approach to humanitarian aid as secular and professional (see Peterson 2011: 167). Moreover, in its literature, the organization promotes

30. Personal translation from Arabic website of IIRO.

31. Petersen, *For Humanity or for the Ummah*, 146. See also Alex De Waal, *Who Fights? Who Cares? War and Humanitarian Action in Africa* (Trenton, NJ: Africa World Press, 2000); and Mohamed M.A. Salih, *Islamic NGOs in Africa: The Promise and Peril of Islamic Voluntarism*, Occasional Paper 246 (Copenhagen: University of Copenhagen, 2002).

both discourse and activities involving a conception of aid as secularized, creating a boundary between aid and Islam. For instance, Peterson (2011: 183) notices that "on its web site the organization calls itself an *International Relief and Development Charity* in effort to downplay that it is an organization established and run by Muslims." According to Smith and Sosin (2001:655), "Islamic Relief claims to be legitimate providers of aid because they are professional, not because they are religious. It is about the services it provides, not the values it possesses." Religion is accepted insofar as it remains personal and does not affect the goal and effectiveness of the humanitarian intervention. Peterson describes well the role of religion in the humanitarian action of IRWW when she called it "secular religiosity" (2011: 189), meaning a religion relegated to the spheres of personal motivation and underlying values. Here, religion is acceptable as the source of individual values, underlying principles and motivation, but not as public rituals and collective practices influencing the ways in which aid is provided (Peterson 2011: 189). Islam is thus considered just as an "ethical reference" (Benedetti 2006: 855). Peterson describes IRWW as "secularizing" aid while IIRO "sacralize" it.

The moderate international approach of organizations such as the IRWW can be seen as a religious reaction to the 20th century wave of globalization, which caused an expansion in the scale and speed of worldwide flows of capital, goods, people, and ideas across national borders. One of the results that came out of this change in the international landscape was the development of the notion of "global governance," which has been defined as "the political interaction of transnational actors aimed at solving problems that affect more than one state or region when there is no power of enforcing compliance" (Pippa Norris 2000: 2). The global civil society and the political role of the contemporary humanitarianism are associated with the global governance of societies (Duffield 2001). Islamic societies have not been alien to this global trend. Through their participation in this contemporary humanitarianism, many transnational IHOs have both internalized and helped to mold this notion of global governance and they have re-appropriated it in a way that matches their ideological basis. Such is the case of the transnational moderate IHOs, of which I argue the IRWW is an example. These IHOs have a *cosmopolitan approach*—cosmopolitanism being used here to point to those who identify with a broader identity such as their continent, or with the world as a whole—as opposed to those who narrowly identify with ethnic, religious, and cultural characteristics. While the *ummatic* approach sees the world in terms of two antagonist identities—

Islamic versus Western Judeo-Christian identity—the cosmopolitan-centric approach broadens identities beyond national, religious and ideological boundaries to a "world community." It therefore homogenizes identities, in contrast to the *ummatic* approach that is based on identity polarization.

In line with this view, the most important feature of the Islamic Relief Worldwide humanitarian action is its focus on the professionalism of its intervention rather than on its religious identity or political agenda. IRWW follows the principles of independence, humanity, and universality, and its humanitarian discourse is development-centric. IRWW actions are not driven by the interests of any specific state and, according to the organization's officials, aid is given to all disadvantaged people across the globe, irrespective of their faith, race, gender, or any other affiliation. Globally, the humanitarian action of IRWW is similar to the mainstream secular humanitarianism portrayed by such organization as Médecins Sans Frontières, Care International, and Oxfam. Even more, while these secular organizations have salient political positions on issues related to human suffering, including open critiques of authoritarian governments, IRWW does not so openly engage in politics. The organization seems not to link its humanitarian activities with any clear political agenda.

In a world dominated by a "single story" of Islam, portraying it as a religion of violence and Islamic NGOs as the non-sword arm of terrorism, the type of humanitarian aid carried out by IRWW exemplifies a modern, open, and civilized model of Islamic organization that may serve politically in restoring the global image of Islam. An additional value-added to Islamic religion in the work of IRWW is that Islamic humanitarianism is considered as an innovative approach to alleviate suffering. Hani El-Banna suggests, "Our presence at numerous international conferences during 2006 reflected the recognition of the added value that Islamic Relief can bring to discussions on humanitarian issues."[32]

National–Fundamentalist IHOs: The Case of the Charitable Wing of the Muslim Brotherhood, Egypt

The Muslim Brotherhood of Egypt can be seen as an organization pertaining to the fundamentalist IHO group while focusing its activities at the

32. Islamic Relief, Annual Report, 2006.

national level.[33] Formed in 1928 in Ismailiyah, Egypt by Hassan al-Banna (1906–49), it intended to resist the cultural and political domination of Egypt during the British colonization. More than 80 years after the creation of the movement, Al-Banna's thinking largely continues to guide the actions of the Egyptian Brotherhood, its sympathizers, and much of moderate Islamism today. The movement initially combined political activism and humanitarian action through the provision of social welfare for the poor. After the first post-revolutionary elections, the Muslim Brotherhood won both the majority in the parliament and the presidency, and had its leader Mohamed Morsi invested as president of Egypt in June 2012. He was ousted in a military coup in 2013 and the movement was outlawed in the same year.

As a national movement created and animated by Egyptians, the Muslim Brotherhood's activism is mostly circumscribed to the national territory of Egypt. The ideology underlying the activism of the movement is that underdevelopment in Egypt has to do with the abandonment of religion in social life and in political governance, which has brough Egypt to religious, cultural, political, economic, social, legal and moral decadence and impotence.[34] The movement has always claimed that Egyptians must go back to the true religion of Islam and move away from the corrupt aspirations and conduct inspired by Western culture. Although the ideological line of the Muslim Brotherhood is described as moderate,[35] the Islamic content of their humanitarian action is not subject to doubt. Among other things, this is exemplified by an overwhelming use of Islamic quotes from the Quran and Hadith (traditions of the Prophet), not to mention their sponsorship of proselytism.

The ideological founding of the Muslim Brotherhood traces back to a nineteen century Islamist movement that, parallel to the *ummatic* vision of the Muslim world, adopted instead a theory of Islamic nationalism. This movement was established by the Indian scholar Sayyid Ahmad Khan (1817–98), who opposed Al-Afghani's pan-Islamism and denied the author-

33. It's noteworthy to mention that the Muslim Brotherhood movement is plural. The same ideology expanded in many Arab countries, but the one that interests us is the Egyptian movement.

34. Richard P. Mitchell, *The Society of the Muslim Brothers* (New York: Oxford University Press, 1969), 212.

35. Janine Clark, *Islam, Charity, and Activism* (Bloomington: Indiana University Press, 2004), 14.

ity of the Caliphate over Indian Muslims. Sayyid Ahmad Khan subsequently inspired Islamic nationalisms through the thought and work of such Islamic leaders as Mohamed Iqbal (1877–1938) in Pakistan and Hassan al-Banna in Egypt. Islamic nationalism is a reformist theory that espouses the idea that: (a) Muslim societies should be organized in a form of modern nation-states; and (b) Shari'a (Islamic Law) should be adapted to the modern context as a constitution and a system of governance.

While after colonization most Muslim states fell under the control of secularists who marginalized the Islamist movements and criticized Shari'a as being anachronistic to modern societies, the adepts of Islamic nationalism, such as militants within the Muslim Brotherhood, strive to demonstrate the viability of Shari'a by establishing organizations able to develop a social welfare system (schools, hospitals, poverty reduction projects, etc.) at the grassroots level. Often, these organizations provide better services than the government. The success of these projects is thus credited to Shari'a, which Islamic nationalists believe shows it as a better alternative to corrupted, ineffective, and thus unviable secular political systems. The quintessential example of these organizations is the Egyptian Muslim brotherhood.

Since its establishment, the Muslim Brotherhood in Egypt started with an overlapping discourse of humanitarianism and political Islamism. It originally stated its purpose as achieving social justice, providing social security to every citizen, contributing to popular service, resisting ignorance, disease, poverty, and vice, and encouraging charity work (Auda 1993: 386). Starting as a religious social organization preaching Islam, teaching the illiterate, and setting up hospitals, it grew and diversified by establishing schools and charity services which provided money, food, and clothing for the marginalized. These socioeconomic programs were not ends in themselves; the movement emphasized that a society based on Islamic precepts should "promote social security for citizens, narrow the socioeconomic gap between classes, undertake welfare spending to assist those in need, encourage economic solidarity among citizens, respect private property, and enforce the requisite that each able-bodied person must be economically productive" (Abed-Kotob 1995: 326–27).

The humanitarian action of the Muslim Brotherhood in Egypt is purported to demonstrate to people a better form of governance than what they see as the corrupted secular system. Ideally, through its humanitarian activism, the movement shows a harmonious Islamic society without exploitation or oppression (Lesch 1992: 183). It then uses it as a quintessential example of what a society should be when it is ruled according to the Islamic law. Humanitarianism is therefore an instrument of political campaigning to gain power.

The policy behind the humanitarian action of the Muslim Brotherhood is therefore to "represent the foundations of an alternative society" (Clark 2004: 16). By offering successful social welfare services in the name of Islam to their fellow citizens, they represent an ideological and practical alternative to the present system. They display an "Islamist vision of a new society and Islamist Identity" (16).

National–Moderate IHOs: The Case of the Islamic Council for Development and Humanitarian Services (ICODEHS), Ghana

The Islamic Council for Development and Humanitarian Services, popularly known as ICODEHS, is a Ghanaian, development-oriented IHO created and run by Ghanaians for the Ghanaians. Founded in Accra in 1991 by Sheikh Mustapha Ibrahim, it has opened branches across the whole country. The organization defines its objectives in five points: (a) create awareness for the needs and aspirations of the people; (b) generate action toward social change; (c) help organize people to develop programs and projects from the grassroots; (d) help effect social change through education; and (e) facilitate and support the self-help initiatives of rural and local communities by assisting them in resource development.

Almost all national-moderate IHOs such as ICODEHS still have some activities related to Islam. However, from their statement of objectives, it is clear that the main goal of the organization is to ensure the development of society as a whole. ICODEHS is non-sectarian (that is, ecumenical) in its provision of aid. As one of its major activities, ICODEHS is noted for providing donations in cash and in kind toward the welfare of Muslims and non-Muslims alike across the country (Samwini 2003: 142). As a moderate organization, it also maintains a clear-cut, unambiguous position toward terrorism: in a message posted on the website of the organization, the founder and general administration of the organization emphasizes that "African Muslims and their counterparts worldwide ought to bear in mind that irresponsible acts of violence that often claim the lives of innocent non-Muslims and even sometimes Muslims alike, is senseless and only seeks to soil the good image of Islam."[36]

---

36. See https://icodehs.org/

In recent years the ICODEHS has increasingly emphasized its religious activities such as the construction of mosques. Yet, the organization's general humanitarian activism remains still development-oriented. This is clear from the messages of the Chairman of the organization, emphasizing the importance of agriculture and women in labor. Activities such as setting up the teacher training college, the nursing school and a university are aimed at promoting education in Ghana, especially among the poor and vulnerable, irrespective of the applicants' religion, gender or tribe. In all of its humanitarian action, ICODEHS does not display any political agenda pursued behind its statutory aims. Yet, its intervention may still have an inadvertent political function insofar as, among all the local IHOs in Ghana, ICODEHS is the only member of the Civil Society Coordinating Council (CivisoC) of SAPRIN-Ghana, thus representing the voice of the Ghanaian Muslims in the country.[37] The humanitarian activism of ICDOHES also exhibits a positive view of Islam.

CONCLUSION

IHOs have come to symbolize the money funnels of terrorist financing in the world. Allegations in the media, intelligence reports, and scholarly studies have continuously linked the spread of Islamic insurgencies in Iraq, Somalia, Yemen, and recently in Mali and Syria to the proliferation of IHOs despite the shortage of evidence to prove such a relationship. Although the accusation is often caveated to index "mainstream Islamic charities," or some specific charitable organizations, the risk of falling into the fallacy of overgeneralization is high given the absence of any comprehensive framework of analysis that determines which organization does or does not serve as venue to financing terrorism.

This chapter has tried to shed light on the widely taken-for-granted linkage between IHOs and terrorist financing. It challenges the monolithic view of IHOs, emphasizing the diversity that characterizes them. It suggests a framework of understanding this diversity and the way it impacts the politicization of aid. The typology that I suggest breaks down the IHOs into four

37. The Civil Society Coordinating Council (CivisoC) is a network of 21 members representing organizations of workers, women, students, Muslims, farmers, fishermen, and small and medium-scale industries, as well as environmentalists and other NGOs. SAPRIN-Ghana is a network encompassing virtually all of the major NGOs, churches and trade union umbrella organizations in the country. In total, there are more than 300 organizations affiliated with SAPRIN.

categories according to their *scale of intervention* and *religious pervasiveness*. The categories that result from this classification portray different types of IHOs with a patterned set of objectives, which differ from one another in predictable ways. Therefore, each category politicizes aid in a different manner. Whereas fundamentalist IHOs follow an *ummah-centric* or *nationalist* approach to politics and use humanitarian aid as a means of campaigning for the adoption of an Islamic way of life, moderate IHOs lean more toward a cosmopolitan or local civil-society approach and follow a development-centric approach.

The typology offered herein is by no mean exhaustive. Some IHOs may not fit neatly into these ideal types. However, this framework offers a starting point for analysis. It is possible to use this typology to conceptualize other IHOs based upon variables such as the geographic distribution of the organization itself, or its financial and operational capabilities. In particular, the ideal types offered herein are limited in a few ways. For example, they employ a relatively static picture of a given IHO for purposes of analysis, while there has been a strong tendency among IHOs to adopt a more moderate stance, particularly after 9/11.

The argument also does not take into account the influence of the local environment in which the organizations intervene, downplaying the variations that may exist between organizations that belong to the same category or variations between the national branches of one transnational organization. In-depth studies of the categories taken individually, transformations of organizations within these ideal types across time, the internal variations, and the relationships among organizational types both within and across these categories will be helpful in advancing our understanding of IHOs.

References

Abed-Kotob, Sana. "The Accommodationists Speak: Goals and Strategies of the Muslim Brotherhood of Egypt." *International Journal of Middle East Studies* 27, no. 3 (1995): 321–39.

Ahmed, Chanfi. "Networks of Islamic NGOs in Sub-Saharan Africa: Bilal Muslim Mission, African Muslim Agency (Direct Aid), and al-Haramayn." *Journal of Eastern African Studies* 3, no. 3 (2009): 426–37.

Ahmed, Hassan Makki M. *Sudan: The Christian Design; A Study of the Missionary Factor in Sudan's Cultural and Political Integration (1843–1986)*. Leicester, UK: Islamic Foundation Leicester, 2007.

Al-Bishr, Mohammed Ben Saud. *Letter to the West: A Saudi View*. Ghaina'a Publications, 2008.

Alterman, Jon B., and Karin Von Hippel, eds. *Understanding Islamic Charities*. Washington, DC: Center for Strategic and International Studies, 2007.

Anderson, J. Brady. "Faith and US Foreign Assistance Policy." *Review of Faith and International Affairs* 6 (2008): 21–24.

Anderson, M. *Do No Harm: Supporting Local Capacities for Peace through Aid*. Boston: Collaborative for Development, 1996.

Auda, Gehad. "The Islamic Movement and Resource Mobilization in Egypt: A Political Culture Perspective." In *Political Culture and Democracy in Developing Countries*, edited by Larry Diamond. Boulder: Lynne Rienner, 1993.

Benedetti, Carlo. "Islamic and Christian Inspired Relief NGOs: Between Tactical Collaboration and Strategic Diffidence." *Journal of International Development* 18, no. 6 (2006): 849–59.

Benthall, Jonathan. "Humanitarianism and Islam after 11 September." In *Humanitarian Action and the 'Global War on Terror': A Review of Trends and Issues*, edited by J. Macrae and A. Harmer. London: Overseas Development Institute, 2003.

Benthall, Jonathan. "The Rise and Decline of Saudi Overseas Humanitarian Charities." Center for International and Regional Studies, Georgetown University in Qatar, Doha, 2018.

Benthall, Jonathan. "Islamic Charities, Faith Based Organizations, and the International Aid System." In *Understanding Islamic Charities*, edited by J. Alterman and K. Von Hippel. Washington, DC: Center for Strategic and International Studies, 2007.

Benthall, Jonathan, and Jerome Bellion-Jourdan. *The Charitable Crescent: The Politics of Aid in the Muslim World*. London: I.B. Tauris, 2003.

Berger, Julia. "Religious Nongovernmental Organizations: An Exploratory Analysis." *Voluntas: International Journal of Voluntary and Nonprofit Organizations* 14 (2003): 15–39.

Burr, J. Millard, and Robert O. Collins. *Alms of Jihad: Charity and Terrorism in the Islamic World*. New York: Cambridge University Press, 2006.

Chandler, David. "Rhetoric without Responsibility: The Attraction of Ethical Foreign Policy." *British Journal of Politics and International Relations* 5, no. 3 (2003): 295–316.

Clark, Janine. *Islam, Charity, and Activism*, Bloomington: Indiana University Press, 2004.

Cockayne, James. "Islam and Humanitarian Law: From a Clash to a Conversation between Civilizations." *International Review of the Red Cross* 84, no. 847 (2002): 597–625.

Comras, Victor. "Al Qaeda Finances and Funding to Affiliated Groups." In *The Po-*

litical Economy of Terrorism Finance and State Responses: A Comparative Perspective, edited by Jeanne K. Giraldo and Harold A. Trinkunas. Palo Alto: Stanford University Press, 2006.

Curtis, Devon. *Politics and Humanitarian Aid: Debates, Dilemmas and Dissension.* HPG Report 10. London: Overseas Development Institute, 2001.

Dajani, Amjad. *Islamic Nationalism vs. Islamic Ummahtism/al-Ummahtya: Conceptualizing Political Islam.* London: Mediterranean and Middle Eastern Studies Program, Department of Theology and Religious Studies, Kings College London, 2011.

De Waal, Alex. *Famine Crimes: Politics and the Disaster Relief Industry in Africa.* Oxford: Oxford African Rights and the International African Institute, in association with James Currey, 1997.

De Waal, Alex. *Who Fights? Who Cares? War and Humanitarian Action in Africa.* Trenton, NJ: Africa World Press, 2000.

Duffield, Mark. *Global Governance and the New Wars: The Merging of Development and Security.* London: Zed Books, 2001.

Ehrenfeld, Rachel. *Funding Evil: How Terrorism Is Financed—and How to Stop It.* New Rochelle, NY: Multieducator, 2003.

Eyben, Rosalind, and Clare Ferguson, eds. *Realising Human Rights for Poor People: Strategies for Achieving the International Development Targets.* London: Department for International Development, 2000.

Ferris, Elizabeth. "Faith-Based and Secular Humanitarian Organizations." *International Review of the Red Cross* 87, no. 858 (June 2005).

Fischer, F. William. "Doing Good? The Politics and Anti-Politics of NGO Practices." *Annual Review of Anthropology* 26 (1997): 439–64.

Fowler, Alan. *Non-Governmental Organisations in Africa: Achieving Comparative Advantage in Relief and Micro-Development.* Discussion Paper no. 249. Brighton: Institute of Development Studies, 1988.

Hashmi, Sohail H. "Is There an Islamic Ethic of Humanitarian Intervention?" *Ethics and International Affairs* 7, no. 1 (1993): 55–73.

Huntington, Samuel. "Transnational Organizations." *World Politics* 25, no. 3 (1973): 333–68.

Jeavons, Thomas. "Identity Characteristics of Religious Organizations: An Exploratory Proposal." In *Sacred Companies,* edited by N. J. Demerath III, Peter Dobkin Hall, Terry Schmitt, and Rhys H. Williams. New York: Oxford University Press, 1998.

Kaag, M. "Aid, *Ummah* and Politics: Transnational Islamic NGOs in Chad." In *Islam and Muslim Politics in Africa,* edited by Benjamin Soares and R. Otayek. Basingstoke: Palgrave Macmillan, 2007.

Kaag, M. "Transnational Islamic NGOs in Chad: Islamic Solidarity in the Age of Neoliberalism." *Africa Today* 54, no. 3 (2008): 3–18.

Levitt, Matthew. *Hamas: Politics, Charity, and Terrorism in the Service of Jihad.* New Haven: Yale University Press, 2006.

Looney, Robert. "The Mirage of Terrorist Financing: The Case of Islamic Charities." *Strategic Insights* 5, no. 3 (2006).

Ly, Pierre-Emmauel. "The Charitable Activities of Terrorist Organizations." *Public Choice* 131, nos. 1–2 (2007): 177–95.

Martens, Kerstin. "Mission Impossible? Defining Nongovernmental Organizations." *International Journal of Voluntary and Non-Profit Organizations* 13, no. 3 (2002): 271–85.

McCleary, M. Rachel. *Global Compassion: Private Voluntary Organizations and U.S. Foreign Policy since 1939*. Oxford: Oxford University Press, 2009.

Mckinlay, R. D., and R. Little. "A Foreign Policy Model of U.S. Bilateral Aid Allocation." *World Politics* 30, no. 1 (1977): 58–86.

Mitchell, Richard P. *The Society of the Muslim Brothers.* New York: Oxford University Press, 1969.

Norris, Pippa. Global "Governance and Cosmopolitan Citizens." In *Globalization and Governance*, edited by Joseph S. Nye Jr. and Elaine Kamarck. Washington, DC: Brookings Institution Press, 2000.

Petersen, Marie Juul. *For Humanity or for the Ummah? Ideologies of Aid in Four Transnational Muslim NGOs.* Copenhagen: University of Copenhagen Press, 2011.

Qutb, Sayyid. *Social Justice in Islam.* Translated by John B. Hardie. New York: Islamic Publication International, 2002.

Rana, Jawad. "Social Welfare and Religion in the Middle East: A Lebanese Perspective." *Social Policy & Administration* 44, no. 7 (2010): 872–74.

Redfield, Peter. "Doctors, Borders, and Life." *Crisis: University of North Carolina at Chapel Hill Cultural Anthropology* 20, no. 3 (2005): 328–61.

Ridgeon, Lloyd. "Islam." In *Major World Religions: From Their Origins to the Present,* edited by Lloyd V. J. Ridgeon. New York: Routledge Curzon, 2003.

Salih, Mohamed M. A. *Islamic NGOs in Africa: The Promise and Peril of Islamic Voluntarism.* Occasional Paper 246. Copenhagen: University of Copenhagen, 2002.

Sami, Zubeida. "The Quest for the Islamic State: Islamic Fundamentalism in Egypt and Iran." In *Studies In Religious Fundamentalism,* edited by Lionel Calpan. Albany: State University of New York Press, 1987.

Samwini, Nathan. *The Muslim Resurgence in Ghana since 1950: Its Effects upon Muslims and Muslim-Christian Relations.* Birmingham: University of Birmingham, 2003.

Slim, Hugo. *Not Philanthropy but Rights-Based Humanitarianism and the Proper Politicisation of Humanitarian Philosophy in War.* Oxford: Centre for Development and Emergency Practice, Oxford Brookes University, 2000.

Tarrow, Sidney. "Transnational Politics: Contention and Institutions in International Politics." *Annual Review of Political Science* 4 (2001): 1–20.

Wiktorowicz, Quintan, and Farouki S. Taji. "Islamic NGOs and Muslim Politics: A Case from Jordan." *Third World Quarterly* 21, no. 4 (2000): 685–99.

Yaylaci, Ismail. "Communitarian Humanitarianism: The Politics of IHOs." Paper presented at the Workshop on Religion and Humanitarianism, American University of Cairo, June 3–5, 2007.

Judaism in the Middle East

Introduction

Judaism is one of the oldest world religions with a long diaspora tradition; during much of that time the religion was not associated with state power. The chapters in this section address the late-modern state of Israel as it contends with its own *Jewish* character, that is, as a modern secular polity with a specifically Jewish (e.g., religious) cultural and institutional identity. While early state leaders often emphasized the Jewish identity of the state as related to cultural and historical heritage more than to religion, the chapters in this volume highlight some of the ways in which religion, *qua religion*, is important in the Israeli political context.

The chapters in this section highlight the following observations: (1) The judiciary has become a key actor in regard to the religion-state nexus in Israel. Israel draws upon several sources in the construction of its state apparatus and institutional framework, including British common law, Ottoman civil law, and Jewish religious traditions. In the Ottoman *millet* system, as modified by Israel into a nation-state context, religious courts are one of only a few primary loci of religious authority within the state. For constitutional questions, the appellate process ultimately ends at the High Court of Justice (HCJ), which is primarily guided by secular law, although Jewish tradition is also meant to inform HCJ decisions. The role of courts in Israel's modified *millet* system means that conflicts between religious and secular principles in cases that originate in religious court jurisdiction find their way to the HCJ. That is, both religious courts and secular courts have become one (although not the only) key locus of conflict resolution regarding the nexus of religion and state, and religion and secularism.

(2) Religious communities *matter*. Their crises are our crises in a sense. Their gains or losses of something as significant as the perceived success or failure of prophecy—for certain communities, a world-building or world-destroying matter—must be understood by scholars to be significant to

study on its own terms, and for topics and themes which may be closer to ourselves. It is also suggestive of analysis of cases across communities in which prophecy remains prescient, or, perhaps, in which the prophecies of one community contradict those of another. Rather than viewing these phenomena through a secular lens in which such things may be seen as regrettably "nonmodern" cultural artifacts on their way to being less important to communities around the world, we may be better off approaching them as empirical matters of great import to real people, and to real politics.

Patricia Sohn situates the discussion of religion, state, and religious freedom in Israel in terms of international legal discourses regarding freedom of religion. She draws upon Saba Mahmood and Gad Barzilai in their respective works regarding the secularizing and individualizing trends in international legal debates as well as in international legal instruments (e.g., treaties and conventions). She agrees with these scholars that the privileging of the secular and the individual in international legal norms undermines the ability of religiously and communally oriented peoples to assert their (religious) interests. She notes that these secular-individual and religious-communal dyads raise a *problematique* in relation to freedom of religion. Likewise, while Mahmood's work emphasizes religious minorities in this context, such as Christian communities in Egypt, Sohn addresses the *problematique* to a context of majority religion, Judaism in the Israeli case.

Sohn suggests that democratic principles do not run counter to religion, per se; that is, in country contexts in which the majority population prefers the incorporation of religion in the state in some meaningful way, such an arrangement *is* the democratic solution. She makes this suggestion with the caveat that substantial human rights violations should not be allowed to this end; that is, such an arrangement should not run to the extreme of tyranny of the majority, or of the community. Nevertheless, the Israeli case is one in which religious authorities have had limited but official roles within the state since immediately before the state's establishment. Both majority and minority populations tend to prefer this arrangement, as it provides institutional autonomy for minorities and a grounded historical, cultural, and religious identity for the majority. Thus, it provides a useful case for analysis of tensions, synthesis, syncretisms, and outright conflict caused by the coexistence, within one state, of secular institutions together with a smaller number of both judicial and executive branch offices overseen by state religious officials.

Eti Peretz and Jonathan Fox discuss the issue of the balance between democratic and Jewish values in the Israeli judiciary. In particular, they do so by addressing the question, was Israeli High Court of Justice (HCJ) president Aharon Barak against religious authorities in his decision making? Barak was a highly reputed HCJ president and is an important legal scholar, internationally as well as nationally within Israel. When the Israeli Knesset passed a new Basic Law in 1985 defining Israel as a Jewish and democratic state, Peretz and Fox tell us, the bar was raised for the (typically secularly oriented) Israeli HCJ in terms of the difficult balancing act expected of it. Some critics of Barak have suggested that he led the HCJ against religious authorities in a unique way. Peretz and Fox tackle this question, empirically, collecting an original data set of all HCJ cases related to religion and state over the tenure of two HCJ presidents, Meir Shamgar (1983–95) and Aharon Barak (1995–2006).

Peretz and Fox outline some of the legal-philosophical issues regarding Israel as a Jewish and a democratic state. Indeed, they tell us, Barak himself argued that the main role of the HCJ was to balance the various and conflicting principles within its polity and legal system. In Israel's case, achieving such congruity between disparate principles included, in particular, the need to balance the particularistic impulse involved in being a Jewish state with a specific national identity tied to a specific religion; its own "civic religion," both secular and connected to religious symbols; and a democratic state valuing civil rights, including freedom of religion, equality, and other democratic values. Peretz and Fox detail some of the criticisms of Barak in the national and international legal literatures. He comes under critique for "creative interpretation," although supporters read him, to the contrary, as more restrained and walking a fine line in an effort to reconcile these diverging (social and ideological) forces and principles. Indeed, Peretz and Fox argue, how to achieve the appropriate balance in these principles remains a topic of "severe disagreement" and ongoing debate.

The authors address disagreements regarding the relative levels of religiosity among the Israeli Jewish population, as well as societal support for various components of the current status quo on religion-state relations. Debates regarding the relative merits of democracy, theocracy, a Torah state, and other potential forms of government advocated by different constituencies are also discussed. The relative willingness of various constituencies to interact with the (secular) state, or with one another, is outlined in some detail. Positions regarding support for religious law, more involvement of religion in the state, or less involvement of religion in the state are all related to their various constituencies. On the most extreme religious end of the spectrum, a very small constituency does not even acknowledge the existence of the secular state. On the opposite extreme secular end of the spectrum, a role for religion in the public sphere is altogether rejected. Ultimately, based upon an empirical study of two HCJ administrations, Perez and Fox argue that Barak should not be characterized as antireligion in his judicial decision-making.

Motti Inbari addresses the responses of three different Jewish messianic religious thinkers in Israel to the Israeli disengagement from Gaza as ideal-typical approaches to failures in prophecy. That is, messianic movements viewed the expansion of Israeli territory as "a partial fulfillment of Biblical prophecy for Jewish redemption." Thus, decreases in territory have been read by messianic movements in Israel as a "failure of prophecy." When faced with such perception of catastrophic failure in what one has understood to be a reflection of prophetic successes, how does a messianic-religious worldview approach failure in the same? Inbari draws upon social science theories from the discipline of psychology, in particular, cognitive dissonance theories, to categorize and explain responses in this case.

Theories of cognitive dissonance, Inbari tells us, would lead us to expect that people will make strong efforts to justify their beliefs in cases of "clear disconfirmation." Inbari expands upon this framework, suggesting, empirically, that Jewish messianic responses to the disconfirmation found in the Gaza disengagement reflect three patterns: (1) acceptance of failure and renunciation of prophecy; (2) rejection of failure and deepening commitment to prophecy; and (3) acceptance of possible failure and significant changes in one's own political behavior. Inbari analyzes the rabbinical narratives of three major contemporary Jewish messianic authorities, that is, religious leaders and thinkers within their communities (not state religious officials). He estimates that the Jewish messianic religious movement on both sides of the Green Line is made up of approximately 200,000 persons.

Inbari outlines the development of messianic Zionism, beginning with Rabbi Yitzhak Hacohen Kook (1865–1935), and the 1948 and 1967 wars. While Orthodox Jewish communities have not always supported the idea of a secular state at all, including Israel as a secular state, religious Zionists approached secular Zionism, loosely speaking, as acting by the hand of the Divine even when its outer shell was that of a secular movement, Inbari tells us. They viewed their own ideal goal as the establishment of the Davidic monarchy and, with their help, the transformation of the Zionists, who were making that dream a reality, from secular to religiously observant people. That is, the goal of religious Zionists was always the establishment of a Torah state; that goal was abandoned in the years after the 1948 war and the establishment of Israel as a state. After the 1967 war, and the trauma of the 1973 war and "imminent territorial defeat," the dream was revived and fueled with the establishment of Gush Emunim, which, Inbari notes, became the dominant stream within messianic Zionism. This movement sought to avoid territorial concessions through the creation of Jewish settlements.

Inbari compares original social-psychological works such as those of Leon Festinger, Henry Riecken, and Stanley Schachter (*When Prophecy Fails*, 1956)[1] with later works on prophetic movements, as well as theories of cognitive dissonance. Festinger, Riecken, and Schachter tell us, according to Inbari, that a clearly falsified belief will be held more intensely after falsification, and that the group will increase proselytization. Their study was done in the context of UFO[2] communities. Later studies on new religions and prophetic movements suggested that the proselytization, rationalization, and reaffirmation framework of Festinger et al. was insufficient and that proselytization, in particular, happened only rarely. Inbari finds, in the case of the messianic Zionist movement, that proselytization continues to be "an important mechanism for easing dissonance." Cognitive dissonance theories, in which it is assumed that significant attempts will be made to resolve tensions when falsification occurs, continue to be important, although Inbari finds variety in the methods of resolution used in his three ideal-typical responses.

THE ISRAELI STATE PROVIDES a fascinating and instructive case of religion as having a (limited) place in the apparatus of an otherwise secular state. The studies in this section of the volume address the context of Judaism as a majority community and in which religion is part of the judicial apparatus, as well as in some parts of the executive branch of the state at the national, district, and municipal levels. Courts are critical actors in this religion-state nexus for reasons of institutional heritage. There is tremendous ideological and theological diversity in Israel. Religious communities matter a great deal to real politics at the national and international levels. And, finally, the case of Judaism offers a complex and rich locus for exploring significant frameworks from social theory with regard to law and courts, religion and states, popular religious movements, and messianism.

1. Leon Festinger, Henry Riecken, and Stanley Schachter, *When Prophecy Fails* (Minneapolis: University of Minnesota Press, 1956).

2. UFO is an acronym for *unidentified flying object*.

Global Trends in Religion and State

Secular Law and Freedom of Religion in Israel

Patricia Sohn

University of Florida—Gainesville

Saba Mahmood has suggested that international human rights legal norms and differential levels of relative sovereignty between Western and Middle Eastern states have led to a tendency in scholarly and activist circles to conceptualize religious rights in terms of the individual rather than the group, to downplay or eschew attention to *religious* liberty, per se, and instead to address "minority rights" in specifically *secularized* terms.[1] For Mahmood, in the Middle East, where the addressing of religious communities as politically significant has been less apt to be contested than in the post-Enlightenment West, it is the term "minority" that has at times been more likely to be controversial.[2] As religion, community rights have been addressed more and less effectively, albeit while contesting the term "minority." The effectuating of the civil rights and religious freedoms, per se, of smaller religious communities have been more problematic in the region, according to Mahmood, to the extent that the local state perceived itself to be engaging in a secularization

Parts of this chapter have appeared previously in the first edition of *Judicial Power and National Politics: Courts and Gender in the Religious-Secular Conflict in Israel* (2008) and are published here with permission of the State University of New York Press. Thank you to Eyup Civelek, Katrina Siason, and Victoria Puerto. All translations from Israel High Court of Justice cases into English are my own.

1. Saba Mahmood, *Religious Difference in a Secular Age* (Princeton: Princeton University Press, 2016), 16–19.

2. Mahmood, *Religious Difference in a Secular Age*, 66–68, 74.

program, as with the Copts in Egypt;[3] or where the religious community was seen as crossing a politically sensitive divide, even if coincidentally, as with the Bahais in Egypt (whose religion was founded in Persia, but whose administrative center is located in Israel).[4]

Scholars such as Gad Barzilai have argued that liberals tend to overvalue the individual, to undervalue communities, and particularly to underestimate the impact of potentially hegemonic community cultures (by contrast to non-hegemonic community cultures) upon the individual.[5] Liberal approaches have implications for the application of existing rights frameworks, which tend to the liberal-individual in orientation. In considering rights frameworks and their application(s) *in situ* around the world, by contrast, Barzilai suggests the need to attend to nonruling, non-liberal communities, which may have developed "distinctive identities" and "unique perceptions of the common good."[6] Such an approach enjoins thinking about rights not only in terms of individuals but in terms of "communal legal cultures":

> Communal legal culture, as we now understand it, is not only about social being and legal consciousness but about the ways in which collective identities of nonruling communities are expressed in law and toward law.[7]

Indeed, where the focus on the individual in the construction of rights frameworks has undermined the legitimacy of communal identities, community legal and political frameworks, and the ability of communities to protect their subjectivity (and perhaps also their autonomy) as communities, it contributes "to the delegitimization of democracies," according to Barzilai.[8] Here, Barzilai is addressing feminists, Orthodox religious communities, and Palestinians. For the communities that he addresses, law has more often tended to be mobilized as state law rather than as international law. State law has been adopted or appropriated in these contexts, both willingly and due to lack of an alternative, such that communities have been forced to

3. Mahmood, *Religious Difference in a Secular Age*, 81.

4. Mahmood, *Religious Difference in a Secular Age*, 152–53.

5. Gad Barzilai, *Communities and Law: Politics and Cultures of Legal Identities* (Ann Arbor: University of Michigan Press, 2005), 14–15, 17, 33, 36.

6. Barzilai, *Communities and Law*, 39.

7. Barzilai, *Communities and Law*, 39.

8. Barzilai, *Communities and Law*, 36.

mobilize liberal individual rights frameworks in defending the rights of the community as a community.[9] In this sense, the globalization of rights frameworks has not decreased state sovereignty, but it has influenced the domestic construction and application of rights frameworks toward one set of liberal individual norms—for better and for worse, when considered in terms of communal rights as conceived in communal terms.[10]

Joining the insights of Mahmood and Barzilai, the *secular* nature of this normative or philosophical move in legal terms may have negative implications for minority rights in contexts in which identity is felt and expressed in religious or communal terms, or both, rather than in secular and individualist terms. Indeed, the secular and the individualist, and the religious and communal, are, with unfortunate consequences, dyads that seem to go together frequently and to oppose one another in basic normative approaches to questions of rights. The *problematique* raised by the *secular* and *individualist* nature of international legal norms today matters in legal terms because religious liberty is also a right in international human rights conventions. It matters because religious approaches are ubiquitous, empirically still today, and many religious constituencies experience their identities and ideas about political culture and political institutions in communal rather than in individualist terms. That is, if domestic and international civil and human rights frameworks are to retain salience in the long run, they should attend to the existing cultural frameworks and expectations *in situ* regarding the place of community in society and in political institutions.[11]

The *problematique* matters, also, in normative terms if one does not accept the secularization thesis discussed in prior chapters as an inherent good. This chapter takes the approach that the secularization thesis is *not* an inherent good for the domestic nation-state-level construction of legal rights, nor for the construction of international legal norms regarding religious liberty/freedom of religion. Rather, religion as expressed in both individual and communal practices and ideals should be seen as a primary expression of the human condition—empirically speaking—and one in which rights frameworks should actively situate themselves to protect reli-

9. Barzilai, *Communities and Law*, 175.

10. Barzilai, *Communities and Law*, 310, see also 47.

11. Patricia J. Woods and Haluk Karadag, "Rights or Riots? Regional Institutional and Cultural Legacies in the MENA Region, and the Case of Turkey," *Journal of Power, Politics & Governance* 3, no. 1 (2015): 65–70.

gious freedoms, *particularly where religious liberty and communal autonomy coincide with and do not conflict with fundamental individual rights*. It is important to note that religious freedom has been (and should be) constructed in terms of liberty to practice as well as right of exit.[12] That is, the comments herein are made with the recognition that communities can be as oppressive as national-level states—and perhaps even more insidiously so. Communities, thus, should not have unfettered freedoms in the face of individual autonomy and privacy; nor, however, should communal identities, liberties, and institutional autonomy be ignored to the exclusive privileging of the (nonreligious) liberal-individual as they are in many Western legal frameworks today.

Both religion and community are here to stay, empirically, around the world. Rather than seeking to suppress each of them with a top-down, secular liberal-individualism, religious liberty and communal autonomy should be addressed in domestic and international civil and international rights frameworks in a way that actively works out an appropriate balance between individual autonomy and rights *qua* community, per se, internationally, and domestically by context.

Logically speaking, the implication of the secular and individualist approach to religious liberty and religious (minority) communities is that religious communities may not be able to attain or enforce human rights (including freedom of religious practice) because they are religious, which runs counter to the secularization impetus of the international human rights norms (as well as the secularization projects of many states). Moreover, they may not be able to attain or enforce human rights because they are communally oriented, which runs counter to the individualization impetus of the liberal legal norms that inform human rights laws. Or, both.[13]

This chapter explores the question of secular law and freedom of reli-

---

12. "Universal Declaration of Human Rights," United Nations General Assembly, December 10, 1948, Article 18: "Everyone has the right to freedom of thought, conscience and religion; this right includes freedom to change his religion or belief, and freedom, either alone or in community with others and in public or private, to manifest his religion or belief in teaching, practice, worship and observance."

13. In many ways, Saba Mahmood's study, *Politics of Piety: The Islamic Revival and the Feminist Subject* (Princeton: Princeton University Press, 2005), presents such tensions as the women's mosque movement in Cairo (successfully) seeks to situate its autonomy, as individuals and as groups, within a wider context that is assiduously religious and communal in nature.

gion as they relate to the relationship between religion and state in the case of Israel. Addressing religious-secular tensions in Israel, the chapter highlights important aspects of the religion-state relationship. Israel, like many countries in the Middle East, follows a form of political institutionalization at least partially modeled upon the Ottoman *millet* system in which legal autonomy is granted to religious communities in certain areas of law.[14] This autonomy stands for majority and minority populations. The chapter addresses conflicts and debates within the majority Jewish population, where the question remains controversial due primarily to a politically active secular minority, and within the territorial boundaries of the Israeli state.

THE ISRAELI CASE

In 1988, a heated conflict erupted between state religious authorities in Israel and the Israel High Court of Justice (HCJ). This clash, which I call the religious-secular conflict, became nothing less than a culture war in the Israeli state and the wider society.[15] It became so heated that, by the mid-1990s, the president of the High Court began to receive death threats. In 1999, at least 200,000 ultra-Orthodox men descended upon the High Court building calling the High Court president a traitor to his people and decrying the "tyranny" of his unelected rule over the country. Meanwhile, some 50,000 secular demonstrators confronted them in a counterprotest. From a failed HCJ attempt in 1969 to challenge religious authorities (*Shalit v. Min. of Interior*), justices on the court knew the stakes for both institutional and social stability in mounting an attack on the autonomy of state religious institutions. And, yet, it did just that in two cases in 1988, cases that marked only the beginning of nearly 15 years of intense legal battles.

Religious personal status law was one of four areas of formal jurisdiction granted to state religious authorities in the 1947 Status Quo Agreements between David Ben Gurion, founding prime minister, and Orthodox Jewish communities in Palestine. Religious personal status law grants citizen

14. Mahmood, *Politics of Piety*, 80–81; Patricia J. Woods, *Judicial Power and National Politics: Courts and Gender in the Religious-Secular Conflict in Israel* (Albany: State University of New York Press, 2008), 33.

15. See, for example, Martin Edelman, *Courts, Politics, and Culture in Israel* (Charlottesville: University of Virginia Press, 1994); and Pinhas Shifman, "Family Law in Israel: The Struggle between Religious and Secular Law," *Israel Law Review* 24 (1990): 537–52.

rights and responsibilities differently along gender lines. Thus, a tension arose between the (gendered) principles of religious law and secular principles, the latter of which assumed that law should be applied equally to all citizens in most instances; that is, norms regarding assumed gender parity in (most) legislation were present strongly enough that there was a felt tension on this issue. The tension between religious and secular principles did not become profound or highly politicized until the *Shalit* case in 1969, in which the religious identity of the mother was the key legal issue in regard to the citizenship of Benjamin Shalit's children. After *Shalit*, a quiet period ensued for nearly 20 years in terms of religious-secular questions in the HCJ. In the late 1980s, however, open conflict erupted and remained a central part of the national political landscape for nearly 15 years. The tension was reinforced with the adoption of two new rights-oriented Basic Laws in 1992.[16] Ultimately, as a governmental response to the conflict, the courts were restructured so that the religious courts came under the authority of the (presumed secular) Ministry of Justice rather than the Ministry of Religious Affairs. The latter was dissolved in 2003 and five years later was replaced with the narrower portfolio of the Ministry of Religious Services.[17]

Key justices sent signals in extrajudicial academic writings and in court cases as early as the early 1970s that they would welcome litigation on a broad set of rights issues. Social movement lawyers who became part of the *judicial community*[18] in the 1970s and 1980s joined in debates over these

16. Shimon Shetreet, *Justice in Israel: A Study of the Israeli Judiciary* (Jerusalem: Martinus Nijhoff, 1994).

17. See Daphna Hacker, "Religious Tribunals in Democratic States: Lessons from the Israeli Rabbinical Courts," *Journal of Law & Religion* 27, no. 1 (2011): 59–81, note 14: "In 2003, the Israeli government decided to abolish the Ministry of Religious Affairs, which had supervised the religious tribunals, and to transfer this authority to the Ministry of Justice. *See* Government Resolution No. 900: The Abolition of the Ministry of Religion (Oct. 8, 2003). In 2008, the Ministry for Religious Services was established, but the authority over the rabbinical courts remained with the Ministry of Justice. *See* Government Resolution No. 2903 (Jan. 6, 2008)."

18. This argument was first published in Patricia J. Woods (i.e., Sohn), "Courting the Court: Social Visions, State Authority, and the Religious-Law Conflict in Israel," PhD diss., University of Washington, 2001 (Ann Arbor, MI: ProQuest Dissertations Publishing, 2001). See also Patricia J. Woods, "Normes juridiques et changement politique en Israël," *Droit et Société* 55, no. 3 (2003): 605–26; Patricia J. Woods, "Cause Lawyers and Judicial Community in Israel: Legal Change in a Diffuse, Normative Community," in *The Worlds Cause Lawyers Make: Structure and Agency in Legal Practice*, ed. Austin Sarat and Stuart Scheingold (Stan-

issues at conferences, through mutual social movement activities, and in professional work. Justices drew upon the legal reasoning that social movement lawyers developed to support a variety of rights claims. These lawyers, in turn, constructed their arguments in close consideration of trends in thinking not only visible on the bench but from knowledge of the status of normative debates within this intellectual community centered around the justices. In addition, lawyers knew the reputations of individual justices.[19] Perhaps more importantly, justices knew the reputations of lawyers arguing regularly before them, those lawyers then reflecting a position not unlike the status of Marc Galanter's *repeat players*.[20] Indeed, interviews suggested that both justice and lawyer reputation had a significant impact on the willingness of a lawyer to bring a case to the HCJ; lawyer reputation was at least perceived by lawyers and some clerks to have some degree of impact upon judicial attention to the case. Over the course of 15 years or so in the 1970s and 1980s, changing (normative) ideas within the judicial community culminated in new legal arguments and, in the context of religious-secular tensions, changed HCJ decision-making on critical issues; these included, particularly, a new upholding of women's equality in both labor and religion questions and the linking of women's equality with challenges to rabbinical authority within the state.[21]

The key social movements in the religious-secular conflict as it emerged in the HCJ have been the religious pluralism movement, the civil rights movement, and the women's movement. This chapter focuses primarily on the women's movement. The initiators of the argument that became the most successful in challenging state religious authority in Israel included lawyers from the women's movement, the civil rights movement, and a private attorney who would later become a deputy attorney general. The women's movement then used that argument in several landmark cases in succession. That key argument was one linking *administrative legality* with *women's equality*. Administrative legality, the presumption that all citizens must be treated equally by state offices unless specified and detailed otherwise by statute, had been accepted as a basis for equality along ethnic lines in Israel's consti-

ford: Stanford University Press, 2005); and Woods, *Judicial Power and National Politics* (1st ed.).

19. See Lawrence Baum on the place of reputation in legal decisions in the US case. Lawrence Baum, *Judges and Their Audiences: A Perspective on Judicial Behavior* (Princeton: Princeton University Press, 2006).

20. Marc Galanter, "Why the 'Haves' Come Out Ahead: Speculations on the Limits of Legal Change," *Law & Society Review* 9, no. 1 (1974): 95–160.

21. Patricia J. Woods, *Judicial Power and National Politics*.

tutional tradition since the 1950s, under the influence of then HCJ president Simon Agranat.[22] Women's equality was an argument not accepted until the landmark cases discussed herein, which were decided in the late 1980s and early 1990s. The religious pluralism movement has provided the most sustained attention to the religious-secular conflict since that time in terms of litigation, particularly in relation to conversion and issues related to non-Orthodox practices (a topic outside the scope of this chapter).

RELIGION IN THE STATE—ISRAELI EXCEPTIONALISM?

Israel is often offered as an exceptional case both politically and socially.[23] In the case of the religious-secular conflict, however, Israel is far from alone. Early literature on religion and politics highlighted the significance of religion in cases in the Middle East, and in countries with large or majority Muslim populations outside the Middle East. These included examples such as Afghanistan,[24] Egypt,[25] Iran,[26] Pakistan and Saudi Arabia,[27] Malaysia,[28]

22. Regarding administrative law, see Martin Shapiro, *The Supreme Court and Administrative Agencies* (New York: Free Press, 1968); Martin Shapiro, "Codification of Administrative Law: The US and the Union," *European Law Journal* 2, no. 1 (1996); 26–47. Regarding Agranat's use of these principles in the developing jurisprudential rights tradition of the HCJ, see Pnina Lahav, *Judgment in Jerusalem: Chief Justice Simon Agranat and the Zionist Century* (Berkeley: University of California Press, 1997).

23. Yehezkel Dror, "On the Uniqueness of Israel: Multiple Readings," in *Israel in Comparative Perspective: Challenging the Conventional Wisdom*, ed. Michael N. Barnett (Albany: State University of New York Press, 1996), 245–63; Michael N. Barnett, "The Politics of Uniqueness: The Status of the Israeli Case," in *Israel in Comparative Perspective*, 3–25.

24. Eden Naby, "The Changing Role of Islam as a Unifying Force in Afghanistan," in *The State, Religion, and Ethnic Politics: Afghanistan, Iran, and Pakistan*, ed. Ali Banuazizi and Myron Weiner (Syracuse: Syracuse University Press, 1986), 124–54.

25. Farhat Jacob Ziadeh, *Lawyers, the Rule of Law, and Liberalism in Modern Egypt* (Stanford, CA: Hoover Institution Press, 1968).

26. Afsaneh Najmabadi, "Hazards of Modernity and Morality: Women, State and Ideology in Contemporary Iran," in *Women, Islam and the State*, ed. Deniz Kandiyoti (London: Palgrave Macmillan, 1991), 48–76.

27. John L. Esposito and John Obert Voll, *Islam and Democracy* (Oxford: Oxford University Press, 1996); John L. Esposito, "Islamization: Religion and Politics in Pakistan," *Muslim World* 72, no. 3–4 (1982): 197–223.

28. Andrew Harding, *Law, Government and the Constitution in Malaysia* (The Hague, Netherlands: Kluwer Law International, 1996).

Indonesia,[29] and India.[30] Formerly secular states such as Iraq and newly developing authorities as in Palestine contend with the question of what place religious institutions and laws will hold within the state. Perhaps surprisingly, even Europe was shown rather early in the field to include some place for religious law or religious institutions, or both, with regard to the state.[31] Some scholars of constitutional law argued that countries around Africa, Asia, and Europe include some official role for religious authorities in their constitutions.[32] Religious freedom and personal religious expression that strains the sensibilities of Christian majorities in Europe have been areas of political and legal tension in France, Britain, the Netherlands, and Germany, to name only a few.[33] Our starting post-Enlightenment notion that the laws and courts of modern states are formulated through the lens of secular, liberal law[34] is complicated by the existence *and resilience* of religious laws, institutions, and practices within modern states. The latter provide consistent challenges to the former and suggest a need for more attention, which has been aptly although not entirely answered by a growing literature

---

29. Daniel S. Lev, *Islamic Courts in Indonesia: A Study in the Political Bases of Legal Institutions* (Berkeley: University of California Press, 1972).

30. Archana Parashar, *Women and Family Law Reform in India: Uniform Civil Code and Gender Equality* (London: SAGE, 1992); Marc Galanter and Rajeev Dhavan, *Law and Society in Modern India* (Delhi: Oxford University Press, 1989).

31. For examples in Eastern Europe, see Mavis Maclean and Jacek Kurczewski, *Families, Politics and the Law: Perspectives for East and West Europe* (Oxford: Oxford University Press, 1994).

32. Eschel Rhoodie, *Discrimination in the Constitutions of the World* (Columbus, GA: Brentwood, 1984), citing countries including Zaire, Nigeria, Kenya, Ghana, Ethiopia, Zambia, India, Malaysia, Thailand, Northern Ireland, Italy, Cyprus, Denmark, Iceland, and Monaco.

33. Talal Asad, *Formations of the Secular: Christianity, Islam, Modernity* (Stanford: Stanford University Press, 2003); Jacques Robert, "Religious Liberty and French Secularism," *Brigham Young University Law Review* (2003): 637–60; Grace Davie, "Religious Minorities in France: A Protestant Perspective," in *Challenging Religion: Essays in Honour of Eileen Barker*, ed. James A. Beckford and James T. Richardson (London: Routledge, 2003), 159–69; J. Christopher Soper and Joel Fetzer, "Religion and Politics in a Secular Europe: Cutting against the Grain," in *Religion and Politics in Comparative Perspective: The One, the Few, and the Many*, ed. Ted Jelen and Clyde Wilcox (Cambridge: Cambridge University Press, 2002).

34. Susan Silbey, "'Let Them Eat Cake': Globalization, Postmodern Colonialism, and the Possibilities of Justice," *Law and Society Review* 31, no. 2 (1997): 207–36; Boaventura de Sousa Santos, *Toward a New Common Sense: Law, Science and Politics in the Paradigmatic Transition* (New York: Routledge, 1995).

on related topics. More recent works outlined in the introductory chapter to this volume affirm these general findings.[35]

Rabbinical authority gained state-sanctioned status in Mandatory Palestine under the Palestine Council of 1921.[36] The new Israeli state adopted this official status, granting rabbinical authorities a position within the state under the Status Quo Agreements. Rabbinical authority was institutionalized in the Israeli state through the Ministry of Religion until 2003, with the national system of rabbinical courts, religious parties, and a broad religious bureaucracy. Since the culmination of the religious-secular conflict, as seen in the HCJ from the late 1980s to the early 2000s, the rabbinical courts have been moved to the Ministry of Justice. Religious personal status law is based upon principles of communal religious law, which distinguishes between rights and responsibilities by community and by gender; likewise, rabbinical authority was organized in the last century—with rare exceptions emerging from the landmark legal cases in the late 1980s and 1990s—on a gendered basis. Gender was a central area of contest in the religious-secular conflict, and mobilized women were key players.

While minor changes had been made in rabbinical jurisdiction before 1988, mainly through the Knesset, until the late 1980s no state institution successfully challenged rabbinical jurisdiction over rabbinical offices, women's status in religious matters, or personal status law.[37] Indeed, rab-

35. See the introduction to this volume for discussion of some of these works.

36. Joel S. Migdal, *State in Society: Studying How States and Societies Transform and Constitute One Another* (Cambridge: Cambridge University Press, 2001).

37. Most changes in the early years of the state were legislative: Women's Equal Rights Law (1951); Adoption Law (1951, based loosely on halakhic principles); Capacity and Guardianship Law (1962); Succession Law (1965, based loosely on halakhic principles); Dissolution of Marriage Law (1969); and Spouse Property Rights Law (1973). The case law on the subject of religion and state is extensive. See Amnon Rubinstein, *The Constitutional Law of the State of Israel* [in Hebrew] (Jerusalem: Schoken, 1996), chapters 4, 5, and 6. However, the cases in which the authority of the religious establishment was ultimately challenged or undermined have been far fewer. A few important HCJ cases include H.C. 26/5 *Kutik v. Wolfson* 5 P.D. 1341 (1951); H.C. 262/62 *Peretz v. Local Council of Kfar Shmaryahu* 16 (3) P.D. 2101 (1962); H.C. *Haklai v. The Minister of the Interior* 17 (1963); H.C. 58/68 *Shalit v. The Minister of the Interior et al.* P.D. 23(2) 477 (1969). With the exception of *Shalit,* however, these cases did not undermine the institutional autonomy of rabbinical authorities. In addition, other cases were brought to the High Court relating to religious law and religious authorities, but usually were not successful in the court. In a few cases that were successful in the court, the decision did not constitute a judicial challenge to religious authorities because of clear legislation, or

binical authorities, Orthodox, and ultra-Orthodox communities accepted many small changes in other important issue areas with only minor complaint as long as the changes did not affect their immediate communities and neighborhoods. With the central issue of religious personal status/family law, however, religious authorities, Orthodox, and ultra-Orthodox communities produced a mass countermovement, responding to what they perceived to be an HCJ attack. Based upon my interviews with several key religious officials, a fervent defense of religious personal status/family law among Orthodox religious officials was rooted in the deeply held conviction that the religious requirements for marriage and divorce for all Israeli Jews must be coterminous with the requirements for full membership (e.g., religious, cultural, social, political) in the Jewish People (first) and the Jewish part of the Israeli national community (second). Orthodox Jewish officials emphasized that they held no claim of equivalent authority with regard to non-Jewish Israeli citizens, who are free to manage their religious personal status laws autonomously in the Orthodox view. Not surprisingly, religious constituencies appeared to believe that they managed their interreligious relations—by respecting one another's *religious* rights and autonomy on *religious* grounds—better than did secularists. Indeed, a long-standing (today perhaps unofficial) interreligious council of the Old City of Jerusalem was mentioned in regard to Orthodox Jewish respect for interreligious relations. For secularists, such a religious approach counters the fundamental principles of the secular liberal state,[38] as well as secular assumptions that religion leads to conflict rather than coexistence.

RELIGION AND THE COURTS IN ISRAEL

The civil courts in Israel are separated into three different levels: magistrate (trial) courts, district appeals courts, and the Supreme Court. The Supreme Court functions both as the highest court of appeal for trial cases, and as the HCJ. The Supreme Court hears regular appeals based upon falsified or new evidence, or if a third party has been convicted of the crime in question

---

because of a decision that corresponded with the preferences of Orthodox leaders.

38. On differences among religious and secular approaches to the Holy Places in Jerusalem, see, for example, Izhak Englard, "The Legal Status of the Holy Places in Jerusalem," *Israel Law Review* 28 (1994): 589–600.

(ordinary appeals). As the HCJ, it decides whether lower courts have acted within their jurisdiction, within the parameters of natural justice, or in other exceptional cases where it sees fit to intervene in the interest of justice.[39] The HCJ is Israel's constitutional court; it addresses questions relating to government overstepping of legal authority. (Israel has a constitutional tradition in jurisprudence rather than a written constitution.) Next to the civil courts there exist three other complete court systems in Israel: religious, military, and labor courts. Each of these includes trial and appellate levels. Cases can, under certain conditions, be appealed from these separate tribunals to the civil district courts, the Supreme Court, or to the HCJ. In the case of rabbinical court decisions, cases can be appealed only on grounds of inappropriate jurisdiction, or lack of a reasonable opportunity to appeal within the religious court system. Since these inherently involve questions of appropriate use of governmental authority and power, cases appealed from the rabbinical courts go directly to the HCJ.

In Israel, religious courts had almost exclusive authority over personal status or family law until 1995, and authority over most areas of family law since then. In an agreement dating from the year before the establishment of the state of Israel, the future government promised rabbinical authorities a position within the state under the Status Quo Agreements. David Ben Gurion, Rabbi Maimon Fishman of the Religious Zionist Movement, and Izhak Greenberg wrote a letter to the Secretariat of Agudat Israel in which it was agreed that the Orthodox communities would participate in and support the new state. In return, the state would guarantee freedom of conscience and Orthodox authority over four areas: (1) *kashrut* (kosher dietary laws); (2) religious marriage and control over personal status issues in general; (3) maintaining the Sabbath; and (4) Jewish religious education (in practice, this area of authority has been relevant primarily for religious populations).

The religious authority that was embedded in the Ministry of Religion (until 2003), the national system of rabbinical courts, religious parties, and the broad religious bureaucracy crosses lines between state and society, political and social institutions. The rabbinical courts are clearly part of the state; religious political parties constitute a borderland between state and society; and the rabbinate and much of the religious bureaucracy is largely independent of the state, although it gets significant funding from the state.

---

39. Asher Maoz, "Enforcement of Religious Courts' Judgments under Israeli Law," *Journal of Church and State* 33, no. 3 (1991): 473–94; Shetreet, *Justice in Israel*.

Minor changes were made in rabbinical jurisdiction between 1945 and the early 1970s (around the time of *Shalit*) through at least six Knesset laws and four major High Court cases. Before the 1970s, the HCJ demonstrated its uneasiness with the authority of the religious establishment in four major cases: *Kutik v. Wolfson* (1951)[40] in which it determined that paternity would be decided in civil, not religious courts; *Peretz v. The Local Council of Kfar Shmaryahu* (1962),[41] in which it was decided that the Reform movement is allowed to use public religious facilities; *Haklai v. The Minister of the Interior* (1963),[42] granting the right to civil marriage to those barred for religious reasons from religious marriage; and *Shalit v. The Minister of the Interior* (1969).[43]

The *Shalit* case was the most fundamental challenge to the religious establishment. It offered strong language from the court about the appropriate (or inappropriate) place of religion in the state. Benjamin Shalit asked the HCJ to force the Ministry of the Interior to register his children as Jewish. Shalit's wife, the children's mother, was not Jewish. But, Shalit contended, the religious law (*halakhah*) for deciding Jewishness, by which a child is Jewish if his/her mother is Jewish, had no place in the laws of an ostensibly secular, civil state. The case caused an uproar in Israel in political circles and in society at large. Termed the "Who is a Jew" case, *Shalit* highlighted many of the inconsistencies that had previously remained under the surface. If Israel was a Jewish state, then who gets to define who is a Jew? If the Orthodox have an official monopoly on defining Judaism in Israel, which was true at the time, then what about immigrants or natives who are from the Reform or Conservative movements? Later questions would arise as well: What about Jews from Ethiopia who had historically not been in close contact with rabbinical Judaism, and thus might not follow Orthodox rabbinical practice? What about immigrants from the former Soviet Union, some of whom were not *halakhically* Jewish, and others of whom might be

40. H.C. 26/5 *Kutik v. Wolfson* 5 P.D. 1341 (1951). For a more detailed discussion of rights-related landmark cases in the early years of the HCJ, see David Kretzmer, "Forty Years of Public Law," *Israel Law Review* 24, no. 3 (1990): 341–67.

41. H.C. 262/62 *Peretz v. Local Council of Kfar Shmaryahu* 16 (3) P.D. 2101 (1962).

42. H.C. *Haklai v. The Minister of the Interior* 17 (1963).

43. H.C. 58/68 *Shalit v. The Minister of the Interior et al.* P.D. 23(2) 477 (1969). Other cases were brought to the High Court relating to religious law and religious authorities, but usually were not successful in the court. In a few cases that were successful in the court, the decision did not constitute a HCJ challenge because of clear legislation.

halakhically Jewish in Orthodox terms but had not been practicing (by ideological choice or by state enforcement)?

In language that appealed to principles of natural law, the HCJ asserted that the religious law defining Jewishness had no place in the laws of the civil state. However, the decision became a debacle in which the HCJ's legitimacy was called into question, and the Knesset quickly changed the law to favor the rabbinical definition of Jewishness. The HCJ avoided making decisions that would challenge religious authorities within the state until the late 1980s.

Some argue that the HCJ changed its policy and began challenging rabbinical authorities in the late 1980s because of personal attitudes. Aharon Barak, president of the High Court from 1995 to 2006, was accused by some scholars and laypeople (particularly among the ultra-Orthodox) of tyrannical rule, of attempting to enforce a tyranny of judges, and of foisting Western secular values on a non-Western and nonsecular public. This answer corresponds with attitudinal answers in public law: in order to find out why justices decide the way they do, scholars need to look at the ideological positions of the justices.[44] However, Barak did not join the HCJ as a justice until 1979, after an initial change on the HCJ from legal positivism to activism in many areas. And he did not become president of the HCJ until 1995, significantly after the HCJ entered the religious-secular conflict, per se. Thus, the timing does not support the suggestion that the person of Aharon Barak was critical to the HCJ decision to enter the fray on the question of religious-secular tensions. Attitudinal changes among several major justices who were important prior to Barak do appear to have had a significant impact on these changes. None of these comments are to downplay the eloquence and significance of Barak as an influential and important legal thinker in Israel and abroad. However, the changes seen in the HCJ entry into the religious-secular conflict in the late 1980s were in the works long before that; that is, it was at least a fifteen-year to two-decade *process* leading to this particular change in HCJ decision-making. Thus, Barak was not the "culprit" suggested by critics.

44. C. Herman Pritchett, *The Roosevelt Court: A Study in Judicial Politics and Values, 1937–1947* (London: Macmillan, 1948); Jeffrey A. Segal and Albert D. Cover, "Ideological Values and the Votes of US Supreme Court Justices," *American Political Science Review* 83, no. 2 (1989): 557–65; Jeffrey A. Segal, "Measuring Change on the Supreme Court: Examining Alternative Models," *American Journal of Political Science* 29, no. 3 (1985): 461–79.

Based largely on the works of Shimon Shetreet,[45] Pinhas Shifman,[46] Asher Moaz,[47] Izhak Englard,[48] Menachem Elon,[49] Menahem Hofnung,[50] and Gad Barzilai,[51] this chapter begins with the assumption that the polarization of the Knesset after the 1977 elections did increase the tendency of social actors to bring cases to the HCJ. Indeed, my interviews with members of the judicial community suggested that the Knesset was viewed by many civil rights attorneys as achieving very little on certain important political issues, and therefore both social actors and politicians did, in fact, newly turn to the courts for solutions to problems or to pursue their agendas in increasing numbers.[52] The ability of any individual to bring certain types of rights cases against government institutions directly to the HCJ after a change in the rules of standing that expanded individual access to the HCJ in 1986 further increased the flow of cases to the HCJ.[53]

WOMEN'S MOVEMENT LEGAL MOBILIZATION

Bias and inequality under the law in the context of ethnicity had long been held illegal in the HCJ when social movements began to bring cases challenging religious authorities (and winning) in the 1980s. The major change

45. Shetreet, *Justice in Israel.*

46. Shifman, "Family Law in Israel."

47. Asher Moaz, "Enforcement of Religious Courts' Judgements under Israeli Law," *Journal of Church and State* 33, no. 3 (1991): 473–94.

48. Izhak Englard, *Religious Law in the Israeli Legal System* (Jerusalem: Alpha, 1975).

49. Menachem Elon, *Jewish Law: History, Sources, Principles* (New York: Jewish Publication Society, 1994).

50. See Menaḥem Hofnung, "Israeli Constitutional Politics: The Fragility of Impartiality," *Journal of Israel Affairs* 5 (1998): 34–54; Menachem Hofnung, "The Unintended Consequences of Unplanned Constitutional Reform: Constitutional Politics in Israel," *American Journal of Comparative Law* 44, no. 4 (1996): 585–604.

51. Gad Barzilai, *Wars, Internal Conflicts, and Political Order: A Jewish Democracy in the Middle East* (Albany: State University of New York Press, 1996).

52. See also Yoav Dotan and Menachem Hofnung, "Legal Defeats—Political Wins: Why Do Elected Representatives Go to Court?," *Comparative Political Studies* 38, no. 1 (2005): 75–103; and Shetreet, *Justice in Israel,* 104.

53. Shetreet, *Justice in Israel.*

that occurred in legal thinking on the court came with *Nevo*[54] and *Shakdiel*,[55] in which the HCJ took, for the first time, women's equality to be part of the wider principle of equality long held dear by the HCJ. However, the earliest cases involved women and labor and began not in the HCJ but in the labor courts, regional and then national. Several labor law cases were critical in developing legal reasoning on women's equality, reasoning that would ultimately be used in challenging religious authorities for many years to come. Some of the cases in which the women's equality argument was initially made, and then made successfully, happened through the work of the same attorney or sets of attorneys. Concurrently with the first landmark legal case, *Nevo*, the case of Leah Shakdiel was heard in the HCJ and decided two years earlier. *Shakdiel* set the initial precedent regarding women's equality that would be used to challenge religious jurisdiction for nearly 15 years.

Leah Shakdiel was elected to the Yeruham Religious Council in 1986.[56] Religious councils administered public works that have to do with religion in a town or municipal region. The local council was to be distinguished from municipal councils, which are equivalent to city governments. The religious council was responsible for the maintenance of ritual baths, any public religious place in the city, public religious events, and the like. It was not responsible for interpretation of matters of religious or *halakhic* (Jewish legal) import.

In 1985, the Shas political party asked the HCJ to review the makeup of all of the religious councils in Israel. It was decided in November 1985 that all religious councils would have to register with the Ministry of Religion to have their membership approved and their mandates renewed. Having received the Yeruham list in February 1986, Leah Shakdiel, a member of the Yeruham Religious Council, sent a letter to the Ministry of Religion in March 1986 inquiring after the status of their review in the ministry. A ministry official responded; the HCJ decision written by Menachem Elon includes the following quote from that letter:

> If I understand your letter correctly, it appears that you are also a member of the Local Council. Regarding this situation, I can already inform you that this is not within the realm of possibility. The religious council

54. H.C. 104/87 *Nevo v. The Jewish Agency et al.* P.D. 44 (4) 749 (1990).
55. H.C. 153/87 *Shakdiel v. The Minister of Religion, et al.* P.D. 42(2) 309 (1988).
56. H.C. 153/87 *Shakdiel v. The Minister of Religion, et al.* P.D. 42(2) 309, 227.

> has no members (*female*) but rather only members (*male*) and I understand that there is not a desire to create this kind of precedent.[57]

A committee of representatives of the prime minister, the Ministry of Religion, and the Ministry of the Interior reviewed the case and issued a stop order on Shakdiel's participation in the Yeruham Religious Council. Shakdiel appealed this order to the HCJ. Several groups offered support in the Shakdiel case, although only Shakdiel is listed as plaintiff. The Israel Women's Network, Na'amat, and the Association for Civil Rights in Israel all provided some type of legal advocacy in the case.

A committee of ministers was convened to decide whether Shakdiel could be a member of the Yeruham Religious Council. It decided that Shakdiel could not serve because she was a woman. In the HCJ case, the respondents argued that, in the history of the state, it had always been understood that local religious bodies have a close relationship with the rabbinate.[58] It was also custom that women could not participate in such bodies. The work of the religious council had a "halakhic-religious" air, and, as such, women neither had the skills nor were they appropriate to the job.[59] The HCJ case file includes several letters from religious council members opposing Shakdiel's acceptance to the council, as well as a letter of support from the local municipal council, which is the body that nominated her in the election.

The Shakdiel case was argued by attorney Yehoshua Shofman (later deputy attorney general under the Ehud Barak administration). Shofman was not a member of the women's movement but rather was an attorney for the Association for Civil Rights in Israel. In their petition for an *order nisi* on March 11, 1987, Shofman based the petition on several legal claims, the first of which was the following: "It is the right of a woman to hold an office in a religious council; in particular, it is the right of a woman not to have her holding of an office in a religious council frustrated *by virtue of [her] being a woman*" (*bashal hiota isha*). Shofman also argued that it is the right of the residents of Yeruham to have their religious council, which makes decisions relating to their rights in religious context, put in working order as

57. The letter is available in the HCJ case file for H.C. 153/87 *Leah Shakdiel v. The Minister of Religion, et al.* P.D. 42. See also the published case decision, 227.

58. The rabbinate is one of the central institutions of the Jewish religious bureaucracy in Israel, largely funded by the state, but also largely independent of it.

59. H.C. 153/87 *Leah Shakdiel v. The Minister of Religion, et al.* P.D. 42(4) 1988, 231.

quickly as possible. The petition included a lengthy discussion of the parameters of jurisdiction of the Committee of Ministers. That committee, Shofman argued, could not appropriate powers not granted to them by law just because of an ad hoc agreement between political parties.[60]

In a 57-page decision penned by Justice Elon, the HCJ argued that religious councils do not require members to be experts on religious law or interpretation. Rather, religious councils administer public works such as the ritual baths, religious schools, public religious events, maintain public religious buildings, and the like.[61] As members of the religious community who are subject to the decisions of the religious council, and as women who are particularly affected by issues such as the administration of ritual baths, there was no legal justification to keep women off local councils *by virtue of [her] being women.* While women may not have participated in these bodies by custom, in the state of Israel they could not be denied participation in what amounted to local governmental bodies. The HCJ thus made a fine but emphatic distinction between religious and civil work. The religious council was charged with overseeing the administrative functions of religious places and events; no male member had ever been required to be an expert Torah scholar. There could be no justification for requiring so of Shakdiel because she was a woman. In fact, Elon wrote, Shakdiel emphasized that were the religious councils charged with making *halakhic* decisions, she never would have brought a case to court.

Again, the language of the court is important. In *Shakdiel,* the HCJ used the words "by virtue of being a woman" no fewer than 10 times. Once it referred to the inability to choose who can sit on the council by virtue of being a man.[62] In addition, it used the word *hiota,* to be, in various constructions with *isha,* woman, and the words *bashal, mshum, akh bashal, prat,* and *ci* to indicate a line of causality: it was unacceptable to disallow a representative to sit on the council due to the fact that she was a woman. The word *hiota,* which refers to being-ness, I have translated "by virtue of [her] being a woman."[63] These are not, of course, the only mentions of *woman* or

60. See the HCJ case file for H.C. 153/87 *Leah Shakdiel v. The Minister of Religion, et al.* P.D. 42(4) 1988, petition to grant an *order nisi* against the Minister of Religion and Committee of Ministers, dated March 11, 1987.

61. H.C. 153/87 *Leah Shakdiel v. The Minister of Religion, et al.* P.D. 42(4) 1988, 236.

62. H.C. 153/87 *Leah Shakdiel v. The Minister of Religion, et al.* P.D. 42(4) 1988, 274–75.

63. H.C. 153/87 *Leah Shakdiel v. The Minister of Religion, et al.* P.D. 42(4) 1988, 227, 231 (twice), 233, 275 (twice), 276, 237, 272, and 274.

man in the case decision. However, what is important about this phrase is that it reflects the syntactic construction used by Shofman in the petition: a woman cannot be denied the right to serve on a religious council *akh bashal hiota isha* (only by virtue of her being a woman).

The unanimous decision in favor of Shakdiel ended with the following two sentences: "*One cannot forget that rabbinical authorities also function under the auspices of the law, and the principle of equality that is incumbent on everyone is also binding on them. Equality can emerge only as the principle of equality is put into practice.*"[64] This statement reflected an unequivocal position in favor of equality and made clear that equality included gender equality. The gender equality argument could be expected, henceforth, to appear as an HCJ challenge to rabbinical authorities in any area in which rabbinical authorities overstepped this inclusive notion of equality. Indeed, the HCJ reasoning in the *Shakdiel* case was mirrored in a decision, four days later, in the case of a woman who had been elected to the Tel Aviv Local Council, a case known as *Poraz.*[65]

The principle of equality was confirmed in three cases in 1994 (*Bavli, Lev,* and *Hoffman*), although the last case, *Hoffman,* reflected a less strident appeal to the principle than the first two. *Bavli*[66] involved a woman seeking equal division of property in a divorce case. Because she and her husband were married in 1972, prior to the adoption of an equal division of property law in Israel, the Rabbinical Court of Tel Aviv-Yaffo decided that she did not have the right to any division of property but only to maintenance (alimony), as allowed in *halakhic* law. In a private petition not related to any social movement, Bavli's attorneys cited *Shakdiel* together with the Women's Equal Rights Law of 1951, which was given new force by the *Shakdiel* and *Nevo* precedents.[67] The HCJ ultimately linked women's equality with both the concept of equality and principles of equity in contract law, expanding still further the application and reach of the principle of women's equality.

> Equal division of property, as a judicial principle, arises from a combination of the principle of equality, which is usually like mother's milk in the

64. H.C. 153/87 *Leah Shakdiel v. The Minister of Religion, et al* P.D. 42(4) 1988, 276, emphasis added.

65. "Poraz" case: H.C. 953/87 *The Labor Party, Tel Aviv Branch Office, et al. v. The Tel-Aviv-Yaffo Municipal Council et al.* P.D. 42 (1988).

66. H.C. 1003/92 *Haia Bavli v. The Rabbinical Court of Tel Aviv-Yaffo* (1992).

67. See the plaintiff's petition in the HCJ file for H.C. 1003/92 *Haia Bavli v. The Rabbinical Court of Tel Aviv-Yaffo.*

> constitutional view of this court, the Women's Equal Rights Law of 1951, principles of contract law . . . and the laws of formulation of equity . . . asks to grant just and appropriate possession to both in a couple of property accumulated through their joint efforts, each as appropriate to his/her efforts.[68]

In another case, the HCJ asserted international human rights principles over what it saw as lesser legal principles. In *Leah Lev et al. v. the Municipal Rabbinical Court of Tel Aviv-Yaffo,* Lev appealed an *order nisi* barring her from exiting the country because she was required to practice *shalom bayit* as part of her divorce proceedings. *Shalom Bayit* means, literally, "peaceful house"; under this *halakhic* principle, a spouse in a divorce case may request that the other spouse return to the matrimonial home in order to try to salvage the marriage. Women's organizations have protested this practice as oppressive and dangerous to women, particularly in cases of domestic abuse. Indeed, many women in women's shelters in Israel have fled *shalom bayit* orders.

In this case, Lev wanted to leave the country. The husband based his request for an *order nisi* barring her from leaving the country on the following: "The woman is managing, through leaving the country, an affair with a foreign man, a resident of the United States, and she intends in the near future to leave (emigrate from) Israel and work to become a resident of the United States with the children, together with this man."[69] The Rabbinical Court of Tel Aviv-Yaffo barred her from leaving the country. The HCJ argued that "*in its jurisdiction, it is incumbent upon the Rabbinical Court to respect human rights*"[70] (emphasis added); freedom to leave the country was a basic human right. The HCJ applied the Basic Law: Human Dignity and Freedom to the situation. In weighing the conflicting legal principles of *shalom bayit* and the human right of freedom of movement, the HCJ averred that the rabbinical court did not have the right to forbid exit from the country just to keep a person from injuring *shalom bayit.* The basic human right overrode a lesser legal principle. A lower court could not make an *order nisi*

---

68. H.C. 1003/92 *Haia Bavli v. The Rabbinical Court of Tel Aviv-Yaffo*, 254–55.

69. H.C. 3914/92 *Leah Lev et al. v. The Municipal Rabbinical Court of Tel Aviv-Yaffo* 94(1) (1994), 1.

70. H.C. 3914/92 *Leah Lev et al. v. The Municipal Rabbinical Court of Tel Aviv-Yaffo* 94(1) (1994), 8.

refusing exit of the country based on relations between spouses.[71] The HCJ treated the Rabbinical Court of Tel Aviv-Yaffo as part of the larger (nonreligious) judicial system.

In *Lev*, the HCJ gave arguably its strongest statement regarding the place of rabbinical courts within the Israeli legal system, which, as should be clear, has been a major source of contention in the debates over the place of religion in state law, as well as questions of freedom of religion. After a long discussion regarding the freedom and constraints with which a court may choose appropriate procedure, the HCJ, with Barak writing the majority opinion, stated unequivocally:

> The rabbinical court functions under the auspices of the law with which the Israeli courts limit it. These constraints bind it. It cannot deviate from them or overstep their bounds.[72]

CONCLUSIONS

Returning to the *problematique* offered at the outset of this chapter, have the Orthodox and ultra-Orthodox Jewish communities in Israel been able to sustain their communal autonomy and freedom of religious belief and practice under domestic and international rights regimes that privilege the individual rather than the communal, and the secular rather than the religious? Have secular communities been able to assert their freedom *from* religion in a state in which religious authorities govern, since 1995, most rather than all issues of personal status/family law (and prior to that almost all areas of personal status/family law)? Have women, who might be part of either set of communities, been able to see their rights enforced? The answer to each of these questions is, yes and no.

The interests of religious communities continue to be maintained by the 1947 Status Quo Agreements. Orthodox and, since the 1970s, some ultra-Orthodox authorities govern most areas of personal status law for the country today. Sabbath (limited application); kashrut (some towns, restaurants, and shops are excluded); and religious education (now, almost

71. H.C. 3914/92 *Leah Lev et al. v. The Municipal Rabbinical Court of Tel Aviv-Yaffo* 94(1) (1994), 2.

72. H.C. 3914/92 *Leah Lev et al. v. The Municipal Rabbinical Court of Tel Aviv-Yaffo* 94(1) (1994), 12.

exclusively for Orthodox religious communities rather than for the whole Jewish population) are under the jurisdiction of religious authorities with less extensive application in regard to nonreligious populations today. Orthodox, secular, and other constituencies have been able to change the legal arena by putting some issues of divorce in a secular Shalom Court, created by a coalition of groups including primarily grassroots women's organizations and the Directorate General of the Rabbinical Courts in 1995. That is, women's organizations and religious authorities worked with one another successfully in order to achieve some compromises.[73] Such coalition work across significant divides was critical to alleviating tensions on religious-secular issues at the time. Women have been successful in expanding women's autonomy, rights, or presence in the areas of women's participation in local religious councils, equal division of property in divorce, and, to some extent, religious rituals at the Western Wall of the Temple Mount.

That is, while the question of religion having a place within the state has raised some significant controversy at the national level, particularly in the years from 1988 to the early 2000s, religious authorities and secular constituencies have been able to navigate the *freedom of religious practice–freedom from religious compulsion* tension inherent in the principle of *freedom of religion* in a meaningful, if imperfect, balance. The HCJ certainly drew upon a human rights framework dependent upon individualist principles (rather than communal) and secular principles (rather than religious). At the same time, in some ways, the rabbinical courts themselves represented the other end of the spectrum, with some attention to communal and robust attention to religious rights and dynamics. The alternative extreme choices of absolutely no role for religion in the state, on the one hand, or, on the other hand, theocracy are equally inappropriate in a state in which the people largely prefer some (at least limited) role for religion in both the public sphere and the state, per se.[74] In keeping with the critiques of scholars such as Mahmood and Barzilai, rights are defined primarily through the lens of the individual

73. The establishment of the Shalom Court system as an outcome of coalition work and compromise among women's movement organizations and religious officials in Israel is a fact claim that emerged from my interviews with women's movement members as well as officials within the Directorate General of the Rabbinical Courts in Israel. It is, apparently, not a fact that is well known in the Israeli populace, which quickly became accustomed to the new options available to it with this new court system.

74. Patricia J. Woods, "Fault Lines," in *The Cambridge Companion to Judaism and Law*, ed. Christine Hayes (New York: Cambridge University Press, 2017).

with all of the problems that entails, and most rights are defined in secular terms. However, religious autonomy exists in some areas as influenced by the Ottoman institutional legacy. And human rights protections are carefully enforced to the extent possible. Nonetheless, the tensions that were felt in the long 1990s, for lack of a better phrase, while not resolved completely, find their way to the HCJ level less frequently today. That is, Israel provides a positive example of ways in which religious authorities and secular forces can coexist in a context in which religious institutions have some limited role within the state.

References

Asad, Talal. *Formations of the Secular: Christianity, Islam, Modernity*. Stanford: Stanford University Press, 2003.

Barnett, Michael N. "The Politics of Uniqueness: The Status of the Israeli Case." In *Israel in Comparative Perspective: Challenging the Conventional Wisdom*, edited by Michael N. Barnett. Albany: State University of New York Press, 1996.

Barzilai, Gad. *Communities and Law: Politics and Cultures of Legal Identities*. Ann Arbor: University of Michigan Press, 2005.

Barzilai, Gad. "Courts as Hegemonic Institutions and Social Change." *Politika* 3 (1998): 31–51.

Barzilai, Gad. *Wars, Internal Conflicts, and Political Order: A Jewish Democracy in the Middle East*. Albany: State University of New York Press, 1996.

Baum, Lawrence. *Judges and Their Audiences: A Perspective on Judicial Behavior*. Princeton: Princeton University Press, 2006.

Davie, Grace. "Religious Minorities in France: A Protestant Perspective." In *Challenging Religion: Essays in Honour of Eileen Barker*, edited by James A. Beckford and James T. Richardson. London: Routledge, 2003.

Dotan, Yoav, and Menachem Hofnung. "Legal Defeats—Political Wins: Why Do Elected Representatives Go to Court?" *Comparative Political Studies* 38, no. 1 (2005): 75–103.

Dror, Yehezkel. "On the Uniqueness of Israel: Multiple Readings." In *Israel in Comparative Perspective: Challenging the Conventional Wisdom*, edited by Michael N. Barnett. Albany: State University of New York Press, 1996.

Edelman, Martin. *Courts, Politics, and Culture in Israel*. Charlottesville: University of Virginia Press, 1994.

Elon, Menachem. *Jewish Law: History, Sources, Principles*. New York: Jewish Publication Society, 1994.

Englard, Izhak. "The Legal Status of the Holy Places in Jerusalem." *Israel Law Review* 28 (1994): 589–600.

Englard, Izhak. *Religious Law in the Israeli Legal System.* Jerusalem: Alpha, 1975.

Enloe, Cynthia H. *Bananas, Beaches, and Bases: Making Feminist Sense of International Politics.* Berkeley: University of California Press, 2014.

Enloe, Cynthia H. *Does Khaki Become You? The Militarization of Women's Lives.* London: Pandora Press, 1988.

Esposito, John L. "Islamization: Religion and Politics in Pakistan." *Muslim World* 72, nos. 3–4 (1982): 197–223.

Esposito, John L., and John Obert Voll. *Islam and Democracy.* Oxford: Oxford University Press, 1996.

Galanter, Marc. "Why the 'Haves' Come Out Ahead: Speculations on the Limits of Legal Change." *Law & Society Review* 9, no. 1 (1974): 95–160.

Galanter, Marc, and Rajeev Dhavan. *Law and Society in Modern India.* Delhi: Oxford University Press, 1989.

Goetz, Anne Marie. "Feminism and the Claim to Know: Contradictions in Feminist Approaches to Women in Development." In *Gender and International Relations,* edited by Rebecca Grant and Kathleen Newland. Bloomington: Indiana University Press, 1991.

Gordon, Evelyn. "Gender Bias Gets Ho-Hum Reaction." *Jerusalem Post,* October 24, 1990.

Hacker, Daphna. "Religious Tribunals in Democratic States: Lessons from the Israeli Rabbinical Courts." *Journal of Law & Religion* 27, no. 1 (2011): 59–81.

Harding, Andrew. *Law, Government and the Constitution in Malaysia.* The Hague, Netherlands: Kluwer Law International, 1996.

Hofnung, Menaḥem. "Israeli Constitutional Politics: The Fragility of Impartiality." *Journal of Israel Affairs* 5 (1998): 34–54.

Hofnung, Menaḥem. "The Unintended Consequences of Unplanned Constitutional Reform: Constitutional Politics in Israel." *American Journal of Comparative Law* 44, no. 4 (1996): 585–604.

Kretzmer, David. "Forty Years of Public Law." *Israel Law Review* 24, no. 3 (1990): 341–67.

Lahav, Pnina. *Judgment in Jerusalem: Chief Justice Simon Agranat and the Zionist Century.* Berkeley: University of California Press, 1997.

Lev, Daniel S. *Islamic Courts in Indonesia: A Study in the Political Bases of Legal Institutions.* Berkeley: University of California Press, 1972.

Maclean, Mavis, and Jacek Kurczewski. *Families, Politics and the Law: Perspectives for East and West Europe.* Oxford: Oxford University Press, 1994.

Mahmood, Saba. *Politics of Piety: The Islamic Revival and the Feminist Subject.* Princeton: Princeton University Press, 2005.

Mahmood, Saba. *Religious Difference in a Secular Age.* Princeton: Princeton University Press, 2016.

Maoz, Asher. "Enforcement of Religious Courts' Judgments under Israeli Law." *Journal of Church and State* 33, no. 3 (1991): 473–94.

Migdal, Joel S. *State in Society: Studying How States and Societies Transform and Constitute One Another*. Cambridge: Cambridge University Press, 2001.

Naby, Eden. "The Changing Role of Islam as a Unifying Force in Afghanistan." In *The State, Religion, and Ethnic Politics: Afghanistan, Iran, and Pakistan*, edited by Ali Banuazizi and Myron Weiner. Syracuse: Syracuse University Press, 1986.

Najmabadi, Afsaneh. "Hazards of Modernity and Morality: Women, State and Ideology in Contemporary Iran." In *Women, Islam and the State*, edited by Deniz Kandiyoti. London: Palgrave Macmillan, 1991.

Parashar, Archana. *Women and Family Law Reform in India: Uniform Civil Code and Gender Equality*. London: SAGE, 1992.

Pritchett, C. Herman. *The Roosevelt Court: A Study in Judicial Politics and Values, 1937–1947*. London: Macmillan, 1948.

Rhoodie, Eschel. *Discrimination in the Constitutions of the World*. Columbus, GA: Brentwood, 1984.

Robert, Jacques. "Religious Liberty and French Secularism." *Brigham Young University Law Review* (2003): 637–60.

Rubinstein, Amnon. *The Constitutional Law of the State of Israel*. Jerusalem: Schoken, 1996.

Santos, Boaventura de Sousa. *Toward a New Common Sense: Law, Science and Politics in the Paradigmatic Transition*. New York: Routledge, 1995.

Segal, Jeffrey A. "Measuring Change on the Supreme Court: Examining Alternative Models." *American Journal of Political Science* 29, no. 3 (1985): 461–79.

Segal, Jeffrey A., and Albert D. Cover. "Ideological Values and the Votes of US Supreme Court Justices." *American Political Science Review* 83, no. 2 (1989): 557–65.

Shapiro, Martin. "Codification of Administrative Law: The US and the Union." *European Law Journal* 2, no. 1 (1996): 26–47.

Shapiro, Martin. *The Supreme Court and Administrative Agencies*. New York: Free Press, 1968.

Shetreet, Shimon. *Justice in Israel: A Study of the Israeli Judiciary*. Jerusalem: Martinus Nijhoff, 1994.

Shifman, Pinhas. "Family Law in Israel: The Struggle between Religious and Secular Law." *Israel Law Review* 24 (1990): 537–52.

Silbey, Susan. "'Let Them Eat Cake': Globalization, Postmodern Colonialism, and the Possibilities of Justice." *Law and Society Review* 31, no. 2 (1997): 207–36.

Soper, J. Christopher, and Joel Fetzer. "Religion and Politics in a Secular Europe: Cutting against the Grain." In *Religion and Politics in Comparative Perspective: The One, the Few, and the Many*, edited by Ted Jelen and Clyde Wilcox. New York: Cambridge University Press, 2012.

"Universal Declaration of Human Rights." United Nations General Assembly, December 10, 1948.

Woods, Patricia J. "Cause Lawyers and Judicial Community in Israel: Legal Change in a Diffuse, Normative Community." In *The Worlds Cause Lawyers Make: Structure and Agency in Legal Practice*, edited by Austin Sarat and Stuart Scheingold. Stanford: Stanford University Press, 2005.

Woods, Patricia J. "Courting the Court: Social Visions, State Authority, and the Religious-Law Conflict in Israel." PhD diss., University of Washington. Ann Arbor, MI: ProQuest Dissertations Publishing, 2001.

Woods, Patricia J. "Fault Lines." In *The Cambridge Companion to Judaism and Law*, edited by Christine Hayes. New York: Cambridge University Press, 2017.

Woods, Patricia J. *Judicial Power and National Politics: Courts and Gender in the Religious-Secular Conflict in Israel.* 2nd ed., rev. Albany: State University of New York Press, (2008) 2017.

Woods, Patricia J. "Normes juridiques et changement politique en Israël." Translated by Margarita Vassileva and Thierry Delpeuch. *Droit et Société* 55, no. 3 (2003): 605–26.

Woods, Patricia J., and Haluk Karadag. "Rights or Riots? Regional Institutional and Cultural Legacies in the MENA Region, and the Case of Turkey." *Journal of Power, Politics & Governance* 3, no. 1 (2015): 63–79.

Yishai, Yael. *Between the Flag and the Banner: Women in Israeli Politics.* Albany: State University of New York Press, 1997.

Yuval-Davis, Nira. "National Reproduction and 'the Demographic Race' in Israel." In *Women-Nation-State*, edited by Nira Yuval-Davis and Floya Anthia. London: Macmillan, 1989.

Zamir, Itzhak. "Administrative Law: Revolution or Evolution." In *Public Law in Israel*, edited by Itzhak Zamir and Allen Zysblat. Oxford: Clarendon Press, 1990.

Zemach, Yaacov S. *Political Questions in the Courts: A Judicial Function in Democracies—Israel and the United States.* Detroit: Wayne State University Press, 1976.

Ziadeh, Farhat Jacob. *Lawyers, the Rule of Law, and Liberalism in Modern Egypt.* Stanford, CA: Hoover Institution Press, 1968.

High Court of Justice Cases

(Year of Decision in Brackets)

H.C. 1003/92 *Haia Bavli v. The Rabbinical Court of Tel Aviv-Yaffo* (1992).

H.C. *Haklai v. The Minister of the Interior* 17 (1963).

H.C. 257/89 *Hoffman et al. v. The Guardian of the Western Wall* P.D. 48 (2) 263 (1994).

H.C. 26/5 *Kutik v. Wolfson* 5 P.D. 1341 (1951).
H.C. 953/87 *The Labor Party, Tel Aviv Branch Office, et al. v. The Tel-Aviv-Yaffo Municipal Council et al.* P.D. 42 (1988) ("Poraz").
H.C. 3914/92 *Leah Lev et al. v. The Municipal Rabbinical Court of Tel Aviv-Yaffo* 94 (1) (1994).
H.C. 104/87 *Nevo v. The Jewish Agency et al.* P.D. 44 (4) 749 (1990).
H.C. 262/62 *Peretz v. Local Council of Kfar Shmaryahu* 16 (3) P.D. 2101 (1962).
H.C. 153/87 *Shakdiel v. The Minister of Religion, et al.* P.D. 42(2) 309 (1988).
H.C. 58/68 *Shalit v. The Minister of the Interior et al.* P.D. 23(2) 477 (1969).

The Balancing of Democratic and Jewish Values in the Israeli Court System, 1983–2006

Eti Peretz and Jonathan Fox

Bar Ilan University

In the amendment to the Basic Law passed by the Knesset in 1985, Israel is defined as a Jewish and democratic state. The dualism inherent in the joined tenets, "Judaism and democracy," has spiritual, social, and even existential implications. This dualism surfaced in its strongest form in the legislative branch of government and in the court system: in practice, the state of Israel is a combination of a secular democratic state with religious laws that bind the entire public. Examples of this state of affairs are the laws stipulating that marriage and divorce will be carried out according to religious rules and prohibiting the raising of pigs on the national territory. This combination of the two elements creates a constant tension between the religious and the secular in the country.

This chapter explores the struggle between Judaism and democracy as expressed in decisions and rulings of the Israeli High Court of Justice between 1983 and 2006, illustrating the rise in the power and status of religion in the judicial branch of government and, indirectly, in Israeli politics and society. It does so by comparing rulings regarding tradition and religion that were issued during Justice Aharon Barak's residency as the High Court of Justice president—during the years 1995–2006—to those issued during the residency of the previous court president, Justice Meir Shamgar, during the years 1983–95. It also illustrates the rise in the power and status of religion in Israeli politics and society between 1983 and 2006.

This chapter examines in particular the validity of the common perception that the Israeli High Court of Justice became antireligious during

Barak's tenure. While there is no systematic evidence as to how common this perception is, it is widely accepted in several sectors of Israeli society. Specifically, many argue that by adopting Barak's activist judicial policy, the court became a significant representative of liberal ideologies that oppose Jewish tradition and religious values.[1] The existence of these claims is proof of the unending tension in Israeli society between Judaism and democracy. In order to evaluate these claims, we use data collected on all Israeli High Court of Justice decisions on cases concerning traditional and religious communities or questions.

The findings show that the Barak era was not particularly antireligious. In fact, Justice Shamgar's presidency was characterized by more antireligious rulings as a proportion of all rulings than that of Justice Barak's tenure. Also, Barak's individually penned decisions and court rulings during his presidency were no more antireligious than those made before his presidency, nor were they more antireligious than the individual decisions of his predecessor. However, data analysis shows that there were considerably more rulings during Barak's tenure concerning religion, a phenomenon suggesting the growing importance of religion and its institutions in Israeli society.

THE BARAK CONTROVERSY

One of the common claims against Justice Barak posits that his liberal and secular attitude caused him to believe that freedom of expression is a central right even when it includes expressions or acts that injure the feelings of the religious public.[2] Barak disputes this claim, maintaining that the state of Israel's values include the values of its *Halakhic* tradition (i.e., pertaining to Jewish law). According to Barak, a justice's role is to do everything he can to create a balance between Israel's values as a Jewish state and its values as a democratic state. This role of the courts in balancing various and often con-

---

1. See, for example, Patricia Woods, who outlines the arguments of some critics of Barak. She argues, by contrast, that Barak was not the cause, but that his thinking contributed to this change, and that religious constituencies criticized him vociferously based upon the idea that he was the culprit. Patricia J. Woods, *Judicial Power and National Politics: Courts and Gender in the Religious-Secular Conflict in Israel*, 1st ed. (Albany: State University of New York Press, 2008).

2. Aharon Barak, "Hofesh Ha'Bituy U'Migbalotav," *Kesher* 8 (1990); Mordechai Heller, "Minuy Shoftim: Ha'Pitron Le'Mashber Ha'Elion," *Tchelet* 8 (2001): 55.

flicting principles constitutes a central policy of the courts especially when balancing state religion policy with other issues such as religious freedom and other civil liberties.[3]

Barak is generally perceived as one of the most transformative judicial figures in Israeli history. This tendency toward innovation includes his tenures as a High Court justice and the court's president, as well as in his earlier capacity as Israel's attorney general. These positions afforded Barak decades to impose his influence upon Israel's judiciary.[4] Given his degree of influence in the legal field, it is not surprising that he is also among the most controversial jurists in Israeli history. His "activism" has received considerable attention (positive and negative) both in Israel and abroad.

Many claims against him have been raised both in Israel and internationally. In particular, his activist and creative interpretation of the law attracts harsh criticism. For example, Richard Posner claims that Justice Barak abuses the term "interpretation" and that his rulings are "remote from a search for the meaning intended by the authors of legislation"; he argues further that Barak's rulings focus rather on Barak's personal opinions of the proper relations between government and society; and that in Barak's court it is "very difficult to tell whether a judgment of unconstitutionality was anything more than the judges' opinion that it was a dumb statute, something they would not have voted for if they were legislators."[5]

Stanley Fish similarly argues that Barak's judicial philosophy allows justices a considerable amount of room for interpretation. Fish quotes Barak's basic philosophy, "as the text ages, the law by its nature, weakens the control of the author over the text he or she [or they] created, and strengthens the control of the legal system—which tries to bridge the gap between law and society's changing needs—in the form of objective purpose."[6] That is, since laws are socially based, the interpretation of the law diverges from the intent of its writers as time passes, so that the law can be in line with current social

3. David M. Beatty, "The Forms and Limits of Constitutional Interpretation," *American Journal of Comparative Law* 49, no. 1 (Winter 2001): 79–120; Jonathan Fox and Deborah Flores, "Religions, Constitutions, and the State: A Cross-National Study," *Journal of Politics* 71, no. 4 (2009): 1499–1513.

4. Ariel Bendor and Ze'ev Segal, "The Hat Maker: Discussions with Justice Aharon Barak with Ze'ev Segal" (Kinneret Zmora-Bitan: Dvir Publications, 2009).

5. Richard A. Posner, "Enlightened Despot," *The New Republic* 53, April 23, 2007.

6. Stanley Fish, "Intention Is All There Is: A Critical Analysis of Aharon Barak's Purposive Interpretation in Law," *Cardozo Law Review* 29 (2008): 1129.

reality. According Stanley Fish, this "creative interpretation . . . moves further and further away from what the text meant for those who produced it and closer and closer to what the interpreter thinks the text ought to mean today."[7]

Whether Barak's judicial activism is in fact disproportionally antireligious is the topic of this chapter, but it is obvious that many feel that during his judicial career Barak undermined the role of Judaism in state affairs.[8] For example, in 2006 Zionist rabbis held a conference on the issue "Who is smarter, Aharon Barak or Maimonides?" with the clear assumption that the twelfth-century rabbi was the smarter of the two.[9] Opposition from Haredi (ultra-Orthodox) circles has been even more overt. For example, Rabbi Ovadia Yosef, the Haredi leader of Israel's Sephardi community and former chief rabbi of Israel, called Barak's court "wicked, stubborn and rebellious."[10]

On February 8, 1999, after a series of court rulings that angered Haredi leaders, Rabbi David Yosef, Rabbi Ovadia Yosef's son, characterized High Court of Justice president Barak as a Jew-hater and said the courts are anti-Semitic. The following day, Haredi former MK Moshe Gafni described the court decisions as judicial dictatorship, adding that an anti-Semite is one who makes trouble for Judaism—and one could say that about Barak.[11]

In a 1999 Haredi demonstration against the High Court of Justice, organized by Haredi rabbi and former MK Menahem Porush, he stated that "we came here to call on the High Court of Justice to end its persecution of Judaism and of the Great Rabbis."[12] On another occasion, Porush criticized the court's "antisemitic decisions."[13] While this controversy waxed in February 1999 after a series of rulings—including rulings that undermined the

---

7. Fish, "Intention Is All There Is," 1129.

8. Woods, *Judicial Power and National Politics*. Woods outlines the arguments of social actors and legal scholars holding this position. See especially chapter 4.

9. Matthew Wagner, "Rabbis Tout Jewish Alternative to Israeli Courts: 'Who Is Smarter, Aharon Barak or Maimonides?,'" *Jerusalem Post*, October 18, 2006, 1.

10. H. Dellos, "Loud Rallying Cries for Divisive Crisis of Faith," *Courier Mail*, February 16, 1999.

11. Shira Shoenberg, "Slurs Not Uncommon in Israeli Political Discourse," *Jerusalem Post*, January 19, 2002.

12. H. Dellos, "Loud Rallying Cries for Divisive Crisis of Faith," *Courier Mail*," February 16, 1999.

13. Lee Hockstader, "Israeli Court Sharpens Discord between Secular, Ultra-Orthodox Jews," *Washington Post*, February 14, 1999.

exemption of Haredi teenagers from the military draft; allowed kibbutzim (collective farms) to operate on the Sabbath; and mandated that representatives of the Conservative and Reform Jewish movements should be allowed to serve on local Jewish councils[14]—these criticisms had been common during Barak's tenure. As noted in more detail below, Barak was also heavily criticized in academic and legal circles.

THE CONTROVERSY OVER JUDAISM'S ROLE IN ISRAEL

Since Israel's foundation, the question of the role that Judaism should play in the state has been a matter of controversy. This is an important theme for the empirical research carried out in this chapter, since it provides the setting in which the High Court of Justice must render decisions regarding religion.

In states with a clear religious majority, there is often pressure for the state to support religion and integrate it into government and society.[15] This is certainly true for Israel.[16] Major controversies include whether businesses should remain closed on the Sabbath; whether all marriages should be conducted under religious auspices; the role of non-Orthodox Judaism in Israel; the question of who is to be considered Jewish; and state enforcement of Jewish dietary laws.[17] While many argue that these religious issues contradict Israel's democratic principles,[18] others posit that, with the exception of the marriage issue, Israeli law is within the bounds of Western democratic standards.[19]

14. Hockstader, "Israeli Court Sharpens Discord."

15. Jonathan Fox, *A World Survey of Religion and the State* (New York: Cambridge University Press, 2008).

16. Benjamin Neuberger, "Dat, Medina U'Politika"—Mimshal U'Politika be'Medinat Israel (Tel-Aviv: Open University, unit 6 (1994): 7; Woods, *Judicial Power and National Politics*, 7–9.

17. Woods, *Judicial Power* (2008); Asher Cohen, "Israeli Assimilation," Rappaport Center for Assimilation Research and Strengthening Jewish Vitality (Ramat Gan: Bar Ilan University, 2002); Eliezer Don-Yehiya and Charles Liebman. *Religion and Politics in Israel* (Bloomington: Indiana University Press, 1984).

18. See, for example, Baruch Kimmerling, *The Invention and Decline of Israeliness* (Berkeley: University of California Press, 2000); Benjamin Neuberger, *Religion and Democracy in Israel* (Jerusalem: Floersheimer Institute, 1997); Amnon Rubinstein, Ha'Mishpat Ha' Konstitutzioni Shel Medinat Israel, A, (1991), 225.

19. Don-Yehiya and Liebman, *Religion and Politics*; Jonathan Fox and Jonathan Rynhold,

Some key themes and structural features define the nature of the controversy. The first is about the nature of the Jewish state itself. On the one hand, a majority of the Israeli public does not accept a complete separation between firm religious roots and Jewish nationalism.[20] And indeed, some of Israel's national symbols invoke religious objects, such as the state's blue-white flag (the colors of the prayer shawl); and the menorah, which was once the symbol of the Temple. These symbols are perceived as national emblems indicating the Jewish people's historic continuity. This "civic religion" stresses the fact that there is a consensus among Jews in Israel that Israel is a Jewish state. A 1985 amendment to Israel's Basic Law in the Knesset (Israel's parliament) formalized this relationship by declaring Israel a Jewish democratic state. On the other hand, there is a severe disagreement over the extent to which the principles of Judaism should be integrated into state law and the extent of state support for and integration with Jewish religious institutions.[21] There is also controversy regarding the interpretation of this 1985 amendment to Israel's Basic Law. Many argue that this article does not constitute a formal establishment of Judaism as the state religion.[22] Others argue that in practice, state and religion are deeply intertwined and, accordingly, Orthodox Judaism effectively serves as Israel's established religion.[23] In practice, the current arrangement is a compromise known as the Status Quo Agreements where, in theory, the state of affairs that existed at Israel's independence remains in force. In practice, this arrangement has been altered over time.[24]

"A Jewish and Democratic State? Comparing Government Involvement in Religion in Israel with Other Democracies," *Totalitarian Movements and Political Religions* 9, no. 4 (2008): 507–31; Steven V. Mazie, *Israel's Higher Law: Religion and Liberal Democracy in the Jewish State* (Lanham, MD: Lexington Books, 2006).

20. Woods, *Judicial Power* (2017), 9.

21. Woods, *Judicial Power* (2008); Menachem Elon and Ben Shimon, *Ma'amad Ha'isha: Mishpat V'Shiput, Masoret U'Tmura: Arachea Shel Chevra Yehudit Ve'Democratit* (Tel Aviv: Ha'Kibuta Ha'Meuchad, 2005); Imanuel Gutman, "Dat Be'Politika Ha'Yisraelit—Gorem Me'Ached U'Me'Faleg," in *Ha'Ma'Arechet Ha'Politit Be'Israel*, ed. M. Lisk and Imanuel Gutman (Tel-Aviv: Am Oved, 1976), 357–410; Gutman, "Dat Be'Politika Ha'Yisraelit"; Neuberger, "Dat, Medina U'Politika."

22. Danuel J. Elazar, *Israel: Building a New Society* (Bloomington: Indiana University Press, 1986).

23. Woods, *Judicial Power* (2008); Alan Dowty, *The Jewish State: A Century Later* (Berkeley: University of California Press, 1987); Neuberger, *Religion and Democracy*.

24. Don-Yehiya and Liebman, *Religion and Politics*; Fox and Reynhold, "A Jewish and Democratic State?"

Another important issue is the relative size of different categories in the secular-religious spectrum, and their political weight. These categories are not clearly defined, as they repose on slightly different definitions by the Central Bureau of Statistics and by the Guttman Institute and the Israel Democracy Center on the other. These different definitions influence heavily the distribution and weight of each of the four categories into which they divide Israeli society.

The secular camp[25] includes between 21 percent[26] and 40percent[27] of Jewish Israelis. According to the 1993 Guttman Institute National Survey and the Israel Democracy Institute, 21 percent regard themselves as completely nonobservant, while 40 percent includes secular Jews with certain religious traditions. This group believes in a Jewish identity based only upon common origin, history, culture, and fate. Most members wish to preserve this identity in a Jewish national, political framework. For many of them, the affinity to Judaism lacks religious content and they are not committed to faith per se, or to a religious lifestyle. Of these, most feel that the current status quo regarding religion and state affairs has the state too heavily involved in religion, and support significant changes. Some support the total separation between religion and state affairs and prefer the European solution in which the state supplies religious services, but the nonreligious citizen is not bound by any religious law or sanction.[28]

The second group is the "*mesorati*" or traditional sector.[29] Its size ranges between 14 percent[30] and 79 percent.[31] According to Central Bureau of Statistics, about 14 percent of Israelis define themselves as "traditional-religious" people and 25 percent define themselves as "traditional-nonreligious," while according to the 1993 Guttman National Survey Institute and the Israel Democracy Institute, 14 percent regard themselves as "strictly observant," 24 percent as "observant to a great extent," and 41 percent as "somewhat observant."

25. Benjamin Neuberger, "Dat, Medina U'Politika," 7; Charles S. Liebman, ed., *Religion, Democracy, and Israeli Society* (London: Hardwood Academic, 1997); Social Pole, *Central Bureau of Statistics* (2006), 7, http// www.cbs.gov.il

26. Liebman, *Religion, Democracy, and Israeli Society*.

27. Social Pole, *Central Bureau of Statistics* (2006), 7.

28. Neuberger, "Dat, Medina U'Politika."

29. The term *mesorati* can also be translated as "conservative"; the term as used in relation to the traditional camp in Israel is not related to the conservative movement in the West.

30. Social Pole, *Central Bureau of Statistics* (2006), 7.

31. Liebman, *Religion, Democracy, and Israeli Society*; Social Pole, *Central Bureau of Statistics* (2006), 7.

This sector does not perceive Judaism as a merger of religion and nationality, and thus claims that the state of Israel's character cannot be secular. This part of the public opposes the idea of separating religion from state affairs. It tends to support the existing status quo with regard to state religion policy.[32] According to survey results, *mesorati* Jews tend to oppose civil marriages but seek an honorable solution for those who cannot marry under religious auspices. They also oppose formal recognition of non-Orthodox Jewish movements, but they require a "flexible" Orthodoxy. For example, they tend to support legislation that forbids raising pigs and marketing them but oppose closing down football fields on the Sabbath.[33]

The third sector is the religious Zionists, who make up approximately 10 percent of the population.[34] They perceive religion and nationality as one entity. They define themselves as genuine Zionists who share Zionist criticism of the Diaspora but reject secular Zionist criticism of religion. According to this constituency, separating religion from state affairs is a prescription for catastrophe. Their vision is a state in which the religious law is the state law, not only in matters of matrimony as is the case today but also in the civic and criminal domains.[35] This group defines Israel as a "Jewish State" in both the national and religious meanings of the term. While the current state of affairs does not meet this ideal, members of this sector, with some notable exceptions, tend to abide by the majority of the state's laws.[36]

The fourth sector includes the 7 percent of the population that define themselves as ultra-Orthodox.[37] This group does not perceive Israel as a Jewish state despite the fact that the majority of the group does acknowledge the existence of the state. In the eyes of the ultra-Orthodox communities, the state as a concept does not offer a religious value; many perceive the (secular) state as one of the heretical aspects of secular modernity that must be challenged.[38] Despite doubts about the state's legitimacy, the ultra-Orthodox sector is politically active and supports several political parties, most of which pursue an agenda of increasing government involvement in religion (and the reverse). Those supporting such platforms tend to believe

32. Woods, *Judicial Power* (2008); Neuberger," Dat, Medina U'Politika."

33. Social Pole, *Central Bureau of Statistics* (2006), 7.

34. Social Pole, *Central Bureau of Statistics* (2006), 7, http// www.cbs.gov.il

35. Woods, *Judicial Power* (2008).

36. Neuberger, "Dat, Medina U'Politika."

37. Social Pole, *Central Bureau of Statistics* (2006), http// www.cbs.gov.il

38. Woods, *Judicial Power* (2008).

that the law of the state should be the religious law and that any other secular government or system of secular legislation is illegitimate. The extreme sector of the ultra-Orthodox current does not even acknowledge the state of Israel as a legitimate entity. It boycotts elections, does not acknowledge official courts or any other state institutions, and refuses to accept state services or money. This extreme ultra-Orthodox minority blames Zionism for polluting the Holy Land, perceives the state as a "rebellious state," and calls government "the impure rulers." This minority objects to any religious legislation created by a secular parliament, because that would mean secularizing the Torah; thus, it does not advocate the involvement of religious communities in the state at all. The Torah is the ultimate law; it does not need recognition from secularists, who they see as heretics.[39]

RELIGION AND THE ISRAELI HIGH COURT OF JUSTICE UNDER BARAK

One of the Israeli High Court of Justice's roles is to balance the tension between Israel's Jewish and democratic components.[40] As is the case with opinions on religion's proper role in Israel, opinions over how well the court executes this task vary considerably. However, all agree that under Chief Justice Barak's tenure, the court was particularly active on religious issues by curbing the power of state religious authorities.

Many argue that this activism improperly undermines the role of Judaism in Israel. For example, High Court justice Menachem Elon believes in the creation of a synthesis between Judaism and democracy. However, he stresses that when there is no way to reconcile the two, Judaism takes precedence. According to Elon, the use of the Jewish sources that he calls "Hebrew Law" is a necessity for the state of Israel's legal system. Elon opposes the judicial activism that Justice Barak led while residing as the High Court of Justice president. He argues that the Barak court supported democracy too

---

39. Neuberger, "Dat, Medina U"Politika"; Aviezer Ravitzki, *Haketz Ha'Megule U'Medinat Ha'Yehudim: Meshichiyut, Tzionut Ve'Radikalism Dati Be'Israel* (Tel-Aviv: Am Oved Publications, 2006).

40. Ariel Rozen-Tzvi, "Medina Yehudit Ve'Demokratit: Abahut Ruchanit, Nikur Ve'Simbioza—Ha'Efshar Le'rabea et Ha'Maagal?," in *Dat, Liberalism Ve'Chevra*, ed. Ariel Porat (Tel-Aviv: Ramot, 2001), 230.

strongly at the expense of Judaism.[41] Haim Shain concurs and states that the decisions of Barak's court systematically led to a decrease in the state's Jewish-democratic character. Furthermore, he argues that Barak acted to decrease severely religious influence upon acceptable public norms. He accuses Barak of repressing the authority of Israel's rabbinical courts.[42] Hillel Nayar similarly accused Barak of underestimating Judaism's importance as a source of Israel's basic values to the extent that he both undermined the legislature's intention and redefined those values both in theory and in fact.[43]

Two important issues on which the Barak court's activism played out are the related issues of the rabbinical monopoly over marriage and divorce among Jews, and the general power and independence of Israel's rabbinical courts. The 1948 Status Quo Agreements granted Orthodox communities authority over several issues, including personal status law in exchange for their recognition of the emerging state. Likewise, Israel's 1953 Rabbinical Court Judicial Law determines that Jews can marry only through rabbinical officials and get divorced only through a rabbinical court. This law effectively gives rabbinical courts a monopoly over these issues, where Jewish law is applied.

Chava Bavli petitioned against the rabbinical court's unequal division of assets, claiming that this contradicted Israel's Women's Rights Law (1951). The ruling occurred while Justice Shamgar was president of the High Court (Barak was a regular sitting justice at that time). The court ruled in favor of Chava Bavli and required equal division of marital assets. Based upon this precedent, Barak later set the rule that all religious courts must follow civil rather than religious law as interpreted by Israel's High Court of Justice in

41. Elon, *Ma'amad Ha'isha: Mishpat Ve'Sshiput.*

42. Haim Shain, "The Jewish State–Concluding Summary," *Hod Ha'Sharon: Shaare Mishpat* (2005): 146–48.

43. Hillel Nayar, "Aharon Barak's Revolutionary Doctrine," *Tchelet* 3 (1998): 11–43; for others who similarly argue that the Barak Court rulings undermined Israel's Jewish character, see Daniel Statman and Gideon Sapir, "Freedom of Religion, Freedom from Religion, and Protecting Religious Feelings," *Mehkarei Mishpat* 21, no. 2 (2004): 5–87; Wagner, "Rabbis Tout Jewish Alternative"; Y. Goell, "Here Come the Judges," *Jerusalem Post*, May 12, 2003, 6; L. Hockstader, "Israeli Court Sharpens Discord between Secular, Ultra-Orthodox Jews," *Washington Post*, February 14, 1999, 29; Shain, "The Jewish State," 146–48; and Kobi Nahshoni, "Harav Sherman: 'Hatzaat Barak tigrom lehitbolelut,'" accessed January 15, 2015, http://www.ynet.co.il/articles/0,7340,L-3542958,00.html

these matters.[44] This ruling resulted in a significant backlash from the rabbinical courts, but also a significant amount of support.[45] It is important to point out that in numerous cases Barak's court sided with the rabbinical courts, leading to the conclusion that the court was by no means one-sided.[46]

THE RISE OF RELIGION IN ISRAELI AND WORLD POLITICS

One explanation for the perception that Barak's court was antireligious is that religion became a more high-profile matter during Barak's tenure. If so, it is not the rulings involving religious questions that changed, but rather their absolute number, the awareness of them, and consequently, the reaction to them. This approach recognizes the fact that religion is becoming a higher profile and more contentious issue in Israeli and world politics, and this circumstance happens to coincide with Barak's tenure.

Many voices in the contemporary literature dealing with religion and world politics make precisely this argument. For example, Mark Juergensmeyer argues that as secular governments have failed to provide economic prosperity and social justice, religion is becoming an increasingly important source of legitimacy, thus fueling religious opposition movements.[47] David Rapoport similarly argues that since the late 1970s, religion has become the primary ideology of violent opposition forces, replacing nationalism and ethnicity in this role.[48] Monica Toft, Daniel Philpott, and Timothy Shah

44. H.C. 1000/92, *Chava Bavli vs. Supreme Rabbinical Court*, Verdict 92(32)221, 1994. Woods, *Judicial Power* (2008); Elon, *Ma'amad Ha'isha: Mishpat Ve'Sshiput*; Naomi Levitski, *Your Honor: Aharon Barak—Bibliography* (Jerusalem: Keter Publications, 2001), 35.

45. Francess Radai, "Diokano Shel Ha'Nasi Aharon Barak: Shivion Be'Medina Yehudit Ve'Democratit," *Mishpatim* (Law faculty periodical, Jerusalem) (2009): 254; Ariel Rozen-Tzvi, "Medina Yehudit Ve'Demokratit."

46. Levitski, *Your Honor: Aharon Barak*, 2001.

47. Mark Juergensmeyer, *The New Cold War? Religious Nationalism Confronts the Secular State* (Berkeley: University of California Press, 1993); Mark Juergensmeyer, *Global Rebellion: Religious Challenges to the Secular State, from Christian Militias to al Qaeda* (Berkeley: University of California Press, 2008).

48. David C. Rapoport, "The Fourth Wave: September 11 in the History of Terrorism," *Current History* 100, no. 650: (2001): 419–24; David Rapoport, "The Four Waves of Modern Terrorism," in *Attacking Terrorism: Elements of a Grand Strategy*, ed. A. Cronin and J. Ludes, 46–73 (Washington, DC: Georgetown University Press, 2004).

argue that in a process that lasted centuries, the modern state marginalized religion, removing it from its former status as an equal partner with the state.[49] This triggered an institutional and social evolution process wherein religion found new bases for support in society, to replace the support that centuries ago came from partnerships with governments. By the late 1960s, this process was sufficiently mature for religious actors, who had previously been inwardly focused on preserving their traditions, to become once more outwardly focused and return to the political arena. Juergensmeyer, Rapoport, Toft et al., and Philpott argue that this trend became especially significant around the late 1970s to the mid-1980s.[50]

While religion has always been a factor in Israeli politics, its increased prominence can be traced to this same period. Shas, the political party credited with transforming religious parliamentary politics in Israel, was formed in 1984. Gideon Aran and Ron Hassner specifically argue that the rise of Jewish religious political violence is consistent with the timing described in Rapoport's theories.[51]

The rise of Shas to political power in 1984 also coincides with the beginning of Justice Shamgar's residency as the High Court of Justice president in 1983. Barak became president in 1995. Thus, if the explanation for the perception of Barak's court as antireligious is based upon the increased prominence of religion in Israeli politics, unrelated to Barak, we would expect the proportion of pro- and antireligious rulings in Shamgar's and Barak's courts to be similar. If, on the contrary, it is based upon an actual bias in Barak's court, we would expect more antireligious rulings during the term of Barak's presidency as compared to the Shamgar's tenure.

PREVIOUS STUDIES

A previous statistical study of this topic by Manof—the Center for Jewish Information, claimed that the High Court of Justice and Justice Barak's judi-

49. Monica Duffy Toft, Daniel Philpott, and Timothy Samuel Shah, *God's Century: Resurgent Religion and Global Politics* (New York: W. W. Norton, 2011); D. Philpott, "Has the Study of Global Politics Found Religion?," *Annual Review of Political Science* 12 (2009): 183–202.

50. Juergensmeyer, *New Cold War?*; Juergensmeyer, *Global Rebellion*.

51. Gideon Aran and Ron E. Hassner, "Rejoinder," *Terrorism and Political Violence* 25, no. 3 (2013): 416–18, 357–61. There is little controversy regarding this issue of timing.

cial activism had led to a secular revolution.[52] According to this claim, Justice Barak used judicial tools to advance social ideas that are foreign to tradition and religion. However, we contend that the Manof study has serious methodological flaws to the extent that the study's results are unreliable. One major issue is that the study missed a number of cases that we found to be relevant. At least 28 relevant cases were not included in the Manof study. Two-thirds of these, according to Manof's definitions, were pro-religion.[53] We argue further that the study improperly included all cases where the High Court of Justice reviewed appeals from Israel's religious court system, and it considered any overturning of a ruling by the religious courts to be antireligious. This move is inappropriate methodologically for two reasons: first, because this type of data would only be meaningful in comparison with how often the High Court of Justice overturned rulings from secular courts. If the proportion of "overturns" to "upholds" is similar for appeals from both court systems, there would be no bias. Second, courts rarely hear appeals in cases where there is little chance of the case being overturned. Accordingly, a more correct analysis would examine how many cases are overturned as a proportion of all attempted appeals, rather than of all appeals actually heard by the court.

Another issue is that the Manof study examines the High Court rulings during Barak's tenure exclusively, in what can be termed as a judicial vacuum. Without a comparison to previous rulings, it is impossible to determine whether the rulings during Barak's tenure as court president are in any way different or similar to the court's position before that period. Thus, even barring other methodological issues, the Manof study does not have sufficient scope to address the issue of whether Barak's court reflected a *change* in court policy.

RESEARCH DESIGN

The study examines all rulings, 69 cases altogether, that deal with religion and tradition made during Justice Barak's tenure as the High Court of Jus-

52. Isaac Hurvitz and Dikla Dahan, "Dat U'Bagatz—Dimuy U'Metziut" (Jerusalem: Manof, the Jewish Information Center, 2004).

53. Margit Cohen, Eli Linder, and Mordechai Kremnitzer, "Religion and the High Court of Justice: Image and Reality—Part One: A Critical Examination of the Publication by Manof," Jerusalem: Center for Jewish Information, 2003.

tice president, beginning August 14, 1995 and ending September 14, 2006.[54] These were the only rulings found relevant to the study's stated domain out of 1,275 total rulings listed in the Nevo rulings database.[55] The study also examines 42 rulings on religion and tradition during Justice Shamgar's tenure.[56] These rulings were made from November 28, 1983 to August 13, 1995. They were the only relevant to the study's goal, out of 557 rulings listed in the Nevo database. While the database includes the individual rulings of each justice in each case, in addition to the final case decision, in this study we examine the rulings of the court and the individual rulings of Justices Barak and Shamgar (but not of other justices). While the numbers themselves are relatively small, it is noteworthy that the latter period saw just over a 50 percent increase in the number of cases that fall within the domain of our study.

In order to locate the relevant rulings, we searched using terms such as "Judaism," "tradition," "Hebrew," and "religion" in the Nevo database. The cases in which these words appeared were examined for content relevant to religion. For example, when examining cases involving Orthodox Jewish institutional authority, cases that were directly connected to religion, such as issues of *kashrut* (Jewish dietary law), were included; on the other hand, cases that were of civilian character, such as wills, inheritances, and common-law marriages, that had no connection to issues of religion in the state and did not reflect in a clear manner the controversy of religion and state affairs, were not included.

We categorized whether a ruling was pro- or antireligious using the same criteria as Isaac Hurvitz and Dana Dikla.[57] Thus, a negative decision—one against religion—is one that meets any of these four criteria: (1) a ruling or decision that rejects a value, norm, or a traditional religious institution; one that negates or contradicts the relevant value, even if there is no religious petitioner; (2) a ruling or decision that includes an explicit negation of Jewish values and a rejection of the Hebrew law; (3) a ruling or decision that implies a change in the state of Israel's religious toward secular norms; (4) a ruling that reduces the authority of Israel's religious courts.

54. In the first stage 75 relevant rulings have been located until after another sifting the number was diminished to the current one.

55. Nevo. an Israeli search engine in Hebrew, of the legal database.

56. Of the 43 relevant rulings the number was diminished to the current one.

57. Hurvitz and Dikla, "Dat U'Bagatz—Dimuy U'Metziut."

On the contrary, a positive decision—one in favor of religion—is one that meets any of these four criteria: (1) a ruling or decision whose essence means the adoption of a traditional or religious value; (2) a ruling or decision that adopts the Hebrew law; (3) a ruling or decision that rejects a law or action that undermines a traditional or religious value or institution; (4) a ruling or decision that implies a change in the state of Israel's religious status quo in favor of religious norms.

Finally, a neutral decision is one that meets any of these three criteria: (1) a ruling or decision that does not determine whether a traditional or religious value should be rejected; (2) a ruling or decision that refers to a religious value or institution, but its reasons are basically technical and not based on principle. Moreover, these same references are employed usually under the same circumstances in other petitions as well; (3) A ruling or decision that deals with the status quo in Israel but no decision regarding change is being made.

All cases are subsequently placed in one of the following eight categories of religious cases: (1) religion and political agreements; (2) safeguarding holy places; (3) freedom of religion and ceremony; (4) injuring religious feelings; (5) Orthodox institutions' authority; (6) the court's attitude toward other trends within Judaism; (7) the court's attitude toward other ethnic groups regarding religious issues; and (8) petitions against the Ministry of Interior.

DATA ANALYSIS AND DISCUSSION

Table 1 shows the voting record during the Barak and Shamgar eras. The most striking finding is that while Barak's court ruled against religion in 52.2 percent of the cases, approximately half of his total rulings on religious issues, Shamgar's court leaned distinctly toward antireligious decisions, ruling against religious interests in 61.9 percent of the cases.[58] There was some substantial differentiation in the court's overall behavior regarding specific types of issues. For instance, during both periods, the court ruled in favor of pro-religious and religious-political agreements in 80 percent of the cases

58. Court Ruling—A court ruling on a legal action where an answer (statement of defense) has been served, shall include the following particulars: a brief (a concise summary of the case); the findings of the court about the key facts of the case; the disputed issues; the ruling; and the reasoning behind it. http://www.sederdin.com/articles/civil-law-dic/

TABLE 1. Final Rulings of the High Court—by Topics and Periods of Tenure, according to Incidence and Percentage Rates

		Court Ruling					
		Anti-religious		Pro-religious		Neutral	
Topic	Period of Tenure	*N*	%	*N*	%	*N*	%
Religion and Political Agreements	Barak	2	25	6	75	0	0
	Shamgar	0	0	2	100	0	0
Safeguard Holy Places	Barak	3	75	1	25	0	0
	Shamgar	2	100	0	0	0	0
Freedom of Religion and Worship	Barak	3	60	1	20	1	20
	Shamgar	3	60	2	40	0	0
Injuring Religious Sentiments	Barak	1	16.7	5	83.3	0	0
	Shamgar	1	100	0	0	0	0
Authority of Orthodox Institutions	Barak	15	62.5	9	37.5	0	0
	Shamgar	16	69.6	7	30.4	0	0
Court's Approach toward the Various Groups in Judaism	Barak	9	75	3	25	0	0
	Shamgar	3	37.5	4	50	1	12.5
Court's Approach toward Ethnic Groups on Religious Issues	Barak	3	42.9	4	57.1	0	0
	Shamgar	1	100	0	0	0	0
Petitions against the Interior Ministry	Barak	0	0	3	100	0	0
	Shamgar	0	0	0	0	0	0
Total	Barak	36	52.2	32	46.4	1	1.4
	Shamgar	26	61.9	15	35.7	1	2.4

and in favor of protecting religion from insult in 71.4 percent of the cases. On the other hand, it ruled against maintaining holy places 83.3 percent of the time and against the authority of Orthodox religious institutions in 66 percent of the cases.[59]

The rulings regarding Orthodox institutions received the most attention—47 of the 111 High Court of Justice religion-related rulings (42.3%)—which tended to go against these institutions. Here too, the Shamgar court was more antireligious, having ruled against the Orthodox institutions in 16 (69.6%) of the cases, while the Barak's court ruled against these institutions in 15 (62.5%) cases.

59. Regarding maintaining holy places, this references a 1967 law that prohibits the desecration of holy places; the law actually applies only to Jews, and the rulings refer to petitions filed against construction work carried out on the Temple Mount by the Muslim Waqf and which include covering in the dirt of the antiquities and building prayer platforms there.

The personal voting records of Justices Barak and Shamgar in religion-related cases confirms the above tendency.[60] Shamgar, during the period covered by this study, heard 20 religious cases and voted against religion in 12 (60%) of them. Barak heard 43 such cases and voted against religion on 25 (58.1%) occasions. Thus, the personal records of the two are very similar. It is noteworthy that the number of cases that fall within our domain heard by each High Court president changed, reflecting over a 100% increase.

In addition, of the 10 other justices who heard at least 10 religion cases during this period, five of them have voting records equally or more antireligious than Justices Barak and Shamgar. These include Justices Mishael Cheshin (18 of 29 cases, 62.1%), Dalia Dorner (14 of 24 cases, 58.3%), Tova Strasberg-Cohen (9 of 15 cases, 60%), Gavriel Bach (10 of 14 cases, 71.4%), and Eliahu Mazza (10 of 17 cases, 58.8%). Only four of these justices had pro-religious voting records. Justice Dorit Beinish voted for the religious side in 9 of 17 (52.9%) cases, as did Justice Ayala Procaccia in 10 of 15 (66.7%) cases, Justice Theodor Or in 9 of 17 (52.9%) cases, and Justice Eliyahu Tal (the only religious justice) in 7 of 11 (63.6%) cases. Finally, Justice Itzchak Zamir voted against religion in 7 of 13 (53.5%) cases. Thus, in the larger perspective, Justice Barak's voting record on religion was not particularly distinct from his predecessors, nor was it exceptional among his colleagues. However, he did, in fact, participate in far more religious cases than any other justice on the High Court of Justice during this period. During Barak's presidency, 251 decisions were passed on religious issues, compared to Shamgar's presidency, in which only 132 such decisions were passed. That is, a 90 percent increase in rulings on religious issues.

Thus, the perception of Barak as being *particularly* antireligious is not confirmed by the evidence. We posit several potential reasons for this discrepancy between perception and reality. First, religion both in Israel and worldwide became a more high-profile issue in the course of the relevant decades. During the two periods analyzed here, the Israeli High Court of Justice's record of rulings on religious issues tends toward more rulings against religion than in favor, especially with regard to the prerogatives of Orthodox religious institutions. While this trend was stronger in Shamgar's court than in Barak's (even though Barak's court saw many more cases in our compilation of cases), it is likely that Israeli society was more sensitive

60. The perspective of each judge sitting in separate panels—personal decisions. It is important to note that in most cases only some of the 15 High Court justices hear a case. That is, no justice hears all cases.

to the issue during Barak's period as court president; second, religion was a more prominent part of the court docket during Barak's period as president. Barak's court ruled on 69 relevant cases as opposed to Shamgar's 42. Barak's court also heard more cases on a wider variety of religious issues than did Shamgar's court, where more than half of the cases focused on Orthodox religious institutions. This increase in the number of cases from the Shamgar to the Barak period lends support to the theory that this period experienced a global religious revival.

It is important to note that this study has limitations, including the fact that it covers only 23 years of the Israeli High Court of Justice's work; an examination of the court's history since its founding would likely produce additional insights. Moreover, this study treats all cases equally, while some cases are more politically relevant than others. Lastly, the changing social and political context in which the High Court operated should be taken into consideration: in the wake of waves of immigration from Europe, Russia, and Ethiopia, the immigrant's Jewish origins were being questioned. This resulted in conflicts between new immigrants and religious institutions, compelling the High Court of Justice to relate to the issues they raised. This situation led to a very stormy period at the High Court of Justice and this circumstance makes it difficult to compare findings to those of quieter periods.

CONCLUSIONS

Empirical findings suggest that the reality of Justice Barak's court was, if anything, less antireligious than that of his predecessor Justice Shamgar. In addition, Barak held a number of opinions that specifically supported religion, including his position that sometimes human rights must be sacrificed in favor of freedom of religion and the rights of religious people.[61]

Barak had a marked tendency to seek compromise with religious institutions whenever possible, in order to avoid exacerbating social tensions. This is more consistent with Naomi Levitski's contention that Barak was not a judicial activist.[62] Nevertheless, even during Barak's period as president, a slight majority of relevant rulings went against religious interests. Barak's

61. Aharon Barak, *Shofet Be'Chevra Democratit* (Haifa: Haifa University Press, 2004).
62. Levitsky, *Your Honor: Aharon Barak.*

individual opinions also run counter to religion more often than not, but his record is similar to that of his predecessor, Justice Shamgar, as well as to those of several other justices who served during this period. Even so, if perceptions were based upon reality, Justice Shamgar and his court should have been considered more markedly antireligious.

We posit that the best explanation for misleading perceptions is that they are driven by a shifting political climate rather than by a shifting judicial policy. In both Israeli and international politics, religion has become increasingly prominent as an issue. In Israel, ultra-Orthodox political parties such as Shas have become more politically active, decade by decade, and sensitive to issues of the political-religious status quo. Likewise, new immigration waves into Israel, which also corresponded with a global increase in the salience of religion in politics, affected both the number of High Court cases related to religion and public sensitivity to them.

In conclusion, it may be said that the Israeli High Court has contributed to institutional continuity in a shifting political environment while confirming the strong role that religious constituencies play in a formally secular state.

References

Aran, Gideon, and Ron E. Hassner. "Rejoinder." *Terrorism and Political Violence* 25, no. 3 (2013): 416–18.

Barak, Aharon. "Hofesh Ha'Bituy U'Migbalotav." *Kesher* 8 (1990).

Barak, Aharon. "Shilton Hachok Ve'Elyonut Ha'Chuka." *Mishpat U'Mimshal* 5 (1999).

Barak, Aharon. *Shofet Be'Chevra Democratit.* Haifa: Haifa University Press, Keter, Nevo, 2004.

Beatty, David M. "The Forms and Limits of Constitutional Interpretation." *American Journal of Comparative Law* 49, no. 1 (Winter 2001): 79–120.

Bendor, Ariel, and Ze'ev Segal. *The Hat Maker: Discussions with Justice Aharon Barak with Ze'ev Segal.* Kinneret Zmora-Bitan: Dvir Publications, 2009.

Berger, Peter. "Hamoderniyut Ve'HaEtdgar He'Chadash shel Ha'Dat." *Tchelet* (2008): 32.

Buruma, Ian. "An Islamic Democracy for Iraq?" *New York Times Magazine*, December 5, 2004, 42–49.

Cohen, Asher. "Israeli Assimilation." Rappaport Center for Assimilation Research and Strengthening Jewish Vitality. Ramat Gan: Bar Ilan University, 2002.

Cohen, Margit, Eli Linder, and Mordechai Kremnitzer. "Religion and the High

Court of Justice: Image and Reality—Part One: A Critical Examination of the Publication by Manof." The Center for Jewish Information. Jerusalem: The Israel Democracy Institute, 2003.

Don-Yehiya, Eliezer, and Charles Liebman. *Religion and Politics in Israel*. Bloomington: Indiana University Press, 1984.

Dowty, Alan. *The Jewish State: A Century Later*. Berkeley: University of California Press, 1987.

Elazar, Daniel J. *Israel: Building a New Society*. Bloomington: Indiana University Press, 1986.

Elon, Menachem, and Ben Shimon. *Maamad Haisha: Mishpat Ve'Sshiput, Masoret U'tmura: Arachaea Shel Chevra Yehudit Ve'Ddemocratit*. Tel-Aviv: Ha'Kibutz Ha'Meuchad, 2005.

Fish, Stanley. "Intention Is All There Is: A Critical Analysis of Aharon Barak's Purposive Interpretation in Law." *Cardozo Law Review* 29 (2008): 1109–46.

Fox, Jonathan. "State Religious Exclusivity and Human Rights." *Political Studies* 56 (2008): 928–48.

Fox, Jonathan. *A World Survey of Religion and the State*. New York: Cambridge University Press, 2008.

Fox, Jonathan, and Deborah Flores. "Religions, Constitutions, and the State: A Cross-National Study." *Journal of Politics* 71, no. 4 (2009): 1499–1513.

Fox, Jonathan, and Jonathan Rynhold. "A Jewish and Democratic State? Comparing Government Involvement in Religion in Israel with Other Democracies." *Totalitarian Movements and Political Religions* 9, no. 4 (2008): 507–31.

Goell, Y. "Here Come the Judges." *Jerusalem Post*, May 12, 2003, 6.

Gutman, Imanuel. "Dat Be'Politika Ha'Yisraelit—Gorem Me'Ached U'Me'Faleg." In *Ha'Ma'Arechet Ha'Politit Be'Israel*, ed. M. Lisk and Imanuel Gutman, 357–410. Tel-Aviv: Am Oved, 1976.

Heller, Mordechai. "Minuy Shoftim: Ha'Pitron Le'Mashber Ha'Elion." *Tchelet* 8 (2001): 55.

Hockstader, L. "Israeli Court Sharpens Discord between Secular, Ultra-Orthodox Jews," *Washington Post*, February 14, 1999, 29.

Huntington, Samuel, P. *The Clash of Civilizations and the Remarking of World Order*. New York: Simon and Schuster, 1996.

Hurvitz, Isaac, and Dana Dikla. "Dat U'Bagatz—Dimuy U'Metziut." Jerusalem: Manof, the Jewish Information Center, 2004.

Juergensmeyer, Mark. *Global Rebellion: Religious Challenges to the Secular State, from Christian Militias to al Qaeda*. Berkeley: University of California Press, 2008.

Juergensmeyer, Mark. *The New Cold War? Religious Nationalism Confronts the Secular State*. Berkeley: University of California Press, 1993.

Kadosh, S., and E. De Hus. "Nasi Beit Ha'Mispat Ha'Elion Bedimus Aharon Barak." *Alei Mishpat* 7 (2009): 131–46.

Kimmerling, Baruch. *The Invention and Decline of Israeliness*. Berkeley: University of California Press, 2000.

Levitski, Naomi. *Haelyonim: Be'Tochechey Beit Ha'Mishpat Ha'Elion*. Bnei Brak: Hakibbutz Ha'Meuchad, 2006.

Levitski, Naomi. *Your Honor: Aharon Barak—Bibliography*. Jerusalem: Keter Publications, 2001.

Liebman, Charles S., ed. *Religion, Democracy, and Israeli Society*. London: Hardwood Academic, 1997.

Mazie, Steven V. *Israel's Higher Law: Religion and Liberal Democracy in the Jewish State*. Lanham, MD: Lexington Books, 2006.

Nahshoni, K. *Harav Sherman: "Hatzaat Barak tigrom lehitbolelut."* Accessed January 15, 2015, http://www.ynet.co.il/articles/0,7340,L-3542958,00.html

Nayar, Hillel. "Aharon Barak's Revolutionary Doctrine." *Tchelet* 3 (1998): 11–43.

Neuberger, Benjamin. "Dat, Medina U'Politika"—*Mimshal U'Politika be'Medinat Israel*. Tel-Aviv: Open University, Unit 6 (1994): 7.

Neuberger, Benjamin. Dat U'Medina Be'Medinot Democratiot. 2002. http://www.openu.ac.il/Adcan/adcan37/adcan

Neuberger, Benjamin. *Religion and Democracy in Israel*. Jerusalem: Floersheimer Institute, 1997.

Paz, Uri. "Ha'Check LeLo Kisuy Shel Aharon Barak." *Maariv*, February 26, 2007.

Philpott, D. "Has the Study of Global Politics Found Religion?" *Annual Review of Political Science* 12 (2009): 183–202.

Posner, M. Richard. "Enlightened Despot." *The New Republic* 53, April 23, 2007.

Radai, Frances. "Diokano Shel Ha'Nasi Aharon Barak: Shivion Be'Medina Yehudit Ve'Democratit." *Mishpatim* (Law faculty periodical, Jerusalem) (2009): Nevo. P.225–58.

Rapoport, David C. "The Fourth Wave: September 11 in the History of Terrorism." *Current History* 100, no. 650: (2001): 419–24.

Rapoport, David. "The Four Waves of Modern Terrorism." In *Attacking Terrorism: Elements of a Grand Strategy*, edited by A. Cronin and J. Ludes, 46–73. Washington, DC: Georgetown University Press, 2004.

Ravitzki, Aviezer. *Haketz Ha'Megule U'Medinat Ha'Yehudim, Meshichiyut, Tzionut Ve'Radikalism Dati Be'Israel*. Tel-Aviv: Am Oved Publications, 2006.

Rozen-Tzvi, Ariel. "Ha'Halacha Ve'Hametziut Ha'Chilonit," In *Dat Liberalism, Mishpacha Ve'Chevra*, ed. Ariel Porat. Tel-Aviv: Ramot, 2001.

Rozen-Tzvi, Ariel. "Medina Yehudit Ve'Demokratit: Abahut Ruchanit, Nikur Ve'Simbioza—Ha'Efshar Le'rabea et Ha'Maagal?" In *Dat, Liberalism Ve'Chevra*, ed. Ariel Porat. Tel-Aviv: Ramot, 2001.

Rubinstein, Amnon. *Ha'Mishpat Ha' Konstitutzioni Shel Medinat Israel* [Israel Constitutional Law]. Tel Aviv: Shocken, 1991.

Shain, Haim. "The Jewish State–Concluding Summary." *Hod Ha'Sharon: Shaare Mishpat*, (2005): 146–48.

Statman, D., and G. Sapir. "Freedom of Religion, Freedom from Religion, and Protecting Religious Feelings." *Mehkarei Mishpat* 21, no. 1 (2004): 5–87.

Toft, Monica Duffy, Daniel Philpott, and Timothy Samuel Shah. *God's Century: Resurgent Religion and Global Politics*. New York: W. W. Norton, 2011.

Wagner, Matthew. "Rabbis Tout Jewish Alternative to Israeli Courts: 'Who Is Smarter, Aharon Barak or Maimonides?'" *Jerusalem Post*, October 18, 2006.

Woods, Patricia J. *Judicial Power and National Politics: Courts and Gender in the Religious-Secular Conflict in Israel*. 1st ed. Albany: State University of New York Press, 2008.

Woods, Patricia J. *Judicial Power and National Politics: Courts and Gender in the Religious-Secular Conflict in Israel*. 2nd ed. Albany: State University of New York Press, 2017.

High Court of Justice Verdicts

H.C. 1514/01 *Yaakov Gur Arye vs. The Second Authority for Television and Radio*, 84(4)267, 2001.

H.C. 6427/02 *Ha'Tnua Le'Eichut Ha'Shilton Be'Israel vs. the Knesset* (unpublished). This is a petition against the legitimacy of the law postponing Yeshiva students' military service based on the fact that they study Torah. According to the petitioners, the Tal Law offends the parity right.

H.C. 5026/04 *Design Charle Delux Rahitim Be'Am + 18 Rozentzweig Zvika, Heterey Avoda Beshabat*. Petition regarding the legitimacy of the law forbidding employing workers on the Sabbath, A 84 (1) 38, 2005.

H.C. 46(2) 464 *Chevra Kadisha Gachsha Kehilat Yerushalyim N., Kestenbaum*, 1992.

H.C. *Shavit, N. Chevra Kadisha Gachsha Rishon Le'Tzion* 53(3)600, 1999.

H.C. 1000/92 *Chava Bavli vs. Supreme Rabbinical Court*, Verdict 92(2)221, 1994.

H.C. 96/5016 *Chorev vs. the Ministry of Transportation* 84 51(4) 1, 1997.

H.C. 953/87 *Poraz vs. Tel-Aviv—Jaffa Municipality* 42 (2) 309, 1988.

H.C. 5070/95 *Naamt, Tnuat Nashim Ovdot Veminadvot Neged Sar Hapnim* 56(20) 721, 2002.

H.C. 1031/93 *Alian Chava vs. Minister of the Interior* 49(4) 662, 1995.

H.C. 2597/99 *Tais Rodrigez Tooshbayim Neged Sar Hapnim* 48(5) 412, 2004.

H.C. 257/89 *Hofman vs. the Wailing Wall Supervisor* 48(2) 265, 1994.

H.C. 14/86 *Laor Neged Ha'Moatza LeBikoret Sratim U'Machazot* 41(1) 421, 1987.

Psychology in Religion and Politics

The Role of Cognitive Dissonance in Religious Readings of the Israeli Disengagement Plan

Mordechai (Motti) Inbari

University of North Carolina—Pembroke

Political ideologies tend to serve as a backbone of identity, and many people chose to define themselves through their ideology. In this chapter, I shall examine how an external event cracked group solidarity and challenged the identity of the followers of a specific ideology. I shall examine the ways in which the rabbinical leadership of messianic religious Zionism confronted Israel's Disengagement Plan—where in 2005 Israel had demolished all of its settlements in the Gaza Strip together with four additional settlements in Samaria. Messianic religious Zionist ideology argues that Israeli territorial expansion represents a partial fulfillment of biblical prophecy for Jewish redemption. Therefore, territorial retreats could be understood as contradicting God's order and a failure of prophecy.

Eric Ericson, in his masterful biography of Martin Luther, described ideology as a militant system with uniform members and uniform goals; at least it is a "way of life," a worldview that is consonant with existing theory, available knowledge, and common sense. Yet, it is significantly more: it is a utopian outlook, a cosmic mood, or a doctrinal logic, all shared as self-evident beyond any need for demonstration.[1]

If political ideologies claim to be of such a solid foundation, how would people who follow a specific ideology respond to clear evidence that contra-

1. Eric Ericson, *Young Man Luther: A Study in Psychoanalysis and History* (New York: W. W. Norton, 1958), 41.

dicts their theories? What are the mechanisms that can lead to ideological change? In this chapter, I examine the role of the psychological condition of cognitive dissonance in challenging political and religious ideologies. The theory of cognitive dissonance argues that people will make strong efforts to justify their beliefs in case of clear disconfirmation. A strong disconfirmation to a set of ideological beliefs can lead to illogical responses intended to justify previous actions and beliefs. Therefore, the study of how people react to their ideology and the levels of flexibility that they can allow may be a benefit from the field of psychology.

In this chapter, I present three reactions by key rabbinical elite figures of messianic religious Zionism to the Israeli withdrawal from Gaza. The ideology of this movement has two layers. First, it is the belief that the Whole Land of Israel belongs to Jews only, and, second, that the Jewish state represents a phase toward the coming of the Messiah. The responses of the movement, as described in this chapter, to the disengagement reflected three options: (1) acceptance of total failure and renunciation of prophecy/ideology; (2) rejection of the possibility of failure while deepening commitment to prophecy even if it seems like failure; and (3) acceptance of possible failure—however, in order to prevent its complete collapse, strong changes in the believers' political behavior emerged.

The article analyzes the rabbinical narratives of three major authorities: Rabbis Shlomo Aviner, Shmuel Tal, and Itzhak Ginzburg. All of these rabbis have many followers, and their theologies represent ideological divisions inside their community. Messianic religious Zionism is a mass movement within Israeli society. It is hard to estimate its exact size, for it has followers inside and outside the Green Line in West Bank settlements. I would argue that followers of the movement range from about 100,000 to 200,000 people.

MESSIANIC RELIGIOUS ZIONISM

Very soon after its emergence, religious Zionism undertook a process aiming to understand how the development of the secular Zionist movement actually represented a stage in an unfolding messianic process. These approaches are identified, in particular, with the religious philosophy of Rabbi Avraham Yitzhak Hacohen Kook (1865–1935). Many Orthodox Jews found it difficult to identify with the emerging Zionist movement and to act within classic

Zionist definitions. Zionist rhetoric spoke of the need to normalize the Jewish people and make it a nation like all the others. The purpose of Zionism was described as being to build a safe haven for the Jewish people. All of these definitions are inconsistent with Jewish religious tradition, which emphasizes a distinction between Israel and the other nations and proclaims that the Land of Israel has a unique theological function. Accordingly, many of those who developed the religious Zionist approach integrated the religious purpose as part of the Zionist idea.

These thinkers used the traditional rabbinical technique of *pshat* and *drash* (the literal meaning as opposed to the exegetical meaning) to justify supporting Zionist political activity. While ostensibly adopting the general Zionist definition of the movement's purpose, this approach imbued it with specific religious meaning: While Zionist activity calls for action in the material realm, simultaneously its innermost core aspires to eternal spiritual life—and this constituted the "real" foundation for the Zionist movement's operations and aims, even if the movement itself was not aware of it.[2] The argument contended that the long-awaited messianic era was about to arrive and would be realized once secular Zionism chose the true path: the complete worship of God. Zionism would then advance to its second phase, known as the revival of the biblical Davidic monarchy, the reinstitution of sacrifices on the Temple Mount, and the reestablishment of the Sanhedrin.[3]

Although this position was present within religious Zionist circles almost from their inception, it occupied only a marginal position in the wider Zionist movement. Moreover, while the vision of transformation to a Torah nation was advocated by certain religious Zionist voices during the period immediately preceding the establishment of the state of Israel (1948), it was soon abandoned by religious Zionists themselves.[4] The situation changed with the Israeli victory in the Six-Day War (June 1967) in which Israel captured additional areas of its biblical homeland. These dramatic events led to the strengthening of religious Zionism's activist wing, dominated mainly by the younger generation of the National Religious Party.[5] Additionally, it

2. Dov Schwartz, *Faith at a Crossroads—A Theological Profile of Religious Zionism* (Leiden: Brill, 2002), 156–92.

3. Motti Inbari, "Religious Zionism and the Temple Mount Dilemma: Key Trends," *Israel Studies* 12, no. 2 (2007): 29–47.

4. Asher Cohen, *The Tallit and the Flag—Religious Zionism and the Vision of the Torah State during the Early Days of the State* [in Hebrew] (Jerusalem: Yad Ben Zvi, 1998), 48–55.

5. Yoni Garb, "The Young Guard of the National Religious Party and the Ideological

created a groundswell of opinion that would ultimately fuel the establishment of the Gush Emunim settlement movement, which would soon after become the dominant stream within religious Zionism.[6]

The Six-Day War created a new reality in the Middle East. In the course of the war, Israel occupied East Jerusalem, the West Bank, the Gaza Strip, the Golan Heights, and the Sinai Peninsula. These areas were not annexed to Israel and have continued to have the status of occupied territories administered by Israel pending their return in the framework of a peace agreement. Immediately after the war, Israel did not, on the whole, initiate Jewish settlement in the occupied areas, with the exception of East Jerusalem, which was formally annexed to the state of Israel. From the outset, however, this principle was not strictly applied, and soon after the war a number of Jewish settlements were established in the occupied territory.[7]

In 1973, Egypt and Syria launched a surprise attack on Israel. Although Israel would eventually push back the attacking armies, the Israeli public was shocked and outraged at both the large number of fatalities Israel suffered and by the military's poor performance, at least at the beginning of the war. Immediately following the war, US Secretary of State Henry Kissinger undertook intensive diplomatic activity aimed at attaining a cease-fire between the sides that would invariably include Israeli territorial concessions. It was against the backdrop of these two events—the trauma of the war and the expectation of imminent territorial retreat—that the Gush Emunim ("Block of the Faithful") movement was founded in February 1974. Led by young religious Zionist activists, Gush Emunim was supported by both Orthodox bourgeois urban circles and secular supporters of the Whole Land of Israel movement.[8] Gush Emunim sought to prevent territorial concessions and to push for the application of Israeli sovereignty to

---

Roots of Gush Emunim," in *Religious Zionism: The Era of Change*, ed. Asher Cohen and Yisrael Harel [in Hebrew] (Jerusalem: Bialik Institute, 2005), 171–200; Eliezer Don Yihya, "Stability and Change in the Camp Party—the National Religious Party and the Young Revolution" [in Hebrew], *State, Government and International Relations* 14 (5740–1980): 25–52.

6. Gideon Aran, "A Mystic-Messianic Interpretation of Modern Israeli History: The Six Day War as a Key Event in the Development of the Original Religious Culture of Gush Emunim," *Studies in Contemporary Jewry* 4 (1988): 263–75.

7. Gershom Gorenberg, *The Accidental Empire—Israel and the Birth of the Settlements, 1967–1977* (New York: Times Books, 2006), 72–98.

8. Dov Schwartz, *Religious Zionism: History and Ideology* (Boston: Academic Press, 2009).

Judea, Samaria, and the Gaza Strip. It attempted to actualize its objectives by settling Jewish communities in the occupied territories. As a result of its activities, the number of Israeli citizens living in the settlements has risen steadily. As of 2010, the settlements' population was estimated at 300,000, and some 40 percent of the Judea and Samaria territory was included in the settlements' municipal areas of jurisdiction.[9]

At the time of its establishment, Gush Emunim did not project a messianic vision. However, immediately following its inception, Gush Emunim was joined by a group of Merkaz Harav Yeshiva's graduates under the spiritual leadership of Rabbi Zvi Yehuda Hacohen Kook, who soon assumed leadership roles in the movement. The members of this group held a religious perspective, which motivated them to political action. They believed that the return of the Jews to the Land of Israel under the auspices of the secular Zionist movement reflected the first stage in God's will to redeem His people. Accordingly, the spectacular Israeli victory in the Six-Day War of 1967 was perceived as a manifestation of the divine plan, and as a preliminary stage in the process of redemption.[10]

In general, Merkaz Harav followers, then as now, see themselves as implementing the philosophy of Rabbi Avraham Yitzhak Hacohen Kook.[11] They try to integrate the senior Kook's philosophy into Israeli reality, emphasizing two key concepts: the holiness of the Land of Israel and the holiness of the state of Israel. According to the junior Kook, the Land of Israel—comprised of land within the 1948 borders, the territories acquired in 1967, and even Transjordan—is one unit, a complete organic entity imbued with its own will and holiness. This entity is connected and united with the entire Jewish people—present, past, and future—so that the people and the land are in a complete oneness. Therefore, no one has a right to give away part of the land.[12] Since the unity of the Whole Land of Israel came as a result of the actions of the Zionist movement, it could, therefore, be understood as a tool that was and could be further implemented to actualize God's will. As such,

9. Idith Zertal and Akiva Eldar, *Lords of the Land: The War over Israel's Settlements in the Occupied Territories, 1967–2007* (New York: Nation Books, 2007).

10. Moshe Hellinger, "Political Theology in the Thought of 'Merkaz HaRav' Yeshiva and Its Profound Influence on Israeli Politics and Society since 1967," *Totalitarian Movements & Political Religions* 9, no. 4 (2008): 533–50.

11. Schwartz, *Faith*, 156–92.

12. Aviever Ravitzky, *Messianism, Zionism, and Jewish Religious Radicalism* (Chicago: University of Chicago Press, 1993), 122–44.

the Israeli state, though secular, should be sanctified as it is part of the messianic process.[13]

According to the Merkaz Harav philosophy, the sanctity of the Whole Land of Israel and the sanctity of the state of Israel are expected to complement and complete one another. However, this has not always been reflected in Israeli reality. After the peace process between Israel and Egypt (1978) and the resulting Israeli withdrawal from Sinai (1982), many Gush Emunim supporters were forced to confront the increasing erosion of their basic beliefs regarding the character and destiny of the state of Israel. The Israeli withdrawal from Sinai together with the subsequent Madrid talks (1991) and Oslo process (1993), which together led to an Israeli withdrawal from parts of the West Bank, provoked a theological crisis for followers of Merkaz Harav's philosophy. The Disengagement Plan (2005) brought this crisis to new heights. The fundamental religious dilemma the plan presented was of a profound character: How can a state that uproots settlements and hands over parts of the biblical Land of Israel to Arab rule be considered "absolutely sacred," as it had been? What sublime religious meaning can be attributed to the actions of a secular state that threatens to destroy, by its own hands, the chance of realizing the messianic hope? Could it be that viewing the Jewish state as a fulfillment of the divine will was a mistake? These theological dilemmas constitute the background for the discussion of prophetic failure.

MESSIANIC DISAPPOINTMENT

The subject of prophetic failure is critical to an understanding of the development of any messianic faith. The most quoted study in this field is *When Prophecy Fails*.[14] In it, Leon Festinger, Henry Riecken, and Stanley Schachter studied Mrs. Marian Keech's small UFO cult, a cult that believed in an imminent apocalypse and later developed a cognitive mechanism to explain why the event did not occur. Festinger's team came to two conclusions: (1) beliefs that are clearly falsified will be held even more intensely

13. Ravitzky, *Messianism*, 136–41.

14. Leon Festinger, Henry Riecken, and Stanley Schachter, *When Prophecy Fails: A Social and Psychological Study of a Modern Group That Predicted the Destruction of the World* (New York: Harper-Torchbooks, 1956).

after falsification; and (2) the group will increase active proselytization. The team used the term "cognitive dissonance" to refer to the distress caused when two contradictory ideas, or cognitions, are held simultaneously. In the case of a messianic or millennial individual or group, cognitive dissonance is said to occur when a fervently held belief appears to be contradicted by empirical evidence. Cognitive dissonance theory argues that persons will be highly motivated to resolve the tension between the contradictory ideas.[15] Since Festinger, Riecken, and Schacter's pathbreaking study, cognitive dissonance theory has become significant in many disciplines for answering certain types of questions. However, the study of prophetic movements has developed since Festinger, Riecken, and Schacter.

In order to understand how prophetic movements survive after disconfirmation, I would like to draw upon Lorne Dawson's formula,[16] which is based upon his own work together with the accumulated knowledge from Joseph Zygmunt,[17] Gordon Melton,[18] and Jon Stone.[19] His analysis contains three survival methods: intensified *proselytization*, various *rationalizations*, and acts of *reaffirmation*. Whereas Festinger and his team argued that proselytization is a key component for the movement's survival, many case studies that were published after *When Prophecy Fails* proved that proselytization seldom happens.[20] However, in the messianic religious Zionist case, I have noticed proselytization as an important mechanism for easing dissonance.

Rationalizing is the key tool for dealing with failure, and there are a few ways it can develop. The use of mysticism to spiritualize prophecy is a major one: mystical interpretations can deny the failure and argue that prophecy

---

15. Festinger, Riecken, and Schachter, *When Prophecy Fails*; see also Jon R. Stone, ed., *Expecting Armageddon: Essential Readings in Failed Prophecy* (London: Routledge, 2000).

16. Lorne Dawson, "Clearing the Underbrush: Moving beyond Festinger to a New Paradigm for the Study of Failed Prophecy," in *How Prophecy Lives*, ed. Diana Tumminia and William Statos Jr. (Leiden: Brill, 2011), 69–98.

17. Joseph F. Zygmunt, "Prophetic Failure and Chiliastic Identity: The Case of the Jehovah's Witnesses," *American Journal of Sociology* 75, no .6 (1970): 926–48.

18. Gordon Melton, "Spiritualization and Reaffirmation: What Really Happens When Prophecy Fails," *American Studies* 26, no. 2 (1985): 17–29.

19. Jon R. Stone, "Prophecy and Dissonance: A Reassessment of Research Testing the Festinger Theory," *Nova Religio* 12, no. 4 (2009): 72–90.

20. There are many exceptions to this rule, such as early Christians, the followers of Sabbetai Zvi, Jehovah's Witnesses, and Lubavitch Hasidim. See Dawson, "Clearing the Underbrush," 73.

has been maintained on divine or ethereal levels. The liberating power of mysticism, especially in Jewish history, lies in the fact that it is rooted in a paradox, exposing inner truth despite outward appearances.[21] Thus, mystical interpretation enables the rejection of reality as it appears externally and the acceptance, instead, of covert spiritual fulfillment.

Another method of rationalization can claim that the prophecy was a test of faith, and that God is putting the believers in miseries in order to examine their strength. A third way or rationalization can be with blaming failure on human errors like misinterpretation, or blaming others for misunderstanding or interfering with the fulfillment of prophecy. Reaffirmation comes with the inward work to increase social solidarity through special educational activities, celebrations, and rituals.[22]

All the components described above are to be found in the different ways in which settlers' rabbis respond to their failure. However, conditions in this case are somewhat different: although the territorial withdrawals create *fear* of a failure of faith because of the vision for the Whole Land of Israel being shattered, it has not yet become apparent beyond doubt that *redemption itself* has failed. Therefore, in this specific case study, messianic believers have an option to take the necessary actions that will prevent failure of the redemptive process. I argue that the messianic religious Zionist's response to failure of faith due to territorial compromises in certain circumstances may go in one of these ways:

1. There may be a logical explanation to an acknowledged failure of prophecy, in which they admit that a religious mistake had been made, and thus they retreat from their expectant messianic perspective.
2. Alternately, they may have the opposite reaction in which followers reject the idea that the prophecy failed, instead arguing that messianic realization is indeed taking place but in the unseen sphere. Therefore, they may argue that, since messianic failure is definitely not certain, that nothing should be changed in theology and practice.
3. Finally, they may acknowledge the failure of their original messianic prophecy and yet still be strengthened in religious zeal in order to prevent complete collapse. The followers of this pattern can be described

21. Gershom Scholem, *Major Trends in Jewish Mysticism* (New York: Shocken Books, 1960), 1–39.

22. Lorne Dawson, "Clearing the Underbrush."

as "hastening the end." They may call for deeper involvement in political action in order to fulfill prophecy.

Below, this chapter identifies the circumstances that lead to each of these three distinct responses.

PROPHECY WAS A MISTAKE—RABBI SHMUEL TAL'S RESPONSE

Following the disengagement, a response reflecting messianic retreat and a disconnection from the prophetic ideology of religious Zionism, together with a rapprochement with the Haredi (ultra-Orthodox) world, was founded in the approach of Rabbi Shmuel Tal, leader of the Torat Chayim Yeshiva. This yeshiva was originally situated in the Gaza Strip; following the Disengagement Plan, it relocated to Samaria (West Bank). Of the figures discussed in this chapter, Rabbi Tal was, therefore, the only one who was affected in an immediate and personal way by the withdrawal from the Gaza Strip. The institution that he headed followed suit.

Shmuel Tal studied at Netiv Meir Yeshiva, the Western Wall Yeshiva, and Mercaz Harav Yeshiva. Rabbi Tal underwent a profound ideological transformation through and in response to the disengagement. Initially, he was an enthusiastic supporter of the approach that views Zionist revival through the prism of a messianic process, but Tal withdrew from the messianic interpretation. Following this change, he presented an alternative religious program based on the demand for disengagement from cooperation with secular Zionism.

After the disengagement, Tal gave an interview for the Haredi weekly *Hamishpacha* (The Family) in which he justified his conscious retreat. Tal claimed that he was offering a new approach for the adherents of religious Zionism based upon a rejection of the affinity of the state and the aspiration to build a spiritual world based upon the Torah and in accordance with the teachings of the leading rabbis of the Haredi community. As if to underscore this shift of allegiance, Tal's yeshiva decided not to celebrate Independence Day in order to emphasize its disconnection from Zionist culture.

Tal emphasized that an undeniable process had taken place whereby Jews had returned to the Land of Israel and are engaging in Torah study on an unprecedented scale. Thanks must be given to God for this reality, which should not be negated. However, he refused to celebrate Independence Day because "dominion has become apostasy." Tal argued that religious Zionism sought to adopt the positive elements of the state while rejecting its negative aspects. However, he came to realize that the national leadership in the broadest sense of the term, including the media, academia, and culture, as well as the courts and government, all challenge the dominion of God. Joy at the existence of the state is incompatible with the criminal leadership of that state. Accordingly, a decision is required: "Is God the King, or, Heaven forbid, does dominion rest with the regime that denies Him and fights against all He holds sacred and dear?" The faithful cannot be partners in the establishment of a system that fights against God to its last breath. The state is effectively controlled by a "rabble."[23]

Shmuel Tal emphasized that his disconnection is from secular leadership and culture, but not from the Jewish people as a whole; his yeshiva continues to be active in efforts to encourage secular Jews to "return" to the fold of the faithful. He articulated that the secular leadership is utterly incompatible with a commitment to the Kingdom of God; therefore, he preferred disengagement: "We must stop leaning on those who beat us; we must stop praying for their well-being and maintaining them," he declared in the interview.

Tal compared Israeli media outlets such as Channel Two television and the newspaper *Yediot Acharonot* to the Arab satellite station Al-Jazeera and the Egyptian newspaper *Al-Manar*. He claimed that the Israeli universities are identical to the Palestinian Bir Zeit University. He argued that those who consider themselves part of the state must use its newspaper and its university; it then becomes impossible to distinguish between different streams, all of which become part of a single entity: "Then they are influenced, and consume their culture and their worldview. They lack the tools to distinguish between good and evil. Confusion is rife, and this confusion wins many victims among the national-religious youth."

Tal rejects the possibility of working from within to change the secular system. For him, those who do so merely become part of this very system. Accordingly, he affiliated with the Haredi camp. During the period preceding the disengagement, Tal met with ultra-Orthodox leaders who advised him on how to act in order to highlight his disassociation from the religious-Zionist public. The Haredi leadership moved into the vacuum that followed the disengagement and managed to co-opt Tal's yeshiva.[24]

23. Rabbi's news website, no longer available.

24. Rabbi's news website, no longer available.

The path taken by Rabbi Shmuel Tal highlights the profound transformation in his religious beliefs that led him to reject the messianic identification of Zionist action. This example reflects a tendency to retreat into a religious enclave as well as a pattern of increasing religious extremism. For Tal, the retreat into the enclave is a withdrawal into mental passivity; the disconnection from Zionism is accompanied by a general disassociation from political activism. Tal decided to renounce the prophetic vision of religious Zionism, to admit a mistake in the collaboration with the secular state, and to turn into a non-Zionist.

PROPHECY FULFILLED IN THE UNSEEN—RABBI SHLOMO AVINER'S STATIST SCHOOL

This section addresses the "statist" school personified by Rabbi Shlomo Aviner, one of the leading rabbis of messianic religious Zionism who maintains a significant number of followers. Aviner lives in Beit El and serves as one of the rabbis of the settlement. Aviner is a creative and prolific writer whose works relate to diverse themes. He studied at Mercaz Harav Yeshiva and considers himself a classic student and follower of Zvi Yehuda Kook.

In order to understand his public comments on the disengagement, his response to the Oslo Accords (1993) highlights his statist views. The signing of the Oslo Accords caught Rabbi Aviner by surprise. Initially, he focused on theodicy—the need to reconcile evil with God's plans and to combat the despair provoked by the agreements. Later, he offered operative suggestions, based on his statist agenda, particularly concerning the need for the settlers to intensify their efforts to educate the general public regarding the importance of defending the Land of Israel.

His immediate response to the Oslo Accords was to find theological justifications for the crisis. In his first opinion column after the signing of the agreement, Aviner based his discussion on the Talmud and recalled that the process of redemption is likened to the early dawn, when darkness and light intermingle. This process has its weak moments and crises alongside victories. Aviner acknowledged that Rabbi Kook (senior) taught that God would not abandon His people, and that redemption is making certain progress even if it cannot be discerned. However, retrogressions may occur along the way and, in any case, they are all merely part of God's plan of action. Aviner linked redemption to an egg in a bird's nest. The chick emerges suddenly from the egg but has been growing there for some time. Therefore, those who follow God's plan by settling the Land and studying Torah, even in times of uncertainty, will receive their reward.

Aviner added that no one should be surprised by crises; the process of resurrecting the nation is long and complex. The problems that arise are a test of perfect faith. Difficulties forge strength, and, accordingly, the public should continue on its path without making any changes. However, it should be expected that things will only get harder.[25] Aviner called for the strengthening of the settlements in Judea and Samaria and in Gaza. He urged people to develop their spiritual strength and to ignore a reality that can lead to doom and despair. This, he argued, was the ultimate test of faith. If the settlers adhered to their beliefs and hope and continued in their actions, it would guarantee that the evil decree would be nullified.

Moreover, Aviner stressed, the settlement movement could expect countless difficulties and challenges. The new reality symbolizes destruction, albeit of a partial nature: "The destruction of part of the Land, part of Zionism."[26] Zionism fails to understand the value of the Land and is sacrificing it for the sake of peace, defined as a temporary alleviation and period of calm, explained the rabbi.

According to Aviner, the faithful should emerge reinvigorated by such difficulties. God does not impose tests in order for humans to fail them; the purpose of the test is to galvanize the faithful. "When destruction and crisis appear, the forces of repair are created at the same time. Indeed, from out of the destruction an even taller building emerges." Aviner employs dialectical reasoning to argue that evil leads to the emergence of something enhanced and improved. God could not bring evil if this were not the case. His conclusion: "We must fight with all our might to prevent crises and defeats, but if they occur, despite our best efforts, we must not despair."

His response was to stress that nothing would or could change in the religious activity. While he did not know how to overcome the challenge, he was certain in the justness of his course: "We will surely overcome; God does not abandon His people."[27] Thus, Aviner's initial response was to strengthen the settlers and to argue that the Oslo Accords fit into God's plans: it is basically a test of faith.

As time passed, Aviner's response to the crisis of faith created by the

25. Shlomo Aviner, *Its Land and Its People: The Struggle for the Land of Israel* [in Hebrew] (Beit El: Hava Library, 1994), 1–2.

26. Aviner, *Its Land and Its People*, 7.

27. Aviner, *Its Land and Its People*, 7–9.

Oslo Accords seems to have focused increasingly on the need to reinforce the settlers' educational message.[28] Accordingly, Aviner was a leading proponent of the need to strengthen educational activities and launch an informational campaign. The proper response was struggling to strengthen the settlements and engaging in outreach and education even in a situation of despair and crisis.

A decade later, after the disengagement from Gaza, Aviner argued that the settlers' way must remain as before and the settlement endeavors should continue. He argued that the destruction of the settlements in the Gaza Strip do not represent a messianic failure in any way and the attitude toward the state of Israel should not change despite the state's destruction of the settlements.

He argued for a distinction between the state of Israel and its leaders. The state has a sacred status as a manifestation of "the dominion of God's throne." It must not be injured, along with the army, which bears special sanctity and must not be harmed at any price. On the other side, Aviner argued that the struggle against the leaders who hold power is legitimate as long as it is waged within the parameters of a legitimate public campaign. Accordingly, religious practice and settlement activities should continue unchanged:

> Redemption is a wonderful thing that will not be spoilt by fools. The state and the army are a wonderful thing that we will not allow fools to spoil. We will continue to mobilize for the state and the army, for redemption is such a wonderful thing—even if there are some darknesses within, nothing has changed! It has only got harder, and we shall continue to build our Land, to be built in it, through the wonders of the Lord God of Israel, Perfect of Knowledge, the Redeemer of Israel.[29]

Aviner rejected the call to disobey orders and to resist the eviction of the settlements by physical means. He also opposed those who called on young people to refuse to serve in the Israeli Defense Forces.[30] He said that although it was the army that dismantled the settlements, the army is involved not only in expulsion but also in protecting the people and the Land. Accordingly, Aviner argued, the balance of its actions slant to the

28. Aviner, *Its Land and Its People*, 31–32.

29. Shlomo Aviner, *In Love and Faith* 526, 19 Av 5765–2005 [in Hebrew].

30. Shmuel Eliyahu, "As Live As It Gets," *Olam Katan* 56 (5766–2006) [in Hebrew].

positive side. Accordingly, for him, military service is a commandment, and, despite the disengagement, young religious Zionists must continue to serve in the army. It is also important for the sake of the future—if the religious soldiers left the army, "evil could run unchecked." Aviner argued that it is an act of devotion to serve in the army, even when it is engaged in expelling Jews.[31] On the basis of the value of statism, and the perception of the nation as an expression of God's will to redeem His people, Aviner urged his followers not to disengage from the society. He urged them to continue to act within it in order to influence the mechanisms of government.

To conclude, in Aviner's reaction to the territorial withdrawals we witness a few components: a call for intensified proselytization, and a major campaign entitled Settling in the Hearts to create outreach to secular Israelis.[32] In addition, his rationalization methods included a mystical interpretation that prophecy is still valid, therefore nothing has to be changed in the religious and the political path of his movement. The cooperation with secular Zionism must remain intact. In addition, the territorial loss has to be viewed as a test of faith for the true believers. In order to pass the test, they need to continue with their beliefs and actions.

HASTENING THE END—THE PATH OF RABBI YITZHAK GINZBURG

For Rabbi Yitzhak Ginzburg, the ultimate spiritual goal of the Zionist path ought to lead to a theocratic regime as a manifestation of God's dominion on earth; however, the way to achieve this goal must undergo dramatic change. According to Ginzburg, only a theocratic revolution can guarantee the success of the final destination.

During the period leading up to the implementation of the Disengagement Plan, the rabbi made a series of sermons in which he analyzed the political situation from the perspective of Kabbalistic theory. The sermons were published on the rabbi's website and later appeared in book form under

31. Aviner, *In Love and Faith*.

32. Michael Feige explains in great detail the attempts of the settler's community to establish their enterprise in the consensus of the majority of the Israelis. See *Settling in the Hearts: Jewish Fundamentalism in the Occupied Territories* (Detroit: Wayne State University Press, 2009).

the title *It Shall Be Saved Therefrom*.[33] The struggle against the Disengagement Plan evidently led Ginzburg to adopt increasingly extreme positions and reinforced his view that the only way to avoid contact with the Israeli state was to retreat into a religious enclave, while at the same time offering a course of action designed to present a political and social alternative.

Yitzhak Ginzburg is the head of Od Yosef Chai Yeshiva in Yitzhar, the most extreme rabbinical institution in the West Bank. Officially Ginzburg is a Chabad rabbi; however, most of his followers are known as the "hill dwellers," young adults of a unique spiritual agenda that combines an ascetic and tough lifestyle with neo-Chassidic tendencies.[34]

Ginzburg drew upon the image of a core and a shell, which emerges from Lurianic Kabbalistic thought. The leitmotif in his book is that "the shell preceded the fruit." According to the Kabbala, the shell is a negative reality that conceals the divine spark. Ginzburg likened the condition of Israel to a nut, which includes four shells surrounding the fruit itself: "We have found that the nut offers an appropriate allegory for the situation of the Return to Zion, a reality which, we believe, contains a sweet fruit, but which at present is visible to us mainly in its shells."[35] Accordingly, the objective of his essay is to provide a clear identification of the Zionist shells in order to find the strength to break these. Ginzburg claims that the nut has three tough and inedible shells, while the fourth, thin shell, is attached to the nut and eaten together with it. He views the reality of the state of Israel according to this metaphor.

The outer shell, Ginzburg says, furthest from the fruit, is secular Zionist consciousness. The characteristic of this shell is the "spirit of disassociation from Jewish tradition," or the abandonment of religious values. This shell also includes religious Zionism, because the movement has failed to change its secular counterpart. Its practical actions have fed secularization and provided it with devoted support without diverting secularism from its distancing of people from the religion.

The shell of the spirit of Zionism is followed by the shell of the insti-

---

33. Yitzhak Ginzburg, *It Shall Be Saved Therefrom* (Kfar Chabad: Gal Eini Institute, 5766–2006).

34. Shlomo Kanniel, "The Hill Settlers—A Biblical Israelite?" [in Hebrew], in *Religious Zionism: An Era of Change*, ed. Asher Cohen and Israel Harel (Jerusalem: Bialik Institute, Jewish National Fund, and World Council for Torah Education, 5764–2004), 533–58.

35. Yitzhak Ginzburg, "The Shell Preceded the Fruit," in *It Shall Be Saved Therefrom* (Kfar Chabad: Gal Eini Institute, 5766–2006), 13–14.

tutions established to manage public life. Ginzburg declares that virtually every institution in Israel is tainted and alienated from Jewish sanctity and the guidance of Torah. It is particularly the case for the justice system, which, according to the rabbi, has gradually come to control and direct every aspect of public life. He argues that the High Court promotes permissiveness, sanctifies the individual ego, mocks the sanctity of the family unit, and encourages equality between Jews and Gentiles—an unacceptable value from Ginzburg's perspective.

The third shell is that of the government. The government is the product of the choice made by the people, therefore, this shell is not a rigid one. It is subject to changes and influences. However, Ginzburg claims that whatever direction the voters take, it can be seen that the government ultimately chooses to act in accordance with the same policy of compromise and withdrawal, reflecting weakness both in the face of the Gentiles and in the face of the surrounding shells.

The fourth shell, which is consumed together with the fruit, is the army. On the one hand, this shell gains its nourishment from the outer shells, absorbing their values. On the other, the army seeks to protect the honor and sanctity of Israel. Its function is to grant Israel a more powerful standing in the Land and in Exile. Accordingly, the reform of this shell lies in its subjugation to Torah, and not in its breaking. According to Ginzburg, this shell nourishes the outer shells more than it is nourished by them; for example, senior governmental positions are held by leaders who emerged through the military system. He claims that the distortion of values in the army, and particularly the concept of the "purity of the weapon," feeds the weakness that denies the public true protection.

The shell of the army has a deceptive quality because, Ginzburg argues, it draws upon the positive value of protecting Jewish life in order to realize negative goals. If the army is completely subordinate to the surrounding shells, it becomes the executor of the wicked policy of the impure shells. The way to reform the army and disconnect it from the other shells is by refusing to obey orders, "out of the clear recognition that the Lord's Torah and commandments take precedence of human commands."[36] According to Ginzburg, the call for soldiers to disobey their orders must be accompanied by numerous mentions of God's name, of the commitment to the Torah, and of the special bond with the Land.

36. Yitzhak Ginzburg, "We Shall Stand by the Name of Our God."

According to Ginzburg, the function of the shell is to protect the fruit until it has grown. The shell then becomes superfluous, and, in fact, its ongoing existence may choke the fruit. The function of the shell is to permit the fruit to grow in a hostile and dangerous world. Ginzburg likens the fruit to the "Assembly of Israel," a rabbinical term describing the Jewish people as a whole. He explains that during exile the vision emerged of redemption, whereby the people would live in accordance with Torah and with God's Messiah as its head. However, the world was unable to accept this innovation calmly and, therefore, redemption began to "enter by stealth." This explains Zionism through which, Ginzburg claims, a process of redemption was consolidated around a secular frame of reference based upon the return of Jewish dominion and the goal of normalcy and equality with the other nations. Ginzburg does not accept these Zionist goals as an end in their own right. Rhetorically, he asks, "Through two thousand years, did we really seek no more than to free ourselves of the tyrant?" He argues that the liberation of the fruit from the shell will come when the Assembly of Israel experiences the establishment of an ordinary state, does not find joy in this innovation, and, subsequently, recognizes that only full and true redemption will give meaning and hope.[37]

On the basis of his analysis of reality, the rabbi offers his audience a plan of action. He emphasizes the need to break the three outer shells and to dismantle the fourth. The spirit of Zionism, which is manifested mainly in the media, must be neutralized; Ginzburg sees this spirit as the main element that castrates and chokes any expectation of true and complete redemption. The shell of the courts should be broken through an intellectual demolition of the arguments of the courts, highlighting the ridiculous character of these positions by contrast to the wise laws of Torah. The third shell, that of government, should be uprooted by overthrowing any government, whether of the right or the left, until a Torah-based regime is installed in Israel.

Rather than form a new political party, Ginzburg advocated a complete separation from the system by means of retreat into an enclave. He argued that because political parties follow the rules of the political game, they are subordinated by the system.

The rejection of state support and the retreat into an enclave are seen by Ginzburg as the only way to offer a real alternative. He claims that the secular establishment cynically exploits the spirit of volunteering and self-

37. Ginzburg, *Saved Therefrom*, 25.

sacrifice that characterizes the religious Zionist public. Accordingly, this public must detach itself from society at large and "act for its own sake—for the House of Israel that declares God's name."[38]

The ideal of separatism is based upon the central argument that the faithful must not collaborate with the establishment. Ginzburg advocates an abandonment of the establishment and the founding of alternative frameworks.[39] The following are the details of this approach, as described by Ginzburg:

1. The prohibition against collaboration includes the rejection of the use of curricula that "inseminate a poison that is the opposite of the Torah and sanctity." Accordingly, Ginzburg proposed the establishment of a separate educational establishment with independent funding sources to promote the aspiration to independence and separatism. Such an educational system would include a program of secular studies from a religious perspective with the goal of corroborating the truths embodied in the Torah. Ginzburg even advocated for the establishment of independent universities as part of the central goal of disconnection from the public education system.
2. A further principle of disconnection was the approach to Israeli sovereignty as reflected in celebrations of Israel's Independence Day. According to Ginzburg, the refusal to collaborate should include a boycott of Independence Day celebrations.
3. The Israeli welfare services treat Jews and Arabs equally. According to Ginzburg, Arabs are the enemy. Thus, there can be no cooperation with policies that provide them with assistance. Ginzburg rejects the approach of the Israeli public health system, which strives to heal any person without distinction and prides itself on this approach. Accordingly, he has advocated for the establishment of a Jewish hospital, "in which our enemies will neither be cured by us nor cure us."[40]
4. A further plan of action related to the refusal to collaborate with the secular system of justice. Ginzburg claimed that any legal system that is not rooted in Torah serves only to add prestige to the Other Side, the mystical term for the forces of evil; accordingly, the faithful should

38. Ginzburg, *Saved Therefrom*, 116.
39. Yitzhak Ginzburg, "A Time to Break Forth and a Time to Build."
40. Ginzburg, *Saved Therefrom*, 121.

not appear before such courts. Ginzburg called for the establishment of a justice system based on the Torah that could cope with contemporary challenges and compete with the arbitration system that is already widely used among the religious public.

5. Ginzburg prohibited the use of the secular media or cooperation with the media. He claimed that merely listening to an apparently neutral newscast causes grave harm, because the pleasant and authoritative tone of the newsreader creates an atmosphere that leaves no room for God's presence as part of reality. He called for the establishment of independent media that would be both loyal and profound and that would follow an editorial line based on a distinction between good and evil.
6. Ginzburg called for the rejection of Arab labor and an insistence that all work should be performed by Jews only. He feared that those who were involved in building the Land would ultimately demand partnership in the fruit of their labors.
7. Ginzburg's position on the subject of the army was more nuanced than in other fields. He did not call upon his followers to disconnect from the army or to establish an alternative militia. It is true that, in one source, he supports the establishment of the "Army of the Lord," and mentioned the Temple Guard as the first component of a messianic army.[41] For the present, however, his main concern was to encourage insubordination. Soldiers should actively declare their rejection of the Israeli Defense Forces' moral code, which Ginzburg claimed increased the spilling of Jewish blood. If a soldier lacked the courage to oppose the army actively, he should at least engage in passive action, including the refusal to take part in uprooting Jews from their Land.[42]

To summarize, Ginzburg argued that a major setback in the prophetic vision had taken place as the result of Israeli withdrawals from the territories. It did not mean that the prophecy had failed, however. For him, some radical corrective means were urgently required. They contained the withdrawal into the religious enclave and the development of alternatives to

41. Motti Inbari, *Jewish Fundamentalism and the Temple Mount—Who Will Build the Third Temple?* (Albany: State University of New York Press, 2009), 157–59.

42. Yitzhak Ginzburg, "It Is a Time of Trouble for Jacob, but He Shall Be Saved," in *It Shall Be Saved Therefrom*, 121–23.

the secular regime. According to his view, once the alternatives were strong enough, the movement could take over the secular state. We see in this line of thought acts of rationalization focused mainly upon overcoming disappointment by political action.

DISCUSSION

The disengagement from Gaza left its mark on Israeli society and demanded ideological attention on the part of messianic movements. The actions of the state forced religious leaders to review their ideologies as tension was developing. A theo-political response was required. In this chapter, I have drawn upon psychological theories of cognitive dissonance in order to analyze the ideological transformation of three leading rabbis.

Cognitive dissonance theory addresses the distress caused when two contradictory ideas or cognitions are held simultaneously. In this case, the two contradictions were the perceived sanctity of the state and its evil acts, establishing a cognitive dissonance. The theory argues that those involved will be strongly motivated to resolve the tension between the contradictory ideas. Cognitive dissonance occurs because of a gap between expectation and experience that must be addressed. To a believer, it is hard to see the fault of his faith, and this tension pushes him to action in order to reduce the tension.

All rabbis discussed in this chapter are Orthodox Jews. Facing prophetic failure, they turned to Orthodoxy as a source of stability. Thus, we saw that the option of renouncing God or declaring His death was not a possibility for any of the rabbis, nor was it viewed as a possible solution to the cognitive dissonance engendered by the conflict between the reality of disengagement and the prophetic vision of the state as maintaining the Land of Israel in a way sanctified by God. The rabbis provide an example of the extent to which the secularization thesis discussed in the introduction of this volume does not fit the case of messianic religious Zionist movements in Israel.

Ideological change is one resolution of cognitive dissonance; however, it requires admitting lifelong ideological mistakes, which are hard to confess (or, internally, cognitively, to accept). In the case of Rabbi Tal, an ideological change occurred. His change was found in tearing down old practices and opinions; he was able to overcome denial and decided to transform himself after a period of doubt and uncertainty. An attempt to refuse change is one of the resolutions of cognitive dissonance. The case of Rabbi Aviner is an example of an attempt to keep the ideology alive when confronted with a major disconfirmation. Aviner's denial was manifested through the use of rationalizations and by establishing a massive proselytization movement. The cognitive dissonance theory can also help us understand the process of religious radicalization that leads to militancy and violence. It is a response to an unresolved dissonance, an attempt to reduce stress through subversion and revolution. Rabbi Ginsburg's response is more reflective of this type of process than the others.

Cognitive dissonance theory emerged in the late 1950s in the study of millennial movements and prophetic disconfirmation. It has developed much since that time. It is used for education, psychotherapy, social behavior, and consumer behavior. Ralph W. Hood, a specialist in the psychology of religion, suggests that more than 1,000 follow-up studies in university laboratories have confirmed the basis of the theory.[43]

The case of the rabbis has shown us that cognitive dissonance is a very powerful psychological force. It has a paralyzing effect on people. Reality does not always meet ideology, and political movements need constantly to adjust. The theory of cognitive dissonance is a tool to realize the inner mechanisms of dealing with crisis, and it can be applied to better understand the social conditions that bring or prevent change among individuals and social movements.

This chapter offered an example of the relationship between politics and religion, and the ways in which political events influence religious ideology. Psychology may help us understand why certain political players prefer passive resistance to events they dislike, whereas others would be more militant in their response. Moreover, this chapter has highlighted that nonrational and irrational ideologies, or those inconsistent in some way with empirical events, can still find followers and justifications among the politically and religiously motivated even after clear signs of disconfirmation.

References

Aran, Gideon. "A Mystic–Messianic Interpretation of Modern Israeli History: The Six Day War as a Key Event in the Development of the Original Religious Culture of Gush Emunim." *Studies in Contemporary Jewry* 4 (1998): 263–75.

43. Ralph W. Hood Jr., "Where Prophecy Lives: Psychological and Sociological Studies of Cognitive Dissonance," in *How Prophecy Lives*, ed. Diana Tumminia and William Statos Jr. (Leiden: Brill, 2011), 21–40.

Aviner, Shlomo. *Its Land and Its People: The Struggle for the Land of Israel*. Beit El: Hava Library, 1994.

Aviner, Shlomo. *In Love and Faith*. [In Hebrew.] 526, 19 Av 5765–2005, 1994.

Cohen, Asher. *The Tallit and the Flag—Religious Zionism and the Vision of the Torah State during the Early Days of the State*. [In Hebrew.] Jerusalem: Yad Ben Zvi, 1998.

Dawson, Lorne. "Clearing the Underbrush: Moving beyond Festinger to a New Paradigm for the Study of Failed Prophecy." In *How Prophecy Lives*, edited by Diana Tumminia and William Statos Jr., 69–98. Leiden: Brill, 2011.

Don Yihya, Eliezer. "Stability and Change in the Camp Party—the National Religious Party and the Young Revolution." [In Hebrew.] *State, Government and International Relations* 14 (1980): 25–52.

Eliyahu, Shmuel. 2006. "As Live As It Gets." [In Hebrew.] *Olam Katan* 56.

Ericson, Eric. 1958. *Young Man Luther: A Study in Psychoanalysis and History*. New York: W. W. Norton.

Feige, Michael. *Settling in the Hearts: Jewish Fundamentalism in the Occupied Territories*. Detroit: Wayne State University Press, 2009.

Festinger, Leon, Henry W. Riecken, and Stanley Schachter. *When Prophecy Fails: A Social and Psychological Study of a Modern Group That Predicted the Destruction of the World*. Minneapolis: University of Minnesota Press, 1956.

Garb, Yoni. "The Young Guard of the National Religious Party and the Ideological Roots of Gush Emunim." [In Hebrew.] In *Religious Zionism: The Era of Change*, edited by Asher Cohen and Yisrael Harel, 171–200. Jerusalem: Bialik Institute, 2005.

Ginzburg, Yitzhak. *It Shall Be Saved Therefrom*. Kfar Chabad: Gal Eini Institute, 2006.

Ginzburg, Yitzhak. "A Time to Break Forth and a Time to Build." Personal blog.

Ginzburg, Yitzhak. "We Shall Stand by the Name of Our God." Personal blog.

Gorenberg, Gershom. *The Accidental Empire—Israel and the Birth of the Settlements, 1967–1977*. New York: Times Books, 2006.

Hellinger, Moshe. "Political Theology in the Thought of 'Merkaz HaRav' Yeshiva and Its Profound Influence on Israeli Politics and Society since 1967." *Totalitarian Movements & Political Religions* 9, no. 4 (2008): 533–50.

Hood, Ralph W., Jr. "Where Prophecy Lives: Psychological and Sociological Studies of Cognitive Dissonance." In *How Prophecy Lives*, edited by Diana Tumminia and William Statos Jr., 21–40. Leiden: Brill, 2011.

Inbari, Motti. *Jewish Fundamentalism and the Temple Mount—Who Will Build the Third Temple?* Albany: State University of New York Press, 2009.

Inbari, Motti. "Religious Zionism and the Temple Mount Dilemma: Key Trends." *Israel Studies* 12, no. 2 (2007): 29–47.

Kanniel, Shlomo. "The Hill Settlers—A Biblical Israelite?" [In Hebrew.] In *Religious Zionism: An Era of Change*, edited by Asher Cohen and Israel Harel, 533–58. Jerusalem: Bialik Institute, Jewish National Fund, and the World Council for Torah Education, 2004.

Melton, Gordon. "Spiritualization and Reaffirmation: What Really Happens When Prophecy Fails." *American Studies* 26, no. 2 (1985): 17–29.

Ravitzky, Aviever. *Messianism, Zionism, and Jewish Religious Radicalism*. Chicago: University of Chicago Press, 1993.

Scholem, Gershom. *Major Trends in Jewish Mysticism*. New York: Shocken Books, 1960.

Schwartz, Dov. *Faith at a Crossroads—a Theological Profile of Religious Zionism*. Leiden: Brill, 2002.

Schwartz, Dov. *Religious Zionism: History and Ideology*. Boston: Academic Press, 2009.

Stone, Jon, ed. *Expecting Armageddon: Essential Readings in Failed Prophecy*. London: Routledge, 2000.

Stone, Jon R. 2009. "Prophecy and Dissonance: A Reassessment of Research Testing the Festinger Theory." *Nova Religio* 12, no. 4 (2009): 72–90.

Zertal, Idith, and Akiva Eldar. 2007. *Lords of the Land: The War over Israel's Settlements in the Occupied Territories, 1967–2007*. New York: Nation Books.

Zygmunt, Joseph F. "Prophetic Failure and Chiliastic Identity: The Case of the Jehovah's Witnesses." *American Journal of Sociology* 75, no. 6 (1970): 926–48.

Hinduism, Buddhism, and Syncretic Religions in Asia

Introduction

The section covering Asian religions includes chapters on Hinduism, Buddhism, and syncretic religions in China. These are among the world's oldest religious movements—sometimes also referred to as philosophies or ways of life—resulting from a composite picture of separate traditions and commingling beliefs, practices, and references to significant scriptures.

What we identify today with the term **Hinduism** is a diversity of beliefs and practices whose origin has been traced to South Asia between the twentieth and fifteenth centuries BC. Today, Hinduism remains a powerfully influential set of beliefs and practices across South and Southeast Asia and via the strong diaspora originating from this region well beyond the Asian continent. While it remains difficult to summarize the features of such a composite set of beliefs, some defining elements include the following. First, Hinduism is best represented as a wide range of theological approaches to the divine, including monotheism, polytheism, and almost all points between the two. Thus, Hindu theological positions on divinity may vary from belief and worship of one God with acceptance of the existence of other gods; to notions of divinity as a pantheon of gods embodied in human forms on earth; to god as permeating the universe and more. Second, this widely ranging set of theological views share a common core across beliefs and practices, principally based upon the primary sacred texts, known as the *Vedas*. This collection of verses and hymns, originally written in Sanskrit, contains revelations received by ancient saints and sages; among these are the doctrines of *Samsara* (the continuous cycle of life, death, and reincarnation) and *Karma* (the universal law of cause and effect), while the concept of *Dharma* (the performance of duty) was only introduced in later texts.

Some of these common bases have been used in the late-modern era as a cornerstone to foster a common *political* identity via the concept of *nation*. Third, Hindu religion, on the one hand, has been effectively used to build a national independence movement, nationalism, as well as explicitly secular nation-state building projects in the context of modern India. On the other hand, the otherwise secular state has self-consciously and effectively used *Hindu* nationalism to cultivate the project of the late-modern state. Hindu nationalism, thus, defies *laic* approaches to and explanatory models for religion and state.

Pratick Mallick portrays Hindu nationalism (*Hindutva*) as intrinsically entangled in Hinduism—a "metaphysics on an imagery of designating the entire society in the name of religion"—to subsequently discuss the many linkages between religious reformism and national Hindu reformism in both India's contemporary history and today's domestic and foreign policy. Indeed, today's two major Indian political parties have roots in nationalist movements: the Indian National Congress Party, which spearheaded national anticolonialism in the British Empire; and the Bharatiya Janata Party, which reflects current Hindu nationalist positions. Mallick offers an engaging historical narrative tracing the roots of Hindu nationalism in contemporary Indian secular politics to eighteenth- and nineteenth-century political philosophers and culminating in the twentieth-century greats, including Mahatma Gandhi. The emphases by Mallick include the historical and political-philosophical trajectory from colonization to independence; the role of Indian migration and education in the colonizer's institutions, which is to say *collaboration* and not only conflict among colonizer and colonized; interaction among Hindu, Muslim, and Christian thinkers, theologies, and philosophies; as well as the cultural influences of Western thought on Indian migrants.

Mallick begins with Raja Ram Mohan Roy (1772–1833), who was known locally and among those familiar with India as India's John Stuart Mill. Roy was a political liberal in an era when that political philosophy was new, still, in Europe itself. He was a champion of moral rights as well as the rights to life, liberty, and the pursuit of property. He was a monist in his approach to the divine, meaning that his version of Hindu religion and theology was one characterized by monotheism. He was influenced by the Christian scriptures as well as by Arabic and Persian Islamic texts in both his theological and political-philosophical discussions; all three of these sources are, needless to say, deeply monotheistic. Moreover, inasmuch as Roy accurately marks the historical roots of Hindu nationalism in India, as Mallick suggests, it is a foundation that is based upon a creative collaborative effort consciously reflecting a synthesis—*an intentional syncretism*—of religious and secular sources each from multiple cultures, religions, and political-philosophical traditions of East and West. That is, Indian political philosophers appeared earnestly eager to synthesize Eastern and Western approaches to both religion and politics from the earliest days of "nationalism" as an idea. Indeed, a desire for synthesis and coexistence appears to be one significant trait among Indian approaches to the colonial and postcolonial periods.

Distinguishing among influential religious thinkers, political philosophers, and leaders who sought varying degrees of "modernization," and various linkages among Hinduism as religion and as politics, Mallick then turns to the migration of Indians to the West, as well as that of a few Westerners to India, as influential in the development of Hindu nationalism. Notions of popular sovereignty ripe in Europe at the time were influential among all of these actors in both collaborative and critical veins. That is, some Indians saw travel and education in the West as constructive in building upon such ideas and applying them to India. Others viewed the use of non-elite Indians in less elevated roles in Western societies with dismay, or noted Western resistance to similar notions of popular sovereignty as applied to the Indian context in critique. Mallick connects Hindu nationalism, likewise, specifically with the Indian independence movements from the nineteenth and twentieth centuries in Europe. Throughout his article, he addresses nineteenth-- and twentieth-century thinkers and leaders such as Sir Syed Ahmad Khan (1817–98); Bal Gangadhar Tilak (1856–1920); Swami Vivekananda (1863–1902); Damodar Savarkar (1883–1966); Shyamji Krishna Verma (1857–1930); Lala Har Dayal (1884–1939); and Mohandas Karamchand Gandhi (Mahatma Gandhi) (1868–1948); critical moments such as the Sepoy Mutiny (1857); and important actors, movements, or phenomena, including the Maratha Empire, the Mughal Empire, the Theosophical Society, Brahmanism, and the changing role of the "caste" system in the development of Hindu nationalism. What emerges from his review is the intrinsic, irrevocable, mutually constitutive bond between Hindu nationalism—a constitutive part of Indian ethnic, territorial, and political identity—and Hinduism.

The history of **Buddhism** closely relates to the history of Hinduism, having begun in the sixth century BC in South Asia at a time of Hinduist prevalence in the region. Hinduism is epistemologically firm, founded on acceptance of the Vedic scriptures, perceived as eternal emanations from the universe as "heard" by sages. The Vedas, much like the holy scriptures in Abrahamic religions, were "received" by priests; these held the universe was governed by a supreme being known as Brahman. In this context, the purpose of one's life was to live in accordance with a given divine order. Because of their narrowly foundational approach and the fact that they were recited in Sanskrit, a language that ordinary people did not understand, the Veda scriptures were questioned since antiquity with different schools of thought—including Charvavka, Jainism, and Buddhism—rejecting their authority in some parts of Asia.

According to the Buddhist tradition, Siddhartha Gautama, a Hindu prince who had been kept within his palace until adulthood, being unsatisfied with his life of privilege and becoming awakened to the reality outside of his world, eventually set out to understand the source of human suffering. After rejecting his position and wealth, and after having experimented with multiple paths toward enlightenment, including mendicancy, meditation, and ascetism, he ultimately understood human sufferance as coming from insistence on permanence in a world of constant change. People's insistence on a fixed "self," on properties they thought of as "theirs," and relationships with others that they believed were "immutable" clashed with the impermanent nature of life. The way to escape suffering was to recognize and act upon these natural tendencies, something that brought Siddhartha to elaborate a body of teachings he began popularizing via the Four Noble Truths and the Eightfold Path. These consisted in pragmatic knowledge and advice allowing one to move from illusion and suffering to enlightenment and joy.[1] What would be described as a cognitive-behaviorist theory in modern parlance proved extraordinarily effective and swiftly expanded worldwide. Although Buddhism does not have a strong institutional structure and only holds loose control over the political scene of a few Asian countries, it is today followed by more than 500 million people and, as recognized by the chapters in this section, influences national and international politics through multiple, if only indirect, leverage.

1. The four noble truths are (1) life is suffering; (2) the cause of suffering is craving; (3) the end of suffering comes with an end to craving; (4) there is a path that leads one away from craving and suffering. The eightfold path serves as a guide to live without attachment to what causes suffering. It requires (1) Right View; (2) Right Intention; (3) Right Speech; (4) Right Action; (5) Right Livelihood; (6) Right Effort; (7) Right Mindfulness; (8) Right Concentration.

Religious syncretism, the process by which elements of distinct religions are merged into a unitary worldview, in China, is often traced back to the Yuan dynasty (1279–1368 AD), when precise references to the explicit concept of the "three teachings combine into one" (Daoism, Confucianism, and Buddhism) could be found. However, the newer among these religions, Buddhism, had to fight against Chinese indigenous challenges to find a place for itself from its beginning, thus creatively adapting to the religious environment it encountered. Some of these indigenous challenges, which eventually blended into today's Chinese syncretic religious practices, had a much longer history; the practice of Qi Gong, for example, has roots that go as far back as 4,000 years ago.

Wasana Wongsurawat discusses some of these beliefs in modern Chinese history, including in the forms that blended animistic or folk traditions at a grassroots level, typically inspired by a collective faith in the supernatural, with eclectic moral teachings coming from Confucianism, Buddhism, and Daoism. She does so while tackling the general, sensitive, and prominent topic of contemporary relations between the Chinese Communist Party (CCP) and religion. One of the key arguments made in the chapter is that both the CCP and Chinese syncretic religious movements—such as secret societies, village militia, and redemptive societies—share a number of common features. The other is that, once established in power, the CCP has reneged on many of its original alliances with these movements and persecuted those that could have represented a dangerous competitor—Qi Gong in its Falun Gong variance being the most notable example—while creating a limited and well-monitored space within which religion is accepted.

Syncretic religious movements in China are typically inspired by a collective faith in the supernatural, which is usually based upon eclectic moral teachings of Confucianism, Buddhism, Daoism, and, at times, local animistic traditions. On the other side, the CCP often organized its support base through folk beliefs and local practices, merged with the foundation of socialist ideas imported from European thinkers—including Karl Marx, Friedrich Engels, and Vladimir Lenin. Local syncretic religious movements and the Chinese Communist Party have much more in common than it would appear at first glance. In particular, Wongsurawat argues, they come into being as a coping mechanism in times of need for various social groups facing misadventures against which they could not expect adequate support from the government. This applies to specific subgroups for syncretic movements—including village militias organized to fight off bandits, community soup kitchens in times of famine, or fictive kinship associations for mutual support among single male migrant laborers—and to rural masses more generally in the CCP case. Both are multicultural movements with the ability to manipulate the support of peasants through institutionalized organs, connections, and networks. They also behave in similar ways: both are very quick to include or exclude (and persecute) certain groups among their followers, expand mass support bases, and to ensure security and stability to their ruling elites.

Hence, the CCP first exploited syncretic religious movements to align itself with the peasant masses. However, once the CCP successfully established the People's Republic of China in 1949, its administration officials set out almost immediately to distance the party from what they viewed as backward superstitious elements within the peasant culture, whose members were also persecuted during the Great Proletarian Cultural Revolution (1966–76). With the reform period (1979 onward), the CCP's hostility toward religions waned, and a degree of religious freedom was accorded to practitioners of five state-recognized religions—Buddhism, Daoism, Catholicism, Protestantism, and Islam—as well as certain syncretic religious movements, for example, Qi Gong schools. Wongsurawat stresses that two firm conditions remained in place: (1) the state maintained the right to monitor and control these five religious organizations; and (2) people's first and foremost pledge of allegiance was required to continue to be to the Chinese Communist Party. Religious syncretic movements that did not abide by this second rule, such as Falun Gong, were quickly, effectively, and ruthlessly wiped out.

Jue Liang's chapter offers witness to one of the many mechanisms through which religion influences society, even in the case of one of the world's least politically organized religions—Buddhism—in one of the most secular societies in the world: China. The chapter begins with a description of the Vajrasattva Teaching Assembly at Larung Gar, a yearly Buddhist assembly catering to well-schooled and affluent Han Chinese in one of the largest and most famous Tibetan Buddhist institutions. Liang then refers to a collection of personal stories of past attendants as a way to highlight the increasingly important role that Buddhism is playing among Chinese elites. In a sense, the chapter complements Wasana Wongsurawat's discussion, as it picks one of the five religions tolerated by the Chinese Communist Party to show its influence on contemporary Chinese society.

In a collection of interviews with participants, *Flowing Tides in the Ocean of Wisdom*, most disciples depict "Tibetan Buddhism (and Buddhism in general) as scientific (not superstitious), transcending ethnic and national boundaries (not confined to one place or one time), and rooted in the long history of Chinese civilization (as opposed to being understood as a foreign belief)." The accounts also reflect generational debates in China—including foundational questions on the meaning of life after the upheavals of the Cultural Revolution, and as people approach the reformist path of Deng Xiaoping—and are therefore a reflection of change in the secular society as much as they are of the image of Buddhism in that secular society. Liang's chapter consistently hints at the idea that the passage of generations of affluent and intellectually well-endowed Chinese Buddhist adepts through institutions such as Larung Gar stands as a testimony to the indirect impact that religion can still have in a society that is widely seen as secular or outright atheist.

Manus Midlarsky and Sumin Lee's chapter deals with several topics attached to Buddhism and its relation to competing religions in a number of cases throughout Asia. The article proposes several research directions, first and foremost asking why, faced with competition from other religions, Buddhism turned violent in Sri Lanka, Myanmar, and Thailand, but not in South Korea. Among the reasons investigated include the difference between Theravadan Buddhism (primarily focused on community), common throughout South and Southeast Asia, including Sri Lanka, Myanmar, and Thailand; and Mahāyānan Buddhism (principally focused on personal growth), practiced in East Asia, including Korea. This difference as causal is dismissed, however; the supposedly peaceful version of Buddhism (Mahāyānan) is also prevalent in Tibet and Japan, where its proponents have staged violent resistance against Chinese occupation and Catholic proselytism, respectively. Ethnicity is taken as an alternative explanation for the different modalities in which Buddhism has engaged with competing religions: in Myanmar, Thailand, and Sri Lanka, the Muslim communities are ethnically different from the majority of the population, while in South Korea there is no ethnic difference between Buddhists and adepts of competing religions. Thus, in line with a strong body of literature, the authors agree that it is the overlapping of ethnic and religious features that seems to be largely conducive to violence and even ethnic cleansing.

There are additional factors, however. In the Korean case, Buddhists have seemed to be able to reach "spiritual distancing" rather than promoting "physical distancing," the concept of "distancing" being understood as a form of conflict resolution on a continuum that can go from physical violence (which, in its most extreme form, can reach physical elimination) to withdrawal to the interiority of religious beliefs. Thus, Korean "distancing," understood as a withdrawal to interior beliefs, performed a substitutive function to the physical "distancing" enacted in the other cases.

Midlarsky and Lee argue that this move was also possible because, by the time Christianity reached the Korean Peninsula in the eighteenth century, Buddhism had already been weakening for a long time. Beginning from the late Koryo dynasty (918–1392), Buddhist monks were accused of loosening morals, as they became associated with the hated Mongols; they were accused of being alienated from the state, and poorly supervising temples. Several historic events further weakened the Buddhist position: after the founding of the Yi dynasty in 1392, Confucianism was introduced as the official state religion and Buddhism was restrained. While Buddhist monks had a revival of popularity when they joined the ranks of the Righteous Volunteer Army to fight the Japanese invasion of Korea during the Imjin War of 1592–98, this rise in public esteem did not last long. Following the brief period, Buddhism began a gradual but steady decline with temples throughout the country falling into disrepair, or simply being abandoned.

Following the Japanese colonization of Korea in 1910, a contamination process began by which Japanese Buddhist practices infiltrated Korean Buddhism, most notably in the practice of allowing monks to marry. This development contributed to a sense of Buddhism becoming associated with the Japanese colonizers. Hence, by the time the Japanese had left the peninsula and Christianity had arrived, Buddhism had long lost its grip over society and was not capable of staging a forceful reaction against its new competitor. Although that did not preclude Korean Buddhists from trying a vigorous revival—the number of Christians at that point was only 2 percent of the population—violence was avoided also thanks to the fact that physical distancing with the Japanese had already been accomplished.

THE ASIAN RELIGION CASES are marked by dynamics of cultural cross-fertilization, syncretism, and coexistence. When compared with Abrahamic religions, they appear less obviously related to dynamics of power and political organization. Yet they influence the international political scene in multiple and, at times, unexpected ways, as evidenced by the case of Buddhism-inspired violence in South and Southeast Asia; or the enormous popularity of Qi Gong practices in China; the ferocious persecution of Falun Gong;

and the continued training of affluent Chinese citizens in Tibetan Buddhist traditions near the border between Tibet, Qinghai, and Sichuan.

Likewise, the historical trajectory of Hindu nationalism reflects perhaps one of the clearest cases of the religious–nationalist–political nexus at work in the Asian continent. This phenomenon bears witness to a conscious effort to bring together multiple religious practices and theological traditions both within and across religions, as well as multiple political traditions, both within and across East and West, in the interest of nation building. The movement that many Westerners think of as beginning with Gandhi has a much longer history and continues to be a defining factor in Indian politics to the present. Hindu nationalism, thus, defies strictly secularist approaches to, and explanatory models for, religion and state in Asia.

Diaspora Hinduism and Hindutva

A Historiography of Modern Indian Politics

Pratick Mallick

Acharya Prafulla Chandra College—New Barrackpore

Hindu nationalism (*Hindutva*)[1] is an issue of popular discourse, discussion, electoral equations, and political and social choices in India. As an area of contestation of ideals, Hindu nationalism is termed as a metaphysics on the imagery of an entire society designated in the name of religion. Across this chapter, I will make the case that in the history of Hindu nationalism, political demands always maintained a religious component, rather than being separated or alienated from religion, and asked for a modernization of both political and religious concepts. The work of some intellectuals and activists was particularly meaningful in promoting Hindu nationalism as intrinsically linked to Hinduism. Thus, if we read between the lines of India's political philosophers, we can identify a strong religious component in the affirmation of the country's identity, one that continues to shape contemporary Indian domestic and foreign policy.

The centrality of this component became evident when the Indian National Congress (hereinafter, the Congress) failed to satisfy questions of people who frowned upon its *modus operandi* of protesting British rule. As a consequence, an alternative, bifurcated stream of politics surfaced parallel to the Congress. On the one side, leaders like Lala Lajpat Rai (1865–1928), Bal Gangadhar Tilak (1856–1920), and Bipin Chandra Pal (1858–1932), commonly

1. Literally, Hindu-ness. The term refers to the notion that one's national identity as a South Asian person would combine Hindu, meaning religion, and Hindu, meaning territory and political sovereignty.

known as Lal-Bal-Pal, went determined to assemble people by numbers; they used rituals and religious festivities as a means to reach their political constituencies. On the other side, the Congress preferred qualitative democracy to quantitative democracy, and remained long unused to the exercise of reaching out to the Indian masses. Yet, as we shall see throughout this chapter, ideological associations between Hinduism and Indian nationalism had already been breeding in the work of Indian political philosophers from earlier on.

INDIA'S RENAISSANCE: FROM THE SEPOY MUTINY TO INDEPENDENCE

The idea of India as a land of Hindus gained strength since the last quarter of the nineteenth century, when European colonialism indirectly spurred the development of a national identity. During this period, the Indians developed the orientation that Hindus should claim this land. Migration both from and returning to India played a fundamental role in fostering patriotism and promoting revolutionary reactions throughout the struggle for independence. Since its origins, therefore, the Hindu nationalist movement united a religious and a territorial notion of Hinduism.

The Sepoy Mutiny of 1857 represented an important stepping-stone to that process, and a true watershed in Indian history, marking a fresh beginning in the conflictual relations between the British colonizers and the Indians.[2] Significantly, even if the Mutiny did not take place in Bombay, it prompted the lawyer and independent activist Vinayak Savarkar to refer to it as the Indian War of Independence. In the decades that followed, militants like Savarkar, who had been exposed to the ideas of European patriots like Giuseppe Mazzini, deeply influenced the Indian nationalist movement. In particular, in exploring the Sepoy Mutiny of 1857, Savarkar reflected upon Mazzini saying that every revolution had an essence in its foundation and made appreciative comparisons between Shivaji and Mazzini's guerrilla tactics in his book *Hindu-Pad-Padashahi*, while also approving of Mazzini's

2. The Sepoy Mutiny of professional Indian infantrymen was a major uprising against British rule in India via the British East India Company, beginning in Meerut, near Delhi, and quickly expanding to other parts of the country. The rebellion resulted in more than a year of conflict and claimed the lives of some 6,000 British and more than 800,000 Indians. Although the rebellion was eventually suppressed, the episode led the British government to take over management of the country from the British East India Company.

methods of employing secret societies.[3] Before Savarkar, Indian nationalist efforts had begun overseas at the initiative of the diaspora that had gone abroad primarily in search of better prospects, or to evade the British police, or for the sake of higher education.

In analyzing the linkages between Hinduism and Indian nationalism, it is significant that long before the Mutiny took place, some Indians had already began de-idolatrizing Hinduism, and promoting monotheism as a way of better serving Indian interests. Among these was Raja Ram Mohan Roy (1772–1833), often referred to as India's John Stuart Mill. Roy was a liberal in response to the structure of Indian society, which was rudimentary, backward, and somewhat parochial. He was the champion of moral rights as well as of the rights of life, liberty, and the pursuit of property.[4] Being influenced by the teachings of the New Testament, on the one hand, and the Quranic concept of *Tawhid*, the Unity of the Almighty, on the other, Roy refused to accept the polytheism of most Hindus.[5] He thus accepted the metaphysical spiritual monism of the *Upanishads*[6]—that is, he believed in monotheism and preached it emphatically.

Roy wanted the essence of Indian society to excel with the help of the British presence. In his own way, he was eager to herald a new ethos to the Indians through arousing a modern path in Hinduism: "The present system of the Hindus is not well calculated to promote their political interests. It is necessary that some change should take place in their religion, at least for the sake of their political advantage and social comfort."[7] Accordingly, Roy promoted "a rational, ethical, non-hierarchical, and modern Hinduism . . . [and]

3. Savarkar was deeply influenced by Giuseppe Mazzini of Italy on theories of nationalism. Mazzini had emphasized the liberty of every nation even by harnessing the means of guerrilla warfare and secret societies. He had given special significance to collectivism in its methodology. To make Mazzini more relevant to the issue of India's freedom struggle, Savarkar translated Mazzini's writings into Marathi. See J. Sharma, *Hindutva: Exploring the Idea of Hindu Nationalism* (Chennai: Context [imprint of Westland Publications], 2019), 145, and introduction to *Mazzini Charitra*, 1906.

4. V. P. Varma, *Modern Indian Political Thought* (Agra: Lalshmi Narain Agarwal [1961] 2006), 21–27.

5. B. N. Seal, *Rammohun Roy: The Universal Man* (Calcutta: Sadharan Brahmo Samaj, 1924).

6. R. M. Roy, *Upanishads: Isha, Kena, Katha and Mundaka*, trans. into English, 1816–19.

7. Quoted by S. Tharoor in his *The Hindu Way: An Introduction to Hinduism* (New Delhi: Aleph Book Company, 2019), 172.

founded a reform movement, the *Brahmo Samaj* . . . of his reformist ideas of Hinduism, emerging from a modernistic reading of *Advaita Vedanta*, with early-Victorian Christianity."[8] *Brahmos* believe in one supreme God with no physical description whereas traditional Hindus believe in idolatry. This was the main point of discord between the traditionalist Hindus and Roy on the accusation that his ideas would undermine the values of the society embedded within traditional Hindu values and rituals: "Some Hindu scholars refused to consider Roy to be a Hindu at all, seeing in the *Brahmo* faith a form of Christianity dressed in Indian clothes."[9] On the other side, because of the social and political reach of his message, Roy was particularly popular among the young: the polemic that young Indian nationalists of the nineteenth century pursued to justify their challenge to the British can be primarily traced to his philosophies.

Roy is often compared in India with Maharaja Ranjit Singh (1780–1839) of Punjab, the head of the ruling Sikh Empire at the time, known for his modernizing reforms, support for the arts, infrastructural investments, and overseeing a period of prosperity. Singh approached religion through a multicultural lens and oversaw policies in a period characterized by religious pluralism and tolerance. Like Roy, Singh sought to organize and consolidate. Singh may have been somewhat more of a traditionalist than Roy, supporting religious pluralism in the context of each traditional religion on its own (traditional) terms. It may be argued that Roy, by contrast, sowed the seeds of demands for modernity—seeking something like a consolidation (or modernization) within religion as well—which Indian youths overseas later pressed into a demand for inalienable nationhood, sovereignty, and autonomy.

Beginning from the 1920s, challenging British rule in India was first and foremost ordained by Vinayak Savarkar (1883–1966), the father of the nationalist philosophy of *Hindutva*. Savarkar expressed his thesis on *Hindutva* as a more comprehensive concept than Hinduism alone. Savarkar was an ardent activist who depicted India as a land of *Hindutva*. Concerned with some basic questions, such as "Who is a Hindu?" and "What is Hinduism?,"[10] he eventually resolved that the correct question should be

8. Tharoor, *The Hindu Way*, 172–73.

9. Tharoor, *The Hindu Way*, 174.

10. P. Dixit, "The Ideology of Hindu Nationalism," in *Political Thought in Modern India*, ed. T. Pantham and K. L. Deutsch (New Delhi: SAGE, 1986).

"What is a Hindu?" According to Savarkar, the Hindus are a nation united by the bonds of their love for their common motherland and that of common blood.[11] He wrote, in Sanskrit: "A Hindu means a person who regards this land of Bharatvarsha, from the Indus to the Seas, as his Fatherland as well as his Holy Land, that is the cradle land of his religion."[12] According to Savarkar, *Hindutva* is based on three bonds: *rashtra* (territorial bond); *jati* (racial bond); and *samskriti* (culture).[13] In his staunch attitude toward *Hindutva*, Savarkar supported marriage between all segments of the Hindu populations, who, according to Savarkar, included the Jains, the Sikhs, the Arya Samajists, and the Brahmo Samajists.[14]

Savarkar's social and political orientations were matched with those of the Legendary Trio—Lal-Bal-Pal, that is, Lala Lajpat Rai from the undivided Punjab; Bal Gangadhar Tilak from Maharashtra; and Bipin Chandra Pal from undivided Bengal. Theirs was an alternative mode of reacting to the British policy of exploitation of India. They veered from the main course of politics of the Congress and emphasized the importance of mobilizing the common people via modern education, while allowing them to maintain some of their superstitions and caste-driven social structure. Tilak also sought to displace the moderate and anglicized nationalist leadership of the Congress by appealing to the religious and cultural sensibilities of the Indian masses.[15] Rai, who often came to India House in London where Savarkar lived, shared the stage with him in many public meetings in Caxton Hall, London, promoting liberal ideals and religious reforms. Rai's life was imbued by Hindu revivalism: when he moved to No. 10 Howley Place, his house became known as Indian Downing Street due to the number of revolutionaries visiting him, while house chores were managed by an Irish family, Mr. and Mrs. McNalty, who took an active interest in the vicissitudes of the British Empire and British colonial policies.[16] On his side, Tilak counted on an extended overseas network of supporters and collaborators to the Hinduist national cause, including Joseph Baptista, the Mumbai activist who later became the first president of Indian home rule and mayor

11. V. D. Savarkar, *Hindutva* (Bombay: Veer Savarkar Prakashan, 1969).

12. V. D. Savarkar, *Hindutva* (Poona: Sadashiva Peth, 1942).

13. Savarkar, *Hindutva* (1969).

14. Varma, *Modern Indian Political Thought*, 384–85.

15. S. Seth, "The Critique of Renunciation: Bal Gangadhar Tilak's Hindu Nationalism," *Postcolonial Studies* 9, no. 2 (2006): 137–50.

16. Seth, "Critique of Renunciation," 58.

of Mumbai. Interestingly, Tilak also had many Indians staying overseas to stand by him, including Deepchand Zaveri, a diamond merchant from Surat with extensive business ties in London and Paris; Sitaram Seth of Manchester; and others. He had close relations with the Labour Party, to the point that he donated 2,000 pounds to turn the weekly paper of the Labour Party into a daily.[17]

Another towering figure in Indian nationalism, Swami Vivekananda (1863–1902) appeared to stand on the fence between Brahmaism and traditionalism Hinduism. This approach suited the diaspora, which was very diverse, and allowed Swami to play a vibrant role in promoting unity among all sects of Hindus residing overseas. While Swami was always in support of Brahmaism, his master was just the reverse. Yet the love for his master made him express gratitude for his catholicity[18] during the famous 1893 lecture in which he introduced Hinduism to the Parliament of the World's Religions, helping attract Americans toward Hinduism. In the parlance of Benedict Anderson, it can be claimed that Swami's unique way of promoting Hinduism beyond India made a modernist fusion of religions, with Hinduism sitting at the apex, with an approach of *unbound seriality* instead of the Andersonian claim of *bound seriality*.[19] Swami Vivekananda remains credited with making Hindu religion accepted as a world religion, while also working toward a religious reformism promoting a mild form of monotheism.

THE ROLE OF THE DIASPORA IN PROMOTING HINDU NATIONALISM

Hindu revivalism, which surfaced in the wake of political, economic, and social changes in Indian society at large, was spearheaded by the Indian diaspora. The idea of Hindu nationalism was initially cultivated and promoted by educated nineteenth-century Indians living abroad. They saw the masses in India as parochial and therefore unaware of modernity in terms of natural rights, including the inalienable right to national sovereignty. These Indians overseas became highly motivated toward considering their home country

17. Seth, "Critique of Renunciation," 57–58.

18. Sharma, *Hindutva*, 53.

19. B. Anderson, *Imagined Communities: Reflections on the Origin and Spread of Nationalism* (London: Verso, [1983] 2006).

as their motherland. Moreover, under the then popular concepts of nationalism and popular sovereignty, they began to see it as their responsibility to free their motherland. Simultaneously, their motivation overlapped with the preaching of Hindu religion(s) and philosophies.

The remarkable work of some Hindu intellectuals and political activists allowed Hindu nationalism to gain particular strength in the last quarter of the nineteenth century. Sir Syed Ahmad Khan (1817–98), for example, emphasized that Indian Muslims required a transformation in their orientations toward knowledge and wisdom, in order to overcome the backward posture of their deliberate detachment from the colonial issue. On the other hand, the Marathas[20] had traditionally been conservative in their religious views and supportive of the caste system, particularly concerning the hegemony of Brahmanism.[21] Figures such as Bal Gangadhar Tilak launched various Hindu festivals aimed at mobilizing people, such as the *Ganpati* Festival and the *Shivaji* Festival. These festivals left a lasting impression among the Marathas and were instrumental in the crystallization of the Hindu peoples as a community, linking the local to the national level, by contrast to rule by aliens. Crucially, Tilak had a strong relationship with the Indian diaspora. He wanted young, educated Indians to ignite self-sacrifice in the cause of the motherland; to that effect, he supported many in obtaining scholarships to study abroad.

For all of them, the idea of religiosity and rituals precisely helped to garner the idea of *Indianhood* (a territorial designator) with that of *Hindu-ness* (a religious designator). In this regard, Savarkar's advocacy of *Hindutva,* a concept that energized the patriotism of young Indians overseas and was subsequently instilled into the mindsets of Indians living inland, combined religion and political identity into one, in place of *Hinduism* as a religious designator only.

The British decision to move a significant number of Indians to the less populated lands in the Pacific, Southeast Asia, and South Africa helped

---

20. The Marathas were the ethno-linguistic community that led the Maratha Empire for a century and a half. They were a dominant political force in South Asia until the early nineteenth century. They favored the Hindu religion by contrast to the Mughal Empire of the time, which followed Islam.

21. Brahmanism refers to a religious system in which Brahmins were the highest caste for some forms of Hindu religion. Originally, the Brahmins were the priestly caste. In more recent periods, the term has taken on connotations relating to social hierarchies and may be associated with certain professions.

in propagating the ideas of Hindu nationalism,[22] resulting in the garnering of a feeling of *community* among those who migrated. Those involved in these migrations were neither skilled workers nor academically trained. Their common feeling was the "Indianhood" that they felt as Hindus. In this way, too, *Hindu* identity became practically associated abroad with Indian national identity.

By contrast, most of those who migrated to Western Europe were coming from the national elites, academically prolific, and inclined toward positions of leadership. Education-wise, they were familiar with Western philosophies, democratic ideologies, and classic economic prescriptions, which were further refined in their higher academic pursuits overseas. While their migration, inasmuch as it was experienced as positive, was made possible in part by colonial administrations, nonetheless, they did not find it difficult to diagnose the discrepancy that survived between Western philosophies, particularly relating to nationalism and popular sovereignty, and their own experiences of colonial reign back home. Therefore, the Indian elites became involved in these intellectual pursuits, and decided to take leadership in promoting Indian independence. Many of these educated Indians joined the Indian Civil Service also owing to their desire to lead their peoples.

Overseas educated Indians were keen to organize themselves; however, due to their sense of gratitude toward the British, their pro-Indian nationalism was seldom anti-British. They tended to tolerate British influence as long as this allowed applying its modern philosophies to India. In other words, educated Indians viewed the British presence in India as positive. They, themselves, benefited from the interaction with the British in terms of travel, migration, and education. However, owing to a spillover effect, they also began being influenced by Western models of nationalism, national sovereignty, and popular sovereignty. They remained detached from the majority of the illiterate Indian population, both at home and overseas.

Hindu revivalists overseas also got support from home constituencies. For instance, the *Arya Samaj*[23] movement was significant both at home and overseas, as those who migrated from Punjab tended to subscribe to his views. Predicators from Punjab—or *Updeshaks*—traveled as far as Trini-

22. C. Jaffrelot, ed., *Hindu Nationalism: A Reader* (Ranikhet: Permanent Black, 2007).

23. Arya Samaj is a monotheistic Hindu movement established in the latter part of the nineteenth century. It rejects the use of statues as idols in religious worship.

dad, South Africa, Canada, and the United States, where Lala Lajpat Rai met some Punjabis before and during World War I.[24]

The emergence of the Theosophical Society[25] in the United States also contributed to the Indian nationalist cause. It was significant because, as an initiative, it was created by foreigners residing in the United States, including Europeans of various backgrounds—Ukrainian, British, and Irish, among others. In the Theosophical Society, *Orientalism*[26] overlapped with *Occidentalism*; it applied Western political philosophies outside the West, and including for its own critique, in support of self-determination in India. The journey of the Theosophical Society can be traced to a Ukrainian activist, Madame Helena Blavatsky (1831–1891), who promoted this society in the United States. Later, Annie Besant (1847–1933), a British agnostic socialist, became deeply influenced by Blavatsky and, thereafter, professed a deep religious faith. After the death of Blavatsky in 1891, Besant dedicated herself to the cause of propagating the ideals of the Theosophical Society, and two years later she came to India and became keenly interested in the cause of *Hinduism*.

In India, Besant emphasized the purpose of imparting religious instruction in school as a compulsory curriculum. In 1914 she launched two newspapers, the *Commonwealth* and *New India*, both with a view to spreading her ideals. Her popularity helped her become the thirty-third president of the Indian National Congress in 1917. She also initiated a movement for her Commonwealth of India bill, which was ultimately read in the House of Commons in England in 1925–26.[27] Her Kamla Lectures at the University of Calcutta, as well as her two major books, stand next to her many pamphlets and smaller publications; together they speak of her clear philosophy of Hinduism as an approach to the ideal of nationalism for India.[28]

The importance of the diaspora in advancing the Indian nationalist cause is perhaps best exemplified by the fact that Hindu nationalism found its

24. Jaffrelot, *Hindu Nationalism*, 361.

25. The Theosophical Society was established in New York in 1875 with the aim of advancing the ideas of Theosophy, a new religious movement drawing upon elements of both European and Asian religions. Some of the movement's multinational leaders soon moved to India, where the movement became significant. It included an interest in the occult, Kabbalah, Eastern religions, and was strongly in favor of Indian nationalism and independence.

26. E. W. Said, *Orientalism: Western Conceptions of the Orient* (Gurgaon: Penguin Random House India, [1978] 2001).

27. Varma, *Modern Indian Political Thought*, 57.

28. Besant, *India: A Nation*; Besant, *How India Wrought Her Freedom*.

base in London. While the Theosophical Society contributed in reorienting Hindu revivalism within India in the last quarter of the nineteenth century,[29] at the outset of the twentieth century Shyamji Krishna Verma (1857–1930) founded India House, a symbolic arena for a generation of young Indian patriots abroad. Verma, an erudite scholar in Sanskrit, was a staunch supporter of nationalism and Hindu culture and civilization who instilled his disciples with fervor for nationalism in light of the Hindu culture.

Meanwhile, the nationalist Madam Bhikaji Rustom Cama (1861–1936), an ethnic Parsi, rose to prominence among Indian nationalists in Europe. Dedicated to the oppressed by raising her voice in favor of India's freedom, she became actively involved in revolutionary activities including by popularizing Bande Mataram[30] and *Madan's Talwar*.[31] Her activities in Europe were so alarming to the British that during her stay in London she was given a notice that her return to India would not be possible unless she would make a declaration not to participate in nationalist activities. She refused, thus remaining in exile until shortly before her death.[32] Cases like Madam Cama epitomize on the one hand the integration between Hindu and non-Hindu patriots, and on the other how developments outside India heralded some important messages to domestic Indian constituencies.

Another remarkable Hindu nationalist active in the United States and Europe was Lala Har Dayal (1884–1939), who in 1913 founded the Ghadar Party with Sohan Sigh Bhakna as its first president. "The Ghadar Party (Indian Revolt) was rooted among the South Asian diaspora, drawing in Punjabi Sikh migrant workers who inhabited the regions stretching from Southeast Asia to the western shores of the Americas. The group's network included Hindus and Muslims as well as bhadralok (Bengali Hindu upper-caste) revolutionaries."[33] Between 1915 and 1918, the Ghadar movement suf-

29. S. Bandyopadhyay, *From Plassey to Partition: A History of Modern India* (New Delhi: Orient Longman, 2004).

30. It is equivalent to "Worshipping the Mother," denoting prayer to the motherland of India. This was one of the most used clarion calls for the compatriots to rouse the indignation of the masses against the British.

31. The name means the *Sword of Madan Lal Dhingra*, and it honors the first Indian to have been sentenced to death and hanged overseas, for assassinating a British official.

32. S. Pal, "Remembering Madam Bhikaji Cama, the Brave Lady to First Hoist India's Flag on Foreign Soil," *Better India*, 2016. http://www.google.com/www.thebetterindia.com/69290/madam-bhikaji-cama-flag-stuttgart-India/amp/

33. S. Chattopadhyay, *Voices of Komagata Maru: Imperial Surveillance and Workers from Punjab in Bengal* (New Delhi: Tulika Books, 2018), 3.

fered repression from the British, Canadian, and US governments.[34] Gradually, the energies of this movement merged with other militant formations, including nationalists and communists, and even became sympathetic toward the Russian Bolshevik Revolution of 1917.[35]

When World War I began, Dayal joined the Indian Independence Committee in Berlin and became its head from 1915 to 1917, despite being targeted by the German government. However, in 1920 he became disillusioned with the nationalist cause, eventually opining that Indians should remain within the British Empire.[36] For him as well, what strikes the most in his vision is the interplay of nationalism and religion, and the call to modernity:

> The Vedas of today are the five fundamental sciences of chemistry, physics, biology, psychology and sociology and that the *angas* and *upangas* are their division and subdivision like astronomy, geology, history, economics and politics. . . . Come to the West, the mother of the arts and sciences today. Do not in your methods try to follow in the footsteps of your old *rishis* but set up new ideals of *rishihood* for the future.[37]

He also promoted a moral discourse hinged on the abrogation of vices and corruption:

> Morality . . . is the soul of the nations, and trade, politics, literature and domestic life are its body. Morality gives unity and consistency to the various manifestations of the corporate will of the body politic.[38]

Thus, Dayal was committed to a better future for Indian politics by means of self-amelioration of the Indians themselves.[39]

Meanwhile, at the end of the nineteenth century, Swami Vivekananda was able to foster the Hindu nationalist cause among the Indian diaspora by using a different approach.[40] In 1893, at the First Parliament of the

34. Chattopadhyay, *Voices of Komagata Maru*, 3.

35. Chattopadhyay, *Voices of Komagata Maru*, 3–4.

36. Varma, *Modern Indian Political Thought*, 386.

37. L. H. Dayal, *Writings of Lala Har Dayal* (Banaras: Swaraj Publishing, 1922), 138–39.

38. Dayal, *Writings of Lala Har Dayal*.

39. By self-amelioration it is denoted that Indians should get rid of the hindrances caused by parochialism and become nationalistic by nature.

40. Through Swami Vivekananda the religion of the Hindus reached a world audience.

World's Religions held in Chicago, he addressed the audience, speaking "of the God of all, the source and essence of every faith."[41] The well-known Indologist, A. L. Basham, wrote, "Swami was the first Indian religious teacher to make an impression *outside* India in the last one thousand years or so."[42] Vivekananda addressed the audience arguing that, since every religion produced men of exalted character, there must be truth in every religion. Thus, he nullified the conviction among the preachers that their own religions could be triumphing over others.[43] Vivekananda requested those religious leaders to accept *religious pluralism* and the notion of the convergence of different faiths into some basic principle, that is, the principle of *unity in diversity*.[44] In his words:

> Much has been said of the common ground of religious unity. . . . Do I wish that the Christian would become Hindu? God forbid. Do I wish that the Hindu or Buddhist would become Christian? God forbid.[45]

Vivekananda was also outspoken toward religious tolerance in India; he opined that *Advaitism* (monotheism) was the last word of religion, and the religion of the future enlightened humanity.[46] On the question of the relation between religions, he said:

> We want to lead mankind to the place where there is neither the Vedas, nor the Bible, nor the Koran; yet this has to be done by harmonizing the Vedas, the Bible and the Koran. . . . For our own motherland, a junction of the two great systems, Hinduism and Islam—Vedanta brain and Islam body—is the only hope.[47]

He had many European and American disciples, and the world got the opportunity to learn the greatness of the Hindu religion from him.

41. Swami Prabhananda, "Swami Vivekananda's Contribution to the Parliament of Religions in Retrospect," *Journal of the Asiatic Society* 35, no. 4 (1993).

42. Quoted in Prabhananda, "Swami Vivekananda's Contribution" (1993).

43. Swami Prabhananda, "Swami Vivekananda's Contribution" (1993).

44. Swami Prabhananda, "Swami Vivekananda's Contribution" (1993).

45. First World's Parliament of Religions, Chicago Address, final session, September 27, 1893.

46. Swami Vivekananda, *My India: The India Eternal* (Golpark, Calcutta: R K M Institute of Culture, 1993).

47. Vivekananda, *My India*.

Among other Hindu nationalists active overseas, in the late 1930s a French-born, Nazi sympathizer woman calling herself Savitri Devi (1905–1982) began making headlines in calling Adolf Hitler an incarnation of Vishnu.[48] She considered that "Hinduism is the national religion of India, and there is no real India besides Hindu India."[49] Both Savarkar and Savitri Devi suggested that the religious aspiration or desire to achieve heavenly eternity had been responsible for the enslavement of India for centuries; they, therefore, were determined to change this situation and called for political power for India. Savarkar, in support of Savitri Devi, wrote, "In all walks of life, for a long time, the Hindus have been fed on inertia-producing thoughts which disabled them to act energetically for any purpose of life, other than 'moksha.' . . . And this is one of the causes of the continuous enslavement of our Hindu Rashtra for centuries altogether."[50] Savitri Devi considered that political power is everything in the world.[51] "Social reforms are necessary, not because they will bring more 'humanity' among the Hindus . . . but because they will bring unity, that is . . . power."[52]

Finally, Mohandas Karamchand Gandhi (Gandhiji) (1868–1948) represents the best known personality among Hindu nationalists and activists active overseas. While in England for his higher studies, in his second year he came in contact with the Theosophists whose London branch was more interested in esoteric Hinduism than in Buddhism, and joined the Blavatsky Lodge of the Theosophical Society in 1891. Although he did not actively participate in the activities of the Theosophical Society, he was solicited to contribute to the translation of the *Bhagavad Gita*[53] from Sanskrit, as well as reading it alongside *The Song Celestial* (1886)—a translation of the *Gita* by Edwin Arnold, who was not only a Theosophist but also a "cross-cultural synthesizer" of Buddhism,[54] Hinduism, Christianity, and Victorian science, and who influenced Gandhi to the extent that he came to believe in the unity

48. S. Tharoor, *Why I Am a Hindu* (New Delhi: Aleph Book Company, 2018), 145–46.

49. Quoted in Tharoor, *Why I Am a Hindu*, 146.

50. www.savitridevi.org/hindus-foreword.html

51. Tharoor, *Why I Am a Hindu*, 146.

52. www.savitridevi.org/hindus-06.html

53. The Bhagavad Gita is the Holy Book of Religion of the Hindus. It is a precious book in Hindu rituals.

54. Buddhism was an offshoot from Hinduism. In the sixth century BC, Buddhism emerged in response to the ritualistic and hierarchical customs and status of the Hindus in general and the Brahmins in particular.

among religions instead of their rigid compartmentalization.[55] These activities happened during his student life in London.

Later, as a professional lawyer, when Gandhi went to South Africa, he gained a different kind of knowledge. He met a large number of Indians belonging to different regions, religions, castes, and classes, from indentured laborers to Persians from western India, Muslim traders from Gujarat, and Hindu plantation workers from the Tamil and Telegu-speaking regions of Madras, as well as Christians belonging to the same region.[56] Therefore, Gandhi's *Satyagraha*[57] in South Africa between 1907 and 1914 was an inclusive approach to the communal sense of "Hindu-ness." These *Satyagrahas* made him learn, once more, the unity among religions, particularly the Hindus, Muslims, and Christians.[58] Normative syncretism was perfected by Gandhi to the point that in 1938, "[a] number of . . . distinguished Christian leaders, men of world-wide influence in opulent and imposing sections of the Church, travelled long extra distances in order to visit, and sit at the feet of a Hindu leader, Mr. Gandhi. Their object was to gain from him advice as to how they might learn to follow Christ better."[59] It was his experience in South Africa that made him "leader of a truly mass movement."[60] Thus, Gandhi thought of India as a potential *nation* in diaspora, refuting the idea of India as a society divided into many micronarratives.

HINDU NATIONALISM AND *HINDUTVA* IN INDEPENDENT INDIA

While the Indian diaspora played a key role in sparking Hindu nationalism in the nineteenth century, the Indian self-rule movement could achieve success only by becoming a mass-based movement that encompassed various sections of society at home. Inclusivity across all social classes, both at home and overseas, remains today the defining feature of Hindu nationalist organizations.

55. D. Arnold, *Gandhi: Profiles in Power* (Edinburgh: Pearson Education, 2001).

56. I. Banerjee-Dube, *A History of Modern India* (Delhi: Cambridge University Press, 2015).

57. A spiritual and political nonviolent act of resistance entailing holding fast to truth. The term was coined by Gandhi.

58. S. Sarkar, *Modern India 1885–1947* (Madras: Macmillan India, 1983).

59. J. S. Hoyland, "Gandhi's Satyagraha and the Way of the Cross," in *Mahatma Gandhi: Essays & Reflections*, ed. S. Radhakrishnan (Mumbai: Jaico Publishing, [1957] 2019), 85

60. Sarkar, *Modern India*.

The main ethos of Gandhi's views of religion was instrumental in bringing the masses to a common cause: his use of the philosophy, language, and symbols of Hinduism had the finality "to cede some territory to others."[61] His language of "*Ram Rajya*,"[62] fasting, an ashram pattern of life, or *Bhajans*,[63] have been called his uncritical attempts at making a space for "peaceful resolution of conflicts."[64] His approach to Dalit politics (e.g., the politics of "untouchability," or other forms of subaltern status, including among tribal and rural peoples) was functional to construct a dominant Hindu public sphere in which the idea of self-rule could easily propagate.[65]

In post-independent and democratic India, Gandhi's effort to achieve inclusivity and consensus among the masses of dispossessed will become mainstream among the group of organizations that are part of the *Rashtriya Swayamsevak Sangh*, or RSS family, later organized as the network of the Hindu nationalist organizations known as *Sangh Parivar*. The RSS—National Volunteer Organizations—can be considered the epicenter of the Hindutva movements and activities, both at home and overseas. These include the Vishva Hindu Parishad (VHP) as the religious wing, the Akhil Bharatiya Vidyarthi Parishad (ABVP), as well as wings meant for the peasants, workers, and tribes.[66] The RSS's key constituencies were the masses of dispossessed that formed the bulk of the Indian population at independence, and of their migrants too.

The supporters of *Hindutva* after India independence came under the banner of feminism as well. The VHP, in particular, encouraged women to become activists of *Hindutva*. As far back as 1936, Lakshmi Bai Kelkar, the

61. P. Chatterjee, "The Moment of Manoeuvre: Gandhi and the Critique of Civil Society," in *Debating Gandhi*, ed. A. Raghuram (Delhi: Oxford University Press, 2006); B. Moore Jr., *Social Origins of Dictatorship and Democracy: Lord and Peasant in the Making of the Modern World* (New York: Penguin University Books, 1966).

62. A term coined by Gandhi to refer to a spiritually principled form of governance as embodied in a state.

63. The term means "mutual assistance and support," as embodied in an open-ended and free-form song sung in a communal or worship context. As song, it may or may not include rhythm and other instruments.

64. A. Gudavarthy, *Politics of Post–Civil Society: Contemporary History of Political Movements in India* (New Delhi: SAGE, 2013).

65. Gudavarthy, *Politics of Post–Civil Society*.

66. I. Therwath, "Cyber-Hindutva: Hindu Nationalism, the Diaspora and the Web." In *e-Diasporas Atlas* (Paris: Fondation Maison des sciences de l'homme, 2012), 5–6.

founder of the women's organization *Rashtra Sevika Samiti*, which ran parallel to the men-only RSS, suggested that women are part of the nation and appealed for imparting to women the ideology of the organization for the benefit of the movement itself.[67] The RSS founder, Keshav Baliram Hedgewar, did not give his consent to that but agreed to assist Kelkar in starting the *Rashtra Sevika Samiti*. Hindu nationalist women not only became very visible in the movement, but they also supported gendered politics.[68]

The RSS played, and continues to play, a crucial role in fostering Hindu nationalism and India's national culture and interests beyond India's borders. Following the establishment of the first *shakhas*[69] among migrants (the first on a Kenya-bound ship by Jagdish Chandra Sharda in 1947[70]), these initially remained limited to Africa before spreading to the United Kingdom and the United States. The shakhas often attracted Hindu migrants,[71] and operated with a remarkable degree of operational sophistication, maintaining at home a secret registry with the names of Indians who were eager to migrate abroad, so that they could be convinced to join or launch a new unit.[72] In 1970, some RSS members who were residing in the United States assembled in New York in order to form the VHP of the USA.[73] Its success can be gauged from the growing number of participants over the years; whereas at the first annual conference of 1970 in Canton, Ohio, there were only 35 del-

67. W. K. Andersen and S.D. Damle, *The Brotherhood in Saffron: The Rashtriya Swayamsevak Sangh and Hindu Revivalism* (Gurgaon: Penguin Books, [1987] 2019), 37.

68. K. D. Menon, *Everyday Nationalism: Women of the Hindu Right in India* (Philadelphia: University of Pennsylvania Press, 2010).

69. Shakha is the basic unit of the RSS in its organizational hierarchy. It is expected to function as a small unit at the neighborhood level, which means similar-minded people establishing a bond of solidarity. Membership in a shakha is strictly kept not below 50 and not more than 100 male participants. Each shakha is to be divided into four age groups that are further subdivided into gatas or groups. In general, the shakhas are open thrice a day for seven days in a week. Members are free to choose the slots as per their convenience to participate. Besides, there are monthly and weekly shakhas as well. The latter kind of shakhas is meant for those who fail to attend shakhas daily; see, for example, Andersen and Damle, *Brotherhood in Saffron*, 83.

70. Andersen and Damle, *Brotherhood in Saffron*, 83.

71. S. Burlet, "Re-awakenings? Hindu Nationalism Goes Global," in *Asian Nationalism in the Age of Globalization*, ed. R. Starr (Richmond, Surrey: Curzon Press, 2001), 13.

72. D. Goyal, *Rashtriya Swayamsevak Sangh* (New Delhi: Radhakrshna Prakashan, 1979), 106n91.

73. Andersen and Damle, *Brotherhood in Saffron*, 145–46.

egates, at the tenth session in New York they were as many as 5,000.[74] This explains the role that the VHP played in organizing Indians around the promotion of Hindutva, in the United States as elsewhere. Overall, there were at least 39 countries across the world where such organizations had active roles, with the strongest in the United States, the United Kingdom, and Australia. It is also noteworthy that the RSS cause was joined by the Sikhs, the Buddhists, and the Jains.[75] Madhav Sadashiv Golwalker extended an invitation to the senior leader of the Sikh Akali Dal party, Master Tara Singh, who appreciatively joined hands with the Hindus by emphasizing that they were not a separate community from the Hindus and that their prosperity was possible so long as the Hindu religion was thriving.[76] Similarly, a Jain saint once remarked. "How can he who does not call himself a Hindu also be a Jain?"[77] Undoubtedly, this is how the Hindu organization turned into a conglomerate worldwide, to which Golwalker made a great contribution. Outside of India, the eastern shores of Africa and Southeast Asia have been among the main centers of Hindutva promotion in post-independence years. Diwali—a major Hindu religious festival—became part of public holidays in some 10 countries, including Kenya, Singapore, Myanmar, Mauritius, and Malaysia.

More recently, the Sangh launched *e-shakhas*, promoting Hindutva online. Social networking sites have been promoting social narratives among supporters of Hindutva. "The RSS was quick . . . to tap the potential of the Web in order to bind together a heterogeneous and geographically spread-out community and transform it into an 'imagined community.' Now, members of the RSS can, without actually meeting, share the same ideology, participate in debates, and synchronically perform the same rituals."[78] Other platforms, which do not belong to official Hindutva organizations, still foster pro-Hindutva orientations as a way of life for Indians living abroad.[79] English publications such as the *Voice of India* contribute to Hindutva, with well-known personalities authoring its articles. The Sangh Parivar groups

74. Andersen and Damle, *Brotherhood in Saffron*.

75. Andersen and Damle, *Brotherhood in Saffron*, 158.

76. Andersen and Damle, *Brotherhood in Saffron*, 158.

77. Quoted in Andersen and Damle, *Brotherhood in Saffron*, 158.

78. Therwath, "Cyber-Hindutva," 8.

79. Among the websites (aside from RSS itself) that play a significant role in promoting Hindutva abroad are those of the Organizer, the Hindu Universe, Hindu Janajagruti Samiti, and Haindava Keralam.

publish magazines and various types of writings on Hindutva, which have circulation all over the world.

RECENT PHENOMENA

Today, the role of the Indian diaspora remains central to Indian nationalism and India's national interests. Since 2003, every January 9 is earmarked as *Pravasi Bharatiya Divas* day to mark the contribution of the overseas Indian community in the national development of India and to commemorate Gandhi's return from South Africa in 1915.[80] The aim is to keep a strong bond between overseas Indians and the government of India. During the premiership of Narendra Modi, the engagement with the Pravasis has reached a peak.[81]

Similarly, Hinduism continue to remain at the center stage of the concept of Hindutva. The major political party in India, the Bharatiya Janata Party (BJP), and the political alliance it leads, the National Democratic Alliance (NDA), are tied together with the meaning and narratives of Hindu nationalism as intrinsically attached to Hinduism, so much so that "a central proposition that has undergirded the philosophy of both the Jana Sangh and its successor is that Hinduism is coterminous with the territory of India."[82] In 2014, the Hindu right-wing VHP received an absolute majority in the general elections to the Lok Sabha (lower chamber of parliament). Following its victory, the party declared that the Hindus had taken back the political power they had lost in the twelfth century.

This has also signaled a shift in foreign policy, in the direction of Savarkar's old idea that Hindutva should be a basic parameter of India's foreign policy.[83] Indian nationalist stances have thus strengthened since the presidency of Narendra Modi, and the country seems to be more articulate about its interests and own security. In particular, since Modi's presidency, India-Pakistan bilateral policy has been mostly shaped by the need to answer nationalistic demands from domestic constituencies. While Modi has put more empha-

80. http://www.mea.gov.in/pravasi-bharatiya-divas.htm

81. S. Ambekar, *The RSS Roadmaps for the 21st Century* (New Delhi: Rupa Publications India, 2019), 156.

82. S. Ganguly, *Hindu Nationalism and the Foreign Policy of India's Bharatiya Janata Party, 2014–15*, Paper Series no. 2 (Washington, DC: Transatlantic Academy, 2015), 6.

83. C. Jaffrelot, *The Hindu Nationalist Movement in India* (London: Hurst, 1993), 27.

sis on soft rather than hard power diplomacy—for example, by balancing his increasingly determined stance on Pakistan with strong cultural diplomacy toward Islam, including by establishing cultural centers throughout the Muslim world, and investing in crude oil from the Persian Gulf region—the nationalistic turn was undoubtedly felt.[84] Hindutva as a foreign policy tool has also contributed to other diplomatic efforts toward China: for example, in April 2005 a memorandum of understanding was signed with Beijing to construct a Hinduist temple in the White Horse Temple complex in Luoyang town.[85] Hindutva-based foreign policy works today also via education diplomacy, with *Sangh parivar* ensuring that the content of school textbooks properly represent and dignify Hindu culture, while fostering a mindset of Hindu-ness among the children of Indian expatriates.[86]

CONCLUSION

Historically, the prevalent notion of Hinduism was deliberately extended to that of *Hindutva*, which added territorial and cultural connotations to the religious concept, in an effort to reach out to the masses of dispossessed who were to support the nationalist cause. Hence, since the late nineteenth century, the paths of Hindu nationalism and Hinduism have traveled side by side. India has today evolved into a democracy that constitutionally subscribes to the ideals of secularism, freedom, equality, and fraternity; one in which, though, religion continues to matter both in public and in

84. The soft approach was also instrumental to secure and strengthen Muslim support for the BJP in national elections. Nonetheless, Modi maintains today an image of Hindu extremist among many Pakistanis, a perspective that has strengthened during his presidency.

85. V. Subrahmaniam, "Pratibha Gifts Indian-Style Temple to the People of China," *The Hindu*, May 29, 2010 (updated November 11, 2016), hehindu.com/news/international/Pratibha-gifts-Indian-style-temple-to-the-people-of-China/article16304440.ece

86. This is mostly found in the United States. For example, in California the Vedic Foundation and the Hindu Education Foundation, an affiliate of the HSS of America, initiated a petition protesting against "unfair and inaccurate depiction of Hinduism in school textbooks." The Vedic Foundation recommended as many as 382 edits across eight textbooks, subsequently expressing satisfaction at getting 70% of their edit recommendations accepted by the textbook committee. See Jaffrelot, *Hindu Nationalism*, 363; and S. Padmanabhan, "Debate on Indian History: Revisiting Textbooks in California," *Economic and Political Weekly*, May 6, 2006, 1761.

private spheres. Religion remains today a critical part of national—and nationalist—discourse and identity, helping in the process of establishing a common cultural platform in a country of more than a billion people. Religious aspects of Hindutva are also responsible for shaping several aspects of India's foreign policy, which can align with Hindutva or Hindu nationalism relying on the support base behind the national government.

References

Ambekar, S. *The RSS Roadmaps for the 21st Century*. New Delhi: Rupa Publications India, 2019.

Anderson, B. *Imagined Communities: Reflections on the Origin and Spread of Nationalism*. London: Verso, (1983) 2006.

Andersen, W. K., and S. D. Damle. *The Brotherhood in Saffron: The Rashtriya Swayamsevak Sangh and Hindu Revivalism*. Gurgaon: Penguin Books, (1987) 2019.

Andersen, W. K., and S. D. Damle. "How the Hindu Nationalist RSS Woos Indian-Americans." *Quartz India*, August 8, 2018. http://www.google.com/amp/s/qz.com/india/1350285/rss-and-the-spread-of-hindu-nationalism-in-us/amp/

Appadurai, A. *Modernity at Large: Cultural Dimensions of Globalization*. Minneapolis: University of Minnesota Press, 1996.

Arnold, D. *Gandhi: Profiles in Power*. Edinburgh: Pearson Education, 2001.

Bandyopadhyay, S. *From Plassey to Partition: A History of Modern India*. New Delhi: Orient Longman, 2004.

Banerjee-Dube, I. *A History of Modern India*. Delhi: Cambridge University Press, 2015.

Basu, M. *The Rhetoric of Hindu India: Language and Urban Nationalism*. Noida: Cambridge University Press, 2017.

Besant, A. *How India Wrought for Freedom: The Story of the National Congress Told from Official Records*. Madras: Theosophical Publishing House, 1915.

Besant, A. *India: A Nation; A Plea for Self-Government*. Madras: Vasanatha Press, 1923.

Bhatt, C. "Dharmo Rakshati Rakshitah: Hindutva Movement in UK." *Ethnic and Racial Studies* 23, no. 3 (2000).

Bhatt, C., and P. Mukta, ed. "Hindutva Movement in the West." *Ethnic and Racial Studies* 23, no. 3 (May 2002).

Burlet, S. "Re-awakenings? Hindu Nationalism Goes Global." In *Asian Nationalism in the Age of Globalization*, ed. R. Starr. Richmond, Surrey: Curzon Press, 2001.

Chatterjee, P. "The Moment of Manoeuvre: Gandhi and the Critique of Civil Society." In *Debating Gandhi*, ed. A. Raghuram. Delhi: Oxford University Press, 2006.

Chattopadhyay, S. *Voices of Komagata Maru: Imperial Surveillance and Workers from Punjab in Bengal*. New Delhi: Tulika Books, 2018.

Corbridge, S., and J. Harris. *Reinventing India: Liberalization, Hindu Nationalism and Popular Democracy*. New Delhi: Oxford University Press, 2000.

Dayal, L. H. *Writings of Lala Har Dayal*. Banaras: Swaraj Publishing, 1922.

Dixit, P. "The Ideology of Hindu Nationalism." In *Political Thought in Modern India*, edited by T. Pantham and K. L. Deutsch. New Delhi: SAGE, 1986.

Embree, A. T. *1857 in India: Mutiny or War of Independence?* Boston: D. C. Heath, 1963.

Ganguly, S. *Hindu Nationalism and the Foreign Policy of India's Bharatiya Janata Party, 2014–15*. Paper Series no. 2. Washington: Transatlantic Academy, 2015.

Godbole, V. S. *A Special Tour of Places in London Associated with Indian Freedom Fighters*. Rev. 2010 [Publicity Flier].

Goyal, D. *Rashtriya Swayamsevak Sangh*. New Delhi: Radhakrshna Prakashan, 1979.

Gudavarthy, A. *Politics of Post–Civil Society: Contemporary History of Political Movements in India*. New Delhi: SAGE, 2013.

Helland, C. "Diaspora on the Electronic Frontier: Developing Virtual Connections with Sacred Homelands." *Journal of Computer-Mediated Communication* 12, no. 3. http://jcmc.indiana.edu/vol12/issue3/helland.html

Hoyland, J. S. "Gandhi's Satyagraha and the Way of the Cross." In *Mahatma Gandhi: Essays & Reflections*, ed. S. Radhakrishnan. Mumbai: Jaico Publishing, (1957) 2019.

Jaffrelot, C., ed. *Hindu Nationalism: A Reader*. Ranikhet: Permanent Black, 2007.

Jaffrelot, C. *The Hindu Nationalist Movement in India*. London: Hurst, 1993.

Karnad, B. *Staggering Forward: Narendra Modi and India's Global Ambition*. Gurgaon: Penguin-Viking, 2018.

Katju, M. *Hinduising Democracy: The Vishva Hindu Parishad in Contemporary India*. New Delhi: New Text, 2017.

Kugelman, M. "After the Kashmir Move: India-Pakistan Relations." *YaleGlobal Online*, August 22, 2019. http://yaleglobal.yale.edu/content/after-kashmir-move-india-pakistan-relations

Kwach, J. "All Public Holidays in Kenya You Should Know. In *Gazetted Public Holidays in Kenya 2020*, July 2020. http://www.tuko.co.ke/261515-gazetted-public-holidays-kenya.html

Mazumdar, S. "The Politics of Religion and National Origin: Rediscovering Hindu Indian Identity in the United States." In *Antimonies of Modernity: Essays on Race, Orient, Nation*, ed. V. Kaiwar and S. Mazumdar. Durham: Duke University Press, 2003.

Menon, K. D. *Everyday Nationalism: Women of the Hindu Right in India*. Philadelphia: University of Pennsylvania Press, 2010.

Moore, B., Jr. *Social Origins of Dictatorship and Democracy: Lord and Peasant in the Making of the Modern World*. New York: Penguin University Books, 1966.

Mukhopadhyay, N. *The RSS: Icons of the Indian Right*. Chennai: Tranquebar, an imprint of Westland Publications, 2019.

Padmanabhan, S. "Debate on Indian History: Revisiting Textbooks in California." *Economic and Political Weekly*, May 6, 2006.

Pal, S. "Remembering Madam Bhikaji Cama, the Brave Lady to First Hoist India's Flag on Foreign Soil." *The Better India*, 2016. http://www.google.com/www.thebetterindia.com/69290/madam-bhikaji-cama-flag-stuttgart-India/amp/

Pande, A. *Making India Great: The Promise of a Reluctant Global Power*. Noida: HarperCollins India, 2020.

Parpola, Asko. *Deciphering the Indus Script*. Cambridge: Cambridge University Press, 2009.

Patel, T. "Legacy of Lal-Bal-Pal: The Legendary Trio Who Stood for Swaraj & Swadeshi Ideals!" *The Better India*, 2018. http://www.google.com/amp/s/www.thebetterindia.com/154097/lal-bal-pal-tilak-lajpat-rai-bipin-chandra-pal/amp/

Pirbhai, M. R. "The Demons of Hindutva: Writing a Theology for Hindu Nationalism." *Modern Intellectual History* 5, no. 1 (April 2008): 27–53.

Prabhananda, Swami. "Swami Vivekananda's Contribution to the Parliament of Religions in Retrospect." *Journal of the Asiatic Society* 35, no. 4 (1993). Reprint, Kolkata: Advaita Ashrama, 2013.

Rawat, M. "Pakistan Suspends Trade Ties with India: Who Gains, Who Loses from Imran Khan's Move." *India Today*, August 9, 2019 (updated August 12, 2019). http://www.google.com/amp/s/www.indiatoday.in/amp/news-analysis/story/Pakistan-suspends-trade-with-india-imran-khan-article-370-jammu-kashmir-1578817-2019-08-09

Roy, R. M. *Upanishads: Isha, Kena, Katha and Mundaka*. Translated into English, 1816–19.

Roy Chaudhury, D. "Saudi Arabia Ends a Loan and Associated Oil Supply to Pakistan Following Threats to Split OIL." *Economic Times*, August 12, 2020 (updated August 14, 2020). https://economictimes.indiatimes.com/news/international/world-news/saudi-arabia-ends-a-loan-and-associated-oil-supply-to-pakistan-following-threats-to-split-oic/articleshow/77499372.cms

Said, E. W. *Orientalism: Western Conceptions of the Orient*. Gurgaon: Penguin Random House India, 2001.

Sarkar, S. *Modern India 1885–1947*. Madras: Macmillan India, 1983.

Sasi, A. "On Govt Drawing Board: Tool to Hard Sell Soft Power in Diplomacy." *Indian Express*, February 14, 2018.

Sathiya Moorthy, N. "Neighbours Challenge Political Hindutva's Ram Agenda." *South Asia Journal*, July 25, 2020.

Savarkar, V. D. *Hindutva*. Poona: Sadashiva Peth, 1942.

Savarkar, V. D. *Hindutva*. Bombay: Veer Savarkar Prakashan, 1969.

Savarkar, V. D. *Hindutva*. New Delhi: Hindi Sahitya Sadan, 2020.

Savarkar, V. D. *The Indian War of Independence 1857*. (1909) 2019.

Seal, B. N. *Rammohun Roy: The Universal Man*. Calcutta: Sadharan Brahmo Samaj, 1924.

Seth, S. "The Critique of Renunciation: Bal Gangadhar Tilak's Hindu Nationalism." *Postcolonial Studies* 9, no. 2 (2006): 137–50.

Sharda, J. C. *Memoirs of a Global Hindu*. New Delhi: Vishwa Niketan, 2008.

Sharma, J. *Hindutva: Exploring the Idea of Hindu Nationalism*. Chennai: Context (imprint of Westland Publications), 2019.

Shepherd, K. I. "Shudra, Not Aryans, Built the Indus Valley Civilisation." *dailyo.in*, August 19, 2018. http://www.google.com/amp/s/www.dailyo.in/lite/variety/harappan-civilisation-indus-valley-civilisation-shudras-mohenjodaro-sanskrit-texts-dholavira-rig-veda/story/1/26155.html

Singh, R. *The Ghadar Heroes*. Bombay: People's Publishing House, 1945.

"Snubbed by OIC on J&K, Pak Threatens to Revolt." *Times of India*, August 8, 2020. https://timesofindia.indiatimes.com/india/snubbed-by-oic-on-jk-pak-threatens-to-revolt/articleshow/77425028.cms

Subrahmanian, V. "Pratibha Gifts Indian-Style Temple to the People of China." *The Hindu*, May 29, 2010 (updated November 11, 2016). hehindu.com/news/international/Pratibha-gifts-Indian-style-temple-to-the-people-of-China/article16304440.ece

Tatla, D. S. "Introduction." In *Voyage of Komagata Maru or India's Slavery Abroad by Baba Gurdit Singh*, ed. Darshan Singh Tatla. Chandigarh: Unistar Books, 2007.

Tharoor, S. *The Hindu Way: An Introduction to Hinduism*. New Delhi: Aleph Book Company, 2019.

Tharoor, S. *Why I Am a Hindu*. New Delhi: Aleph Book Company, 2018.

Therwath, I. "Cyber-Hindutva: Hindu Nationalism, the Diaspora and the Web." In *e-Diasporas Atlas*. Paris: Fondation Maison des sciences de l'homme, April 2012.

Varma, V. P. *Modern Indian Political Thought*. Agra: Lalshmi Narain Agarwal, 2006. Original publication, 1961.

Vivekananda, Swami. *Chicago Address, Final Session*. September 27, 1983.

Vivekananda, Swami. *My India: The India Eternal*. Golpark, Calcutta: R K M Institute of Culture, 1993.

Viyogi, N. *The History of Indigenous People of India: The Foundation of Indus Valley Civilization and Their Later History*. New Delhi: Samyak Prakashan, (1995) 2015.

Multiculturalism and Revolution

An Analytical History of the Chinese Communist Party's Relationship with Syncretic Religious Movements

Wasana Wongsurawat
Chulalongkorn University—Bangkok

The Chinese Communist Party's (CCP) relationship with religion may be longer and more eventful than most other aspects of the party's history. In the same way that Chinese communism was never a straightforward replica of the Marxist-Leninist movement in the Soviet Union, the CCP's stance toward and relationship with religions of all sorts has been full of twists, turns, and ever-transforming "Chinese characteristics."[1] Variations in these

---

Research for this article was part of the "Buddhist Pluralism Project" under the leadership of Professor Suwanna Satha-Anand with the generous support of Thailand Science Research and Innovation (TSRI 2018-2021).

1. "With Chinese characteristics" refers to the technical term for a socialist market economy as introduced by Deng Xiaoping at the beginning of the Reform Era and proclaimed by Secretary General Zhao Ziyang in the 13th National Congress in 1987 as "socialism with Chinese characteristics," suggesting that anything "with Chinese characteristics" is not straightforwardly the way it is commonly expected to be. Socialism with Chinese characteristics is open to the world market economy, and similarly the socialist stance toward religion "with Chinese characteristics" would tend to be different from the approach of other socialist parties toward religion. For a concise theoretical discussion of what "socialism with Chinese characteristics" means exactly, see Ian Wilson, "Socialism with Chinese Characteristics: China and the Theory of the Initial Stage of Socialism," *Australian Journal of Political Science* 24, no. 1 (1989): 77–84.

have primarily depended upon the personality of the party leaders as well as the party's position in the context of China's tumultuous political history of the twentieth and twenty-first century. Starting from its establishment a full century ago in 1921, the CCP founding fathers, Chen Duxiu and Li Dazhao, were firmly footed in the Leninist tradition of atheist materialism. Religion was considered a tool of the oppressive classes, the antithesis of political consciousness, and an organized form of superstition.[2] However, this stance lasted only as long as the CCP dominance of the founding fathers. Once Chiang Kai-shek consolidated his leadership of the Kuomintang (KMT), he instigated the purge of Communist members from the party through what has come to be known as the Shanghai Massacre, on April 12, 1927, which included the execution of Li Dazhao in Beijing later that month, and the expulsion of Chen from the CCP in November 1929.

The disagreements between the party's founding fathers and the post-1927 leader, Mao Zedong, toward religion occurred along lines similar to those of the ideological conflicts among the proletarian driving forces of the communist revolution. Chen and Li insisted upon following Moscow's directives, which suggested that the CCP cooperate with the KMT in unifying and developing the country into a fully industrialized state before instigating a communist revolution driven by a majority of industrial workers. Mao and his followers, on the other hand, noted that since the 1927 massacre, it had become impossible to follow Moscow's directives and continue to work with the KMT. The revolution needed to happen much sooner in order to save the lives of remaining CCP comrades, and, therefore, had to be driven by peasants, who represented the majority of the Chinese working class.

Once Mao consolidated his leadership through the Long March and established the Communist headquarters in Yan'an, Shaanxi Province, the peasant-driven revolution became the fundamental policy of the CCP. Throughout the Long March and the establishment of the new government in Yan'an, the CCP under Mao's leadership was forced to reconsider its stance toward religion, and especially toward folk beliefs and the practices of rural masses. In order to better understand and gain support from a significant segment of the Chinese peasantry, it became necessary to recognize some of their beliefs and practices not as backward superstitions but as the foundational basis of folk knowledge, and the natural wisdom of the agrar-

2. Shaoqing Cai, *Zhongguo jindai huidangshi yanjiu* (Beijing: Zhonghua shulu, 1987), 333.

ian proletariat class.[3] This new approach allowed the CCP to incorporate numerous peasant militant groups and local militia—in the forms of secret societies and village militia—into the People's Liberation Army, as well as to benefit from the philanthropic work of redemptive societies.

This compromising stance toward folk religious organizations active among the rural masses, however, ended soon after the CCP's victory on the Mainland and the establishment of the People's Republic of China in October 1949. The CCP's first government in Beijing started to distance itself from superstitious peasant organizations and millenarian movements as soon as it managed to consolidate power throughout Mainland China. Former secret society and millenarian movement members were encouraged to reform themselves in the direction of the anti-superstitious party line, and Mao Zedong's thought was to become the people's main system of belief. This tendency became considerably more extreme with the outbreak of the Great Proletarian Cultural Revolution in the summer of 1966. Party members and military officers who had past connections with secret societies and millenarian movements were purged, along with clergy and known practitioners of organized religions.[4] By the end of the Cultural Revolution in 1976, a large number of temples, churches, mosques, and shrines across Mainland China had been razed to the ground.

The Communist government's stance toward religions appeared to relax with the dawn of the reform era. Deng's regime claimed to grant religious freedom to all citizens of the PRC. It was, however, a restricted freedom like most other freedoms under the dictatorship of the Chinese Communist Party. The state recognized only five organized religions—Buddhism, Daoism, Islam, Catholicism, and Protestantism—and it closely monitored them. Citizens who desired to enjoy this new state-controlled religious freedom could choose to be faithful and practice one among these five officially recognized religions. All other religions were considered superstition (迷信-míxìn).[5]

To be sure, even adepts of these five religions had to abide by gov-

3. Yun Chen, "Zhongguo Minzu Yundong zhi Guoqu yu Jianglai," in *Henan Shizhi Ziliao*, vol. 6 (Zhengzhou: Henansheng defang shizhi pianzuan weiyuanhui, 1984), 4–5.

4. Zhiping Zuo, "Political Religion: The Case of the Cultural Revolution in China," *Sociological Analysis* 52, no. 1 (1991): 99–110.

5. Yushuang Zheng, "Political Constitution and the Protection of Religious Freedom: A Jurisprudential Reading of Article 36 of the Chinese Constitution," in *Christianity in Chinese Public Life: Religion, Society, and the Rule of Law*, ed. Joel A. Carpenter and Kevin R. den Dulk (New York: Palgrave Macmillan, 2014), 79–96.

ernment rules created to ensure that Chinese believers would always owe their first and foremost allegiance to the Chinese Communist government. These rules included, for example, the prohibition against the recognition of the pope as the supreme leader of the Catholic Church; the insistence that Catholic bishops in the People's Republic of China had to be appointed by the Chinese government instead of the Vatican; the ban against recognizing the Dalai Lama as the spiritual leader of Tibetan Buddhists; and more. Yet, according to the strict party line, religion was something allowed, albeit not encouraged. Party members and high-ranking officials of the state, for example, were advised to steer clear of such uncommunist practices.

SYNCRETIC RELIGIOUS MOVEMENTS

Syncretic religious movements are, by definition, less organized, more fluid, diverse, and adaptable than organized religions. The Chinese government interacts with these movements in different ways. Some are considered part of a recognized organized religion, such as the practice of Qi Gong,[6] which is considered a Buddhist practice and has been monitored by the same organizations liaising Buddhist practitioners and the state. Others, such as lineage associations or clan associations, are considered a form of ancestral worship, related to Confucianism,[7] which is not considered a religion in the same way as the five state-sanctioned organized religions mentioned above. Syncretic religious movements were and still are an important part of modern and contemporary Chinese history because they encapsulate the multicultural nature of the Chinese grassroots population, which has been the most pow-

6. Qi Gong is a form of folk Chinese exercise that coordinates breathing with body movements. The logic of Qi Gong is an eclectic mix of Buddhism, Daoism, Chinese medicine, and martial arts. It is one of the most ancient forms of exercise-cum-spiritual practice that has survived to the present day. Qi Gong is believed to have started to develop close to 4,000 years ago, long before the establishment of the first Chinese dynasty. It appears in a wide range of cultural products—literature, religious art, and drama—throughout the dynastic era, and is one of the very few ancient practices adopted and encouraged by the Chinese Communist Party, one that survived the Cultural Revolution more or less unscathed.

7. As Confucius came to be the PRC's most well-known cultural ambassador at the turn of the twenty-first century, the Confucius Institute became the most important organ of cultural diplomacy, and Confucianism came to be regarded as the essence of Chinese culture that could bridge the PRC with the Sinophone and Chinese diaspora, as well as enhance relations with the greater East Asia cultural sphere countries—Japan, Korea, Singapore, and so forth.

erful driving force behind China's numerous political transformations across the era of revolution, that is, in the twentieth century.

In the Chinese context, syncretic religious movements are popular movements at the grassroots level, typically inspired by a collective faith in the supernatural, which is usually based upon eclectic moral teachings of Confucianism, Buddhism, Daoism, and, at times, incorporated within local animistic traditions. These movements often come into being as a coping mechanism for various subgroups facing misfortunes against which they cannot expect adequate support from the state—for example, village militias to fight off bandits, community soup kitchens in times of famine, or fictive kinship associations for mutual support among single male migrant laborers. These movements primarily arise in time of need and fade away when disasters subside. Nonetheless, in times of major crises, when disasters appear to be so numerous and frequent as to push people to think that the ruling regime is no longer beneficial, syncretic religious movements may escalate into rebellions, or they may join forces in support of revolutionary movements that could overthrow the ruling regime and establish new forms of government.

The history of relations between the Chinese Communist Party and syncretic religious movements is particularly interesting and useful to understanding Chinese social and political history in the modern and contemporary period. Its significance is due to the many strong parallels between the CCP and the syncretic religious movements. While syncretic religious movements follow eclectic sets of beliefs and morality, often integrating teachings from Buddhism and Daoism within the context of Confucian traditions and practices, the CCP has developed its own ideology by integrating folk beliefs and local practices with the foundation of socialist ideas imported from European thinkers—including Karl Marx, Friedrich Engels, and Vladimir Lenin. This syncretic intellectual tradition allowed Maoism to become a form of socialist movement, where the communist revolution could be driven by peasants instead of the industrial proletariat, and resulted in an anachronistic variant of Chinese communism, where the society was directly transformed from an agrarian society into a dictatorship of the proletariat without having to complete the industrial revolution first.

Maoist features during the Cultural Revolution also included a strong personality cult similar to the practices of many syncretic religious movements, which deify historical figures or leading members of the movement, or both.[8] Like syncretic religious movements, the Chinese Communist Party

8. Zhiping Zuo, "Political Religion: The Case of the Cultural Revolution in China," 99–110.

is also quick to include or exclude, and to persecute, certain groups among their followers in order to safeguard the movement's political advantage, expand mass support bases, or ensure security and stability for the movement's ruling elite. It would be fair to conclude that some important features that allowed the CCP to win support among the Chinese masses, to be victorious in the Chinese Civil War, and to remain in power across the Chinese Mainland to the present are the same features that allowed many syncretic religious movements—in their various incarnations as peasant rebellions, millenarian movements, or cult associations—to succeed in their otherwise often short-lived political life cycles.

Reciprocally, after the consolidation of the CCP, syncretic religious movements have been able to survive to this day precisely by integrating themselves into the vast pro-establishment network of mass organizations supporting the CCP's ruling elite. The key to political success in the world's most populous nation lies in the ability to manipulate the support of multicultural movements through party organs and through connections, network building, cooperation, and co-organization with grassroots civil society groups, including syncretic religious movements.

The pages that follow include an investigation of three major types of syncretic religious movements that had been influential in major political transformations in twentieth-century China, as well as the history of their relationships with the Chinese Communist Party. These three types of syncretic religious movements are (1) secret societies, (2) village militia, and (3) redemptive societies.

SECRET SOCIETIES

Chinese secret societies are a form of fictive kinship networks created in support of male migrant laborers who travel afar to make a living and remit money in support of their families and ancestral hometowns. There is no definite evidence that could pinpoint when the first secret society came into being in China, but it is generally agreed that secret societies became a widespread phenomenon in south China sometime in the eighteenth century. The main trigger behind the emergence of secret societies in China was probably the expansion of the economy and the population at uneven rates. These developments resulted in shortages of arable land and widespread unemployment. Consequently, large sectors of the adult male population were forced to travel far away to find employment. This situation was extreme for people living in a cultural context that perceived the abandonment of ancestral tombs as the worse sort of sin. Incidentally, this cultural attitude explains why Chinese migrant laborers often insist, till our day, upon identifying themselves as sojourners—meaning that they intend to return home once business is accomplished—and regularly remit money home to support their families and continue the upkeep of ancestral tombs.

In addition to managing filial duties at home, migrant laborers experienced the problem of the lack of support networks, particularly for male migrants. Since many male migrant laborers were either yet to be married—and prospects for marriage were often nonexistent for the poor who needed to abandon the tombs of their ancestors in order to support themselves—or were migrating alone while leaving their wives and children behind, they were often categorized by the pejorative "guāng gùn" [光棍], or "bare stick." From the perspective of the state, these men were among the most problematic groups within the population, because they moved around and seemingly had nothing to lose. They were, therefore, more prone to enter into criminal activity, to join gangs of bandits, or to instigate rebellions. From the perspective of the bachelors themselves, life without the support of their family networks was also miserable. In a Confucian culture where the family serves as the most fundamental unit of society, all basic human necessities—such as finding housing, employment, health care, security—are usually met by relying on family networks.

Secret societies came into being in the absence of such family support networks, first as a sworn brotherhood of a few migrant laborers with something in common—hometown, clan name, or dialect. They would take an oath to be loyal and support each other as though they had been born of the same biological family. Over time, these brotherhoods expanded in number and became secret societies, which could include hundreds of sworn brothers operating across many provinces. Members of larger secret societies might not know each other personally, but they could recognize a sworn brother of the same society through certain symbolic gestures—for example, hand signals, the way one held a teacup, or smoked a cigarette. Once fellow secret society brothers identified one another, they were bound by the oath they had taken upon joining the society to be loyal and support each other as though they were real brothers. Hence, secret societies served the purposes of the nonpresent family network for male migrant laborers when they were far away from their real families and ancestral hometowns.

The spiritual aspect of Chinese secret societies is also intriguing. First, most secret societies use some version of the "Oath of the Peach Garden" from the *Romance of the Three Kingdoms* as the oath that all incoming members must take during the initiation ceremony. This oath appears in the historical epic when the three heroes, Liu Bei, Guan Yu, and Zhang Fe, become sworn brothers. This legendary sworn brotherhood shared a fundamental ideology and the highest political objective in life: Liu Bei was the true heir of the Han, predestined to ascend the throne as emperor and follow the ongoing wars of the three kingdoms. In the end, Liu Bei's faction was not the winner. Nonetheless, Liu Bei, Guan Yu, and Zhang Fei remained among the greatest literary heroes, and the aspiration to establish a regime of a Han ruler to govern the majority Han population in China would eventually become the foundation of the modern Chinese nationalist movement of Sun Yat-sen and his followers. Because the phenomenon of secret societies arose in the eighteenth century, when China was under the rule of the Qing dynasty—a Manchu minority ruling class—the Oath of the Peach Garden took on a special meaning for migrant laborers of the south, who had to memorize and utter the words of the oath in their initiation into each secret society.

Like the sworn brothers of the *Romance of the Three Kingdoms*, the sworn brothers of eighteenth-century secret societies were also in a situation in which the Han majority population of China was ruled by a minority ethnic group.[9] Thus, they too could aspire to recover the glory of the fallen Han-majority dynasty. This is why most secret societies would claim that their ultimate political agenda was to "fǎn qing fù míng" [反清復明], which is to overthrow the Qing dynasty and revive the Ming dynasty.

Secret societies also have a significant Buddhist element in their legend of origins. Most secret societies claimed to descend from the first secret society that was organized by a group of monks from the Shaolin Temple. According to the legend, a group of seven monks fled Shaolin Temple and traveled south, fleeing persecution from the Manchu troops that had recently

9. Since the Qing dynasty, which was predominantly Manchu, ruled the Han Chinese majority in the eighteenth century, secret society members felt inspired by the heroes of the *Romance of the Three Kingdoms* who fought numerous battles in the hope to return Liu Bei, who was supposedly the true heir, to the throne of the Han dynasty. Secret society members in the Qing era imagined themselves fighting for a comparable purpose, to overthrow the Manchu and reestablish a regime of a Han Chinese emperor to rule over the Han majority of China.

overthrown the Ming dynasty and established the Qing dynasty in the late seventeenth century. The monks did not want to lend their services to what they perceived as the barbaric regime of non-Han rulers, so they fled beyond the reach of the new dynasty and attempted to find support from the Ming loyalist population in the south. They sought, eventually, to overthrow the Qing and reestablish the Ming as rightful rulers of China. This Buddhist element is crucial in the protonationalist narrative of Chinese secret societies. Monks cannot participate in imperial examinations; similarly, devoted Buddhist practitioners would tend not to seek official positions through the imperial examination system since the main ideology featured in the exams was predominantly Confucian rather than Buddhist.

Once the Manchu, and most other non-Han dynasties throughout the dynastic history of China, established themselves in China, they enhanced their ruling power by holding imperial examinations as a tool to recruit talented Han intellectuals into the new dynasty's bureaucratic system. In other words, the Han literati could be bribed into submission and thereby proffer support for the foreign regime by tempting them with official positions through imperial examinations. In this sense, it was the grassroot population, especially those too poor for the Confucian education necessary to participate in the examinations, who were the last to maintain hope of carrying on the "fǎn qing fù míng" [反清復明] aspiration even after the Manchus had successfully expanded the Great Qing Empire to the southernmost reaches of China proper.

With the rise of British dominance in the China trade following the Opium Wars and the coolie trade in the late nineteenth century, an exodus of millions of Chinese male laborers to destinations throughout the British Empire occurred. Consequently, Chinese secret society networks quickly expanded worldwide.[10]

The prominent anti-Manchuism that featured in the ideology of secret societies came to heavily influence Sun Yat-sen's nationalism and would later become the first of his 'Three Principles of the People' [三民主義]. Sun joined the Heaven and Earth Society [天地會—tiān dì huì] during the period that he sojourned to live and work with his elder brother in Hawai'i. The idea that working class sojourners could be the driving force of a new Han Chinese regime led Sun Yat-sen to call upon the Chinese dias-

10. David Ownby, "The Heaven and Earth Society as Popular Religion," *Journal of Asian Studies* 54, no. 4 (1995): 1023–46.

pora to support revolutionary movements. This move resulted in significant financial support from overseas Chinese tycoons. The most popular slogan among Chinese revolutionaries became "The overseas Chinese are the mothers of the revolution" [華僑為革命之母].[11] The Xinhai Revolution,[12] for example, significantly benefited from the support of provincial military units and railroad workers, whose ranks were overwhelmingly dominated by secret society members. Sun Yat-sen clearly acknowledged the revolution's debt of gratitude to secret societies when he participated in an official ceremony at the imperial tomb of the first Ming emperor, Emperor Hongwu.[13] The latter was the most important secret society icon after the sworn brother heroes of *The Romance of the Three Kingdoms*, during which Sun read a report to the late emperor on the success of the revolutionaries. The revolutionaries were able to overthrow the Manchus and establish a new regime where the Han majority would be ruled by fellow Han people in a Han-majority government. This ceremony appeared to be among the top priorities of Sun Yat-sen's provisional government; it was carried out within weeks of the establishment of the Republic of China in January 1912.[14]

Secret societies continued to play an important role in twentieth-century Chinese politics. After the republic disintegrated into a state of warlordism following the death of General Yuan Shikai and the conclusion of the First World War, secret societies across Mainland China aligned themselves with various competing political groups. Some joined the warlords while others joined Sun Yat-sen's Guangdong-based Kuomintang-led government.

11. Jianli Huang, "Umbilical Ties: The Framing of Overseas Chinese as the Mother of Revolution," in *Sun Yat-sen, Nanyang and the 1911 Revolution*, ed. Lee Lai To (Singapore: ISEAS, 2011), 75–129.

12. The "Xinhai Revolution" is one of the more popular titles for the Chinese Revolution that broke out on October 10, 1911 in Wuchang, spread across much of south and central China, and resulted in the collapse of the Qing dynasty and the subsequent establishment of the Republic of China on January 1, 1912. "Xinhai" is the corresponding year in the sexagenary cycle calendar—a system of naming years in a 60-year cycle, which was popular across East Asia from ancient times up to the early twentieth century—of 1911 in the Christian era.

13. One of the most widespread Chinese secret societies in Southeast Asia in the late nineteenth to early twentieth century was the Hóngmén [洪門] or Hóngzi [洪子]. Society members referred to themselves as the sons of Emperor Hongwu who was regarded as the proto-nationalist hero who overthrew the Mongols and established the great Ming dynasty of the Han majority.

14. Prasenjit Duara. *Rescuing History from the Nation: Questioning Narratives of Modern China* (Chicago: University of Chicago Press, 1995), 131.

Shortly after the Northern Expedition, Chiang Kai-shek enlisted the support of the Shanghai-based secret society boss, Du Yuesheng, in purging Communists and Communist sympathizers from the Kuomintang in what became known as the Shanghai Massacre of 1927.[15] After several thousand comrades were slaughtered in the first two weeks of April that year, the old CCP leadership was in some disarray. It gave a chance to the younger leader who advocated peasant organization and agrarian socialism, Mao Zedong, to rise to the forefront of the movement. Mao's proposal to rely on the peasant masses as the main driving force of the revolution became the main CCP policy, allowing its survival through the Long March (1934–36). It was also through the treacherous course of the Long March that party leaders came to appreciate syncretic religious movements as primitive forms of peasant organizations. They received much support from secret society groups as well as village militia, both throughout the Long March and after they established the new Communist headquarters in Yan'an, Shaanxi Province. It was during this period that many prominent secret society members joined the ranks of the People's Liberation Army,[16] including He Long, who had been a prominent member of the Elder Brother Society [哥老會] of Hunan, and who later rose to become one of the 10 marshals of the People's Liberation Army.[17]

VILLAGE MILITIA

Village militia provide another interesting form of grassroot social movement with syncretic religious inspiration. Unlike secret societies, which came into being as a form of imagined family network, village militias were rooted in their localized hometown identities. The majority of village militia units begun popping up across the southern provinces of China in the latter half of the Qing dynasty. There are two major reasons for the initial need and existence of village militias in the late nineteenth century. First, it was due to the territorial expansion of the Great Qing Empire [大清國] in the

15. Elizabeth Perry, *Shanghai on Strike: The Politics of Chinese Labor* (Stanford: Stanford University Press, 1993).

16. Stuart R. Schram, "Mao Tse-Tung and Secret Societies," *China Quarterly* 27 (1966), 4.

17. Robert Elegant, *China's Red Masters: Political Biographies of the Chinese Communist Leaders* (New York: Twayne, 1951).

late eighteenth century. This territorial change resulted in the overextension of imperial troops as well as state bureaucratic personnel, forcing the state to rely upon the local gentry in governing communities at the grassroots level. It also allowed villages to establish their own self-protection units to serve as security forces where imperial troops were scarce. Second, and perhaps more important, as political turmoil mounted toward the end of the nineteenth century after the defeats of the two Opium Wars and widespread rebellion and unrest, the Qing government could no longer afford the manpower needed for the protection of small villages across the vast rural countryside of the southern provinces. Thus, the local population had to rely upon their own grassroot organizations for the protection of their hometowns.

Village militia usually included a group of working-age men who came together and trained each other in the use of weapons and martial arts. Each locality would have their own martial specialty depending upon whatever the local expertise happened to be. Village militia usually evolved around some form of spiritual faith. It often came in the form of syncretic religious movements—usually a mixture of Buddhism, Daoism, and local animism—that provided superstitious assurance for the village fighters in the form of magical amulets, talismans of invulnerability, and so forth. The main purpose of the village militia units in the late nineteenth century was to protect their hometowns from security threats, including bandit attacks, rebellions, and other forms of local political unrest. A kind of local militia, a village militia readily transformed itself into a grassroots political force and contributed to increasing political turmoil across China in late nineteenth to early twentieth century. Many joined the Taiping Rebellion[18] and later contributed to the Xinhai Revolution. Following the disintegration of the republic after the end of the First World War, a large number of village militia transformed themselves into units within the local warlords' armies.

---

18. The Taiping Rebellion refers to a rebellion led by a Hakka scholar from Guangdong named Hong Xiuquan, who claimed to be the younger brother of Jesus Christ. He called upon his Han compatriots to overthrow the Qing dynasty and establish the Heavenly Kingdom of Great Peace (太平天國—Tài Píng Tiān Guó) with Hong as the political and spiritual leader. The Taiping Rebellion broke out in 1850 in the southern provinces of Guangdong and Guangxi. The movement spread quickly to the Yangzi River valley and was able to capture Nanjing in 1853. From then on Nanjing was established as the heavenly capital of the Taiping Kingdom until it fell to the modernized army of the Qing general Zeng Guofan in 1864. Hong Xiuquan committed suicide shortly before the fall of his capital and the Taiping Rebellion was subsequently successfully suppressed.

Around the same time the CCP became interested in incorporating secret societies into the party, they developed a similar attitude toward the village militia they had encountered through the Long March. In a manner similar to that of the secret societies, the Maoist leadership treated village militia as another primitive form of peasant organization that could be used to resist oppressive feudal and capitalist classes. Hence, such militia were viewed as natural allies of the Chinese Communist Party.

Unlike secret societies, which were primarily composed of transient laborers, the village militia of the southern provinces—Fujian, Guangdong, Guangxi, Yunnan, and Sichuan—were closely tied to the history of their hometowns. The local gazettes [地方誌] of most townships in these areas would include the history of the contributions of the village militia within each locality.[19] There are records of these local militias joining the Second United Front and contributing to guerrilla warfare against Japanese troops during the War of Resistance. In the civil war that followed, some village militia supported the KMT and others supported the CCP. Nonetheless, the history of village militia more or less ended with the establishment of the People's Republic of China, as the remnants of the units after the civil war were either disbanded or incorporated into the People's Liberation Army or other CCP party mechanisms.

REDEMPTIVE SOCIETIES

Redemptive societies are philanthropic branches of millenarian movements. They are a type of syncretic religious movement that comes into action during times of disaster. As with secret societies and village self-protection units, redemptive societies exist to provide support for communities at the grassroots level under circumstances in which one cannot expect support from the state. Redemptive societies usually run soup kitchens, orphanages, homeless shelters, and the like in war zones, or in areas severely affected by natural disasters, famine, epidemics, and other such apocalyptic scenarios. Redemptive society members are usually influenced by a mixture of the popular organized religions—Confucianism, Buddhism, and Daoism—and local versions of animism, often coming together in the belief that, with

19. Bao'an xian difangzhi bianzuan weiyuanhui, *Bao'an Xianzhi* (Guangzhou: Guangdongren chubanshe, 1997), 607.

the end of the world coming soon, people must help one another survive difficult times and remain alive for the utopia that will arise once disasters subside.

Redemptive societies could be at odds with the state for several reasons. First, their millenarian beliefs tend to lead to the expectation that the state is about to collapse, since the end of the world is imminent in any case. Hence, as mentioned, redemptive societies tend to act as philanthropic branches of millenarian movements. That is, while millenarian movements might be staging rebellions to overthrow the ruling regime in preparation of apocalyptic scenarios, redemptive societies tend to focus more on providing support to the casualties of such unrest with the expectation that the ruling regime will be overthrown by the rebels anyway. Second, redemptive society members tend to believe in a universalistic sort of syncretic religion. They operate for the survival of all human beings in the face of apocalyptic disaster and, ideally, without any form of nationalistic, ethnic, or cultural discrimination. Although redemptive societies may not necessarily fight the ruling regime, they can still be detrimental to the state's nationalist propaganda attempts. A clear example of this phenomenon is given by Prasenjit Duara's study of redemptive societies in northeast China on the eve of the War of Resistance in the 1930s.[20] Duara's study demonstrated the extent to which the universalistic faith of redemptive societies in northeast China made them more prone to support Japanese pan-Asian propaganda rather than the Chiang Kai-shek's government's Chinese particularist and nationalist propaganda. Consequently, the Chinese Nationalist government regarded redemptive societies with suspicion and considered them to be a threat to national security instead of possible allies in providing humanitarian support to citizens in times of war.

The universalistic appeal of redemptive societies places them on a common ground with the Chinese Communist movement in the early 1930s. In addition to sharing similar attitudes of universalistic support for grassroots people—the international proletariat in the case of the CCP, and the human race for redemptive societies—redemptive societies and millenarian movements were also regarded by the CCP as primitive forms of peasant organizations and potential allies against the KMT and other oppressive classes during the Chinese Civil War.

20. Prasenjit Duara, "Transnationalism and the Predicament of Sovereignty," *American Historical Review* 1, no. 4 (1997): 1030–51.

THE CHINESE COMMUNIST PARTY AND SYNCRETIC RELIGIOUS MOVEMENTS IN THE PEOPLE'S REPUBLIC OF CHINA

The CCP considered the three syncretic religious movements to be potential allies, beginning from the establishment of the new Chinese Soviet headquarters in Yan'an in the mid-1930s and until the conclusion of the Chinese Civil War and the establishment of the People's Republic of China in 1949. The eclectic beliefs of syncretic religious movements allowed them to appeal to large sectors of rural China in the mid-twentieth century. The Chinese Communist Party's capacity to align with these groups also allowed them to organize the peasant masses for the revolution more effectively. Perhaps more importantly, the Chinese Communist movement under the leadership of Mao Zedong had the ability to mix, match, and adapt a great variety of beliefs and ideologies into the movement for the sake of widening the support base among the rural agrarian population. Multiculturalism in religion and spirituality has always been a very powerful driving force behind popular uprisings in Chinese history, from peasant rebellions that toppled dynasties throughout the imperial period to the peasant-driven Communist revolution that solidified CCP rule throughout Mainland China.[21] Nonetheless, once the CCP established itself as the mainstream ruling power of the People's Republic of China, multiculturalist mass movements, especially syncretic religious organizations of the likes of secret societies, village militias, and redemptive societies, almost instantly became possible threats to the CCP's dominant position.

From the establishment of the PRC and throughout the Maoist period, the CCP government systematically distanced the narrative of the revolution away from syncretic religious movements. Village militia that had supported the revolution were, for the most part, co-opted into the People's Liberation Army. Leading secret society members who joined the party were encouraged to forsake the "backward superstitious beliefs" so as truly to embrace the teachings of Marx, Lenin, and Mao Zedong's thought. Furthermore, there was no need for redemptive societies any longer, since the CCP, as the dictatorship of the proletariat, could serve the Chinese peasant masses and improve their quality of life in a way that feudalistic dynastic rule and the bourgeois KMT government had not. In other words, grassroots social

21. Jean Chesneaux. *Les Sociétés S,ecrêtes en Chine* (Paris: Juliard, 1965).

movements inspired by syncretic religions had only been necessary because earlier governments had not been able to properly care for the basic needs of the rural masses. Now that the CCP was in charge and claimed to represent the peasant masses, there was no need for the fictive kinship network of secret societies, village self-protection units, or philanthropic redemptive societies.

The CCP's ambivalent stance toward syncretic religious movements during the first decade of the establishment of the PRC turned into hostility during the Great Proletarian Cultural Revolution (1966–76). Former members of the secret societies and village self-protection units, even those who had joined the party or attained high ranks within the People's Liberation Army, came under attack as bandits and superstitious remnants of the feudal era. Even Marshal He Long was denounced as "the biggest bandit" in December 1966 and subsequently perished while under house arrest in June 1969. Practitioners of organized religions fared worse through the Cultural Revolution with widespread destruction of religious architecture and artifacts, and an almost nationwide purge of clergymen of all religions. Confucian-related practices, especially ancestral worship, came under severe attack. Thousands of lineage ancestral shrines across southern China were practically wiped out in the early 1970s. Ironically, it was the practitioners in Hong Kong, Taiwan, and overseas Chinese communities that managed to preserve Chinese religious traditions through the disaster of the Cultural Revolution. Many of them returned, mostly from Hong Kong and Southeast Asia, to the Mainland during the reform period to support the reestablishment of Chinese religious institutions and ancestral shrines, and to reintroduce the complex rituals of ancestral worship to their ancestral homeland. However, syncretic religious movements, especially those that had been most active in the revolutionary years of the early twentieth century—including the three types of movements investigated earlier in this study—never recovered their past glory in Mainland China.

QI GONG MOVEMENTS AND THE SURPRISING CASE OF THE FALUN GONG PURGE

While most pre-Maoist syncretic religious movements did not recover in the Chinese Mainland despite the allowance of limited religious freedom in the reform period, the CCP tolerated some movements that resembled some of the old syncretic religious movements in pre-Maoist China. One such movement that enjoyed more success than others, and a spectacular boom in the 1990s, was the Qi Gong movement. Qi Gong is a native Chinese form of exercise that combines breathing patterns with routines of body movements. The practice of Qi Gong goes as far back as Chinese civilization itself. There is no known single inventor of Qi Gong, and there have always been great variations among the numerous schools of Qi Gong in thousands of localities across the Chinese Mainland. Qi Gong fits the general definition of a syncretic religious movement in that it is often practiced in combination with a mixture of Buddhist and Daoist ideologies. In premodern times, Qi Gong was adopted as a form of martial art. Many village self-protection units practiced Qi Gong, and local Qi Gong masters had the reputation of possessing supernatural powers. Such masters could, at times, become icons of worship for locals, especially in time of political turmoil.

Interestingly, in the modern Chinese context, Qi Gong escaped the Cultural Revolution's purges; this, despite many superstitious traditions attributed to Qi Gong. Mao Zedong had very high regard for Qi Gong from his adolescent years; he encouraged good Chinese Communists—party members, members of the armed forces, and even Red Guards—to practice Qi Gong as a good way to keep fit, and as a brilliant form of folk wisdom native to China and practiced by Chinese people from time immemorial. Hence, while organized religions such as Buddhism and Daoism were systematically attacked, and while most syncretic religious movements were the target of brutal purges during the Cultural Revolution, Qi Gong continued to develop as one of the very few politically accepted forms of Chinese cultural heritage with its quasi-religious or spiritual overtones, or both.

In the reform period, the state categorized Qi Gong as an activity connected with Buddhism, and all Qi Gong schools came under the supervision of the same state organs that oversaw Buddhist religious organizations and Buddhist practitioners in China. Qi Gong continued to flourish throughout the 1980s. It was even promoted by state organs as a cheap and effective form of exercise that could help enhance the health and fitness of Chinese masses. By the early 1990s, there was a "Qi Gong craze" across the PRC. One particular school emerged as most successful, the Falun Gong school of Master Li Hongzhi [李洪志]. Li's version of Qi Gong, which he called "Falun Gong" [法轮功] or "Falun Dafa" [法轮大法], is a combination of Qi Gong with Buddhist meditation and Daoist morality. Li first introduced Falun Gong to the public in 1992, holding classes in his hometown of Changchun in Jilin Province in northeastern China.

Initially, Falun Gong was extremely successful. It was exceedingly popular and rapidly gained an exceptionally large following. The practice was also lauded by local officials and provincial branch members of the Chinese Communist Party. Li received many awards from local and provincial government units for his success in enhancing the health of the Chinese people with his Qi Gong instruction through the Falun Gong method. By 1995 Falun Gong had become a national phenomenon that had millions of followers across the country. Li was then contacted by the Ministry of Health and the China Qigong Research Society, main state organ that oversaw the administration of Qi Gong schools throughout the country. He was given the request that he join them in establishing a "Falun Gong Association," which would further promote the practice of Falun Gong while allowing the state to monitor the movement properly. The movement appeared to be growing so fast that it might soon surpass the Chinese Communist Party in membership and popularity with the Chinese masses. Li, however, disagreed with this suggestion regarding the direction of development for Falun Gong. He did not want to join the state in establishing a Falun Gong Association since he no longer desired or needed to charge fees from his followers. He wanted to allow everyone who wanted to learn Falun Gong to be able to practice free of charge by making his teachings available through various media for free. His plan meant there would be no way that the government could monitor or control the rising numbers of Falun Gong followers; it was a possibility that the movement might quickly become a threat to national security from the CCP's perspective.

Tension rose between Li Hongzhi and the government's China Qigong Research Society to the point that Li decided to withdraw from the association altogether in 1996.[22] Consequently, Falun Gong could no longer be monitored by the state. This change resulted in the outbreak of a major anti–Falun Gong propaganda campaign by the CCP government. The government news agencies began broadcasting accusations that Falun Gong was an illegal cult and a threat to national security. Government-recognized Buddhist organizations also started to question the validity of Falun Gong and discouraged Buddhist practitioners from becoming involved in Falun Gong. Li's followers struck back, first on April 22, 1999, by organizing a mass demonstration in front of the office of a youth magazine of Tianjin Nor-

22. James Tong, "Anatomy of Regime Repression in China: Timing, Enforcement Institutions, and Target Selection in Banning the Falungong, July 1999," *Asian Survey* 42, no. 6 (2002): 795–820.

mal College that had published an article accusing Falun Gong of being a superstitious cult and suggesting that the practice of Falun Gong could be harmful to China's youth. This first mass demonstration was met by more than 300 police officers, and 45 of the demonstrators were arrested by the end of the day.

The arrests in Tianjin sparked indignation among Falun Gong followers nationwide. Three days later, on April 25, 1999, over 10,000 Falun Gong supporters descended upon the government headquarters at Zhongnanhai demanding an explanation from Premier Zhu Rongji. The premier did eventually come out to meet protesters and engaged in negotiations. Seemingly to the satisfaction of both parties and the mass of Falun Gong protestors at Zhongnanhai, the day ended without incident. Nonetheless, the incident on April 25, 1999 greatly disturbed CCP leaders at the highest levels. President Jiang Zemin decided that Falun Gong was the greatest threat to national security since the student demonstrations in Tiananmen Square in 1989. The top echelons of the CCP agreed that Falun Gong must be swiftly and systematically destroyed for the sake of national stability and the party's own political security. On June 10, 1999, the 610 Office (named after its date of establishment) was specifically established for the suppression of Falun Gong. The 610 Office was not connected or supervised by any other state organ and reported directly only to the Politburo; it had nationwide jurisdiction and extensive legal capabilities that allowed it to arrest and persecute anyone related to the Falun Gong, including members of the CCP. The massive 610 Falun Gong purge started toward the end of July 1999 with the arrest of more than 4,500 leading members of the Falun Gong across 29 provinces, and 300,000 members of the CCP with connections to the Falun Gong were forced to publicly denounce the group. By this time, Li Hongzhi had managed to flee the country, but the arrests of his followers continued with great efficiency. By October that year, more than 20,000 Falun Gong–related arrests had been carried out; Falun Gong was officially proclaimed an illegal cult, banned in China; and all known followers faced prison sentences and attitude adjustment camps.

In a matter of six months, the Falun Gong, which had once boasted millions of followers on the Chinese Mainland, had been completely destroyed. Thousands of followers fled the country, while those who remained were subject to severe punishments. There have been rumors of Falun Gong arrestees being tortured, executed, and their organs harvested for the black market. While the Chinese government vehemently denied these allegations, there has yet to be an international human rights investigation into this matter, and Falun Gong followers who managed to flee the country continue to publish horror accounts of their persecution in the PRC.

Since the end of 1999, Falun Gong has become a global movement with followers and practitioners in countries across the globe. Yet they have not gained momentum or even a significant increase in followers worldwide since their exodus from the PRC. Despite regularly organizing demonstrations against the CCP government in major world cities such as New York, London, Sydney, and, recently, Hong Kong, by the end of the 2000s Falun Gong was no longer a threat to the PRC's national security or the CCP's dominant political position.[23]

CONCLUSION: WHY CERTAIN SYNCRETIC RELIGIOUS MOVEMENTS COME INTO CONFLICT WITH THE CCP

Why did the CCP, under the leadership of President Jiang Zemin, suppress the Falun Gong in such a severe manner as it did throughout the Chinese Mainland in 1999? Since the purge, it appears that Falun Gong has been completely destroyed as a movement inside the PRC, while most other Qi Gong movements are still alive and well. Even other syncretic movements that appear, to the observer, far more deviant and which had histories of persecution during the Cultural Revolution, such as secret societies in former colonial territories, have not faced persecution since the return of Hong Kong and Macau in 1997 and 1999.

The first and perhaps most obvious answer is loyalty and control. It appears that the CCP leadership tolerates religious organizations that are willing to be monitored and influenced by the state. Syncretic religious movements that have been categorized with one or another state-sanctioned religion are also tolerated and even encouraged if they prove to have other practical purposes, such as enhancing the health and well-being of the population, as in the case of Qi Gong. Even in cases where universal religious freedom continues to apply according to the local colonial tradition—that is, in Hong Kong and Macau—secret societies can continue to survive and flourish without being monitored and controlled directly by the state if they are willing to express undivided loyalty toward Beijing. Thus, throughout

23. Tong, "Anatomy of Regime Repression in China."

the Hong Kong anti-Beijing demonstrations of 2019 and 2020, Hong Kong secret societies openly expressed support for Beijing to the point of beating up demonstrators on a few occasions. Secret societies in Macau had also signaled their patriotism and loyalty to Beijing and the CCP government. It therefore appears that the central government tolerates these organizations, seeing them as part of local culture and cooperative remnants of colonial rule.[24]

Clearly, the Falun Gong's most critical downturn came when Li Hongzhi refused to allow the state to interfere in his relationship with his followers by refusing to charge a fee for his teachings, and by withdrawing from the China Qigong Research Society. It was at that point that the negative propaganda against Falun Gong practitioners began. Matters worsened with the show of force of tens of thousands of Li Hongzhi's followers demonstrating in front of Zhongnanhai. From that point forward, Falun Gong moved from being an unmonitored Qi Gong movement to becoming a full-blown threat to national security.

Beneath the surface reasoning of loyalty and control, there is also an important parallel between the Chinese Communist Party and movements like the Falun Gong. Multiculturalist grassroots movements have always had momentous political influence in China. Throughout imperial history, major peasant rebellions have consistently arisen in one or another form of syncretic religious movement.

The "all-inclusive" ideology of millenarian peasant movements is something that CCP leaders in the Maoist era adopted. While frequently hearkening back to Marxist-Leninist ideals, it was Mao Zedong's thought that propelled the CCP's success in the Chinese Civil War. Since the main driving force behind the Chinese Communist revolution was the agrarian masses, this revolution was considerably more similar to the millenarian peasant revolts in the late nineteenth century than it was to the proletariat uprising of the Russian Revolution. Not surprisingly, the CCP took advantage of grassroots syncretic religious organizations in support of their efforts to overthrow the Nationalist regime and establish the People's Republic of China. Nonetheless, as Chinese history would prove time and again, syncretic religious movements are better for toppling regimes than for maintaining one. Hence, once the CCP became the established government of

24. Martin Purbrick, "Patriotic Chinese Triads and Secret Societies: From the Imperial Dynasty to Nationalism and Communism," *Asian Affairs* 50, no. 3 (2019): 305–22.

China, the party line consistently disapproved and discouraged religious faith, and particularly syncretic religious movements of all sorts. Oppression of these movements reached extreme levels during the Cultural Revolution when Maoism became the undeclared state religion, even though such oppression proved to be disastrous for China's socioeconomic development throughout the decade between 1966 and 1976.

CCP leaders of the reform era saw the need to remove Maoism from the position it had held as a sort of undeclared state religion under the Cultural Revolution. This change, it was decided, could best be achieved by allowing other faiths and religions to emerge after the decade of banning and eradication. Some religions, even certain syncretic religious movements, thus became tolerated. Chinese people could enjoy limited religious freedom if they accepted the state's right to monitor and control their religious organizations, and pledged allegiance to the Chinese Communist government only. It is here where the relationship between the CCP and syncretic religious movements stands at present, a time in which the CCP no longer aspires to revolution.

References

Bao'an xian difangzhi bianzuan weiyuanhui. *Bao'an Xianzhi*. Guangzhou: Guangdongren chubanshe, 1997.

Cai, Shaoqing. *Zhongguo jindai huidangshi yanjiu*. Beijing: Zhonghua shulu, 1987.

Chen, Yun. "Zhongguo Minzu Yundong zhi Guoqu yu Jianglai." In *Henan shizhi ziliao*, vol. 6. Zhengzhou: Henansheng defang shizhi pianzuan weiyuanhui, 1984.

Chesneaux, Jean. *Les sociétés secrêtes en Chine*. Paris: Juliard, 1965.

Duara, Prasenjit. *Rescuing History from the Nation: Questioning Narratives of Modern China*. Chicago: University of Chicago Press, 1995.

Duara, Prasenjit. "Transnationalism and the Predicament of Sovereignty." *American Historical Review* 1, no. 4 (1997): 1030–51.

Elegant, Robert. *China's Red Masters: Political Biographies of the Chinese Communist Leaders*. New York: Twayne, 1951.

Huang, Jianli. "Umbilical Ties: The Framing of Overseas Chinese as the Mother of Revolution." In *Sun Yat-sen, Nanyang and the 1911 Revolution*, edited by Lee Lai To, 75–129. Singapore: ISEAS, 2011.

Ownby, David. "The Heaven and Earth Society as Popular Religion." *Journal of Asian Studies* 54, no. 4 (1995): 1023–46.

Perry, Elizabeth. *Shanghai on Strike: The Politics of Chinese Labor*. Stanford: Stanford University Press, 1993.

Purbrick, Martin. "Patriotic Chinese Triads and Secret Societies: From the Imperial Dynasty to Nationalism and Communism." *Asian Affairs* 50, no. 3 (2019): 305–22.

Schram, Stuart R. "Mao Tse-Tung and Secret Societies." in *China Quarterly* 27 (1966).

Tong, James. "Anatomy of Regime Repression in China: Timing, Enforcement Institutions, and Target Selection in Banning the Falungong, July 1999." *Asian Survey* 42, no. 6 (2002): 795–820.

Wilson, Ian. "Socialism with Chinese Characteristics: China and the Theory of the Initial Stage of Socialism." *Australian Journal of Political Science* 24, no. 1 (1989): 77–84.

Zheng, Yushuang. "Political Constitution and the Protection of Religious Freedom: A Jurisprudential Reading of Article 36 of the Chinese Constitution." In *Christianity in Chinese Public Life: Religion, Society, and the Rule of Law*, edited by Joel A. Carpenter and Kevin R. den Dulk, 79–96. New York: Palgrave Macmillan, 2014.

Zuo, Zhiping. "Political Religion: The Case of the Cultural Revolution in China." *Sociological Analysis* 52, no. 1 (1991): 99–110.

"Trading Western Suits for Monastic Robes"

Remaking Tibetan Buddhism in the Chinese Religious Revival

Jue Liang

Denison University—Granville

As arguably the largest Buddhist learning center in the world, Larung Gar (Tib. Bla rung sgar, Chn. 喇荣佛学院) regularly houses thousands of monastics and attracts tens of thousands more whenever public teaching gatherings take place. Of the four annual public teaching gatherings at Larung Gar, the Vajrasattva Teaching Assembly (Chn. 金刚萨埵法会) specifically caters to Han Chinese Buddhists.[1] People come from all over China, and from all walks of life, from government employees to businesspersons, from university professors to homemakers. The more well-to-do ones usually arrive in strapping SUVs, carrying provisions for themselves and for a donation. The less resourceful endure their long ride in a packed van or bus, and generate their share of good merit by donating time or labor at the teaching assembly. However they arrive, this monumental crowd

1. The Vajrasattva Assembly takes place from the eighth to the fifteenth day of the fourth month of the Tibetan calendar, or the Saga Dawa (Tib. Sa ga zla ba), usually considered a holy time as celebrations of the Buddha's enlightenment and nirvāṇa take place during this month. The other three are the Vidyadhāra Assembly (Chn. 持明法会; it takes place from the first to the eighth day of the first month of the Tibetan calendar), the Samantabhadra Assembly (Chn. 普贤云供法会; from the first to the eighth day of the sixth month of the Tibetan calendar), and the Great Bliss Assembly (Tib. Bde chen zhing grub, Chn. 极乐法会; from the eighteenth to the twenty-sixth of the ninth month of the Tibetan calendar). Of the four, the Vidyadhāra and Samantabhadra Assemblies are generally not open to the public, while the Great Bliss Assembly has mostly Tibetan attendees.

would be beyond the wildest imagination for those who first reached Larung almost 40 years ago, when it was a humble encampment with only dozens of Tibetan followers.

Founded by Khenpo Jigme Phuntsok (Tib. Mkhan po 'Jigs med phun tshogs, Chn. 晋美彭措堪布, 1933–2004),[2] or Khenpo Jigphun, in the early 1980s, Larung Gar began as a small residence for him and his few disciples. But its influence and size quickly grew. First came the Tibetan disciples, attracted by the acclaimed Treasure revealer and Buddhist teacher; then the Han Chinese and even foreign disciples arrived, many of whom had heard Khenpo Jigphun's name from his well-attended and well-publicized pilgrimage to Mount Wutai (Tib. Ri bo rtse lnga, Chn. 五台山) in 1987.[3] By the 1990s, Larung Gar had attracted thousands of non-Tibetan pilgrims and disciples (most of them Han Chinese), a feat never accomplished by any other Tibetan Buddhist institution. At its peak around 2010, it was considered the largest Buddhist monastic institution in the world, regularly housing over 50,000 monastics, a significant portion of which came from Han Chinese regions in China, or neidi (Chn. 内地).

While Larung Gar's rise to eminence took place in tandem with the larger religious revival in China since the early 1980s,[4] its unprecedented success remains a case of singular significance. Considering the degree of discontinuity in and the erasure of religious activities that China found itself in after the Cultural Revolution, the national and global popularity achieved

2. For a brief biography of Khenpo Jigme Phuntsok, see Antonio Terrone, "Khenpo Jigme Phuntsok," *Treasury of Lives*, October 2013, accessed June 13, 2020, http://treasuryoflives.org/biographies/view/Khenpo-Jigme-Puntsok/10457

3. This pilgrimage to Mount Wutai is discussed in Terrone, "Khenpo Jigme Phuntsok." Also see David Germano, "Re-membering the Dismembered Body of Tibet: Contemporary Tibetan Visionary Movements in the People's Republic of China," in *Buddhism in Contemporary Tibet: Religious Revival and Cultural Identity*, ed. Melvyn C. Goldstein and Matthew Kapstein (Berkeley: University of California Press, 1998), 85–87.

4. This revival is credited to the end of the Cultural Revolution in 1976 and the beginning of the economic reform in 1979 in general, and to the restoration of religious freedom in Article 36 of the constitution in 1982, after the 3rd Plenary Session of the 11th Central Committee of the Communist Party of China, in particular. In addition to Article 36, the issuance of an internal communication, Document No. 19, entitled "The Basic Viewpoint and Policy on the Religious Question during Our Country's Socialist Period," also marks a new attitude of religious tolerance. For a complete English translation of Article 36 and Document No. 19, see Donald E. MacInnis, *Religion in China Today: Policy and Practice* (Maryknoll, NY: Orbis Books, 1989), 8–26, 34–35.

by Larung Gar in a short time period of three decades is remarkable and rivaled by few other religious institutions in China. Moreover, as a Tibetan Buddhist institution, Larung Gar is the first of its kind to have a pervasive and persisting influence on Han Chinese Buddhists. While the Yuan and Qing dynasties (founded by Mongol and Manchu rulers, respectively) recognized Tibetan Buddhism as the state religion and venerate Tibetan Buddhist masters, Han intellectuals and literati have historically viewed this form of Buddhism as suspect, if not outright degenerate.[5] It was only in the Republic period (1912–49) that we see regular exchanges between Chinese and Tibetan Buddhist lineages, but this exchange trickled away with the founding of the People's Republic of China.[6]

What makes the success story of Larung Gar different? What explains its massive appeal? And what can this story tell us about Buddhism and the religion question in China? This chapter sets out to answer these questions. Building on current scholarship on the history of Larung Gar and the spread of Tibetan Buddhism in the Han Chinese population,[7] I am especially inter-

5. Weirong Shen, "Magic Power, Sorcery and Evil Spirit: The Image of Tibetan Monks in Chinese Literature during the Yuan Dynasty," in *The Relationship between Religion and State (chos srid zung 'brel) in Traditional Tibet*, ed. Christoph Cüppers (Lumbini: Lumbini International Research Institute, 2004), 189–227.

6. For a discussion on Sino-Tibetan Buddhist interaction in the early twentieth century, see Gray Tuttle, *Tibetan Buddhists in the Making of Modern China* (New York: Columbia University Press, 2005); also see Nicole Willock, *Lineages of the Literary: Tibetan Buddhist Polymaths of Socialist China* (New York: Columbia University Press, 2021).

7. While there are a number of studies on Larung Gar, its history, and its significance in the Tibetan Buddhist world, only a few of them choose to focus on the Han Chinese Tibetan Buddhist community at Larung. For a discussion on how economic forces and the institutionalization of religious charisma intersect and create a "Sino-Tibetan Buddhist alliance," contributing to the spread of Tibetan Buddhism in China, see Dan Smyer Yü, *The Spread of Tibetan Buddhism in China: Charisma, Money, Enlightenment* (London: Routledge, 2014). David Germano's "Re-membering the Dismembered Body of Tibet" also pays attention to the fact that Khenpo Jigme Phuntsok attracted disciples not only from Tibetan areas but also from other areas of China and foreign disciples as well. Khenpo's revelatory activities also expand beyond the limit of the Tibetan geographical landscape. The most recent volume dedicated to the invention of a "new" Tibetan Buddhist tradition in Chinese society today is Joshua Esler's *Tibetan Buddhism among Han Chinese: Mediation and Superscription of the Tibetan Tradition in Contemporary Chinese Society* (Lanham, MD: Lexington Books, 2020). The primary concern for *Tibetan Buddhism among Han Chinese* is the interactive, dynamic relationship between the worldview of Han Chinese Tibetan Buddhist practitioners and Tibetan Buddhist cultural values. While Esler centers his investigation around the lived experience of Han Chinese Tibetan Buddhists, and examines how their cultural world is

ested in how Tibetan Buddhism is communicated and presented to Han Chinese disciples, and how these disciples narrate their own experience of conversion, of finding religion in a secular age. For the Tibetan Buddhist leaders of our age, the survival of Buddhism requires a reinvention of what Buddhism is, which calls for a careful reading of the zeitgeist as well as an inheritance from its past. Using a hitherto unstudied collection of 125 first-person accounts of Han Chinese disciples who have arrived at Larung to study and practice,[8] I examine the reason for their conversion as presented in the collection and query the purpose behind compiling their life stories. I argue that, by advocating for an inclusive and intellectual vision, Larung Gar establishes itself as a modern institution, and Tibetan Buddhism as a universal religion. Tibetan Buddhism (and Buddhism in general) is depicted as scientific (not superstitious), transcending ethnic and national boundaries (not confined to one place or one time), and rooted in the long history of Chinese civilization (as opposed to being understood as a foreign belief).

In the following sections, I first introduce demographic information about these Han Chinese intellectual disciples, discuss the shared elements in their stories of converting to Buddhism, and then move on to analyze what their interpretation of Tibetan Buddhism is, and what attracted them to it. Studying the collection as a whole, I propose that this discourse of Buddhism as a scientific, transnational, and at the same time historically rooted religion is not an unprecedented practice. Based on the Buddhist concept of *upāya*, or expedient means, the Buddhist teaching always needs to be delivered in a manner that is appropriate to the circumstances it finds itself in. In the case of Larung Gar, its success lies precisely in its skillful adaption to the changing social and political reality of its time.

COLLECTING THE LIFE STORIES OF INTELLECTUAL BUDDHISTS

In the collection titled *Zhihai langhua* 智海浪花 (*Flowing Tides in the Ocean of Wisdom*, hereafter *Flowing Tides*)[9] its compiler (and one of the abbots in

---

shaped by but also superscribes onto the Tibetan Buddhist cultural world, I choose to read its primary sources as carefully crafted discourses that do not reflect (at least not only) the lived experiences of Han Chinese practitioners, but a version of Tibetan Buddhism that is considered particularly fit to be presented to a Han Chinese, intellectual audience.

8. In the following discussion, unless otherwise noted, I use the terms "Han Chinese disciples," "Han Chinese Tibetan Buddhists," and "intellectual Buddhists" interchangeably.

9. Suodaji Kanbu 索达吉堪布, *Zhi hai lang hua: Jiang shu 125 wei zhi shi fen zi de xue*

charge of the Han Chinese Tibetan Buddhist population at Larung Gar after Khenpo Jigme Phuntsok's passing), Khenpo Sodargye (Tib. Mkhan po Bsod dar rgyas, Chn. 索达吉堪布, b. 1962), presents relatable stories of modern, highly educated Buddhist practitioners to the Han Chinese audience.[10] In his personal experience, ordinary people have long worshipped the crowning achievements of scientists, while at the same time they dismiss or even denigrate many Buddhist practitioners, who are equally accomplished in their pursuit of the true nature of all things:

> If we say that the use of science is to guide human beings out of their misconception about what themselves, society, life, and the universe really are, then the Buddhadharma is undeniably the highest, most superior form of science. What other forms of scientific knowledge can, like Buddhism, immediately cut to the illusory nature of things, disguised by

---

fo li cheng 智海浪花：讲述125位知识分子的学佛历程 [Flowing tides in the ocean of wisdom: Stories of 125 intellectuals about learning the dharma] (Hong Kong: Xin yi tang, 2001). This collection has been reprinted by multiple Buddhist monasteries across China and other publishers, attesting to the popular demand for it. Thirty-one stories from the collection are also republished in a 2014 publication, with some alterations including name changes. Suodaji Kanbu, *Xing hao you fan nao: 31 wei li xiang zhe de xin ling zhi lü* 幸好有烦恼：31位理想者的心灵之旅 [Fortunate to be troubled: The spiritual journey of 31 idealists] (Beijing: Zhong guo you yi chu ban gong si, 2014).

10. *Flowing Tides* is not the first book that attempts to capture and make sense of the phenomenon of a "Buddhism fever" among Han Chinese intellectuals. Two other collections contain relevant biographical materials of these Han Chinese Tibetan Buddhists: see Chen Xiaodong 陈晓东, *Ning ma de hong hui: Jin ri la rong shan zhong de yi kuai mi cheng jing tu* 宁玛的红辉：今日喇荣山中的一块密乘净土 [Blazing brilliance of the Nyingma school: A Pure Land of tantric Buddhism in the Larung Valley today] (Lanzhou: Gan su min zu chu ban she, 1999), and Wu, Yutian 吴玉天, *Fang xue yu da shi: Xi zang mi zong kao cha fang tan ji shi* 访雪域大师：西藏密宗考察访谈纪实 [Visiting Buddhist masters in the land of snow: Documentation and interviews on tantric Buddhism in Tibet] (Lanzhou: Gan su min zu chu ban she, 2005). Chen's *Blazing Brilliance of the Nyingma School* was written in 1997, around the same time as *Flowing Tides*, and provides 30 vignettes of individuals and events taking place at Larung at the time, from eminent masters like Khenpo Jigme Phuntsok to ordinary practitioners, both Tibetan and non-Tibetan. Wu's *Visiting Buddhist Masters in the Land of Snow*, on the other hand, is an autobiographical account of the author's visit to Tibetan Buddhist sites and his interactions with Tibetan lamas. Compared to these two, *Flowing Tides* represents the biggest collection of narrative accounts about Han Chinese Tibetan Buddhists at Larung, and the most authoritative one, as it is compiled by Khenpo Sodargye, the lama for all Han Chinese disciples.

their manifold manifestations? What other scientists can, like the Buddha, gain insight into the true nature of the universe through only direct perception (Skt. *pratyakṣa,* Chn. 现量), without relying on any physical tools for experiment or mental inferences based on discriminating thoughts?

. . .

If we preach with the Buddha's words to the letter, the incomparably sacred Dharma might not attract much secular interest. However, if demonstrated by [the conversion of] the intellectuals, who are widely respected, [the Dharma] will no doubt resonate with many.[11]

For this reason, Khenpo Sodargye decided to share the stories of these "intellectual Buddhists" (Chn. 知识分子佛教徒), most of whom have worked or studied abroad or have a college degree, or both, with a wider audience, so as to "remove the misunderstanding about Buddhists in common folks due to ignorance."[12] At the beginning of each account, he provides background information about the protagonist, introducing them to the readers; in the end, he concludes with an analysis of their views of Buddhism as well as some occasional personal reflection. The core narrative consists of stories of how these intellectuals transformed from being casually interested in Buddhism to finally taking refuge and becoming professional practitioners; some even became full-time monastics and stayed on at Larung or other monasteries. In other words, they have traded their Western suits for Buddhist monastic robes.

These accounts provide us with a glimpse behind the mass interest in Buddhism, especially Tibetan Buddhism, from the 1980s onward, and the perspective from these new Buddhists, as related by themselves. While the veracity of many of these accounts can hardly be determined (Khenpo Sodargye admitted to having changed some of the names and biographical details; many of the practitioners who lived at Larung in the 1990s have already left; I am only able to identify one case where the protagonist is related to a public figure[13]), they remain important to our understanding as

11. Suodaji Kanbu, *Flowing Tides,* 1–2.

12. Suodaji Kanbu, *Flowing Tides,* 4.

13. This is the story of Zhang Lei 张雷, who is the brother of Zhang Chaoyang张朝阳 or Charles Zhang, the founder and CEO of Sohu Inc. (Chn. 搜狐), a Chinese internet company.

a discourse Larung leaders adopted and presented to the public. This discourse has certainly worked: the collection became a bestseller and is still cited by many Han Chinese Buddhists I interviewed at Larung from 2017 to 2020, almost two decades after its publication. Thirty-one stories from it were selected and reproduced as a smaller collection in 2014.[14] Khenpo Sodargye carries on with an impressive number of popular Buddhism books in Chinese and has become arguably the best-selling author in this category and one of the most celebrated Buddhist teachers in China today.[15]

The 125 accounts contain life stories of intellectual Buddhists of both genders and include both monastics and laypeople. They are from all over China (a few from abroad), from the northeastern province of Heilongjiang to the southern part of Guizhou, from as far west as Xinjiang and as far east as Shanghai. Table 1 gives some insight into the gender and monastic status of these disciples.

As advertised in the preface, most of these disciples are well educated (table 2). Over half of them hold a bachelor's degree, and almost one-quarter of them have earned postgraduate degrees, forming an unusually highly educated group. (For comparison, 326 in every 100,000 people in China were enrolled in higher education institutions in 1990, and 723 in 100,000 in 2000—roughly 0.3% and 0.7%, respectively.[16]) They are predominantly Han Chinese in ethnicity. Of the 125 included, only two are Chinese Mongols, two are Koreans in China, and one is Manchu. They also have some international exposure in their background: one comes from Belgium and a number of these practitioners have lived or are living or studying abroad

---

14. Suodaji kanbu, *Fortunate to Be Troubled*, also see note 7 above.

15. The author page of Khenpo Sodargye (Suodaji Kanbu) on douban.com (Chn. 豆瓣网, the Chinese equivalent of Goodread) records 62 books. Before 2000, most of his books are translations of Tibetan Buddhist literature, including commentaries, instructions to laypeople, and hagiographies of Buddhist masters or the life story of the Buddha. Since the publication of the *Flowing Tides* in 2001, Khenpo Sodargye has continued his translation and scholastic writing, but he has also expanded the genre as well as the scope of his writing. This latter category includes popular introductory books to Buddhism such as *Xinling de nuoya fangzhou* 心灵的诺亚方舟 [Noah's ark of the mind], *Ku caishi rensheng* 苦才是人生 [Living through suffering], and *Zuo caishi dedao* 做才是得到 [Achieving through doing], as well as his own commentary on Confucian classics such as the *Classic of Filial Piety* 孝经 and *Disciplines for Pupils and Children* 弟子规.

16. "Education Statistical Yearbook of China," *EPS China Data*, accessed August 2, 2020, http://www.epschinadata.com/

TABLE 1. Gender and Monastic Status in *Flowing Tides*

Gender	Lay/Monastic	Number
Male	Lay	29
Male	Monastic	45
Female	Lay	29
Female	Monastic	22

Note: There are slightly more male protagonists in *Flowing Tides* than there are females. This is not necessarily a representation of the gender ratio of Han Chinese disciples at Larung. Larung is known for its attention to female monastic education and has attracted more female than male pilgrims in general. The higher number of male Buddhists interviewed for this volume could be attributed to the male monastic identity of Khenpo Sodargye, who is bound by the *vinaya*, or monastic disciplines, and will need to exercise extra caution when interacting with women, monastic or not. For a discussion on female monastic education at Larung, see Jue Liang and Andrew S. Taylor, "Tilling the Fields of Merit: The Institutionalization of Feminine Enlightenment in Tibet's First Khenmo Program," *Journal of Buddhist Ethics* 27 (2020): 231–62.

TABLE 2. Education Level in *Flowing Tides*

Highest Academic Degree	
High School	1
Associate Degree (Chn. 大专)	29
Bachelor's Degree	64
Master's Degree	15
Doctorate	15
n/a	1

(including the United States, the United Kingdom, Singapore, and South Korea). In short, these intellectual Buddhists are well above average in education level, and are well traveled and relatively affluent.[17] They wield more social and economic capital and inhabit the middle to upper echelons of Chinese society.

17. Although the income level is not a topic of much interest in the collection, in relating their personal encounter with Buddhism, many discuss their previous professions as highly paid. However, financial stability or prosperity does not ultimately satisfy their need for a spiritual life. In one case, a laywoman named Minglan 明兰 could easily afford transpacific flights from her home in Canada to Larung just to attend an exam on the seven treatises in her advanced Dharma class. On another occasion, Khenpo Sodargye mentioned a donation of one million RMB by Yuanbo 圆波 to build an assembly hall for Han Chinese monastics, commending his generosity. Suodaji Kanbu, *Flowing Tides*, 278–79, 644–51.

THE PATH LEADING TO BUDDHISM

In this section, I will sketch out some common narrative threads shared by the experience of many protagonists in *Flowing Tides*. These include their reason behind converting to Buddhism, a shared image of Buddhism as they perceive it, and their collective impression of religious life and activities in the two decades between 1980 and 2000.

For many protagonists in *Flowing Tides* as well as millions of people who reached adulthood shortly after the Cultural Revolution, the national discussion on the meaning of life (Chn. 人生意义大讨论) in the early 1980s marks one of the most memorable ideological shifts in their formative age. Peng Lie 彭列, a former farming expert from northeastern China, cites this discussion as the force that prompted him to reflect on the meaning of life and to ultimately find the answer in Buddhism, as he recalls his high school years:

> At that time, the *gaokao*[18] should be the most important life event that determines my fate. But the nationwide discussion on the meaning of life had a greater impact on me. It was a discussion that swept the nation from 1979–1980. Initiated by an open letter to the editorial office of *China Youth* 中国青年 by Pan Xiao 潘晓,[19] entitled "Why Does the Path of Life Grow Narrower and Narrower,"[20] many propaganda units organized public debates on the different views of life. What is the meaning of life? There were so many widely different opinions on this matter. I read almost all of the articles on this issue. Although I had to complete a lot of practice tests in order to prepare for the gaokao, I'd rather lose some sleep and get to an answer to the meaning of life, so that

18. *Gaokao* 高考, or the National College Entrance Examination, is a nationwide, annual standardized test that is a prerequisite for entering any public higher education institutions in China. For the longest time, the gaokao has been the singular determinant of high school graduates' fates—if and where they will go to college, what they will major in, and whether there will be tuition aid or scholarships.

19. Pan Xiao is a pseudonym combining parts of the names of the two authors who have contributed to this open letter, Pan Wei 潘炜 and Huang Xiaoju 黄晓菊. Both were invited by *China Youth* to write about their own views on life. *China Youth* is a magazine founded and supervised by the Communist Youth League of China (Chn. 共青团中).

20. Pan Xiao, "Why Does the Path of Life Grow Narrower and Narrower?," 人生的路啊，怎么越走越窄, *China Youth* 5 (May 1980).

> I could improve my understanding of life and society. The discussion on life's meaning spread wider and wider by the day, people wrote in with piles and piles of letters to the editorial office; finally, *China Youth* had to suspend the discussion. As you can see, different views on life and the world are questions people have passionately inquired after for the past centuries; however, no satisfactory answer was found. It is after I started learning about the Dharma that I realized the key to life's meaning has been perfectly laid out in Buddhist scriptures and treatises.[21]

Others in *Flowing Tides* share Peng's sentiment. Ling Ming 林明, a biostatistics PhD from the University of Michigan, regards her intellectual achievements as meaningless compared to her understanding of the truth of life or the purpose of humankind. Having studied biology as an undergraduate at Peking University, one of the most elite universities in China, she continued her postgraduate research in the United States. However, her dissatisfaction with the explanatory power of modern science only increased as she progressed in her studies. She was in particular tormented by the fraught ethics of animal testing and finally decided to come to Larung in search of an antidote to the materialistic world and to her growing sense of alienation.[22] Another monk, Yuanlian 圆莲, also remarked that, ever since college, he had long wondered about the ultimate purpose of human life. This sense of emptiness could not be fulfilled by the loving care of his parents or by his prestigious status as a college student. He began to search for an answer by reading extensively, from *qigong* 气功 manuals to Daoist and Buddhist scriptures. It was finally through encountering the *Diamond Sutra* (Chn. 金刚经) that he found what he was looking for.[23]

It is not uncommon for people to survey different religious or spiritual practices before finally settling on one. In *Flowing Tides*, many of the intellectual Buddhists were also familiar with popular qigong practices at the time[24] or with organized religions like Christianity. Of the 125 subjects, 28

21. Suodaji Kanbu, *Flowing Tides*, 331–32.

22. Suodaji Kanbu, *Flowing Tides*, 41–46.

23. Suodaji Kanbu, *Flowing Tides*, 433.

24. In his book *Qigong Fever*, David Palmer offers a history of the rise and fall of *qigong* from 1949 to 1999. At the founding of the People's Republic of China, qigong started as an officially backed medical practice to counter Western medicine. After a forced hiatus (along with virtually all other cultural practices) during the Cultural Revolution, it came back in a revitalized form that centers around demonstrations of paranormal feats and claimed to be

of them explicitly relate their experience practicing *qigong*. A former *qigong* practitioner, Zhixian 智贤, mentions that *qigong* practices provide a bridge between modern methods and traditional techniques of the body and open up previously concealed potential within oneself.[25] While for some, qigong is an entry point to which a lifelong spiritual journey begins, other former qigong practitioners (and Khenpo Sodargye) see it in a less positive light, arguing that "compared to the Dharma, most qigong practices are not the most superior (Chn. 究竟)."[26] As for those who were exposed to Christianity, some considered its tenets uninspiring and criticized it for its idolatry, while acknowledging that philanthropic efforts by church organizations are worth emulating.[27]

For these disciples, Buddhism emerged as the most attractive religious or spiritual path for them. What exactly about Buddhism makes it stand out? In the next section, I will analyze three prominent features of the version of Buddhism as propagated in the *Flowing Tides*. Buddhism is scientific rather than superstitious, is transcultural rather than locally confined, and has coexisted with other elements of traditional Chinese culture for a long time.

BUDDHISM, A SCIENTIFIC, TRANSCULTURAL, AND TRADITIONAL RELIGION

In the accounts of their conversion to Buddhism, these Han Chinese intellectuals discuss different reasons that make Buddhism their choice for religious practice. For them, Buddhism provides a convincing case that answers life's most important question, and is particularly well suited to the needs of their time. Three themes emerge in their characterization of Buddhism (and in Khenpo Sodargye's commentary as well). Buddhism is compatible with or even transcends modern science; its reach goes beyond the Chinese cultural milieu, captivating Eastern and Western minds alike; at the same

---

able to withstand rigorous scientific investigation. By the 1990s, qigong has become a national movement, giving rise to many renowned masters and networks of practitioners, wealth, and power. David A. Palmer, *Qigong Fever: Body, Science and Utopia in China* (London: Hurst, 2007).

25. Suodaji Kanbu, *Flowing Tides*, 271.

26. Suodaji Kanbu, *Flowing Tides*, 268.

27. Suodaji Kanbu, *Flowing Tides*, 429.

time, the long history of Buddhism in China also attests to its legitimacy and status as a homegrown tradition.

The first defining characteristic of Buddhism for these intellectuals is that it is scientific, that is, Buddhism as a method of inquiry is compatible with, if not more advanced than, science. An apology for Buddhism against criticism from those who sided with science runs through *Flowing Tides* as a common theme. In "Analyzing Buddhism with Scientific Methods," a lay Buddhist, Wu Jin 吴金, laid out the following claim:

> When I began to analyze Buddhist teachings with a scientific worldview and methodology, I discovered that standing in front of me is such a massive treasure house. If I were to make a judgment with my limited knowledge of modern science, I will say that "science," as represented by the modern disciplines of engineering, science, and liberal arts, will culminate in the Buddhadharma. I really do hope that the descent of Maitreya will be the ultimate result of scientific developments.[28]

To prove his point, Wu quotes a famous statement from the *Heart Sutra*: form is no different from emptiness; emptiness is no different from form; form is emptiness; emptiness is form (色不异空，空不异色，色即是空，空即是色).[29] Here, the "form" represents everything in the universe except for the mind, while "emptiness" stands not for nonexistence, but for the true nature of things. Expressed in the language of physics, "emptiness" is analogous to energy, while "form" is the manifestation of said energy. In this way, the form/emptiness teaching expresses the law of conservation of energy.[30] He further debunked the claim that "science proves that Buddhism is superstition" by arguing that science is not a static body of knowledge, but a method for an objective, fair exploration. The fact that we cannot explain supernatural phenomena using the knowledge we have does not make these phenomena superstitious.[31] Buddhism even meets the reproducibility

28. Suodaji Kanbu, *Flowing Tides*, 324–325.

29. The *Heart Sutra* is considered the pinnacle of the Perfection of Wisdom (Skt. *prajñāpāramitā*) teachings in Mahāyāna Buddhism, and is the most well-known and widely recited Buddhist scripture in East Asian Buddhism. For a complete translation, see Donald S. Lopez, *The Heart Sutra Explained: Indian and Tibetan Commentaries* (Albany: State University of New York Press, 1988), 19–20.

30. Suodaji Kanbu, *Flowing Tides*, 325.

31. Suodaji Kanbu, *Flowing Tides*, 327.

requirement for scientific research—the experiences of Buddhist practitioners past and present are the perfect example.[32]

In "My Scientific View of Buddhism," another monk, Huixian 慧贤, clarifies the teaching on interdependence and emptiness using the example of visual processing. In order to form a visual image of leaves, two elements are needed—the perception of light and its reflection of leaves in the eyes, and the processing of such a perception in the brain. This process is not a direct reproduction of leaves in the brain, but a reconstruction of the image of leaves through the medium of light. The processing of sensory information and the subsequent conviction of things as really existing are based on the sense faculties and mediated experience; for Huixian, this aligns well with the Buddhist theory of perception, which breaks down the cognitive process into a tripartite system of attribute, sensory basis, and consciousness (Skt. *guṇa-āyatana-vijñāna*, Chn. 尘-根-识).[33] In the eyes of these intellectual Buddhists, Buddhism, a tradition founded over two millennia ago, not only corresponds with discoveries in modern science, its profound wisdom could also very well transcend the limitations of scientific inquiry and lead us into further advancement of knowledge.

A second aspect that makes Buddhism an attractive option for these intellectuals is that it not only is compatible with the scientific method of inquiry but also attracts practitioners far and wide. In keeping with the zeitgeist of opening up and reform, many protagonists in *Flowing Tides* have been in contact with, studied, or even lived in Western countries. For them, the interest in Buddhism and other "Eastern" spiritual traditions among their Euro-American friends and colleagues attests to the transcultural, timeless appeal of Buddhism.

The first story in *Flowing Tides*, titled "The Dharma That Traverses the World," features Aizesheng 艾泽生 (Edgerton?),[34] a Belgian Buddhist who had received a doctorate degree in traditional Chinese medicine in China and was an extraordinarily diligent practitioner. In his conversation with Khenpo Sodargye, Aizesheng sums up his reason for coming to China and practicing Buddhism:

32. Suodaji Kanbu, *Flowing Tides*, 329.

33. Suodaji Kanbu, *Flowing Tides*, 28–29.

34. Since the accounts in *Flowing Tides* are provided only in Chinese without English originals, it is unlikely that Aizesheng's full name can be discovered, or that he can be identified.

> With the arrival of the Digital Age, distances between different regions are shortened, and exchanges between Eastern and Western cultures are more widespread. More and more Westerners came to know Buddhism and became Buddhists. They are in particular impressed with the spirit of compassion and equality in Buddhist teachings. In a modern society, not only is material production highly developed, people also demand a more advanced form of civilization. In the past decade, various types of organizations are founded abroad with a dedicated purpose of protecting the environment and animal rights; many people actively took part in them. The number of people who became vegetarians and refrained from killing animals is also growing. In response to this trend, some airlines started to offer vegetarian options on international flights. Families built birdhouses to feed the birds in their backyard, so that they will not kill other insects. Philanthropic institutions took care of homeless animals. Even the Queen of Netherlands was criticized by animal protection agencies for her hunting activities. We can see that the moral principles of kindness in this world have no conflict with Buddhist teaching. With an increasing number of people who aspire to integrity and pursue the truth of life, the prophecy of Master Padmasambhava is gradually coming to realization. I do not doubt that in the near future, the Dharma will captivate the attention of fortunate ones all over the world, and eventually lead countless sentient beings to their own Pure Land.[35]

Another monk from Taiwan, Lianguang 蓮光, also refers to the widespread interest in yoga, Zen, and Tibetan Buddhism in the West. He laments the loss of the true Buddhist transmission in the land where it had blossomed for a long time:

> Nowadays in monasteries in India and Nepal, many Westerners are studying the Dharma. I have even witnessed an American Buddhist passing his Geshe exam in Sera Monastery in Southern India.[36] The more civilized a country becomes, the more prosperous the Dharma is:

35. Suodaji Kanbu, *Flowing Tides*, 20.

36. For a discussion of the community of Western monks and their study of Tibetan Buddhist scholasticism, including perspectives from the first Westerner to receive a Geshe Lharampa degree (the highest scholastic degree in the Geluk school of Tibetan Buddhism), Georges Dreyfus, see Georges Dreyfus and Ven. Jampa Kaldan, "A Remarkable Feat by Extraordinary Men: The Western Geshe in Two Acts," *Mandala* (April–May 2007), 27–29.

> such is the global trend of our time. Looking back to China now, even though it was a major Buddhist country, [its cultural traditions like] calligraphy and the art of tea—not to mention Zen—are all carried off by the Japanese and given names in Japanese such as *shodō* and *sadō*, so that many foreigners think these traditions originated from Japan.[37]

Yuanshang 圆上, a statistics PhD turned Buddhist nun, encountered Buddhism from a different direction. She first encountered a book on past life recollections during hypnotic therapy, composed by a Yale-graduated psychiatrist, Dr. Brian Weiss.[38] Titled *Many Lives, Many Masters*, this book changed Yuanshang's previous conviction that reincarnation is all made up superstition, and changed her attitude toward Buddhism.[39] Compared to Aizesheng and Lianguang, who view Buddhism as a superior spiritual path that can win over Western minds in itself, Yuanshang took a more circuitous path that led her first to Western psychiatry and then to Buddhism.

In addition to attracting many Western practitioners, Buddhism is also perceived not as a foreign religion, but as an essential part of traditional Chinese culture. Few of the Han Chinese intellectual Buddhists distinguish between the Tibetan and Chinese forms of Buddhism. When Tibetan Buddhism is singled out for discussion, it is usually with an emphasis on its scholastic tradition,[40] its lineage of renowned masters and vast literature,[41] and its supposedly unbroken and unadulterated transmission, especially the tantric teachings and practices.[42] Many of these Han Chinese Bud-

37. Suodaji Kanbu, *Flowing Tides*, 294–95.

38. Brian Weiss, *Many Lives, Many Masters* (London: Piatkus, 1994).

39. Suodaji Kanbu, *Flowing Tides*, 36.

40. For example, Huang Xi 黃曦, a Han Chinese Buddhist, is particularly drawn to the debate tradition in Tibetan Buddhism, and considers debating the best way to approach the ultimate truth. In the preface to his life story, Khenpo Sodargye comments that Tibetan Buddhism preserves "the most superior tradition of philosophical debate," which is quintessential in determining the true meaning of Buddhist teaching. Suodaji Kanbu, *Flowing Tides*, 36, 652.

41. Many protagonists in *Flowing Tides* mention reading hagiographies of Tibetan Buddhist masters like Milarepa, Tsongkhapa, and Mipham Rinpoche. Suodaji Kanbu, *Flowing Tides*, 136, 211.

42. A monk named Lianguang summarizes the reasons behind the popularity of Tibetan Buddhism as follows: (1) Tibetan Buddhism uses logics and debate to establish the true teaching; (2) it contains a detailed, gradual system of practice that cuts through illusions and ignorance; (3) there are many practices distinct to Tibetan Buddhism that are not shared by

dhists have studied with both Chinese and Tibetan Buddhist masters or made pilgrimages to Chinese and Tibetan Buddhist monasteries and sacred sites alike, or both.[43] It is not uncommon for them to adopt an eclectic body of Buddhist knowledge that includes Chan or Zen teachings, Pure Land chantings, and Tibetan Buddhist yogic practices. In other words, the Buddhism in *Flowing Tides* is one that transcends the ethnic boundaries of Han and Tibetan, and one that boasts a long history of almost 2,000 years in China. For example, Cao Liangbo's 曹良波 entry into Buddhism was classical Chinese art and literature:

> The paintings and poems of my favorite Tang poet, Wang Wei, is infused with Zen aesthetics. His Zen paintings in particular, by using light-toned shades in ink paintings, reveal a mind that is peaceful, expansive, and pure. This produced an intensive curiosity about Buddhism in me. Moving forward in the history of Chinese art, one would come to the remarkable realization that many famous writers, poets, artists—from Bai Jüyi, Liu Zongyuan, Du Mu, Ouyang Xiu, Su Dongpo, Huang Tingjian, Lu You, Dong Qichang, Zhu Da, to Liang Qichao, Xü Beihong, Master Hongyi, and Feng Zikai—are all deeply familiar with Buddhist teachings. In other words, we can no longer speak about their artistic style if we remove Buddhist influence and elements in their works.
>
> When assuming a higher vantage point, I discovered that, to my surprise, since it arrived in China in the Eastern Han Dynasty, Buddhism has integrated itself into the deepest level of the Chinese national character and the undercurrents of Chinese civilization. It has become an indivisible part of our spiritual, cultural, and material life. Buddhist culture manifests itself everywhere, whether it is within the realm of arts—architecture, painting, poetry, fiction, plays, calligraphy, or fashion—or any aspect of social life.[44]

---

other Buddhist traditions, and are particularly effective at dispelling obstacles on the path to liberation. Suodaji Kanbu, *Flowing Tides*, 293–294.

43. Many in *Flowing Tides* mention their meetings with Master Qingding 清定, former abbot of Zhaojue Monastery 昭觉寺 in Chengdu and a Buddhist master who is well versed in both the Chinese and Tibetan Buddhist traditions. Some even took refuge with Master Qingding or were ordained by him. Suodaji Kanbu, *Flowing Tides*, 18, 164, 210, 222, 324, 747, 760, 812, 902.

44. Suodaji Kanbu, *Flowing Tides*, 144–45.

Some even talk about Buddhist teaching and traditional Chinese culture as if they are indistinguishable. Wu Ming 吴铭, a lay Buddhist with a PhD degree, bemoans the lack of an education in "traditional culture" (Chn. 传统文化), especially about how learned people of the past viewed the world and human life. For Wu, the deeper he dives down into Buddhist wisdom, the more he realizes the hubris and superficiality of so-called modern civilization. Criticizing ancient culture without understanding its depth is like seeing only a few leaves, but not the towering tree.[45]

The propagation of Buddhism can further be coupled with other Chinese religious and philosophical systems. As discussed in the previous section, many protagonists explored other spiritual options before coming to Buddhism, and it is not uncommon for them to see these options as compatible with, or even reinforcing, each other. When Ling Ming discusses her mission to promote the spread of Buddhism, it entails combining the power of love and compassion evident in both Tibetan Buddhism and Confucian teachings on humanity (Chn. 仁) and human relations.[46]

Altogether, these three characteristics of Buddhism—scientific, transnational, and traditional—form a timely answer to the spiritual crisis and the nationwide discussion going on in China. Like qigong and New Confucianism, Buddhism traces its history back to classical Chinese culture, which was regaining its popularity at the time. It is also not a form of superstition that belongs to an Old China that will need to be eradicated with the founding of a New China. As for the "Tibetan" part of Tibetan Buddhism taught and practiced at Larung, which used to be seen with suspicion, if not contempt, by Han Chinese intellectuals, it can be addressed by emphasizing the historical interactions between Sino-Tibetan Buddhist traditions, and by obscuring the boundaries between Tibetan and Chinese Buddhism.[47]

45. Suodaji Kanbu, *Flowing Tides*, 720.

46. Suodaji Kanbu, *Flowing Tides*, 46.

47. Khenpo Sodargye has also authored another apologetic treatise in response to 19 questions raised by Master Jiqun 济群, a prolific Chinese scholar-monk in the Weiyang Chan transmission. This work explicitly engages with questions or stereotypes Han Chinese practitioners traditionally associated with Tibetan Buddhism. These include the lack of vegetarianism and sexual celibacy in some Tibetan Buddhist monastics, the question of proper transmission in tantric practice, the possibility of enlightenment within this life, and the relationship between esoteric and exoteric Buddhism. Suodaji Kanbu, *Zang mi wen da lu* 藏密问答录 [Questions and answers on Tibetan esoteric Buddhism] (Seda: Se da la rung wu ming fo xue yuan, 2002).

CONCLUDING REMARKS

Despite its humble beginning as a small encampment—a "Gar" (Tib. sgar) in its literal sense—Larung has hosted many generations of Han Chinese and Tibetan Buddhists since it began offering these teaching assemblies in the 1990s. The size of the group grew significantly over time, from a few hundreds to over 100,000, until a recent limitation on enrollment size and number of participants at teaching gatherings.[48] Some of the participants today witnessed their parents or grandparents doing just the same thing; some of them were deprived of that. The sacred sites may have shifted place, digital counters worn on the fingers may have replaced the 108-bead rosaries, but the tradition itself is again found, and even revitalized, in its new emanation.

The case of Larung Gar and other institutions points to the fact that Buddhism and other religions do not remain undercurrents in a supposedly secular or atheist Chinese society. Rather, religion remains integral to people's lives and worldviews. Even as Buddhist institutions like Larung Gar face immense challenges in continuing and expanding their influence, their skillful adaption to the social, cultural, and political landscape in China proves time and again the felt need for a religious life. By employing the Buddhist concept of expedient means and rebranding Buddhism, especially Tibetan Buddhism, as a scientific, transnational, and at the same time quintessentially Chinese religion, the leaders at Larung Gar deliver a vision of Buddhism that has succeeded in responding to the needs of its time.

References

Chen, Xiaodong 陈晓东. *Ning ma de hong hui: Jin ri la rong shan zhong de yi kuai mi cheng jing tu* 宁玛的红辉：今日喇荣山中的一块密乘净土 [Blazing brilliance of the Nyingma school: A Pure Land of tantric Buddhism in the Larung Valley today]. Lanzhou: Gan su min zu chu ban she, 1999.

48. One of the abbots at Larung Gar told us in a 2018 interview that the official enrollment number at Larung Gar is capped at 5,000 monastics, including 3,500 nuns and 1,500 monks. Limitations on gathering size have also been in place since 2018, resulting in a reduction of the crowd size as well as publicity. For a discussion of the gender situation at Larung, see Jue Liang and Andrew S. Taylor, "Tilling the Fields of Merit: The Institutionalization of Feminine Enlightenment in Tibet's First Khenmo Program," *Journal of Buddhist Ethics* 27 (2020): 231–62; also see Padma 'tsho (Baimacuo) and Sarah Jacoby, "Gender Equality in and on Tibetan Buddhist Nuns' Terms," *Religions* 11, no. 543 (October 2020): 1–19.

Dreyfus, Georges, and Ven. Jampa Kaldan. "A Remarkable Feat by Extraordinary Men: The Western Geshe in Two Acts." *Mandala* (April–May 2007): 27–29.

"Education Statistical Yearbook of China." *EPS China Data*. Accessed August 2, 2020. http://www.epschinadata.com/

Esler, Joshua. *Tibetan Buddhism among Han Chinese: Mediation and Superscription of the Tibetan Tradition in Contemporary Chinese Society*. Lanham, MD: Lexington Books, 2020.

Germano, David. "Re-membering the Dismembered Body of Tibet: Contemporary Tibetan Visionary Movements in the People's Republic of China." In *Buddhism in Contemporary Tibet: Religious Revival and Cultural Identity*, edited by Melvyn C. Goldstein and Matthew Kapstein, 53–94. Berkeley: University of California Press, 1998.

Liang, Jue, and Andrew S. Taylor. "Tilling the Fields of Merit: The Institutionalization of Feminine Enlightenment in Tibet's First Khenmo Program." *Journal of Buddhist Ethics* 27 (2020): 231–62.

Lopez, Donald S. *The Heart Sutra Explained: Indian and Tibetan Commentaries*. Albany: State University of New York Press, 1988.

MacInnis, Donald E. *Religion in China Today: Policy and Practice*. Maryknoll, NY: Orbis Books, 1989.

Padma 'tsho (Baimacuo), and Sarah Jacoby. "Gender Equality in and on Tibetan Buddhist Nuns' Terms." *Religions* 11, no. 543 (October 2020): 1–19.

Palmer, David A. *Qigong Fever: Body, Science and Utopia in China*. London: Hurst, 2007.

Pan Xiao. "Why Does the Path of Life Grow Narrower and Narrower?" 人生的路啊，怎么越走越窄. *China Youth* 5 (May 1980).

Shen, Weirong. "Magic Power, Sorcery and Evil Spirit: The Image of Tibetan Monks in Chinese Literature during the Yuan Dynasty." In *The Relationship between Religion and State (chos srid zung 'brel) in Traditional Tibet*, edited by Christoph Cüppers, 189–227. Lumbini: Lumbini International Research Institute, 2004.

Smyer Yü, Dan. *The Spread of Tibetan Buddhism in China: Charisma, Money, Enlightenment*. London: Routledge, 2014.

Suodaji Kanbu 索达吉堪布. *Xing hao you fan nao: 31 wei li xiang zhe de xin ling zhi lü* 幸好有烦恼：31位理想者的心灵之旅 [Fortunate to be troubled: The spiritual journey of 31 idealists]. Beijing: Zhong guo you yi chu ban gong si, 2014.

Suodaji Kanbu 索达吉堪布. *Zang mi wen da lu* 藏密问答录 [Questions and answers on Tibetan esoteric Buddhism]. Seda: Se da la rung wu ming fo xue yuan, 2002.

Suodaji Kanbu 索达吉堪布. *Zhi hai lang hua: Jiang shu 125 wei zhi shi fen zi de xue fo li cheng* 智海浪花：讲述125位知识分子的学佛历程 [Flowing tides in the ocean of wisdom: Stories of 125 intellectuals about learning the Dharma]. 2 vols. Hong Kong: Xin yi tang, 2001.

Terrone, Antonio. "Khenpo Jigme Phuntsok." *Treasury of Lives*, October 2013. Accessed June 13, 2020. http://treasuryoflives.org/biographies/view/Khenpo-Jigme-Puntsok/10457

Tuttle, Gray. *Tibetan Buddhists in the Making of Modern China*. New York: Columbia University Press, 2005.

Weiss, Brian. *Many Lives, Many Masters*. London: Piatkus, 1994.

Willock, Nicole. *Lineages of the Literary: Tibetan Buddhist Polymaths of Socialist China*. New York: Columbia University Press, 2021.

Wu, Yutian 吴玉天. *Fang xue yu da shi: Xi zang mi zong kao cha fang tan ji shi* 访雪域大师:西藏密宗考察访谈纪实 [Visiting Buddhist masters in the land of snow: Documentation and interviews on tantric Buddhism in Tibet]. Lanzhou: Gan su min zu chu ban she, 2005.

Distancing the Other

Religious Violence and Its Absence in South Korea

Manus I. Midlarsky and Sumin Lee

Rutgers University, New Brunswick

In this chapter, we contrast the peaceful displacement of formerly dominant Buddhism in South Korea with the role of Buddhism in initiating violence against religious contenders in Sri Lanka, Myanmar, and Thailand. We then address the puzzle presented by South Korean religious exceptionalism. Religious dominants typically have not acceded peacefully to challenge. The European Wars of Religion of the sixteenth and seventeenth centuries and the more recent Sunni-Shia conflicts, especially in the Middle East, are cases in point. Yet Christianity, which in 1945 claimed 2 percent of the South Korean population, rose to nearly 28 percent in 2015. That was met peacefully by Buddhists, who, from a predominant position in 1945, have become a minority, totaling only 15.5 percent of the South Korean population in 2015, fewer than the number of Protestants. Elsewhere, in Sri Lanka, Myanmar, and Thailand, Buddhists have committed violence against Muslims, perceived to be religious challengers to Buddhism.

The framework developed here is based on the concept of "distancing the other." Distancing can consist in targeting the other for warfare or even extermination, as in genocide, the most extreme form of distancing, by which the other simply no longer exists. In South Korea, a far more benign form of distancing emerged in which the interiority of religious faith became a form of distancing from the atheistic Communist North and the Japanese form of Buddhism practiced during the Japanese occupation.

THE CONCEPTUAL FRAMEWORK: DISTANCING

Distancing is a form of conflict resolution in which religion can play an important role. The conflict can be resolved by violence, or simply by withdrawal to the interiority of religious beliefs. Vertical distance is a form of hierarchical inequality between individuals at the top of the hierarchy and those at the bottom. In the vertical form of inequality, the hierarchical dimension is typically wealth or income. This is the traditional form of inequality that has occupied much attention in the literature until recently. Horizontal inequality, on the other side, exists on the basis of ethnicity, religion, or any other basis for collective identification. Although wealth or income can be a factor distinguishing groups, often the basis for violence between collectivities is discrimination in access to political office, discriminatory legislation favoring one group over another, or any other way in which one group is favored over others.

Violence often erupts between groups based on a perception of inequality by one group relative to the other, as suggested by existing theories on horizontal inequality and conflict,[1] and confirmed by empirical analyses of this relationship.[2] These robust findings stand in contrast to the findings of

1. See Frances Stewart and Arnim Langer, "Horizontal Inequality and Conflict: An Introduction and Some Hypotheses," in *Horizontal Inequalities and Conflict: Understanding Group Violence in Multiethnic Societies*, ed. Frances Stewart (Houndmills, Basingstoke UK: Palgrave Macmillan, 2008), 3–24; Arnim Langer and Graham K. Brown, "Cultural Status Inequalities: An Important Dimension of Group Mobilization," in *Horizontal Inequalities and Conflict*, 41–53; Frances Stewart and Arnim Langer, "Horizontal Inequalities: Explaining Persistence and Change," in *Horizontal Inequalities and Conflict*, 54–82; and Frances Stewart, Graham K. Brown, and Arnim Langer, "Major Findings and Conclusions on the Relationship between Horizontal Inequalities and Conflict," in *Horizontal Inequalities and Conflict*, 285–300.

2. See Lars-Erik Cederman, Kristian Skrede Gleditsch, and Halvard Buhaug, *Inequality, Grievances, and Civil War* (Cambridge: Cambridge University Press, 2013); Gudrun Østby, "Polarization, Horizontal Inequalities and Violent Civil Conflict," *Journal of Peace Research* 45, no. 2 (2008): 143–62; Joshua R. Gubler and Joel Sawat Selway, "Horizontal Inequality, Crosscutting Cleavages, and Civil War," *Journal of Conflict Resolution* 56, no. 2 (2012): 206–32; Henrikas Bartusevičius, "A Congruence Analysis of the Inequality-Conflict Nexus: Evidence from 16 Cases," *Conflict Management and Peace Science* 36, no. 4 (2019): 339–58; and Andreas Wimmer, Lars-Erik Cederman, and Brian Min, "Ethnic Politics and Armed Conflict: A Configurational Analysis of a New Global Data Set," *American Sociological Review* 74, no. 2 (2009): 316–37.

the relationship between vertical inequality and mass violence, which typically do not reach high levels of significance.[3]

The studies of horizontal inequality typically examine the static relationship between groups that yields the violence. But the concept of distancing suggests a more dynamic condition in which *individuals* formerly existing in a condition of vertical inequality are then grouped into communities that are subsequently subjected to horizontal inequality. Certainly, Jews in Germany prior to 1933 existed in a vertical relationship with the government, but they were then singled out for discrimination, thereby establishing a horizontal inequality between the Jewish and German communities. When carried to its extreme, such as in the ghettos of Eastern Europe where the Nazi forced the Jews to congregate in 1940–45, the distancing process facilitated the annihilation of Jewish communities.[4] The ultimate distancing was infinite, for the murdered Jews no longer existed.

While colonial regimes did commit genocides, they more often established horizontal inequality between societal groups—the occupier and the occupied. In these settings, the relationship between the two groups is mostly based on identity, rather than income level or individual accomplishments. Horizontal inequality is still one of the clear legacies of colonialism in formerly colonized countries. The combination of physical proximity and sociopolitical distance between occupiers and occupied *within* formerly occupied territory is one of the toxic leftovers of colonialism. Hence, physical, even psychological distancing is necessary to begin self-government with a clean slate.

THE ROLE OF RELIGION IN DISTANCING THE OTHER

In attempting to distinguish between the violence committed by Buddhists against Muslims in Sri Lanka, Myanmar, and Thailand from the peaceful behavior of Buddhists toward Christians in South Korea, one immediately needs to examine the different forms of Buddhism involved in the four locations.

3. Manus I. Midlarsky, "Rulers and the Ruled: Patterned Inequality and the Onset of Mass Political Violence," *American Political Science Review* 82, no. 2 (1988): 491–509.

4. Manus I. Midlarsky, *The Killing Trap: Genocide in the Twentieth Century* (Cambridge: Cambridge University Press, 2005); and Manus I. Midlarsky, "Genocide and Religion in Times of War," in *Oxford Research Encyclopedia of Politics* (Oxford: Oxford University Press, 2019).

Theravadan Buddhism is common throughout South and Southeast Asia, including Sri Lanka, Myanmar, and Thailand, while Mahāyānan Buddhism is mostly practiced in East Asia, including South Korea. A key difference between the two inheres in the meanings of the two names. Theravada translates into "Doctrine of the Elders,"[5] while Mahāyāna implies the great vehicle for personal spirituality and salvation.

A major expectation of Mahāyāna Buddhism is an existence based on compassion and improving happiness and social well-being in the here and now for all sentient beings.[6] Mahāyāna Buddhists also view the Buddha in Trikaya Doctrine as a benevolent supernatural entity, in contrast to the historical Buddha.[7] In Trikaya, Buddha has three bodies: his Nirmanakaya or body in this world; his Dharma body, in which he is eternal beyond all dualities in reality; and Sambhogaya, in which his body manifests itself for bodhisattvas in a celestial domain.[8] Theravada does not have the Trikaya concept, and views the Buddha as a historical figure.[9]

Emphasis on the community is more common in the Theravadan tradition. This might imply that Theravadan Buddhism would be more active in defense of the community from perceived or actual threat than the Mahāyānan. Yet this latter presumably more pacific form of Buddhism is also common in Tibet, where Buddhist monks have led the opposition to the Chinese efforts at assimilating Tibet in their own image, yielding much violence. And in Japan the Mahāyānan tradition gave rise to Zen Buddhism, which in its early attacks against Catholic missionaries entailed considerable violence. Thus, the existence of two variants of Buddhism, one violent against Muslims who in the Buddhist perception appear to challenge its predominance, and the other peaceful, giving way to a large Christian presence, does not assist in distinguishing between the presence or absence of violence.

---

5. Elders, here, refers to senior monks, who are committed to preserving tradition. In Richard F. Gombrich, *Theravada Buddhism: A Social History from Ancient Benares to Modern Colombo* (Abingdon, UK: Routledge, 2006).

6. Damien Keown, *Buddhism: A Very Short Introduction* (Oxford: Oxford University Press, 2013).

7. Keown, *Buddhism*; and Taigen D. Leighton, *Faces of Compassion: Classical Bodhisattva Archetypes and Their Modern Expression* (Somerville, MA: Wisdom Publications, 2012).

8. John Snelling, *The Buddhist Handbook: A Complete Guide to Buddhist Schools, Teaching, Practice, and History* (Rochester, VT: Inner Traditions, 1998).

9. Leighton, *Faces of Compassion*.

THE ROLE OF ETHNICITY IN DISTANCING THE OTHER

Ethnicity is another possible explanation for the different modalities in which Buddhism has engaged with competing religions. In Myanmar and Thailand, the Muslim communities are ethnically different from the majority of the population. In Sri Lanka, Tamil-speaking Muslims are also seen as pertaining to a distinct ethnic group, which the Sinhalese majority associates with the Tamil community. Similarly, the Rohingya in Myanmar are not only Muslim but also originally Bengali in ethnicity, while Muslims in Thailand are mostly Malay descendants, with some of them supporting Malay separatist movements. On the other side, in South Korea there is no ethnic difference between Buddhists and adepts of competing religions. This might signify that religion is not the primary feature distinguishing violent from pacific variants of Buddhism, whereas ethnicity could be the distinguishing factor.

Yet two elements suggest the primacy of religion over ethnicity. First, outside of South Korea, in certain cases, Buddhist monks have been at the forefront of attacks against Muslims. Those who focus on nationalism would of course emphasize the ethnic differences stemming from Muslims' diverse geographic origins, notably today's Bangladesh in the case of Myanmar, Tamil Nadu (for more recent Muslim arrivals) in Sri Lanka, and Malaysia (in the southernmost provinces) in the instance of Thailand. To be sure, there often exists cooperation between the two opponents of Islam—nationalist and religious—as in Myanmar where the ousted military has made common cause with militant Buddhist monks, but it is the religious community that typically has been in the forefront of attacks on Muslims.[10]

Second, distancing in South Korea could just as easily refer to the ethnically different Japanese who recently departed South Korea. Yet having already left, their departure would no longer be desired as apparently is the case for Muslims in the violent cases of Sri Lanka, Myanmar, and Thailand. The choice of a different religion after the Japanese occupation could not be associated with the undesirability of an ethnically alien occupier, but could be seen to stem from the unwillingness to be associated with any version of Buddhism (Zen) practiced by the Japanese. Further, Christianity has the positive attraction of being associated with the dynamic economies of the West, in contrast to the moribund Communism of North Korea. Thus,

10. Min Zin, "Anti-Muslim Violence in Burma: Why Now?," *Social Research: An International Quarterly* 82, no. 2 (2015): 375–97.

the growing Christian presence has created considerable distancing from both North Korea and Japan. Distance actually begun during the Japanese occupation, when the occupiers co-opted the Buddhist temples into their administration. Accordingly, many Koreans claimed no religion, resulting in the 2015 National Census record of 56 percent of South Koreans identifying themselves as nonreligious.

Yet, as we shall see, it is the overlapping of ethnic and religious elements that is most toxic in enabling ethnic cleansing, and even the genocide of religiously different people.

VIOLENT DISTANCING: THE CASES OF SRI LANKA, MYANMAR, AND THAILAND

Sri Lanka

While many Tamil arrived in Sri Lanka from India during the British colonial period, an indigenous Tamil community (known as Moors) predated those arrivals. The language laws of 1956 mandated the Sinhala language in all governmental activities, thus disadvantaging Tamil speakers, who had learned English during the British colonial period and were employed in governmental services. Until that year, official business was conducted in English, the official language of Ceylon under British rule. Crucially, the Tamil community was far more receptive to learning English than the majority of Sinhalese. Educated by American missionaries, English-speaking Tamils were employed by the colonial bureaucracy, and were overrepresented compared to their population size. Perhaps because of the British colonial experience in India with its large Tamil-speaking community, the British were receptive to the Tamil presence. Unlike the previous Portuguese and Dutch colonizers, the British viewed Muslims in a positive way:

> The British found in the Moors a community of enterprising active, hardworking, dynamic, and business minded people who were in the British view the polar opposite of the slovenly, indolent and unenterprising majority Sinhalese. Therefore, the Moors were viewed with favour as a class of beneficial economic functionaries in an emerging commercial economy.[11]

11. Ameer Ali, "Muslims in Harmony and Conflict in Plural Sri Lanka: A Historical

By the time the language laws mandated Sinhalese as the official language of Sri Lanka, Tamils occupied roughly 50 percent of the national bureaucracy positions.[12] Without proficiency in Sinhalese, the most educated of the Tamil community lost their positions, and other legislation stripped the Tamil business community of much of their livelihood.

Tamil opposition to the national government led to the rise of the ruthless extremist Liberation Tigers of Tamil Eelam, which at one point mounted the largest number of suicide attacks in the world by the Black Tigers, so called because they wore black clothing in the expectation of their imminent deaths. After a failed Indian intervention in Sri Lanka in 1987 on behalf of the Tamil community, the Sinhalese government mounted a major offensive against the Tamils in the Jaffna Peninsula, ultimately defeating the Liberation Tigers of Tamil Eelam and killing most of its members and supporters in 2009. The Hindu Tamils were no longer a threat to the national government or the Buddhist establishment. Although Muslims typically spoke the Tamil language, they did not participate in the uprising against the Sinhalese-led government.

The only remaining religious group with some prominence in the business community was the Tamil-speaking Muslims. "Muslim Sri Lankans are now at the receiving end of Islamophobia rhetoric, even violence, from Sinhala Buddhist nationalist organizations, driven by a belief that the Muslim community represents a threat to Buddhism."[13] Additionally, "Muslims are the only Sri Lankan ethnic group bearing a religious rather than a linguistic, ethnic or racial name, i.e. faith is not only a theological marker but also an identity marker, which means there remain tensions and fault lines along racial and religious lines."[14] All of this stands in stark contrast to the earlier efforts of the Sinhalese leadership to co-opt Muslims in a joint effort against the Tamil extremists. Having won this battle against the Tamil extremists, the Muslim community as the only remaining large minority now is identified in bold relief.

Summary from a Religio-Economic and Political Perspective," *Journal of Muslim Minority Affairs* 34, no. 3 (2014): 234.

12. Neil DeVotta, *Blowback: Linguistic Nationalism, Institutional Decay, and Ethnic Conflict in Sri Lanka* (Stanford: Stanford University Press, 2004), 120.

13. James John Stewart, "Muslim–Buddhist Conflict in Contemporary Sri Lanka," *South Asia Research* 34, no. 3 (2014): 241.

14. A. R. M. Imtiyaz and Amjad Mohamed-Saleem, "Muslims in Post-War Sri Lanka: Understanding Sinhala-Buddhist Mobilization against Them," *Asian Ethnicity* 16, no. 2 (2015): 191.

During the Sinhalese-Tamil conflict "Muslims, with their political support for the Sinhalese-dominated major parties, gained some socioeconomic as well as political concessions from successive ruling parties."[15] These concessions by the Sinhalese government included the establishment of segregated Muslim schools, a training college for Muslims, the provision of mosques, the institutionalization of holidays, and legal provisions under the marriage act. Having Arab countries' economic and military support and keeping the Muslims on their side against the Tamil struggle was a major policy goal of the Sinhalese government.[16]

Two Buddhist nationalist groups, Bodu Bala Sena (BBS, Buddhist Strength Army) and Sinhala Ravaya (Voice of the Sinhala People) were active. Both have the primary concern of ensuring that Buddhism remains the dominant religion of Sri Lanka. "The argument behind these claims is that Muslims are taking over the country and are now establishing mosques and other religious sites with the intention of displacing Buddhists from those areas. It is therefore claimed that the presence of these Muslim sites represents a threat to the stability of Buddhism throughout the country."[17]

Sinhala Ravaya produces a huge amount of anti-Muslim propaganda. They attack Muslims' halal practices: "The killing of animals in this way leads Buddhist nationalists to challenge Islam. It is argued that killing an animal using halal techniques is unkind and un-Buddhist. In particular, nationalists now almost exclusively focus on the slaughter of cattle. . . . Sinhala Ravaya activists have, for example, been implicated in an attack on a beef stall in Tangle."[18]

Both religious and economic grievances are strong. Religiously,

> the proliferation of mosques with foreign funds and presence of Muslim shrines in the country, calling for prayer over loudspeakers, slaughtering of cattle for sale and consumption, halal certification of food products and preaching of Islamic religious extremism are prominent issues.[19]

15. Imtiyaz and Mohamed-Saleem, "Muslims in Post-War Sri Lanka," 192.
16. Imtiyaz and Mohamed-Saleem, "Muslims in Post-War Sri Lanka," 192–93.
17. Stewart, "Muslim-Buddhist Conflict in Contemporary Sri Lanka," 248.
18. Stewart, "Muslim-Buddhist Conflict," 253.
19. Ali, "Muslims in Harmony and Conflict in Plural Sri Lanka," 239.

Economically,

> the export of Sinhalese female labour to the Middle East particularly as house maids, the emergence of Muslims as successful businessmen and entrepreneurs, Muslim possession of property in urban areas and a disproportionate increase in Muslim population . . . seem to be the major problems.[20]

There is a strong parallel with the Muslims of Bosnia within the former Yugoslavia. Until the 1960s Muslims were simply identified by their religion, like the Serbian Orthodox or the Croatian Roman Catholics. But in 1960, their request for ethnic identification was granted by the federal Yugoslav government. This new status now meant that Bosnian Muslims could compete with other ethnicities for federal goods and services. That new competition, in which ethnicity and religion were merged into one concept, ultimately created enabling conditions for the 1994 genocide of Muslims in Srebrenica, at the hands of the Bosnian Serbs.

But even in the merging of ethnic and religious elements, it was their religion that made the Bosnian Muslims vulnerable. As the Bosnian Serb leader Radovan Karadzic (later convicted of war crimes) remarked,

> It is clear that the path to salvation of Serbs of the Muslim faith is the return to Orthodoxy. . . . They were temporarily—in respect to eternity what is a few hundred years—of another faith either because of the pressure of the occupiers or personal comfort. . . . it does not mean that they do not have in them much of what is Serb, Christian, and Orthodox.[21]

Only religious conversion could have saved the murdered Muslims at Srebrenica, much as conversion to Buddhism by the Sri Lankan Muslims could save them from persecution and perhaps worse.

---

20. Ali, "Muslims in Harmony and Conflict," 239.

21. Paul Mojzes, "The Camouflaged Role of Religion in the War in Bosnia and Herzegovina," in *Religion and the War in Bosnia*, ed. Paul Mojzes (Atlanta: Scholars Press, 1998), 87–88.

Myanmar

Unlike Sri Lanka, where religion rose to the fore only recently, religion was a paramount concern for Buddhists immediately after independence. During colonial times the Karen, a non-Buddhist minority in Burma, were disproportionately represented in the colonial British army. A majority of Karen had converted to Christianity. This Karen dominance of the army continued into the independence period, becoming evident with the choice of a Karen, Lieutenant General Smith Dun, as the first commander in chief of the Burmese army, although he was substituted by a Burman shortly after independence.[22]

Many Rohingya Muslims in Myanmar descend from Bengalis situated within British India. Publics in Myanmar consider the Rohingya's origin as Bengali Muslims from Bangladesh and they are often referred to as "intruders from neighboring Bangladesh."[23]

> For the ruling military-led governments, religious difference, like ethnic difference, marked individuals and groups as outside the national community and as potential threats to the integrity of the country. Partly as a result of this, Burmese nationalism became increasingly conflated with Buddhist religious identity, conveying a sense that to be authentically a citizen of Myanmar was to be Buddhist (and ethnically Burman).[24]

The anti-Muslim attitudes and activities of Buddhist monks originated in colonial times.[25] Promised partial independence, the Rohingya allied with Britain when the Japanese invaded in 1942, leading to intercommunal strife in the Arakan (Rakhine) region. Many Burmese Buddhists, on the other hand, welcomed the Buddhist Japanese as allies against Britain, in a move

---

22. Thant Myint-U, *The River of Lost Footsteps: A Personal History of Burma* (New York: Farrar, Straus and Giroux, 2006), 261.

23. Zin, "Anti-Muslim Violence in Burma," 375.

24. Matthew J. Walton and Susan Hayward, "Contesting Buddhist Narratives: Democratization, Nationalism, and Communal Violence in Myanmar," *Policy Studies: East-West Center* 17 (2014): 6.

25. Nyi Nyi Kyaw, "Islamophobia in Buddhist Myanmar," in *Islam and the State of Myanmar: Muslim-Buddhist Relations and the Politics of Belonging*, ed. Melissa Crouch (Oxford: Oxford University Press, 2010), 192.

that contributed to the demise of the British Empire, and yielded an independent Burma. As a result of these opposing views, the Arakanese Muslims and Buddhists became deeply polarized,[26] while continuing cohabitation in the same political space. At the end of the war, the British reneged on the promise of partial independence for the Rohingya.[27]

The 1982 Burmese Citizenship Law deprived the Rohingya of citizenship: "Muslims were banned from entering the public sector, in contrast to the pre- and post-independence period when Muslims engaged in the public sector as prominent politicians and cabinet ministers."[28] Compounding the exclusion from the public sector is the economic condition of Arakan State. Its population is "largely agrarian and remains one of Burma's poorest, with over 43.5 percent living below the poverty line, second only to Chin State, according to a 2011 study by UNDP."[29]

There are two Buddhist nationalist groups, the 969 and MaBaTha, that "justify discrimination (and sometimes even violence) against Muslims as a necessary response to the imminent threat of Islam's expansion in Asia, and its encroachment upon the Buddhist community."[30] These Buddhists argue for the necessity to defend the *sasana*, which refers not only to the tenets of the religion itself, but to the entire Buddhist community consisting of monks, nuns, and laypeople. Further, "defending Buddhism, therefore, requires not only protecting the integrity of the state, but also ensuring that the state and its leaders create an environment conductive to the well-being of the religion."[31]

The MaBaTha (Organization for the Protection of Race and Religion) has more targeted political strategies and a more centralized structure than the 969. This group is discriminatory and "spreads a virulently anti-Muslim message and reinforces notions of an exclusively Buddhist nation."[32] They

---

26. Benjamin Schonthal, "Making the Muslim Other in Myanmar and Sri Lanka," in *Islam and the State in Myanmar: Muslim-Buddhist Relations and the Politics of Belonging*, ed. Melissa Crouch (Oxford: Oxford University Press: 2016), 234–57.

27. Azeem Ibrahim, *The Rohingyas: Inside Myanmar's Hidden Genocide* (Oxford: Oxford University Press, 2016), 7.

28. Kyaw, "Islamophobia in Buddhist Myanmar," 193.

29. Human Rights Watch, *"The Government Could Have Stopped This": Sectarian Violence and Ensuing Abuses in Burma's Arakan State* (New York: Human Rights Watch, 2012).

30. Walton and Hayward, "Contesting Buddhist Narratives," 20.

31. Walton and Hayward, "Contesting Buddhist Narratives," 21.

32. Walton and Hayward, "Contesting Buddhist Narratives," 15.

control religious education across the country, and they teach their extremist anti-Muslim interpretation of Buddhism.[33] Commonly, monks argue that Myanmar is being taken over by Muslims; they claim that Muslims will take over the country by marrying and forcibly converting Buddhist women. Both MaBaTha and 969 draw upon the concept of "just war" in order to defend engaging violence, which they use to protect the Buddhist community against non-Buddhist insurgency groups and foreign elements.[34]

Several events confirm the involvement, or at least the collusion, of the state in perpetrating or allowing violence against Muslims. For example, in 2012 the rape and murder of an ethnic Rakhine woman led to a retaliatory mob of Rakhine killing 10 Muslims.[35] Late in 2012 at least 200 people were killed and 147,000 people displaced, 138,000 of whom were Rohingya. The state did not intervene until the fourth day of violence, and later "the evidence strongly suggests not only that a calculated decision was made by the State authorities to allow the massacres to take place, but also that security forces participated in some instances."[36] A program of "undeterred propagation of hate speech coupled with clear political coordination" was lethal.[37] Crucially, ethnic cleansing was also supported by Buddhist monks. "In a two-day public demonstration that began in Mandalay on 2 September, thousands of people, including hundreds of Buddhist monks, took part in support of President Thein Sein's proposal to resettle the Rohingyas to a third country. The monks urged the people to save their motherland by supporting the president's proposal."[38]

Thailand

Like in Myanmar, the ethnic and religious elements are also merged in the case of Thailand. This was not a consequence of spontaneous Muslim

33. Ibrahim, *The Rohingyas*, 14.

34. Walton and Hayward, "Contesting Buddhist Narratives," 25.

35. Nehginpao Kipgen, "Addressing the Rohingya Problem," *Journal of Asian and African Studies* 49, no. 2 (2014): 236.

36. Penny Green, Thomas Macmanus, and Alicia De la Cour Venning, *Countdown to Annihilation: Genocide in Myanmar* (London: International State Crime Initiative, Queen Mary University of London. 2015), 76.

37. Zin, "Anti-Muslim Violence in Burma," 378.

38. Kipgen, "Addressing the Rohingya Problem," 242.

migration during the colonial period, as in Myanmar, but rather the product of the Anglo-Siamese Treaty of 1909, which "effectively cemented the northernmost borders of the Malay-Muslim world, and was seen as an act of Anglo-Siamese complicity that forcibly incorporated seven Malay sultanates into Siam."[39] This essentially colonial act by Britain set the stage for the later Thai-Muslim confrontation.

Because Thailand was never colonized, scholars such as Benedict Anderson suggest that the absence of a colonial history inhibited an authentic nationalist movement in that country:[40]

> And because the different ethnic groups in Thailand did not have a shared history of fighting western colonial powers, other means were necessary to integrate them into Thai society. This integration was seen in the aim of the Thai state to give all citizens a common identity—a Thai identity. . . . Such Thaicizing efforts have ranged from austere policies of assimilation to less drastic integration and more flexible approaches of defining Thai-ness through civil society.[41]

A nationalist revolution occurred in 1932 that led to efforts to assimilate the Muslim Malays into Thai society. It began by teaching Malays the Thai national anthem, Thai history, and the Thai language.[42] A militantly nationalist regime emerged in 1938 that had a forced assimilation policy; Thai leader Pibul Songkhram strongly discriminated against the Malay language and culture. This, in turn, led to the emergence of a separatist insurgency in southern Thailand. A military-orchestrated shift in political power in 1947 made the Thai government resistant to any regional linguistic, cultural, or religious autonomy in the south.

Additionally,

---

39. Joseph C. Liow, *Muslim Resistance in Southern Thailand and Southern Philippines: Religion, Ideology, and Politics* (Washington, DC: East-West Center, 2006), 26.

40. Duncan McCargo, "Buddhism, Democracy and Identity in Thailand," *Democratization* 11, no. 4 (2004): 155–70.

41. Saroja Dorairajoo, "Peaceful Thai, Violent Malay (-Muslim): A Case Study of the 'Problematic' Muslim Citizens of Southern Thailand," *Copenhagen Journal of Asian Studies* 27, no. 2 (2009): 69.

42. Andrew D. W. Forbes, "Thailand's Muslim Minorities: Assimilation, Secession, or Coexistence?" *Asian Survey* 22, no. 11 (1982): 1056–73.

> the kind of modernization carried out by the Chakri [Thai] kings was analogous to that pursued by colonial governors under formal imperialism. In this sense, the incorporation of the Buddhist sangha [community] into a political order organized along principles of internal colonialism is an important element of the legacy of the absolute monarchy.[43]

Internal colonialism in Thailand is understood as the deepening economic disparities between the main urban center (Bangkok) and the rural hinterland, manifesting in the economic underdevelopment of the (Malay-Muslim) south.[44]

A new government under General Prem Tinsulanonda (1980–88) supported Muslim cultural rights and religious freedoms, offered the guerillas a general amnesty, and implemented an economic development plan for the south.[45] However, episodic outbreaks of violence activities still occurred in the Muslim south.[46] In 2004, when Thai police arrested four *ustaz* (Islamic teachers) as the masterminds behind the ongoing two years of unrest and turmoil, four Buddhist monks were murdered. In turn, in April 2004, Thai forces attacked a group of young Thai Malay men inside the historic Krue Se mosque, who were being sought as police "assailants." Thirty-two men were killed (out of a total of 106) inside the mosque.[47] "The attack had a symbolic historical and cultural significance that cannot be overemphasized. In Malay-Muslim folklore, the 400-year-old Krisek Mosque [Krue se Mosque] is emblematic of Malay-Muslim identity."[48]

In the months following the attack at Krue Se, violence, including fatalities, increased. Insurgents were partially responsible but governmental forces played the dominant role.[49] The Buddhist majority of the country supported the government's strong reaction. Buddhist monks, although

---

43. McCargo, "Buddhism, Democracy, and Identity in Thailand," 157.

44. Aurel Croissant, "Unrest in South Thailand: Contours, Causes, and Consequences since 2001," *Contemporary Southeast Asia: A Journal of International and Strategic Affairs* 27, no. 1 (2005): 27.

45. Croissant, "Unrest in South Thailand."

46. Dorairajoo, "Peaceful Thai, Violent Malay (-Muslim)," 66.

47. Charles Keyes, "Muslim 'Others' in Buddhist Thailand," *Thammasat Review* 13, no. 1 (2008): 28.

48. Liow, *Muslim Resistance in Southern Thailand and Southern Philippines*, 37.

49. Keyes, "Muslim 'Others' in Buddhist Thailand," 29.

not primary agents, were nonetheless armed participants in the conflict.[50] Attacks on monks in the southern region led to retaliation against Malay-Muslims, as "the significance of a Thai Buddhist monk's identity becomes fused with Thai Buddhism and Thai nationalism. When someone attacks a monk, they are attacking these two principles, and violent reactions are intense when someone attacks such ideals."[51] "In the recent upsurge of violence in the south of Thailand, the Malay Muslims have become even more un-Thai by challenging the integrity of Thailand's borders and threatening national security."[52]

In contrast to Sri Lanka and Myanmar, a number of well-organized Islamic militant groups are actively fighting for the establishment of an independent Islamic caliphate in southern Thailand. The Thai government has responded with a heavy hand, and groups such as Human Rights Watch have documented numerous human rights abuses on all sides of the conflict. Nine in every 10 victims of violence in the region have been civilians.

NONVIOLENT DISTANCING: SOUTH KOREA

The growth of Christianity in South Korea (19.7% Protestant, 7.9% Catholic, against 15.5% of Buddhists in the 2015 census) is remarkable when compared to its far more limited gains in Japan (currently approximately 1%), another East Asian country heavily influenced by US culture. To understand this exceptional development, we need to delve into Korean history, and especially the Korean relationship with Japan, for it is in this nexus that an answer can be found.

From the fourth until the fourteenth centuries, Buddhism enjoyed an unrivaled position as the leading ideology and national faith. Yet, even in the late Koryo dynasty (918–1392), several reasons contributed to the decline of Buddhism. There was a loosening in the moral and spiritual legitimacy of Buddhism, as monks were involved in luxurious and even scandalous lives. Politically, they became associated with the hated Mongols; economically, the monks' alienation from the state and ineffective supervision of temples

50. Michael K. Jerryson, *Buddhist Fury: Religion and Violence in Southern Thailand* (Oxford: Oxford University Press, 2011), 4.

51. Jerryson, *Buddhist Fury*, 53.

52. Dorairajoo, "Peaceful Thai, Violent Malay (-Muslim)," 70.

frustrated civil officials.[53] Two specific events further weakened the dominant position of the Buddhists.

First, after the founding of the Yi dynasty in 1392, Confucianism became the official state religion. Buddhism was restrained in several ways, including by introducing stricter selection procedures for Buddhist monks; limiting the number of temples and hermitages; reducing the number of officially sanctioned Buddhist sects; reorganizing the ecclesiastical system; and banning Buddhist monks from entering the capital city.[54] Buddhist clerics fell into the lower social strata and anti-Buddhism sentiment became widespread among the general public.[55] Despite these efforts, many members of the Korean elite continued to remain Buddhist. The Chosŏn Court often utilized the expertise of the few remaining monks.[56]

Second, the Japanese invasion of Korea sparked the highly destructive Imjin War of 1592–98. Spurred by Japanese outrages, which included destroying temples and abducting or killing monks, many monks joined the "Righteous Volunteer Army."[57] In this context, "the state ordered the monks to rise up against the Japanese [promising] to give certificates and prizes."[58] Eight thousand monk-soldiers from across the country enlisted for the war in June-December 1592. Yet, if any rise in popularity resulted from this, it did not last long: "Following the Imjin wars, Buddhism began a gradual but steady decline not only economically but also spiritually. Many temples throughout the country fell into disrepair or were simply abandoned."[59]

---

53. Key P. Yang and Gregory Henderson, "An Outline History of Korean Confucianism: Part I: The Early Period and Yi Factionalism," *Journal of Asian Studies* 18, no. 1 (1958): 86.

54. Robert E. Buswell, "Buddhism in Korea," in *The Religious Traditions of Asia: Religion, History and Culture*, ed. Joseph M. Kitagawa (Abingdon, UK: Routledge, 2002), 352.

55. Pori Park, "Korean Buddhist Reforms and Problems in the Adoption of Modernity during the Colonial Period," *Korea Journal* 45, no. 1 (2005): 88.

56. Chosŏn used monk-healers to assist in public health clinics, monk-artisans to produce papers for the officials, and even requested monks to organize a fighting force when the Japanese invaded in 1592. Monk soldiers were frequently used by the monarchs. See Don Baker, "The Religious Revolution in Modern Korean History: From Ethics to Theology and from Ritual Hegemony to Religious Freedom," *Review of Korean Studies* 9, no. 3 (2006): 263.

57. Karel Werner, "Buddhism and Peace: Peace in the World or Peace of Mind?," *International Journal of Buddhist Thought and Culture* 5, no. 1 (2005): 27.

58. Hwansoo Kim, "Buddhism during the Chosŏn Dynasty (1392–1910): A Collective Trauma?," *Journal of Korean Studies* 22, no. 1 (2017): 122.

59. Henrik Hjort Sørensen, "Buddhism and Secular Power in Twentieth-Century Korea," in *Buddhism and Politics in Twentieth-Century Asia*, ed. Ian Harris (London: Continuum, 1999), 127–52.

Meanwhile, Christianity first began its influence as Korean envoys encountered ideas brought by Jesuit missionaries from Peking in the eighteenth century.[60] Christianity was banned by the regime, as it was opposed to ancestor worship, while Confucianism and Buddhism bonded against the common foe.

In the late nineteenth century, an unequal treaty between Korea and Japan—the Kanghwa Treaty—opened the doors of three Korean ports, and granted extraterritorial rights to Japanese settlers. This not only opened the way for Christian missions but also provided Japanese Buddhists with the opportunity to proselytize.[61] In 1877 Japanese missionaries—Higashi Buddhists—first arrived, sent in order to

> serve Japanese nationals in Korea and, more importantly, to function as a buffer zone against which to ease the animosity of Koreans against Japan's military and economic encroachment. The Higashi Buddhists were pleased to accede to the government's needs and embarked on their mission in Korea to support the foreign expansion.[62]

A new religion arose containing elements of Buddhism, Confucianism, and shamanism—the Tonghak—that moved to the forefront of anti-Japanese activities, culminating in the 1894 Tonghak Peasant Rebellion. In response to this rebellion, the Japanese army was stationed for the first time on the Korean Peninsula. An additional response consisted of the Gabo Reforms that removed old prohibitions against Buddhist monks and allowed them access to the capital city, from which they had been banned since 1449. The withdrawal of anti-Buddhist decrees in this period led to a Buddhist revival in Korea, although the "return to pluralism . . . also allowed other religions, among them various forms of Christianity, to gain a foothold in Korean society, sometimes at the expense of Buddhism."[63]

After the Japanese victory in the First Sino-Japanese War of 1894–95 a second wave of Japanese missionaries arrived in Korea: the Nishi Hoganji

60. Suk-Jay Yim, Roger L. Janelli, and Dawnhee Yim Janelli, "Korean Religion," in *The Religious Traditions of Asia: Religion, History, and Culture*, ed. Joseph M. Kiragawa (Abingdon, UK: Routledge, 2002), 343.

61. Hwansoo Kim, "'The Future of Korean Buddhism Lies in My Hands': Takeda Hanshi as a Sōtō Missionary," *Japanese Journal of Religious Studies* 37, no. 1 (2010): 99–135.

62. Park, "Korean Buddhist Reforms and Problems," 91–92.

63. Boudewijn Walraven, "Buddhist Accommodation and Appropriation and the Limits of Confucianization," *Journal of Korean Religions* 3, no. 1 (2012): 114.

branch of the Jodo Shin school and the Jodo school. The government, now pro-Japanese (the Kim Hongjip cabinet), established a headquarters for organizing Korean Buddhism. In 1902 the *Kuknae Sach'al Hyonse Chuk* (Law for the Operation of the Temples in the Country) was the first law for the regulation of Buddhist temples. Japanese Buddhist missionaries strongly supported this regulation. Uncontested Japanese power on the peninsula resulted from the defeat of Russia in the 1904–05 Russo-Japanese War. A third wave of Japanese missionaries from the Soto, Shinbone, and Rinzai schools arrived in Korea. "Seeking to serve the Japanese immigrant communities, priests soon began establishing offices and temples in major cities throughout Korea as branches of their homeland sect."[64] Korean clerics were sent to Japan in order to study Buddhism, before and after the annexation.

A pro-Japanese monk, Yi Hoegwang, established the Won school with the aid of priests of the Japanese Soto Zen school in order to induce the Korean temples to accept the sovereignty of Japanese Buddhism.[65] An effort to unify and revive the dwindling strength of Korean Buddhism led to the formation of the Wonjong organization that opposed the *Pulgyo yonguhoe* (Association of Buddhist Studies), which was a pro-Japanese organization.[66] However, the Wonjong ended up electing the pro-Japanese Yi Hoegwang as its leader.

Japanese colonization was formalized with the annexation of Korea in 1910, which lasted until 1945. One year after annexation, the Temple Ordinance selected 33 temples as the main Buddhist institutions. "The governor-general in Seoul had the sole mandate to appoint the abbots of the Korean temples, and he was free to interfere as he pleased in their economy and landholdings. The result of this was that only declared pro-Japanese abbots were appointed for the temples, a move which estranged the majority of the Korean *sangha* [Buddhist community]."[67] Religion was thus exploited in order to support Japanese imperialism in Korea. The Temple Ordinance survived beyond the end of Japanese rule in 1945.

64. Kim, "'The Future of Korean Buddhism Lies in My Hands,'" 101.

65. Henrik Hjort Sørensen, "The Attitude of the Japanese Colonial Government towards Religion in Korea (1910–1919)," *Copenhagen Journal of Asian Studies* 8, no. 1 (1993): 53–54.

66. Nam-lin Hur, "Han Yong'un (1879–1944) and Buddhist Reform in Colonial Korea," *Japanese Journal of Religious Studies* 37, no. 1 (2010): 75–97.

67. Sørensen, "The Attitude of the Japanese Colonial Government," 54.

OCCUPATION

During the Japanese occupation, pro-Japanese Korean monks attempted a merger with a major Japanese sect:

> Yi Hoe-gwang went so far as to negotiate a combination of the Korean church with the Japanese Sōtō sect, but most Korean Sŏn monks regarded the gradualistic teachings of the Sōtō sect as anathema to the subitist [sudden awakening] orientation of their own tradition, and managed to block the merger.[68]

This merger attempt was immediately countered by a nationwide campaign to restore a spirit of independence among Korean Buddhists.[69]

Efforts at reform soon followed in an attempt to revitalize Buddhism with the common goal of modernization.[70] A primary goal of the movement was to equip clerics with the knowledge of modern society necessary to effectively disseminate Buddhist teachings. Han Yong'un argued for the "unification of doctrinal orientation of the sangha, simplification of practices, centralization of the sangha administration, and reformation of sangha policies and customs."[71] He even advocated monks' marriage as he felt this was necessary if Buddhism was to maintain any viable role in modern secular society. The Pulgyo Yushin Hoe (the Buddhist Reform Association) led by Han Yong'un was, however, generally hostile toward pro-Japanese supporters among the Korean sangha and they successfully ousted Kang Taeryon, a leading pro-Japanese abbot, from his post (Sorenson 1999). In 1926 the Japanese government legalized the marriage of Buddhist monks, setting the ground for a question that would later become a major issue in independent Korea: Would the Korean sangha continue to allow clerical marriages as did the Japanese?

Although the Korean sangha did execute reforms, they focused mainly on monastic education.[72] At the same time, efforts of the Korean sangha fell short of expectations as they ran into limits imposed by the Temple

68. Buswell, "Buddhism in Korea," 353.
69. Hur, "Han Yong'un (1879–1944) and Buddhist Reform in Colonial Korea," 76.
70. Park, "Korean Buddhist Reforms and Problems," 88.
71. Park, "Korean Buddhist Reforms and Problems," 96.
72. Park, "Korean Buddhist Reforms and Problems," 96.

Ordinance. A single Buddhist national association was created in 1915 that controlled the affairs of the 33 temples. Among them, 10 temples opened their own schools for education, influenced by modern Japanese Buddhist schools.[73]

A signal event of this period was the March 1st Independence Movement that in 1919 staged nationwide rallies in favor of Korean independence. This movement is seen as "probably the most important production of inter-religious cooperation in modern Korean history."[74] Among the 33 signatories of the Declaration of Korean Independence, only two were Buddhist monks. This fact alone "shows the degree of political conformism Buddhism demonstrated in colonial Korea."[75] Yet Buddhists were still divided on the issue of the Japanese occupation.

As a consequence of the March 1st Independence Movement, the Japanese colonial regime softened some of its coercive policies. A limited degree of political freedom was granted. Many youths now opposed the Buddhists' overt and covert collaboration with the Japanese government. Buddhist youth associations embarked on a campaign against the Temple Ordinance, the Japanese coercive regulations imposed on Korean temples, and demanded self-government of the Buddhist order. However, "Korean monks regarded cleric [*sic*] marriage, their having fewer regulations, and living in cities as a more convenient way for them to relate to and assist lay people, as compared to living in monasteries as celibate monks."[76]

WARTIME AND POSTINDEPENDENCE

In 1931, Japan occupied Manchuria; six years later the Second Sino-Japanese War begun, followed by the Pacific War in 1941. In occupied Korea, the teaching of the Korean language and culture was abolished, to the point that

73. Sørensen, "The Attitude of the Japanese Colonial Government," 55.

74. Chong-suh Kim, "Religious Pluralism of Korea Today," *Seoul Journal of Korean Studies* 15 (2002): 166.

75. Vladimir Tikhonov, "One Religion, Different Readings: (Mis) interpretations of Korean Buddhism in Colonial Korea, Late 1920s-Early 1930s," *Journal of Korean Religions* 1, no. 12 (2010): 165.

76. Pori Park, "The Buddhist Purification Movement in Postcolonial South Korea: Restoring Clerical Celibacy and State Intervention," in *Identity Conflicts: Can Violence Be Regulated?*, ed. J. Craig Jenkins and Esther E. Gottlieb (Abingdon, UK: Routledge, 2007), 131.

Koreans were forced to convert their own names into Japanese names, and any semblance of Korean nationalist ideology was suppressed. By the end of Japanese rule, some monks were seen as compromised by their acceptance of the Japanese policy of "Japan and Korea Are One Entity."[77] Many of those who opposed this policy fled to small sanctuaries in the countryside, where the colonial regime could not reach. While many Protestant leaders were co-opted by the Japanese regime,[78] Protestant churches gained popular support as they mostly sympathized with Korean nationalism and helped the work of the modernists.[79]

The Committee for the Preparation of Korean Buddhist Renovation, whose leaders belonged to the right-wing group Youth Party for Korean Independence, led efforts for the decolonization of Korean Buddhism, including by abolishing "the colonial products of the 'Temple Ordinance' and its detailed regulations, as well as the main branch monastery system."[80] Division within the Korean Buddhist sangha persisted until early 1948, while "the right-left polarization of the society, a consequence of the international Cold War ideology, also became a crucial element in the conflict of Korean Buddhists."[81] Despite the efforts of Korean Buddhists, the US military government did not abolish the Temple Ordinance, which was instead used to control the Japanese temples remaining in Korea.[82]

AFTER THE KOREAN WAR

The Buddhist Purification Movement arose in 1952, ending in 1962, unifying the entire religious order including both Bhiksuni and Daecheo, the married monks (Jogye Order of Korean Buddhism). However, conflict arose between the celibate monks and those who were married. Efforts began to eliminate married clerics who were tolerated under the practices of Japanese Buddhism and were considered to be Japanese collaborators. The Taego-

77. Park, "Korean Buddhist Reforms and Problems," 109.

78. Chengpang Lee and Myungsahm Suh, "State Building and Religion: Explaining the Diverged Path of Religious Change in Taiwan and South Korea, 1950–1980," *American Journal of Sociology* 123, no. 2 (2017): 472.

79. Lee and Suh, "State Building and Religion," 471.

80. Park, "Buddhist Purification Movement in Postcolonial South Korea," 133.

81. Park, "Buddhist Purification Movement in Postcolonial South Korea," 134–35.

82. Park, "Buddhist Purification Movement in Postcolonial South Korea," 135.

Chong (a liberal sect of married monks) flourished under Japanese patronage. On the other hand, the Chongye-Chong (which maintained celibacy during the occupation) tried to restore the meditative, scholastic, and disciplinary orientations of traditional Korean Buddhism, Son Buddhism. "In declaring the holy 'Dharma War,' they [the Chogye order] sought to restore the celibate tradition of the sangha (monastic community), with the Vinaya rules re-instituted. In tandem, the celibate faction made wholesale accusations of married clerics being the very product of colonized Buddhism."[83]

The married clerics argued that "they practiced *taejung Pulgyo* (Buddhism for the General Public) and modern Buddhism, while adapting to the conditions of the time. . . . In other words, cleric [*sic*] marriage was a way to respond to the urgencies of the time, to facilitate interactions between the laity and the populace."[84]

At the end of the Korean War, President Syngman Rhee supported and himself led the reform against married clerics. In 1954 he commanded that married clerics leave the Buddhist order. Thus, "the married clerics became the main target of de-colonization [as] President Rhee stated that his nation, which was in the process of restoring the freedom and independence of Korean people at the price of life, would not tolerate those who were pro-Japanese. . . . He further insisted that everyone should cherish patriotism by abandoning Japanese customs and habits. He stated that those who were Buddhist clerics in a Japanese fashion should gradually return to lay life and help restore the sacred celibate tradition. *All the married clerics were thus regarded as Japanese collaborators.*"[85]

As noted by Nam-lin Hur, clerical marriage had become the towering symbol of colonial Buddhism, causing the leaders of the "movement of Buddhist purification" to take vengeance against the married monks "polluted" by Japanese Buddhism.[86] While this resulted in present-day South Korean Buddhism being mostly represented by the Chogye order, this internal conflict did much to weaken Buddhism in the face of increasingly proselytizing Christianity.

During the Rhee administration, Christianity had consistently extended

83. Park, "Buddhist Purification Movement in Postcolonial South Korea," 132.

84. Park, "Buddhist Purification Movement in Postcolonial South Korea," 135.

85. Park, "Buddhist Purification Movement in Postcolonial South Korea," 135, emphasis added.

86. Hur, "Han Yong'un (1879–1944) and Buddhist Reform in Colonial Korea," 94.

its influence. President Rhee himself was Christian, thus affording "Western missionaries and native churches [with] various types of institutional privileges to spread the Christian message."[87] In supporting the anticommunist ideology of the Rhee administration, many Western Christian leaders and missionaries promoted themselves as spiritual guides and "launched an ideological crusade against the communist force."[88] The government also supported Christianity's crusade against communism by providing preferences on accessing institutions such as the military chaplaincy program.

After Rhee was ousted for political corruption and electoral fraud, and after Park Chung Hee seized power, Christianity continued to grow rapidly as it served the military regime's key goal: modernization. Park, himself a Buddhist, promoted an enlightenment campaign called the "New Village Movement" (*Saemaeul Un-dong*), which "discursively pitched 'science' against 'superstition' and systematically drove people away from their age-old customs throughout the 1970s."[89] Christianity was used to promote this discourse, with Protestant-led enlightenment campaigns focused on creating self-reliant Christian rural communities backed by spiritual evangelism and ideological criticism of communism.[90]

Buddhism also benefited from state-led modernization as the government banned folk religions. Buddhism absorbed the massive exodus from shamanism and other folk religions and "allowed a syncretic coexistence with various folk religious customs."[91]

Both Buddhism and Christianity served the Park regime's anticommunism policies. Buddhists promoted the notion of *Huguik Bulgyo* (state-protecting Buddhism). Christian military chaplaincy was used to translate religion into military strength; until now the military remains the most Christianized sector in society.[92] Religiously inspired patriotism was emphasized by the government, also called the "weaponization of religious faith."[93] "In these religious narratives, the Japanese occupation of Korea, national

87. Lee and Suh, "State Building and Religion," 478.

88. Lee and Suh, "State Building and Religion," 479.

89. Lee and Suh, "State Building and Religion," 491.

90. Ŭn Hŏ, "5–16 kunjŏnggi chaegŏn kungmin undong ŭi sŏnggyŏk" [The characteristic of the state-rebuilding mass campaign under the May 16th military government], *Yŏksa Munje Yŏn'gu* 11 (December 2003): 11–51.

91. Lee and Suh, "State Building and Religion," 492.

92. Lee and Suh, "State Building and Religion," 492.

93. Lee and Suh, "State Building and Religion," 494.

division, and the Korean War followed by the Cold War, were featured as dark forces, as 'external' victimizers under which the Korean nation, church, and individuals suffered."[94]

Against this backdrop, both Christianity and Buddhism have been growing in the postwar era.[95] Currently, religious toleration is high as no single religious community is strong enough to dominate others.[96] Scholars also point to the existence of an external enemy—communism in North Korea—and to secular goals such as a hope for unification as having served common goals for which different religions can bond.[97]

Since the 1960s, there have been sincere efforts at interreligious dialogues between Buddhism and Christianity.[98] One example is the Religious Leaders' Pilgrimage of National Reunification in 1996. This was the first time that religious leaders in Korea—the Buddhists, Catholics, Protestants, and Won Buddhists—gathered, agreeing to establish the Religious Council for National Reconciliation and Reunification. Another recent example is the Asoka Declaration by the Korean *sangha* in 2011. This declaration "fully acknowledges other religions' values as a means of liberation or salvation" and "states that other religions' teachings ought to be respected as much as the Buddha's teachings."[99] Tobŏp, the chair of the Reconciliation and Harmony (*Hwajaeng*, 和諍)[100] Committee, argued that one should move beyond the passive dimension of recognition and tolerance of other religions and learn from their teachings. He claims Christianity and other religions are in partnership with Buddhism toward the Truth. This declaration has been assessed as "Korean Buddhism's most radical and constructive institutional attempt ever to take up the challenge of Christianity."[101] While

94. Jin-Heon Jung, "Some Tears of Religious Aspiration: Dynamics of Korean Suffering in Post-war Seoul, South Korea," *MMG Working Paper* 12, no. 19 (2012): 8.

95. Lee and Suh, "State Building and Religion."

96. Baker, "The Religious Revolution in Modern Korean History."

97. Kim, "Religious Pluralism of Korea Today."

98. Kim, "Religious Pluralism of Korea Today."

99. Bernard Senécal, "Jesus Christ Encountering Gautama Buddha: Buddhist-Christian Relations in South Korea," *Journal of Korean Religions* 5, no. 1 (2014): 90.

100. *Hwajaeng* is a philosophy of Wŏnhyo (617–686), one of the Great Masters of Korean Buddhism. *Hwajaeng* emphasizes "the harmonization of all disputes" and "the harmony of all existences in their mutual non-obstruction." See Young Woon Ko, "Wŏnhyo's Theory of 'Hwajaeng' and Buddhist-Christian Dialogue," *Journal of Korean Religions* 5, no. 1 (2014): 15–26.

101. Senécal, "Jesus Christ Encountering Gautama Buddha," 89–90.

Buddhists were faced with opposition from within the sangha, other religions, especially Catholicism, welcomed this progressive and comprehensive movement by the Korean Buddhists.

CONCLUSION

Buddhism in Korea was long associated with the Japanese occupation, which was established following Japan's victories in interstate wars. Once the Japanese occupation ended and North Korea stood as an opponent, Christianity in its various forms, with its emphasis on modernism and anticommunism, appeared more attractive to many South Koreans. Conflict within the Buddhist sangha, without any counterpart within Christian denominations, also rendered Buddhism less attractive. And without the presence of the Japanese in Korea after World War II, the ethnic dimension was mooted. These findings are consistent with those of Matthias Basedau, Birte Pfeiffer, and Johannes Vüllers associating increased religious conflict with overlapping religious, ethnic, and other societal differences, as we found in Sri Lanka, Myanmar, and Thailand.[102]

A major contribution to the effort of finding pacific substitutes for interreligious violence is the internalization of religious tenets as a substitute for external efforts to proselytize, often violently. The history of the Sufi component in Islam is instructive in this respect: with the rise of Islamic extremism, Sufi leaders have emphasized the role of *jihad* as an internal purification of the individual Muslim's faith.[103] This stands in strong contrast to the extremists' emphasis on *jihad* as a war against "infidel" enemies. Remarkably, Sufi India has been nearly free of domestically originated Islamic terrorism directed at the federal government. This emphasis on the individual interiority of belief is a complement to governmental and religious leaders' efforts to resolve domestic conflicts.[104]

Buddhism too, especially within the Mahāyāna tradition common in

---

102. Matthias Basedau, Birte Pfeiffer, and Johannes Vüllers, "Bad Religion? Religion, Collective Action, and the Onset of Armed Conflict in Developing Countries," *Journal of Conflict Resolution* 60, no. 2 (2016): 226–55.

103. Leon Carl Brown, *Religion and State: The Muslim Approach to Politics* (New York: Columbia University Press, 2000); and Yoginder Sikand, *Muslims in India since 1947: Islamic Perspectives on Inter-Faith Relations* (London: Routledge Curzon, 2004).

104. Nukhet A. Sandal, *Religious Leaders and Conflict Transformation: Northern Ireland and Beyond* (Cambridge: Cambridge University Press, 2017).

East Asia, can foster this pacific form of religion. While this may be more difficult in the Theravadan form, which emphasizes the welfare of the Buddhist community, efforts can be made to incorporate this interiority of belief, as has been done in Cambodia and Laos, where Theravadan Buddhism is dominant and where there are significant pockets of minority religions.

The long duration of insurgencies in the three Southeast Asian countries analyzed in this chapter also distinguishes them from South Korea, whose Communist insurgency ended with the Korean War. The burgeoning Christianity in the South distances this society from the Communist North. Ironically, the Korean War imposed a pacifying clarity on the Korean Peninsula.

The colonial legacy in all three cases of Buddhist-inspired violence against Muslims was crucial. It established a horizontal inequality between groups that persists to this day. After the Japanese departure from South Korea, any legacy of an earlier inequality between pro-Japanese Buddhists and nationalistic Korean Buddhists was overtaken and mooted by the rise of Christianity and the concomitant decline of Buddhism. At the same time, Christian and Buddhist institutions united in their joint efforts to combat the remnants of Japanese colonialism, and any residual influence of atheism from Communist North Korea. Therefore, a psychological distancing from both the Japanese occupiers and the atheistic Communist North became predominant in South Korea. To this day, religious elements in the South, and even more generally in the North, are wary of the unification project.

References

Ali, Ameer. "Muslims in Harmony and Conflict in Plural Sri Lanka: A Historical Summary from a Religio-Economic and Political Perspective." *Journal of Muslim Minority Affairs* 34, no. 3 (2014): 227–42.

Baker, Don. "The Religious Revolution in Modern Korean History: From Ethics to Theology and from Ritual Hegemony to Religious Freedom." *Review of Korean Studies* 9, no. 3 (2006): 249–75.

Bartusevičius, Henrikas. "A Congruence Analysis of the Inequality–Conflict Nexus: Evidence from 16 Cases." *Conflict Management and Peace Science* 36, no. 4 (2019): 339–58.

Basedau, Matthias, Birte Pfeiffer, and Johannes Vüllers. "Bad Religion? Religion, Collective Action, and the Onset of Armed Conflict in Developing Countries." *Journal of Conflict Resolution* 60, no. 2 (2016): 226–55.

Brown, Leon Carl. *Religion and State: The Muslim Approach to Politics*. New York: Columbia University Press, 2000.

Buswell, Robert E. "Buddhism in Korea." In *The Religious Traditions of Asia: Religion, History and Culture*, edited by Joseph M. Kitagawa, 347–54. Abingdon, UK: Routledge, 2002.

Cederman, Lars-Erik, Kristian Skrede Gleditsch, and Halvard Buhaug. *Inequality, Grievances, and Civil War*. Cambridge: Cambridge University Press, 2013.

Croissant, Aurel. "Unrest in South Thailand: Contours, Causes, and Consequences since 2001." *Contemporary Southeast Asia: A Journal of International and Strategic Affairs* 27, no. 1 (2005): 21–43.

DeVotta, Neil. *Blowback: Linguistic Nationalism, Institutional Decay, and Ethnic Conflict in Sri Lanka*. Stanford: Stanford University Press, 2004.

Dorairajoo, Saroja. "Peaceful Thai, Violent Malay (-Muslim): A Case Study of the 'Problematic' Muslim Citizens of Southern Thailand." *Copenhagen Journal of Asian Studies* 27, no. 2 (2009): 61–83.

Fair, C. Christine. *Urban Battle Fields of South Asia: Lessons Learned from Sri Lanka, India, and Pakistan*. Santa Monica, CA: Rand Corporation, 2005.

Forbes, Andrew D. W. "Thailand's Muslim Minorities: Assimilation, Secession, or Coexistence?" *Asian Survey* 22, no. 11 (1982): 1056–73.

Gombrich, Richard F. *Theravada Buddhism: A Social History from Ancient Benares to Modern Colombo*. Abingdon, UK: Routledge, 2006.

Green, Penny, Thomas Macmanus, and Alicia De la Cour Venning. *Countdown to Annihilation: Genocide in Myanmar*. London: International State Crime Initiative, Queen Mary University of London. 2015.

Gubler, Joshua R., and Joel Sawat Selway. "Horizontal Inequality, Crosscutting Cleavages, and Civil War." *Journal of Conflict Resolution* 56, no. 2 (2012): 206–32.

Hŏ, Ŭn. "5–16 kunjŏnggi chaegŏn kungmin undong ŭi sŏnggyŏk'" [The characteristic of the state-rebuilding mass campaign under the May 16th military government]. *Yŏksa Munje Yŏn'gu* 11 (December 2003): 11–51.

Human Rights Watch. *"The Government Could Have Stopped This": Sectarian Violence and Ensuing Abuses in Burma's Arakan State*. New York: Human Rights Watch, 2012.

Hur, Nam-lin. "Han Yong'un (1879–1944) and Buddhist Reform in Colonial Korea." *Japanese Journal of Religious Studies* 37, no. 1 (2010): 75–97.

Ibrahim, Azeem. *The Rohingyas: Inside Myanmar's Hidden Genocide*. Oxford: Oxford University Press, 2016.

Imtiyaz, A. R. M., and Amjad Mohamed-Saleem. "Muslims in Post-War Sri Lanka: Understanding Sinhala-Buddhist Mobilization against Them." *Asian Ethnicity* 16, no. 2 (2015): 186–202.

Jerryson, Michael K. *Buddhist Fury: Religion and Violence in Southern Thailand*. Oxford: Oxford University Press, 2011.

Jung, Jin-Heon. "Some Tears of Religious Aspiration: Dynamics of Korean Suffering in Post-war Seoul, South Korea." *MMG Working Paper* 12, no. 19 (2012): 7–31.

Keown, Damien. *Buddhism: A Very Short Introduction*. Oxford: Oxford University Press, 2013.

Keyes, Charles. "Muslim 'Others' in Buddhist Thailand." *Thammasat Review* 13, no. 1 (2008): 19–42.

Kim, Chong-suh. "Religious Pluralism of Korea Today." *Seoul Journal of Korean Studies* 15, no. 1 (2002): 153–75.

Kim, Hwansoo. "Buddhism during the Chosŏn Dynasty (1392–1910): A Collective Trauma?" *Journal of Korean Studies* 22, no. 1 (2017): 101–42.

Kim, Hwansoo. "'The Future of Korean Buddhism Lies in My Hands': Takeda Hanshi as a Sōtō Missionary." *Japanese Journal of Religious Studies* 37, no. 1 (2010): 99–135.

Kipgen, Nehginpao. "Addressing the Rohingya Problem." *Journal of Asian and African Studies* 49, no. 2 (2014): 234–47.

Ko, Young Woon. "Wŏnhyo's Theory of 'Hwajaeng' and Buddhist-Christian Dialogue." *Journal of Korean Religions* 5, no. 1 (2014): 15–26.

Kyaw, Nyi Nyi. "Islamophobia in Buddhist Myanmar." In *Islam and the State of Myanmar: Muslim-Buddhist Relations and the Politics of Belonging*, edited by Melissa Crouch, 183–210. Oxford: Oxford University Press, 2010.

Langer, Arnim, and Graham K. Brown. "Cultural Status Inequalities: An Important Dimension of Group Mobilization." In *Horizontal Inequalities and Conflict: Understanding Group Violence in Multiethnic Societies*, edited by Frances Stewart, 41–53. Houndmills, Basingstoke, UK, 2008.

Lee, Chengpang, and Myungsahm Suh. "State Building and Religion: Explaining the Diverged Path of Religious Change in Taiwan and South Korea, 1950–1980." *American Journal of Sociology* 123, no. 2 (2017): 465–509.

Leighton, Taigen D. *Faces of Compassion: Classical Bodhisattva Archetypes and Their Modern Expression*. Somerville, MA: Wisdom Publications, 2012.

Liow, Joseph C. *Muslim Resistance in Southern Thailand and Southern Philippines: Religion, Ideology, and Politics*. Washington, DC: East-West Center, 2006.

McCargo, Duncan. "Buddhism, Democracy and Identity in Thailand." *Democratization* 11, no. 4 (2004): 155–70.

Midlarsky, Manus I. "Genocide and Religion in Times of War." In *Oxford Research Encyclopedia of Politics*. Oxford: Oxford University Press, 2019.

Midlarsky, Manus I. *The Killing Trap: Genocide in the Twentieth Century*. Cambridge: Cambridge University Press, 2005.

Midlarsky, Manus I. "Rulers and the Ruled: Patterned Inequality and the Onset of Mass Political Violence." *American Political Science Review* 82, no. 2 (1988): 491–509.

Mojzes, Paul. "The Camouflaged Role of Religion in the War in Bosnia and Herzegovina." In *Religion and the War in Bosnia*, edited by Paul Mojzes, 74–98. Atlanta, GA: Scholars Press, 1998.

Myint-U, Thant. *The River of Lost Footsteps: A Personal History of Burma*. New York: Farrar, Straus and Giroux, 2006.

Østby, Gudrun. "Polarization, Horizontal Inequalities and Violent Civil Conflict." *Journal of Peace Research* 45, no. 2 (2008): 143–62.

Park, Pori. "The Buddhist Purification Movement in Postcolonial South Korea: Restoring Clerical Celibacy and State Intervention." In *Identity Conflicts: Can Violence Be Regulated?*, edited by J. Craig Jenkins and Esther E. Gottlieb, 131–48. Abingdon, UK: Routledge, 2007.

Park, Pori. "Korean Buddhist Reforms and Problems in the Adoption of Modernity during the Colonial Period." *Korea Journal* 45, no. 1 (2005): 87–113.

Sandal, Nukhet A. *Religious Leaders and Conflict Transformation: Northern Ireland and Beyond*. Cambridge: Cambridge University Press, 2017.

Schonthal, Benjamin. "Making the Muslim Other in Myanmar and Sri Lanka." In *Islam and the State in Myanmar: Muslim-Buddhist Relations and the Politics of Belonging*, edited by Melissa Crouch, 234–57. Oxford: Oxford University Press, 2016.

Senécal, Bernard. "Jesus Christ Encountering Gautama Buddha: Buddhist-Christian Relations in South Korea." *Journal of Korean Religions* 5, no. 1 (2014): 81–107.

Sikand, Yoginder. *Muslims in India since 1947: Islamic Perspectives on Inter-Faith Relations*. London: Routledge Curzon, 2004.

Snelling, John. *The Buddhist Handbook: A Complete Guide to Buddhist Schools, Teaching, Practice, and History*. Rochester, VT: Inner Traditions, 1998.

Sørensen, Henrik Hjort. "The Attitude of the Japanese Colonial Government towards Religion in Korea (1910–1919)." *Copenhagen Journal of Asian Studies* 8, no. 1 (1993): 49–69.

Sørensen, Henrik Hjort. "Buddhism and Secular Power in Twentieth-Century Korea." In *Buddhism and Politics in Twentieth-Century Asia*, edited by Ian Harris, 127–52. London: Continuum, 1999.

Southwick, Katherine. "Preventing Mass Atrocities against the Stateless Rohingya in Myanmar: A Call for Solutions." *Journal of International Affairs* 68, no. 2 (2015): 137–56.

Stewart, Frances. "Horizontal Inequality and Conflict: An Introduction and Some Hypotheses." In *Horizontal Inequalities and Conflict: Understanding Group Violence in Multiethnic Societies*, edited by Frances Stewart, 3–24. Houndmills, Basingstoke, UK: Palgrave Macmillan, 2008.

Stewart, Frances, Graham K. Brown, and Arnim Langer, "Major Findings and Conclusions on the Relationship between Horizontal Inequalities and Conflict." In

Horizontal Inequalities and Conflict: Understanding Group Violence in Multiethnic Societies, edited by Frances Stewart, 285–300. Houndmills, Basingstoke, UK: Palgrave Macmillan, 2008.

Stewart, Frances, and Arnim Langer. "Horizontal Inequalities: Explaining Persistence and Change." In *Horizontal Inequalities and Conflict: Understanding Group Violence in Multiethnic Societies*, edited by Frances Stewart, 54–82. Houndmills, Basingstoke, UK: Palgrave Macmillan, 2008.

Stewart, James John. "Muslim–Buddhist Conflict in Contemporary Sri Lanka." *South Asia Research* 34, no. 3 (2014): 241–60.

Tikhonov, Vladimir. "One Religion, Different Readings: (Mis) interpretations of Korean Buddhism in Colonial Korea, Late 1920s-Early 1930s." *Journal of Korean Religions* 1, no. 12 (2010): 163–88.

Walraven, Boudewijn. "Buddhist Accommodation and Appropriation and the Limits of Confucianization." *Journal of Korean Religions* 3, no. 1 (2012): 105–16.

Walton, Matthew J., and Susan Hayward. "Contesting Buddhist Narratives: Democratization, Nationalism, and Communal Violence in Myanmar." *Policy Studies: East-West Center* 71 (2014): 1–56.

Werner, Karel. "Buddhism and Peace: Peace in the World or Peace of Mind?" *International Journal of Buddhist Thought and Culture* 5, no. 1 (2005): 7–33.

Wimmer, Andreas, Lars-Erik Cederman, and Brian Min. "Ethnic Politics and Armed Conflict: A Configurational Analysis of a New Global Data Set." *American Sociological Review* 74, no. 2 (2009): 316–37.

Yang, Key P., and Gregory Henderson. "An Outline History of Korean Confucianism: Part I: The Early Period and Yi Factionalism." *Journal of Asian Studies* 18, no. 1 (1958): 81–101.

Yim, Suk-Jay, Roger L. Janelli, and Dawnhee Yim Janelli. "Korean Religion." In *The Religious Traditions of Asia: Religion, History, and Culture*, edited by Joseph M. Kiragawa, 333–46. Abingdon, UK: Routledge, 2002.

Zin, Min. "Anti-Muslim Violence in Burma: Why Now?" *Social Research: An International Quarterly* 82, no. 2 (2015): 375–97.

Contributors

EDITORS

Simone Raudino is Visiting Professor at the Kyiv School of Economics, Ukraine, and cofounder of the interfaith organization Bridging Gaps, Hong Kong (PhD, International Political Economy, University of Hong Kong, 2014). Since 2005, he has alternated work for governmental organizations—the United Nations, the Democratic Party (United States), and the European Union—with entrepreneurial and academic activities. He is the author of *Development Aid and Sustainable Economic Growth in Africa: The Limits of Western and Chinese Engagements* (Palgrave Macmillan, 2016), and coeditor of *Global Economic Governance and Human Development* (Routledge, 2018).

Patricia Sohn is Associate Professor of Political Science and Jewish Studies at the University of Florida (PhD, Interdisciplinary, Near and Middle East Studies–Modern Middle East Politics, University of Washington, 2001). She has been a Visiting Scholar with the Center for Middle Eastern Studies, Harvard University, and at several additional universities in the United States and internationally. She has received national and collegiate fellowships from institutions including the Social Science Research Council (US), the National Science Foundation (Law and Social Sciences dissertation grant, Woods Co-PI, SES#9906136), the University of Florida, and the University of Washington. She is the author of *Judicial Power and National Politics: Courts and Gender in the Religious-Secular Conflict in Israel* (State University of New York Press, 2017 [2nd ed.; 1st ed., 2008]).

COMMENTATOR

Mark Tessler is Samuel J. Eldersveld Collegiate Professor in the Department of Political Science and Research Professor in the Center for Political Studies, Institute for Social Research, University of Michigan (PhD, Political Science, Northwestern University, 1969). Professor Tessler is one of the very few American scholars to have attended university and lived for extended periods in both the Arab world and Israel. He has conducted field research in Tunisia, Israel, Morocco, Egypt, and Palestine (West Bank and Gaza). He is the author, coauthor, or editor of 15 books, including *A History of the Israeli-Palestinian Conflict* (Indiana University Press, 2009), which has won several national awards; *Islam and Politics in the Middle East: Explaining the Views of Ordinary Citizens* (Indiana University Press, 2015); and *Religious Minorities in Non-Secular Middle Eastern and North African States* (Palgrave MacMillan, 2020). His pioneering research on public opinion in the Arab world includes cofounding and codirecting the Arab Barometer survey project, which has conducted rigorous, nationally representative, and publicly available surveys in Arab countries since 2006. Professor Tessler is cofounder and past president of the American Institute for Maghrib Studies, established in 1984, and a member of the Council of American Overseas Research Centers. He is also cofounder and past president of the Association for Israel Studies, established in 1985.

CONTRIBUTORS

Mutaz Al-Khatib is Associate Professor of Methodology and Ethics at Hamad Bin Khalifa University, Doha, Qatar (PhD, Omdurman Islamic University, 2009). He serves on the editorial boards of *Studies in Islamic Ethics* and *Journal of Islamic Ethics*, both published by Brill. His research interests include ethics and moral philosophy, Islamic law (*fiqh*), and Ḥadīth criticism. He was producer of *Al-Sharia and Life*, Al-Jazeera Television (2004–13), and a founding member of the Intellectual Forum for Innovation (1999). He served as Editor-in-Chief of the "Islam and Contemporary Affairs" section of IslamOnline.net (2003–8). He has been a Visiting Fellow at the Center for Modern Oriental Studies, Berlin (2006), and a Visiting Scholar at the Forum Transregionale Studien, Berlin (2012–13). He is author of *The Textual Critical Approach of Hadith: A Study in the Methods of Traditionalists & Legal Theorists* (Beirut, 2011; in Arabic). He is author or editor of several books, and over 30 academic articles, primarily in Arabic, on hadith criticism and contemporary *fiqh*, the higher objectives of Sharia, and Islamic ethics. He is currently working on a special issue related to Islamic ethics and moral philosophy.

Antoine Arjakovsky is a Research Director at the Collège des Bernardins, Paris, and Founding Director of the Institute of Ecumenical Studies at the Ukrainian Catholic University, Lviv (PhD, History, École des Hautes Etudes en Sciences Sociales, Paris, 2000). He was the Director of the French Collège Universitaire at the Lomonossov University (Moscow). He has published extensively on religion and politics, and the history of Russian religious thought, including *The Way: Religious Thinkers of the Russian Emigration in Paris and Their Journal, 1925–1940* (Notre Dame University Press, 2013), and *What Is Orthodoxy?* (Angelico Press, 2018). His publications have appeared in French, English, Russian, and Ukrainian.

C. K. Martin Chung is Assistant Professor in the Department of Government and International Studies at Hong Kong Baptist University (PhD, European Studies, University of Hong Kong, 2014). Previously, he was Research Assistant Professor of the European Union Academic Programme, Hong Kong, and a lecturer at the University of St. Joseph, Macau. His first monograph, *Repentance for the Holocaust: Lessons from Jewish Thought for Confronting the German Past* (Cornell University Press, 2017), explores the role of religious ideas in German *Vergangenheitsbewältigung* (coming to terms with the past). In *Reconciling with the Past: Resources and Obstacles in a Global Perspective* (Routledge, 2017, coedited with Annika Frieberg), he analyzes the ideas of apology and confession in Chinese and European contexts and the problem of their political application at present. His articles have appeared in *Parliamentary Affairs, International Journal of Transitional Justice* and *Jahrbuch für Politik und Geschichte.*

Abdourahmane (Rahmane) Idrissa is Senior Researcher in the African Studies Center at Leiden University, and Assistant Professor at Leiden University, Netherlands (PhD, Political Science, University of Florida, 2009). He has been a research fellow in the Society, Work and Development Institute, University of the Witwatersrand (2017) and the Global and Economic Governance Program, Oxford University and Princeton University (2009–11). He founded and runs a political economy think tank in Niger. He is published in English and French under the names Rahmane Idrissa and Abdourahmane Idrissa, respectively, in the areas of political economy, political Islam, and political theory. He is the author of *The Politics of Islam in the Sahel: Between Persuasion and Violence* (Routledge, 2017). He is coauthor of: *L'Afrique pour les Nuls*, 2015, and *The Historical Dictionary of Niger* (4th ed.; Scarecrow Press—Rowman & Littlefield, 2012).

Mordechai (Motti) Inbari is Professor of Religion at the University of North Carolina at Pembroke (PhD, Institute of Contemporary Jewry, Department of Modern Jewish History, Hebrew University of Jerusalem, 2006). He is the author of four books: *Jewish Fundamentalism and the Temple Mount*, 2009; *Messianic Religious Zionism Confronts Israeli Territorial Compromises*, 2012; *Jewish Radical Ultra-Orthodoxy Confronts Modernity: Zionism and Women's Equality*, 2016; and *The Making of Modern Jewish Identity: Ideological Change and Religious Conversion*, 2019. He has served as a Visiting Fellow at the University of Florida (2006–7) and at the Schusterman Center for Israel Studies, Brandeis University (2008–9).

Marco Ferraro is a PhD candidate in political science at METU University (Orta Doğu Teknik Üniversitesi, or Middle East Technical University, Ankara, Turkey). His academic interests are related to nationalism, post-truth, and post-secularism. Since 2004, he has been working in international organizations focusing on democracy, rule of law, and communication.

Jonathan Fox (PhD in Government and Politics, University of Maryland, 1997) is the Yehuda Avner Professor of Religion and Politics at Bar Ilan University, Israel, and Director of the Religion and State project (www.religionandstate.org). He has published extensively on various aspects of religion and politics, including government religion policy, discrimination against religious minorities, and religious conflict. His recent books include *Thou Shalt Have No Other Gods before Me: Why Governments Discriminate against Religious Minorities* (Cambridge University Press, 2020), and *An Introduction to Religion and Politics: Theory and Practice* (Routledge, 2018).

Sumin Lee is a Doctoral Candidate in the Department of Political Science, Rutgers University–New Brunswick. Her dissertation is entitled "Gender Justice for Whom: Domestic Accountability for Wartime Sexual Violence." It examines a state's strategic use of accountability mechanisms during and after internal conflicts as a means to win support from domestic and international audiences. Her research interests also include geospatial variations of warring actors' use of violence and of accountability.

Jue Liang is Visiting Assistant Professor in the Religion Department at Denison University. Her current book project, "Conceiving the Mother of Tibet: The Life, Lives, and Afterlife of the Buddhist Saint Yeshe Tsogyel," examines the literary tradition surrounding the matron saint of Tibet, Yeshe Tsogyel, in the fourteenth and fifteenth centuries. It presents the blossoming of this literary tradition in tandem with Nyingma Buddhists' efforts to trace their religious pedigree and define what counts as authentic Buddhism. She is also working on a second project entitled "Who Is a Buddhist Feminist: Theorizing Gender and Religion in Contemporary Tibet." It is a study of the history, discourse, and social effects of the khenmo program, a gender-equality initiative that has been taking place at Tibetan Buddhist institutions in China for the past three decades.

Manus I. Midlarsky is the Moses and Annuta Back Professor of International Peace and Conflict Resolution at Rutgers University, New Brunswick, and Director of the Center for the Study of Mass Violence. His more recent publications are *Origins of Political Extremism: Mass Violence in the Twentieth Century and Beyond* (Cambridge University Press, 2011) and *The Killing Trap: Genocide in the Twentieth Century* (Cambridge University Press, 2005). He also published the edited volume *Handbook of War Studies III: The Intrastate Dimension* (University of Michigan Press, 2009), the third in this Handbook series; as well as articles in journals including the *American Political Science Review, American Journal of Political Science, Journal of Politics, Journal of Conflict Resolution, Journal of Peace Research, International Studies Quarterly, Journal of Personality,* and *Oxford Research Encyclopedia of Politics.* The original *Handbook of War Studies*, 1989, was reissued in the Routledge Revivals Series as were *The Internationalization of Communal Strife*, 1992, and *The Onset of World War*, 1988, reissued in that series, 2014.

Eti Peretz received her PhD from the Department of Political Science, Bar Ilan University, Israel (2018). Her dissertation is entitled "Religious Freedom in Western Democracies Toward Religious Cults and Minorities: 1990–2008."

Pratick Mallick is Assistant Professor of Political Science at Acharya Prafulla Chandra College (government sponsored), West Bengal, India. He has been a Research Assistant in an Indian Council of Social Science Research project in the Department of Humanities and Social Sciences, Indian Institute of Technology–Kharagpur. He is currently working on an edited volume on politics in India.

Wasana Wongsurawat is Associate Professor of modern Chinese history at the Department of History, Faculty of Arts, Chulalongkorn University, Bangkok, Thailand. She specializes in the transnational history of modern China, including the history of the Chinese overseas and China–Southeast Asia interactions. She has been the editor and coeditor of edited volumes, including *Dynamics of the Cold War in Asia: Ideology, Identity and Culture* (Palgrave, 2009) and *Sites of Modernity: Asian Cities in the Transitory Moments of Trade, Colonialism and Nationalism* (Springer, 2016). She is the author of *The Crown and the Capitalists: The Ethnic Chinese and the Founding of the Thai Nation* (University of Washington Press, 2019).

Ibrahim Yahaya Ibrahim is a Consulting Senior Sahel Analyst for the International Crisis Group, Dakar, Senegal (PhD Political Science, University of Florida, 2018). He has been a Fulbright Fellow (2011–13) and a consultant for Freedom House (2016 and 2017). He has given invited papers at institutions including University of North Carolina, Chapel Hill; University of California, Berkeley; USAID, and others. He has worked for Albasar International Foundation (2009–11) and was Research Specialist in the Department of Arabic and Ajami Manuscripts, Institute of Research in Human Sciences, University of Abdou Moumouni Dioffo (2007–9). He is author of the dissertation, *Political Contestation and Islamic Discourse in the Sahel: Comparative Analysis of Mali, Mauritania, and Niger*. He works in French, English, Arabic, Hausa, and Zarma/Songhay.

Index

Action, 7, 137; in relation to Conflict, 50, 140, 164–65; over Contemplation, 47, 82; and Disaster, 349; Governmental versus Religious, 46, 128; Humanitarian, 152, 209, 215–17; Human versus Divine, 174; and Knowledge, 86; Legal, 273; Life-Promoting, 5; Missionary (Da'wa), 210; Mobilizations or Programs for, 131, 157, 166, 205, 218, 283, 285, 404; and Religion and State, 127, 153, 212, 219, 221, 273, 286, 300; Religious Meaning, 218, 220, 286, 288–89; Right, 308; Social, 15; Thought and, 13, 47, 52

Administration, 205; China, 310; Colonial, 320; Court, 230, 248; and NGO, 220; Public, 8, 107; Religious, 249, 385, 398; Religious Schools, 354; Rhee, 401–2; Russian, 107; State, 150; Zelensky, 118

Administrative, Functions, 249; Legality, 238; Political, 46; Religious, 211, 233

Afghan-Soviet War, 153

Africa, 14, 17, 19, 21, 25, 32, 57, 60–61, 147–48, 155, 168–69, 171–72, 205, 215, 220, 240, 320, 321, 327, 329–31, 391

Afterlife, 5, 69, 80, 151, 177, 214

Agrarian, 338, 341, 347, 351, 357, 390

Aid, Humanitarian, 200, 203, 204, 206, 207, 208, 213, 215, 217, 222

Al Ghazali, Abu Hamad, 179

Al Ghazali, Muhammad, 189

Al Qaeda, 18, 55, 202–3, 213, 269

Al Qaradawi, Yusuf, 175, 182, 186, 189

Ancien Régime, 10, 89

Apostasy (*Riddah*), 150–52, 154, 173–74, 176–91, 193–95, 290

Appleby, R. Scott, 52, 54–55, 57

Armenia (Armenians), 59

Asia, 14, 25, 38, 46, 126, 202, 240, 305, 307–8, 311–14, 319–21, 323, 325, 329–30, 340, 345–46, 350, 352, 354, 357, 371, 383, 386, 390–97, 405

Ataturk, Mustafa Kemal, 19, 58

Authority, 10; Divine, 4, 68; Ecclesiastical, 102, 135; Jurists,180; Legal, 243; and Meaning, 69; and Ottoman Millet, 227; and Privatized Religion, 13; Rabbinical, 238, 241–42, 268, 272–73; Religion and Conflict, 51; Religion and State, 15, 48, 218–19, 237, 244, 274; and Scriptures (Veda), 308; Spiritual and Temporal, 11, 45–47, 135; and State Sovereignty, 211

Balkans, 17, 20, 59, 202

Barak, Aharon, 229–30, 245, 252, 259–63, 267–77

Barzilai, Gad, 228, 233–34, 246, 253

Belief (in God), 4–5, 20–22, 152, 187, 305; Anti-Science, 91; Ascetic, 82; Believer, 55; Believers, statistics, 49; Change in, 191; and Cognitive Dissonance, 287; and Conflict, 50, 161, 386; and Consociational, 143; and Customs, 54; False, 185, 351 (on Nietzsche and False Belief, *see* Nietzsche); and Falsified, 231, 286; and Folk, 309, 338; Foreign, 363; Freedom of (*see* Freedom of Religion); and Interiority, 312, 381, 404–5; and Ireland, 124, 132, 140; Loss of or lack of (and Disbelief), 98, 181, 183, 187–88, 194; and Markets, 106; Messianic, 294; Millenarian, 350; and Peace, 61; Populism, 71, 99, 110; and Practices, 305, 338; and Prophecy, 230, 286; Religious, 14, 31, 45, 188, 210, 213, 214–15, 252, 282, 291, 309, 311; Rights, 235; and Sectarianism, 136–37; and Secularization Thesis, 13, 31; Syncretic, 341, 351; Systems, 47, 49, 51–52, 339; and Values, 97, 207

Benoist, Alain de, 47

Bible, 49, 53, 103, 325
Blueprint, 7, 16, 128–29, 131, 142–43. *See also* Clifford Geertz
Bosnia and Herzegovina, 57, 388
Buddhism, 25, 46, 49, 53, 305, 307–12, 326, 339, 340–41, 348–49, 353, 360–77, 380, 382–84, 386–88, 390–91, 394–405, 415
Burkina Faso, 155, 162, 168, 171

Candide, 6
Case Study (Case Studies), 23–25, 67–68, 71, 147, 152, 154, 157, 201, 206, 212, 287–88, 392
Catholic (Catholicism), 13, 20, 40, 59, 68, 72–73, 91–92, 99–100, 106, 116–17, 120–25, 127–35, 138, 140, 310–11, 318, 339–40, 383, 388, 394, 403–4, 413
Causal, 25, 36, 38–40, 42–43, 52, 60; Causality, 249; Causation, 45; Relationship(s), 17, 110
Cavanaugh, William, 52
China, 14, 56, 58–59, 62, 305, 309–12, 332, 337, 339–42, 344–58, 360–62, 364, 366, 368–72, 375–77
Chinese Communist Party (CCP), 309–10, 337–39, 341–42, 347, 349–52, 354–58
Christianity, 4, 9, 22, 25, 38, 46, 49, 57, 67, 71, 78, 80, 86, 91–92, 114, 117, 120–23, 124, 129, 131, 134, 158, 185–86, 188, 193, 240, 312, 317, 326, 339, 369, 370, 380, 384, 389, 394, 396, 401–4, 405
Church (Churches), 3, 13, 15, 17, 20, 45–48, 57, 59, 67, 71, 91–93, 99–102, 117, 120, 122–33, 134–38, 140–43, 169, 246, 327, 339, 340, 370, 398, 400, 402–3
Church of Satan, 49
Civil Society, 11, 46, 166, 171, 221, 328 342, 392; and Democratic Institutions, 109; Global, 216; National, 209
Cleavages, 20, 73, 93, 125, 136
Cold War, 14, 16, 50, 55–56, 62, 139, 269–70, 400, 403
Communal, 25, 67, 73, 105, 121, 135, 228, 234–35, 241, 252–53, 327–28, 389; Intercommunal, 73, 120–21, 123–24, 126, 133, 389; and Legal Culture, 233
Comparative, 12, 16–18, 25, 36–37, 40–42, 53, 82, 121, 162, 171, 203, 239–40, 246, 261
Conceptual (Conceptualization), 7, 15, 23–24, 31, 35, 40, 42, 46, 48, 68, 70, 77, 80, 85, 88, 92, 94, 113, 148, 153, 190, 209, 213, 222, 232, 381
Confidence, and Faith and Reason, 115; Methodological, 23; Political, 109
Conflict, Religion and, 45, 48, 51–52, 55–58, 60
Confucian (Confucianism), 40, 312, 340–41, 343, 352, 366, 396; Education, 345; "Islamo-Confucian Bloc," 17; New, 376; State Religion, 312, 395; and Syncretism, 309, 349–50
Consociational, 125, 143
Contemplation (Contemplate, Contemplative), 47, 82, 194
Court (Courts), 231, 240, 245, 290; Chosŏn Court, 395; Religious, 227; Sharia Law and, 153, 156, 158–59, 162, 168–70, 175–76, 195. *See also* High Court of Justice
Culture (Cultural), 7, 16–17, 34, 52, 265, 284, 307; Buddhist, 375, 395; Chinese, 340, 370, 374, 376; and Community, 233; Confucian, 343; Culture Wars, 22, 236; Eastern, 373; and Essentializing Arguments, 41; European, 97; Hindu, 322–23, 325, 332; as Idol(s), 133; and Korea, 396, 399; and Liberalism, 111; Local, 154, 357; Malay, 392; and Meaning, 80; and Modernization Theory, 35, 42; National, 92, 329; Peasant, 310; Political, 17, 234; and Populism, 108; and Religiosity, 39; Religious (Religion), 104, 214; and Religious Authorities, 48; Sunni, 163; and Synthesis, 154; U.S. 394; Western, 218, 373

Daoism, 309–10, 339–41, 348–49, 353. *See also* Taoism
Da'wa, 191, 204, 213
Democide, 58
Democracy (Democracies), 8, 16–18, 25, 148, 166, 172, 239, 246, 263–65, 328; and Buddhism, 392–93; French Model, 165; and Gender, 39–41, 166; India, 314, 332; and Islam, 41, 166; Liberal, 13, 22, 163, 165, 264; Middle East and North Africa Attitudes, 148; and Minorities, 133; and Moral Framework, 56; Multiparty, 163; and Postliberal(ism), 111; Religion, 9, 116, 118, 229, 259–60, 267; and Sharia, 162; (as) Western, 7, 108
Descartes, René, 48, 112

Diaspora (Diasporas), 100, 152, 227, 266, 305, 314, 316, 318–20, 323–24, 327–28, 331, 340
Discourse (Discourses), 54, 75, 87, 90–93, 95, 102, 116, 149, 207, 211, 216–17, 219, 262, 402; and Genealogy, 48, 54; Gnostic, 72, 104; Hindutva, 314, 324; Interchurch, Cross-Denominational, or Ecumenical, 140, 142; Juridical (Fiqh), 190; Legal, Domestic or International, 228; and Liberalism, 87–88; Marginalized, 86; National, 59, 161, 162–63, 332; Quranic, 175, 186; Religious, 60, 76, 94, 99, 156, 169, 210, 366; Scientific and Transnational, 363
Disengagement, 230, 281–82, 286, 289, 290–91, 293–95, 300
Dissonance, Cognitive, 230–31, 281–82, 287, 300–301
Divine (Divinity), 4, 7, 26, 84, 230, 285–86, 288, 308; Action, 174; Authority (Europe), 68, 133; and Hinduism, 305, 306; Humanity, 72, 107, 113–14; Intervention, 72, 135; Principles, 56; Rebirth, 112; and Revelation, 192; Right of Kings, 10–11, 46; Rulings, 190; Spark, 295; Will, 176; Wrath (or Judgment), 55, 132
Domination (Dominating), 15, 47, 86, 90, 106, 116, 130, 143, 149, 160, 175, 202, 217–18, 346, 387, 403
Durkheim, Émile, 8, 12; anomie and suicide with urbanization and decreasing salience of religion as social bond, 12
Dynasty, 340; Chosŏn, 395; Han, 344–45, 357, 375; Koryo, 312, 394; Ming, 344–46; Qing, 344–48; Yi, 312, 395; Yuan, 309, 362; Zhou, 62

Eastern Europe, 14, 17, 20, 57, 59, 202, 240, 382, 388
Ecumenical (Ecumenicalism), 93, 99, 116–18, 124–25, 142, 220; Council(s), 100
Elites, 54, 67, 72, 75, 89, 92, 93, 105, 107–8, 150, 205, 310; Knowledge, 87–88, 90, 94–95, 320; Merchant, 149; Urban (Cosmopolitan), 109
Emergentist, 72, 115. *See also* Ferry, Jean-Marc
Enlightenment, Buddhist, 308, 360, 362, 367, 376, 402; Buddhist-Feminine, 376, 377; Liberal, 7, 52, 56, 84, 86–88; Post-Enlightenment, 7, 52, 232, 240; Protestant-Led, 402
Epistemology (Epistemologies, Epistemological), 13–15, 17–18, 45, 48, 51, 55–56, 76, 307
Equality, 32, 39–40, 56, 93, 174, 229, 238–40, 247, 250, 296–97, 332, 373, 377; and Inequality, 61, 201, 246, 381–82, 405
Esoteric, 49, 67, 70–71, 159, 326, 376
Esposito, John, 18, 239
Essence (Essences), 67–68, 70, 83, 86, 273, 315–16, 325
Ethic, 6, 17, 69, 116; Ethical, 46–47, 92, 95, 115–16, 193, 195, 216, 316; Ethico-Legal, 190; Ethics, 46, 52, 94, 115–16, 150, 175, 367, 369, 377, 395
Ethos, 25, 54, 137, 142; and Gandhi, 327; Greek, 78; and Hindutva, 316
Europe (European), 8, 10, 12, 20, 25, 67–71, 76, 85, 87–89, 91, 94–95, 97–98, 105, 110, 115, 117, 118, 191, 265, 315, 321, 324, 341; Discourse(s), 86; (Normative) Imagination, 70, 73; Wars of Religion 14, 380
European Union, 76, 86–87, 90, 93, 108
Experience, Religious, 45

Fascism, 49, 109–10; Protofascist or Quasi-Fascist, 81, 111
Ferry, Jean-Marc, 72, 115. *See also* Emergentist
Fiqh, 150–51, 173–74, 179–80, 182, 190–93, 195
Folk Religion (Folk Religions), 339–40; Beliefs and Practices, 309, 338, 341; Customs, 402; Folklore, 393; Knowledge or Wisdom, 338, 353; Misunderstandings within, 365
France, 10, 18, 20–21, 92, 108, 161, 240
French Revolution, 8, 14, 186
Fundamentalism (Fundamentalist), 49, 71, 98, 110, 117, 209, 294, 299

Galtung, Johan, 50–51
Gandhi, Mohandas Karamchand (Mahatma) (Gandhiji), 306–7, 313, 326–28, 331
Geertz, Clifford, 7, 14; 'Model of' and 'Model for,' 7; Blueprint, 7, 16
Gender, 52, 215, 217, 221, 232, 237, 241, 260, 329, 366–67; and Equality, 39–40, 93, 250, 377; and Feminine, 367, 377; and Identity, 17
Genealogy, 48, 54, 68–69, 75–79, 82–86, 90, 94–95, 109

Genocide, 58–59, 380, 382, 385, 388, 390–91
Germany, 3, 20, 58–59, 122, 240, 382
"God is Dead," 3, 7, 9, 13, 19, 26, 67, 79, 121; "Death of God," 4–10, 12, 14, 19, 31, 68–70, 73, 77, 85, 91, 96
God, and Creation, 71, 129; the Father, 72, 103, 118; and Heavens, 71–72, 102
Greek (Greeks), 59, 62, 80; Greek Catholics, 100; Liturgy, 99; Moral Concepts, 68–69, 77–79, 131; Virtues, 78
Growth, Personal, 6, 311
Guénon, René, 46–47
Gumi, Abubakar, 148, 157–62, 166, 169

Hadd (legal punishment), 173, 182, 187, 188
Harmony, 385, 387–88, 403; lack thereof (Disharmony), 113
Healing, 49, 59, 99–100, 117
Hermeneutics, 56
High Court of Justice, 227–30, 236–39, 241–54, 259, 262–63, 267–68, 270–71, 274–76, 296; Justices, 236–38, 245, 261, 272, 275, 277
Hinduism, 25, 49, 305–7, 314–18, 320, 322, 325–26, 328, 331–32
Hindutva, 306, 314, 316–18, 320, 322–23, 327–28, 330–32
Ḥirābah. *See* Rebellion
Hobbes, Thomas, 11, 56, 110
Holocaust, 58–59, 62
Homogenization, 7; Homogeneous, 59
Hóngmén (Hóngzi), 346
Humanitarian, 148, 152–53, 200–220, 350
Humility, 68, 79–80
Huntington, Samuel, 17, 34, 211; and Max Weber, 17–18
Hurd, Elizabeth, 8, 10, 15–16, 25, 74, 120, 122–23
Hypothesis (Hypotheses), 24, 32, 37–38, 40–42, 381

Ideas, 13, 33, 42, 47, 50, 56, 67, 69–71, 76, 80, 83, 98, 127, 147–48, 154, 157, 188, 207, 214, 216, 234, 238, 271, 287, 300, 307, 309, 315, 317, 320–21, 341, 396; Ideational, 14, 25, 70
Identity (Identities), 13, 14, 17–18, 20, 32, 46, 50, 52–53, 60–62, 69, 71–72, 75–76, 92–93, 95, 111, 115, 128, 133, 152, 189, 191, 204, 207, 210–11, 213–14, 216–17, 220, 227–29, 233–35, 237, 265, 281, 287, 306–7, 314–15, 320, 332, 347, 361, 367, 382, 386, 389, 392, 393–94, 399
Ideology, 6, 15, 50, 52, 68, 70, 76, 85–91, 95, 108–9, 116, 131, 148, 156, 159, 160, 164, 204, 207, 218, 239, 269, 281–82, 284, 289, 301, 314, 322, 329–30, 341, 344–45, 357, 392, 394, 400, 402
Ijtihad, 173, 186
Illusions (and Normative Thought or Theology), 48, 105, 110, 374
Immanent (Immanence), 71, 98, 115
India, 218–19, 240, 306–7, 313–32, 371, 373, 385–86, 389, 404
Inequality. *See* Equality
Institutions (Institutional), 6, 13–15, 19–22, 24–25, 34–36, 40, 46–49, 51–52, 55, 68–72, 75, 88, 91–95, 102, 105–7, 109, 124–25, 127, 147, 150, 154, 158, 160, 163, 170, 202–4, 209–12, 227–28, 231, 234–36, 239–41, 243, 246, 248, 254, 260, 264, 267, 270, 272–77, 283, 289, 295–96, 306, 308, 310–11, 352, 354, 361–63, 366–68, 373, 377, 386–87, 397, 402–3, 405
Interchurch. *See* Interfaith
Interfaith (Interchurch), 100, 120, 123–37, 140–43
International Humanitarian Organizations (IHOs), 152–53, 200–213, 215–17, 220–21
International Islamic Relief Organization (IIRO), 152, 201, 212–16
International Relations, 8, 10, 13–15, 22, 25, 31, 120, 284
Ireland, 20, 68, 72–74, 120–37, 140–43
Islam (Islamic), 15, 17–18, 20, 22–23, 25, 32, 37–42, 46, 49, 57, 71, 118, 147–89, 191–95, 200–222, 235, 239–40, 306, 310, 319, 325, 331, 339, 384, 387, 389–90, 393–94, 412
Islamic Relief Worldwide, 152
Islamist, 17, 57, 148–49, 153, 163, 165, 168, 204–6, 218–20
Italy (Italian), 76, 79, 92–93, 105, 240, 316

Jihad (Jihadism, Jihadist), 71, 97, 148, 153, 155–57, 170–72, 175–76, 188–89, 194, 201–2, 204, 404
Judaism, 17, 25, 32, 38, 57, 71, 185, 193, 227, 231, 244, 259–60, 262–68, 272–74
Juergensmeyer, Mark, 8, 55, 60, 269–70

Juncture (Junctures) (Historical), 13, 25
Just War, 56, 391

Khomeini, Ayatollah Ruhollah, 19
Knowledge (Economies of, Philosophical, Religious, as a Value), 5, 11–12, 46–47, 51–52, 67, 69–70, 76, 83–88, 90–91, 95, 98, 105, 153, 161, 214, 238, 281, 287, 293, 308, 319, 327, 338, 364, 371–72, 375, 398

Laic (Laïc), 71, 74, 98, 166, 306; Laicism, 71, 120, 123; Laïciste, 165; Laicists, 122; Laïcité, 92–93, 163, 167–68, 170
Larung Gar, 360–67, 369, 376–77
Latin America, 14, 19
Legitimacy, 14, 47, 56, 75, 102, 245, 266, 269, 394; Traditional Sources, 11, 233, 371
Leviathan, 11, 56
Liberal (Liberalism, Liberalization) 49, 72, 85, 91, 114, 148, 156–57, 242, 267; Arts and Sciences, 371; Democracy, 13, 22, 79, 90, 95, 165, 264; Economic, 112; Elites, 75–76; Enlightenment, 7; Freedoms and Rights, 163, 166, 169; Globalization, 85, 87–88, 90, 94–95; and Hindutva, 316, 318; Law, 168, 233–35, 239, 240; Myth, 106; Neoliberal (*see* Neoliberal); Political, 306; Postliberal, 107, 116; Religion, 22, 49, 86, 118, 401; and Secularism, 260; Ultraliberal, 107, 110
Liberating, Mysticism, 288; Secular Neutrality, 15
Liberty, 56, 175; of Conscience, 118; and Hindutva, 306, 316; Human, 114; Religious, 232, 234–35, 240
Locke, John, 11, 56
Logos, Textual, 54

Machiavelli, Nicolò, 56, 110
Maghreb, 17, 21, 33, 152
Mahmood, Saba, 22, 228, 232–36, 253
Mali, 155, 157, 162, 168, 170–71, 221
Manchu, 344–46, 362, 366; Manchuria, 399
Manichean, 55, 93–94
Maqasid, 151, 175–76, 192, 195–96
Martin, David, 13
Marx, Karl, 8; 12, 104–5, 309, 341, 351; Marxism, 49, 86, 88, 337, 357
Masonry, Masonic, 49
Material (Materialism, Materialist), 85, 105, 117, 214, 369; Analysis, 25; Biographical, 364; Conditions, 34; Disciplines, 70; and Empirical, 25; Exclusion, 20; Leninist (Atheist), 338; Philosophies, 110; Precedent, 9; Production, 373; Realm, 283, 375; Resources, 82, 210; and Spiritual Dialectic, 68; Strategies, 68; Violence, 71
Meaning, 5, 10, 33, 47, 69–71, 79–80, 82–85, 93, 112, 148, 151, 153, 156–57, 160, 174–75, 186, 191, 228, 253, 261, 266, 271, 306, 311, 314, 331, 344, 368–69, 374, 383
Mecca (Meccan), 54, 183–84, 194; Historical (Pagan) Elites, 54
Messianic, 111, 230–31, 281–89, 291, 293, 299–300
Metanoia, 131. *See also* Greek Moral Concepts
Metaphysical, 45, 51, 55–57, 62, 69, 77, 79–81, 84–85, 90–91, 94, 97, 316; Metaphysics, 51, 69–70, 72, 79–81, 83–84, 94, 306, 314
Method (Methods, Methodology, Methodological), Analytical, Juridic, and Research, 23–25, 41–43, 45, 48–51, 53, 56–57, 62, 75, 77, 83, 179, 181, 190–92, 195, 209, 271, 287, 316, 371–72; of Rationalization, 12, 287–88, 294
Metropolitan, 20, 100. *See also* Urban
Middle Class(es), 12, 150, 162, 163–65
Middle East and North Africa (MENA), 14, 16–19, 25, 32, 40–41, 60, 147–48, 152–54, 171, 204–5, 227, 232, 234, 236, 239, 246, 284, 380, 388
Millenarian (Millenary), 108, 117, 339, 342, 349–50, 357
'Model of' and 'Model for.' *See* Geertz, Clifford
Modernization (Modernize, Modernism), 7–8, 12, 16, 20, 31–36, 39, 42, 307; and Evolutionary Social Theories (e.g., Progress), 12–13; Theory, 16, 31–35, 39, 42
Modesty, 68
Monastery, Sera, 373; System in Chinese Buddhism, 400; Zhaouje, 375
Monastic, 360–61, 365–67, 376–77, 398, 401
Mongol, 312, 346, 362, 366, 394
Monotheism, 305–6, 316, 319, 325
Moral (Morality), 5, 9, 45, 47, 76, 83–85, 89, 93–95, 123, 128, 141, 164, 169, 173, 190, 193–95, 218, 239, 306, 316, 324, 341, 353, 373, 394; Arenas of, 68; and Asceticism,

Moral (Morality) (*continued*)
76; Certitude, 4; Dialectic, 90; Good, 69; Greek (*see* Greek Moral Concepts); Justification(s), 57; Morality, Herd, 6; Neomoralism, 117; Philosophy, 69; Populist, 75, 91; Questions, 4; Religious, 6, 45, 47, 214, 309, 312; Superiority, 56; System, 79; Wars or Struggles regarding, 62, 69, 75, 90
Mujahedeen, 153
Muslim Brotherhood, 152, 201, 217–20; Egyptian Charitable Branch, 152
Myanmar, 53, 311, 330, 380, 382–85, 389, 390–92, 394, 404
Mystical, 51, 287–88, 294, 298; Mysticism, 114, 287–88. *See also* Sufi (Sufism)
Myth (Myths), 47, 52, 76, 81, 94–96, 102, 104, 106; of the Cavern, 83; and Girardet, Raoul, 104; Mythical (Mythological), 92, 108–9; Mythologize, 84; Political, 91

Narrative (Narratives), 15, 60, 79, 116, 125, 132, 206, 346, 364; Buddhist, 365, 368, 389–91; Hindutva, 327, 330–31; Laicist or Secularist, 120, 123; Liberal, 106; Nationalist or Protonationalist, 55, 327, 345; and Populism or Neopopulism, 71, 87, 91, 94; Religious, 102, 104, 230, 282, 402; Revolutionary, 351
Neoliberal (Neoliberals), 68, 71–72, 88, 99, 105–6, 108, 112, 205
Neo-Personalist, 72, 115–16
Neo-Positive, 25
Nietzsche, Friedrich, 4, 7, 9–12, 19, 67–69, 73, 83, 86, 121; False Belief, 9–10; and Genealogy (*see* Genealogy); Herd Madman, 3, 26; Material-Historical Account, 8, 10, 12, 26; Meaningful Existence, 5; Mentality (Last Man), 6–7; and Metaphysics, 70, 77, 79–81, 84; Nihilism, 4–6, 9, 81, 83; and Populism, 68, 89–91, 95; Priestly Type, 67, 69, 78–81, 95; Prototype of Man, 67–69, 77–80, 82, 90, 94; and Religion (Belief, Decline, Otherworldly, Systems, Value), 4–5, 10–12, 69, 75; and Secularism, Secularization, 8, 10, 19, 76; Self-Deification, 6–7, 70; Tragedy, 5, 9, 77; Übermensch, 5–7, 67, 70; Warrior Type, 69
Niger, 148–49, 150, 155, 157–72, 212
Nigeria, 148–49, 155–62, 168–71, 205, 240
Nihilism. *See* Nietzsche, Friedrich: Nihilism
Non-Governmental Organizations (NGOs), 200, 203–6, 209, 213, 215, 217
Normative, 7–8, 10, 16, 20, 22, 26, 31, 35, 40, 48, 54–56, 62, 68–70, 74, 79, 94, 234, 237–38, 327
North Africa. *See* Middle East and North Africa (MENA)
Noumena, 71, 98

Occult, 321; Occultism, 49
Ochs, Peter, 52
Omar, A. Rashied, 57
Ontology (Ontological), 4, 9, 11–12, 18, 56, 81; Ontological(ly), 15
Organizations, Social (Societal), 11, 47, 56
Overman. *See* Nietzsche, Friedrich: Übermensch

Pagan (Pagans), 54, 182, 187; Paganism, 49, 193
Pahlavi, Reza Shah, 46
Parties, Religious, 15, 74, 241, 243, 283–84
Perfection (Perfect, Religious Context), 5, 292–93, 327,369, 371–72
Philosophy (Philosopher), 4, 5, 7, 10–11, 25, 45, 68–70, 81–82, 94, 112, 114, 208, 261, 282, 285, 286, 306, 317, 322, 327, 331, 403
Political Religions, 69–70, 77, 86, 91, 94–95, 264, 285
Pope John-Paul II, 117, 138–39
Popular, 161; Populism, Religious, 91, 95; Populist, 67, 68, 75–77, 79, 86–90, 92–96, 99, 107, 116–17; Populists, 69, 70–72; and Religious Movement(s), 70
Postconflict Societies, 59
Post-Soviet. *See* Soviet Union: Post-Soviet
Power, 12–13, 45, 50, 54, 71–72, 75, 78, 80–82, 84, 97, 103, 107–10, 114, 126, 128, 133, 143, 216, 220, 249, 259, 268, 270, 288, 293, 309, 312, 339, 342, 345, 351, 370, 392, 397, 402; Distribution of, 73–74; Explanatory, 31, 38–40, 43, 369; Global, 90; of Love and Compassion, 376; of Markets, 106; Political, 5, 10–11, 102, 326, 331; Relations, 48; Secular, 11; Separation of, 147; State versus Religious, 150, 157, 159, 190, 227, 243, 267; Supernatural, 353; Temporal, 4, 46–47

Preferences, 242, 402
Primordial, Fears, 5
Process (Processes) 6–9, 11–12, 14, 16, 19, 32–35, 39, 46, 48, 52, 69–70, 73–74, 76–77, 81, 88, 90, 94, 104, 111, 121–23, 129, 140–41, 165, 168, 179, 191, 201, 203, 210, 227, 245, 270, 282, 285–86, 288–89, 291–92, 297, 301, 309, 312, 315, 332, 372, 382, 401
Protestant (Protestantism, Protestants), 17, 40, 59, 68, 72–73, 100, 112, 116, 120–25, 129–30, 132–35, 140–41, 240, 310, 339, 380, 394, 400, 402–3
Protests, 17, 20, 140, 167–70, 203–4, 236, 251, 314, 332, 355
Prussia, 3, 10
Psychology, 4, 5, 10, 35, 82, 230, 281–82, 301, 324
Public Opinion, 17–18, 32, 100, 148, 168–69, 172, 412
Punjab, 317, 321, 323
Pure Science, 23

Qi Gong, 309–10, 312, 340, 352–54, 356–57
Quran (Koran), 53, 151 152 175–82, 186, 188, 191–92, 194, 210, 213, 218, 316, 325, 396; Quranic, 151–52, 175–76, 178–79, 181, 192, 316

Ramadan, 188, 189, 215
Rational (Rationality), 12, 70, 86–87, 98, 105, 107–8, 110–11, 114–15; and Antirationalist, 67, 70, 90, 94–95; and Irrational or non-rational, 10, 86, 96, 104, 301; Rationalism (Rationalist), 7, 10, 52, 86, 96; Rationalize, 190
Real, the, 69
Rebellion (Rebellions), 11, 55, 59, 191, 269–70, 315, 341, 342–43, 348, 350, 351, 357; Ḥirābah, 191; Peasant Rebellions, 341–42, 357, 396; Taiping Rebellion, 348; Tonghak Peasant Rebellion, 396
Reconciliation and Harmony Committee, 403
Redeem (Redeemer), 285, 293–94
Redemption, 230, 281, 285, 288, 291, 293, 297
Regime Change, 10
Religion, 45–46; Freedom of, 150–52, 175–76, 177, 189, 228–29, 232, 234, 252–53, 268, 273–74, 276; and Identity, 20; Majority, 331, 344; Minority, 311; in Politics, 15; Popular, 46; Regulation of, 19; Separation from State, 18; State Religions, Statistics, 19; Strong, 54–56; Syncretic (Syncretism), 25, 305, 307, 309–10, 312, 327, 337, 340–42, 348–56, 356–58, 402; Weak, 55–56
Religiosity, 18–22, 36, 39, 41, 67, 91, 94, 207, 209, 210, 216, 229, 320
Renaissance, 56, 214, 315
Revelation (Revelatory), 114, 129, 192, 305, 362
Revival, Buddhist, 312, 360–61, 396; Hindu, 318–19, 321–22, 329; Islamic, 205, 235; National (Domestic) Prophetic/Messianic, 276, 283, 289; Religious, 152; Revivalism, 201
Revolution, Bolshevik or Russian. *See* Russian (Bolshevik) Revolution
Revolutions of 1848, 10
Rhetoric, 14, 68, 72, 90, 297, 386
Riddah. *See* Apostasy
Riots, 20, 168–70, 234. *See also* Rebellion
Romanticism, 12, 56, 103–4
Rousseau, Jean Jacques, 11, 56
Rural, 8, 126, 220, 310, 328, 338–39, 348, 351–52, 393, 402
Russia (Russian), 20, 58, 72, 99–100, 102, 104–5, 107–9, 113, 117, 276, 324, 357, 397
Russian (Bolshevik) Revolution, 324, 357

Sadaqa, 152, 201, 207
Sahel, 147–48, 152, 155–58, 162, 168, 171–72, 202
Salafist (Salafists, Salafism), 148–50, 156–58, 162–72
Savarkar, Damodar, 307, 315–18, 320, 322–23, 326, 331
Science, The Gay, 3, 8
Scientism, 111
Scientology, 49
Sectarian (Sectarianism, Sectarianized), 58, 73–74, 120, 122–24, 132, 135–38, 140–42, 207, 220, 390
Secular (Secularism), 6, 8–11, 14–20, 22, 25, 31–32, 46–48, 52, 55, 67–70, 73–74, 76–77, 84, 86–87, 92–93, 95, 97–98, 101, 110, 114, 117, 121–23, 127–29, 134–35, 142–43, 147, 149, 153, 160, 170–71, 190, 205, 215–17, 219, 227–45, 252–54, 259–60, 262, 265–69, 271–72, 277, 282–86, 289–91, 294–95, 297–99, 300, 306–7, 310–11, 363, 365, 377, 395, 398, 403;

Secular (Secularism) (*continued*)
Christian, 15, 73–74, 120–21, 123, 125, 128–29, 131, 140, 141–42; Forces (Secularists), 10, 15, 17, 19, 164–65, 167–68, 219, 242, 254, 267; Secularization, 7–8, 10, 15, 16, 18, 22, 25, 32–33, 35–36, 67, 73–74, 76, 94, 120–23, 125, 128–29, 131, 134, 140–42, 158,161, 163, 165–66–167, 170, 186, 206, 210–11, 227, 240, 295, 332; Secularization Thesis, 8, 12–14, 16–17, 234, 300
Secularization Thesis. *See* Secular-Secularization Thesis
Shaman (Shamanism), 49, 396, 402
Shamgar, Meir, 229, 259–60, 268, 270, 272–77
Sharia (al-Shari'a), 153, 156, 158–59, 162, 168–70, 175–76, 182, 192, 195, 196. *See also* Court: Sharia Law; Democracy: Sharia
Shaw, Tamsin, 10
Social Justice, 56, 219, 269
Social Movement (Social Movements), 7, 49, 147–48, 153–54, 237, 238, 246, 250, 301, 347
Sodargye, Khenpo, 364–67, 370, 372, 374, 376
Solidarity, 12, 107, 180, 205, 214–15, 219, 281, 288, 329
South Korea, 311, 380, 382–85, 394, 399–401, 403–5
Sovereignty, 11, 47, 108, 129, 232, 234, 314, 350, 397; Popular, 75, 307, 317, 319–21
Soviet Union, 14, 16–17, 20, 58, 86–87, 102, 202, 205, 244, 337, 351; Post-Soviet, 108
Spirit (Spirituality, Spiritual), 6, 11, 17, 21, 45–47, 49, 51–52, 67–70, 72, 101–2, 111–113, 115, 129–30, 141, 158–59, 172, 205–7, 214, 259, 283, 285, 287–89, 292, 294–95, 311, 327, 328, 340, 344, 348, 351, 353, 362, 364, 367, 369–70, 372–76, 383, 394–95, 398, 402; and Monism, 316
Sri Lanka, 53, 311, 380, 382–90, 394
State, Contract, 10–11, 14, 56; Controlled (Religious Institutions), 15; Islamic, 148, 157, 164, 170, 189; Modern, 9, 14, 36, 115, 227, 240, 270, 306; Power, 12, 46, 150, 159, 190, 227; *Superiorem Non Recognoscens*, 11–12
Sufi (Sufism), 149, 159–62, 167, 170, 174, 404
Super Men. *See* Nietzsche, Friedrich: Übermensch
Superior Men. *See* Nietzsche, Friedrich: Übermensch
Swaggart, Jimmy, 49
Symbol (Symbols), 55, 71, 76, 79, 92, 96–97, 142, 192, 229, 264, 328, 401; and Populist, 91, 95
Symbolic, 393; Arena, 322; Gestures, 343
Syncretic (Syncretism). *See* Religion: Syncretic

Taiping Rebellion. *See* Rebellion
Taoism (Taoist), 72, 114. *See also* Daoism
Taxonomy (Taxonomies), 25, 152–53, 200, 206, 209
Taylor, Charles, 97
Teleology (Teleological), 55
Temporal (Temporality), 4, 11, 33, 45–47,49, 51–52, 57, 151, 177, 181–82, 190–91
Thailand, 53, 240, 311, 380, 382–85, 391–94, 404
Theocracy, 46, 189, 253; Theocratic, 25; Theocratic State, 148, 157, 164, 170, 229, 294
Theology (Theological), 26, 49, 52, 59, 67–68, 73–74, 102, 110–11, 115, 121, 124, 127–28, 131, 133, 135, 140–42, 147–54, 156, 159–64, 174, 206–10, 231, 282–83, 285, 286, 288, 291, 305–6, 313, 386, 395
Theosophic (Theosophy), 49; Theosophical Society, 307, 321–22, 326
Thesis, 25, 234, 322; and Antithesis, 338; and Hypothesis, 38, 41; and Synthesis, 111, 147, 154, 228, 267, 307
Thirty Years War, the, 73
Tibet (Tibetan), 59, 310–11, 313, 340, 360–67, 371, 373–77, 383, 415
Torah, 229–30, 249, 267, 280, 283, 289, 292, 295–99
Tradition (Traditions, in religious or religious-secular context), 53–54, 68, 71, 74, 86–87, 102, 108, 111, 117–18, 120, 123–24, 127, 129, 131, 133, 143, 149–50, 154, 157–58, 160–62, 172, 174–75, 177, 179, 181–82, 184–85, 193, 201, 218, 227, 259–60, 265, 270–73, 283, 295, 305, 308–9, 313, 317–19, 352–53, 356, 362, 370–72, 374–77, 381, 383, 395–96, 398, 401, 404; Animist, 341; and Traditional Doctrine, 46, 49, 97–98, 169
Transcendent (Transcendence, Transcendental), 45, 49, 60, 71, 80, 97, 98–99, 113–15; Rights, 56
Troubles, the, 73, 120–21, 124–26, 131–33, 139–40

Übermensch. *See* Nietzsche, Friedrich: Übermensch
Uighurs, 59
Ukraine, 20, 68, 71–72, 97, 99–105, 109, 118
United Kingdom, 21, 48, 58, 73, 121, 152, 201, 215, 329–30, 367
Urban (Urbanization), 8, 12, 33, 35, 159, 161–62, 164, 167, 264, 388, 393; Space, 169

Veda (Vedas), 305, 308, 317, 324–25
Verma, Shyamji Krishna, 307, 323
Virtues: Moral or Religious Concepts, 80, 109–12, 117, 175; a Policy of, 116. *See also* Greek Moral Concepts
Voltaire, 6
Volunteerism, 47, 328; Activist, 47; Army, Righteous Volunteer, 312, 395; Volunteers (Volunteering), 204, 210, 297

Waqf, 152, 201, 207, 274
War, Just. *See* Just War
Warrior (Warrior Tradition), 47, 69
Weber, Max, 8, 12; and Samuel Huntington, 17–18; and Mark Tessler, 17
Weltanschauung, 7, 8, 19
Westphalia, Peace of, 11, 15; Westphalian System, 107
Wilson, Brian, 13
Witchcraft, 49
Worldview, 15, 51, 55–56, 230, 281, 290, 309, 362, 371, 377. *See also* Belief-Values; Culture; Ethos; Myth, as in mythos

Yugoslavia, 59

Zakat, 152, 201, 205, 207
Zelensky, Volodymyr, 71–72, 99, 102–5, 118